ILLINOIS CRIMINAL PROCEDURE

Third Edition

VOLUME 1

Related LEXIS® Law Publishing Titles:

Illinois Criminal Defense Motions–by Richard Kling (1 vol. hardbound)

For additional information, or to place an order, please contact:

LEXIS® Law Publishing
P.O. Box 7587
Charlottesville, VA 22906-7587
Phone: (800) 562-1197
FAX: (800) 643-1280

ILLINOIS CRIMINAL PROCEDURE

Third Edition

VOLUME 1

Edited by

Ralph Ruebner

LEXIS® LAW PUBLISHING
CHARLOTTESVILLE, VIRGINIA

8108320

Contributors

Ralph Ruebner, Editor
Professor of Law
The John Marshall Law School

Anne M. Herbert, Editorial Assistant
Attorney, Chicago, Illinois
Law Clerk to Illinois Appellate Justice Thomas R. Rakowski

Authors

Leonard L. Cavise
Associate Professor of Law
DePaul University College of Law

Honorable Kenneth L. Gillis
Former Judge of the Circuit Court
Cook County; Attorney, Chicago

Iain D. Johnston
Attorney, Chicago

Richard S. Kling
Clinical Professor of Law
Illinois Institute of Technology,
Chicago-Kent College of Law

Timothy P. O'Neill
Professor of Law
The John Marshall Law School

Phyllis J. Perko
Attorney, West Dundee, Illinois
Former Deputy Director,
State's Attorneys' Appellate
Service Commission

Ralph Ruebner, Author
Professor of Law
The John Marshall Law School

v

Preface

The first and second editions of this book were well received by bar and bench. A number of appellate opinions by Illinois reviewing courts have referred to it as authority.

Our book is unique because it blends critical analysis and opinions of well-known academicians who have rich backgrounds in criminal litigation, a distinguished jurist who recently retired from the bench, and two highly regarded practitioners. The views expressed by each author are his or her own and not necessarily those of the editor.

Timothy P. O'Neill, a professor of law at The John Marshall Law School, is a former public defender in Cook County. Professor Howard B. Eisenberg, who authored Chapter 2, Confessions, in the first edition has left Illinois and serves as the Dean of Marquette University Law School in Wisconsin. I revised his chapter for the second and third editions. The Honorable Kenneth L. Gillis is a former judge of the Circuit Court of Cook County and was a highly respected defender and prosecutor. Richard S. Kling is a clinical professor of law at the Illinois Institute of Technology, Chicago-Kent College of Law and is a former Cook County public defender. Leonard L. Cavise is an associate professor of law at DePaul University College of Law and a former appellate and trial defender in Cook County. Phyllis J. Perko is in the private practice of law and is highly regarded for her expertise as an appellate litigator. She previously served as state deputy director of the Illinois State's Attorneys' Appellate Service Commission, assistant appellate defender, and law clerk to the Honorable Thomas J. Moran, justice of the Illinois Supreme Court. Iain D. Johnston is currently an associate with a Chicago law firm and previously served as an assistant attorney general and law clerk to the Honorable Philip G. Reinhard, then Justice of the Illinois Appellate Court and now judge of the United States District Court, Northern District, Rockford, Illinois.

I wish to single out the superb work of Ms. Anne Herbert who assisted me in revising the first and second editions. This book is intended to guide Illinois judges and practitioners through a complex and ever-changing area of the law. It may also be used as a textbook by law students and criminal justice students. An annual supplement will be available.

Ralph Ruebner, Editor
Chicago, 1999

Contents

VOLUME 1

Contents

CHAPTER 2 CONFESSIONS

CHAPTER 3   CHARGING

Contents

CHAPTER 4 PRETRIAL PROCEDURES AND PRACTICES

Contents

VOLUME 2

Preface

CHAPTER 5   TRIAL RIGHTS AND PROCEDURES

Contents

Contents

CHAPTER 6   SENTENCING

Contents

CHAPTER 7   APPEALS AND COLLATERAL REMEDIES

1

ARRESTS, SEARCHES, AND SEIZURES

Timothy O'Neill

§ 1.01 Introduction: The Scope of Article 1, Section 6 of the Illinois Constitution

Article I, section 6 of the Illinois Constitution states:

> The people shall have the right to be secure in their persons, houses, papers and other possessions against unreasonable searches, seizures, invasions of privacy or interceptions of communications by eavesdropping devices or other means. No warrant shall issue without probable cause, supported by affidavit particularly describing the place to be searched and the persons or things to be seized.[1]

The same general subject is covered by the Fourth Amendment of the United States Constitution:

> The right of the people to be secure in their persons, houses, papers, and effects, against unreasonable searches and seizures, shall not be violated, and no Warrants shall issue, but upon probable cause, supported by Oath or affirmation, and particularly describing the place to be searched, and the persons or things to be seized.[2]

The Illinois Supreme Court has characterized the language in both constitutions as "nearly identical."[3] Indeed, the comparable section in the Illinois Constitution of 1870 was even closer to the language of the Fourth Amendment.[4] The 1970 amendment was intended to "include guarantees of

---

1. ILL. CONST. art. I, § 6 (1970).

2. U.S. CONST. amend. IV.

3. People v. Tisler, 103 Ill. 2d 226, 469 N.E.2d 147, 152 (1984).

4. Article II, section 6 of the 1870 Constitution stated:
   > The right of the people to be secure in their persons, houses, papers and effects, against unreasonable searches and seizures, shall not be

freedom from unreasonable eavesdropping and invasions of privacy."[5] The Illinois Supreme Court has interpreted this amendment as extending greater protection to individuals against invasions of the right to privacy than that afforded under the federal constitution.[6]

Thus Illinois, like the federal government, seeks to protect those interests in which individuals have exhibited a reasonable expectation of privacy. To determine what is a reasonable expectation of privacy, courts apply a two-pronged test. First, it must be determined if the person in fact possesses a "subjective expectation of privacy."[7] Second, the expectation must be "one that society is prepared to recognize as reasonable."[8] Moreover, the interest protected must be personal to the individual.[9]

Article I, section 6 guarantees that the individual will be protected against unreasonable seizures by the government. Thus, an individual may not be arrested without probable cause.[10] However, a police officer may stop and

---

　　　　violated; and no warrant shall issue without probable cause, supported
　　　　by affidavit, particularly describing the place to be searched, and the
　　　　persons or things to be seized.

5. 7 *Record of Proceedings,* SIXTH ILL. CONST. CONVENTION 2683, *cited in Tisler,* 103 Ill. 2d 226, 469 N.E.2d at 155.

6. In re May 1991 Will County Grand Jury, 152 Ill. 2d 381, 604 N.E.2d 929 (1992). Recognizing a person's reasonable expectation to privacy in remaining free from close scrutiny of his personal characteristics, the Illinois Supreme Court held that the Illinois Constitution requires that "some showing of individualized suspicion as well as relevance must be made before physical evidence of a noninvasive nature, such as an in-person appearance in a lineup or fingerprinting, is demanded of a witness," *id.,* 604 N.E.2d at 935–36, that a search warrant supported by probable cause is required to obtain pubic hair samples, and that probable cause must also be established before head hair may be pulled, cut, or combed to obtain samples. *Id.,* 604 N.E.2d at 936.

7. Rakas v. Illinois, 439 U.S. 128, 143 n.12 (1978); People v. Collins, 106 Ill. 2d 237, 478 N.E.2d 267, 279, *cert. denied,* 474 U.S. 935 (1985).

8. *Rakas,* 439 U.S. at 143 (quoting Katz v. United States, 381 U.S. 337, 361 (1967) (Harlan, J., concurring)); People v. Collins, 106 Ill. 2d 237, 478 N.E.2d 267 (1985); People v. Holt, 91 Ill. 2d 480, 440 N.E.2d 102, 108 (1982). *See also* People v. Smith, 152 Ill. 2d 229, 604 N.E.2d 858, 864 (1992) (setting forth two part test: "[f]irst, a person must have exhibited an actual (subjective) expectation of privacy . . . [; and] [s]econd, this expectation must be one that society . . . recognize[s] as 'reasonable' "), *cert. denied,* 507 U.S. 1040 (1993).

9. *Rakas,* 439 U.S. at 133–34; People v. Janis, 139 Ill. 2d 300, 565 N.E.2d 633 (1990) (reasonable expectation of privacy in gravel area part of commercial establishment from which public excluded).

10. People v. Creach, 79 Ill. 2d 96, 402 N.E.2d 228, 231, *cert. denied,* 449 U.S. 1010 (1980).

temporarily detain an individual for a limited investigation absent probable cause to arrest if the officer is able to point to specific and articulable facts that, taken with reasonable inferences drawn from the officer's experience, would reasonably warrant the investigative intrusion.[11] In this context, *reasonable* means that the "facts and circumstances must be specific and articulable."[12] In other situations, it may be difficult to ascertain whether a particular police-citizen interaction has risen to the level of a "seizure" for constitutional purposes.[13]

The protections of both the Fourth Amendment and Article I, section 6 apply only to searches and seizures conducted pursuant to government authority; these provisions have no effect on private intrusions.[14] Moreover, these provisions prohibit only those searches and seizures that are "unreasonable." Warrantless searches and seizures are per se unreasonable under both the Fourth Amendment and Article I, section 6, unless they fall within a few specifically established and well-delineated exceptions.[15] In Illinois some of these exceptions are search by consent, search incident to arrest, and search predicated on probable cause where there are exigent circumstances that make it impractical to obtain a warrant.[16]

§ 1.02   The Concept of Probable Cause: Definition

In Illinois probable cause is needed before any arrest[17] or search[18] can be executed. Probable cause for arrest exists if "the facts and circumstances within

---

11. 725 ILCS 5/107-14; Terry v. Ohio, 392 U.S. 1, 20–21 (1968); People v. McGowan, 69 Ill. 2d 73, 370 N.E.2d 537 (1977), *cert. denied*, 435 U.S. 975 (1978).

12. *McGowan,* 69 Ill. 2d 73, 370 N.E.2d at 539–40.

13. *See* Florida v. Royer, 460 U.S. 491 (1983); United States v. Mendenhall, 446 U.S. 544 (1980).

14. Illinois v. Andreas, 463 U.S. 765 (1983); Burdeau v. McDowell, 256 U.S. 465 (1921); People v. Heflin, 71 Ill. 2d 525, 376 N.E.2d 1367 (1978), *cert. denied*, 439 U.S. 1074 (1979).

15. Katz v. United States, 389 U.S. 347, 357 (1967); People v. Pakula, 89 Ill. App. 3d 789, 411 N.E.2d 1385, 1389 (3d Dist. 1980).

16. People v. Hoffstetter, 128 Ill. App. 3d 401, 470 N.E.2d 1247 (5th Dist. 1984); People v. Gardner, 121 Ill. App. 3d 464, 459 N.E.2d 676 (2d Dist. 1984).

17. ILL. CONST. art. 1, § 6 (1970); 725 ILCS 5/107-2. *Reasonable grounds* in section 107-2 is synonymous with *probable cause*. People v. Davis, 98 Ill. App. 3d 461, 424 N.E.2d 630 (1st Dist. 1981).

18. ILL. CONST. art. 1, § 6 (1970). The Illinois Supreme Court, however, has ruled that neither probable cause nor individualized suspicion was constitutionally required to justify mandatory testing for the human immunodeficiency virus (HIV). People v. Adams, 149 Ill. 2d 331, 597 N.E.2d 574 (1992). In determining

the arresting officer's knowledge are sufficient to warrant a man of reasonable caution in believing that an offense has been committed and that the person arrested has committed the offense."[19] Probable cause requires more than mere suspicion[20] but something less than evidence necessary to result in conviction.[21] Courts recognize that in the warrantless arrest situation, police must deal with "ambiguous circumstances."[22] Thus each case must be governed by its own facts and circumstances.[23] In dealing with the concept of probable cause,

---

the constitutionality of an Illinois statute which required a person convicted of prostitution to undergo mandatory HIV testing, the court found that while a search had occurred for Fourth Amendment purposes, the "important public health mission" of the state outweighed an "individual's interest in requiring some degree of individualized suspicion." *Id.,* 597 N.E.2d at 582. Additionally, requiring a showing of probable cause or individualized suspicion is impractical since "there are no outward manifestations of the disease, or of a person's status as a carrier of HIV, apart from the individual's membership in a high-risk group." *Id.,* 597 N.E.2d at 583. Thus, the court concluded that a probable cause requirement "would only jeopardize the State's goal of accurately identifying HIV carriers among those members of the population who are primarily at risk of exposure to the virus." *Id. See also* 730 ILCS 5/5-5-3(g).

19. People v. Creach, 79 Ill. 2d 96, 402 N.E.2d 228, 230, *cert. denied,* 449 U.S. 1010 (1980) (quoting People v. Robinson, 62 Ill. 2d 273, 342 N.E.2d 356, 358 (1976)). *See* Dunaway v. New York, 442 U.S. 200, 208 n.9 (1979); Brinegar v. United States, 338 U.S. 160, 175–76 (1949); Carroll v. United States, 267 U.S. 132, 162 (1925). Both federal and state requirements for probable cause, as well as the concept of reasonable grounds used in section 107-2 of the Illinois Code of Criminal Procedure, are synonymous. People v. Garmon, 196 Ill. App. 3d 549, 554 N.E.2d 378 (1st Dist. 1990); People v. Bell, 96 Ill. App. 3d 857, 421 N.E.2d 1351 (1st Dist. 1981). *See* People v. Gaston, 259 Ill. App. 3d 869, 631 N.E.2d 311, 315 (1st Dist. 1994) ("Probable cause exists when the police possess enough evidence to lead a reasonable man to believe that a crime has been committed and that the defendant committed it").

20. People v. Moody, 94 Ill. 2d 1, 445 N.E.2d 275 (1983).

21. People v. Lippert, 89 Ill. 2d 171, 432 N.E.2d 605, *cert. denied,* 459 U.S. 841 (1982); People v. Frye, 113 Ill. App. 3d 853, 447 N.E.2d 1065 (4th Dist. 1983). *See also* People v. Batac, 259 Ill. App. 3d 415, 631 N.E.2d 373, 378 (2d Dist. 1994) (probable cause found in *probability* of criminal activity, not prima facie showing).

22. *Moody,* 94 Ill. 2d 1, 445 N.E.2d at 278.

23. People v. Sims, 167 Ill. 2d 483, 658 N.E.2d 413, 422 (1995) (police had probable cause to arrest defendant based on statements given to police by two witnesses that defendant told them he was involved in crime and corroborated by conditions at crime scene), *cert. denied,* 517 U.S. 1172 (1996); People v. Rainey, 302 Ill. App. 3d 1011, 706 N.E.2d 1062, 1065 (3d Dist. 1999) (defendant turning away from police officer and "furtively" placing something in his mouth not enough to justify warrantless arrest); People v. Merriweather, 261 Ill. App. 3d 1050, 634

therefore, courts ". . . deal with probabilities. These are not technical; they are the factual and practical considerations of everyday life on which reasonable and prudent men, not legal technicians, act."[24] Moreover, in later assessing whether probable cause existed, a purely objective inquiry into the reasonableness of the police officer's conduct is utilized; that is, in retrospect it is irrelevant what the officer subjectively believed.[25]

Similarly, probable cause to search is established if the totality of facts and circumstances would justify a reasonable person in believing that a crime had been committed and that evidence of the crime is located in a particular place.[26] The probability of criminal activity, as opposed to proof beyond a reasonable doubt, is the standard for determining whether probable cause is present in a specific case.[27] Again, Illinois courts determine whether such a probability exists through common sense considerations of the facts rather than by technical legal rules.[28]

In *Ornelas v. United States*,[29] the Supreme Court held that the question of whether probable cause or reasonable suspicion exists is determined based on

---

N.E.2d 361, 365 (2d Dist. 1994) (no probable cause while police executing search warrant for second floor to search defendant who stepped out of first floor apartment but did not act suspiciously or attempt to flee); People v. Salvator, 236 Ill. App. 3d 824, 602 N.E.2d 953, 963 (4th Dist. 1992) (distinctive odors can be persuasive evidence of probable cause, officers may detect controlled substances by their smell); People v. Smith, 215 Ill. App. 3d 1029, 576 N.E.2d 186 (1st Dist. 1991) (officer had probable cause to arrest based on general description of suspect, vicinity, and facial characteristics); People v. Agnew, 152 Ill. App. 3d 1037, 504 N.E.2d 1358 (2d Dist. 1987) (officer's hunch that cigarettes in defendant's possession were stolen insufficient basis for arrest); People v. Houston, 151 Ill. App. 3d 102, 502 N.E.2d 1111 (1st Dist. 1986) (no probable cause to arrest where defendant not in possession of car used at shooting and witness's description of defendant uncertain).

24. *Moody,* 94 Ill. 2d 1, 445 N.E.2d at 278 (quoting Brinegar v. United States, 388 U.S. 160, 175 (1949)). *See also* People v. Cabrera, 116 Ill. 2d 474, 508 N.E.2d 708, *cert. denied,* 484 U.S. 929 (1987).

25. People v. Moody, 94 Ill. 2d 1, 445 N.E.2d 275 (1983); People v. Clark, 185 Ill. App. 3d 231, 541 N.E.2d 199 (2d Dist. 1989).

26. People v. Smith, 95 Ill. 2d 412, 447 N.E.2d 809 (1983); People v. Clark, 92 Ill. 2d 96, 440 N.E.2d 869 (1982); People v. Wolsk, 118 Ill. App. 3d 112, 454 N.E.2d 695 (1st Dist. 1983).

27. People v. Tisler, 103 Ill. 2d 226, 469 N.E.2d 147 (1984); People v. Exline, 98 Ill. 2d 150, 456 N.E.2d 112 (1983).

28. People v. Tisler, 103 Ill. 2d 226, 469 N.E.2d 147 (1984); People v. Mitchell, 45 Ill. 2d 148, 258 N.E.2d 345, *cert. denied,* 400 U.S. 882 (1970).

29. 517 U.S. 690, 696–97 (1997). Illinois courts have indicated they would follow *Ornelas. See* People v. Kidd, 175 Ill. 2d 1, 675 N.E.2d 910, 922 (1996), *cert.*

two principal components: first, what are the totality of the facts and circumstances that occurred leading up to the stop or search; and second, whether the totality of the facts and circumstances, when viewed from the perspective of an objectively reasonable police officer, adds up to probable cause or reasonable suspicion. The second component is a mixed question of law and fact. Therefore, on appeal, the trial court's determination is reviewed *de novo*.[30]

§ 1.03 Types of Information That Can Be Used to Establish Probable Cause

First-hand knowledge is not the only kind of information that can be used to establish probable cause. First, it is proper for a police officer to consider hearsay provided by other police officers.[31] As long as the other officers are engaged in a common investigation, the information can be used to establish probable cause.[32] Second, it is proper for a police officer to consider hearsay provided by citizens. However, this information can only be considered if it meets a standard of reliability. Until recently, it was considered crucial to distinguish between hearsay from professional informants and hearsay from ordinary citizens. Understanding why this distinction is no longer so crucial will illuminate important changes that have occurred in this area.

Until recently in Illinois, a magistrate asked to determine whether probable cause existed for the issuance of a warrant used the *Aguilar-Spinelli* test to evaluate hearsay evidence the police wanted to use to establish probable cause. This test evolved from two United States Supreme Court cases—*Aguilar v.*

---

denied, 520 U.S. 1269 (1997); People v. Wardlow, 287 Ill. App. 3d 367, 678 N.E.2d 65, 67 (1st Dist. 1997), *aff'd*, 183 Ill. 2d 306, 701 N.E.2d 484 (1998); People v. Aguilar, 286 Ill. App. 3d 493, 676 N.E.2d 324, 326 (1st Dist. 1997); People v. Patterson, 282 Ill. App. 3d 219, 667 N.E.2d 1360, 1366 (1st Dist. 1996).

30. *Ornelas*, 517 U.S. at 691.

31. People v. Poe, 48 Ill. 2d 506, 272 N.E.2d 28, *cert. denied*, 404 U.S. 942 (1971); People v. Wrona, 7 Ill. App. 3d 1, 286 N.E.2d 370 (3d Dist. 1972). *See also* People v. Peak, 29 Ill. 2d 343, 194 N.E.2d 322 (1963) (officers working together may rely on each other's information to establish probable cause); People v. McCoy, 135 Ill. App. 3d 1059, 482 N.E.2d 200 (2d Dist. 1985) (prior arrests and convictions may be considered in making probable cause determination). *Cf.* People v. Corral, 147 Ill. App. 3d 668, 498 N.E.2d 287 (4th Dist. 1986) (mere knowledge, on part of state officers, that federal agents had information that narcotics could be in car stopped by state officers not substantial enough connection between two agencies to establish probable cause based on *Peak* doctrine).

32. *Poe*, 48 Ill. 2d 506, 272 N.E.2d at 31. *See* Whitely v. Warden, 401 U.S. 560 (1971); People v. Fox, 155 Ill. App. 3d 256, 508 N.E.2d 475, 480 (2d Dist. 1987) (knowledge concerning probable cause may be imputed to all officers working together, even if knowledge was not conveyed to arresting officer).

Texas[33] and *Spinelli v. United States.*[34] To determine whether a hearsay tip was reliable under this test, two elements had to be established. First, the judicial officer had to determine how the informant learned of the information—that is, whether the informant possessed an adequate "basis of knowledge." Second, the judicial officer had to decide whether there was sufficient reason to believe that the informant was credible—that is, whether the informant exhibited sufficient evidence of veracity and prior reliability. Each "prong" in this test had to be independently satisfied; the failure to satisfy either of the two prongs meant the information could not be considered.[35] Thus, under the *Aguilar-Spinelli* test, prior reliability had to be specifically established when information came from professional informants.[36] On the other hand, ordinary citizens who provided information were presumed to be reliable.[37]

In 1984 the Illinois Supreme Court said that it would follow the lead of the United States Supreme Court in abandoning the *Aguilar-Spinelli* test in favor of the test enunciated in *Illinois v. Gates.*[38] In *Gates,* the Court expressed its dissatisfaction with the way the two-pronged *Aguilar-Spinelli* rule had been implemented by lower courts. The Court explained that it had never intended the rigid compartmentalization that had developed around the two *Aguilar-Spinelli* standards. Although both the veracity of the informant and the inform- ant's basis of knowledge are relevant to a determination of whether the hearsay

---

33. 378 U.S. 108 (1964).

34. 393 U.S. 410 (1964).

35. People v. Tisler, 103 Ill. 2d 226, 469 N.E.2d 147, 154 (1984). *See also* People v. Drewes, 278 Ill. App. 3d 786, 663 N.E.2d 456, 457–58 (3d Dist. 1996) (where officer unavailable to testify as to informant's reliability or to corroborate informant's tip, prosecutor had not met burden of establishing reliability).

36. People v. Thomas, 62 Ill. 2d 375, 342 N.E.2d 383 (1975); People v. McNeil, 52 Ill. 2d 409, 288 N.E.2d 464 (1972); People v. Hawthorne, 45 Ill. 2d 176, 258 N.E.2d 319, *cert. denied,* 400 U.S. 878 (1970).

37. People v. Hoffman, 45 Ill. 2d 221, 258 N.E.2d 326, *cert. denied,* 400 U.S. 904 (1970); People v. Hester, 39 Ill. 2d 489, 237 N.E.2d 466, *cert. granted,* 394 U.S. 1957 (1969), *cert. dismissed,* 397 U.S. 660 (1970). *See* People v. Aguilar, 286 Ill. App. 3d 493, 676 N.E.2d 324, 326–27 (1st Dist. 1997) (information support- ing arrest coming from victim or eyewitness to crime entitled to particularly great weight); People v. Hood, 262 Ill. App. 3d 171, 634 N.E.2d 404, 408 (2d Dist. 1994) (probable cause to arrest existed where citizen/informants had no motive to lie and substantial part of their statements independently verified); People v. Smith, 258 Ill. App. 3d 1003, 630 N.E.2d 1068, 1080 (1st Dist. 1994) (informa- tion considered reliable where supplied by victim of crime or eyewitness to it).

38. 462 U.S. 213 (1983); *Tisler,* 103 Ill. 2d 226, 469 N.E.2d at 157. *But see* People v. Lawson, 298 Ill. App. 3d 997, 700 N.E.2d 125, 130 (1st Dist. 1998) (warrant- less arrest made by police in reliance on radio bulletin invalid because police officer issuing bulletin did not have probable cause to make arrest).

statements are reliable, establishing the existence of each is not a sine qua non for a finding of probable cause. In its place, the *Gates* Court established a flexible "totality of the circumstances" test and stated:

> The task of the issuing magistrate is simply to make a practical, common-sense decision whether, given all the circumstances set forth in the affidavit before him, including the "veracity" and "basis of knowledge" of persons supplying hearsay information, there is a fair probability that contraband or evidence of a crime will be found in a particular place.[39]

---

39. Illinois v. Gates, 462 U.S. 213, 238 (1983). *See* People v. Kidd, 175 Ill. 2d 1, 675 N.E.2d 910, 921–22 (1996) (informant's tip together with details police discovered at crime scene amounted to probable cause), *cert. denied*, 520 U.S. 1269 (1997); People v. Prince, 288 Ill. App. 3d 265, 681 N.E.2d 521, 528–29 (1st Dist. 1997) (assuming defendant was detained, police had sufficient probable cause to do so where they had been provided with a description of a man, which defendant matched, who ran past a witness shortly after the shooting, and they received an anonymous call implicating defendant and offering details of the crime, which police independently corroborated); People v. Patterson, 282 Ill. App. 3d 219, 667 N.E.2d 1360, 1367 (1st Dist. 1996) (police corroboration of informant's statements coupled with independent investigation amounted to probable cause); People v. Rogers, 231 Ill. App. 3d 774, 596 N.E.2d 1291 (4th Dist. 1992) (although police viewed their source of information as one criminally involved in illegal drug transactions and an unreliable source, probable cause existed where police were present when source participated in a "controlled buy"); People v. Milam, 224 Ill. App. 3d 642, 587 N.E.2d 30 (3d Dist. 1992) (informant's tip established probable cause to stop car where informant had given reliable information on 10 prior occasions, officer saw car, and occupants matched informant's detailed description); People v. Canet, 218 Ill. App. 3d 855, 578 N.E.2d 1146 (1st Dist. 1991) (informant's tip became reliable when independent police investigation corroborated tip details). *But see* People v. Damian, 299 Ill. App. 3d 489, 701 N.E.2d 171, 173–74 (5th Dist. 1998) (no probable cause to issue warrant because controlled buy done six weeks earlier and there was no reason to believe defendant engaged in ongoing criminal activity); People v. Anaya, 279 Ill. App. 3d 940, 665 N.E.2d 525, 530–31 (1st Dist. 1996) (compilation of otherwise innocuous factors including hard-sided luggage, individual traveling from city known to be source of drugs, and individual nervous when asked questions by police could apply to very large category of presumably innocent travelers and did not constitute probable cause); People v. Yarber, 279 Ill. App. 3d 519, 663 N.E.2d 1131, 1137-38 (5th Dist. 1996) (uncorroborated anonymous tip of innocent details not sufficient for probable cause), *cert. denied*, 519 U.S. 1150 (1997); People v. Halmon, 225 Ill. App. 3d 259, 587 N.E.2d 1182 (1st Dist. 1992) (uncorroborated anonymous tip not sufficient for probable cause); People v. Crespo, 207 Ill. App. 3d 947, 566 N.E.2d 496 (2d Dist. 1991) (informant's tip did not provide probable cause because informant not reliable and tip not corroborated).

Thus, it is no longer necessary to make a rigid distinction between hearsay from a professional informant and hearsay from an ordinary citizen. The proper inquiry is whether or not a consideration of the totality of the circumstances convinces the magistrate that probable cause indeed exists.[40]

The Illinois Appellate Court was faced with the issue whether police officers can lawfully arrest a suspect based on a polygraph exam.[41] The polygraph exam showed the suspect was lying.[42] When confronted with the results of the exam, the suspect refused to alter his statement.[43] The police then arrested the

---

40. People v. Turner, 143 Ill. App. 3d 417, 493 N.E.2d 38 (1st Dist. 1986) (statements by co-offenders can establish probable cause). *See* People v. Hall, 164 Ill. App. 3d 770, 518 N.E.2d 275 (1st Dist. 1987) (information supplied by inmate presumed reliable absent indication that informant was paid by police), *cert. denied,* 488 U.S. 867 (1988). *See also* People v. House, 141 Ill. 2d 323, 566 N.E.2d 259 (1990) (co-defendant's custodial statement provided probable cause to arrest defendant); People v. Weston, 271 Ill. App. 3d 604, 648 N.E.2d 1068, 1073 (1st Dist. 1995) (indicia of reliability of information from informant's tip found in statement against penal interest of the declarant); People v. Almendarez, 266 Ill. App. 3d 639, 639 N.E.2d 619, 622 (1st Dist. 1994) (co-defendant's statement against interest which was not in response to promise of leniency furnished probable cause to arrest defendant), *cert. denied,* 514 U.S. 1006 (1995); People v. Caine, 258 Ill. App. 3d 599, 630 N.E.2d 1037, 1040 (1st Dist. 1994) (test for whether accomplice's statements provide probable cause is "whether they provide sufficient information and reliability such that a reasonably prudent person, having the knowledge possessed by the officer at the time of his arrest would believe the defendant committed the offense"); People v. Halmon, 225 Ill. App. 3d 259, 587 N.E.2d 1182 (1st Dist. 1992) (statement by third party not implicating self did not provide probable cause); People v. Earley, 212 Ill. App. 3d 457, 570 N.E.2d 1235 (5th Dist. 1991) (officer had probable cause where defendant's sister told police that defendant was using narcotics, sister had searched defendant's luggage, had given police cocaine, and had described defendant's car and license plate); People v. Miller, 212 Ill. App. 3d 195, 570 N.E.2d 1202 (2d Dist. 1991) (co-offender's statement provided sufficient probable cause where statement was against penal interest and information was consistent with officers' observations); People v. Mackey, 207 Ill. App. 3d 839, 566 N.E.2d 449 (1st Dist. 1990) (statement by person driving murder victim's vehicle to the effect that defendant, who was living with driver, had given him vehicle was sufficient to establish probable cause); People v. Calhoun, 126 Ill. App. 3d 727, 467 N.E.2d 1037 (5th Dist. 1984) (implicating statements of co-offenders provided probable cause for warrantless arrest).

41. People v. Haymer, 154 Ill. App. 3d 760, 506 N.E.2d 1378 (1st Dist. 1987).

42. *Id.,* 506 N.E.2d at 1380.

43. *Id.*

---

suspect.[44] The court held the fact that a suspect failed a polygraph exam cannot be used in determining probable cause to arrest.[45]

In *People v. Green,* the court held that information provided by a private citizen is presumed reliable, and police officers may make an investigatory stop based on that information.[46] In *Green,* the court held that a bus driver's tip that three passengers were smoking marijuana on the bus provided sufficient probable cause to justify the officers' investigatory stop.[47] Furthermore, the defendant's flight when approached by the officers provided probable cause that the defendant was committing or had committed a crime.[48]

In *People v. McPhee,*[49] the court held that an officer's seizure of a package at a Federal Express facility at the Los Angeles International Airport, which was based on three factors: (1) the package was not delivered by truck or courier; (2) the package was paid for in cash and had handwritten on it "air bills"; and (3) the package was going from one individual to another, without more, was insufficient to constitute probable cause.[50] However, in *People v. Shapiro,*[51] the court determined that probable cause existed to support the seizure of a package based on the United States Postal Service profile that included the following six factors: "(1) heavy brown paper wrapping; (2) heavily taped seams; (3) handwritten address label; (4) sent from one individual to another; (5) mailed from a zip code different from the address; and (6) a fictitious address."[52]

In *Whren v. United States,*[53] the Supreme Court unanimously determined that the police may stop a car where they have probable cause to believe that

---

44. *Id.*

45. *Id.,* 506 N.E.2d at 1384.

46. People v. Green, 153 Ill. App. 3d 888, 506 N.E.2d 367 (3d Dist. 1987).

47. *Id.,* 506 N.E.2d at 368.

48. *Id.,* 506 N.E.2d at 368–69. *Compare* People v. Wardlow, 183 Ill. 2d 306, 701 N.E.2d 484, 487 (1998) (joining the majority of jurisdictions in holding that an individual's flight upon the approach of police in a high-crime area is, alone, not enough to justify an investigatory stop), *cert. granted,* 119 S. Ct. 1573 (1999); People v. Rainey, 302 Ill. App. 3d 1011, 706 N.E.2d 1062, 1065 (3d Dist. 1999) (defendant turning away from police officer and "furtively" placing something in his mouth held not to justify warrantless arrest, but might be enough for *Terry* stop).

49. 256 Ill. App. 3d 102, 628 N.E.2d 523 (1st Dist. 1993).

50. *Id.,* 628 N.E.2d at 531.

51. 177 Ill. 2d 519, 687 N.E.2d 65 (1997).

52. *Id.,* 687 N.E.2d at 69–70.

53. 517 U.S. 806, 813 (1996) (must have probable cause to believe that driver has or is about to commit traffic offense; however, subjective motivations of police in stopping car so they could search it for contraband did not affect Fourth Amend-

the driver committed a traffic offense despite the officer's subjective motivations in securing a search of the vehicle on other grounds.[54] In *People v. Thompson*,[55] the Fifth District, in interpreting *Whren*, explained that the officer's subjective motivations cannot make an otherwise lawful stop unlawful, nor can the motivations invalidate the stop.[56] However, the officer's motivations may be relevant to questions of the reasonableness of the initial stop and scope of any subsequent search of persons or the vehicle.[57]

In *Pennsylvania v. Mimms*,[58] the United States Supreme Court held that an officer may order the driver to exit his vehicle during a traffic stop in the interest of officer safety. The Court, using the same officer safety rationale, later extended the per se rule of *Mimms* to include passengers.[59] In *People v. Gonzalez*, the Illinois Supreme Court adopted the holdings of the United States Supreme Court, stating that it is reasonable for a police officer to control the movements of all individuals during a traffic stop.[60]

§ 1.04 Seizures

Both Article I, section 6 of the Illinois Constitution and the Fourth Amendment of the United States Constitution prohibit unreasonable seizures.[61] Not

---

ment analysis). *See also* Ohio v. Robinette, 519 U.S. 33, 35, 39–40 (1996) (decision to ask individual to exit car after officer decided not to issue citation for traffic offense that provided probable cause for initial stop did not make seizure unlawful); People v. Orsby, 286 Ill. App. 3d 142, 675 N.E.2d 237, 239–40 (2d Dist. 1996) (where police stopped car on minor traffic offenses because subject of narcotics investigation within, sufficient probable cause to initially stop vehicle and subsequent search and seizure did not violate Fourth Amendment).

54. *Whren*, 517 U.S. at 813.

55. 283 Ill. App. 3d 796, 670 N.E.2d 1129, 1135 (5th Dist. 1996) (search of passenger after officer released traffic offender when officer could articulate no safety concerns could be unreasonable and in violation of the Fourth Amendment).

56. *Id.*, 670 N.E.2d at 1131, 1134.

57. *Id.*, 670 N.E.2d at 1134.

58. 434 U.S. 106 (1977) (Court weighed public interest in officer safety against individual's right to be free from arbitrary interference before setting bright line rule that police may order driver to exit vehicle).

59. Maryland v. Wilson, 519 U.S. 408 (1997) (police may order passengers out of vehicle even where officer has no suspicion that passenger has been involved in a crime).

60. 184 Ill. 2d 402, 704 N.E.2d 375, 382–83 (1998) (police may order passenger who exited vehicle to remain with the vehicle). *See also* People v. Boyd, 298 Ill. App. 3d 1118, 700 N.E.2d 444 (4th Dist. 1998).

61. ILL. CONST. art. 1, § 6 (1970); U.S. CONST. amend. IV.

every encounter between a police officer and a citizen is a seizure under these constitutional provisions. A person is "seized" only when his or her freedom of movement is restrained by an officer's physical force or show of authority.[62] A seizure is determined by ascertaining whether, in view of all the circumstances surrounding the incident, a reasonable person would have believed that he or she was not free to leave.[63] Circumstances that might suggest that a seizure has occurred include, but are not limited to: (1) the threatening presence of several officers; (2) the display of a weapon by an officer; (3) the physical touching of the citizen; and (4) the use of language or tone of voice indicating that compliance with the officer's request might be compelled.[64]

The United States Supreme Court has held that no "seizure" occurs under the Fourth Amendment when the police merely pursue an individual and this show of authority fails to cause the person to submit.[65] To constitute a seizure there must be *either* the application of physical force, however slight, *or* submission to the officer's "show of authority."[66]

Police-citizen encounters can be roughly divided into three categories. First, there are seizures sufficiently intrusive to be labeled arrests. Arrests may not be made without probable cause.[67] Second, there are seizures that are too brief to be arrests but occur when police officers detain an individual for a limited investigation based on specific and articulable facts that suggest to the officer that the individual is about to commit or has committed an offense.[68] Such a

---

62. United States v. Mendenhall, 446 U.S. 544, 553 (1980). *See* California v. Hodari D., 499 U.S. 621 (1991); People v. Long, 99 Ill. 2d 219, 457 N.E.2d 1252 (1983). *But see* People v. Billingslea, 292 Ill. App. 3d 1026, 686 N.E.2d 603, 605–06 (1st Dist. 1997) (although officer's actions in blocking defendant's path was show of force indicating officer's intent to restrain, he was not seized because he chose not to submit to officer's direction and instead turned away).

63. *Mendenhall,* 446 U.S. at 553; Michigan v. Chesternut, 486 U.S. 567 (1988) (no seizure occurs when police cruiser slowly follows a pedestrian); People v. Downey, 198 Ill. App. 3d 704, 566 N.E.2d 300 (2d Dist. 1990) (citing *Chesternut*).

64. *Mendenhall,* 446 U.S. at 554; People v. Downey, 198 Ill. App. 3d 704, 556 N.E.2d 300 (2d Dist. 1990).

65. *Hodari D.,* 499 U.S. at 626.

66. *Id. See also* Brower v. Inyo County, 489 U.S. 593 (1989) (stopping of motorist with a roadblock is a "seizure"); People v. Ward, 302 Ill. App. 3d 550, 707 N.E.2d 130, 137–38 (1st Dist. 1998) (defendant not seized when police "nudged" him to awake him; reasonable person in his shoes would feel free to leave).

67. See the probable cause discussion in sections 1.02–1.03 of this chapter. Florida v. Royer, 460 U.S. 491 (1983); Dunaway v. New York, 442 U.S. 200 (1979); People v. Wipfler, 68 Ill. 2d 158, 368 N.E.2d 870 (1977).

68. Terry v. Ohio, 392 U.S. 1 (1968); 725 ILCS 5/107-14. *See Whren,* 517 U.S. 806, 819 (1996) (individuals in car detained based on probable cause that the driver

stop can be justified by less than probable cause. Third, there are police-citizen encounters that do not rise to the level of seizures because they involve no restraint of movement through show of force or authority.[69]

§ 1.05 — Arrests

An arrest in Illinois occurs when (1) the police inform an individual of a violation, (2) the individual submits to police control, (3) the police intend to effect an arrest, and (4) the individual understands the police.[70] Both the intent of the police officer and the understanding of the arrestee are essential elements.[71] Whether the police have advised the suspect that he or she was free to leave and the timing of such advice are also considered.[72] Yet the understanding

---

committed traffic offense); People v. Orsby, 286 Ill. App. 3d 142, 675 N.E.2d 237, 240 (2d Dist. 1996) (where officers had probable cause to stop defendant's vehicle, subjective motivations did not make the otherwise lawful seizure illegal); People v. Edwards, 285 Ill. App. 3d 1, 673 N.E.2d 752, 753–54 (3d Dist. 1996) (individual lawfully further detained at a checkpoint for seat belt infraction despite the statute's language prohibiting stopping vehicles solely for seat belt infraction because the second stop was an extension of the first and not merely due to the fact defendant was not wearing his seat belt). *But see* People v. Arteaga, 273 Ill. App. 3d 943, 655 N.E.2d 290, 291–92 (3d Dist. 1995) (defendant seized when police ordered him to wait while checking validity of his driver's license where defendant stopped to determine whether he possessed valid temporary registration and police ascertained he did when first approached car).

69. Florida v. Royer, 460 U.S. 491 (1983); United States v. Mendenhall, 446 U.S. 544, 553 (1980). *See* People v. Murray, 137 Ill. 2d 382, 560 N.E.2d 309 (1990) (recognizing these three categories); People v. Crocker, 267 Ill. App. 3d 343, 641 N.E.2d 1237, 1239 (3d Dist. 1994) (no seizure where police approach individual on street or in public place and merely ask him or her questions).

70. People v. Holveck, 141 Ill. 2d 84, 565 N.E.2d 919 (1990); People v. Wipfler, 68 Ill. 2d 158, 368 N.E.2d 870 (1977); People v. Clark, 9 Ill. 2d 400, 137 N.E.2d 820 (1956); People v. Bailey, 259 Ill. App. 3d 180, 630 N.E.2d 1158 (1st Dist. 1994); People v. Mannon, 217 Ill. App. 3d 381, 577 N.E.2d 532 (3d Dist. 1991); People v. Stofer, 180 Ill. App. 3d 158, 534 N.E.2d 1287 (1st Dist. 1989); People v. Hollins, 169 Ill. App. 3d 304, 523 N.E.2d 1309 (3d Dist. 1988); People v. Holloway, 131 Ill. App. 3d 290, 475 N.E.2d 915 (1st Dist. 1985).

71. People v. Wipfler, 68 Ill. 2d 158, 368 N.E.2d 870 (1977); People v. Ussery, 24 Ill. App. 3d 864, 321 N.E.2d 718 (3d Dist. 1974); People v. Smith, 5 Ill. App. 3d 341, 275 N.E.2d 480 (1st Dist. 1971).

72. People v. Melock, 149 Ill. 2d 423, 599 N.E.2d 941 (1992) (although finding that the suspect was not placed under arrest, the court commented that the polygraph examiner's notification to the suspect that he was free to leave was merely a part of the interrogation technique given after questioning was nearly complete without regard to the suspect's constitutional rights and noted the likelihood that

of the arrestee is measured not against the arrestee's subjective beliefs but rather against "what a reasonable man, innocent of any crime, would have thought had he been in the defendant's shoes."[73]

Section 107-2 of the Illinois Code of Criminal Procedure[74] provides that a valid arrest may be made when a warrant has been issued[75] or when there are reasonable grounds to believe that the person to be arrested is committing or has committed a crime.[76] "Reasonable grounds" have been held to be synonymous

---

such advice was not perceived as an indication that the suspect was actually free to leave). *But see* People v. McKinney, 277 Ill. App. 3d 889, 661 N.E.2d 408, 411–12 (1st Dist. 1996) (defendant under arrest at station where held 34 hours before confession even though police said free to leave; denied access to mother, held in interrogation room which police entered and exited via key, defendant had to ask to use bathroom, and slept on floor during night).

73. *Wipfler,* 68 Ill. 2d 158, 368 N.E.2d at 873 (quoting Hicks v. United States, 382 F.2d 158, 161 (D.C. Cir. 1967)). *See* Michigan v. Chesternut, 486 U.S. 567 (1988); People v. Fair, 159 Ill. 2d 51, 636 N.E.2d 455, *cert. denied,* 513 U.S. 1020 (1994). *See* People v. Williams, 164 Ill. 2d 1, 645 N.E.2d 844, 849 (1994) (reasonable innocent person in defendant's position would not have considered self under arrest when voluntarily agreed to accompany officer to station, was advised of *Miranda* rights, was not handcuffed, door to large interview room was left open, and companion allowed to remain in same room), *cert. denied,* 515 U.S. 1136 (1995); People v. Johnson, 159 Ill. 2d 97, 636 N.E.2d 485, 493 (listing essential elements of the arrest as "intent of police to make the arrest and the defendant's understanding, based on an objective standard of reasonableness, that he is in fact under arrest"), *cert. denied,* 513 U.S. 968 (1994); People v. Sneed, 274 Ill. App. 3d 274, 653 N.E.2d 1340, 1347 (1st Dist. 1995) (15-year-old defendant seized without probable cause prior to formal arrest where police detained him at high school, transported him to police station and sequestered him for 6½–8 hours in interrogation room, defendant never told he could leave or allowed to speak to parent or youth guardian; defendant's confession inadmissible and conviction reversed); People v. Barlow, 273 Ill. App. 3d 943, 654 N.E.2d 223, 228–29 (1st Dist. 1995) (defendant under illegal arrest even though voluntarily went to police station where left in locked interview room for seven hours and kept in custody another 15 hours before confessing, while police attempted to verify defendant's original statement; case remanded for attenuation hearing); People v. Marts, 266 Ill. App. 3d 531, 639 N.E.2d 1360, 1366 (1st Dist. 1994) (despite defendant's low intelligence, his prior breakdown, and being read *Miranda* warnings, defendant was arrested only after making incriminating statements).

74. 725 ILCS 5/107-2.

75. 725 ILCS 5/107-2.

76. People v. Edwards, 144 Ill. 2d 108, 579 N.E.2d 336 (1991) (police had probable cause to arrest at the time they entered house with search warrant), *cert. denied,* 504 U.S. 942 (1992); People v. Moody, 94 Ill. 2d 1, 445 N.E.2d 275, 279 (1983)

(reasonable grounds are based on objective, not subjective, factors; inquiry is geared to what facts objectively show, not what officer on scene subjectively believed); People v. Turnipseed, 274 Ill. App. 3d 527, 653 N.E.2d 1258, 1260 (1st Dist. 1995) (police had probable cause to arrest defendant where responding to call concerning a woman with gun, defendant met description, was arguing with neighbors over drug debt, and neighbors told police defendant had gun and had threatened to use it); People v. Koutsakis, 272 Ill. App. 3d 159, 649 N.E.2d 605, 608 (3d Dist. 1995) (length of time, 14–20 minutes, detaining defendant after being stopped for minor traffic offense unreasonable; stalling was used so another officer could arrive at scene with drug dog); People v. McBee, 228 Ill. App. 3d 769, 593 N.E.2d 574 (1st Dist. 1992) (probable cause existed where officer overheard offer to sell cocaine and saw defendant pass a clear plastic bag); People v. MacFarland, 228 Ill. App. 3d 107, 592 N.E.2d 471 (1st Dist. 1992) (probable cause existed where officers knew defendant was with victim shortly before murder); People v. Chavez, 228 Ill. App. 3d 54, 592 N.E.2d 69 (1st Dist. 1992) (officers had probable cause based on wound on defendant's leg and defendant's ripped, muddy, and bloody clothes); People v. Bobe, 227 Ill. App. 3d 681, 592 N.E.2d 301 (1st Dist. 1992) (probable cause existed based on police case report and corroboration by detectives of informant's information); People v. Kolichman, 218 Ill. App. 3d 132, 578 N.E.2d 569 (1991) (officers had probable cause to arrest defendant for disorderly conduct where they observed defendant stagger, drool, hold onto counter for support, his face was flushed, and he spoke incoherently), cert. denied, 505 U.S. 1224 (1992); People v. Trice, 217 Ill. App. 3d 967, 577 N.E.2d 1195 (1st Dist. 1991) (police had probable cause upon corroboration of facts given by anonymous 911 caller); People v. Pittman, 216 Ill. App. 3d 598, 575 N.E.2d 967 (4th Dist. 1991) (police had probable cause to arrest defendant found in close proximity to marijuana and drug paraphernalia); People v. Jones, 215 Ill. App. 3d 652, 575 N.E.2d 561 (3d Dist. 1991) (officer had probable cause to arrest when saw defendant throw cocaine out window); People v. Thompson, 215 Ill. App. 3d 514, 575 N.E.2d 256 (4th Dist. 1991) (probable cause based on loaded handgun found under passenger seat in easy reach of defendant); People v. Mason, 213 Ill. App. 3d 163, 571 N.E.2d 1127 (3d Dist. 1991) (probable cause existed where officers were informed that victim's rental car was in the possession of three unknown men, license check revealed it was owned by rental agency, defendant and passengers acted nervously, and defendant could not give full name of man who had loaned them car); People v. Bulman, 212 Ill. App. 3d 795, 571 N.E.2d 850 (1st Dist. 1991) (probable cause existed after investigation established licensee was driving and smelled strongly of alcohol); People v. Harvey, 209 Ill. App. 3d 733, 568 N.E.2d 381 (1st Dist. 1991) (probable cause existed where defendant last seen with deceased, defendant signed hotel registration card, and missing bed sheets found in defendant's car); People v. McCleary, 208 Ill. App. 3d 466, 567 N.E.2d 434 (1st Dist. 1990) (probable cause based on eyewitnesses' description, evidence of weapon, and suspect living a short distance from scene); People v. Taylor, 165 Ill. App. 3d 64, 518 N.E.2d 662 (4th Dist. 1987) (prior law enforcement experience of officer

17

with "probable cause."[77] Generally, the legality of an arrest is tested by the presence or absence of probable cause, not by the presence or absence of a warrant.[78]

---

relevant in determining existence of probable cause). *But see* People v. Garmon, 196 Ill. App. 3d 549, 554 N.E.2d 378 (1st Dist. 1990) (no probable cause to arrest when defendant tried to sell $1,500 camera equipment for $50, had no receipt, and claimed he purchased from someone else for $50); People v. McGhee, 154 Ill. App. 3d 232, 507 N.E.2d 33, 36 (1st Dist. 1987) (information that defendant was in victim's company previous night held insufficient to create probable cause to arrest, whether with or without warrant).

77. In re D.G., 144 Ill. 2d 404, 581 N.E.2d 648 (1991) (mere possession of $1,000 by minor did not create probable cause); People v. Drake, 288 Ill. App. 3d 963, 683 N.E.2d 1215, 1219 (2d Dist. 1997) (no probable cause to arrest car passenger who had no knowledge of contraband found in trunk; mere presence in car as passenger insufficient to establish probable cause); People v. Bates, 218 Ill. App. 3d 288, 578 N.E.2d 240 (1st Dist. 1991) (coerced confession by co-defendant insufficient to provide probable cause); People v. Graham, 214 Ill. App. 3d 798, 573 N.E.2d 1346 (1st Dist. 1991) (defendant arrested without probable cause where defendant's initial encounter was on sidewalk outside dormitory with four officers present, college officials directed police to defendant, defendant's arm grabbed by police who led him to police car, defendant seated between two officers, and defendant driven directly to station, frisked, and questioned); People v. Beamon, 213 Ill. App. 3d 410, 572 N.E.2d 1011 (1st Dist. 1991) (defendants were under arrest without probable cause where roused from bed by five officers, not told they could refuse to accompany police, were taken into interrogation rooms, and were 18 and 17 years old with no prior experience); People v. McGhee, 154 Ill. App. 3d 232, 507 N.E.2d 33 (1st Dist. 1987) (information that defendant was in victim's company previous night held insufficient to create probable cause to arrest, whether with or without warrant); People v. Dace, 153 Ill. App. 3d 891, 899, 506 N.E.2d 332, 337 (3d Dist. 1987) (knowledge that victim was last seen with defendant may create suspicion, but it is insufficient for probable cause). *But see* People v. Ward, 302 Ill. App. 3d 550, 707 N.E.2d 130, 138 (1st Dist. 1998) (police had probable cause to arrest defendant where he arose from couch and threatened to kick officer's ass and police did not rely solely on verbal threats but also on defendant's demeanor and conduct); People v. Boyd, 298 Ill. App. 3d 1118, 700 N.E.2d 444, 450 (4th Dist. 1998) (police had probable cause to detain defendant based on their detection of strong odor of marijuana emanating from car in which defendant was passenger); People v. Fortney, 297 Ill. App. 3d 79, 697 N.E.2d 1, 7 (2d Dist. 1998) (police had reasonable grounds/probable cause that defendant was driving under the influence where defendant fell against the back of her car upon exiting it; her eyes were watery, glassy, and bloodshot; there was a very strong smell of alcohol on her breath; and police learned she drank four glasses of champagne earlier that evening).

78. People v. Weathers, 18 Ill. App. 3d 338, 309 N.E.2d 795 (1st Dist. 1974). The legislature has made additions to section 107-2(3) which state that "[a] peace officer who executes a warrant of arrest in good faith beyond the geographical

An objectively reasonable stop or other seizure is not invalid simply because the officer acted out of an improper or dual motivation.[79] However, an arrest may not be used as a mere pretext to avoid the warrant requirement of the Fourth Amendment.[80]

If an arrest warrant is to be used, the issue of the existence of reasonable grounds or probable cause[81] must be resolved by a detached judicial officer.[82] If there are reasonable grounds or probable cause, a warrant may be issued.[83] This decision is based primarily on information contained in a sworn statement or affidavit that is presented to the judicial officer. In Illinois, this document is called a complaint.[84]

Illinois law provides that the complaint for an arrest warrant must be in writing.[85] It should state the name of the accused, and if the name is unknown, any name or description by which the person can be identified with reasonable

---

limitation of the warrant shall not be liable for false arrest." 725 ILCS 5/107-2(3). This complements the addition to section 107-9(d)(8), which provides that the search warrant must "[s]pecify any geographical limitation placed on the execution of the warrant, but such limitation shall not be expressed in mileage." 725 ILCS 5/107-9(d)(8).

79. People v. Guerrieri, 194 Ill. App. 3d 497, 551 N.E.2d 767 (5th Dist. 1990). *See also* People v. Woidtke, 224 Ill. App. 3d 791, 587 N.E.2d 1101 (5th Dist. 1992) (defendant's arrest for obstruction of peace officer not a pretext to interrogate him about murder); People v. Sorrells, 209 Ill. App. 3d 1064, 568 N.E.2d 497 (4th Dist. 1991) (probable cause to stop defendant for traffic violation although officers were acting on anonymous tip of drug activity and did not obtain warrant); People v. Mendoza, 208 Ill. App. 3d 183, 567 N.E.2d 23 (2d Dist. 1991) (probable cause to arrest for illegal immigration status, even if arrest is pretext to question defendant about homicide).

80. People v. Hattery, 183 Ill. App. 3d 785, 539 N.E.2d 368 (1st Dist. 1989). *Cf.* People v. Perez, 258 Ill. App. 3d 465, 631 N.E.2d 240, 245 (5th Dist. 1994) (even slight traffic violation, if proven at hearing, not considered a pretextual stop for subsequent Cannabis Control Act violation).

81. In Illinois, reasonable grounds and probable cause are synonymous for purposes of arrest. People v. Wright, 56 Ill. 2d 523, 309 N.E.2d 537 (1974); People v. Davis, 98 Ill. App. 3d 461, 424 N.E.2d 630 (1st Dist. 1981); People v. Walls, 87 Ill. App. 3d 256, 408 N.E.2d 1056 (1st Dist. 1980).

82. 725 ILCS 5/107-9(a).

83. 725 ILCS 5/107-9(c).

84. 725 ILCS 5/107-9(a).

85. 725 ILCS 5/107-9(b). People v. Cleaves, 169 Ill. App. 3d 252, 523 N.E.2d 720 (5th Dist. 1988) (fact that suspect was in vicinity of burglary, was known to be on parole, and was evasive when questioned was insufficient to support probable cause).

certainty should be given.[86] It should state the offense with which the accused is charged[87] and the time and place of the offense as definitely as possible.[88] Finally, the complaint must be subscribed and sworn to by the complainant.[89] It is important to note that the words of the complaint itself need not establish probable cause. The judicial officer is free to orally examine the complainant or any other witness and to use this information with the complaint to determine whether probable cause exists.[90]

In an isolated number of cases, courts have granted motions to suppress evidence obtained from searches executed incident to arrests based on stale or flawed warrants.[91] However, where the police are not at fault for the error or flaw, evidence seized pursuant to the arrests based on information then known to be correct by the police does not provide a basis for suppressing evidence.[92]

Although the Illinois Supreme Court has held that, if possible, it is "desirable"[93] that an arrest be made with a warrant, an arrest without a warrant is generally proper, providing the police have probable cause.[94] Thus, a warrant-

---

86. 725 ILCS 5/107-9(b)(1).

87. 725 ILCS 5/107-9(b)(2).

88. 725 ILCS 5/107-9(b)(3).

89. 725 ILCS 5/107-9(b)(4).

90. 725 ILCS 5/107-9(c).

91. People v. Mourecek, 208 Ill. App. 3d 87, 566 N.E.2d 841, 845 (2d Dist. 1991) (fact that officer relied on stale electronically communicated information warranted suppression); People v. Joseph, 128 Ill. App. 3d 668, 470 N.E.2d 1303, 1306 (1st Dist. 1984) (reversing trial court's denial of motion to suppress where defendant was arrested based on computer search which showed defendant was wanted on bond forfeiture warrant; at the suppression hearing, the court's records showed that bond had been posted four days earlier); People v. Decuir, 84 Ill. App. 3d 531, 405 N.E.2d 891, 892 (3d Dist. 1980) (motion to suppress granted where defendant arrested pursuant to a warrant that had been recalled and quashed two weeks prior due to lack of probable cause, even though arrest warrant was from another jurisdiction).

92. People v. Rayford, 281 Ill. App. 3d 596, 667 N.E.2d 534, 537 (1st Dist. 1996) (motion to suppress evidence obtained pursuant to arrest was properly denied where defendant was lawfully arrested for possession of a stolen car and information in computer was current since owner had not informed police that the stolen car had been recovered).

93. People v. Johnson, 45 Ill. 2d 283, 259 N.E.2d 57, 60 (1970), *cert. denied,* 407 U.S. 1914 (1972).

94. People v. Johnson, 94 Ill. 2d 148, 445 N.E.2d 777 (1983) (standards applicable to police officer's probable cause assessment for warrantless arrest are at least as stringent as standards applied to magistrate's decision; anything less would encourage police to avoid obtaining warrant); People v. Lekas, 155 Ill. App. 3d

less arrest in a public place is always proper, as long as probable cause exists.[95] An arrest may be made anywhere within the jurisdiction of this state.[96] Therefore, officers are authorized to pursue suspects outside the city limits.[97] Moreover, the warrantless arrest of a person in his or her home is proper if the police entered the home with probable cause and in "hot pursuit."[98] Finally, officers entering a private dwelling are not required by the constitution or by the Illinois Criminal Code to state their purpose prior to entry if they are in the process of making an authorized arrest.[99]

391, 508 N.E.2d 221, 237 (1st Dist. 1987) (rejects state argument that as long as officers have probable cause to arrest, arrest warrant is no longer required in Illinois), *cert. denied*, 485 U.S. 942 (1988). *See also* People v. Adams, 131 Ill. 2d 387, 546 N.E.2d 561 (no probable cause); People v. Young, 206 Ill. App. 3d 789, 564 N.E.2d 1254 (1st Dist. 1990) (same); People v. Lucy, 204 Ill. App. 3d 1019, 562 N.E.2d 1158 (5th Dist. 1990) (same); People v. Gordon, 198 Ill. App. 3d 791, 556 N.E.2d 573 (1st Dist. 1990) (same); People v. Downey, 198 Ill. App. 3d 704, 556 N.E.2d 300 (2d Dist. 1990) (same).

95. United States v. Watson, 423 U.S. 411 (1976) (warrantless felony arrest in public held to be proper); People v. Holdman, 73 Ill. 2d 213, 383 N.E.2d 155 (1978), *cert. denied*, 440 U.S. 938 (1979); People v. Wolff, 182 Ill. App. 3d 583, 538 N.E.2d 610 (3d Dist. 1989).

96. 725 ILCS 5/107-5(c). *See* People v. Niedzwiedz, 268 Ill. App. 3d 119, 644 N.E.2d 53, 55–56 (2d Dist. 1994) (DUI arrest of defendant following private citizen's tip valid extraterritorial citizen's arrest by uniformed officer outside jurisdiction even though he called for backup); People v. Gutt, 267 Ill. App. 3d 95, 640 N.E.2d 1013, 1016 (2d Dist. 1994) (officer making extraterritorial valid citizen's arrest after observing defendant fail to signal when making left-hand turn had authority to ask defendant to submit to breathalyzer test).

97. People v. Pollard, 216 Ill. App. 3d 591, 575 N.E.2d 970 (4th Dist. 1991). *See* People v. Williams, 267 Ill. App. 3d 82, 640 N.E.2d 981, 988 (2d Dist. 1994) (evidence of defendant's offenses occurring in midst of valid, extraterritorial arrest admissible even though committed outside jurisdiction of arresting officer); Prairie Grove v. Sutton, 260 Ill. App. 3d 682, 633 N.E.2d 162, 164 (2d Dist. 1994) (traffic arrest outside officer's jurisdiction valid because officer observed crime occurring within his jurisdiction). *Compare* People v. Stanley, 264 Ill. App. 3d 94, 637 N.E.2d 1072, 1074 (3d Dist. 1994) (although officer within jurisdiction at time he aimed radar gun at defendant's car, invalid arrest because defendant outside officer's jurisdiction).

98. United States v. Santana, 427 U.S. 38 (1976); People v. Barbee, 35 Ill. 2d 407, 220 N.E.2d 401 (1966); People v. Coleman, 194 Ill. App. 3d 336, 550 N.E.2d 1263 (2d Dist. 1990) (*dictum*).

99. People v. Pietryzk, 153 Ill. App. 3d 428, 505 N.E.2d 1228 (1st Dist. 1987).
    Illinois has recently passed legislation allowing police officers to enter private dwellings without knocking and announcing their office under certain circumstances. The new Act amends section 108-8 of the Code of Criminal Procedure:

However, Illinois, following the lead of the United States Supreme Court in *Payton v. New York,*[100] mandates that a warrantless arrest in a private residence is unlawful unless it is accompanied by exigent circumstances.[101] This rule necessitates two considerations: (1) what constitutes a private residence and (2) what constitutes exigent circumstances.

As to the private residence requirement, it is clear that it includes an apartment[102] and a hotel room[103] as well as a traditional home.[104] Moreover, a hotel room occupant does not waive the Fourth Amendment right by having

---

Sec. 108-8. Use of force in execution of search warrant. (a) All necessary and reasonable force may be used to effect an entry into any building or property or part thereof to execute a search warrant.

(b) Upon a finding by the judge issuing the warrant that any of the following exigent circumstances exist, the judge may order the person executing the warrant make entry without first knocking and announcing his office:

(1) the presence of firearms or explosives in the building in an area where they are accessible to any occupant;

(2) the prior possession of firearms by an occupant of the building within a reasonable period of time;

(3) the presence of surveillance equipment, such as video cameras, or alarms systems, inside or outside of the building;

(4) the presence of steel doors, wooden planking, crossbars, dogs, or other similar means of preventing or impeding entry into the building.

725 ILCS 5/108-8.

100. 445 U.S. 573 (1980).

101. People v. Abney, 81 Ill. 2d 159, 407 N.E.2d 543 (1980); People v. Ford, 228 Ill. App. 3d 212, 592 N.E.2d 544 (1st Dist. 1992) (exigent circumstances justified warrantless arrest where officers had co-defendant's statement and reasonably believed defendant armed and dangerous). *But see* People v. Graves, 135 Ill. App. 3d 727, 482 N.E.2d 223 (4th Dist. 1985) (upholds warrantless arrest in defendant's doorway, absent exigent circumstances, when defendant answered door not knowing police officers were persons knocking and officers had probable cause).

102. People v. Wormack, 91 Ill. App. 3d 169, 414 N.E.2d 177 (1st Dist. 1980).

103. People v. Olson, 198 Ill. App. 3d 675, 556 N.E.2d 273 (2d Dist. 1990) (extends to guest in a hotel room which is registered to another person). *See also* People v. Eichelberger, 91 Ill. 2d 359, 438 N.E.2d 140, *cert. denied,* 459 U.S. 1019 (1982); People v. Bankhead, 27 Ill. 2d 18, 187 N.E.2d 705 (1963); People v. Wilson, 86 Ill. App. 3d 637, 408 N.E.2d 988 (2d Dist. 1980).

104. *See* People v. White, 117 Ill. 2d 194, 512 N.E.2d 677 (1987) (where homeless suspect had stayed at brother's home a short time and then fled to escape police, brother's home considered suspect's home for Fourth Amendment purposes), *cert. denied,* 485 U.S. 1006 (1988).

the room door "cracked open."[105] However, a warrantless arrest can be made in the hallway outside one's hotel room; Illinois courts consider this area a public place.[106] Moreover, the entrance to a hotel room has also been construed as a public place. Therefore, it was proper for the police to knock on the defendant's door, allow her to open it, announce their office, and make a warrantless arrest.[107]

Note that the United States Supreme Court has held that an overnight guest in an apartment possessed a sufficiently reasonable expectation of privacy to fall under the protection of *Payton*.[108] The United States Supreme Court found that even though the guest has no legal interest in the premises or legal authority to control entrance of others, hosts generally respect the privacy interests of their guests.[109] Further, society as a whole recognizes that a house guest has a legitimate expectation of privacy in his host's home.[110] Thus, the house guest's expectation of privacy is reasonable[111] and an expectation we all share.[112]

In *Minnesota v. Carter*, the United States Supreme Court held that a person in an apartment for a short period of time may have no legitimate expectation of privacy.[113] A distinction is made between an overnight social guest and a person who is only on the premises for a purely commercial purpose.[114] In *Carter*, a police officer looked through a gap in closed blinds and observed the defendants bagging cocaine in an apartment.[115] The defendants argued that the officer's observation was an unreasonable search in violation of their Fourth

---

105. People v. Eichelberger, 91 Ill. 2d 359, 438 N.E.2d 140 (1982).

106. People v. Blount, 101 Ill. App. 3d 443, 428 N.E.2d 621 (1st Dist. 1981), *cert. denied,* 459 U.S. 847 (1982). *See also* People v. Pietryzk, 153 Ill. App. 3d 428, 505 N.E.2d 1228 (1st Dist. 1987) (stairwell in abandoned building is not "private place").

107. People v. Schreiber, 104 Ill. App. 3d 618, 432 N.E.2d 1316 (1st Dist.), *cert. denied,* 459 U.S. 1214 (1983).

108. Minnesota v. Olson, 495 U.S. 91 (1990).

109. *Id.* at 99.

110. *Id.* at 100.

111. *Id.*

112. *Id.*

113. 119 S. Ct. 469 (1998) (defendants on premises with consent of homeowner to bag cocaine did not have legitimate expectation of privacy). *See also* New York v. Burger, 482 U.S. 691, 700 (1987) (property used for commercial purposes is treated differently than residential property for Fourth Amendment purposes.)

114. *Carter*, 119 S. Ct. at 474.

115. *Id.* at 471.

Amendment rights.[116] The Court disagreed, holding that since the defendants were not overnight social guests, but merely present for a business transaction and were only in the home for a matter of hours, they did not have a reasonable expectation of privacy.[117]

A distinction is made concerning the common interior and hallways of a locked apartment building. It has been held that tenants do have an expectation of privacy in these areas and that it is improper for the police to effect an entry merely to make a warrantless arrest.[118]

It should also be noted that a warrantless arrest in a private residence is always proper, however, if police have a right to be in that residence. Thus, if police have probable cause to arrest and voluntary consent to enter is properly given by an occupant of a dwelling, a warrantless arrest can be effected within.[119]

As to the exigent circumstances requirement, the Illinois Supreme Court in *People v. Abney*[120] suggested several examples, including:

1. the need for prompt police action;

2. the absence of any deliberate or unjustified delay by the officer during which time a warrant could have been obtained;

3. the belief that the suspect was armed and exhibited some sign of a violent character;

4. proof that the officer was acting on a clear showing of probable cause based on reasonably trustworthy information;

5. evidence that the defendant was clearly identified;

6. strong reason to believe that the defendant was present on the premises;

7. a peaceful entry;[121] and

---

116. *Id.* at 472.

117. *Id.* at 474.

118. People v. Trull, 64 Ill. App. 3d 385, 380 N.E.2d 1169 (4th Dist. 1978). *But see* People v. Williams, 275 Ill. App. 3d 249, 655 N.E.2d 1071, 1076 (1st Dist. 1995) (porch of apartment is not an area where defendant has a reasonable expectation of privacy for Fourth Amendment purposes).

119. People v. Bean, 84 Ill. 2d 64, 417 N.E.2d 608, *cert. denied,* 454 U.S. 1821 (1981); People v. Ellis, 187 Ill. App. 3d 295, 543 N.E.2d 196 (1st Dist. 1989), *cert. denied,* 498 U.S. 942 (1990).

120. 81 Ill. 2d 159, 407 N.E.2d 543 (1980).

121. People v. Abney, 81 Ill. 2d 159, 407 N.E.2d 543 (1980); People v. Gaines, 220 Ill. App. 3d 310, 581 N.E.2d 214 (1st Dist. 1991) (citing *Abney* factors).

8. The Illinois Supreme Court, citing *Abney* with approval, suggested that courts also consider the likelihood that the suspect will escape if not promptly apprehended.

Obviously, the presence of exigent circumstances has to be determined on a case-by-case basis. Thus, exigent circumstances have been found to exist when police went to the defendant's residence immediately after receiving the victim's statement one and one-half hours after he had been attacked; there was no deliberate delay by the police; and the defendant was armed and suspected of being dangerous.[122] Exigent circumstances were also found to exist when obtaining a warrant would have been impracticable because of the late hour; it was reasonable to believe the defendant was armed; and the arrest was made peaceably.[123] However, exigent circumstances were not found where, despite the fact that the offense was serious, there was no evidence to believe the defendant would flee during the time it would take to obtain a warrant and there was some doubt that the defendant was even on the premises at the time of entry.[124] Likewise, no exigent circumstances were found where the arrest took place a day after the alleged robbery; there was no chance the defendant would escape; and the police forcibly entered the defendant's apartment with guns

---

122. *Abney*, 81 Ill. 2d 159, 407 N.E.2d at 547–49.

123. People v. Krohn, 100 Ill. App. 3d 37, 426 N.E.2d 540 (3d Dist. 1981). *See* People v. Eichelberger, 91 Ill. 2d 359, 438 N.E.2d 140, 145 (1982) (fact that officers reasonably believed crime was being committed in their presence justified warrantless entry; no unjustified delay; entry was peaceful); People v. Mitran, 194 Ill. App. 3d 344, 550 N.E.2d 1258 (2d Dist. 1990) (exigent circumstances found where police believed occupant of apartment needed aid and saw an occupant make a quick movement toward gun); People v. Knight, 139 Ill. App. 3d 188, 486 N.E.2d 1356 (1st Dist. 1985) (exigent circumstances based on brutality of crime, prompt police action, risk of flight and arrest of co-offenders in same building), *cert. denied*, 480 U.S. 905 (1987); People v. McNair, 102 Ill. App. 3d 322, 429 N.E.2d 1233 (1st Dist. 1981) (exigent circumstances found to exist where there was no unjustified police delay, crime was murder, there was strong showing of probable cause, defendant was suspected of being violent, and entry was peaceful).

124. People v. Wormack, 91 Ill. App. 3d 169, 414 N.E.2d 177 (1st Dist. 1980). *See also* People v. White, 171 Ill. 2d 194, 512 N.E.2d 677 (1987) (exigent circumstances were not present to justify warrantless arrest occurring almost two weeks after murders, where police had probable cause days before), *cert. denied*, 485 U.S. 1006 (1988).

drawn.[125] In *People v. Brown*,[126] the court held that evidence seized during the warrantless search of defendant's apartment should have been suppressed.[127] In this case, police saw co-defendant standing on defendant's porch after hearing a gunshot. They attempted to pursue him but he escaped into the apartment. The police were unable to access the apartment due to a steel-fortified door.[128] The court stated that a warrantless entry at this time would have been justified under the hot pursuit doctrine.[129] Instead, the police surrounded the area and sought a search warrant. Nearly three hours later, the police again attempted to enter the apartment without a warrant. They were successful this time. However, the court found that exigent circumstances no longer existed.[130] First, the police believed it safe enough to obtain a search warrant. Second, the violent activity which the police observed had occurred three hours earlier and although discharge of a firearm violates city ordinance, it is not a grave crime. Co-defendant made no attempt to escape and the police had no evidence that anyone else was in the apartment and in danger. Finally, there was no evidence the co-defendant would destroy any evidence.[131]

Once a defendant is under arrest, he must be presented before a judicial magistrate without unnecessary delay. The standard for unnecessary and unreasonable delay will depend on the circumstances of each case.[132] As a general

---

125. People v. Rembert, 89 Ill. App. 3d 371, 411 N.E.2d 996 (1st Dist. 1980). *See* People v. Foskey, 136 Ill. 2d 66, 554 N.E.2d 192 (1990) (exigent circumstances did not exist where there was only small likelihood that object of conspiracy would be accomplished; fear by police that defendant might flee if tipped off was insufficient exigency to justify warrantless arrest where police, through their own actions, created the exigency); People v. Lagle, 200 Ill. App. 3d 948, 558 N.E.2d 514 (5th Dist. 1990) (no exigent circumstances to justify warrantless arrest in home); People v. Motton, 139 Ill. App. 3d 661, 487 N.E.2d 1117 (1st Dist. 1985) (no exigent circumstances where police believed he could not get arrest warrant for six hours but made no attempt in three-hour period after probable cause established to obtain warrant, where no hot pursuit or indication of flight); People v. Klimek, 101 Ill. App. 3d 1, 427 N.E.2d 598 (2d Dist. 1981) (mere fact that offense was "recent" does not per se provide police with exigent circumstances to make warrantless arrest).

126. 277 Ill. App. 3d 989, 661 N.E.2d 533 (1st Dist. 1996).

127. *Id.*, 661 N.E.2d at 539.

128. *Id.*, 661 N.E.2d at 538.

129. *Id.*

130. *Id.*, 661 N.E.2d at 539.

131. *Id.*

132. People v. Shannon, 149 Ill. App. 3d 525, 501 N.E.2d 166 (1st Dist. 1986).

rule, a defendant must be presented before a magistrate with reasonable promptness given the circumstances of the case.[133] Illinois courts have held that delays of 29 hours[134] and 36 hours[135] are not unreasonable. The Illinois Code of Criminal Procedure provides that a person arrested without a warrant shall be "taken without unnecessary delay before the nearest and most accessible judge in that county."[136] It is unclear just what constitutes "unnecessary delay."[137] Recently, the United States Supreme Court held that a system that provides a combined probable cause-arraignment proceeding within 48 hours of a warrantless arrest is presumptively reasonable under the Fourth Amendment; however, the arrestee may challenge this presumption based on the facts of the particular case.[138] Conversely, a period of *more* than 48 hours—including weekends—is presumptively unreasonable, but the state may rebut this with a showing of extraordinary circumstance.[139]

§ 1.06 — Investigation Stops Based on Less than Probable Cause

The Illinois Code of Criminal Procedure provides that a peace officer may stop any person in a public place for a reasonable period of time when the officer reasonably infers from the circumstances that a person is committing, is about to commit, or has committed an offense as defined by the code.[140] After

---

133. *Id.,* 501 N.E.2d at 169.

134. People v. Martin, 121 Ill. App. 3d 196, 459 N.E.2d 279 (2d Dist. 1984).

135. People v. Shannon, 149 Ill. App. 3d 525, 501 N.E.2d 166 (1st Dist. 1986).

136. 725 ILCS 5/109-1(a).

137. *See, e.g.,* People v. Matthews, 205 Ill. App. 3d 371, 562 N.E.2d 1113 (1st Dist. 1990); People v. Dove, 147 Ill. App. 3d 659, 498 N.E.2d 279 (4th Dist. 1986).

138. Riverside County, Calif. v. McLaughlin, 500 U.S. 44, 56 (1991).

139. *Id.* at 57.

140. 725 ILCS 5/107-14. *But see* People v. Fenton, 154 Ill. App. 3d 152, 506 N.E.2d 979, 981 (3d Dist. 1987) (private citizen cannot make noncustodial inquiries or make *Terry* stops of another private citizen), *rev'd,* 125 Ill. 2d 343, 532 N.E.2d 228 (1988) (police officer's identification of defendant admissible even though officer out of his jurisdiction; officer was a private citizen and there was no search within meaning of the Fourth Amendment because officer identified defendant as defendant got out of car).

In *People v. Payne,* 277 Ill. App. 3d 1000, 661 N.E.2d 1163 (2d Dist. 1996), the court held that the legislature clearly intended to allow police officers to stop vehicles and make arrests when an officer perceives a violation of the Child Passenger Protection Act (625 ILCS 25/1 *et seq.*).

identifying himself or herself,[141] the officer may demand the name and address of the person and an explanation of his or her actions.[142] The detention and questioning is then conducted near the place the person was stopped.[143] This statute is predicated on the principles established by the United States Supreme Court in *Terry v. Ohio.*[144]

This so-called "*Terry* stop" comes within the bounds of the Fourth Amendment and thus must be found to be reasonable.[145] Something less than probable cause will justify this type of intrusion. A police officer reasonably infers that such a stop is necessary when he or she possesses "knowledge of sufficient articulable facts at the time of the encounter to create a reasonable suspicion that the person in question has committed, or is about to commit, a crime."[146] The officer must have a particularized and objective basis for determining that

---

141. People v. Vollrath, 95 Ill. App. 3d 866, 420 N.E.2d 760 (3d Dist. 1981) (failure of uniformed officers in squad car to identify themselves violated section 107-14 and mandated suppression of evidence). *But see* People v. Solis, 135 Ill. App. 3d 991, 482 N.E.2d 207 (2d Dist. 1985) (failure of peace officer to identify himself held not erroneous when defendant knew and recognized officer).

142. 725 ILCS 5/107-14. *See* People v. Smith, 266 Ill. App. 3d 362, 640 N.E.2d 647, 649 (4th Dist. 1994) (officer's request for identification from passenger in vehicle lawfully stopped for traffic violation within scope of community caretaking or public safety function, therefore, no legal justification required and no seizure in violation of Fourth Amendment; under these circumstances, an officer is not required to give *Miranda*-type warnings nor advise passenger of right to refuse to cooperate with his request). *But see* People v. Branch, 295 Ill. App. 3d 110, 692 N.E.2d 398, 402 (2d Dist. 1998) (officer lacked authority to ask for identification and run warrant check on backseat passenger where there was no suspicion of criminal activity).

143. 725 ILCS 5/107-14. *But see* People v. Fenton, 154 Ill. App. 3d 152, 506 N.E.2d 979, 981 (3d Dist. 1987) (private citizen cannot make noncustodial inquiries or make *Terry* stops of another private citizen), *rev'd,* 125 Ill. 2d 343, 532 N.E.2d 228 (1988) (police officer's identification of defendant admissible even though officer out of his jurisdiction; officer was a private citizen and there was no search within meaning of the Fourth Amendment because officer identified defendant as defendant got out of car).

144. 392 U.S. 1 (1968); People v. Lee, 48 Ill. 2d 272, 269 N.E.2d 488 (1971) (legislative intent was to codify *Terry*).

145. People v. Smithers, 83 Ill. 2d 430, 415 N.E.2d 327 (1980).

146. *Id.,* 415 N.E.2d at 330; People v. Green, 153 Ill. App. 3d 888, 506 N.E.2d 367 (3d Dist. 1987). *See also* United States v. Sokolow, 490 U.S. 1 (1989) (no particular factor need indicate criminal activity as long as the totality of factors yields articulable suspicion).

such a stop is necessary and is entitled to consider the "whole picture" in making such a determination.[147]

Obviously, the facts of a particular case are all-important in reviewing the propriety of a *Terry* stop. For example, in *People v. McGowan*,[148] the Illinois Supreme Court considered a case in which two black-clad men were walking at 12:50 A.M. through an industrial area that had recently been the scene of a significant number of burglaries. A tavern two blocks away was the only business open in the vicinity. On these facts, the court found that the police properly stopped the men based on the reasonable inference that they had committed or were about to commit a burglary. *People v. Smithers*[149] concerned

---

147. United States v. Cortez, 449 U.S. 411, 417–18 (1981). *See also* United States v. Sokolow, 490 U.S. 1 (1989) (use of "drug courier profile" is only *a* factor used in determining whether, under the totality of the circumstances, a stop was justified); People v. Evans, 296 Ill. App. 3d 1, 689 N.E.2d 142, 149–51 (1st Dist. 1997) (detention of defendant justified because police had reasonable suspicion that defendant was transporting illegal drugs; transportation of defendant approximately 150 yards to DEA office proper, particularly in light of fact defendant refused to provide identification and could provide no other means for officers to ascertain contents of baggage).

148. 69 Ill. 2d 73, 370 N.E.2d 537 (1977), *cert. denied,* 435 U.S. 975 (1978).

149. 83 Ill. 2d 430, 415 N.E.2d 327 (1980); People v. Scott, 148 Ill. 2d 479, 594 N.E.2d 217 (1992) (defendant matched description of man who had followed a woman shortly before murder and defendant seen following another woman in general vicinity three days later), *cert. denied,* 507 U.S. 989 (1993); People v. Safunwa, 299 Ill. App. 3d 707, 701 N.E.2d 1202, 1207 (2d Dist. 1998) (request for and verification of license held to be minimal intrusion not sufficient to invalidate *Terry* stop notwithstanding fact initial justification for stop, belief defendant matched description of arrest warrant target, dissipated before police officer requested the license); People v. Green, 298 Ill. App. 3d 1054, 700 N.E.2d 1097, 1102 (2d Dist. 1998) (stop and frisk of defendant in hotel lobby justified where crime committed in immediate vicinity of hotel, defendant matched description of suspect, defendant was apprehended in same hotel lobby where suspect was previously seen entering and exiting, and guns were a specific concern at this location in dealing with drug dealers). *See also* People v. Moore, 294 Ill. App. 3d 410, 689 N.E.2d 1181, 1185 (2d Dist. 1998) (*Terry* stop upheld where police had been told by two informants that cocaine was sold from a particular apartment, it was delivered there by a man in a black bra and red car, defendant was seen in front of the building several times in a red car wearing a black bra, the car was registered to defendant, defendant was known to police as involved in drug sales, and defendant attempted to drive away from the apartment when the raid began); People v. Ware, 264 Ill. App. 3d 650, 636 N.E.2d 1007, 1010 (1st Dist. 1994) (both *Terry* stop and frisk valid where defendant hurried from address to which police responded to a report of disturbance at, officer noticed bulge in defendant's pocket, and location was site of frequent weapons arrest); People v. Bynum, 257

a call to the police stating there was a "man with a gun" at a local tavern. When the police officer arrived at the tavern, he saw a man walking toward him. The man then reversed direction and headed toward the tavern's rear exit. The

---

Ill. App. 3d 502, 629 N.E.2d 724, 730 (1st Dist. 1994) (*Terry* stop valid where defendant, after seeing officer, discarded bag in flower garden and attempted to leave scene); People v. Chatmon, 236 Ill. App. 3d 913, 604 N.E.2d 399 (2d Dist. 1992) (officer justified in approaching stopped vehicle to determine why vehicle was parked where statute prohibited "stopping, standing or parking on any controlled-access highway except under certain circumstances"); People v. Taggart, 233 Ill. App. 3d 530, 599 N.E.2d 501 (2d Dist. 1992) (officer acted in response to a radio dispatch over police communication channels of a suspicious vehicle), *cert. denied,* 509 U.S. 945 (1993); People v. O'Brien, 227 Ill. App. 3d 302, 591 N.E.2d 469 (2d Dist. 1992) (*Terry* stop proper where defendant speeding); People v. Adams, 225 Ill. App. 3d 815, 587 N.E.2d 592 (4th Dist. 1992) (absence of license plates proper basis for *Terry* stop); People v. Smith, 224 Ill. App. 3d 511, 586 N.E.2d 785 (1st Dist. 1992) (*Terry* stop valid where defendant was known to officer to have been carrying weapon one month earlier and defendant changed direction and quickened pace after he made eye contact with officer); People v. Matlock, 223 Ill. App. 3d 498, 585 N.E.2d 238 (5th Dist. 1992) (*Terry* stop proper where defendant on private property bearing a posted no trespassing sign and officer knew owner, knew no one was at home, and knew residence had recently been burglarized and vandalized); People v. Morales, 221 Ill. App. 3d 13, 581 N.E.2d 730 (2d Dist. 1991) (*Terry* stop valid where officer saw defendant cupping hands and exchanging something with another man); People v. Freeman, 219 Ill. App. 3d 240, 579 N.E.2d 576 (3d Dist. 1991) (*Terry* stop proper based on defendant's clothing, direction of travel, time, and officer's knowledge of defendant's reputation); People v. Conard, 213 Ill. App. 3d 1068, 572 N.E.2d 1203 (3d Dist. 1991) (officer validly stopped defendant based on dispatch); People v. Erby, 213 Ill. App. 3d 657, 572 N.E.2d 345 (2d Dist. 1991) (officer had reasonable suspicion necessary to detain defendant while another officer checked out defendant's story); People v. Cardenas, 209 Ill. App. 3d 217, 568 N.E.2d 102 (1st Dist. 1991) (*Terry* stop valid where police knew of defendant's prior convictions, parole, description, and pattern); People v. Payton, 208 Ill. App. 3d 658, 567 N.E.2d 540 (1st Dist. 1991) (*Terry* stop valid where police saw defendant in early morning hours drive very slowly, stop, exit car, walk behind residence, resist officer's chase for 10-15 minutes; return to house 45 minutes later, jump in car and drive away); People v. Smith, 208 Ill. App. 3d 44, 566 N.E.2d 939 (5th Dist. 1991) (*Terry* stop valid where officer received "suspicious person" call in 1700 block and stopped defendant in 1400 block, defendant fit description, and time and place of stop close to scene of offense); People v. Dall, 207 Ill. App. 3d 508, 565 N.E.2d 1360 (4th Dist. 1991) (*Terry* stop valid where police observed defendant, after 2 a.m., carrying a duffle bag and running faster than a jog in burglary area). Other cases finding sufficient facts to support a *Terry* stop: People v. Starks, 190 Ill. App. 3d 503, 546 N.E.2d 71 (2d Dist. 1989), *cert. denied,* 498 U.S. 827 (1990); People v. DeHoyos, 172 Ill. App.

officer asked the bartender if the man had been involved in a fracas and the bartender answered affirmatively. On these facts, the Illinois Supreme Court found that a *Terry* stop was justified.

Stops have also been found improper in a variety of circumstances. A police stop of a man resembling the description of the perpetrator of an armed robbery that occurred twenty-four hours earlier and fourteen blocks away was found to be unreasonable.[150] Likewise, the fact that a man fit the general description of the perpetrator of a robbery that occurred three hours earlier and two and one-half miles away was found to be insufficient reason for a *Terry* stop.[151]

3d 1087, 527 N.E.2d 319 (1st Dist. 1988); People v. Dyer, 141 Ill. App. 3d 326, 490 N.E.2d 237 (5th Dist. 1986).

150. People v. Byrd, 47 Ill. App. 3d 804, 365 N.E.2d 443 (1st Dist. 1977). *See also* People v. Washington, 269 Ill. App. 3d 862, 646 N.E.2d 1268, 1272 (1st Dist. 1995) (description that robbery suspect was "male black wearing a blue coat and black hat" fleeing westbound was too vague and incomplete to justify *Terry* stop of a person who was wearing a "dark blue hat and a blue Chicago Bears starter jacket" who was not fleeing or acting suspiciously).

151. People v. Moorhead, 17 Ill. App. 3d 521, 308 N.E.2d 381 (1st Dist. 1974). *See also* People v. Moore, 286 Ill. App. 3d 649, 676 N.E.2d 700, 703–04 (3d Dist. 1997) (defendant talking to and possibly exchanging money with person inside of van parked outside of tavern known for gang and narcotic activities insufficient); People v. Rosemeier, 259 Ill. App. 3d 695, 631 N.E.2d 356, 358 (2d Dist. 1994) (car clocked at 45 m.p.h., where average speed of cars on road was 55–70 m.p.h., was not "reasonable, articulable cause" for believing defendant committing or about to commit traffic offense); People v. Harper, 237 Ill. App. 3d 202, 603 N.E.2d 115 (2d Dist. 1992) (observations of defendant entering and exiting an apartment building which was a "known dope house" did not constitute articulable suspicion that a crime had been committed and the ensuing *Terry* stop was improper); In re D.D.H., 221 Ill. App. 3d 150, 581 N.E.2d 849 (5th Dist. 1991) (*Terry* stop improper when based only on defendant walking up and down aisles of store and waving at officer); People v. Faletti, 215 Ill. App. 3d 61, 573 N.E.2d 867 (3d Dist. 1991) (automobile's single momentary crossing of center-line without more not sufficient for *Terry* stop); People v. Reusch, 209 Ill. App. 3d 991, 568 N.E.2d 941 (3d Dist. 1991) (no suspicion that driver unlicensed, automobile unregistered, or that vehicle or occupant violating the law); People v. Swisher, 207 Ill. App. 3d 125, 565 N.E.2d 281 (4th Dist. 1990) (car occupant's ducking down or making rapid movement and leaning forward in car insufficient); People v. Fox, 203 Ill. App. 3d 742, 561 N.E.2d 132 (5th Dist. 1990) (insufficient evidence for stop); People v. Hunt, 188 Ill. App. 3d 359, 544 N.E.2d 118 (3d Dist. 1989) (officer's knowledge of criminal activity in area is not per se sufficient to justify a stop); People v. McVey, 185 Ill. App. 3d 536, 541 N.E.2d 835 (3d Dist. 1989) (insufficient evidence to justify stop); People v. Jones, 181 Ill. App. 3d 576, 537 N.E.2d 395 (2d Dist. 1989) (same).

With *People v. Wardlow*,[152] the Illinois Supreme Court joined the majority of jurisdictions in holding that an individual's flight upon the approach of a police officer in a high-crime area alone is insufficient to justify a *Terry* stop. There must be an independently suspicious circumstance to create a reasonable suspicion of involvement in criminal activity.[153] In *Wardlow*, police were "caravanning" in a high-crime area with the purpose of investigating narcotics sales.[154] The defendant did not appear to be breaking any laws, but fled after looking in the direction of the officers. The officer testified that he turned his vehicle around and watched the defendant run through a gangway and then through an alley, carrying a white opaque bag under his arm. Police cornered him coming out of the alley and, without asking any questions or identifying himself, one of the officers conducted a protective pat-down search. He then squeezed the bag and discovered a gun.[155] The court held that the officer was acting upon a mere hunch, and that he did not have a reasonable articulable suspicion that someone had committed or was about to commit a crime.[156] When police act upon hunches, the risk of arbitrary and abusive police practices exceeds tolerable limits.[157]

In a recent Illinois appellate decision, the court held that a police officer who saw the defendant turn away from him and then "furtively" place something in his mouth did not have probable cause to make a warrantless arrest, but stated that the officer may have had reasonable articulable suspicion for a *Terry* stop.[158]

A *Terry* stop can be supported by an anonymous tip corroborated by other evidence.[159]

---

152. 183 Ill. 2d 306, 701 N.E.2d 484 (1998), *cert. granted*, 119 S. Ct. 1573 (1999).

153. *Id.*, 701 N.E.2d at 489.

154. *Id.*, 701 N.E.2d at 484.

155. *Id.*

156. *Id.*, 701 N.E.2d at 489.

157. *Id.*, *citing* Brown v. Texas, 443 U.S. 47, 52 (1979).

158. People v. Rainey, 302 Ill. App. 3d 1011, 706 N.E.2d 1062, 1065 (3d Dist. 1999) (the court found that the actions of the defendant in this case were stronger justification for governmental intrusion than those of the defendant in *Wardlow*, but they did not support probable cause).

159. Alabama v. White, 496 U.S. 325 (1990) (*Terry* stop justified because totality of circumstances, coupled with independent corroboration of significant aspects of anonymous tip, provided sufficient indicia of reliability. Police received anonymous tip that woman would be leaving particular apartment building at specified time and that she would drive brown Plymouth station wagon to Dobey's Motel; anonymous caller further advised police that she would be carrying about an ounce of cocaine in a brown attache; by surveilling the apartment building and following her, police were able to corroborate facts: she left the building, she got

In *People v. Branch*[160] the defendant was driving an automobile, owned by another individual, that had a license-applied-for sticker in the rear window. There were two passengers. The defendant was stopped because an officer could not read the sticker. However, as the officer approached the car he was able to read it, yet, he proceeded to the window and asked the defendant for identification and registration. The officer advised the two passengers that they were required by law to wear their seat belts. He then asked each of them for identification. After deciding to give warnings for failure to wear seat belts and improper display of the sticker, the officer returned to his car and ran a computer warrant check on each identification. The officer learned that one of the occupants had an outstanding warrant and then arrested him. The officer then informed the other two that he was going to search the car incident to arrest. The passenger whom the defendant had identified as the owner (but he was not) told the officer he could search the entire car. When the officer entered the car he smelled marijuana and located marijuana in it. He then arrested the defendant and the other passenger. On searching the defendant, he found a gun.[161]

The trial judge suppressed the evidence finding an unlawful seizure. The judge reasoned that the officer required the defendant to wait while he ran a computer check but the officer had no reason to detain the defendant because he had given him a facially valid license.[162] The supreme court disagreed.

---

into brown Plymouth, these events occurred within time frame predicted by caller, and finally, even though the police stopped her before she reached the hotel, she took the most direct route possible to the hotel. Court believed that because caller was able to predict defendant's future behavior so well and so much of tip was verified, there was sufficient indicia of reliability to justify stop); People v. Brodack, 296 Ill. App. 3d 71, 693 N.E.2d 1291, 1295 (2d Dist. 1998) (*Terry* stop of DUI defendant upheld where police received tip that car was "all over the road" and police observed defendant's vehicle which matched the description in general location, coupled with fact defendant failed to pull to side when lights and sirens activated). *Compare* People v. Pantoja, 184 Ill. App. 3d 671, 540 N.E.2d 892 (2d Dist. 1989) (*Terry* stop invalid; no corroboration of anonymous tip) *and* People v. Moraca, 124 Ill. App. 3d 561, 464 N.E.2d 312 (2d Dist. 1984) (*Terry* stop invalid; no corroboration of anonymous tip) *with* In re J.J., 183 Ill. App. 3d 381, 539 N.E.2d 764 (2d Dist. 1989) (in person citizen complaint not as vigorously scrutinized as anonymous tip; *Terry* stop proper). *But see* People v. Ertl, 292 Ill. App. 3d 863, 686 N.E.2d 738, 745–47 (2d Dist. 1997) (phone call to police from defendant's wife stating he was in her driveway and she knew he owned a gun but did not know if he had it with him held insufficient to justify *Terry* stop; not a reliable tip since based on prior experience rather than direct observation of current criminal conduct).

160. 295 Ill. App. 3d 110, 692 N.E.2d 398 (2d Dist. 1998).

161. *Id.*, 692 N.E.2d at 400.

162. *Id.*

Although noting several recent cases have so concluded, it reasoned that a long line of cases allow an officer to run a quick warrant check of the driver when presented with a facially valid identification.[163] It concluded that this reasoning was more sound and that it was unwise to adopt a per se rule forbidding an officer from running a warrant check even when presented with a facially valid license.[164] Nonetheless, the court held that it was improper to run a check on the backseat passenger because the officer had no reason to suspect that that person was involved in any criminal activity. Accordingly, it affirmed the suppression based on this latter violation.[165]

In *City of Chicago v. Morales*,[166] the Illinois Supreme Court held that the Chicago Gang Congregation (gang loitering) ordinance was unconstitutional, finding that it violated due process because it was impermissibly vague on its face and arbitrarily restricted personal liberties.[167] As to vagueness, the court noted that an ordinance is vague when it fails to delineate any specific standard of conduct. The ordinance must be sufficiently definite so that reasonable persons know whether the conduct they are engaging in is lawful or not. The ordinance must also define the offense so as not to encourage arbitrary and discriminatory enforcement. Adequate notice of the proscribed conduct is necessary so that due process requirements are met. In other words, ordinary persons will not be required to guess at the law's meaning. The court noted that it has repeatedly held that broadly worded statutes prohibiting loitering without any additional unlawful conduct are unconstitutional.[168] However, a court may uphold the ordinance if it combines a second act to form prohibited conduct.[169]

The gang loitering ordinance was not sufficiently definite so that the ordinary person would know what conduct was unlawful. Instead, it criminalized acts of loitering in public places without distinguishing between innocent conduct and conduct that causes harm. The meaning of the term *loitering* itself was not sufficient to inform the average citizen of any criminal implications. Even the definition of loitering in the ordinance was not helpful because people with legitimate and lawful purposes may not always be able to make their purpose apparent to an officer stopping them.[170] The court rejected the State's argument that an additional element was present based on either (1) loitering with a gang

---

163. *Id.*, 692 N.E.2d at 401.

164. *Id.*

165. *Id.*, 692 N.E.2d at 402.

166. 177 Ill. 2d 440, 687 N.E.2d 53 (1997), *aff'd*, 119 S. Ct. 1849 (1999).

167. *Id.*, 687 N.E.2d at 59.

168. *Id.*, 687 N.E.2d at 60.

169. *Id.*, 687 N.E.2d at 61.

170. *Id.*

member was required or (2) failure to obey a police order to disperse was required. With regard to the first argument, the court stated that the ordinance does not prohibit the act of loitering with a gang member but instead requires only that an officer reasonably believe that one person in a group is a gang member.[171] Reasonable belief is insufficient to support a criminal conviction. Moreover, this element itself is vague. An individual standing on a corner with a group of people has no way of knowing whether an approaching officer believes that one of the group is a gang member.[172] With regard to the second element, this was also insufficient; it is essentially the same situation held unconstitutional in the case of *Shuttlesworth v. City of Birmingham*.[173] The mere addition of this element failed to provide adequate notice of any particular proscribed conduct.[174]

With regard to arbitrary enforcement, the court found that there was absolute discretion given to individual officers to decide whether any given person was loitering. Moreover, the police were given complete discretion to determine whether any member of the group was a gang member.[175] Although the Chicago Police Department issued guidelines for enforcement of the ordinance and standards and guidelines for establishing probable cause for determining when an individual is a gang member, the guidelines too failed to save the ordinance. The guidelines did nothing to cure the lack of definition of the term *loitering*. Additionally, the record demonstrated that the police did not follow the guidelines in a uniform manner.[176]

The court further found that the ordinance also violated substantive due process because it was an arbitrary exercise of the city's police power. Numerous protected rights were impermissibly infringed upon, including the right to travel, the right to locomotion, the right to freedom of movement, and the right to associate with others.[177]

A separate, although related, issue is whether the police are justified in searching a person properly stopped for questioning under *Terry*. It is clear that the mere fact that a person has been properly stopped pursuant to *Terry* is not a per se justification for a search. Rather, the Illinois Code of Criminal Procedure permits an officer to search the person for weapons only if he or she

---

171. *Id.*, 687 N.E.2d at 62.

172. *Id.*

173. 382 U.S. 87, 90 (1965) (holding that broadly worded statute prohibiting loitering without additional unlawful conduct unconstitutional).

174. *Morales*, 177 Ill. 2d 440, 687 N.E.2d at 62.

175. *Id.*, 687 N.E.2d at 63.

176. *Id.*, 687 N.E.2d at 64.

177. *Id.*, 687 N.E.2d at 65.

"reasonably suspects that he or another is in danger of attack."[178] Again, the officer's belief is not judged by the probable cause test; the officer's belief that he or she or another is in danger need only be reasonable.[179]

People v. Lawson[180] exemplifies that the decisions to stop and to search are severable. In this case the court held that the police had reason to effect a *Terry* stop on the defendant because there was a reasonable suspicion of criminal conduct. However, the court suppressed the fruits of the search because it found no basis for determining that the defendant was armed and dangerous.[181] In *People v. Rivera*,[182] the appellate court held that the mere fact that a police

---

178. 725 ILCS 5/108-1.01. *See* People v. Smith, 224 Ill. App. 3d 511, 586 N.E.2d 785 (1st Dist. 1992) (pat-down reasonable where defendant had belt around neck which extended down underneath sweatshirt and was known by police to have been carrying weapon previous month); People v. Morales, 221 Ill. App. 3d 13, 581 N.E.2d 730 (2d Dist. 1991) (bulge in stopped suspect's clothing justified frisk); People v. Freeman, 219 Ill. App. 3d 240, 579 N.E.2d 576 (3d Dist. 1991) (pat-down of defendant known by officer to have reputation for carrying guns was justified); People v. Mathis, 211 Ill. App. 3d 678, 570 N.E.2d 634 (1st Dist. 1991) (pat-down reasonable where officers responded to call that violent crime was occurring and observed suspect running from building); People v. Dall, 207 Ill. App. 3d 508, 565 N.E.2d 1360 (4th Dist. 1991) (consent to search during *Terry* stop justified search of duffle bag). *But see* People v. Galvin, 127 Ill. 2d 153, 535 N.E.2d 837 (1989) (evidence insufficient to justify pat-down); People v. Rivera, 272 Ill. App. 3d 502, 650 N.E.2d 1084 (1st Dist. 1995) (*Terry* stop justified on minimal articulable suspicion; however, *Terry* requires more than generalized belief that drug dealers may carry weapons to justify frisk; thus, making defendant unzip his jacket violated *Terry* and also constituted an impermissible search); People v. Kramer, 208 Ill. App. 3d 818, 566 N.E.2d 756 (3d Dist. 1991) (pat-down search of vehicle's occupants after police checked identifications and found them satisfactory was not justified); People v. Brown, 190 Ill. App. 3d 511, 546 N.E.2d 95 (2d Dist. 1989) (defendant's conduct in moving hand from dashboard to floor following lawful *Terry* stop not sufficient to justify pat-down); People v. Morgan, 138 Ill. App. 3d 99, 484 N.E.2d 1292 (4th Dist. 1985) (officer had no reasonable belief that defendant would attack him after defendant was told he could leave area, therefore subsequent search of defendant was invalid).

179. People v. Smithers, 83 Ill. 2d 430, 415 N.E.2d 327 (1980).

180. 61 Ill. App. 3d 133, 377 N.E.2d 1280 (1st Dist. 1978).

181. *See also* People v. Smithers, 83 Ill. 2d 430, 415 N.E.2d 327 (1980) (reasonable basis for pat-down search where bartender identified patron who had been involved in bar fight during which gun was spotted); People v. Cleaves, 169 Ill. App. 3d 252, 523 N.E.2d 720 (5th Dist. 1988) (searches need not be limited to pat downs, and officer may look under clothing if that is necessary to discover weapons); People v. Watson, 145 Ill. App. 3d 492, 495 N.E.2d 1153 (1st Dist. 1986) (officer did not have reasonable basis to justify pat-down search).

182. 272 Ill. App. 3d 502, 650 N.E.2d 1084 (1st Dist. 1995).

officer believes "narcotic arrests often or sometimes or always involve weapons" is insufficient, alone, to support reasonable suspicion necessary to justify a *Terry* frisk.[183]

Even if the stop is justified under *Terry*, evidence will be suppressed when the search exceeds the proper scope of a *Terry* search.[184] Moreover, even if the *Terry* pat-down is proper, this does not mean the officer can remove any object he or she feels.[185] To justify the conduct of the police officer in removing an item, he or she must both subjectively believe the item is a weapon *and* that belief must be reasonable based upon articulable reasons.[186]

In *People v. Flowers*,[187] the Illinois Supreme Court held the frisk of the defendant following a *Terry* stop resulting in discovery of a pipe and cocaine unreasonable. The court noted that the sole justification for a *Terry* search was to protect police and others in the vicinity. The scope of the frisk is limited to a search for weapons.[188] In this case, there were no facts to support a reasonable suspicion that defendant was armed and dangerous. The officer himself testified that he had no reason to suspect defendant was armed. When the police initially investigated the anonymously called-in burglary, all of the houses in the area were found secure and the defendant was not seen until fifteen minutes later. At that time, there was no evidence that he attempted to avoid the police or that

---

183. *Id.*, 650 N.E.2d at 1090.

184. *See, e.g.,* People v. Cox, 295 Ill. App. 3d 666, 693 N.E.2d 483, 487 (4th Dist. 1998) (frisk illegal after lawful stop where police told defendant they were going to search him for a stolen wallet and then he attempted to discard cocaine he had in his pocket, where no evidence police inquired of defendant whether he was involved in robbery or whether he was armed); People v. Harper, 237 Ill. App. 3d 202, 603 N.E.2d 115 (2d Dist. 1992) (search of interior of defendant's mouth exceeded the permissible scope of a proper *Terry* search).

185. People v. Rickey, 206 Ill. App. 3d 302, 564 N.E.2d 256, 261 (4th Dist. 1990).

186. People v. Pence, 225 Ill. App. 3d 1061, 588 N.E.2d 1245 (3d Dist. 1992) (pat-down unjustified where defendant was calm and cooperative and officer did not feel defendant was dangerous); People v. Morales, 221 Ill. App. 3d 13, 581 N.E.2d 730 (2d Dist. 1991) (during pat-down when officer discovered squeezable bulge, search may not proceed under *Terry*); People v. Creagh, 214 Ill. App. 3d 744, 574 N.E.2d 96 (1st Dist. 1991) (pat-down search not justified where bulge in defendant's pants was soft and did not resemble gun); People v. Conard, 213 Ill. App. 3d 1068, 572 N.E.2d 1203 (3d Dist. 1991) (pat-down not justified where officers outnumbered defendant who offered little resistance and coin purse in coat lining could not have reasonably been a weapon); In Interest of F.R., 209 Ill. App. 3d 274, 568 N.E.2d 133 (1st Dist. 1991) (pat-down unjustified since officer did not have suspicion of danger of attack and no reasonable ground to suspect soft crumpled up potato chip bag contained weapon).

187. 179 Ill. 2d 257, 688 N.E.2d 626 (1997).

188. *Id.*, 688 N.E.2d at 629–30.

he engaged in any suspicious behavior. Contrarily, he completely cooperated with the police and gave them a plausible explanation for being in the area. He further gave consent to the police to search his bag after he truthfully told them there were only clothes in it. Defendant even showed the police the contents of his pockets.[189]

The court found it problematic that the officer stated he routinely frisked individuals he stopped for investigative questioning: frisk was automatic. The court emphatically stated that this was not proper. *Terry* is a narrow scope exception to the probable cause rule that is designed to strike a balance between protecting police and society and an individual's right to be free from unreasonable searches and seizures. *Terry* does not permit an officer to engage in the practice of routine frisks without any thought whatsoever as to whether the individual is armed.[190]

Further elaborating on what a police officer may seize during a *Terry* pat-down, the United States Supreme Court in *Minnesota v. Dickerson*[191] held that any contraband detected through the sense of touch which is "immediately apparent" to the officer as contraband may be admitted. The Court made this finding analogizing it to a plain view seizure during a legal search. Since the officer is feeling the contraband during a lawful *Terry* search, the Court concluded that there is no invasion of the suspect's expectation of privacy and thus, a warrantless seizure of contraband discovered through the sense of touch is constitutional.[192]

Illinois adopted *Dickerson* in *People v. Mitchell*.[193] The Illinois Supreme Court first rejected defendant's contention that the Illinois Constitution provides more expansive protection than the federal constitution finding that section 6 of Article I is interpreted the same as the federal search and seizure provision. It relied on *People v. Tisler*.[194] The court further rejected defendant's argument that a search and seizure incorporates the right to privacy clause and held that that clause does not cover the conduct at issue.[195] Ultimately, the court

---

189. *Id.*, 688 N.E.2d at 630.

190. *Id.*, 688 N.E.2d at 631.

191. 508 U.S. 366 (1993).

192. *Id.* at 373–77; People v. Blake, 268 Ill. App. 3d 737, 645 N.E.2d 580, 582–83 (2d Dist. 1995) (merely appearing nervous at officer's approach insufficient suspicion to justify frisk which went beyond what was necessary to determine if object was weapon, and police gave no explanation of how tightly rolled mass could distinctively feel like marijuana as opposed to other legitimate substances).

193. 165 Ill. 2d 211, 650 N.E.2d 1014 (1995).

194. 103 Ill. 2d 226, 469 N.E.2d 147 (1984). *See Mitchell*, 165 Ill. 2d 211, 650 N.E.2d at 1018.

195. *Mitchell*, 165 Ill. 2d 211, 650 N.E.2d at 1019.

held that the plain touch doctrine does not violate the Illinois Constitution's section 6 guarantee.[196] The court further noted that the plain touch doctrine is not new but in fact derives from the plain view doctrine which has been embodied in Illinois law since 1943.[197]

The court also held that there is no inadvertency requirement for plain touch purposes.[198] However, it did state that an "officer's belief [that an object is contraband] must be objectively reasonable, in light of his past experience and training, and capable of verification."[199] The object though, must be readily identifiable by touch as contraband.[200] In this case, the court found both the stop and seizure were justified because the police observed crack pipes and scouring pads in the front seat of defendant's car, thus, the police had probable cause to believe that what he felt, a piece of rock inside a small baggy in defendant's shirt pocket, was rock cocaine.[201]

Once the police have effected a valid *Terry* stop and have conducted a search for weapons, if justified, their options are limited. If they have discovered evidence that would establish probable cause, then they may make an arrest.[202] Under certain limited circumstances, it might be proper to transport a person stopped pursuant to *Terry* to a location several miles away for an identification "show-up."[203] However, if no probable cause is established, the individual must

---

196. *Id.*, 650 N.E.2d at 1020.

197. *Id.*

198. *Id.*, 650 N.E.2d at 1022.

199. *Id.*

200. *Id.*

201. *Id.*, 650 N.E.2d at 1025.

202. People v. Henderson, 266 Ill. App. 3d 882, 640 N.E.2d 1344, 1347 (1st Dist. 1994) (investigative *Terry* stop of car matching description of vehicle used in armed robbery ripened into probable cause to arrest where officer observed trunk lid punched, steering column peeled, and defendant stated he was owner but a registration check showed he was not); People v. Jones, 214 Ill. App. 3d 256, 574 N.E.2d 772 (2d Dist 1991) (officer had probable cause to search envelope that fell from defendant's wallet during *Terry* stop based on defendant's attempts to cover envelope with shoe); People v. Erby, 213 Ill. App. 3d 657, 572 N.E.2d 345 (2d Dist. 1991) (officer had probable cause to arrest defendant after learning person meeting defendant's description had purchased items from store with credit card in different name than defendant gave officers); People v. Cardenas, 209 Ill. App. 3d 217, 568 N.E.2d 102 (1st Dist. 1991) (probable cause to arrest established after officers discovered evidence in plain view during *Terry* stop).

203. United States v. Sharpe, 470 U.S. 675 (1985) (20-minute delay did not turn *Terry* stop into arrest); People v. Lippert, 89 Ill. 2d 171, 432 N.E.2d 605 (1982) (transporting defendant two or three miles in sparsely populated rural area does not contravene statute's provision that questioning must be in the vicinity; several

be released. Specifically, only probable cause sufficient for arrest—and not the reasonable suspicion sufficient for a *Terry* stop—can justify seizing a person and transporting him or her to a police station for custodial interrogation.[204]

---

minutes required for transportation does not violate reasonable period of time provision); People v. Smith, 208 Ill. App. 3d 44, 466 N.E.2d 939 (5th Dist. 1991) (extension of *Terry* questioning proper upon enigmatic answers); People v. Bujdud, 177 Ill. App. 3d 396, 532 N.E.2d 370 (1st Dist. 1988) (while officer's display of weapons is factor in determining whether stop is investigatory or custodial, presence of weapons alone will not convert *Terry* stop into arrest); People v. Rodriquez, 153 Ill. App. 3d 652, 505 N.E.2d 1314, 1318 (2d Dist. 1987) ("Movement of a suspect in the general vicinity of the stop is permissible without converting what would otherwise be a temporary seizure into an arrest."); People v. Runnion, 150 Ill. App. 3d 879, 502 N.E.2d 439 (2d Dist. 1986) (*Terry* stop did not become arrest when officer held defendant for 10 minutes while another officer searched area for evidence of crime); People v. Jackson, 145 Ill. App. 3d 789, 495 N.E.2d 1359 (3d Dist. 1986) (fact that officer had weapon drawn does not convert *Terry* stop to arrest where officer had information that suspect might be armed); People v. Dyer, 141 Ill. App. 3d 326, 490 N.E.2d 237 (5th Dist. 1986) (20-minute to one-hour detention did not convert *Terry* stop to arrest). *But see* People v. Hardy, 142 Ill. App. 3d 108, 491 N.E.2d 493 (4th Dist. 1986) (police officer's retention of suspect's driver's license and request that suspect follow him to police station converted *Terry* stop into arrest).

204. Dunaway v. New York, 442 U.S. 200 (1979); People v. Townes, 91 Ill. 2d 32, 435 N.E.2d 103, *cert. denied,* 459 U.S. 878 (1982); People v. Sturdivant, 99 Ill. App. 3d 370, 425 N.E.2d 1046 (1st Dist. 1981). *See also* People v. Anaya, 279 Ill. App. 3d 940, 665 N.E.2d 525, 530–31 (1st Dist. 1996) (although initial encounter was consensual, once defendant refused to give consent to the search of her luggage, police violated the Fourth Amendment when they nonetheless proceeded to search her luggage without "reasonable and articulable suspicion"); People v. Mitchell, 228 Ill. App. 3d 167, 592 N.E.2d 175 (1st Dist. 1992) (defendant did not consent to remain in locked interrogation room with over 30 hours of intermittent interrogation); People v. Halmon, 225 Ill. App. 3d 259, 587 N.E.2d 1182 (1st Dist. 1992) (same as *Mitchell*); People v. Walls, 220 Ill. App. 3d 564, 581 N.E.2d 264 (1st Dist. 1991) (defendant who was lawfully brought to police station for questioning was detained without probable cause when kept overnight and questioned again several times in the morning); People v. Gordon, 198 Ill. App. 3d 791, 556 N.E.2d 573 (1st Dist. 1990) (defendant's detention at station illegal seizure because not told under arrest, not permitted to make phone call and not allowed to communicate with anyone); People v. Berrios, 178 Ill. App. 3d 241, 533 N.E.2d 64 (1st Dist. 1988) (no probable cause to hold defendant at police station); People v. Rodriquez, 153 Ill. App. 3d 652, 505 N.E.2d 1314 (2d Dist. 1987) (stop is converted to arrest when reasonable person would conclude that he or she was not free to leave scene; acts of handcuffing a suspect, reading him his *Miranda* warnings, and placing him in back of squad car were sufficient to convert a stop to an arrest). *But see* People v. Bell, 233 Ill. App. 3d

The extent of a *Terry* stop is flexible, however, depending on the circumstances of the case. In *People v. Paskin*,[205] a lone officer stopped two burglary suspects in a rural area.[206] While waiting approximately four minutes for backups, the officer drew his gun and ordered the defendants to approach him and to lie face down in the road.[207] The appellate court held that the officer's actions did not constitute an arrest given the brief detention, the officer's need to protect himself and to quickly investigate his suspicions, and the fact that the defendants were not taken to another location.[208]

40, 598 N.E.2d 256 (2d Dist. 1992) (defendant not under arrest when accompanied officers to station for questioning); People v. Perez, 225 Ill. App. 3d 54, 587 N.E.2d 501 (1st Dist. 1992) (defendant remained at station because he was cooperating as informant and was free to leave at any time); People v. Woodson, 220 Ill. App. 3d 865, 581 N.E.2d 320 (1st Dist. 1991) (no probable cause but no illegal detention for 12 hours where defendant initiated and voluntarily accompanied officers to station, allowed phone calls, and visited sister), *cert. denied,* 505 U.S. 1208 (1992); People v. Bulman, 212 Ill. App. 3d 795, 571 N.E.2d 850 (1st Dist. 1991) (defendant who had been involved in serious car accident voluntarily answered home's front door and voluntarily agreed to go to police station to fill out accident report); People v. Paskins, 154 Ill. App. 3d 417, 506 N.E.2d 1037 (3d Dist.) (ordering suspects to lie facedown on roadside with officer's gun drawn did not convert investigatory stop into formal arrest), *cert. denied,* 484 U.S. 868 (1987); People v. Staten, 143 Ill. App. 3d 1039, 493 N.E.2d 1157 (2d Dist. 1986) (detention of defendant in squad car was permissible under *Terry* where officer reasonably believed that crime had been committed); People v. Vena, 122 Ill. App. 3d 154, 460 N.E.2d 886 (2d Dist. 1984) (placing handcuffed defendant in squad car did not constitute arrest because (1) there was no intrusive purpose on part of police, (2) defendant's freedom was completely restrained whether he was inside or outside squad car, (3) no effort was made to impose intrusive investigation on defendant, and (4) no public stigma attached to defendant as result of being placed in squad car).

205. 154 Ill. App. 3d 417, 506 N.E.2d 1037 (3d Dist. 1987).

206. *Id.,* 506 N.E.2d at 1040.

207. *Id.,* 506 N.E.2d at 1038.

208. *Id.,* 506 N.E.2d at 1041. *See also* People v. Ross, 289 Ill. App. 3d 1013, 682 N.E.2d 87, 90 (1st Dist. 1997) (production of firearms owner identification card created independent basis to continue and expand initial *Terry* stop of defendant, thus it was proper for police to ask defendant whether there was a gun in the car after being provided with identification card); People v. Easley, 288 Ill. App. 3d 487, 680 N.E.2d 776, 780, 783 (3d Dist. 1997) (police justified in detaining defendants for an additional two minutes until canine unit arrived, where at time defendant presented identification police observed a business card decorated with marijuana leaves, defendant was perspiring and nervous, a computer check showed defendant had a prior drug conviction, police observed ashtray closed upon return to car where previously open, and defendants told police they were

In contrast to *Paskins,* in *People v. Rodriquez,*[209] giving a defendant his *Miranda* warnings, handcuffing him, and placing him in a squad car was held to constitute an arrest. The *Rodriquez* court conceded, however, that handcuffing a defendant and putting him in a squad car is not indicative per se of an arrest.[210]

Note that the *Terry* principle has also been extended to apply to the detention of objects; thus, articulable suspicion can justify the brief detention of luggage for the purpose of allowing a dog to sniff it for drugs.[211]

In *People v. Shapiro,*[212] defendants were charged with possession of a controlled substance with intent to deliver after a heavy, brown paper wrapped package was delivered to their house pursuant to a controlled delivery. The package was addressed to one of the defendants. En route from Oregon, the suspicious package was stopped at O'Hare Airport because it matched three of the United States Post Office's drug package profile criteria. Pursuant to Post Office policies, the package was shipped to St. Louis for inspection. Once it arrived in St. Louis, it was positively sniffed by dogs for controlled substances. A search warrant was obtained based on this, and the package was searched. A controlled delivery was set up thereafter and an anticipatory search warrant obtained. The package was successfully delivered before the police executed the warrant. Shapiro moved to suppress the evidence, which the trial judge granted, finding that the police lacked probable cause to detain and investigate

---

traveling to a festival to advocate legalization of hemp; the dissent argued that the officer lacked probable cause to detain defendants after he had issued a verbal warning, checked the driver's license, and run a warrant check; the fact that defendant possessed a business card with a marijuana leaf on it and that they were going to a festival were lawful activities protected by the First Amendment and amounted only to mere suspicion).

209. 153 Ill. App. 3d 652, 505 N.E.2d 1314, 1319 (2d Dist. 1987).

210. *Id.*

211. United States v. Place, 462 U.S. 696 (1983); People v. Evans, 296 Ill. App. 3d 1, 689 N.E.2d 142, 149 (1st Dist. 1997) (detention of defendant's luggage proper where he arrived on flight often used in drug trafficking, acted nervous, gave conflicting answers to law enforcement questions, said luggage was his but did not know combination or how he was going to open it); People v. Guenther, 225 Ill. App. 3d 574, 588 N.E.2d 346 (2d Dist. 1992) (*Place* rationale extended to allow canine sniff in a private home where officers had probable cause to believe contraband present); People v. Boyd, 215 Ill. App. 3d 894, 576 N.E.2d 116 (1st Dist. 1991) (evidence sufficient to justify detention of luggage for a canine sniff test); People v. Statham, 209 Ill. App. 3d 352, 568 N.E.2d 183 (1st Dist. 1991) (same). *But see* People v. Sherman, 190 Ill. App. 3d 814, 547 N.E.2d 476 (1st Dist. 1989) (evidence insufficient to satisfy detention of luggage); People v. Nelson, 188 Ill. App. 3d 619, 544 N.E.2d 1111 (1st Dist. 1989) (same).

212. 177 Ill. 2d 519, 687 N.E.2d 65 (1997).

the package. The appellate court affirmed, albeit on different grounds. It concluded that while the initial detention was proper, the nature and extent of the detention and investigation that led to probable cause was unreasonable. The supreme court affirmed, stating that resolution of the case hinged on the constitutionality of the original decision to detain the package and the reasonableness of its detention and investigation.

With regard to the detention, the court stated that simply because something is deposited in the mail system does not mean there are no Fourth Amendment protections. In fact, "effects deposited with the United States mail enjoy the same search and seizure protections as if they were located within a private residence."[213] However, it does not mean that packages can never be investigated as long as reasonable suspicion of a criminal activity exists and the nature and duration of the detention is not unreasonable.[214] The Post Office, based on its experience, had developed a six characteristic drug package profile. In this case, based on the brown wrapping, the heavy tape, and the fact that the package was hand-addressed from one individual to another, the Post Office had reasonable suspicion to detain the package. These factors were sufficient to give rise to a reasonable articulable suspicion that the package contained narcotics, warranting a minimally intrusive detention and investigation.[215]

With regard to the nature and extent of the detention, the court concluded that it was more than minimally intrusive and, therefore, was unreasonable. The government did not expeditiously conduct an investigation when it detained the package. In fact there was no investigation at all at the time of detention. Instead, the package was shipped to St. Louis. The court pointed out that O'Hare Airport is located in Chicago and that there was sufficient opportunity, if not ample, to have the package investigated there. Accordingly, there was no investigatory diligence exhibited by the Post Office and the detention of the package was unreasonable.[216]

§ 1.07 — Roadblocks

Roadblocks have been utilized by law enforcement in different situations, either as emergency measures to find or stop a fleeing suspect,[217] or in planned nonemergency situations to investigate all motorists for a particular viola-

---

213. *Id.*, 687 N.E.2d at 69.

214. *Id.*

215. *Id.*, 687 N.E.2d at 70.

216. *Id.*, 687 N.E.2d at 71.

217. Brower v. County of Inyo, 489 U.S. 593 (1989) (driver of stolen car was killed when he crashed into police roadblock that had been set up to stop him).

tion.[218] The United States Supreme Court has held a Fourth Amendment seizure occurs when a vehicle is stopped at either type of roadblock.[219] With the planned checkpoint roadblock, motorists may be seized without probable cause or individualized articulable suspicion.[220] The courts use a three-part balancing test to determine the constitutionality of such seizures, balancing the state's interest, the extent to which the interest is advanced, and the degree of intrusion upon the individual motorist.[221]

One such roadblock that has frequently passed the three-part test is the checkpoint set up to deter drunk drivers.[222] The states have an important interest in eradicating the drunk driving problem.[223] The intrusion involved in stopping cars is minimal considering the short duration and lack of psychological intensity of the encounter.[224] In *People v. Bartley,*[225] the Illinois Supreme Court emphasized the need to prevent "roving patrols" by circumscribing the police officers' discretion. Checkpoints selected pursuant to specific departmental guidelines that involve the stopping of every vehicle for a very short period of time are constitutional.[226]

In *People v. Scott,*[227] the Illinois Appellate Court held that a roadblock that gave police officers the unbridled discretion to determine which motorists would be directed to proceed through the checkpoint was unreasonable, and therefore the defendant's conviction for driving under the influence was re-

---

218. Michigan v. Sitz, 496 U.S. 444, 450–52 (1990) (DWI checkpoints set up along state roads held constitutional); United States v. Martinez-Fuerte, 428 U.S. 543 (1976) (permanent highway checkpoint for illegal aliens near Mexican border found proper); People v. Bartley, 109 Ill. 2d 273, 486 N.E.2d 880, 886–89 (1985) (DWI checkpoint constitutional seizure due to compelling state reason and minimal intrusion). *But see* Delaware v. Prouse, 440 U.S. 648 (1979) (random stops made in an effort to apprehend unlicensed and unsafe vehicles disapproved because no evidence stops would be effective and they were too discretionary).

219. *Brower,* 489 U.S. at 599; *Martinez-Fuerte,* 428 U.S. at 556.

220. *Brower,* 489 U.S. at 599; *Martinez-Fuerte,* 428 U.S. at 556.

221. Brown v. Texas, 443 U.S. 47, 50–51 (1979).

222. *Sitz,* 496 U.S. at 455; *Bartley,* 109 Ill. 2d 273, 486 N.E.2d at 888–89.

223. *Sitz,* 496 U.S. at 455; *Bartley,* 109 Ill. 2d 273, 486 N.E.2d at 888–89.

224. *Sitz,* 496 U.S. at 452.

225. *Bartley,* 109 Ill. 2d 273, 486 N.E.2d at 880.

226. *Sitz,* 496 U.S. at 453. *See also* United States v. Trevino, 60 F.3d 333, 337–38 (7th Cir. 1995) (checkpoint to detect possible safety and traffic violations not unreasonable even though no warning signs posted where police were in uniforms, official vehicles were parked in sight of approaching motorists, checkpoint was administered in accordance with department guidelines, and every approaching vehicle was stopped), *cert. denied,* 516 U.S. 1061 (1996).

227. 277 Ill. App. 3d 579, 660 N.E.2d 555 (3d Dist. 1996).

versed.[228] In this case, police set up a roadblock on Main Street, stopping every third vehicle. An officer was stationed at Garfield Street, a street just before the roadblock, to prevent individuals from evading the roadblock. Although the officer was required to allow residents of Garfield to proceed up that street, there was no standard for how the officer was to make this determination.[229] The defendant, who lived on Garfield, attempted to turn onto that street. The officer stopped him and, without asking for identification, ordered him through the roadblock.[230] The defendant went through it and failed a sobriety test. On appeal, he contended the stop of his vehicle was improper.[231] The court agreed, finding that the officer stationed at Garfield had the sole discretion to determine who would proceed through the roadblock.[232] The procedure allowed the officer to randomly, and without restriction, decide who would be allowed to traverse Garfield and avoid the roadblock.[233] Because the defendant was a resident of Garfield, he should not have been forced through the roadblock.

The state argued that the officer could reasonably have believed the defendant was attempting to evade the roadblock because he turned just before it. The court rejected this argument, relying on *Murphy v. Commonwealth*,[234] in which the Virginia court stated: "[u]nder the government's view, every citizen who turned onto a road within sight of a checkpoint, for whatever legitimate reason, would be subject to an investigative detention. This result we cannot sanction."[235] In this case, the defendant turned prior to the roadblock; he lived on Garfield and was on his way home. The police did not have a reasonable suspicion that he was attempting to evade the roadblock simply because he turned onto Garfield prior to the roadblock.[236]

The United States Supreme Court has also upheld a permanent checkpoint for detecting illegal aliens near the Mexican border.[237] Other checkpoints, however, including a checkpoint to apprehend unlicensed vehicles, and a checkpoint to determine compliance with a city's vehicle sticker requirement,

---

228. *Id.*, 660 N.E.2d at 557.

229. *Id.*

230. *Id.*

231. *Id.*, 660 N.E.2d at 558.

232. *Id.*

233. *Id.*, 660 N.E.2d at 559.

234. 9 Va. App. 139, 384 S.E.2d 125 (1989).

235. *Id.* at 146, 384 S.E.2d at 129.

236. *Scott*, 277 Ill. App. 3d 579, 660 N.E.2d at 559.

237. United States v. Martinez-Fuerte, 428 U.S. 543 (1976).

were found to violate the Fourth Amendment.[238] In *People v. Adams*,[239] the court held that the City of Waukegan's roadblock set up to determine whether individuals were city residents and whether they had a current city vehicle sticker was an unreasonable search and seizure.[240] Although recognizing that the vehicle sticker requirement is a legitimate revenue-raising purpose, it "hardly equates with the 'compelling' public safety purpose of a DUI checkpoint and does not qualify as a 'grave' public concern sufficient to warrant this type of police intrusion."[241] The public interest was "minuscule." The ordinance was administrative and regulatory in nature rather than being related to protecting the health and safety of the public, or preventing crime. The court found no other jurisdiction upholding a similar search. Further, there was ample evidence of subjective intrusion factors.[242] First, the location where the roadblock was set up was left to the discretion of the sergeant in the field. It was not established by a "politically accountable" or "policy-making level" official.[243] Further, the police were stopping only those vehicles that did not display a city sticker. Moreover, there was no evidence that the stops were based on preexisting, written, standardized guidelines. Additionally, there was no evidence the public was given advance notice of the roadblock. Finally, the state presented no evidence of the effectiveness of the procedure in enforcing the sticker requirement.[244] The court opined that there were less intrusive methods of enforcement. In conclusion, the court found that the interest of sticker enforcement was less than compelling when weighed against the intrusion to ordinary motorists.[245] In sum, there was insufficient evidence to demonstrate that the roadblock was: (1) authorized by policy-level or politically accountable officials; (2) operated pursuant to sufficient specific, standardized, preexisting guidelines to limit officer discretion; (3) operated in a safe manner; (4) publicized clearly and in advance; and (5) actually effective in advancing the interest on which it was based.[246]

---

238. Delaware v. Prouse, 440 U.S. 648 (1979); People v. Adams, 293 Ill. App. 3d 180, 687 N.E.2d 536 (2d Dist. 1997).

239. 293 Ill. App. 3d 180, 687 N.E.2d 536 (2d Dist. 1997).

240. *Id.*, 687 N.E.2d at 536.

241. *Id.*, 687 N.E.2d at 543.

242. *Id.*, 687 N.E.2d at 540.

243. *Id.*, 687 N.E.2d at 541.

244. *Id.*, 687 N.E.2d at 541–42.

245. *Id.*, 687 N.E.2d at 542.

246. *Id.*, 687 N.E.2d at 543.

§ 1.08 — Police-Citizen Encounters That Are Not Seizures

Not every confrontation between a citizen and police constitutes a seizure of that person. Only when the officer, by means of physical force or show of authority, has in some way restrained the liberty of a citizen will an encounter be classified as a seizure.[247] The Illinois Supreme Court has approvingly cited the United States Supreme Court's plurality opinion in *Florida v. Royer*,[248] which stated that a police officer does not violate the Fourth Amendment by merely approaching a person in public, asking if he or she will answer questions, questioning the person if he or she will listen, or introducing the person's answers as evidence in a criminal prosecution.[249]

---

247. People v. Long, 99 Ill. 2d 219, 457 N.E.2d 1252 (1983) (citing Terry v. Ohio, 392 U.S. 1, 19 n.16 (1968)). *See also* Florida v. Bostick, 501 U.S. 429, 435 (1991) (law enforcement practice of boarding buses at scheduled stops to obtain consent to search luggage of passengers does not constitute seizure within meaning of the Fourth Amendment. Although confines of bus were limited, officers were blocking aisle, and bus was soon scheduled to depart, police presence was not coercive because defendant would not have felt free to leave bus even if police had not been present. "[D]egree to which a reasonable person would feel [free to leave] is not an accurate measure of the coercive effect of the encounter" because "the person is seated on a bus and has no desire to leave." Court remanded to determine whether police conduct would have communicated to reasonable person that he was not free to decline police requests or otherwise terminate encounter); People v. Booker, 209 Ill. App. 3d 384, 568 N.E.2d 211 (1st Dist. 1991) (no seizure when police asked defendant to accompany them to station to provide additional information; however, this was transformed into an unlawful seizure when the detention lasted for an unreasonable length of time); People v. Alcantara, 179 Ill. App. 3d 105, 534 N.E.2d 405 (1st Dist. 1989) (no seizure); People v. Daniels, 134 Ill. App. 3d 911, 481 N.E.2d 314 (4th Dist. 1985) (no seizure when officer told defendant that he needed to talk with him and would appreciate it if defendant would come to the police station, and defendant agreed to do so). *But see* People v. Besser, 273 Ill. App. 3d 164, 652 N.E.2d 454, 457 (4th Dist. 1995) (motion to suppress properly granted where police searched Greyhound bus; *Bostick* distinguished because detention not brief, police did not advise passengers they were free to ignore officers' questions, police used trained dog to search some areas of bus, and police would not allow anyone to leave bus with unclaimed luggage; a reasonable person would not have felt free to decline officers' requests).

248. 460 U.S. 491 (1983) (plurality).

249. *Long*, 99 Ill. 2d 219, 457 N.E.2d at 1256 (citing *Royer*, 460 U.S. at 497); People v. Bradley, 292 Ill. App. 3d 208, 685 N.E.2d 426, 428 (4th Dist. 1997) (officer's request of defendant to produce driver's license after a stop to check license-applied-for sticker did not constitute a seizure), *cert. denied*, 524 U.S. 931 (1998); People v. Erby, 213 Ill. App. 3d 657, 572 N.E.2d 345 (2d Dist. 1991) (officers approaching parked vehicle, shining light into vehicle, and asking questions of

This community caretaking function, also known as the public safety function, was endorsed by the Illinois Supreme Court in *People v. Murray.*[250] The *Murray* court noted that the *Mendenhall* factors did not indicate that this type of police/citizen encounter was a seizure.[251] This community caretaking function is permissible as long as it is reasonable and only minimally intrudes on the privacy and mobility of the citizen.[252]

The test for whether a police officer is acting in a community care-taking function is whether the officer has used any force or coercion or has seized the individual by some way of restraining his liberty.[253] "Once a seizure has occurred, an officer is not acting in his community caretaker function, even if his original intention had nothing to do with the detection or investigation of a crime."[254]

Decisions on whether a stop has occurred will often depend on the specific facts of the case in question. For example, it was held in one case that no stop occurred where a police officer had silently followed the defendant in a truck; the defendant voluntarily pulled over to the side of the road; the officer approached the truck to question the vehicle's occupants; the officer ran a license check when the defendant could not produce a driver's license; and the defendant was then allowed to return to his truck.[255]

---

occupants did not constitute seizure). *See also* People v. Robinson, 167 Ill. 2d 397, 657 N.E.2d 1020, 1026 (1995) (defendant not unreasonably detained in doorway of apartment where police identified themselves, advised him they were there because they had reports of drug sales, and asked him basic questions such as who lived in apartment and whether he lived there, he willingly answered police officers' questions, and he was only briefly detained).

250. 137 Ill. 2d 382, 560 N.E.2d 309 (1990).

251. *Id.*, 560 N.E.2d at 313.

252. *See* People v. Murray, 137 Ill. 2d 382, 560 N.E.2d 309 (1990) (upholding officers waking defendant who was asleep in his car parked on the side of the road to ask for identification). *See also* People v. Quigley, 226 Ill. App. 3d 598, 589 N.E.2d 133 (4th Dist. 1992) (upholding stop of defendant's car to inquire about altercation with another driver).

253. People v. Murray 137 Ill. 2d 382, 560 N.E.2d 309, 311-12 (1990). *See, e.g.*, City of Highland Park v. Lee, 291 Ill. App. 3d 48, 683 N.E.2d 962, 966 (2d Dist. 1997) (use of emergency lights was show of authority in attempt to restrain liberty that reasonable person would not feel free to ignore and constitutes a seizure requiring probable cause or reasonable suspicion, rejecting *People v. Quigley*, 226 Ill. App. 3d 598, 589 N.E.2d 133 (4th Dist. 1992)).

254. *City of Highland Park*, 291 Ill. App. 3d 48, 683 N.E.2d at 966–67 (rejecting *Quigley* to the extent that *Quigley* disregarded *Murray* and the prohibition against a seizure without an articulable suspicion or probable cause).

255. People v. Long, 99 Ill. 2d 219, 457 N.E.2d 1252, 1253–54, (1983). *See* People v. Hines, 12 Ill. App. 3d 582, 299 N.E.2d 581 (1st Dist. 1973) (merely asking

This issue of "stop versus no stop" is particularly vexing with regard to police-citizen encounters in airports when police suspect illegal drug activity. The shift in the position taken by Illinois courts can be seen by first examining *People v. DeLisle,*[256] which was decided in 1982. In this case the First District Appellate Court found an airport encounter between drug agents and a traveler to be unconstitutional although the traveler matched the so-called "drug courier profile."[257] The court refused to adopt the seizure test articulated by Justice Stewart in *United States v. Mendenhall*[258] that held that no seizure occurs in such a confrontation unless objective reasons exist suggesting that the person stopped is not free to proceed.[259] Because only one other Supreme Court justice concurred with this formulation, the First District rejected it.

Yet two years later the First District came to the opposite conclusion in *People v. Brett.*[260] Under factual circumstances very similar to *DeLisle,* the court held that the defendant's belief that he was being detained by the drug officers was both unreasonable and irrelevant. Instead, the court focused on Justice Stewart's test in *Mendenhall*—which since *DeLisle,* it noted, had been adopted by a majority of the United States Supreme Court[261]—and held that objectively the defendant was free to leave before any contraband was discovered on his person. The court noted that it was true that the defendant was "immobilized" at the point the agents approached him in the airport, spoke with him, and asked to see his ticket. However, the defendant was free to leave once the agents returned his ticket and merely requested that he go with them to a place where they could search his luggage. Because objectively he was free to

---

defendant to approach car is not stop for purposes of Fourth Amendment); People v. Howlett, 1 Ill. App. 3d 906, 274 N.E.2d 885 (1st Dist. 1971) (questioning per se is not stop under Fourth Amendment). *But see* People v. Sinclair, 281 Ill. App 3d 131, 666 N.E.2d 1221, 1225-26 (3d Dist. 1996) (a seizure occurred where police stopped a car, required the driver and passenger to produce identification, instructed individual to exit the car, patted down individual, ordered him to keep his hands on his head, and directed the actions of the driver and other passengers, because a reasonable person in similar circumstances would not believe that he was free to leave).

256. 104 Ill. App. 3d 297, 432 N.E.2d 954 (1st Dist. 1982).

257. The drug courier profile is a list of characteristics law enforcement authorities claim to be indicative of criminal narcotics activity. *See* United States v. Mendenhall, 446 U.S. 544 (1980); Pierce v. DeLisle, 104 Ill. App. 3d 297, 432 N.E.2d 954 (1st Dist. 1982).

258. 446 U.S. 544 (1980).

259. *Id.* at 555.

260. 122 Ill. App. 3d 191, 460 N.E.2d 876 (1st Dist. 1984).

261. *Id.,* 460 N.E.2d at 879 (citing Florida v. Royer, 460 U.S. 491, 502 (plurality), 513–19 (Blackmun, J., dissenting)).

leave, no stop occurred and he was not "seized"; he therefore consented to the search. The First District has continued to adhere to this position.[262]

---

262. People v. Miller, 124 Ill. App. 3d 620, 464 N.E.2d 1197 (1st Dist. 1984) (no seizure occurred where no indication that defendant was restrained and agent told defendant that he did not have to consent to search). *See also* Michigan v. Chesternut, 486 U.S. 567 (1988); People v. Hobley, 159 Ill. 2d 272, 637 N.E.2d 992, 1000 (where defendant consented to accompany detectives to headquarters, was not handcuffed, and was not taken anywhere without his consent, reasonable person in defendant's position would have believed free to leave; probable cause arose after polygraph examiner told defendant he had reason to believe he was lying, and defendant then confessed), *cert. denied,* 513 U.S. 1015 (1994); People v. Green, 301 Ill. App. 3d 767, 704 N.E.2d 437, 439 (4th Dist. 1998) (encounter between defendant and police not investigatory stop where defendant approached police and stopped to speak with him at police's request; there were no coercive circumstances or show of authority or force); People v. Prince, 288 Ill. App. 3d 265, 681 N.E.2d 521, 527–28 (1st Dist. 1997) (defendant not under arrest at time of confession where he agreed to go to station with police after police had entered his girlfriend's house with consent, he was not restrained, and he was told he was free to leave); People v. Olivarez, 279 Ill. App. 3d 90, 664 N.E.2d 156, 161 (1st Dist. 1996) (no seizure where officers approached individuals in public train station, identified themselves as officers, requested the opportunity to ask a few questions, informed the individuals that they were free to leave, and never attempted to prevent their departure through threats or a show of authority); People v. Booth, 265 Ill. App. 3d 462, 637 N.E.2d 580, 584 (1st Dist. 1994) (arrest did not occur until juvenile implicated himself, where not handcuffed, searched, fingerprinted or photographed, was read *Miranda* rights and informed of right to have his mother or youth officer present; although detectives did not tell defendant he was free to leave, they did not say he was not free to leave); People v. McClom, 262 Ill. App. 3d 826, 635 N.E.2d 677, 682 (1st Dist. 1994) (even though detective patted defendant down before taking him to station, no arrest occurred because defendant voluntarily accompanied detective, no weapons were drawn, and no threatening language was used); People v. Statham, 209 Ill. App. 3d 352, 568 N.E.2d 183 (1st Dist. 1991) (upholding officers' stop of defendant after departing airplane when defendant agreed to speak to officers and did not indicate a desire to end the conversation or leave); People v. Price, 195 Ill. App. 3d 701, 552 N.E.2d 1200 (1st Dist. 1990) (no seizure during airport encounter); People v. Clark, 185 Ill. App. 3d 231, 541 N.E.2d 199 (2d Dist. 1989) (defendant not seized where officer merely approached defendant's vehicle, tapped on the window, and indicated to defendant to roll down the window after identifying himself as police officer).

§ 1.09 Search Warrants

The requirements for obtaining and executing a search warrant have been codified in Illinois.[263] A judge may issue a search warrant on the written complaint of any person, under oath or affirmation, that states facts sufficient to show probable cause and that particularly describes the place or person, or both, to be searched and the things to be seized.[264] A number of considerations flow from this.

First, the broad purpose of this law is to circumscribe the power of the government to conduct searches by preventing "fishing expeditions" by the police.[265] Thus, the determination of whether the complaint establishes probable cause must be made by a neutral and detached judicial officer, not by a police officer.[266] Moreover, the judge must not act merely as a rubber stamp for the police[267] but must independently determine from the information given in the complaint the persuasiveness of the facts relied on by the police in reaching the conclusion that probable cause exists.[268]

The judge must base his or her decision solely on the sworn statements or affidavits presented.[269] The complaint for which a search warrant is issued must state the facts the complainant bases his or her belief on with sufficient certainty that if the complaint is false, perjury may be charged.[270] A defective complaint cannot be cured by extrinsic evidence.[271] Thus, the complaint

---

263. 725 ILCS 5/108-1 through 5/108-14.

264. 725 ILCS 5/108-3.

265. People v. Dahl, 110 Ill. App. 3d 295, 442 N.E.2d 321, 325 (4th Dist. 1982).

266. People v. Greer, 87 Ill. 2d 89, 429 N.E.2d 505 (1981).

267. People v. Greer, 91 Ill. App. 3d 304, 414 N.E.2d 831, 832 (5th Dist. 1980), *aff'd,* 87 Ill. 2d 89, 429 N.E.2d 505 (1981) (quoting Aguilar v. Texas, 378 U.S. 108, 111 (1964)).

268. People v. Tate, 44 Ill. 2d 432, 255 N.E.2d 411 (1970); People v. West, 48 Ill. App. 3d 132, 362 N.E.2d 791 (4th Dist. 1977); People v. Close, 60 Ill. App. 2d 477, 208 N.E.2d 644, 648 (3d Dist. 1965).

269. People v. Tisler, 103 Ill. 2d 226, 469 N.E.2d 147 (1984); People v. Greer, 87 Ill. 2d 89, 429 N.E.2d 505 (1981).

270. People v. George, 49 Ill. 2d 372, 274 N.E.2d 26, 29 (1971); People v. Savanna Lodge No. 1095, L.O.O.M., 407 Ill. 227, 95 N.E.2d 328, 330 (1950).

271. People v. Moore, 90 Ill. App. 3d 760, 413 N.E.2d 516 (4th Dist. 1980). *See, e.g.,* People v. Lawlor, 291 Ill. App. 3d 97, 683 N.E.2d 214, 216–17 (2d Dist. 1997) (seizure order pursuant to rule 413 technical irregularity that could not be overcome by state's contention that order was "in all practicality" a search warrant; although order based on an affidavit, a complaint, and review by a neutral and detached magistrate, no probable cause existed sufficient for issuance of search warrant).

must set forth both the facts that would cause a reasonable person to believe a crime has been committed and the facts that would cause a reasonable person to believe the evidence was in the place to be searched."[272] In addition to these factors, the probable cause relied on must not be stale.[273]

A court should evaluate various factors in determining staleness. These factors include: the incriminating nature of the evidence; the suspect's possessory interest in the items; the mobility of the items; the likelihood that the suspect moved or destroyed the items; the relationship between the suspect and the area searched; and, most importantly, the nature of the suspect's criminal conduct.[274] An affidavit that merely states conclusions cannot support the issuance of a search warrant.[275]

Illinois courts stress that, in reading the complaint to determine whether probable cause exists, a judge should utilize "a pragmatic analysis of everyday life on which reasonable and prudent men, not legal technicians, act."[276] Affidavits should not be found deficient through hypertechnical scrutiny.[277] To establish probable cause, it is not necessary to establish the need for a search warrant by proof beyond a reasonable doubt.[278] Probability, not a prima facie showing of criminal activity, is the standard for issuance of a search warrant.[279]

---

272. People v. George, 49 Ill. 2d 372, 274 N.E.2d 26 (1971); People v. Casillo, 99 Ill. App. 3d 825, 425 N.E.2d 1379 (3d Dist. 1981).

273. People v. Rehkopf, 153 Ill. App. 3d 819, 506 N.E.2d 435, 437 (2d Dist. 1987).

274. *Rehkopf,* 153 Ill. App. 3d 819, 506 N.E.2d at 437–38. *See also* People v. Thompkins, 121 Ill. 2d 401, 521 N.E.2d 38 (search warrant for telephone extension cords, hair fiber, and bloodstains based on probable cause despite issuance 83 days after murders took place), *cert. denied,* 488 U.S. 871 (1988); People v. Damian, 299 Ill. App. 489, 701 N.E.2d 171, 173–74 (1st Dist. 1998) (an informant's buy conducted six weeks earlier could not be used to establish probable cause for continuing course of criminal conduct); People v. Sellers, 237 Ill. App. 3d 545, 604 N.E.2d 993 (3d Dist. 1992) (a 15-day delay from the time that the contraband was first observed was not unreasonable, particularly where the defendant was allegedly engaged in a continuing course of conduct); People v. Nally, 216 Ill. App. 3d 742, 575 N.E.2d 1341 (2d Dist. 1991) (delay in executing arrest warrant until after tape recording of conversation between defendant and person wearing police wire permissible).

275. People v. Elias, 316 Ill. 376, 147 N.E. 472 (1925).

276. People v. Bauer, 102 Ill. App. 3d 31, 429 N.E.2d 568, 573 (2d Dist. 1981) (citing People v. Blitz, 68 Ill. 2d 287, 369 N.E.2d 1238, 1240 (1977)).

277. People v. Stewart, 104 Ill. 2d 463, 473 N.E.2d 1227 (1984), *cert. denied,* 471 U.S. 1120 (1985); People v. Gacy, 103 Ill. 2d 1, 468 N.E.2d 1171 (1984), *cert. denied,* 470 U.S. 1037 (1985).

278. People v. Dowd, 101 Ill. App. 3d 830, 428 N.E.2d 894 (1st Dist. 1981).

279. People v. Bibbs, 176 Ill. App. 3d 521, 531 N.E.2d 75 (4th Dist. 1988); People v. Malone, 106 Ill. App. 3d 575, 435 N.E.2d 917 (3d Dist. 1982).

It is clear that the kind of information needed in the complaint need not be restricted to the personal, first-hand knowledge of the officer.[280] Hearsay statements are proper, provided there is a substantial basis for crediting the hearsay.[281] Until recently, an affidavit based on the hearsay of an informant had to pass the stringent *Aguilar-Spinelli* test,[282] which required that hearsay could not be considered unless the affidavit showed the basis of knowledge—how the informant acquired the information—and the veracity of the informant—his or her past record of truthfulness or facts indicating that the present information was reliable. However, the Illinois Supreme Court abolished the *Aguilar-Spinelli* test in favor of the "totality of circumstances" test established by the United States Supreme Court in *Illinois v. Gates*.[283] (This is dealt with in detail in the concluding section in this chapter on the exclusionary rule.)

Illinois Compiled Statutes chapter 725, section 5/108-3 describes two general classifications of items that may be seized pursuant to a search warrant: (1) items inanimate by nature and (2) things that are or once were animate.

First, the statute provides that a warrant may authorize the seizure of "[a]ny instruments, articles or things designed or intended for use or which are or have been used in the commission of, or which may constitute evidence of, the offense in connection with which the warrant is issued; or contraband, the fruits of a crime, or things otherwise criminally possessed."[284] Thus, the statute follows the United States Supreme Court in refusing to distinguish "fruits, instrumentalities, and contraband" from "mere evidence."[285] The statute allows a broad range of material to be seized.

Second, the statute provides that a warrant may authorize the seizure of any kidnap victim, any human fetus, or any human corpse.[286]

Section 108-3 also deals with search warrants directed to the media and states that they are proper only if there is probable cause to believe that the

---

280. People v. Bauer, 102 Ill. App. 3d 31, 429 N.E.2d 568 (2d Dist. 1981).

281. People v. Jackson, 22 Ill. 2d 382, 176 N.E.2d 803 (1961), *cert. denied,* 368 U.S. 985 (1962); People v. Sylvester, 86 Ill. App. 3d 186, 407 N.E.2d 1002 (1st Dist. 1980).

282. Spinelli v. United States, 393 U.S. 410 (1969); Aguilar v. Texas, 378 U.S. 108 (1964).

283. *See* People v. Tisler, 103 Ill. 2d 226, 469 N.E.2d 147 (1984) (adopting Illinois v. Gates, 462 U.S. 213 (1983)).

284. 725 ILCS 5/108-3(a)(1). *But see* People v. Eagle Books, Inc., 151 Ill. 2d 235, 602 N.E.2d 798, 805 (1992) (noting special rule where "materials presumptively protected by the first amendment are involved"; officers should have seized only a single copy of books and magazines prior to an adversary hearing on obscenity, constitutionally improper to conduct "large scale confiscations").

285. Warden v. Hayden, 387 U.S. 294 (1967).

286. 725 ILCS 5/108-3(a)(2).

items will be either destroyed or removed from the state[287] or that the person against whom it is issued has committed or is committing a criminal offense.[288] Thus, the Illinois standard allows for fewer search warrants to be issued against the media than the more lax standard approved by the United States Supreme Court in *Zurcher v. Stanford Daily*.[289]

§ 1.10 — Anticipatory Search Warrants

Anticipatory search warrants, although held to pass constitutional muster,[290] were found by the Illinois Supreme Court in *People v. Ross* to violate the Illinois statute governing search warrants.[291] In response, the Illinois legislature amended section 108-3(a)(1) to specifically allow anticipatory search warrants. This amendment was modeled after federal law and provides:

> (a) Except as provided in subsection (b), upon the written complaint of any person under oath or affirmation which states facts sufficient to show probable cause and which particularly describes the place or person, or both, to be searched and the things to be seized, any judge may issue a search warrant for the seizure of the following:
>
> > (1) Any instruments, articles or things *designed or intended for use* or which *are or* have been used in the commission of, or which may constitute evidence of, the offense in connection with which the warrant is issued; *or contraband, the fruits of crime, or things otherwise criminally possessed.*[292]

Ordinarily, an anticipatory warrant situation involves custom officials or a postmaster who has intercepted a package containing contraband, and police seek a search warrant for the intended recipient, to be used if and when they accept the package.[293]

---

287. 725 ILCS 5/108-3(b)(2).

288. 725 ILCS 5/108-3(b)(1).

289. 436 U.S. 547 (1978) (no showing necessary that newspaper against whom search warrant was issued had committed or was currently committing any criminal offense).

290. People v. Martini, 265 Ill. App. 3d 698, 638 N.E.2d 397 (2d Dist. 1994).

291. 168 Ill. 2d 347, 659 N.E.2d 1319, 1321–22 (1995).

292. 725 ILCS 5/108-3(a)(1) (emphasis denotes amendments).

293. *See, e.g.*, People v. Carlson, 287 Ill. App. 3d 700, 679 N.E.2d 791 (2d Dist. 1998); People v. Nwosu, 284 Ill. App. 3d 538, 672 N.E.2d 366 (1st Dist. 1996).

In *People v. Carlson*,[294] the Illinois Supreme Court held that evidence seized pursuant to an anticipatory search warrant issued and executed prior to its decision in *Ross* was admissible based on the good faith exception to the exclusionary rule. The court first note that in *Ross* it held that such a warrant was *statutorily* invalid, not *constitutionally* invalid.[295] The court specifically held that such warrants do not violate the Fourth Amendment of either the United States Constitution or the Illinois Constitution.[296] In determining that such warrants were valid, the court found such warrants reasonable because police knew a package containing contraband would be delivered to a specific address. If issuance of such warrants were forbidden, the risk of losing track of the package and ultimately losing its contents clearly existed. Further, such warrants are issued based upon probable cause. Evidence is presented to a neutral magistrate that contraband is to be delivered to a certain place, at a certain time, and execution of the warrant is contingent upon that delivery.[297] Thus, the anticipatory warrant was constitutional. After holding that anticipatory warrants were constitutional, the court concluded that the seizure in *Carlson* was proper based on the good faith exception. It first rejected application of the *Krull* good faith exception as it had done in *Krueger*, because this would drastically change Illinois's exclusionary rule.[298] However, it did apply the good faith exception outlined in *Leon*. The police acted in good faith upon the warrant. At the time it was obtained, there was no Illinois law saying such warrants were invalid either statutorily or constitutionally.[299]

In *People v. Favela*,[300] the court upheld an anticipatory search warrant. The defendant alleged that the warrant was invalid because not all conditions precedent had been satisfied. The court stated that while it is "better practice to command on the face of an anticipatory warrant that it not be executed before satisfying conditions precedent . . . , there is no statutory requirement that the issuing judge do so."[301] Here, the only reasonable interpretation of the warrant, based on the police officer's affidavit seeking the warrant, was that it was not to be executed until all conditions precedent were fulfilled. Moreover, the evidence presented at trial showed that all three conditions precedent had in fact been satisfied before the warrant was executed; therefore, its execution was not premature. The conditions precedent were: (1) controlled delivery of

---

294. 185 Ill. 2d 546, 708 N.E.2d 372 (1999).

295. *Id.*, 708 N.E.2d at 374.

296. *Id.*, 708 N.E.2d at 375.

297. *Id.*, 708 N.E.2d at 376.

298. *Id.*, 708 N.E.2d at 377.

299. *Id.*, 708 N.E.2d at 378.

300. 288 Ill. App. 3d 85, 681 N.E.2d 582 (3d Dist. 1997).

301. *Id.*, 681 N.E.2d at 585.

package known to contain marijuana, (2) surveillance of the premises, and (3) opening of one box by defendant before the warrant was executed.[302]

§ 1.11 — Issuance

Any warrant issued is the warrant of the judge who found probable cause to issue it. It is not the warrant of the court in which the judge is currently sitting.[303] Thus, there is no need for the warrant to be docketed with the clerk of court until after the warrant has been either executed or returned "not executed."[304] Section 108-5 requires the time and date of issuance to be included in the warrant and by implication the signature of the judge. The failure to include these items will invalidate the warrant.[305]

§ 1.12 — Execution

A warrant may be executed by any peace officer of the state or any other person specially named by the issuing judge in the warrant.[306] It must be executed within 96 hours from the date and time of issuance.[307] If the warrant is executed,[308] the duplicate copy is to be left at the place the seizure was made,

---

302. *Id.*

303. 725 ILCS 5/108-4.

304. *Id.;* People v. Stansberry, 47 Ill. 2d 541, 268 N.E.2d 431 (docketing warrant after execution not unconstitutional on grounds of encouraging government harrassment of citizen), *cert. denied,* 404 U.S. 873 (1971); People v. Price, 46 Ill. 2d 209, 263 N.E.2d 484 (1970), *appeal dismissed, cert. denied,* 402 U.S. 902 (1971).

305. People v. Taylor, 198 Ill. App. 3d 667, 555 N.E.2d 1218 (3d Dist. 1990). *But see* People v. Blake, 266 Ill. App. 3d 232, 640 N.E.2d 317, 321 (2d Dist. 1994) (inadvertent omissions of time, date, and issuing judge's signature from search warrant were technical irregularities which did not affect substantial rights of accused).

306. 725 ILCS 5/108-5; People v. Carnivale, 61 Ill. 2d 57, 329 N.E.2d 193 (1975) (section 108-5 allows Chicago police officer to execute warrant issued in Chicago outside of city).

307. 725 ILCS 5/108-6; People v. Stansberry, 47 Ill. 2d 541, 268 N.E.2d 431 (delay until next day constitutionally proper), *cert. denied,* 404 U.S. 873 (1971); People v. Ripa, 80 Ill. App. 3d 674, 399 N.E.2d 1000 (2d Dist. 1980) (delay of two days constitutionally proper); People v. Bryant, 127 Ill. App. 2d 110, 261 N.E.2d 815 (1st Dist. 1970) (delay of three days constitutionally proper).

308. *Serving* a search warrant is synonymous with *executing* the warrant. People v. McCullum, 33 Ill. App. 3d 451, 338 N.E.2d 248 (3d Dist. 1975), *aff'd and remanded,* 66 Ill. 2d 306, 362 N.E.2d 307 (1977).

or if possible, with the person against whom the warrant was directed.[309] Any warrant not timely executed is to be returned to the court and marked "not executed." A warrant may be executed at any time of any day or night.[310] Illinois courts have also held that once a search warrant has been executed, police may reenter to retrieve items previously seized, tagged, and inadvertently left behind.[311]

In *Richards v. Wisconsin*,[312] the Supreme Court unanimously held that states cannot create blanket exceptions to the knock and announce requirement in executing search or arrest warrants. Specifically, the Supreme Court rejected a Wisconsin statute that empowered police officers to never knock and announce their presence when executing a search warrant in a felony drug investigation.[313] The Supreme Court held that "[i]n order to justify a 'no-knock entry,' the police must have a reasonable suspicion that knocking and announcing their presence, under the particular circumstances, would be dangerous or futile, or that it would inhibit the effective investigation of the crime by, for example, allowing the destruction of evidence."[314] The Court specifically rejected a more stringent requirement of probable cause to justify a no-knock entry.[315] The Supreme Court reaffirmed *Wilson v. Arkansas*[316] to the extent that police can disregard the knock and announce requirement when executing a warrant, despite lack of permission from the magistrate in the warrant, if the circumstances at the time of execution present a threat of physical violence or where police officers have reason to believe that evidence would likely be destroyed if advance notice was given.[317]

In *United States v. Ramirez*,[318] the Supreme Court held that the Fourth Amendment did not hold the police to a higher standard when they entered premises under a no knock entry and, in the course of entering, destroy property.[319] The Court concluded that it was obvious from the holdings of

---

309. 725 ILCS 5/108-6. *But see* People v. McCullum, 66 Ill. 2d 306, 362 N.E.2d 307 (1977) (absent prejudice, police failure to leave copy of warrant at time of search does not invalidate search).

310. 725 ILCS 5/108-13.

311. People v. Schuldt, 217 Ill. App. 3d 534, 577 N.E.2d 870 (3d Dist. 1991).

312. 520 U.S. 385 (1997).

313. *Id.* at 388.

314. *Id.* at 394.

315. *Id.*

316. 514 U.S. 927 (1995).

317. *Richards,* 520 U.S. at 391. For a discussion of the Illinois statute and related law see § 1.14.

318. 523 U.S. 65 (1998).

319. *Id.* at 68.

Wilson and *Richards* that the lawfulness of an entry did not depend on whether any property was damaged during the course of the entry.[320] Thus, there was no Fourth Amendment violation where the police, who had been told by a confidential informant that the resident kept guns in the garage, while executing a search warrant broke out a garage window to discourage the resident from rushing to the guns.[321]

§ 1.13 — Command

Illinois law requires that the warrant particularly describe the place to be searched and the things to be seized.[322] The purpose of this particularity requirement is to prevent the use of warrants so general that police would have limitless discretion as to where they may search and what they may seize.[323]

Illinois courts have determined that a warrant is sufficiently descriptive if it enables the police, with reasonable effort, to identify the place intended.[324] The defendant has the burden of establishing that, in view of all the relevant facts, the lack of particularity in the description of the premises caused prejudicial ambiguity or confusion.[325] Errors, and even omissions, in portions of addresses will not per se invalidate a search warrant.[326] Moreover, reference to the affidavit attached to the warrant is permissible in determining the validity of

---

320. *Id.* at 70–71.

321. *Id.* at 71–72.

322. 725 ILCS 5/108-3, 5/108-7.

323. Warden v. Hayden, 387 U.S. 294 (1967); Marron v. United States, 275 U.S. 192 (1927); People v. Fragoso, 68 Ill. App. 3d 428, 386 N.E.2d 409 (1st Dist. 1979).

324. People v. Watson, 26 Ill. 2d 203, 186 N.E.2d 326 (1962); People v. Smith, 20 Ill. 2d 345, 169 N.E.2d 777 (1960); People v. Moore, 124 Ill. App. 2d 204, 260 N.E.2d 255 (1st Dist. 1970). *See* People v. Luckett, 273 Ill. App. 3d 1023, 652 N.E.2d 1342, 1345 (1st Dist. 1995) (particularity requirement not met where only general description of multiple occupancy building provided). *But see* People v. Siegwarth, 285 Ill. App. 3d 739, 674 N.E.2d 508, 511–12 (3d Dist. 1996) (warrant description of specific apartment was sufficient to justify a search of the entire apartment, including individually padlocked rooms).

325. People v. Bauer, 102 Ill. App. 3d 31, 429 N.E.2d 568 (2d Dist. 1981).

326. People v. Watson, 26 Ill. 2d 203, 186 N.E.2d 326 (1962) (description in warrant of apartment 604 at 2300 South State was sufficient to justify search of apartment 604 at 2310 South State because building was first one on even side of 2300 block); People v. Holmes, 175 Ill. App. 3d 495, 529 N.E.2d 1043 (1st Dist. 1988) (lack of name on mailbox conflicting with officer's description held not fatal); People v. Hicks, 49 Ill. App. 3d 421, 364 N.E.2d 440 (1st Dist. 1977) (lack of street address of hotel held not fatal); People v. Kissinger, 26 Ill. App. 3d 260, 325 N.E.2d 28 (3d Dist. 1975) (lack of city held not fatal).

the warrant.[327] It is not necessary that the description of the premises in the warrant be "technically correct."[328] Rather, it should at the very least identify the place to be searched to the exclusion of all other places.[329]

Illinois courts demand that the items to be seized be identified "with such particularity that the officer charged with the execution of the warrant will be left with no discretion respecting the property to be taken."[330] Thus,

---

327. People v. Bauer, 102 Ill. App. 3d 31, 429 N.E.2d 568 (2d Dist. 1981); People v. Fragoso, 68 Ill. App. 3d 428, 386 N.E.2d 409 (1st Dist. 1979); People v. Mecca, 132 Ill. App. 2d 612, 270 N.E.2d 456 (1st Dist. 1971).

328. People v. Redmond, 43 Ill. App. 3d 682, 357 N.E.2d 204 (1st Dist. 1976); People v. Edwards, 35 Ill. App. 3d 807, 342 N.E.2d 800 (1st Dist. 1976).

329. People v. Curry, 56 Ill. 2d 162, 306 N.E.2d 292 (1973); People v. Watson, 26 Ill. 2d 203, 186 N.E.2d 326 (1962); People v. Edwards, 35 Ill. App. 3d 807, 342 N.E.2d 800 (1st Dist. 1976). *Compare* Maryland v. Garrison, 480 U.S. 79 (1987) (warrant authorized search of third-floor apartment; during search police realized that third floor contained two apartments and they were in the wrong one; officers' conduct found to be reasonable under the circumstances); People v. Luckett, 273 Ill. App. 3d 1023, 652 N.E.2d 1342, 1347–49 (1st Dist. 1995) (search pursuant to warrant authorizing search of first floor of two flats valid even though two apartments on first floor; *Garrison* did not address whether search valid where police enter one apartment, realize it's wrong one, and then immediately search second apartment; where police could not have reasonably known or discovered there were two apartments on floor, contraband could be easily destroyed, and police action upon discovering two apartments on first floor, they acted reasonably and satisfied "reasonable effects" test announced in *Garrison*); People v. Economy, 259 Ill. App. 3d 504, 631 N.E.2d 827, 833 (4th Dist. 1994) (where warrant's description encompassed entire building at address, it was reasonable to search that portion of first floor defendant used for law offices because controlled substances and related paraphernalia could just as easily have been located there as in residential portion) *with* People v. Bass, 220 Ill. App. 3d 230, 580 N.E.2d 1274 (1st Dist. 1991) (when police went to execute search warrant of first floor apartment and noticed there were two first floor apartments, warrant was invalid); People v. Sanchez, 191 Ill. App. 3d 1099, 548 N.E.2d 13 (1st Dist. 1989) (not reasonable for police to search a second building, adjacent to the one listed in warrant, which had a separate address).

330. People v. Sovetsky, 343 Ill. 583, 175 N.E. 844, 846 (1931); People v. Simmons, 210 Ill. App. 3d 692, 569 N.E.2d 591 (2d Dist. 1991) (general description in warrant invalid); People v. Bishop 71 Ill. App. 3d 52, 388 N.E.2d 1144, 1146–47 (5th Dist. 1979) (warrant invalid where items seized were neither contraband nor inherently related to the offense specified in the general warrant that left determination of property to be seized entirely to the discretion of executing officers). *But see* People v. Siegwarth, 285 Ill. App. 3d 739, 674 N.E.2d 508, 511 (3d Dist. 1996) (warrant valid where items seized were contraband specifically related to

descriptions in warrants of "undetermined amount of United States currency,"[331] "weapon,"[332] and "other articles of merchandise too numerous to mention"[333] are insufficient. However, when property of a specified nature is to be seized, rather than particular property, a description of its characteristics is sufficient.[334]

It is possible that the time lapse between the facts alleged and the issuance of the warrant could cause information to become "stale" and thus insufficient to establish probable cause.[335] "In Illinois, there is no set rule as to when the passage of time extinguishes probable cause."[336] Whether probable cause is

---

accompanying complaint and officers did not believe the warrant to be a "general warrant" but instead believed "they were authorized to seize" only those things listed in accompanying complaint).

331. People v. Holmes, 20 Ill. App. 3d 167, 312 N.E.2d 748 (1st Dist. 1974).

332. *Id.,* 312 N.E. 2d at 752.

333. *Sovetsky,* 343 Ill. 583, 175 N.E. at 846. *See also* People v. Brown, 153 Ill. App. 3d 307, 505 N.E.2d 405 (3d Dist. 1987) (search warrant held overly broad due to following language: "any other equipment, appliances or other property which is found to have been stolen in the commission of, or which constitutes evidence of, the offense of (1) Theft; (2) Burglary"); People v. Albritton, 150 Ill. App. 3d 545, 502 N.E.2d 83 (3d Dist. 1986) (use of terms *jewelry* and *chains* held insufficient and overly broad for search warrant).

334. People v. Curry, 56 Ill. 2d 162, 306 N.E.2d 292 (1973) (description in warrant of "items related to a call girl operation" sufficient); People v. Williams, 40 Ill. 2d 522, 240 N.E.2d 645 (1968) (description in warrant of ".22 caliber firearms, shells, shell casings, and blood stained clothing" found sufficient), *cert. denied,* 393 U.S. 1123 (1969); People v. Mertens, 77 Ill. App. 3d 791, 396 N.E.2d 595 (2d Dist. 1979) (description in warrant of "elephant tusks, handguns, rifles, and shotguns" found sufficient); People v. Raicevich, 61 Ill. App. 3d 143, 377 N.E.2d 1266 (3d Dist. 1978) (description in warrant of one particularly described firearm "and any other handguns which may be stolen" found sufficient), *cert. denied,* 441 U.S. 963 (1979); People v. Miller, 36 Ill. App. 3d 542, 345 N.E.2d 1 (5th Dist. 1975) (description in warrant of "stolen vehicles and vehicles or parts of vehicles with the manufacturers' identifying number altered or removed" found sufficient). *But see* People v. Eagle Books, Inc., 151 Ill. 2d 235, 602 N.E.2d 798 (1992) (warrant authorizing search of adult bookstore and seizure of magazines containing depictions of a multitude of enumerated sexual acts resulted in a constitutionally improper general search requiring suppression of evidence obtained).

335. People v. McCoy, 135 Ill. App. 3d 1059, 482 N.E.2d 200, 205 (2d Dist. 1985).

336. *Id.* (citing People v. Evans, 57 Ill. App. 3d 1044, 373 N.E.2d 524, 529 (2d Dist. 1978)).

extinguished depends "upon all the facts and circumstances of the particular case," particularly the continuity of the offense.[337]

§ 1.14 — Use of Force in Execution

Illinois law provides that "[a]ll necessary and reasonable force may be used to effect an entry into any building or property or part thereof to execute a search warrant."[338] Yet Illinois courts require that before a search warrant is executed, the police officer must knock and announce his or her office.[339] This so-called "knock and announce" rule is not constitutionally mandated nor is it required by statute.[340] Its purpose is to notify the person inside of the presence of police and of the impending intrusion, to give that person time to respond, to avoid violence, and to protect privacy as much as possible.[341] Violation of this rule may render the fruits of the subsequent search inadmissible.[342] In *Wilson v. Arkansas*,[343] the Supreme Court held that the knock and announce principle

---

337. *McCoy,* 135 Ill. App. 3d 1059, 482 N.E.2d at 205 (citing People v. Dolgin, 415 Ill. 434, 114 N.E.2d 389, 393 (1953)).

338. 725 ILCS 5/108-8 has been amended to also allow police officers to enter a private dwelling when executing a search warrant without first knocking and announcing their office.

339. People v. Ouellette, 78 Ill. 2d 511, 401 N.E.2d 507 (1979); People v. Arias, 179 Ill. App. 3d 890, 535 N.E.2d 89 (3d Dist. 1990) (police entry into porch of defendant's residence in order to "knock and announce" is proper); People v. Trask, 167 Ill. App. 3d 694, 521 N.E.2d 1222 (2d Dist. 1988) (police officers waited reasonable time, even though it was not particularly long, after knock and announce before forcible entry).

340. People v. Wolgemuth, 69 Ill. 2d 154, 370 N.E.2d 1067 (1977), *cert. denied,* 436 U.S. 908 (1978); People v. Boykin, 65 Ill. App. 3d 738, 382 N.E.2d 1369 (3d Dist. 1978). *See also* People v. Condon, 195 Ill. App. 3d 815, 552 N.E.2d 413 (2d Dist. 1990), *aff'd,* 148 Ill. 2d 96, 592 N.E.2d 951 (1992), *cert. denied,* 507 U.S. 948 (1993) (Chief Justice Rehnquist and Justice White in a dissent to the denial noted that there is a conflict in both the federal and state courts concerning under what conditions police officers may enter a suspect's home with a search warrant without knocking or announcing their presence).

341. *Ouellette,* 78 Ill. 2d 511, 401 N.E.2d at 510; People v. Saecho, 129 Ill. 2d 522, 544 N.E.2d 745 (1989) ("knock and announce" fulfilled).

342. People v. Rogers, 59 Ill. App. 3d 396, 375 N.E.2d 1009 (4th Dist. 1978); People v. Richard, 34 Ill. App. 3d 621, 339 N.E.2d 400 (2d Dist. 1975). *Cf.* People v. Van Matre, 164 Ill. App. 3d 201, 517 N.E.2d 768 (5th Dist.) (mere failure of police to announce purpose *may* influence whether subsequent entry is constitutionally reasonable), *cert. denied,* 488 U.S. 829 (1988).

343. 514 U.S. 927.

forms a part of the analysis under the Fourth Amendment as to whether an entry was reasonable or not. The Court found that under certain circumstances, law enforcement interests may warrant entry without the necessity of knocking and announcing prior to the actual entry. Although the Court did not set forth a "comprehensive catalog" of situations which would not require police to knock and announce, leaving that job to the trial courts, it did suggest exceptions such as a fleeing felon or where evidence may be destroyed.[344] However, once police have complied with the knock and announce rule, they are then justified in using force if necessary to effect an entrance.[345]

In 1992, the Illinois legislature promulgated a new provision that permitted a "no knock" warrant to issue under certain circumstances.[346] However, three

---

344. *Id.* at 934–36.

345. People v. Mathes, 69 Ill. App. 3d 275, 387 N.E.2d 39 (3d Dist. 1979); People v. Boykin, 65 Ill. App. 3d 738, 382 N.E.2d 1369 (3d Dist. 1978). *See* People v. Riddle, 258 Ill. App. 3d 253, 630 N.E.2d 141, 145 (2d Dist. 1994) (no rigid rules for determining if police have allowed sufficient time before forcing entry into dwelling, but "a person should be afforded sufficient opportunity to respond to authority before a forced entry is made"). In *United States v. Bragg*, 138 F.3d 1194, 1195 (7th Cir. 1998), the court held that the federal "knock and announce" provision requiring agents to announce themselves before breaking down a door did not apply to additional doors in sequence once the agents knocked on the first door. The statute applied per house; not per door. In *United States v. Ramirez*, 118 S. Ct. 992, 995 (1998), the Supreme Court held that property damaged in execution of a no-knock search warrant did not render the entry unlawful.

346. 725 ILCS 5/108-8(b) provided:

> Upon a finding by the judge issuing the warrant that any of the following exigent circumstances exist, the judge may order the person executing the warrant to make entry without first knocking and announcing his office:
>
> (1) the presence of firearms or explosives in the building in an area where they are accessible to any occupant;
>
> (2) the prior possession of firearms by an occupant of the building within a reasonable period of time;
>
> (3) the presence of surveillance equipment, such as video cameras, or alarm systems, inside or outside of the building; and
>
> (4) the presence of steel doors, wooden planking, crossbars, dogs, or other similar means of preventing or impeding entry into the building.

See People v. Seaberg, 262 Ill. App. 3d 79, 635 N.E.2d 126, 133 (2d Dist. 1994) (police requested "no knock" warrant fearing for their safety where evidence demonstrated that defendant possessed .9mm Uzi, kept it loaded, and handled it when transacting cocaine sale three weeks previous).

of the circumstances have been held to be unconstitutional.[347] In response, the legislature again amended the provision.[348]

---

347. Paragraph (b)(2) was held unconstitutional by the Illinois Supreme Court in *People v. Krueger*, 175 Ill. 2d 60, 675 N.E.2d 604 (1996), *cert. denied*, 118 S. Ct. 149 (1997). Based on precedent holding that the mere presence of firearms on premises does not equate with exigent circumstances, the court concluded that in order for exigent circumstances to exist warranting a no knock entry, the police must have a reasonable belief that the firearms would be used against them had they entered with the normal announcement. *Id.*, 675 N.E.2d at 608–09. It was clear from Illinois law, in particular *People v. Condon*, 148 Ill. 2d 96, 592 N.E.2d 951 (1992), and *People v. Ouellette*, 78 Ill. 2d 511, 401 N.E.2d 507 (1979), both discussed below, that entries based on the presence of firearms only violate the constitutional requirement of reasonableness. *Krueger*, 176 Ill. 2d 60, 675 N.E.2d at 609–10.

In *People v. Wright*, 183 Ill. 2d 16, 697 N.E.2d 693 (1998), the supreme court held unconstitutional paragraph (b)(1), pursuant to *Condon* and *Krueger*. It too noted that Illinois has long concluded that the mere presence of firearms, whether accessible or not, alone, does not constitute an exigent circumstance. As *Krueger* stated, the police must have a reasonable belief that the firearms will be used against them should they announce. *Id.*, 697 N.E.2d at 696.

Finally, in *People v. Aaron*, 296 Ill. App. 3d 317, 694 N.E.2d 1093 (2d Dist. 1998), the court held unconstitutional paragraph (b)(4), opining that the rationale of *Krueger* applied to this paragraph as well. The statute only required that barricade-type devices be present. It did not require that the devices impede police entry. The statute failed to take into account the fact that law abiding citizens must at times utilize such devices to protect their property. Accordingly, such devices are not always used to impede police entry. *Id.*, 694 N.E.2d at 1099. In the instant case, the only exigent circumstance was the presence of a wooden barricade blocking the door. There was nothing in the affidavit supporting the no knock warrant that demonstrated the barricade was in place to impede police entry. *Id.* In conclusion, the court stated that the paragraph was based solely on the presence of barricades without consideration of whether the barricades posed a danger to the police, provided an opportunity to dispose evidence, or whether the customary knock and announce would be futile. *Id.*, 694 N.E.2d at 1100. Allowing a no knock warrant to issue based on this violates the constitutional requirements of reasonableness. *Id.*

See also discussion of *Richards v. Wisconsin*, 520 U.S. 385 (1997), in § 1.12.

348. Paragraph 725 ILCS 5/108-8(b) now provides:

(b) The court issuing a warrant may authorize the officer executing the warrant to make entry without first knocking and announcing his or her office if it finds, based upon a showing of specific facts, the existence of the following exigent circumstances:

(1) that the officer reasonably believes that if notice were given a weapon would be used:

(i) against the officer executing the search warrant; or

Yet Illinois courts have also allowed police to dispense with the knock and announce rule if exigent circumstances are present. To establish exigent circumstances, the police must have "particular reasons to reasonably believe in a particular case that evidence will be destroyed."[349] It is not enough for the police to claim exigent circumstances merely because the warrant is for narcotics, for example, and narcotics are by nature easily disposable. There must be particular reasons in that particular case.[350] Exigent circumstances were found to exist in *People v. Conner,*[351] where the police knew the defendant kept buckets of water near toilets to aid in disposing of contraband; that the defendant maintained impregnable security on all ground floor doors and windows; and that during two previous searches, the defendant turned twelve guard dogs loose on the police.

Illinois courts have also approved of ruses used to peacefully gain entrance to a building that is to be searched. In *People v. Bargo,*[352] a police officer

---

(ii) against another person.

(2) that if notice were given there is an imminent "danger" that evidence will be destroyed.

This amendment became effective January 1, 1998. *See* People v. Hancock, 301 Ill. App. 3d 786, 704 N.E.2d 431, 435 (4th Dist. 1998) (no-knock search warrant need not be quashed where defendant was not present at residence at time of entry and there was no property damage; no constitutional rights of defendant's were violated).

349. *Ouellette,* 78 Ill. 2d 511, 401 N.E.2d at 511 (quoting 2 W. LAFAVE, SEARCH AND SEIZURE 134–35 (1978)). *See also* People v. Trask, 167 Ill. App. 3d 694, 521 N.E.2d 1222 (2d Dist. 1988) (exigent circumstances found to exist where officer knew defendant had previously concealed loaded pistol).

350. *Ouellette,* 78 Ill. 2d 511, 401 N.E.2d at 511; People v. Clark, 144 Ill. App. 3d 7, 494 N.E.2d 166 (3d Dist. 1986). *See also* People v. Condon, 195 Ill. App. 3d 815, 552 N.E.2d 413 (2d Dist. 1990), *aff'd,* 148 Ill. 2d 96, 592 N.E.2d 951 (1992) (mere presence of weapons in home per se not sufficient to justify failure to "knock and announce"), *cert. denied,* 507 U.S. 948 (1993); *Riddle,* 258 Ill. App. 3d 253, 630 N.E.2d at 146–47 (presence of guns, drugs, and pit bulls not exigent circumstances because no evidence defendant would use gun against police, defendant had quick means to dispose of drugs, or that dogs were vicious); People v. Masters, 155 Ill. App. 3d 1015, 508 N.E.2d 1163 (4th Dist. 1987) (examples of exigent circumstances).

351. 78 Ill. 2d 513, 401 N.E.2d 513 (1979). *Cf.* People v. Clark, 144 Ill. App. 3d 7, 494 N.E.2d 166 (3d Dist. 1986) (use of battering ram to execute search warrant held improper where no exigent circumstances existed). *See also* People v. Hardin, 179 Ill. App. 3d 1072, 535 N.E.2d 1044 (2d Dist. 1989) (exigent circumstances present when officers had reason to believe person in home at time of executing search warrant was armed).

352. 64 Ill. App. 3d 1011, 382 N.E.2d 83 (1st Dist. 1978).

disguised as a letter carrier gained entry into a home after ringing the doorbell and informing the defendant that he had a package for her. Only after he gained entrance did he announce his office. The court found that this subterfuge did not in any way violate section 108-8.[353]

§ 1.15 — Detention and Search of Persons on Premises

Illinois law allows the person executing a search warrant to "reasonably detain to search" any person on the premises at the time to either protect himself or herself from attack or to prevent the disposal or concealment of any item particularly described in the warrant.[354] The justification for the search is not limited solely to the protection of the police officer;[355] because it is also concerned with the preservation of evidence, it is more akin to a "search incident to arrest."[356] Because of its similarity to a "search incident to arrest," the timing of a section 108-9 search must be strictly construed; it must be conducted at the earliest opportune moment after the officer decides it is necessary.[357] In applying section 108-9, courts have held that the person searched must have a connection with the premises or persons named in the search warrant.[358] Additionally, the officer must show independent probable cause justifying the search of a person not named in the warrant.[359]

---

353. *See also* People v. Witherspoon, 216 Ill. App. 3d 323, 576 N.E.2d 1030 (1st Dist. 1991) (police activated defendant's car alarm to lure defendant from his home to execute a search warrant); People v. Sunday, 109 Ill. App. 3d 960, 441 N.E.2d 374 (2d Dist. 1982) (use of ruse to get defendant outside premises during execution of search warrant found proper).

354. 725 ILCS 5/108-9. *See* People v. Llanos, 288 Ill. App. 3d 592, 681 N.E.2d 598, 601 (1st Dist. 1997) (toolbox that police saw defendant carry onto premises of which defendant had in his possession during search was implicitly covered by search warrant because once box brought onto premises it assumed character of any other container that might conceal narcotics; further, judge issuing search warrant was advised that narcotics were stored in a box; cocaine found inside box admissible).

355. *See* Terry v. Ohio, 392 U.S. 1 (1968).

356. People v. Campbell, 67 Ill. App. 3d 748, 385 N.E.2d 171 (3d Dist. 1979) (citing Chimel v. California, 395 U.S. 752 (1969)).

357. People v. One 1968 Cadillac Automobile, 4 Ill. App. 3d 780, 281 N.E.2d 776 (2d Dist. 1972).

358. People v. Gutierrez, 109 Ill. 2d 59, 485 N.E.2d 845, 846 (1986); People v. Simmons, 210 Ill. App. 3d 692, 569 N.E.2d 591 (2d Dist. 1991) (no probable cause to search defendant nonresident).

359. *Gutierrez,* 109 Ill. 2d 59, 485 N.E.2d at 847 (citing Ybarra v. Illinois, 444 U.S. 85 (1979)). *See also* People v. Edwards, 144 Ill. 2d 108, 579 N.E.2d 336 (1991),

It should be noted that the statute does not say that probable cause must exist before a search can take place under this section. Yet Illinois courts have interpreted the language "reasonably detain to search" to mean that the officer must be prepared to articulate some reasons why he or she believed that the person might have attacked the officer or that the person might have disposed of the items.[360]

The statute clearly applies to people present at the time of the police entry.[361] Decisions differ in the situation of a person entering the premises either during or after the search. Key factors include the connection the person has with the residence and the stage of the search in which the entry occurs.[362] Although it is unclear whether the situation is covered by section 108-9, Illinois follows the holding of the United States Supreme Court in *Michigan v. Summer,*[363] which allows police executing a search warrant to detain and search an occupant of the premises found outside on the steps of the premises.[364]

---

cert. denied, 504 U.S. 942 (1992). *See* People v. Coats, 269 Ill. App. 3d 1008, 647 N.E.2d 1088, 1091 (3d Dist. 1995) (improper to search babysitter at address searched because she was not named in warrant and did not live there; connection with premises too attenuated), *cert. denied,* 516 U.S. 1147 (1996).

360. People v. Miller, 74 Ill. App. 3d 177, 392 N.E.2d 271 (1st Dist. 1979), *cert. denied,* 450 U.S. 915 (1981); People v. Dukes, 48 Ill. App. 3d 237, 363 N.E.2d 62 (1st Dist. 1977).

361. People v. Wolski, 83 Ill. App. 3d 17, 403 N.E.2d 528 (2d Dist. 1980), *cert. denied,* 450 U.S. 915 (1981); People v. Kielczynski, 130 Ill. App. 2d 231, 264 N.E.2d 767 (1st Dist. 1970). *See* People v. Allen, 268 Ill. App. 3d 279, 645 N.E.2d 263, 267 (1st Dist. 1994) (pat-down of passenger in backseat proper for officer's safety as long as probable cause existed to arrest driver of car).

362. People v. Miller, 74 Ill. App. 3d 177, 392 N.E.2d 271 (1st Dist. 1979) (search of defendant improper where defendant came to apartment after police had completed their search and police had no reason to believe she was dangerous); People v. Campbell, 67 Ill. App. 3d 748, 385 N.E.2d 171 (3d Dist. 1979) (search of defendant's purse proper where defendant entered apartment while police were lawfully searching it); People v. Dukes, 48 Ill. App. 3d 237, 363 N.E.2d 62 (1st Dist. 1977) (search of defendant improper where defendant was innocent stranger who mistakenly entered premises being searched); People v. Pugh, 69 Ill. App. 2d 312, 217 N.E.2d 557 (1st Dist. 1966) (search of defendant proper where he entered brother's apartment while police were still engaged in search).

363. 452 U.S. 692 (1981). *But see* Ybarra v. Illinois, 444 U.S. 85 (1979) (search warrant authorizing search of tavern and bartender will not per se justify search of patron).

364. People v. Valentin, 135 Ill. App. 3d 22, 480 N.E.2d 1351 (1st Dist. 1985); People v. Sunday, 109 Ill. App. 3d 960, 441 N.E.2d 374 (2d Dist. 1982).

§ 1.16 — Return to Court of Things Seized

Illinois law requires the police to return all seized items to the judge who authorized the search.[365] An Illinois court has differentiated between per se contraband and derivative contraband. Contraband per se are items which by possession alone constitute an offense. In contract, derivative contraband are articles which have been or are used in an unlawful manner.[366] When an article is not contraband per se, its use must have a rational relationship to an unlawful purpose before it is subject to forfeiture.[367] The police are also required to file an inventory of all items seized.[368] It is clear, however, that violation of these postsearch provisions will not invalidate an otherwise legal search.[369]

§ 1.17 — Challenge to the Accuracy of Warrant Affidavits

Traditionally, Illinois did not allow a defendant to impeach the veracity of the sworn statements on which a warrant was issued.[370] This changed in 1978 when the United States Supreme Court decided *Franks v. Delaware*,[371] which created a limited right to an evidentiary hearing to challenge the truthfulness of facts contained in an affidavit for a search warrant. This right to challenge can be applied to nongovernmental as well as governmental affiants.[372]

---

365. 725 ILCS 5/108-10.

366. People v. Massey, 219 Ill. App. 3d 909, 579 N.E.2d 1259 (5th Dist. 1991) (money not contraband per se and should have been returned).

367. *Id.,* 579 N.E.2d at 1264.

368. 725 ILCS 5/108-10.

369. People v. Curry, 56 Ill. 2d 162, 306 N.E.2d 292 (1973); People v. Hartfield, 94 Ill. App. 2d 421, 237 N.E.2d 193 (5th Dist. 1968).

370. People v. Stansberry, 47 Ill. 2d 541, 268 N.E.2d 431 (1971); People v. Nakon, 46 Ill. 2d 561, 264 N.E.2d 204 (1970); People v. Price, 46 Ill. 2d 209, 263 N.E.2d 484 (1970); People v. Berry, 46 Ill. 2d 175, 263 N.E.2d 487 (1970), *cert. denied,* 401 U.S. 959 (1971); People v. Mitchell, 45 Ill. 2d 148, 258 N.E.2d 345, *cert. denied,* 400 U.S. 882 (1970); People v. Bak, 45 Ill. 2d 140, 258 N.E.2d 341, *cert. denied,* 400 U.S. 882 (1970).

371. 438 U.S. 154 (1978). *See* People v. Vauzanges, 158 Ill. 2d 509, 634 N.E.2d 1085, 1089 (1994) (different standards exist for disclosure of informant's identity at preliminary hearing and trial; at pretrial stage court is concerned with *existence* of informant and with maintaining integrity of judicial process); People v. Sutton, 260 Ill. App. 3d 949, 631 N.E.2d 1326, 1333 (1st Dist. 1994) (*Franks* hearing not to be used for discovery; defendant's request to produce informant so he could cross-examine informant did not provide constitutional basis for production of informant).

372. People v. Born, 113 Ill. App. 3d 449, 447 N.E.2d 426 (2d Dist. 1983).

An affidavit in support of a search warrant is presumed to be valid.[373] However, a trial judge must conduct an evidentiary hearing if a defendant can make a substantial preliminary showing that (1) a false statement, made knowingly or intentionally or with a reckless disregard for the truth, was included by the affiant in the affidavit; and (2) the alleged false statement was necessary to the finding of probable cause.[374] The defendant cannot obtain a hearing with mere denials of the facts alleged in the affidavit; something more than conclusory statements are needed.[375] Affidavits or sworn statements of witnesses should be furnished, or their absence satisfactorily explained.[376] Moreover, the defendant can only attack the veracity of the affiant; the veracity of any informant the affiant may have relied on is irrelevant.[377]

373. People v. Gardner, 121 Ill. App. 3d 464, 459 N.E.2d 676 (2d Dist. 1984); People v. Born, 113 Ill. App. 3d 449, 447 N.E.2d 426 (2d Dist. 1983).

374. People v. Shiflet, 125 Ill. App. 3d 161, 465 N.E.2d 942, 951 (2d Dist. 1984) (citing Franks v. Delaware, 438 U.S. 154 (1978)). *See, e.g.*, People v. Pearson, 271 Ill. App. 3d 640, 648 N.E.2d 1024, 1027 (1st Dist. 1995) (defendant made a substantial showing that police included a false statement in search warrant affidavit where warrant was based solely upon information supplied by confidential informant, detective did not undertake independent investigation to corroborate time of alleged sale or any of informant's charges, and defendant's affidavit and corroborating affidavits provided apparently airtight alibi).

375. People v. Coleman, 91 Ill. App. 3d 646, 415 N.E.2d 553 (1st Dist. 1980); People v. Anderson, 74 Ill. App. 3d 363, 392 N.E.2d 938 (4th Dist. 1979).

376. People v. Martine, 106 Ill. 2d 429, 478 N.E.2d 262 (1985); People v. Redmond, 114 Ill. App. 3d 407, 449 N.E.2d 533, 536–37 (2d Dist. 1983) (quoting *Franks,* 438 U.S. at 171–72). *See* People v. Gomez, 236 Ill. App. 3d 283, 603 N.E.2d 702 (1st Dist. 1992) (the following proof by defendant was sufficient to warrant a preliminary *Franks* hearing: defendant was not party named in officer's affidavit, did not live in apartment where officer's affidavit claimed a drug transaction occurred, and did not have a key to apartment, nor was apartment rented at the time of the alleged drug transaction and the officer had previously filed nine different warrant complaints alleging substantially identical comments between the various defendants and informants participating in alleged drug transactions). *But see* People v. McBee, 228 Ill. App. 3d 769, 593 N.E.2d 574 (1st Dist. 1992) (denial of evidentiary hearing proper where no allegations that officer made false statement); People v. Maiden, 210 Ill. App. 3d 390, 569 N.E.2d 120 (1st Dist. 1991) (mere conclusory statements insufficient to require evidentiary hearing); People v. Rish, 208 Ill. App. 3d 751, 566 N.E.2d 919 (3d Dist. 1991) (denial of evidentiary hearing proper where no affidavits or offers of proof filed).

377. People v. George, 126 Ill. App. 3d 1, 466 N.E.2d 1242 (1st Dist. 1984); People v. Rodriguez, 119 Ill. App. 3d 575, 456 N.E.2d 989 (1st Dist. 1983); People v. Kelly, 118 Ill. App. 3d 794, 455 N.E.2d 826 (1st Dist. 1983). *See also* People v. Agyei, 232 Ill. App. 3d 546, 597 N.E.2d 696 (1st Dist. 1992) (false information

Courts have recognized the difficulty in presenting evidence sufficient to trigger a *Franks* hearing, especially in situations involving an anonymous informant.[378] Illinois courts have found there may be situations in which a defendant is entitled to learn the identity of an informant[379] and have left open the question of whether defendants can ever be provided with discovery to establish the need for a *Franks* hearing.[380]

If a *Franks* hearing is held, the defendant has the burden of proving that the affidavit contains perjury or a reckless disregard for the truth. This must be established by a preponderance of the evidence.[381] A mere showing of falsity is not sufficient to void the warrant. It is voided only if the defendant shows that, minus the falsehood, probable cause is not established by the affiant.[382] If the warrant is voided, the fruits of the search will be suppressed to the same extent as if probable cause were lacking on the face of the warrant.[383]

---

in affidavit did not require quashing of arrest; police had reason to believe the informer because he had given correct information in another narcotics case); People v. Martin, 148 Ill. App. 3d 1061, 500 N.E.2d 528 (1st Dist. 1986) (defendant may impeach the veracity of affiant but not affiant's informant).

378. *Rodriguez,* 119 Ill. App. 3d 575, 456 N.E.2d at 991 (citing United States v. Dorfman, 542 F. Supp. 345 (N.D. Ill. 1982)).

379. People v. Freeman, 121 Ill. App. 3d 1023, 460 N.E.2d 125 (2d Dist. 1984).

380. People v. Rodriguez, 119 Ill. App. 3d 575, 456 N.E.2d 989 (1st Dist. 1983).

381. People v. Shiflet, 125 Ill. App. 3d 161, 465 N.E.2d 942, 951 (2d Dist. 1984) (citing Franks v. Delaware, 438 U.S. 154 (1978)). *But see* People v. Edwards, 144 Ill. 2d 108, 579 N.E.2d 336 (1991) (denial of evidentiary hearing proper because defendant did not show false information was made with reckless disregard for the truth or intentional omission), *cert. denied,* 504 U.S. 942 (1992); People v. Lipscomb, 215 Ill. App. 3d 413, 574 N.E.2d 1345 (4th Dist. 1991) (defendant not entitled to a *Franks* hearing where affidavit did not indicate witness could positively identify defendant and affidavit did not indicate nexus between sexual assault and defendant's blood, hair, and saliva); People v. Cordero, 214 Ill. App. 3d 1007, 574 N.E.2d 800 (1st Dist. 1991) (affidavit not deficient simply because its format was similar to that of other complaints filed by same officer); People v. Elworthy, 214 Ill. App. 3d 914, 574 N.E.2d 727 (1st Dist. 1991) (presence of boilerplate language concerning reliability of informant did not affect affidavit's veracity); People v. Abata, 136 Ill. App. 3d 57, 482 N.E.2d 1119 (2d Dist. 1985) (defendants did not meet preponderance of evidence burden because they merely pled general denial creating only inference that affiant lied or recklessly disregarded truth).

382. People v. Shiflet, 125 Ill. App. 3d 161, 465 N.E.2d 942 (2d Dist. 1984).

383. People v. Redmond, 114 Ill. App. 3d 407, 449 N.E.2d 533, 536–37 (2d Dist. 1983) (citing Franks v. Delaware, 438 U.S. 154 (1978)).

The Illinois Supreme Court was asked to decide whether the omission of material facts is sufficient to void a warrant under the *Franks* case.[384] The court held that if the defendant shows that the omitted information was material and that it was omitted to mislead the magistrate, then the search warrant can be voided under *Franks.*[385]

If a reviewing court finds that a defendant was erroneously granted a *Franks* hearing, courts generally will not consider the evidence received at that hearing.[386] A finding in favor of a defendant at an improperly held hearing will be affirmed, however, if the hearing revealed the search warrant affiant recklessly disregarded the truth or lied in obtaining the warrant.[387] In this situation, courts can consider the evidence received at the hearing.[388]

The kind of evidence needed to trigger a *Franks* hearing is illustrated by *People v. Garcia.*[389] The affidavit requested a search warrant based on the fact

---

384. People v. Stewart, 105 Ill. 2d 22, 473 N.E.2d 840 (1984).

385. *Id.,* 473 N.E.2d at 849. For an earlier case applying *Franks* to a deliberate omission case, see *People v. Reynolds*, 96 Ill. App. 3d 79, 420 N.E.2d 1193 (3d Dist. 1981). *See also* People v. Chaney, 286 Ill. App. 3d 717, 677 N.E.2d 4, 7–8 (1st Dist. 1997) (new *Franks* hearing warranted where trial judge who issued second search warrant was not advised that the officer had previously conducted an unsuccessful search upon a search warrant that was based on the exact same information as that contained in the second warrant). *But see* People v. Hickey, 178 Ill. 2d 256, 687 N.E.2d 910, 923–34 (1997) (defendant not entitled to *Franks* hearing to challenge affidavit for search warrant to obtain blood and saliva samples based on affiant's failure to indicate that DNA search had indicated only preliminary match, affiant allegedly misrepresented and omitted facts concerning defendant's physical characteristics and the difference between them and the victim's description of perpetrator), *cert. denied,* 118 S. Ct. 2375 (1998).

386. People v. O'Neil, 135 Ill. App. 3d 1091, 482 N.E.2d 668 (1st Dist. 1985).

387. *Id.,* 482 N.E.2d at 674. *See* People v. Pearson, 271 Ill. App. 3d 640, 648 N.E.2d 1024, 1027 (1st Dist. 1995) (in determining whether defendant entitled to *Franks* hearing, defendant need only show officer-affiant acted recklessly in using information provided by confidential informant and need not show officer-affiant deliberately made false statements to obtain warrant).

388. *O'Neil,* 135 Ill. App. 3d 142, 482 N.E.2d at 674.

389. 109 Ill. App. 3d 142, 440 N.E.2d 269 (1st Dist. 1982), *cert. denied,* 460 U.S. 1040 (1983). To the extent that *Garcia* went beyond *Franks,* it was discredited in *People v. Lucente,* 116 Ill. 2d 133, 506 N.E.2d 1269 (1987). *Garcia* held that if an affidavit contained any false statements by the affiant, the warrant would have to be quashed. This posture was inconsistent with the limitation in *Franks* that if probable cause was found after excising the untruths, suppression would not result. *See* People v. Griffin, 178 Ill. 2d 65, 687 N.E.2d 820, 828 (1997) (the warrant affidavit, with informant's inculpatory statements excised, read in a common sense and realistic fashion, established probable cause and defendant was not entitled to a *Franks* hearing), *cert. denied,* 118 S. Ct. 2376 (1998).

that the defendant was selling cocaine or a certain drug. The defendant averred that the complaining officer had lied in every factual allegation in the affidavit. The officer alleged that the defendant's car was parked outside his apartment on the date in question. The defendant, however, alleged in a detailed affidavit that on that day he was driving his car from Florida to Chicago. The defendant appealed the trial court's refusal to allow a *Franks* hearing.[390] The appellate court reversed and remanded the case for a *Franks* hearing, holding that to require more of a showing from the defendant would place an "insurmountable burden" on defendants.[391]

Expanding on the *Franks* concept of a substantial preliminary showing necessary to trigger an evidentiary hearing, the Illinois Supreme Court, in *People v. Lucente,*[392] held that a trial judge must balance the statements contained in the warrant affidavit against the statements supporting the defendant's challenge.[393] Factors to be considered in the balancing include: the officer's independent corroboration on the informant's tip; evidence that the informant blatantly lied; the presumed validity of search warrants; the limited exceptions to the validity of search warrants; and the fact that the defendant's guilt or innocence is not being determined.[394] The court stated that under this balancing test, when the informant is confidential, an alibi-type preliminary

---

390. People v. David, 141 Ill. App. 3d 243, 489 N.E.2d 1124 (2d Dist. 1986).

391. *Garcia,* 109 Ill. App. 3d 142, 440 N.E.2d at 273. *See also* People v. Witherspoon, 216 Ill. App. 3d 323, 576 N.E.2d 1030 (1st Dist. 1991) (an alibi-type showing sufficed to hold a *Franks* hearing); People v. Zymantas, 147 Ill. App. 3d 420, 497 N.E.2d 1248 (1st Dist. 1986) (sufficient showing to trigger a *Franks* hearing).

392. 116 Ill. 2d 133, 506 N.E.2d 1269 (1987).

393. *Id.,* 506 N.E.2d at 1277.

394. *Id. See also* People v. Thompkins, 161 Ill. 2d 148, 641 N.E.2d 371, 381 (1994) (informant's subsequent affidavit that she never spoke to police about offense insufficient for *Franks* hearing because police could not have produced her name if she had not spoken with them and police able to corroborate details of her statement), *cert. denied,* 514 U.S. 1038 (1995); People v. Phillips, 265 Ill. App. 3d 438, 637 N.E.2d 715, 721 (1st Dist. 1994) (affidavits from interested parties not rise to level of preliminary showing of falsehood required for *Franks* hearing; showing of reliability of informant not required where informant himself is affiant and appeared before judge issuing warrant); People v. Elworthy, 214 Ill. App. 3d 914, 574 N.E.2d 727 (1st Dist. 1991) (officer's failure to corroborate and officer's omission of 10 to 13 occasions where searches based on informant's information unsuccessful did not establish officer's reckless disregard for truth). *But see* People v. Pearson, 271 Ill. App. 3d 640, 648 N.E.2d 1024, 1027 (1st Dist. 1995) (defendant made substantial showing to merit *Franks* hearing where warrant approved by state's attorney at 11:06 a.m. on September 11th and warrant alleged crime occurred on September 11th; simple deduction showed alleged sale must have occurred between midnight and 11:06 a.m. and averments in warrant

showing may or may not be sufficient to trigger a *Franks* hearing.[395] The court again declined, however, to decide whether an officer can ever be compelled to produce a confidential informant.[396]

§ 1.18 When a Search Is Not a Search

The mere fact that a police officer has recovered incriminating evidence against a person does not necessarily mean that the officer obtained it through a search. "A search implies a prying into hidden places for that which is concealed, and it is not a search to observe that which is open to view."[397] A

---

demonstrated police did not undertake independent investigation to corroborate crime).

395. *Lucente,* 116 Ill. 2d 133, 506 N.E.2d at 1277. *See also* People v. Cordero, 214 Ill. App. 3d 1007, 574 N.E.2d 800 (1st Dist. 1991) (alibi-type showing was sufficient evidence to grant suppression). *See* People v. Arce, 289 Ill. App. 3d 521, 683 N.E.2d 502, 506 (1st Dist. 1997) (denial of *Franks* hearing affirmed even though question existed as to the truthfulness of the informant's statements because warrant based on tip from informant who had worked with police for three and one-half years and defendant would not be able to accompany informant to location sworn to in affidavit without triggering alarm on his electronic home monitoring system; dissent argued defendant was entitled to a *Franks* hearing based on allegations that warrant affidavit contained false statements where defendant made substantial preliminary showing of an alibi; the fact informant was reliable did not address the falsity of the allegations). *But see* People v. McCoy, 295 Ill. App. 3d 988, 692 N.E.2d 1244, 1252 (1st Dist. 1998) (defendant charged with drug offenses was not entitled to *Franks* hearing where affidavits were executed by interested parties, and there were times unaccounted for in affidavits during which time informant could have purchased drugs from defendant).

396. *Lucente,* 116 Ill. 2d 133, 506 N.E.2d at 1273. *See also* People v. Elworthy, 214 Ill. App. 3d 914, 574 N.E.2d 727 (1st Dist. 1991) (disclosure of informant not required where judge reviewed informant's file, was convinced there was an informant, and informant did not participate).

397. People v. McCracken, 30 Ill. 2d 425, 197 N.E.2d 35, 37 (1964); People v. Davis, 33 Ill. 2d 134, 210 N.E.2d 530, 532 (1965); People v. Marvin, 358 Ill. 426, 193 N.E. 202, 203 (1934). *See* People v. Herrington, 163 Ill. 2d 507, 645 N.E.2d 957, 958 (1994) (defendant had no expectation of privacy in conversation under eavesdropping statute while individual to whom he was talking was recording conversation); People v. Calvert, 258 Ill. App. 3d 504, 629 N.E.2d 1154, 1160–61 (5th Dist. 1994) (no reasonable expectation of privacy in conversation at police station, therefore, inadvertent recording of conversation not considered search). *See also* People v. Neal, 109 Ill. 2d 216, 486 N.E.2d 898 (1985) (no Fourth Amendment search when state police unzipped trooper's department-issued raincoat pouch and found incriminating evidence because he had no reasonable

search implies an invasion and a quest with some sort of force, either actual or constructive. Where the police have the right to observe items and activity in open fields owned by the defendant, to seize items abandoned by the defendant, or to find evidence in plain view, no search has occurred because the police have not "pried into hidden places."[398] In a recent case, the Seventh Circuit held that thermal imaging scanning of one's home which detected heat emanating from marijuana crop was not a search within the Fourth Amendment.[399] According to this court, the defendant did not have a reasonable expectation of privacy in heat emitted from his property, since he took no steps to conceal or contain the heat emission.[400]

§ 1.19 — The Open Fields Doctrine

The "open fields" doctrine was first articulated by Justice Holmes in 1924 in *Hester v. United States*.[401] In holding that the police activities on the defendant's land did not violate the Fourth Amendment, Justice Holmes wrote, "[t]he special protection accorded by the Fourth Amendment to the people in their 'persons, houses, papers, and effects,' is not extended to the open fields. The distinction between the latter and the house is as old as the common law."[402] Nor are open fields within the meaning of the Fourth Amendment's use of the

---

expectation of privacy in state-owned property); People v. McKendrick, 138 Ill. App. 3d 1018, 486 N.E.2d 1297 (1st Dist. 1985) (one party to telephone conversation has no reasonable expectation that other party will not reveal what is said); People v. Liberg, 138 Ill. App. 3d 986, 486 N.E.2d 973 (2d Dist. 1985) (no reasonable expectation of privacy and therefore no Fourth Amendment violation when police officers overheard defendant making telephone call from cell in close proximity to officers).

398. *Marvin,* 358 Ill. 426, 193 N.E. at 203; People v. Hobson, 169 Ill. App. 3d 485, 525 N.E.2d 895 (1st Dist. 1988) (no search where police entered open garage to investigate activities for evidence of crime they had probable cause to believe was being committed); People v. Accardi, 284 Ill. App. 3d 31, 671 N.E.2d 373, 375 (2d Dist. 1996) (fly-over not a search requiring a warrant citing *California v. Ciraolo*, 476 U.S. 207 (1986)). *See also* United States v. McDonald, 100 F.3d 1320, 1326–27 (7th Cir. 1996) (police manipulating and feeling the outside of luggage for "bricks" of contraband did not constitute a search), *cert. denied*, 520 U.S. 1258 (1997).

399. United States v. Myers, 46 F.3d 668, 670 (7th Cir.), *cert denied*, 516 U.S. 1033 (1995). *See also* People v. Siwek, 284 Ill. App. 3d 7, 671 N.E.2d 358, 363 (2d Dist. 1996) (videotaping not a search where one party consented to it).

400. *Myers,* 46 F.3d at 670.

401. 265 U.S. 57 (1924).

402. *Id*. at 59.

term *effects*. "[T]he term 'effects' is less inclusive than 'property' and cannot be said to encompass open fields."[403]

The Illinois Supreme Court adopted the open fields doctrine in 1969 in *City of Decatur v. Kushmer*.[404] In this case, the defendant argued that city officials conducted a warrantless entry onto his land and took photographs of his property to charge him with violating a city ordinance prohibiting the storing of any materials that may harbor rats. The land the officials ventured on was a large unenclosed yard adjacent to the defendant's house where he had accumulated a variety of scrap materials. Because the condition of the premises was exposed to public view and was plainly visible from beyond the defendant's property, the court found that the defendant could have no reasonable expectation of privacy as to the area. Furthermore, the mere fact that the officials might have trespassed by entering the land to photograph the condition was held irrelevant to the Fourth Amendment analysis. The trespass did not change the fact that the defendant had no reasonable expectation of privacy as to the open fields surrounding his home.[405]

In 1987, the United States Supreme Court in *United States v. Dunn*[406] established four factors to be used in distinguishing "open fields" from the curtilage surrounding one's home.[407] *Dunn* said a judge should consider:

---

403. Oliver v. United States, 466 U.S. 170, 177 (1984).

404. 43 Ill. 2d 334, 253 N.E.2d 425 (1969).

405. People v. Smith, 288 Ill. App. 3d 820, 681 N.E.2d 80, 82 (1st Dist. 1997) (under open fields doctrine defendant could not claim a legitimate expectation of privacy in any unoccupied or undeveloped area beyond the immediate surroundings of his home; cocaine recovered from a vacant lot was admissible). *See* Miller v. Pollution Control Bd., 267 Ill. App. 3d 160, 642 N.E.2d 475, 483 (4th Dist. 1994) (entry upon land to photograph incriminating conditions visible from neighboring property not an unreasonable search or seizure because no justified expectation of privacy); People v. Lashmett, 71 Ill. App. 3d 429, 389 N.E.2d 888 (4th Dist. 1979) (entry of police onto defendant's farm to check serial number of certain farm equipment, which was located 100 to 125 yards away from defendant's house, held proper under open fields analysis), *cert. denied,* 444 U.S. 1081 (1980). *See also* United States v. Shanks, 97 F.3d 977, 979 (7th Cir. 1996) (police lawfully searched trash placed in alley adjacent to apartment building because trash was not within curtilage of residence), *cert. denied,* 519 U.S. 1135 (1997). *But see* People v. Accardi, 284 Ill. App. 3d 31, 671 N.E.2d 373, 375–76 (2d Dist. 1996) (even though police fly-over to observe contraband did not require a warrant because it was within the scope of the "open fields" doctrine, subsequent physical entry by police onto property to seize contraband was a search and seizure requiring a warrant).

406. United States v. Dunn, 480 U.S. 294 (1987).

407. *Id.* at 301.

(1) the proximity of the area claimed to be curtilage to the home; (2) whether the area is within an enclosure surrounding the home; (3) the nature and uses to which the area is put; and (4) the steps taken by the resident to protect the area from observation by passersby.[408]

At least one Illinois court has used these criteria in concluding that a warrantless search of defendant's property was invalid because it intruded on his curtilage.[409]

§ 1.20 — Abandonment

The person who abandons property no longer has a reasonable expectation of privacy as to that property. Thus, government examination and appropriation of such items does not run afoul of the Fourth Amendment.[410] Illinois courts have found that a person who leaves an automobile to prevent capture by police has abandoned both the car and its contents.[411] Items intentionally dropped by

---

408. *Id.;* People v. Janis, 139 Ill. 2d 300, 565 N.E.2d 633 (1990) (curtilage does not apply to areas immediately adjacent to or surrounding a commercial establishment).

409. People v. Stork, 203 Ill. App. 3d 1028, 561 N.E.2d 419 (5th Dist. 1990).

410. Abel v. United States, 362 U.S. 217 (1960) (warrantless examination of defendant's hotel room, once he had moved out, was not search under Fourth Amendment because defendant no longer had any reasonable expectation of privacy as to room or its contents); People v. Hoskins, 101 Ill. 2d 209, 461 N.E.2d 941, *cert. denied,* 469 U.S. 840 (1984); People v. Wilcher, 145 Ill. App. 3d 309, 495 N.E.2d 1001 (1st Dist. 1986), *cert. denied,* 480 U.S. 948 (1987). *See* People v. Smith, 203 Ill. App. 3d 545, 561 N.E.2d 252 (4th Dist. 1990) (discusses theoretical basis of abandonment doctrine). *See also* People v. Pacheco, 281 Ill. App. 3d 179, 666 N.E.2d 370, 374 (2d Dist. 1996) (where defendant discarded a bag, the bag became abandoned property in which the defendant had no possessory, ownership, or privacy interest, and thus lost any Fourth Amendment protection in the bag); United States v. McDonald, 100 F. 3d 1320, 1328 (7th Cir. 1996) (defendant had abandoned luggage where she refused to admit ownership when questioned about ownership repeatedly by police), *cert. denied,* 520 U.S. 1258 (1997). *But see* People v. Kozlowski, 278 Ill. App. 3d 40, 662 N.E.2d 630, 633–34 (2d Dist. 1996) (defendant did not abandon room despite being late in rent and having had his possessions removed where defendant made late rent payment and was still in possession of key).

411. People v. Jones, 38 Ill. 2d 427, 231 N.E.2d 580 (1967); People v. Washington, 90 Ill. App. 3d 631, 413 N.E.2d 170 (2d Dist. 1980), *cert. denied,* 454 U.S. 846 (1981). *See also* People v. Childs, 226 Ill. App. 3d 915, 589 N.E.2d 819 (4th Dist. 1992) (defendant fled car after being stopped for traffic violation); People v. Arnett, 217 Ill. App. 3d 626, 577 N.E.2d 773 (5th Dist. 1991) (officers had probable cause to believe unlocked car with warm engine within 100 yards of

individuals have been abandoned for Fourth Amendment purposes.[412] Items placed in the trash or garbage have likewise been abandoned,[413] even when the garbage is located on the defendant's property.[414]

However, the mere fact that a person has relinquished control over an item does not result in a finding of abandonment per se. Abandonment is a question of fact based on an examination of a person's act and concurrent intent.[415] Thus, it cannot be said that the owner of a mobile home abandons it when he or she has to live elsewhere because it has been largely destroyed by fire.[416] Moreover, where a person drops an object pursuant to an arrest later shown to be unlawful, that object will not be deemed to have been abandoned.[417]

§ 1.21 — Plain View

"The plain view doctrine authorizes seizure of illegal or evidentiary items visible to a police officer whose access to the object has some prior Fourth Amendment justification and who has probable cause to suspect that the item is connected with criminal activity."[418] The doctrine is grounded on the proposition that once police are lawfully in a position to observe an item firsthand, its owner's privacy interest in that item is lost. Because of the importance of justifying the officer's presence, the United States Supreme Court has said that

---

recent burglary was getaway car and search of glove box for ownership and impounding proper).

412. People v. Sylvester, 43 Ill. 2d 325, 253 N.E.2d 429 (1969); People v. Henderson, 33 Ill. 2d 225, 210 N.E.2d 483 (1965); People v. Brasfield, 28 Ill. 2d 518, 192 N.E.2d 914 (1963), *cert. denied*, 375 U.S. 980 (1964); People v. Pacini, 85 Ill. App. 3d 1076, 407 N.E.2d 897 (1st Dist. 1980).

413. People v. Huddleston, 38 Ill. App. 3d 277, 347 N.E.2d 76 (3d Dist. 1976). *See also* People v. Green, 153 Ill. App. 3d 888, 506 N.E.2d 867 (3d Dist. 1987) (trash can in public restroom considered in plain view).

414. People v. Stein, 51 Ill. App. 3d 421, 366 N.E.2d 629 (1st Dist. 1977). *See also* People v. Clodfelder, 176 Ill. App. 3d 339, 530 N.E.2d 1173 (4th Dist. 1988) (property left at railroad track embankment deemed abandoned).

415. *Huddleston*, 38 Ill. App. 3d 277, 347 N.E.2d at 79. *See also* People v. Lee, 226 Ill. App. 3d 1084, 590 N.E.2d 1000 (3d Dist. 1992) (mere disclaimer of property interest did not amount to abandonment of property).

416. People v. Dorney, 17 Ill. App. 3d 785, 308 N.E.2d 646 (4th Dist. 1974).

417. People v. Roebuck, 25 Ill. 2d 108, 183 N.E.2d 166 (1962).

418. Illinois v. Andreas, 463 U.S. 765, 771 (1983). *See* Coolidge v. New Hampshire, 403 U.S. 443 (1971); People v. Tyler, 210 Ill. App. 3d 833, 569 N.E.2d 240 (5th Dist. 1991) (officer's search of defendant's clothing at hospital not justified under plain view during inventory or to ascertain identity).

plain view is less an independent exception to the warrant requirement than a doctrine relating to the rights of a properly positioned police officer.[419]

Three requirements are needed to justify a warrantless seizure under the plain view doctrine. First, the police must observe the item from a place where they have a right to be.[420] Second, it must be immediately apparent to the police that the item is evidence of a crime.[421] Third, the discovery of the item must be inadvertent.[422]

§ 1.22 — — A Place Where an Officer Has a Right to Be

The requirement of observing the item from a place the officer has a right to be can be met several different ways. First, plain view can justify the seizure of items discovered during a search pursuant to a warrant issued for other

---

419. Texas v. Brown, 460 U.S. 730, 739 (1983) (plurality opinion). *See* People v. Evans, 259 Ill. App. 3d 650, 631 N.E.2d 872, 876 (2d Dist. 1994) (following routine traffic stop, officer did not have probable cause to search small wooden box in defendant's shirt pocket because it was not a "single-purpose" container which had no legitimate purpose; hence, arrest based on drugs found in box and evidence subsequently found in automobile inadmissible). *But see* People v. Hilt, 298 Ill. App. 3d 121, 698 N.E.2d 233, 236 (2d Dist. 1998) (police had probable cause to search defendant's car following a traffic stop in the early morning hours after they observed a baggie with a knotted corner, a unique container that was well known to be used for narcotic transactions; the police had prior experience with such containers; and the stop occurred in an area known for drug transactions at that time of day).

420. People v. Hamilton, 74 Ill. 2d 457, 386 N.E.2d 53 (1979); People v. Holt, 18 Ill. App. 3d 10, 309 N.E.2d 376 (1st Dist. 1974). *See* Coolidge v. New Hampshire, 403 U.S. 443 (1971).

421. People v. Tate, 38 Ill. 2d 184, 230 N.E.2d 697 (1967); People v. Mullens, 66 Ill. App. 3d 748, 383 N.E.2d 1369 (1st Dist. 1978). *See* Coolidge v. New Hampshire, 403 U.S. 443 (1971); People v. Edwards, 144 Ill. 2d 108, 579 N.E.2d 336 (1991) (officer acted reasonably in searching for search warrant items in telephone directory), *cert. denied,* 504 U.S. 942 (1992). *But see* People v. Alexander, 272 Ill. App. 3d 698, 650 N.E.2d 1038, 1047 (1st Dist. 1995) (evidence suppressed since incriminating nature of stolen automobile parts could not have been immediately apparent to officers upon entry into garage).

422. People v. Sexton, 118 Ill. App. 3d 998, 455 N.E.2d 884 (4th Dist. 1983); People v. Smith, 101 Ill. App. 3d 772, 428 N.E.2d 641 (4th Dist. 1981). Although Illinois appears to demand inadvertency, this element did not command a majority in the United States Supreme Court in *Coolidge,* and courts across the country are split. *Compare* United States v. Szymkowiak, 727 F.2d 95 (6th Cir. 1984) (inadvertence is necessary in finding of plain view) *with* United States v. Bellina, 665 F.2d 1335 (4th Cir. 1981) (dictum) (questioning whether element of inadvertence is necessary).

purposes. For example, in *People v. Hester*,[423] the Third District Appellate Court held that the fact that the police were conducting a search pursuant to a warrant authorizing the seizure of marijuana and hash pipes did not preclude them from seizing other incriminating items discovered during the search.[424] A search warrant does not, however, provide the police with carte blanche to go beyond the limits of the warrant to seize such items. In *People v. Gualandi*,[425] for example, a warrant authorized the police to search for items on the first floor of a house. While conducting the search, the police also searched the second floor and found marijuana. The appellate court found that this observation of marijuana could not justify the issuance of a search warrant because the police had no right to go to the second floor.

Second, plain view can justify the seizure of items discovered during a search pursuant to an exception to the warrant requirement. For example, in *People v. Elders*,[426] the police made a warrantless entry into a trailer and recovered contraband. The Fifth District found the warrantless entry justified because the police reasonably believed that an emergency existed and that the entry was necessary to protect a child's life. Because the police were in a place they had a right to be when they saw the contraband, the seizure was justified.[427]

---

423. 22 Ill. App. 3d 118, 319 N.E.2d 301 (3d Dist. 1974).

424. *Accord* People v. Philyaw, 34 Ill. App. 3d 616, 339 N.E.2d 461 (2d Dist. 1975) (seizure of stereo tapes proper under plain view doctrine even though warrant authorizing search merely listed "tools and motor oil").

425. 21 Ill. App. 3d 992, 316 N.E.2d 195 (4th Dist. 1974).

426. 63 Ill. App. 3d 554, 380 N.E.2d 10 (5th Dist. 1978).

427. *See* People v. Lovitz, 39 Ill. App. 3d 624, 350 N.E.2d 276 (2d Dist. 1976), *cert. denied*, 434 U.S. 842 (1977); People v. Clayton, 34 Ill. App. 3d 376, 339 N.E.2d 783 (1st Dist. 1975); People v. Brooks, 7 Ill. App. 3d 767, 289 N.E.2d 207 (1st Dist. 1972). When the initial entry is unlawful, police observations are subject to suppression. People v. Abrams, 48 Ill. 2d 446, 271 N.E.2d 37 (1971); People v. Clark Memorial Home, 114 Ill. App. 2d 249, 252 N.E.2d 546 (2d Dist. 1969). *See also* People v. Dale, 301 Ill. App. 3d 593, 703 N.E.2d 927, 931–32 (4th Dist. 1998) (seizure of drugs that fell out of defendant's clothing while officer watched him pack was not justified by plain view because officer exceeded scope of defendant's consent). *But see* People v. Garcia, 296 Ill. App. 3d 769, 695 N.E.2d 1292, 1299 (1st Dist. 1998) (police who viewed gun through open door while making an arrest on the front porch was justified in entering home where drugs were seen in plain view); People v. Tingle, 279 Ill. App. 3d 706, 665 N.E.2d 383, 389 (1st Dist. 1996) (despite court's finding that defendant was illegally arrested on the sidewalk, where he independently directed officer's attention to his nearby car, the officer's view of a gun in plain view justified seizure of gun from car and subsequent search of remainder of vehicle for other items); People v. Chavez, 228 Ill. App. 3d 54, 592 N.E.2d 69 (1st Dist. 1992) (seizure of stained pants justified where officers present pursuant to consent and knew crime scene was

Third, plain view can justify the discovery of evidence by any of the senses as long as the police are properly engaged in law enforcement activities. Thus, an officer can testify about a conversation he or she inadvertently overhears through an open door.[428] An officer's mere smelling of the odor of burning marijuana can be sufficient to establish probable cause for a search.[429] Seeing an item in a front yard[430] or through a car window[431] is sufficient to justify seizure if the police activity is otherwise lawful.

Illinois courts have also dealt with the use of extrinsic aids to augment the senses. They have held that the use of a flashlight does not remove a situation from the plain view rule.[432] However, although it has been held that the use of binoculars by police does not per se constitute an unreasonable search,[433] it is of "vital importance"[434] whether the police had reason to believe a crime had taken place or was taking place at the time they used them. Police use of an airplane to fly over the defendant's farm to search for stolen farm equipment

---

muddy and bloody); People v. Harrell, 226 Ill. App. 3d 866, 589 N.E.2d 943 (4th Dist. 1992) (second and third search invalid, not pursuant to mother's consent); People v. Bradley, 220 Ill. App. 3d 890, 581 N.E.2d 310 (1st Dist. 1991) (taking of photographs of murder victim was not "seizure" where officers were validly on premises); People v. Galdine, 212 Ill. App. 3d 472, 571 N.E.2d 182 (2d Dist. 1991) (defendant's consent to undercover agents to enter house justified plain view seizure); People v. Torry, 212 Ill. App. 3d 759, 571 N.E.2d 827 (1st Dist. 1991) (bloody clothing in bathroom and on back porch of defendant's apartment properly seized by officer pursuant to sister's valid consent).

428. People v. Brooks, 51 Ill. 2d 156, 281 N.E.2d 326 (1972).

429. People v. Stout, 106 Ill. 2d 77, 477 N.E.2d 498 (1985). *See* People v. Strauser, 146 Ill. App. 3d 128, 496 N.E.2d 1131 (1st Dist. 1986) (smell of raw marijuana emanating from briefcase was enough to establish probable cause). *But see* People v. Cohen, 146 Ill. App. 3d 618, 496 N.E.2d 1231 (2d Dist. 1986) (odor of burning cannabis, while sufficient to provide probable cause, does not justify warrantless entry into private residence absence exigent circumstances).

430. People v. George, 49 Ill. 2d 372, 274 N.E.2d 26 (1971). *See* City of Decatur v. Kushmer, 43 Ill. 2d 334, 253 N.E.2d 425 (1969) (photographing items on defendant's private property exposed to public did not constitute search).

431. People v. Bombacino, 51 Ill. 2d 17, 280 N.E.2d 697, *cert. denied,* 409 U.S. 912 (1972); People v. Elmore, 28 Ill. 2d 263, 192 N.E.2d 219 (1963); People v. Oliver, 129 Ill. App. 2d 83, 262 N.E.2d 597 (4th Dist. 1970).

432. People v. Bombacino, 51 Ill. 2d 17, 280 N.E.2d 697 (1972); People v. Epperly, 33 Ill. App. 3d 886, 338 N.E.2d 581 (2d Dist. 1975); People v. Oliver, 129 Ill. App. 2d 83, 262 N.E.2d 597 (4th Dist. 1970).

433. People v. Hicks, 49 Ill. App. 3d 421, 364 N.E.2d 440 (1st Dist. 1977).

434. People v. Ciochon, 23 Ill. App. 3d 363, 319 N.E.2d 332 (2d Dist. 1974).

has been approved where the equipment was in open view and located in open fields.[435]

§ 1.23 — — It Must Be "Immediately Apparent" That the Item Seized Is Evidence of a Crime

Even if an item is in plain view, the police may not seize it unless it is immediately apparent that it is evidence of a crime.[436] This requirement has provided the courts with some difficulty. Although it was found that it was immediately apparent that a tinfoil package was evidence of a drug crime,[437] the search of an envelope with a glassine window through which the officer believed he saw policy slips was found improper under the plain view doctrine because it was not immediately apparent that the item was criminal evidence.[438] Moreover, the United States Supreme Court has held that the "plain view" authority is not constitutionally valid when a police officer must first physically remove an object to determine if it is evidence of a crime.[439]

The United States Supreme Court in *Texas v. Brown*[440] attempted to define the contours of the immediately apparent requirement. *Brown* dealt with a stop at a routine driver's license checkpoint. While the officer examined the defendant's driver's license, he saw a knotted opaque balloon fall from the defendant's hand. The officer, after seeing plastic vials and white powder in the car, seized the balloon. The Supreme Court held that, even though a balloon is not contraband per se, the seizure was justified under the plain view exception because an experienced police officer, who saw evidence of narcotics in the car and who knew that balloons were often used as containers for narcotics, had probable cause to believe the balloon contained narcotics. Thus, in this situation even an innocent item such as a balloon could be seized because it was immediately apparent that it was criminal evidence.[441]

---

435. See the discussion of the open fields exception in § 1.19 in this chapter. *See also* Florida v. Riley, 488 U.S. 445 (1989) (no reasonable expectation of privacy that fallen-down greenhouse would not be observed by police helicopter at an altitude of 400 feet).

436. Coolidge v. New Hampshire, 403 U.S. 443, 466 (1971) (plurality). *Accord* People v. Sexton, 118 Ill. App. 3d 998, 455 N.E.2d 884 (4th Dist. 1983).

437. People v. Davis, 33 Ill. 2d 134, 210 N.E.2d 530 (1965).

438. People v. Tate, 38 Ill. 2d 184, 230 N.E.2d 697 (1967).

439. Arizona v. Hicks, 480 U.S. 321 (1987).

440. 460 U.S. 730 (1983).

441. *See, e.g.,* People v. Washington, 238 Ill. App. 3d 371, 610 N.E.2d 88 (1st Dist. 1992) (officer's experience justified seizure of plastic sandwich bag protruding from defendant's waistband under plain view doctrine even though officer was unable to see contents of the bag), *cert. denied,* 509 U.S. 929 (1993).

Brown emphasized that an item need not be contraband to be seized under the immediately apparent rationale. Nevertheless, the police must be able to articulate reasons for believing that the seized item is criminal evidence. Thus, it was found improper to seize a television during an arrest of the defendant in his room[442] and improper to seize a brown bag from the defendant's car during a traffic stop.[443] Moreover, it was found improper for the police to seize a motorcycle found in the defendant's van pursuant to a traffic stop, even though the police officer knew the driver was a convicted burglar and that the address given by the driver was a place frequented by persons dealing in stolen motorcycle parts.[444]

The full effect of *Brown* has yet to be determined. However, in a case decided several months after *Brown,* the Fourth District—without specifically citing

---

442. People v. Mullins, 66 Ill. App. 3d 748, 383 N.E.2d 1369 (1st Dist. 1978). *Compare* People v. Jones, 269 Ill. App. 3d 797, 635 N.E.2d 961, 968 (1st Dist. 1994) (once defendant's mother gave police permission to enter, search of basement justified by plain view doctrine and exigent circumstances where officer looked down basement steps and based on knowledge and experience believed red plastic bag he saw constituted evidence of narcotics delivery). *See also* People v. Watkins, 293 Ill. App. 3d 496, 688 N.E.2d 798, 803 (1st Dist. 1997) (plain view doctrine authorizes the warrantless seizure of pager resting on top of pile of money, suggesting use in connection with drug activities, while police conducting search incident to lawful arrest).

443. People v. Collins, 53 Ill. App. 3d 253, 368 N.E.2d 1007 (5th Dist. 1977). *But see* People v. Madison, 264 Ill. App. 3d 481, 637 N.E.2d 1074, 1078 (1st Dist. 1994) (incriminating nature of brown chunks in plastic bag which defendant was holding immediately apparent, therefore, officers had probable cause to enter hood of car and retrieve bag they observed defendant place there); People v. Moore, 259 Ill. App. 3d 574, 631 N.E.2d 470, 472 (3d Dist. 1994) (plain view allows warrantless seizure where following traffic offense officer saw cigarette package with top torn off on dashboard and inside were clear plastic bags of white powder "readily recognizable as cocaine").

444. People v. Nally, 71 Ill. App. 3d 238, 389 N.E.2d 262 (2d Dist. 1979). *See also* People v. Alexander, 272 Ill. App. 3d 698, 650 N.E.2d 1038, 1045 (1st Dist. 1995) (search of garage and seizure of stolen automobile parts not valid under plain view where police had no reasonable belief items were evidence of criminal activity since police only knew that three years prior defendant was implicated in possession of stolen auto parts and had no additional facts to support a reasonable belief that parts in the garage were stolen); People v. Brink, 174 Ill. App. 3d 804, 529 N.E.2d 1 (4th Dist. 1988) ("plain view" not applicable when police had no probable cause to seize items from vehicle in order to obtain serial numbers of items which later proved to be stolen); People v. McGhee, 106 Ill. App. 3d 767, 436 N.E.2d 267 (3d Dist. 1982) (plain view doctrine does not justify search based on discovery of tavern glass smelling of alcohol and lying on its side in defendant's car).

Brown—justified the seizure of a black medical bag under the plain view doctrine by holding that because it was so unlikely that the defendant could legally possess such a bag, it could be found that the incriminating character of the bag was immediately apparent.[445]

§ 1.24 — — The Item Must Have Been Discovered Inadvertently

A plurality of the Supreme Court in *Coolidge v. New Hampshire*[446] held that the plain view doctrine cannot be applied when the police are aware in advance that incriminating evidence will be found at a location. In other words, if the discovery is not inadvertent, the plain view exception does not apply and a warrant is required.

However, the United States Supreme Court explicitly rejected the "inadvertency" requirement in *Horton v. California.*[447] All that is necessary to invoke "plain view" is that it is "immediately apparent" that the item is contraband or evidence of criminality and that the officer is in a place where he has a right to be.[448] At least one Illinois court has approvingly cited *Horton* for this proposition.[449]

§ 1.25 — Drug and Medical Testing

The United States Supreme Court has upheld random drug testing of three classes of employees: (1) those carrying firearms or involved in drug interdiction; (2) those with access to confidential documents; and (3) those occupying

---

445. People v. Sexton, 118 Ill. App. 3d 998, 455 N.E.2d 884 (4th Dist. 1983); People v. Hebel, 174 Ill. App. 3d 1, 527 N.E.2d 1367 (5th Dist. 1988) (plain view doctrine applied to lewd photographs), *cert. denied,* 489 U.S. 1085 (1989). *Compare* Penny v. Penny, 188 Ill. App. 3d 499, 544 N.E.2d 1015 (1st Dist. 1989) (mere fact that officer saw opaque black plastic container in defendant's car did not create probable cause for officer to seize it).

446. 403 U.S. 443 (1971).

447. Horton v. California, 496 U.S. 128 (1990).

448. *Id.* at 136.

449. People v. Gentile, 205 Ill. App. 3d 952, 563 N.E.2d 926, 931–32 (1st Dist. 1990). *See also* People v. Edwards, 144 Ill. 2d 108, 579 N.E.2d 336 (1991) (when officer, flipping through telephone directory, saw victim's name circled, directory became immediately apparent evidence), *cert. denied,* 504 U.S. 942 (1992); People v. Washington, 238 Ill. App. 3d 371, 610 N.E.2d 88 (1st Dist. 1992) (officer's seizure of plastic sandwich bag protruding from defendant's waistband constituted a permissible warrantless seizure under the plain view doctrine), *cert. denied,* 509 U.S. 929 (1993).

safety-sensitive positions.[450] The Supreme Court has also upheld random testing of student athletes. In *Vernonia School District v. Acton*,[451] the Court held that a school's policy which required student athletes to submit to random drug testing was constitutional under both the Fourth and Fourteenth Amendments.[452] Although the Court found that the testing constituted a search within the meaning of the Fourth Amendment, it found that the athletes' expectation of privacy was minimal based on communal undressing, the fact students were subject to pre-season medical examinations, and the fact the students' conduct was strictly regulated by school rules.[453] In addition, the privacy interests were "negligible" and the test results were reported to only a limited number of persons.[454] Finally, the government concern at issue, deterring drug use by students and particularly, athletes, was important, if not compelling.[455] Thus, there is no need to obtain an arrest warrant or search warrant, or establish probable cause before conducting such a test.[456] The Illinois Legislature has enacted an AIDS testing statute which provides for testing of any defendant convicted of unlawful possession of hypodermic needle or syringe.[457] Illinois courts have upheld the constitutionality of this statute, relying on *Von Raab* and *Skinner,* finding it reasonable under the Fourth Amendment.[458] In *People v. Floyd*,[459] the court held that blood tests imposed on involuntarily committed patients, including defendant, at a mental health facility, which were used to

---

450. National Treasury Employees Union v. Von Raab, 489 U.S. 656 (1989); Skinner v. Railway Labor Executives Ass'n, 489 U.S. 602 (1989); People v. Wealer, 264 Ill. App. 3d 6, 636 N.E.2d 1129, 1135 (2d Dist. 1994) (statute requiring persons convicted of certain sex offenses to submit blood and saliva specimens to Illinois State Police for DNA testing and maintenance of a data bank not unreasonable search and seizure). *But see* Hillard v. Bagnola, 297 Ill. App. 3d 906, 698 N.E.2d 170, 178–79 (1st Dist. 1998) (compelled urinalysis of police officer did not violate Fourth Amendment where evidence was sufficient to show reasonable articulable grounds to suspect officer of drug involvement).

451. 515 U.S. 646 (1995).

452. *Id.* at 665–66.

453. *Id.* at 656–57.

454. *Id.* at 658.

455. *Id.* at 661.

456. *Id.* at 653–54.

457. 730 ILCS 5/5-5-3(h) .

458. People v. Adams, 149 Ill. 2d 331, 597 N.E.2d 574 (1992); People v. C.S., 222 Ill. App. 3d 348, 583 N.E.2d 726 (2d Dist. 1991); People v. Thomas, 220 Ill. App. 3d 110, 580 N.E.2d 1353 (2d Dist. 1991).

459. 274 Ill. App. 3d 855, 655 N.E.2d 10 (5th Dist. 1995).

facilitate and monitor psychotropic medication, were not unreasonable searches and seizures because tests served a proper purpose to treat patients.[460]

In *People v. Kirk*,[461] defendant was involved in a car accident that caused the death of his girlfriend. He was taken to the hospital at which time he had been requested to provide blood and urine samples. Upon testing of the samples, it was determined that his BAC was .06 and that cannabis was present in his urine. At the trial for recission of the summary suspension, the urine evidence was barred, the trial court finding that there was no probable cause to request the urine sample. The appellate court disagreed, stating that under section 11-501.1(a), once an officer believes that a driver is chemically impaired, the officer can request any kind of test—breath, urine, or blood. The officer need not have "individualized suspicion" of drugs or alcohol before requesting multiple chemical tests.[462] The court further noted that its decision was supported by section 11-501.6(a) under which an officer can request a chemical test without probable cause if: (1) an accident has occurred that results in serious injury or death; and (2) the driver is issued a ticket. In the instant case, both conditions were met. The court distinguished *Krosse* and *Klyczek* because in those cases the additional tests were requested only after the initial test failed to provide the officer with a favorable result. In the instant case, both tests were requested at the same time.[463]

§ 1.26 — Administrative Inspections

In *Camara v. Municipal Court,* the United States Supreme Court, in upholding housing safety inspections, declared that there can be no ready test for determining the reasonableness other than by balancing the need to search against the invasion which the search entails.[464] The *Camara* Court noted three factors to consider in balancing: (1) whether the practice at issue has a long history of judicial and public acceptance; (2) whether the practice is essential to achieve acceptable results; and (3) whether the practice involves a relatively limited invason of privacy.[465] The *Camara* rationale has been extended to:

---

460. *Id.*, 655 N.E.2d at 21.

461. 291 Ill. App. 3d 610, 684 N.E.2d 437 (4th Dist. 1997).

462. *Id.*, 684 N.E.2d at 440–41.

463. *Id.*, 684 N.E.2d at 442.

464. Camara v. Municipal Court, 387 U.S. 523 (1967).

465. *Id.*

inspection of mines;[466] welfare recipients;[467] fire scenes;[468] border searches;[469] vehicle use regulations;[470] prisoner searches;[471] testing water for hazardous waste.[472]

Following Supreme Court precedent, the Illinois Appellate Court held that a teacher had a reasonable suspicion to confiscate a student's jacket and turn it over to the police.[473] In this case, the defendant was in a behavior disorder class and was not allowed to wear his coat.[474] When the teacher asked him to remove his coat, he refused. He then attempted to confront another student, the teacher intervened, and defendant threw her. The defendant then removed his jacket and placed it on a chair. The teacher, who thought that the defendant had a weapon in the coat, confiscated it. In finding the teacher had reasonable suspicion to confiscate the jacket, the court noted that she had direct knowledge of defendant's recent increased disruptive behavior and of his comments concerning weapons. He also displayed physical aggression towards her and continued to confront another student despite her efforts to stop him.[475] The court also found that the police properly searched the jacket incident to his arrest even though they searched the jacket at the police station rather than at the scene.[476] The police had arrested defendant for aggravated battery, and they had been told by the teacher she believed the jacket contained a weapon. The defendant did not have access to the jacket, and the police decided not to search the jacket in the classroom as enough disruption had already occurred.[477]

If an administrative procedure provides for securing a search warrant, the provision must be complied with.[478] However, a prior suspicion of statutory

---

466. Donovan v. Dewey, 452 U.S. 594 (1981).

467. Wyman v. James, 400 U.S. 309 (1971).

468. Michigan v. Tyler, 436 U.S. 499 (1978).

469. United States v. Ramsey, 431 U.S. 606 (1977).

470. Delaware v. Prouse, 440 U.S. 648 (1979).

471. Bell v. Wolfish, 441 U.S. 520 (1979).

472. People v. Electronic Plating Co., 291 Ill. App. 3d 328, 683 N.E.2d 465, 469 (1st Dist. 1997) (no expectation of privacy in waste waters flushed out of commercial premises into sewer system), *cert. denied*, 523 U.S. 1048 (1998).

473. People v. McKinney, 274 Ill. App. 3d 880, 655 N.E.2d 40, 45 (5th Dist. 1995).

474. *Id.*, 655 N.E.2d at 44.

475. *Id.*

476. *Id.*, 655 N.E.2d at 46.

477. *Id.*

478. People v. Prolerized Chicago Corp., 225 Ill. App. 3d 307, 587 N.E.2d 1175 (1st Dist. 1992).

violation will not make a subsequent warrantless inspection unreasonable.[479] If evidence of criminal activity is discovered during the course of a valid administrative search, it may be seized under the plain view exception.[480] Administrative searches may not be used as a pretext to search for evidence of criminal violations.[481]

§ 1.27 School Searches

In *New Jersey v. T.L.O.*,[482] the United States Supreme Court recognized that the Fourth Amendment, as extended to the states by the Fourteenth Amendment, does protect public school students against unreasonable searches and seizures in school.[483] However, courts must strike a balance between the students' legitimate expectation of privacy and the school's security need to maintain a safe environment in which students can learn.[484] Thus, the proper standard to apply in cases of school searches by a police officer or public school official is not probable cause, but instead the lesser standard of reasonable suspicion.[485] Thus, in order to conduct a search or seizure in a school, the action must be justified at its inception and the search actually conducted must be reasonably related in scope to the circumstances which justified the interference in the first place.[486]

---

479. Colonnade Catering Corp. v. United States, 410 F.2d 197 (1969), *rev'd on other grounds,* 397 U.S. 72 (1970).

480. Michigan v. Clifford, 464 U.S. 287 (1984).

481. People v. Madison, 121 Ill. 2d 195, 520 N.E.2d 374, *cert. denied,* 488 U.S. 907 (1988). *See* People v. Nash, 278 Ill. App. 3d 157, 662 N.E.2d 552, 555 (5th Dist. 1996) (administrative inspection of timber buyers's records unreasonable usurpation of privacy interest where used as tool to further criminal investigation because police already had evidence of criminal activity).

482. 469 U.S. 325 (1985).

483. *Id.* at 333.

484. *Id.* at 337–40.

485. *Id.* at 340–41.

486. *Id.* at 341–42. *See* People v. Dilworth, 169 Ill. 2d 195, 661 N.E.2d 310, 317–18 (where a police officer was assigned to the school as a full-time member of staff and where the search was conducted at the request of a teacher in furtherance of the school's attempt to maintain a proper school environment, reasonable suspicion standard applies; reasonable suspicion existed under the facts of the case for the officer to suspect defendant was carrying drugs in a flashlight and thus, the search of the flashlight was reasonable), *cert. denied,* 517 U.S. 1197 (1996).

In *People v. Pruitt*, 278 Ill. App. 3d 194, 662 N.E.2d 540 (1st Dist. 1996), the court held that the use of metal detectors to screen students before entering school was reasonable under the Fourth Amendment. *Id.*, 662 N.E.2d at 547. No individualized suspicion was required. The metal detectors satisfied the balancing

§ 1.28 Searches of Vehicles

If the police have probable cause to search a vehicle, it can generally be accomplished without a warrant. This exception to the warrant requirement was first established by the United States Supreme Court in 1925 in *Carroll v. United States*.[487] Although the *Carroll* Court found that an individual does possess some privacy interest in an automobile, the Fourth Amendment affords less protection to a vehicle than to other structures. This is true for two reasons. First, the inherent mobility of vehicles suggests that they be treated differently from stationary structures. The United States Supreme Court expressed this idea:

> [T]he guaranty of freedom from unreasonable searches and seizures by the Fourth Amendment has been construed, practically since the beginning of Government, as recognizing a necessary difference between a search of a store, dwelling house or other structure in respect of which a proper official warrant readily may be obtained, and a search of a ship, motor boat, wagon or automobile, for contraband goods, where it is not practicable to secure a warrant because the vehicle can be quickly moved out of the locality or jurisdiction in which the warrant must be sought.[488]

Cases have consistently stressed that a relaxed warrant standard is needed because vehicles can be quickly moved.[489] Second, an individual possesses a lesser expectation of privacy for a vehicle and the things within it. Part of this stems from the individual's realization that vehicles are pervasively regulated in our society. The United States Supreme Court expressed this best in *South Dakota v. Opperman:*

> Automobiles, unlike homes, are subjected to pervasive and continuing governmental regulation and controls, including periodic inspection and

---

test as set forth in *T.L.O.* The action was justified by the reality of violence in the schools. The screening was directed and controlled by school officials. The detectors belonged to the school board and the purpose of the screening was not to investigate or secure evidence of a crime. On the other hand, the intrusion to the students was minimal and all students were required to proceed through the detectors. *Id.* Therefore, the trial court erred in granting two students' motions to suppress weapons seized following the search. *Id.*, 662 N.E.2d at 551.

487. 267 U.S. 132 (1925).

488. California v. Carney, 471 U.S. 386, 400 (1985) (citing *Carroll*, 267 U.S. at 153).

489. South Dakota v. Opperman, 428 U.S. 364, 367 (1976); Cardwell v. Lewis, 417 U.S. 583, 588 (1974); Cady v. Dombrowski, 413 U.S. 433, 442 (1973); Chambers v. Maroney, 399 U.S. 42, 52 (1970); Cooper v. California, 386 U.S. 58, 59 (1967).

licensing requirements. As an everyday occurrence, police stop and examine vehicles when license plates or inspection stickers have expired, or if other violations, such as exhaust fumes or excessive noise, are noted, or if headlights or other safety equipment are not in proper working order.[490]

The way vehicles are constructed suggests some basis for this lesser expectation of privacy. For example, items found in the passenger compartment of a car are often in public view to anyone walking past the vehicle. Clearly there is a lesser expectation of privacy.[491] Yet the automobile exception has also been applied to items found in locked car trunks,[492] a sealed package found in a car trunk,[493] a closed compartment under the dashboard,[494] the interior of a vehicle's upholstery,[495] and sealed packages under a covered pickup truck.[496]

Note that not every police observation related to a vehicle constitutes a "search" under the Fourth Amendment. For example, the United States Supreme Court held that a car owner has no reasonable expectation of privacy in the Vehicle Identification Number (VIN) of a car because it is on the car's dashboard and is visible from outside the car.[497] No "search" would occur if the officer viewed it from the outside.[498] Moreover, even if the officer has

---

490. *Opperman,* 428 U.S. at 368. *Compare* People v. Anderson, 176 Ill. App. 3d 348, 531 N.E.2d 116 (2d Dist. 1988) (owner of car does not surrender all Fourth Amendment protections).

491. *Lewis,* 417 U.S. at 590; People v. Elmore, 28 Ill. 2d 263, 192 N.E.2d 219 (1963); People v. Oliver, 129 Ill. App. 2d 83, 262 N.E.2d 597 (4th Dist. 1970). *But see* People v. Anderson, 176 Ill. App. 3d 348, 531 N.E.2d 116 (2d Dist. 1988) (warrantless search of door edge of defendant's vehicle to look at weight tag was unreasonable where officer's safety was not furthered and defendant had reasonable expectation of privacy in tag).

492. Cady v. Dombrowski, 413 U.S. 433 (1973); People v. Blitz, 68 Ill. 2d 287, 369 N.E.2d 1238 (1977), *cert. denied,* 435 U.S. 974 (1978); People v. Binder, 180 Ill. App. 3d 624, 536 N.E.2d 218 (4th Dist. 1989). *See also* United States v. Webb, 83 F.3d 913 (7th Cir. 1996).

493. United States v. Ross, 456 U.S. 798 (1982).

494. Chambers v. Maroney, 399 U.S. 42 (1970).

495. Carroll v. United States, 267 U.S. 132 (1925).

496. United States v. Johns, 469 U.S. 478 (1985).

497. New York v. Class, 475 U.S. 106, 118 (1986).

498. *Id. But see* People v. Alexander, 272 Ill. App. 3d 698, 650 N.E.2d 1038, 1044 (1st Dist. 1995) (police viewing of VINs on windshields, which were seized pursuant to a later search warrant, in garage in which they illegally entered, suppressed because defendant had reasonable expectation of privacy in garage and windshields; this is different from the situation where an officer views a VIN

to reach into the car and remove papers covering the VIN on the dashboard, this action is so unintrusive, and thus constitutionally permitted, even though it could be considered a "search."[499] On the other hand, the Second District has held that a police officer's act of opening a car door to check a certificate tag containing the gross weight of the vehicle was a "search," intrusive enough to require a showing of reasonableness under the Fourth Amendment.[500]

§ 1.29 — The Scope of the Search

Illinois courts follow the bright line rule established by the United States Supreme Court in *United States v. Ross*[501] that if police have probable cause[502] to believe that a vehicle contains contraband, they may conduct a warrantless search of every part of the vehicle, including all containers, in which there is probable cause to believe that the contraband may be contained. Thus, in *People v. Clark*[503] a police officer, after stopping the defendant's car for a traffic violation, observed a green leafy substance that appeared to be cannabis lying on the floor of the car. The officer then searched the car and found a cigarette box in the front seat containing cannabis. He then took the keys from the

---

after stopping a moving vehicle on the street; this is tantamount to opening a door to search for a VIN).

499. *Class*, 475 U.S. at 119.

500. People v. Anderson, 176 Ill. App. 3d 348, 531 N.E.2d 116 (2d Dist. 1988).

501. 456 U.S. 798 (1982).

502. To establish probable cause in Illinois, "it must be shown that the totality of the facts and circumstances known to the officer at the time of the search would justify a reasonable person in believing that contraband was present in the automobile." People v. Clark, 92 Ill. 2d 96, 440 N.E.2d 869, 871 (1982), *quoted in* People v. Smith, 95 Ill. 2d 412, 447 N.E.2d 809, 811–12 (1983); People v. Chatmon, 236 Ill. App. 3d 913, 604 N.E.2d 399 (2d Dist. 1992) (observation in plain view of partially burned cannabis cigarette gave officer probable cause to search the vehicle); People v. Gaines, 220 Ill. App. 3d 310, 581 N.E.2d 214 (1st Dist. 1991) (police had probable cause to search car used in crime based on victim's description of car, defendant, and license plate number); People v. Lewis, 211 Ill. App. 3d 276, 569 N.E.2d 1221 (4th Dist. 1991) (probable cause based on odor of marijuana, presence of rolling paper, and loose marijuana); People v. Corral, 147 Ill. App. 3d 668, 498 N.E.2d 287 (4th Dist. 1986) (traffic violation, such as speeding, is not sufficient to establish probable cause to search vehicle). *Compare* People v. Schrems, 224 Ill. App. 3d 988, 586 N.E.2d 1337 (2d Dist. 1992) (officer's narcotics training and observation, pursuant to consent, of glass pipe gave probable cause); People v. Kolody, 200 Ill. App. 3d 130, 558 N.E.2d 589 (2d Dist. 1990) (presence of rolling paper in car does not per se establish probable cause).

503. 92 Ill. 2d 96, 440 N.E.2d 869 (1982).

ignition, opened the locked glove compartment, and found three bags of cannabis. The Illinois Supreme Court found the search of the car and the locked glove compartment to be proper. It disposed of the contention that it was improper for the police to have unlocked the glove compartment by citing the following language from *Ross:*

> The scope of a warrantless search of an automobile * * * is not defined by the nature of the container in which the contraband is secreted. Rather, it is defined by the object of the search and the places in which there is probable cause to believe that it may be found.[504]

As long as probable cause exists, the scope of the warrantless search of a vehicle is as broad as that which a magistrate could legitimately authorize by means of a search warrant.[505]

It should be noted that before *Ross* was decided, the propriety of the search of the cigarette box in *Clark* would have been seriously questioned. However, *Ross* overruled *Robbins v. California,*[506] a case in which the United States Supreme Court held that police could make warrantless searches in vehicles only of those containers that clearly revealed the contents to an observer. The *Ross* court emphasized that the police could search any container capable of holding the type of contraband the police had probable cause to believe was in the vehicle:

> [P]rohibiting police from opening immediately a container in which the object of the search is most likely to be found and instead forcing them first to comb the entire vehicle would actually exacerbate the intrusion on privacy interests. Moreover, until the container itself was opened the police could never be certain that the contraband was not secreted in a yet

---

504. *Id.,* 440 N.E.2d at 872 (quoting *Ross,* 456 U.S. at 824).

505. People v. Wolsk, 118 Ill. App. 3d 112, 454 N.E.2d 695 (1st Dist. 1983) (approving warrantless search of passenger area and trunk); People v. Beil, 110 Ill. App. 3d 291, 442 N.E.2d 291 (2d Dist. 1982) (approving warrantless search of inside of car and trunk). *See* People v. Martin, 121 Ill. App. 3d 196, 459 N.E.2d 279 (2d Dist. 1984); People v. Drummond, 103 Ill. App. 3d 621, 431 N.E.2d 1089 (1st Dist. 1981) (warrantless search of defendant's van proper because police had probable cause to believe car was instrument of, or contained evidence of, crime being investigated); People v. Walls, 87 Ill. App. 3d 256, 408 N.E.2d 1056 (1st Dist. 1980); People v. Fletcher, 66 Ill. App. 3d 502, 383 N.E.2d 1285 (1st Dist. 1978). *See also* People v. Binder, 180 Ill. App. 3d 624, 536 N.E.2d 218 (4th Dist. 1988) (warrantless search of defendant's parked car proper where police discovered 12-pack of beer in passenger compartment occupied by persons appearing to be minors).

506. 453 U.S. 420 (1981).

undiscovered portion of the vehicle; thus in every case in which a container was found, the vehicle would need to be secured while a warrant was obtained.[507]

The Illinois Supreme Court explicitly adopted this analysis in *People v. Smith*.[508] In this case, during the warrantless search of a vehicle, the police recovered a "one-hitter box," an item commonly used for the transportation of cannabis. Opening the box, the officer recovered cannabis, a metal pipe, and a quantity of cocaine. The Illinois Supreme Court held that because the police officer had probable cause to believe the vehicle contained drugs, the officer had the right to open the container as well. In *People v. Blakely*,[509] the court held that the area behind the stereo system in an automobile is a container. Therefore, when police make a lawful custodial arrest and search the passenger compartment, they may search this area as well. There is enough room behind the stereo to store a weapon or other item.[510]

The result in *Smith* is consistent with *Ross* because probable cause to search a vehicle automatically provides the police with probable cause to search a container within the vehicle, if the container is capable of holding the contraband being sought. The reverse is not true, however. The mere fact that a container that the police have probable cause to search is found in a vehicle does not provide the police with probable cause to search the vehicle. In that situation, the search of the container will be governed by the same search and seizure principles that would apply if the container had not been found in a vehicle. For example, in *United States v. Chadwick*[511] federal officials in San Diego suspected that a footlocker being shipped on a train to Boston contained narcotics. Officials were alerted in Boston, where they met the train and, before anyone claimed the footlocker, had a trained police dog confirm that the footlocker gave off the odor of a controlled substance. They did not seize the footlocker at that time but waited until Chadwick claimed it and placed it in the trunk of his car. At that time the officials arrested Chadwick, seized the footlocker from the trunk, opened it without a warrant, and recovered a quantity of marijuana. The United States Supreme Court held the warrantless search to be improper; the appropriate procedure would have been to seize and secure the footlocker and then obtain a warrant before searching it. The Supreme Court found the automobile exception inapplicable because there was no probable

---

507. *Ross,* 456 U.S. at 821 n.28, quoted in People v. Smith, 95 Ill. 2d 412, 447 N.E.2d 809, 812 (1983).

508. 95 Ill. 2d 412, 447 N.E.2d 809 (1983).

509. 278 Ill. App. 3d 704, 663 N.E.2d 760 (2d Dist. 1996).

510. *Id.*, 663 N.E.2d at 762.

511. 433 U.S. 1 (1977).

cause to search the entire motor vehicle.[512] Moreover, the Court found that "a person's expectations of privacy in personal luggage are substantially greater than in an automobile."[513]

In *California v. Acevedo*,[514] the United States Supreme Court rejected the *Chadwick-Sanders* scope requirements and held that police are not required to obtain a search warrant to open a closed container found within a car, as long as they have probable cause that the container holds contraband or evidence of criminality. They do not need to have probable cause that contraband or evidence may be found elsewhere in the vehicle. In this case, the police had probable cause that a brown paper bag that defendant had placed in the trunk of his car contained marijuana. Police stopped the car, opened the trunk, and searched the bag.[515]

In *Wyoming v. Houghton*,[516] the United States Supreme Court held "that police officers with probable cause to search a car may inspect a passenger's belongings found in the car that are capable of concealing the object of the search."[517] The Court first relied upon historical evidence, including *Ross*, to find that the Framers would have believed it was reasonable to search containers within an automobile.[518] Cases subsequent to *Ross* have clearly identified that the *Ross* holding applied to all containers in the car, "without qualification as to ownership."[519] Thus, the critical element with regard to a warrantless search is the object of the search—"not that the owner of the property is suspected of crime but that there is reasonable cause to believe that the specific 'things' to be searched for and seized are located on the property to which entry is sought."[520] Further, as with owners, passengers have a reduced expectation of privacy with regard to property that is transported in vehicles. Similarly, there is a particular substantial governmental interest at stake.

> Effective law enforcement would be appreciably impaired without the ability to search a passenger's personal belongings when there is reason to

---

512. *Id.* at 13. *See also* Arkansas v. Sanders, 442 U.S. 753 (1979); People v. Bowen, 164 Ill. App. 3d 164, 517 N.E.2d 608 (5th Dist. 1987) (where officer who conducted vehicle search was unaware of defendant's license suspension, search could not be justified).

513. *Chadwick,* 433 U.S. at 13.

514. California v. Acevedo, 500 U.S. 565 (1991).

515. *Id.* at 579.

516. 119 S. Ct. 1297 (1999).

517. *Id.* at 1304.

518. *Id.* at 1300–1301.

519. *Id.* at 1301.

520. *Id.*, (quoting Zurcher v. Stanford Daily, 436 U.S. 547, 556 (1978)).

believe contraband or evidence of criminal wrongdoing is hidden in the car. As in all car-search cases, the "ready mobility" of an automobile creates a risk that the evidence or contraband will be permanently lost while a warrant is obtained. [Citations.] In addition, a car passenger ... will often be engaged in a common enterprise with the driver, and have the same interest in concealing the fruits or the evidence of their wrongdoing.[521]

§ 1.30 — Where a Vehicle May Be Searched

When a vehicle is stopped on the highway and police have probable cause to make a warrantless arrest, the vehicle may be searched either on the highway or at the police station.[522] Illinois courts have not found delays of up to six hours to be unreasonable enough to invalidate a subsequent warrantless search,[523] yet on one occasion the court found a delay of three days between the seizure and the warrantless search to be unreasonable enough to invalidate the search.[524] The justification for the warrantless search does not disappear merely because the car is in police custody, nor must the police make a showing that it was unreasonable to have to obtain a warrant because the car probably would have been tampered with during that time.[525]

§ 1.31 — Significance of Where a Vehicle Is Found

The vast majority of cases utilizing the automobile exception concern police stops of vehicles in transit. Obviously, there must be a valid reason

---

521. *Houghton*, 119 S. Ct. at 1302.

522. People v. Canaday, 49 Ill. 2d 416, 275 N.E.2d 356 (1971). *See* Colorado v. Bannister, 449 U.S. 1 (1980); Chambers v. Maroney, 399 U.S. 42 (1970); People v. Joyner, 50 Ill. 2d 302, 278 N.E.2d 756 (1972); People v. Ehn, 24 Ill. App. 3d 340, 320 N.E.2d 536 (1st Dist. 1974); People v. Babic, 7 Ill. App. 3d 36, 287 N.E.2d 24 (2d Dist. 1972).

523. People v. Smith, 50 Ill. 2d 229, 278 N.E.2d 73 (delay of six hours did not invalidate search), *cert. denied*, 409 U.S. 1022 (1972); People v. Wiggins, 45 Ill. App. 3d 85, 358 N.E.2d 1301 (1st Dist. 1976) (delay of seven to twelve minutes did not invalidate search); People v. Stewart, 10 Ill. App. 3d 187, 293 N.E.2d 169 (2d Dist. 1973) (delay of two hours did not invalidate search).

524. People v. Emert, 1 Ill. App. 3d 993, 274 N.E.2d 364 (2d Dist. 1971). Illinois courts may not adhere to this position in future cases because the United States Supreme Court found that a three-day delay between the seizure and the warrantless search of closed containers found during the search of a motor vehicle did not invalidate that search. United States v. Johns, 469 U.S. 478 (1985).

525. Michigan v. Thomas, 458 U.S. 259 (1982); People v. Wolsk, 118 Ill. App. 3d 112, 454 N.E.2d 695 (1st Dist. 1983).

for the police to make the stop in the first place before the automobile exception is applicable.[526]

In *People v. Peter*,[527] however, the Illinois Supreme Court confronted a situation where police made a warrantless search of an automobile parked outside the defendant's house. The defendant referred the court to *Coolidge v. New Hampshire*,[528] in which the United States Supreme Court found that the automobile exception did not apply to a situation in which police arrested a defendant at his house and then conducted a warrantless search of his car parked in the driveway. The Supreme Court found the warrantless search improper because of the absence of many factors that underlie the automobile exception. In the *Coolidge* case there was "no alerted criminal bent on flight, no fleeting opportunity on an open highway after a hazardous chase, no contraband or stolen goods or weapons, no confederates waiting to move the evidence, not even the inconvenience of a special police detail to guard the immobilized automobile."[529] The *Peter* court, however, distinguished *Coolidge* and affirmed the warrantless search. The court enumerated exigent circumstances that it found missing in the *Coolidge* case. In *Peter,* the car was discovered inadvertently. The police had probable cause to believe it contained evidence of a crime, and Peter's relatives and friends could have destroyed the evidence in the time it would have taken to obtain a warrant. The court found the warrantless search to be proper although the car had never been mobile.[530]

---

526. People v. Clark, 92 Ill. 2d 96, 440 N.E.2d 869 (1982); People v. Harr, 93 Ill. App. 2d 146, 235 N.E.2d 1 (2d Dist. 1968). *See* People v. Harris, 199 Ill. App. 3d 1008, 557 N.E.2d 1277 (2d Dist. 1990) (stopping a car for a minor traffic violation does not per se justify a search). *Cf.* People v. Strawn, 210 Ill. App. 3d 783, 569 N.E.2d 269 (4th Dist. 1991) (initial stop of automobile with tinted windows proper); People v. Jones, 207 Ill. App. 3d 30, 565 N.E.2d 240 (1st Dist. 1990) (initial stop of automobile with a cracked windshield justified and defendant's furtive movements gave probable cause), *cert. denied,* 502 U.S. 878 (1991). *But see* People v. Fulton, 289 Ill. App. 3d 970, 683 N.E.2d 154, 157–58 (1st Dist. 1997) (seizure of cocaine found in car unlawful where officer who moved defendant's car after arresting him for driving without a license did not have consent to search car); People v. Innis, 237 Ill. App. 3d 289, 604 N.E.2d 389 (4th Dist. 1992) (warrantless search of automobile following a mere traffic violation was improper; circumstances must indicate that a more serious crime has been committed).

527. 55 Ill. 2d 443, 303 N.E.2d 398 (1973), *cert. denied,* 417 U.S. 1920 (1974).

528. 403 U.S. 443 (1971).

529. *Id.* at 462.

530. People v. Peter, 55 Ill. 2d 443, 303 N.E.2d 398 (1973).

§ 1.32 Inventory Search of Car by Police

The Illinois Supreme Court has expressly approved warrantless police searches of vehicles lawfully in police custody. In *People v. Clark,*[531] the court adopted the policy set forth by the United States Supreme Court in *South Dakota v. Opperman.*[532] *Clark* examined a situation in which the police impounded a vehicle and made a search after a routine procedure of securing and inventorying the automobile's contents. *Clark* found such a warrantless search reasonable and recognized three legitimate objectives for the procedure: "protection of police officers from potential danger, protection of the owner's property while his car is in police custody, and protection against later claims that property has been lost or stolen."[533]

However, before an inventory search can be lawfully conducted, it must first be determined that the police had the right to impound the vehicle.[534] It is for the court to determine whether the impoundment preceding the inventory search was proper. The mere existence of a police regulation authorizing the impoundment of all vehicles of arrested persons that are not parked on the owner's property does not per se make the inventory search reasonable.[535] Each inventory search must be independently determined to be reasonable pursuant to constitutional principles. For example, in *People v. Schultz*[536] the defendant was arrested in a local lounge. The police found the defendant's car parked in the lounge's parking lot. They towed the car to police headquarters and conducted an inventory search pursuant to a police department policy authorizing such action. The appellate court suppressed the fruits of this search, finding that the impoundment was unreasonable because the car had nothing to do with the police investigation, and neither the defendant nor the lot owner asked the police to tow the car.[537] Thus,

---

531. 65 Ill. 2d 169, 357 N.E.2d 798 (1976), *cert. denied,* 431 U.S. 918 (1977).

532. 428 U.S. 364 (1976).

533. People v. Clark, 65 Ill. 2d 169, 357 N.E.2d 798, 800 (1976) (citing *Opperman,* 428 U.S. at 368).

534. People v. Braasch, 122 Ill. App. 3d 747, 461 N.E.2d 651 (2d Dist. 1984). In *Braasch,* the court held that in determining the propriety of an inventory search, the threshold question is whether the original impoundment was proper under the Fourth Amendment. *See* People v. Brown, 100 Ill. App. 3d 57, 426 N.E.2d 575 (2d Dist. 1981); People v. Schultz, 93 Ill. App. 3d 1071, 418 N.E.2d 6 (1st Dist. 1981).

535. People v. Schultz, 93 Ill. App. 3d 1071, 418 N.E.2d 6 (1st Dist. 1981).

536. 93 Ill. App. 3d 1071, 418 N.E.2d 6 (1st Dist. 1981).

537. *Accord* People v. Valdez, 81 Ill. App. 3d 25, 400 N.E.2d 1096 (2d Dist. 1980) (improper to tow defendant's car from restaurant parking lot merely because defendant was arrested there).

because the police had no responsibility for either the car or its contents, the impoundment and subsequent search of the car was improper.[538]

In addition, an Illinois court will suppress the fruits of an inventory search if it finds that the inventory was merely a pretext for conducting a search for investigative reasons.[539] The purposes of the search must be consistent with the objectives set out in *Clark*.

As to the scope of the vehicle inventory, it is clear that the police may not only inventory those items in plain view[540] but may also search under the passenger seats[541] and in closed glove compartments.[542] In a case of first impression, the Second District Appellate Court held the inventory search exception also allows police to open a locked car trunk and search within.[543]

It is less clear whether the police may examine the contents of closed containers found during the vehicular inventory search. Illinois courts have traditionally found that, absent exigent circumstances, the inventory exception does not authorize the inspection of closed containers.[544] However, these decisions are now questionable in light of the United States Supreme Court's decision in *Illinois v. Lafayette*.[545] Although *Lafayette* dealt with the search of closed containers as part of the procedure incident to jailing an arrested person at the station house,

---

538. People v. Van Hatten, 52 Ill. App. 3d 338, 367 N.E.2d 556 (4th Dist. 1977). *See* People v. Brown, 100 Ill. App. 3d 57, 426 N.E.2d 575 (2d Dist. 1981) (improper to tow defendant's car from city street parking space following his arrest inside bowling alley).

539. People v. Reincke, 84 Ill. App. 3d 222, 405 N.E.2d 430 (5th Dist. 1980); People v. Fox, 62 Ill. App. 3d 854, 379 N.E.2d 917 (4th Dist. 1978). *See* People v. Ocon, 221 Ill. App. 3d 311, 581 N.E.2d 892 (2d Dist. 1991) (objectively reasonable inventory not made unreasonable by officers' alleged subjective improper motives or their failure to complete required forms); People v. Alewelt, 217 Ill. App. 3d 578, 577 N.E.2d 809 (3d Dist. 1991) (warrantless search of automobile trunk not justified where car was secure at police headquarters); People v. Brink, 174 Ill. App. 3d 804, 529 N.E.2d 1 (4th Dist. 1988) (assertion that search was an "inventory" rejected because police left vehicle unlocked on property over night).

540. People v. Clark, 65 Ill. 2d 169, 357 N.E.2d 798 (1976).

541. People v. Ruffolo, 64 Ill. App. 3d 151, 380 N.E.2d 1204 (3d Dist. 1978).

542. People v. Clark, 65 Ill. 2d 169, 357 N.E.2d 798 (1976).

543. People v. Braasch, 122 Ill. App. 3d 747, 461 N.E.2d 651 (2d Dist. 1984).

544. People v. Bayles, 82 Ill. 2d 128, 411 N.E.2d 1346 (1980) (inventory search of suitcase improper), *cert. denied,* 453 U.S. 923 (1981); People v. Velleff, 94 Ill. App. 3d 820, 419 N.E.2d 89 (2d Dist. 1981) (inventory search of plastic bag improper); People v. Salter, 91 Ill. App. 3d 831, 414 N.E.2d 1252 (1st Dist. 1980) (inventory search of bag improper); People v. Dennison, 61 Ill. App. 3d 473, 378 N.E.2d 220 (5th Dist. 1978) (inventory search of tool box proper).

545. 462 U.S. 640 (1983).

at least one Illinois court has held that *Lafayette* also sanctions the search of a closed container found during an automobile inventory search.[546]

The United States Supreme Court has recently held that the opening of a closed container during a police inventory of a vehicle is valid only if this action is specifically provided for in standardized criteria or an established routine.[547] Such a policy, however, need not be "all or nothing"; that is, the policy may allow police discretion in deciding whether or not to open a closed container during a specific inventory.[548]

§ 1.33   Inventory Search of Arrestee

In *Illinois v. Lafayette,*[549] the United States Supreme Court established a bright line rule concerning the inventory search of closed containers found on arrestees about to be jailed. In *Lafayette,* the police searched the defendant's shoulder bag as part of their standard inventory procedure at the station house and recovered a controlled substance. The Court found this proper under the Fourth Amendment, refusing to hold that a less intrusive method, such as simply inventorying the entire unopened bag, was constitutionally necessary. Illinois courts follow the *Lafayette* decision[550] and have thus overruled a

---

546. People v. Braasch, 122 Ill. App. 3d 747, 461 N.E.2d 651 (2d Dist. 1984).

547. Colorado v. Bertine, 479 U.S. 367 (1987); People v. Krueger, 268 Ill. App. 3d 190, 643 N.E.2d 872, 874 (4th Dist. 1994) (confirming that evidence of standardized police procedures detailing when an inventory search of vehicle is proper, is necessary for such searches to be valid). *See also* People v. Hundley, 227 Ill. App. 3d 1056, 591 N.E.2d 903 (3d Dist.) (opening cigarette case held improper in absence of standardized police procedure mandating the opening of closed containers), *rev'd,* 156 Ill. 2d 135, 619 N.E.2d 744 (1993) (okay under circumstances of case to open cigarette case); People v. Lear, 217 Ill. App. 3d 712, 577 N.E.2d 826 (5th Dist. 1991) (no showing that it was standard procedure to open closed containers in all impounded vehicles). *But see* People v. Walker, 228 Ill. App. 3d 76, 592 N.E.2d 1 (1st Dist. 1992) (search of bag during inventory search of car proper where officer felt trigger guard and butt of shotgun while holding bag).

548. Florida v. Wells, 495 U.S. 1 (1990).

549. 462 U.S. 640 (1983).

550. People v. Dillon, 102 Ill. 2d 522, 468 N.E.2d 964 (1984); People v. Hoskins, 101 Ill. 2d 209, 461 N.E.2d 941 (1984); People v. Hadley, 179 Ill. App. 3d 152, 534 N.E.2d 395 (5th Dist. 1989). *See* People v. Mannozzi, 260 Ill. App. 3d 199, 632 N.E.2d 627, 634 (2d Dist. 1994) (search of defendant's purse at police station proper both as search incident to arrest and as inventory search precedent to incarceration where arrest was for DUI; although DUI is bondable offense, record not clear if officer knew whether defendant could post bond or would be incarcerated). *But see* People v. Tyler, 210 Ill. App. 3d 833, 569 N.E.2d 240 (5th Dist. 1991) (officer improperly searched defendant's clothing under inventory

97

substantial line of cases to the contrary.[551] Illinois courts have also held that once the police have properly inventoried an arrestee's effects, it is proper for the police to take a later, warrantless "second look" at the effects.[552]

§ 1.34   Exigent Circumstances

Under certain special circumstances, police are justified in conducting a warrantless search of premises.[553]

---

search exception where not common police practice and hospital policy was to give clothing to relatives); People v. Nogel, 137 Ill. App. 3d 392, 484 N.E.2d 516 (4th Dist. 1985) (*Lafayette* does not apply when person in custody will not be incarcerated, which implies more than mere administrative detention for booking).

551. *See, e.g.,* People v. Helm, 89 Ill. 2d 34, 431 N.E.2d 1033 (1981) (inventory search of arrestee's purse at police station improper); People v. Bean, 107 Ill. App. 3d 662, 437 N.E.2d 1295 (3d Dist. 1982) (inventory search of wallet at police station improper), *cert. granted and judgment vacated,* 463 U.S. 1202 (1983).

552. People v. Richards, 94 Ill. 2d 92, 445 N.E.2d 319 (1983); People v. Hadley, 179 Ill. App. 3d 152, 534 N.E.2d 395 (5th Dist. 1989); People v. Cain, 171 Ill. App. 3d 468, 525 N.E.2d 1194 (4th Dist. 1988).

553. People v. Williams, 161 Ill. 2d 1, 641 N.E.2d 296, 306 (1994) (guiding principle in determining if exigent circumstances exist validating warrantless entry is reasonableness under the totality of the circumstances confronting the officers at time entry was made). Factors considered relevant to determination of exigency include:

> (1) whether the offense under investigation was recently committed; (2) whether there was any deliberate or unjustifiable delay by the officers during which time a warrant could have been obtained; (3) whether a grave offense is involved, particularly one of violence; (4) whether the suspect was reasonably believed to be armed; (5) whether the police officers were acting upon a clear showing of probable cause; (6) whether there was a likelihood that the suspect would have escaped if not swiftly apprehended; (7) whether there was strong reason to believe that the suspect was on the premises; and (8) whether the police entry, though nonconsensual, was made peaceably.

People v. Foskey, 136 Ill. 2d 66, 554 N.E.2d 192, 197 (1990). *See* People v. Mahaffey, 166 Ill. 2d 1, 651 N.E.2d 1055, 1066–67 (exigent circumstances existed where police had probable cause to arrest defendant, likelihood defendant would flee, entry was peaceful, no evidence of unjustified delay, grave offenses involved, and defendant probably armed), *cert. denied,* 516 U.S. 1002 (1995); People v. Pierini, 278 Ill. App. 3d 975, 664 N.E.2d 140, 144 (1st Dist. 1996) (exigent circumstances existed to make warrantless entry of defendant's apartment and to seize partially smoked cannabis cigarette in plain view, where offense occurred in presence of officer, evidence could easily have been destroyed, and officer acted on clear showing of probable cause); People v. Abt, 269 Ill. App. 3d 831, 646 N.E.2d 1341, 1347 (1st Dist. 1995) (hastily set up controlled drug buy justified as exigency of a felony in officers' presence,

§ 1.35 — Protective Sweep

The Illinois Supreme Court has carved out a warrant exception in *People v. Free.*[554] In this case, the police obtained a warrant to arrest the defendant for murder and attempted murder. They went to his parents' house and for thirty minutes attempted, through the use of a public address system, to call the defendant from the house. When these actions failed, the police lobbed a tear gas canister into the second-story window. The defendant subsequently came out of the house and was arrested. The police then entered the house "to make certain there was no one else present in the building and to make certain that the tear gas projectile did not hit someone or start a fire."[555] During this entry, the police observed incriminating evidence, which resulted in the police obtaining a search warrant and seizing the evidence.

The *Free* court rejected the defendant's argument that the evidence should be suppressed and justified the officers' warrantless entry as a "protective sweep." The court quoted at length from Professor LaFave:

---

allowing entry without warrant); People v. Patterson, 267 Ill. App. 3d 933, 642 N.E.2d 866, 871 (1st Dist. 1994) (exigent circumstances justified warrantless entry to arrest when defendant sold cocaine to officer moments before entry, no real delay when officer could have obtained warrant, narcotics trafficking is considered grave offense, and entry was peaceable). *See also* United States v. Brown, 64 F.3d 1083, 1086 (7th Cir. 1995) (exigent grounds existed to search drug suspect's apartment without warrant where car of suspect who had attempted to conclude drug transaction with defendant was outside apartment, defendant was standing outside apartment, and defendant told police he lived elsewhere causing police to wonder if drug dealer was victim of car theft or worse, and police searched dealer's apartment to see if everything okay). Warrantless searches of the person have also been held constitutionally permissible in certain circumstances. *See* Schmerber v. California, 384 U.S. 757 (1966) (warrantless extraction of blood for blood-alcohol testing was reasonable); People v. Ayres, 228 Ill. App. 3d 277, 591 N.E.2d 931 (3d Dist. 1992) ("evanescent nature" of blood alcohol evidence led court to conclude that a warrant was not needed to conduct involuntary breathalyzer test based upon probable cause). *But see* People v. Brown, 277 Ill. App 3d 989, 661 N.E.2d 533, 538–39 (1st Dist. 1996) (existence of probable cause and recentness of offense of discharging a firearm are alone insufficient to justify a warrantless entry). Warrantless searches of trash have been upheld as constitutionally permissible given exigent circumstances. People v. McNeal, 175 Ill. 2d 335, 677 N.E.2d 841, 847 (where defendant had recently threatened victim with a gun and had been observed depositing a brown paper bag in trash, the search of the trash for the bag and the search of the contents for the gun was reasonable), *cert. denied,* 522 U.S. 917 (1997).

554. 94 Ill. 2d 378, 447 N.E.2d 218, *cert. denied,* 464 U.S. 865 (1983).

555. *Id.,* 447 N.E.2d at 225.

In some situations, the "potentiality for danger surrounding the arrest" may be so high that entry of premises to make a "protective sweep" will be permissible even though the arrest itself was achieved without entry. Typically, the reason no entry was made to arrest is because the police perceived the situation as a very dangerous one and then took steps to cause the prospective arrestee to exit the premises and submit to arrest outside. Even with that person now in custody, the police may have good reason to doubt whether they can withdraw from the area with their prisoner without being fired upon, in which case an entry and "protective sweep" is justified. Such entries have been upheld when a weapon used in a recent crime by the arrestee or a weapon used by someone in firing at the police from those premises is as yet unaccounted for, and also when police have information the defendant was travelling with armed associates or that the defendant was armed and accompanied by another.[556]

Thus, the court found that the police were justified in making a warrantless protective sweep to retrieve the tear gas canister, air out the house, check for fire, and determine whether there were persons present who either were in danger or posed a danger to police.[557]

This type of a procedure was approved by the United States Supreme Court in *Maryland v. Buie*.[558] The Court held that a properly limited protective sweep in conjunction with an in-home arrest is permissible when the searching officer possesses a reasonable belief based on specific and articulable facts that the

---

556. *Id.*, 447 N.E.2d at 227 (quoting 2 F. LaFave, Search and Seizure § 6.4(c) at 431 (1978)).

557. *See* People v. Connolly, 55 Ill. 2d 421, 303 N.E.2d 409 (1973) (warrantless entry found proper where police aided fire fighter extinguishing fire and searched for other possible persons in gas-filled house; term *protective sweep* not used); People v. Parent, 148 Ill. App. 3d 957, 500 N.E.2d 80 (3d Dist. 1986) (court approved warrantless "walk-through" of defendant's apartment after arrest due to exigent circumstances). *See also* People v. Benabe, 180 Ill. App. 3d 235, 535 N.E.2d 949 (1st Dist. 1989) (exigent circumstances justified warrantless entry of defendant's home two days after gang-related shooting); People v. Hill, 169 Ill. App. 3d 902, 524 N.E.2d 604 (1st Dist. 1988) (warrantless entry of motel room justified by exigent circumstances where undercover officer observed drug paraphernalia and concluded there was danger of violence). *But see* People v. Rushing, 272 Ill. App. 3d 387, 649 N.E.2d 609, 613 (1st Dist. 1995) (search of tool box under defendant's bed not valid as protective sweep or exigent circumstances where defendant arrested in bathroom which was searched, and apartment cursorily searched for lost gun; there was no evidence defendant's family posed a threat to the police, and no officer testified they searched the box because of concern for their safety).

558. 494 U.S. 325 (1990).

area that he or she wishes to sweep harbors an individual who poses a danger to those who are at the arrest scene.[559] "This is no more and no less than was required in *Terry.*"[560]

§ 1.36 — Emergency Entry

Under certain limited circumstances, police are justified in making a warrantless entry and conducting a search of the premises to provide aid to persons or property. Illinois courts have justified this under the so-called "emergency doctrine."

In *People v. Bondi*[561] a woman was reported missing by her cousin. A warrantless search by the police on the woman's property resulted in the discovery of the woman's body in a shallow grave. The defendant, her husband, attempted to suppress this evidence. The court ruled that the warrantless search was proper under the emergency doctrine. Quoting Professor LaFave, the court set out three requirements needed to trigger use of the doctrine:

(1) The police must have reasonable grounds to believe that there is an emergency at hand and an immediate need for their assistance for the protection of life or property.

(2) The search must not be primarily motivated by intent to arrest and seize evidence.

(3) There must be some reasonable basis, approximating probable cause, to associate the emergency with the area or place to be searched.[562]

---

559. *Id.* at 334. *See also* People v. Harris, 297 Ill. App. 3d 1073, 679 N.E.2d 850, 858 (1st Dist. 1998) (gun found in oven outside scope of protective sweep); People v. Pierini, 278 Ill. App. 3d 975, 664 N.E.2d 140, 145 (1st Dist. 1996) (officer exceeded scope of protective sweep in searching a duffle bag found in rear bedroom of apartment).

560. *Buie*, 494 U.S. at 334.

561. 130 Ill. App. 3d 536, 474 N.E.2d 733 (5th Dist. 1984), *cert. denied*, 474 U.S. 836 (1985).

562. *Id.,* 474 N.E.2d at 736 (quoting 2 F. LaFave, Search and Seizure § 6.6(a) at 469 (1978)). *See* People v. Greene, 289 Ill. App. 3d 796, 682 N.E.2d 354, 358–59 (2d Dist. 1997) (warrantless entry to screened porch justified where lesser expectation of privacy than in residence proper because police unable to attract defendant's attention when they knocked on screen door and exigent circumstances existed, particularly where someone at residence called 911, hung up, and when the 911 operator called back there as no answer and entry was peaceful: warrantless entry into residence also justified by exigent circumstances after police knocked on front door, spotlighted themselves and called out identification at which point

Applying these factors to the case at bar, the court found that the fact that the woman was reported missing gave the authorities reasonable grounds to believe that she may be in imminent danger of death or serious bodily harm; that the primary intent was to locate her and not to seize evidence against the defendant; and that her residence and property were the most likely places to search for evidence of her whereabouts.

The use of this doctrine has also justified the search of a room where the resident had been reported as missing and the police detected the odor of a dead body;[563] the search of a room where the occupant had been reported as missing, the police received no response to their knocking, and the officers heard movements inside;[564] the search of a person lying on the landing in a hotel who did not respond to police questioning;[565] and the entry and search of a room in which a dog had been heard barking for three days, the police had tried to contact the defendant at home and at work, and the police received no response to their knocking.[566] However, the doctrine was found not to justify the warrantless search of a hotel room merely because the room contained cocaine.[567]

---

defendant locked door and returned to couch and hide something there, and when defendant opened door he denied making a call to 911—these factors gave police reasonable suspicion to believe someone in house was in trouble but unable to get help: drugs found in sofa cushion admissible under plain view doctrine—found pursuant to warrantless entry where police observed defendant put something in couch while lawfully on front porch and police had probable cause to believe drugs in couch based on defendant's actions combined with smell of marijuana in residence). *See, e.g.*, People ex rel. Waller v. Seeburg Slot Machines, 267 Ill. App. 3d 119, 641 N.E.2d 997, 1004 (2d Dist. 1994) (warrantless entry into commercial building justified because broken window large enough to allow access and rash of burglaries had occurred in area).

563. People v. Brooks, 7 Ill. App. 3d 767, 289 N.E.2d 207 (1st Dist. 1972).

564. People v. Clayton, 34 Ill. App. 3d 376, 339 N.E.2d 783 (1st Dist. 1975).

565. People v. Smith, 47 Ill. 2d 161, 265 N.E.2d 139 (1970). *See also* People v. Koniecki, 135 Ill. App. 3d 394, 481 N.E.2d 973 (4th Dist. 1985).

566. People v. Thornton, 286 Ill. App. 3d 624, 676 N.E.2d 1024, 1028–29 (2d Dist. 1997).

567. People v. Vought, 174 Ill. App. 3d 563, 528 N.E.2d 1095 (2d Dist. 1988), *cert. denied*, 492 U.S. 911 (1989). *See also* People v. Krueger, 208 Ill. App. 3d 897, 567 N.E.2d 717 (2d Dist. 1991) (warrantless entry of defendant's home, following automobile accident, not justified under emergency exception because not required to safeguard motorist or ascertain whether he needed assistance), *cert. denied*, 503 U.S. 919 (1992); People v. Griffin, 158 Ill. App. 3d 46, 510 N.E.2d 1311 (5th Dist. 1987) (refusing to invoke "emergency exception").

§ 1.37 — Hot Pursuit

The doctrine of "hot pursuit" was articulated by the United States Supreme Court in *Warden v. Hayden.*[568] In that case, police officers, who had reason to believe that a person who had committed a robbery was hiding in a house, entered the house to search for him. They spread out through the first and second floors and the basement. The defendant was found and arrested in an upstairs bedroom. An officer who continued the search in the basement found in a washing machine some clothing that matched the description of that worn by the robber. The Court held that police in continuous hot pursuit of a subject may enter a building to continue the search for that suspect or for dangerous weapons police reasonably believe are present. This rule is followed in Illinois.[569]

Moreover, at least one Illinois court has extended this concept to provide for a doctrine of "warm pursuit." In *People v. Morrow,*[570] two women who had been abducted and released by their captor contacted the police and led them to a house that they believed had been the scene of the crime. At this point several hours had elapsed since their release. The officers, without a warrant, ventured onto the private property, looked into the garage, and verified that the make and model of a car inside matched the description of the abductors' car previously given by the women. The appellate court found this warrantless search justified. Although conceding that it did not fulfill the elements needed to constitute hot pursuit, the court characterized it as warm pursuit. The court approved of a balancing test between individual rights and the exigencies of the situation. It held that although great necessity might justify a "tumultuous" warrantless entry, moderate necessity would justify a "limited or peaceable intrusion."[571] The court then compared *People v. Simon,*[572] in which the First District Appellate Court justified a warrantless entry accomplished with a battering ram where the suspects were armed and dangerous, with *People v.*

---

568. 387 U.S. 294 (1967).

569. People v. Cole, 54 Ill. 2d 401, 298 N.E.2d 705 (1973); People v. Hall, 1 Ill. App. 3d 949, 275 N.E.2d 196 (1st Dist. 1971); People v. Rivera, 233 Ill. App. 3d 69, 598 N.E.2d 423 (2d Dist. 1992) (officers authorized to make warrantless entry into private premises to effectuate a *Terry* stop where a lawful basis existed to make stop in a public place and suspect reacted by suddenly fleeing to private place to thwart detention at the public location); People v. Maiden, 210 Ill. App. 3d 390, 569 N.E.2d 120 (1st Dist. 1991) (exigent circumstances where defendant recognized officers prior to his hurried entry into house).

570. People v. Morrow, 104 Ill. App. 3d 995, 433 N.E.2d 985 (1st Dist. 1982).

571. *Id.,* 443 N.E.2d at 992–93.

572. 101 Ill. App. 3d 89, 427 N.E.2d 843 (1st Dist. 1981).

Davis,[573] in which a peaceable warrantless residential arrest was justified where the suspects were not armed. Using this balancing test, the court found that the slight intrusion in this case was justified by the warm pursuit of the officers.

§ 1.38 Search of Person Arrested

Once any valid arrest is effectuated, police have the right to make a full search of the arrestee. Both the United States Supreme Court, in its companion cases *United States v. Robinson*[574] and *Gustafson v. Florida,*[575] and the Illinois courts have emphasized that it is the fact of a custodial arrest itself—not any additional belief that the suspect is either armed or carrying contraband—that justifies the search.[576] The Illinois Code of Criminal Procedure provides that when a lawful arrest is made by a police officer, the officer may reasonably search the person arrested to discover the fruits of the crime or any instruments, articles, or things that may have been used in the commission of, or that may constitute evidence of, an offense.[577] Illinois courts refuse to make fine distinctions concerning the chronological order of an arrest and a search incident to arrest. As long as probable cause to arrest exists, it is proper for the police to search an individual before the formal arrest.[578] This is consistent with the rationale behind the "search incident to arrest" exception—that the right to

---

573. 97 Ill. App. 3d 299, 422 N.E.2d 989 (1st Dist. 1981).

574. 414 U.S. 218 (1973).

575. 414 U.S. 260 (1973).

576. People v. Wolsk, 118 Ill. App. 3d 112, 454 N.E.2d 695 (1st Dist. 1983).

577. 725 ILCS 5/108-1.

578. People v. Rossi, 102 Ill. App. 3d 1069, 430 N.E.2d 233 (2d Dist. 1981); People v. De La Fuente, 92 Ill. App. 3d 525, 414 N.E.2d 1355 (3d Dist. 1981); People v. Jones, 56 Ill. App. 3d 414, 371 N.E.2d 1093 (1st Dist. 1977). *See* Rawlings v. Kentucky, 448 U.S. 98 (1980); People v. Kolichman, 218 Ill. App. 3d 132, 578 N.E.2d 569 (1st Dist. 1991) (defendant convicted of possession of controlled substances seized during search incident to arrest for disorderly conduct), *cert. denied,* 505 U.S. 1224 (1992); People v. Dawson, 213 Ill. App. 3d 335, 572 N.E.2d 972 (1st Dist. 1991) (gun validly recovered from bag on windowsill outside apartment where bag in defendant's hands when officers entered apartment); People v. Ott, 209 Ill. App. 3d 783, 567 N.E.2d 1104 (1st Dist. 1991) (probable cause for arrest existed so officers' seizure and reading of note in defendant's wallet permissible). Cf. People v. Harrell, 226 Ill. App. 3d 866, 589 N.E.2d 943 (4th Dist. 1992) (search of bedroom incident to arrest not valid where defendant arrested in unfinished attic); People v. Tyler, 210 Ill. App. 3d 833, 569 N.E.2d 240 (5th Dist. 1991) (search incident to arrest not valid where search not made on day of arrest).

search is predicated on the general need to disarm an arrestee and discover any possible evidence on his or her person.[579]

Recently, the United States Supreme Court, in *Knowles v. Iowa,* refused to extend the *Robinson* bright line rule to situations where a discretionary arrest did not take place.[580] *Knowles* struck down a statute allowing police officers to conduct a full search even after they had decided not to make an arrest, stating that the rationale for a full search does not exist absent an arrest.[581]

The scope of a search incident to arrest is limited to the arrestee's person and the area within his or her immediate control.[582] This scope, of course, offers no bright line rule that can be applied in every situation. In 1974, the Illinois Supreme Court faced a situation in which the defendant was arrested in his kitchen. During the subsequent search, a gun was found in a dog food bag on a shelf approximately seven to ten feet away from the defendant. Although it found the seizure of the gun to be valid, the court held that the validity of such a search depended on the facts of the particular situation. The court said, "[a]mong the factors to be considered . . . are the knowledge that the suspect was armed, the presence of another person who might attempt to assist the suspect, the accessibility of the searched area, and the physical control of the situation exercised by the police."[583]

Thus, it was improper for the police to search under the cushion on a chair in the living room when a defendant was arrested in the doorway between the kitchen and the living room.[584] Likewise, it was improper for the police to arrest a defendant on the first floor of his home, take him upstairs, and then claim that a search of an upstairs bedroom was incident to arrest.[585] However, when a

---

579. United States v. Robinson, 414 U.S. 218, 234–35 (1973). *See* People v. Kincy, 106 Ill. App. 3d 250, 435 N.E.2d 831 (2d Dist. 1982).

580. 119 S. Ct. 484, 488 (1998) (Iowa statute that allowed police officers to do full search incident to a traffic citation held unconstitutional).

581. *Id.* at 487–88.

582. Chimel v. California, 395 U.S. 752, 763 (1969); People v. Montgomery, 112 Ill. 2d 517, 494 N.E.2d 475 (1986) (fingerprints may be taken pursuant to search incident to arrest), *cert. denied,* 479 U.S. 1101 (1987).

583. People v. Williams, 57 Ill. 2d 239, 311 N.E.2d 681, *cert. denied,* 419 U.S. 1026 (1974).

584. People v. Bishop, 60 Ill. App. 3d 940, 377 N.E.2d 585 (4th Dist. 1978).

585. People v. Robbins, 54 Ill. App. 3d 298, 369 N.E.2d 577 (5th Dist. 1977). *See* People v. Machroli, 44 Ill. 2d 222, 254 N.E.2d 450 (1969) (improper for police to search room after arrested defendant had just left it); People v. Alexander, 272 Ill. App. 3d 698, 650 N.E.2d 1038, 1044 (1st Dist. 1995) (where defendant was arrested outside a garage, search of garage exceeded search incident to arrest because unnecessary to prevent defendant from seizing a weapon or destroying evidence; it was apparent that search was designed to find stolen property).

defendant was arrested in a hotel corridor and was permitted to enter his room to get dressed, it was found proper for the police to search all places and items within the defendant's immediate control.[586] Moreover, this exception supported the room-by-room search of an entire house where police suspected that accomplices of the arrestee might be hiding.[587] Illinois courts have held that a *Chimel* search is valid despite the fact that the defendant had been handcuffed prior to the search.[588]

For the search incident to arrest exception to apply, it is not always necessary to conduct the search at the place of arrest. For example, the fact that the search is conducted at a police station, rather than at the place of arrest, does not per se invalidate the search.[589]

There are limits on the kind of search that may be conducted on a person's body. Both the Illinois Supreme Court and the Illinois Code of Criminal Procedure have dealt with the issue of strip searches. A strip search entails having an arrested person remove clothing to allow the police to make a visual inspection of the genitals, buttocks, anus, or if female, breasts.[590] The Illinois Supreme Court has held that such a search is a serious invasion of an arrestee's privacy and that in some cases it may constitute a violation of the Fourth Amendment.[591] In 1979, the Illinois Code of Criminal Procedure was amended to reflect that no person arrested for a traffic, regulatory, or misdemeanor offense may be strip searched unless the case involves weapons or a controlled substance or there is a reasonable belief that the individual is concealing a weapon or a controlled substance.[592] The code also sets out a detailed list of

---

586. People v. Blount, 101 Ill. App. 3d 443, 428 N.E.2d 621 (1st Dist. 1981). *See* Washington v. Chrisman, 455 U.S. 1 (1982).

587. People v. Carmack, 103 Ill. App. 3d 1027, 432 N.E.2d 282 (3d Dist.), *cert. denied,* 459 U.S. 875 (1982).

588. People v. Hoskins, 101 Ill. 2d 209, 461 N.E.2d 941, *cert. denied,* 469 U.S. 840 (1984); People v. Perry, 47 Ill. 2d 402, 266 N.E.2d 330 (1971); People v. Olson, 198 Ill. App. 3d 675, 556 N.E.2d 273 (2d Dist. 1990).

589. People v. Seymour, 84 Ill. 2d 24, 416 N.E.2d 1070, 1074 (1981); People v. Wolsk, 118 Ill. App. 3d 112, 454 N.E.2d 695 (1st Dist. 1983). *See* United States v. Edwards, 415 U.S. 800, 803 (1974). Note that the converse is not true—that is, once a defendant is arrested and removed from a location, that location may not be searched incident to arrest. People v. Kalpak, 10 Ill. 2d 411, 140 N.E.2d 726 (1957).

590. 725 ILCS 5/103-1(d). People v. Whitehead, 140 Ill. App. 3d 433, 488 N.E.2d 1087 (5th Dist. 1986) (requiring suspect to remove his jacket does not constitute strip search).

591. People v. Seymour, 84 Ill. 2d 24, 416 N.E.2d 1070 (1981).

592. 725 ILCS 5/103-1(c).

procedures for strip searching.[593] At least one Illinois court has approved of a warrantless x-ray examination of defendant's body based on exigent circumstances following his arrest.[594]

§ 1.39   Search of Automobile Incident to Arrest

In *New York v. Belton,*[595] the United States Supreme Court held that incident to the arrest of an occupant of an automobile, the police may validly search the entire automobile passenger compartment, as well as any containers within the car. The search does not include the trunk.[596] The arrest alone justifies this search. The Court accepts that these items and areas are within the control of the arrestee in every case.

Illinois has accepted the *Belton* rule.[597] One Illinois court, however, has refused to follow *Belton* when it held that the police had manipulated the timing of defendant's arrest in order to bring the *Belton* exception into play.[598]

---

593. *Id.* § 5/103-1(e), (j).

594. People v. Williams, 157 Ill. App. 3d 496, 510 N.E.2d 445 (5th Dist. 1987).

595. 453 U.S. 454 (1981).

596. *Id.* at 460–61 n.4; People v. Sweborg, 293 Ill. App. 3d 298, 688 N.E.2d 144, 147 (3d Dist. 1997) (reversible error allowing police to search trunk of car legally stopped where search of interior gave no indication of weapon, pat-down search showed no weapons, and computer search showed no criminal record for defendant and defendant refused consent to search); People v. Weatherbe, 122 Ill. App. 3d 654, 462 N.E.2d 1 (2d Dist. 1984) (*Belton* rule does not extend to trunk).

597. People v. Dillon, 102 Ill. 2d 522, 468 N.E.2d 964 (1984); People v. Hoskins, 101 Ill. 2d 209, 461 N.E.2d 941 (1984); People v. Weatherbe, 122 Ill. App. 3d 654, 462 N.E.2d 1 (2d Dist. 1984). *See, e.g.,* People v. Bosnak, 262 Ill. App. 3d 122, 633 N.E.2d 1322, 1326 (2d Dist. 1994) (driver is "recent occupant" within contemplation of *Belton* and police have authority to search passenger compartment incident to arrest of driver, where driver had exited vehicle but was within its immediate vicinity). *Compare* People v. Mourecek, 208 Ill. App. 3d 87, 566 N.E.2d 841 (2d Dist. 1991) (plain view of ammunition clips and lack of identification provided probable cause to arrest and search incident to arrest; thus, discovery of gun on defendant's person proper); People v. Kalivas, 207 Ill. App. 3d 415, 565 N.E.2d 1038 (2d Dist. 1991) (search of automobile valid even though defendant handcuffed and in squad car at time of search); People v. Kolody, 200 Ill. App. 3d 130, 558 N.E.2d 589 (2d Dist. 1990) (*Belton* not applicable).

598. People v. Scudder, 175 Ill. App. 3d 798, 530 N.E.2d 533, 536 (2d Dist. 1988) (arresting officer, as he was leaving to arrest defendant, saw defendant in police station; officer did not arrest him at that time but followed him in squad car and arrested him ten minutes later; court stated that "the police deliberately passed up a convenient opportunity to arrest defendant in order to enable them to later make the arrest in a place they desired to search").

Moreover, the Illinois Supreme Court has held that the rule is applicable in situations other than those involving automobiles. The court has stressed that *Belton's* ruling that containers in the immediate control of the defendant may be searched incident to arrest is always applicable and should not be confined merely to containers found in automobiles.[599]

§ 1.40   Search of Automobile Incident to *Terry* Stop

Something less than the probable cause needed to arrest will justify the search of the interior of an automobile. In *Michigan v. Long*,[600] the United States Supreme Court, applying the principles of *Terry v. Ohio*,[601] held that a warrantless search of the interior of a car was justified where police stopped the driver based on a reasonable belief that he was dangerous and might have access to a weapon. Balancing the potential danger to the police against the type of search made in the case, the Court approved of the *Terry*-type weapon search of the interior of the car.

§ 1.41   Consent Searches

It is proper for the police to conduct a warrantless search if the subject waives his or her rights under the Fourth Amendment.[602] When the state seeks to rely on consent as a justification for a warrantless search, it must prove by a preponderance of the evidence that the consent was freely and voluntarily

---

599. People v. Hoskins, 101 Ill. 2d 209, 461 N.E.2d 941 (1984).

600. Michigan v. Long, 463 U.S. 1032 (1983); People v. Zamora, 203 Ill. App. 3d 102, 560 N.E.2d 1053 (1st Dist. 1990) (finding *Long* inapplicable on facts of case); People v. Froio, 198 Ill. App. 3d 116, 555 N.E.2d 770 (2d Dist. 1990) (applying *Long*). *See* People v. Strawn, 210 Ill. App. 3d 783, 569 N.E.2d 269 (4th Dist. 1991) (*Terry* stop of car with tinted windows valid); People v. Payton, 208 Ill. App. 3d 658, 567 N.E.2d 540 (1st Dist. 1991) (*Terry* search of automobile valid); People v. Rodriquez, 154 Ill. App. 3d 401, 506 N.E.2d 1064 (3d Dist. 1987) (applying *Long*, court allows search of automobile interior prior to questioning and frisking of automobile's occupants).

601. 392 U.S. 1 (1968).

602. Schneckloth v. Bustamonte, 412 U.S. 218 (1973); People v. De Morrow, 59 Ill. 2d 352, 320 N.E.2d 1 (1974); People v. Eiland, 217 Ill. App. 3d 250, 576 N.E.2d 1185 (5th Dist. 1991) (probationer's waiver of Fourth Amendment rights extends only to searches conducted upon a reasonableness standard; thus, probationer's consent to intensive probation conditions allowing warrantless searches reasonable where probation officer had information from police officer and results of urinalysis tests indicated likelihood of facts justifying search).

given.[603] However, a judicial determination that a person voluntarily consented to a search is a question of fact, and the trial court's finding on conflicting evidence and witness credibility will not be disturbed on appellate review unless it is clearly erroneous.[604] Mere acquiescence in the face of an officer's claim of lawful authority is not sufficient.[605] The state's burden of proof on this issue, however, is less stringent than that of waivers of Fifth and Sixth

---

603. People v. Corral, 147 Ill. App. 3d 668, 498 N.E.2d 287 (4th Dist. 1986). *See also* People v. Sanchez, 292 Ill. App. 3d 763, 686 N.E.2d 367, 372 (3d Dist. 1997) (consent to search mobile home upheld where driver, who was not owner, validly consented to search even though driver contended he did not understand or speak English where police testified they conversed with him in English); People v. Perez, 288 Ill. App. 3d 1037, 681 N.E.2d 173, 179 (3d Dist. 1997) (defendant consented to search of vehicle where no threats or pressure was made to consent and videotape showed defendant understood English well enough to give police affirmative responses to several questions and admitted he never told officer to stop search); People v. Carter, 288 Ill. App. 3d 658, 681 N.E.2d 541, 547 (1st Dist. 1997) (consent to search defendant's bag, including teddy bear in which three kilograms of cocaine were found, upheld where defendant was aware she was not under arrest, was not touched or detained by police, and gave permission to search bag); People v. Alvarado, 268 Ill. App. 3d 459, 644 N.E.2d 783, 790 (4th Dist. 1994) (defendant's consent voluntary despite fact he was in handcuffs, had been given *Miranda* warnings, and had requested counsel, because he understood he had right to refuse consent); People v. Harrell, 226 Ill. App. 3d 866, 589 N.E.2d 943 (4th Dist. 1992) (mother's consent voluntary although she was ill and distraught); People v. Breeding, 219 Ill. App. 3d 590, 579 N.E.2d 1128 (1st Dist. 1991) (stop of narcotics suspect at train station consensual because she, as a reasonable person, would have believed she was free to go), *cert. denied,* 505 U.S. 1222 (1992).

604. People v. Hernandez, 278 Ill. App. 3d 545, 663 N.E.2d 86, 90 (1st Dist. 1996).

605. Bumper v. North Carolina, 391 U.S. 543 (1968); People v. Casazza, 144 Ill. 2d 414, 581 N.E.2d 651 (1991) (officers' illegal representation of authority to seize yacht while awaiting search warrant vitiated consent), *cert. denied,* 503 U.S. 919 (1992); People v. Bailey, 273 Ill. App. 3d 431, 652 N.E.2d 1084, 1087–88 (1st Dist. 1995) (defendant's consent invalid where he originally refused to consent to search of bags, police had no reasonable suspicion that defendant's bags contained contraband, and therefore, police could not have legally carried out threat to subject defendant's bags to investigatory detention; court refused to adopt bright line rule that any initial refusal to consent bars subsequent request for consent); People v. Cardenas, 237 Ill. App. 3d 584, 604 N.E.2d 953 (3d Dist. 1992) (consent vitiated by officer's misleading response to defendant implying that it was legal to conduct a search without consent and that it was done all the time); People v. Guenther, 225 Ill. App. 3d 574, 588 N.E.2d 346 (2d Dist. 1992) (defendant's consent not vitiated by officer's comment that they could bring a drug sniffing canine into house). *Compare* People v. Bolden, 150 Ill. App. 3d

Amendment rights.[606] This less stringent standard has been justified on the ground that Fifth and Sixth Amendment trial rights are directly concerned with the reliability of evidence and testimony.[607] Fourth Amendment rights, however, are considered more personal to an individual defendant, and violations of such rights do not affect the reliability of trial evidence. Thus, the voluntariness of a consent to search is a question of fact that is decided through an examination of all the circumstances surrounding the incident.[608] More significantly, it is not necessary that the state demonstrate that the individual actually knew he or she had the right to refuse to consent to the search, although the failure of the police to so warn is a factor to be considered in determining voluntariness.[609] However, once an individual says "no", the person should be allowed to leave and the police cannot continue to intimidate, harass, or badger the person to convince him or her to consent to the search.[610] Other factors to be considered include, but are not limited to, the defendant's age[611] and

---

1075, 502 N.E.2d 304 (1st Dist. 1986) (in which defendant's aunt legitimately consented to allow officers to enter her apartment for purpose of speaking with defendant).

606. *See* Johnson v. Zerbst, 304 U.S. 458, 464 (1938) (prosecutor must prove an "intentional relinquishment of a known right or privilege").

607. Schneckloth v. Bustamonte, 412 U.S. 218, 241–42 (1973).

608. People v. Sommer, 45 Ill. App. 3d 459, 359 N.E.2d 1190 (4th Dist. 1977) (citing *Bustamonte,* 412 U.S. at 248–49). *See In re* M.N., 268 Ill. App. 3d 893, 645 N.E.2d 499, 502–03 (1st Dist. 1994) (juvenile by nonverbal conduct conveyed consent to officer to open vial which contained cocaine packets); People v. Kessler, 147 Ill. App. 3d 237, 497 N.E.2d 1323 (2d Dist. 1986) (nonverbal acts can constitute valid consent).

609. *Bustamonte,* 412 U.S. at 248–49; People v. Haskell, 41 Ill. 2d 25, 241 N.E.2d 430 (1968); People v. Ledford, 38 Ill. 2d 607, 232 N.E.2d 684 (1967). *See also* People v. Brownlee, 293 Ill. App. 3d 315, 687 N.E.2d 1174, 1176 (4th Dist. 1997) (police not required to inform a detained motorist that he is free to go before officer may ask motorist to search vehicle).

610. People v. Sinclair, 281 Ill. App. 3d. 131, 666 N.E.2d 1221, 1226 (3d Dist. 1996) (where defendant was illegally detained beyond the justifable stop, consent was tainted by illegality, and consent was also involuntary). *See also* People v. Sweborg, 293 Ill. App. 3d 298, 688 N.E.2d 144, 147–48 (3d Dist. 1997) (motorist stopped for routine traffic stop did not revoke denial of consent to search trunk when he instructed officer how to remove keys from ignition; motorist not required to specifically deny permission to search guitar case in trunk).

611. People v. Sommer, 45 Ill. App. 3d 459, 359 N.E.2d 1190 (4th Dist. 1977).

intelligence,[612] the propriety of the police conduct,[613] and the general atmosphere surrounding the subject's actions.[614] The findings of the trial court on the issue of voluntariness of consent must be accepted on review unless the findings are clearly erroneous.[615] Illinois decisions in this area are often fact-specific and occasionally contradictory.[616]

---

612. *Id.,* 359 N.E.2d at 1191.

613. People v. Dalpe, 371 Ill. 607, 21 N.E.2d 756 (1939) (no consent found where police procured subject's acquiescence through ruse); People v. McGurn, 341 Ill. 632, 173 N.E. 754 (1930) (no consent found where police violently assaulted subject before obtaining his consent). *See also* People v. Albrecht, 271 Ill. App. 3d 629, 649 N.E.2d 57, 59 (1st Dist. 1995) (no consent where police did not inform defendant that retained attorney present and requesting to speak with him); People v. Graf, 265 Ill. App. 3d 746, 638 N.E.2d 1181, 1184 (2d Dist. 1994) (signed consent form not dispositive if other circumstances show consent was obtained by coercion). *But see* People v. Sanchez, 292 Ill. App. 3d 763, 686 N.E.2d 367, 373–73 (3d Dist. 1997) (40-minute delay after driver consented to search of motor home was reasonable where canine unit was held up while it responded to another request for assistance, police informed driver on two occasions of reason for delay, and driver and passengers did not object to delay).

614. People v. Paull, 176 Ill. App. 3d 960, 531 N.E.2d 1008 (1st Dist. 1988) (statements that officers could get warrant if consent not given and this would look bad for defendant did not rise to level of coercion that would invalidate roommate's consent); People v. Shaver, 77 Ill. App. 3d 709, 396 N.E.2d 643 (2d Dist. 1979) (coercive atmosphere of police station was factor in finding lack of consent); People v. Clark Memorial Home, 114 Ill. App. 2d 249, 252 N.E.2d 546 (2d Dist. 1969) (coercive atmosphere is factor in finding of lack of consent). *See also* People v. Carter, 288 Ill. App. 3d 658, 681 N.E.2d 541 (1st Dist. 1997) (where conversation took place on public walkway in an airport, and one of six police officers present informed individual that she was free to leave at any time, individual was not seized and voluntarily consented to search of luggage.)

615. People v. DeMorrow, 59 Ill. 2d 352, 320 N.E.2d 1, 5 (1974); *Sommer,* 45 Ill. App. 3d 459, 359 N.E.2d at 1191.

616. *Compare* People v. Reed, 37 Ill. 2d 91, 227 N.E.2d 69 (1967) (defendant's response of "Look" to police question, "What about the car?" found to be too equivocal to support finding of consent to search); People v. Zazzetta, 27 Ill. 2d 302, 189 N.E.2d 260 (1963) (defendant's response of "No" to police question about whether he "cared if the officer looked into the car" found not to support finding of consent to search because of coercive atmosphere); People v. Flagg, 217 Ill. App. 3d 655, 577 N.E.2d 815 (5th Dist. 1991) (defendant's consent to search girlfriend's home invalid where officers claimed right to search and were going to search regardless of consent); People v. Purchase, 214 Ill. App. 3d 152, 573 N.E.2d 831 (3d Dist. 1991) (consent not voluntary where officer told wife she would be jailed and baby taken away, and officer claimed to have valid search warrant); People v. Casazza, 202 Ill. App. 3d 792, 560 N.E.2d 386 (3d Dist. 1990)

In *People v. Brownlee*,[617] the court held that the Illinois Constitution does not require a police officer, when the officer stops a car but decides not to issue a citation or after the officer has issued a citation, to tell the driver that he or she is free to leave before asking for consent to search the car.[618] The court interpreted the Illinois Constitution in accord with the interpretation given by the United States Supreme Court to the Fourth Amendment.[619]

When consent is used to justify a warrantless search, the police behavior cannot exceed the scope of the consent.[620] For example, it has been held that where a physician allowed police to seize the records of one patient, police were not entitled to seize the records of other patients as well.[621] In addition, it was held that a consent given to search a trunk did not also include a consent to

---

(consent not voluntary when officers threatened to obtain warrant and to secure person if defendant did not consent), *aff'd*, 144 Ill. 2d 414, 581 N.E.2d 650 (1991), *cert. denied*, 503 U.S. 919 (1992); People v. Barry, 200 Ill. App. 3d 930, 558 N.E.2d 443 (5th Dist. 1990) (consent not voluntary when obtained by threats); People v. Manke, 181 Ill. App. 3d 374, 537 N.E.2d 13 (3d Dist. 1989) (consent not voluntary when defendant coerced by officer's threat to impound car and obtain search warrant if no consent given) *with* People v. Henderson, 33 Ill. 2d 225, 210 N.E.2d 483 (1965) (defendant's response of "Go ahead" to police request to search apartment found to establish consent).

617. 293 Ill. App. 3d 315, 687 N.E.2d 1174 (4th Dist. 1998).

618. *Brownlee*, 293 Ill. App. 3d 315, 687 N.E.2d at 1179.

619. In *Ohio v. Robinette*, 519 U.S. 33, 39–40 (1996), the Court held that the federal provision did not mandate the "first-tell-then-ask" rule.

620. People v. Corral, 147 Ill. App. 3d 668, 498 N.E.2d 287 (4th Dist. 1986); People v. Porter, 141 Ill. App. 3d 71, 489 N.E.2d 1154 (5th Dist.), *cert. denied*, 479 U.S. 951 (1986). *See* People v. Wright, 302 Ill. App. 3d 128, 706 N.E.2d 904, 908 (1st Dist. 1998) (defendant, owner of an auto parts recycling plant, consented to seizure where he voluntarily relinquished police books and certificates of title); People v. Phillips, 264 Ill. App. 3d 213, 636 N.E.2d 1118, 1121 (5th Dist. 1994) (defendant consented to search of motorcycle carrier and officer did not exceed scope when he examined object/bag in pocket of defendant's jacket found to contain drugs); People v. Harrell, 226 Ill. App. 3d 866, 589 N.E.2d 943 (4th Dist. 1992) (consent did not authorize continued search after defendant apprehended; however, evidence found in plain view during initial search admissible); People v. Logsdon, 208 Ill. App. 3d 989, 567 N.E.2d 746 (5th Dist. 1991) (defendant, while hospitalized, consented to police search of house for intruders; no search warrant needed for marijuana in plain view).

621. People v. Schmoll, 383 Ill. 280, 48 N.E.2d 933 (1943); People v. Walters, 187 Ill. App. 3d 661, 543 N.E.2d 508 (2d Dist. 1989) (person's consent to search of automobile does not extend to search of apartment).

search a paper bag found in the trunk.[622] In *Florida v. Jimeno,*[623] however, the United States Supreme Court has held that a suspect's general consent to search his vehicle for drugs allows the police to open all closed containers within the vehicle which might reasonably hold drugs.[624] However, police need not obtain consent to search items that have been abandoned. Thus, Illinois courts have refused to require consent before the police conduct warrantless searches of garbage cans and trash bags because no one has a reasonable expectation of privacy over the contents of such receptacles.[625]

§ 1.42 Third-Party Consent Searches

There are situations in which the fruits of a consensual search may be introduced against a party even though that party never consented to such a search. For example, when a person with an equal right to use or occupy certain property voluntarily consents to a search, any evidence found may be used against all other owners or occupants of the property.[626] In *United States v.*

---

622. People v. Sanders, 44 Ill. App. 3d 510, 358 N.E.2d 375 (5th Dist. 1975). However, this decision may have been undercut by *United States v. Ross,* 456 U.S. 798 (1982). *See also* People v. Baltazar, 295 Ill. App. 3d 146, 691 N.E.2d 1186, 1189–90 (3d Dist. 1998) (search of rented moving truck cargo hold where officer moved couch, saw three cardboard boxes and cut open object wrapped in duct tape that was inside one box exceeded scope of defendant's consent to officer's request to "take a look" inside after defendant was stopped for speeding; objectively reasonable person would have understood exchange to simply mean defendant consented to officer's looking into back of truck to confirm defendant's statements that it contained his personal belongings).

623. 500 U.S. 248 (1991).

624. *Id.* at 248. *See also* People v. Kelk, 231 Ill. App. 3d 797, 596 N.E.2d 1267 (4th Dist. 1992) (driver's consent to officer's request to "look in the car" after he asked the driver whether there were any drugs or weapons in the vehicle served as a general consent to search the car and its contents, including a duffle bag in the passenger compartment). *But see* People v. James, 163 Ill. 2d 302, 645 N.E.2d 195, 203 (1994) (distinguishing *Jimeno*; driver's consent to search vehicle after valid traffic stop did not extend to purse on passenger side belonging to companion).

625. People v. Stein, 51 Ill. App. 3d 421, 366 N.E.2d 629 (1st Dist. 1977); People v. Huddleston, 38 Ill. App. 3d 277, 347 N.E.2d 76 (3d Dist. 1976); California v. Greenwood, 486 U.S. 35 (1988) (warrantless search and seizure of garbage left for collectors outside curtilage of home did not violate Fourth Amendment).

626. United States v. Matlock, 415 U.S. 164 (1974). *See also* People v. Holmes, 180 Ill. App. 3d 870, 536 N.E.2d 1005 (3d Dist. 1989) (11-year-old child competent to give lawful consent).

Matlock,[627] the United States Supreme Court held that common authority to justify such a search is not predicated merely on property rights but rather is concerned with mutual use of property by persons generally having joint access or control for most purposes. Thus, it is reasonable for the police to recognize that the consent of any one property user is sufficient because the other users have assumed the risk that one of their group might permit the area to be searched.[628]

The Illinois Supreme Court recently held in *People v. Bull* that police officers may rely on a third party's apparent consent to search a closed container on the premises.[629] The focus is on whether the third party says he or she has access to the closed container, and not whether the third party opened the container.[630] In *Bull*, the police went to the home of defendant's girlfriend, where defendant had been living, and asked if they could search her home.[631] After signing a consent form, the girlfriend was asked whether there was any area of the premises to which she did not have access, and she responded in the negative. When the police discovered a closed box near the bed, they again asked the girlfriend if she had access to the box. She responded that she did, but told them she did not know what was in the box.[632] The defendant argued that the police

---

627.   415 U.S. 164 (1974).

628.   People v. Simpson, 172 Ill. 2d 117, 665 N.E.2d 1228, 1242–43 (co-defendant gave valid consent to search defendant's apartment because she was defendant's roommate, a leaseholder; current resident, she had "mutual use of property" and, therefore, common authority to consent; whether co-defendant's consent to search storage locker extended to closed bags in locker waived and no plain error because evidence of defendant's guilt overwhelming and error cannot be said to be substantial), *cert. denied,* 513 U.S. 982 (1996); People v. Chambers, 261 Ill. App. 3d 123, 633 N.E.2d 123, 129 (4th Dist. 1994) (consent to enter by third party with common authority over premises justified warrantless arrest of overnight guest), *cert. denied,* 513 U.S. 1194 (1995); People v. Steinberg, 260 Ill. App. 3d 653, 633 N.E.2d 142, 144–45 (2d Dist. 1994) (common authority does not require ownership interest or possession of key but rather mutual use of property). *But see* People v. Ward, 301 Ill. App. 862, 704 N.E.2d 777, 785–86 (1st Dist. 1998) (defendant entitled to a full hearing on his motion to suppress where record silent as to his girlfriend's authority to consent to search of their shared bedroom, the scope of any consent, and the circumstances surrounding any consent).

629.   185 Ill. 2d 179, 705 N.E.2d 824, 834 (1998) (police officers who questioned defendant's girlfriend specifically about her common authority over and access to closed box were justified in relying on her apparent authority, notwithstanding fact that she told police defendant alone used the box).

630.   *Id.,* 705 N.E.2d at 834.

631.   *Id.,* 705 N.E.2d at 832.

632.   *Id.*

officers should have known that her consent was inadequate, but the court disagreed, holding that the police officers could reasonably believe that she had the requisite common authority.[633]

This type of third-party consent is based on the situation in which the nonconsenting owner against whom the evidence is being introduced was not present at the time his or her co-user consented to the search. A different situation occurs when two occupants are present, consent is requested, and one occupant consents while the other objects. Courts have split on this issue.[634] It is an open question in Illinois.[635]

In *United States v. Jensen*,[636] the United States Court of Appeals for the Seventh Circuit upheld the search of the vehicle the defendant was driving prior to his arrest. After police arrested the defendant, the question arose of what to do with the automobile which belonged to his out-of-state stepfather. One officer spoke to the stepfather who asked if the police could take it to the station until he was able to get someone there to pick it up. The police agreed but told him it would be inventoried. He consented to this. Another officer, not aware of this arrangement, asked the defendant if he would consent to a search of the car. The defendant said he could not because it was his stepfather's car.[637] Ultimately, the car was retrieved and inventoried, and the police found thousands of dollars of consumer goods, $8,000 in cash and travelers' checks, and $4,000 in Home Depot checks. When the defendant was confronted with this evidence, he admitted he was involved in a two-year scheme to defraud retail stores across the country. He sought to suppress the evidence, contending his privacy interest in the car was superior to that of his stepfather's. The court disagreed.[638] The defendant's statement that he could not consent because the car was his stepfather's indicated to the police that the defendant and his stepfather at least had common authority over the car. Thus, the defendant expressly acknowledged to the police that his stepfather had the right and power to consent to a search. Further, the defendant essentially told the police that his stepfather's privacy interest in the car was greater than his because he said he

---

633. *Id.*, 705 N.E.2d at 834.

634. United States v. Robinson, 479 F.2d 300, 303 (7th Cir. 1973); Lucero v. Donovan, 354 F.2d 16, 20–21 (9th Cir. 1965); Tompkins v. Superior Court, 59 Cal. 2d 65, 27 Cal. Rptr. 889, 378 P.2d 113 (1963); Silva v. State, 344 So. 2d 559 (Fla. 1977); Dorsey v. State, 2 Md. App. 40, 232 A.2d 900 (1967). *But see* United States v. Sumlin, 567 F.2d 684 (6th Cir. 1977), *cert. denied,* 435 U.S. 932 (1978).

635. People v. McGrew, 128 Ill. App. 3d 464, 470 N.E.2d 1157 (1st Dist. 1984).

636. 169 F.3d 1044 (7th Cir. 1999).

637. *Id.* at 1045.

638. *Id.* at 1048.

had no power to consent to a search. Accordingly, the police had a reasonable belief that the stepfather had authority to consent.[639]

Illinois courts require both actual and apparent authority as the basis of a third-party consent. One court has stated that the state must prove "not only that the consentor had authority to consent, but that 'It reasonably appeared to the searching officer . . . that facts existed which will render consentor's consent binding on the defendant.' "[640] Thus, apparent authority is a necessary but not sufficient factor.[641] Moreover, actual authority is an objective determination; the mere fact that the person against whom the evidence is offered had a subjective expectation of privacy over the area searched is not sufficient to trigger Fourth Amendment protection.[642]

Yet the authority of these decisions is now questionable based on a recent decision of the United States Supreme Court, *Illinois v. Rodriguez*,[643] holding that the exclusionary rule does not apply when the police rely on the consent of a third party whom the police reasonably believe possesses common

---

639. *Id.* at 1049.

640. People v. Taylor, 31 Ill. App. 3d 576, 333 N.E.2d 41, 44 (4th Dist. 1975) (quoting People v. Miller, 19 Ill. App. 3d 161, 310 N.E.2d 808, 815 (4th Dist. 1974)). *See* People v. Garza, 276 Ill. App. 3d 659, 658 N.E.2d 1355, 1361–62 (1st Dist. 1995) (warrantless entry, based on third-party consent to search, valid if "facts available to the officer at the time warranted a reasonably cautious person to believe that consenting party has authority over the premises"; consenting person need not actually possess authority to consent; officer's error in not leaving apartment once discovered not abandoned after receiving consent to enter from building manager but error harmless were evidence recovered not important to defendant's conviction).

641. People v. Miller, 40 Ill. 2d 154, 238 N.E.2d 407, *cert. denied,* 393 U.S. 961 (1968); People v. Bochniak, 93 Ill. App. 3d 575, 417 N.E.2d 722 (1st Dist. 1981), *cert. denied,* 455 U.S. 938 (1982). *See also* People v. Speer, 184 Ill. App. 3d 730, 540 N.E.2d 1089 (2d Dist. 1989) (accepting existence of apparent authority but rejecting theory of ratified authority to justify warrantless search).

642. People v. Stacey, 58 Ill. 2d 83, 317 N.E.2d 24 (1974) (overruling People v. Nunn, 55 Ill. 2d 344, 304 N.E.2d 81 (1973)).

643. Illinois v. Rodriguez, 497 U.S. 177 (1990) (police may have reasonably believed that person had joint access or control over apartment where third person represented that apartment was "our[s]" and that she had clothes and furniture there. Reasonableness of police determination of authority to consent must be adjudged by an objective standard of whether facts available at moment would warrant reasonable person in belief that consenting party had authority over premises. Case was remanded to determine whether police reasonably believed that third party had authority to consent).

authority over premises, but who in fact does not.[644] Not every belief will be found to be "reasonable." One court refused to apply *Rodriguez* to a consent given by a landlord, finding that reliance on a landlord's consent was unreasonable.[645]

The courts have examined third-party searches in a variety of business and personal settings. As to the former, it has been held that a hotel clerk has no authority to consent to a search of a guest's room[646] unless the room has already been vacated by the guest.[647] A property owner may not validly consent to a search of a tenant's premises,[648] even when the owner is a mother renting out a garage to her son who lives next door to her.[649] A receptionist has no right to consent to a general search of the office where he or she is employed because a receptionist lacks common authority over the premises.[650] Likewise, a bus

---

644. *Id.* at 186. *See* People v. Ward, 302 Ill. App. 3d 550, 707 N.E.2d 130, 137 (1st Dist. 1998) (entry into basement apartment valid where another occupant let police in and said defendant was in basement); People v. Patrick, 298 Ill. App. 3d 16, 697 N.E.2d 1167, 1174 (1st Dist. 1998) (arrest of defendant proper where grandmother consented to entry into residence, even though defendant was found in back apartment; where grandmother gestured over her shoulder and said defendant was "back there" at time she opened front door, and she led them to where defendant was; and where police believed residence was a single residence); People v. Mason, 268 Ill. App. 3d 249, 644 N.E.2d 13, 17 (1st Dist. 1994) (search of premises proper where police received consent of man who identified himself as lessee; police reasonably believed he had authority over premises).

645. People v. Kramer, 204 Ill. App. 3d 1011, 562 N.E.2d 654 (2d Dist. 1990).

646. Stoner v. California, 376 U.S. 483 (1964). *See* People v. Bankhead, 27 Ill. 2d 18, 187 N.E.2d 705 (1963); People v. McDonald, 51 Ill. App. 2d 316, 200 N.E.2d 369 (1st Dist. 1964). *See also* People v. Kozlowski, 278 Ill. App. 3d 40, 662 N.E.2d 630, 633 (2d Dist. 1996) (defendant had not lost possessory interest in hotel room or expectation of privacy, and therefore motion to suppress evidence should have been granted; although defendant was behind on rent and hotel owners removed defendant's possessions, room searched after defendant paid back rent and he still possessed key to room).

647. Abel v. United States, 362 U.S. 217 (1960); People v. Vought, 174 Ill. App. 3d 563, 528 N.E.2d 1095 (2d Dist. 1988), *cert. denied*, 492 U.S. 911 (1989).

648. Chapman v. United States, 365 U.S. 610 (1961); People v. Kramer, 204 Ill. App. 3d 1011, 562 N.E.2d 654 (2d Dist. 1990); People v. Sedrel, 184 Ill. App. 3d 1078, 540 N.E.2d 792 (3d Dist. 1989). *But see* People v. Mahaffey, 166 Ill. 2d 1, 651 N.E.2d 1055, 1066 (where defendant was "sublessee" of individual who gave officers consent to search, consent valid where consentor was tenant of apartment), *cert. denied*, 516 U.S. 1002 (1995).

649. People v. Bochniak, 93 Ill. App. 3d 575, 417 N.E.2d 722 (1st Dist. 1981).

650. People v. Polito, 42 Ill. App. 3d 372, 355 N.E.2d 725 (1st Dist. 1976), *cert. denied*, 434 U.S. 873 (1977).

terminal agent has no right to consent to the search of a locker properly rented by another person.[651] In *People v. Manuel*,[652] the court held that judicial approval was not needed to audiotape a telephone conversation, under the eavesdropping statute, between a suspected drug dealer and an informant where the informant gives consent to tape the conversation.[653]

The right of parents to consent to searches of those parts of their home shared with their children has been generally accepted by the courts.[654] Illinois courts have approved of such searches even when the children have taken extraordinary measures to establish exclusive control of certain areas within the parental home. For example, the Illinois appellate court upheld a mother's consent to a police search of her fifteen-year-old son's bedroom in *In Re Salyer*.[655] In this case, the son kept a combination lock on the outside of his door as well as another lock inside. The son contributed money towards the rent, and it was agreed that the mother could not enter without knocking. Nevertheless, the court held that implicit in the legal rights and duties of a parent is the right to exert parental authority over a minor son, including the right to control a room in the parental house in which the son resides.

This case should be distinguished from a situation in which a child has moved out of the parental home but has retained a house key and uses the house for storage. In such a case, an Illinois court found that the child had the right to enter for a limited purpose and thus could not consent to a search of the premises.[656]

---

651. People v. Miller, 19 Ill. App. 3d 161, 310 N.E.2d 808 (4th Dist. 1974). *See also* People v. Speer, 184 Ill. App. 3d 730, 540 N.E.2d 1089 (2d Dist. 1989) (social guest at home is not authorized to consent to search).

652. 294 Ill. App. 3d 113, 689 N.E.2d 344 (1st Dist. 1997).

653. *Id.*, 689 N.E.2d at 350.

654. People v. Nolan, 59 Ill. App. 3d 177, 375 N.E.2d 445 (1st Dist. 1978); People v. Johnson, 23 Ill. App. 3d 886, 321 N.E.2d 38 (1st Dist. 1974). *See also* People v. Henderson, 142 Ill. 2d 258, 568 N.E.2d 1234 (1990) (mother's "passive" consent without an express verbal statement valid where police could reasonably believe consent to enter had been given), *cert. denied*, 502 U.S. 882 (1991); People v. Chavez, 228 Ill. App. 3d 54, 592 N.E.2d 69 (1st Dist. 1992) (mother consented to search of 17-year-old daughter's locked room).

655. 44 Ill. App. 3d 854, 358 N.E.2d 1333 (3d Dist.), *cert. denied*, 434 U.S. 925 (1977). *See also* People v. Bliey, 232 Ill. App. 3d 606, 597 N.E.2d 830 (1st Dist. 1992) (although finding that a mother gave valid consent to search her son's bedroom, the court noted that the presumption of common authority could be overcome when evidence of exclusive possession, such as keeping the room locked during absences and explicitly instructing that no one be allowed into the bedroom, is present).

656. People v. Taylor, 31 Ill. App. 3d 576, 333 N.E.2d 41 (4th Dist. 1975). *See* People v. Weinstein, 105 Ill. App. 2d 1, 245 N.E.2d 788 (1st Dist. 1968) (nonoccupant

A brother[657] or sister[658] may validly consent to a search as long as he or she has common authority over the item or premises to be searched. The same is true of spouses.[659] Friends may give consent only if they have a sufficient interest in the items or premises to be searched.[660]

§ 1.43 Consent Once Removed

In *United States v. Akinsanya*,[661] the United States Court of Appeals for the Seventh Circuit held that the "consent once removed" doctrine adopted in *United States v. Paul*,[662] validated a warrantless search of a drug dealer's apartment. The doctrine is applicable where an undercover agent or government informant "(1) enter[s] at the express invitation of someone with authority to consent; (2) at that point establishe[s] the existence of probable cause to effectuate an arrest or search; and (3) immediately summon[s] help from other officers."[663] In this case, all three elements were met. The defendant consented to the informant's entry into his apartment. Once inside, the informant saw what appeared to be heroin which created probable cause to search. The informant

---

father who possessed key to son's residence did not have equal rights in premises and could not validly consent to search).

657. People v. Heflin, 71 Ill. 2d 525, 376 N.E.2d 1367 (1978).

658. People v. Walker, 34 Ill. 2d 23, 213 N.E.2d 552 (1966).

659. People v. Koshiol, 45 Ill. 2d 573, 262 N.E.2d 446 (1970), *cert. denied,* 401 U.S. 978 (1971).

660. *Compare* People v. Nicks, 23 Ill. App. 3d 443, 319 N.E.2d 524 (4th Dist. 1974); People v. Smith, 108 Ill. App. 2d 172, 246 N.E.2d 689 (2d Dist. 1969), *cert. denied,* 397 U.S. 1001 (1970) *with* People v. Rodriguez, 79 Ill. App. 2d 26, 223 N.E.2d 414 (1st Dist. 1976). *But see* People v. Mendoza, 234 Ill. App. 3d 826, 599 N.E.2d 1375 (5th Dist. 1992) (driver of automobile consented to its search); People v. Ollins, 231 Ill. App. 3d 243, 595 N.E.2d 1295 (1st Dist.) (valid consent given by friend of defendant's mother who was present in apartment at mother's request and was instructed to watch over son), *opinion withdrawn and superseded,* 606 N.E.2d 192 (1st Dist. 1992) (valid consent because individual had specific, delegated authority and control over apartment); People v. Long, 208 Ill. App. 3d 627, 567 N.E.2d 514 (1st Dist. 1990) (girlfriend consented to police entering her apartment). *But see* People v. Pickens, 275 Ill. App. 3d 108, 655 N.E.2d 1206, 1210 (5th Dist. 1995) (overnight guest at defendant's home lacked authority to consent to warrantless search where guest not listed on defendant's lease, did not reside with defendant, did not pay rent or utilities, lived elsewhere, and only occasionally stayed in defendant's home).

661. 53 F.3d 852 (1995).

662. 808 F. 2d 645, 648 (7th Cir. 1986).

663. *Akinsanya*, 53 F.3d at 856.

then promptly called the federal authorities and informed them that he had observed drugs on the premises. According to the court, when defendant gave consent to the informant, he effectively granted consent to the authorities. The consent was not withdrawn merely because the informant stepped out of the apartment immediately before or at the time the authorities entered it.[664]

In *People v. Finley*,[665] a case of first impression, the court held that the doctrine of "consent once removed" as applied in *Galdine* was not applicable. In this case, the police asked an informant to purchase cocaine from the defendant. He went in and was told by the defendant that he did not have the quantity the informant desired. The informant left and went back to the officers who then told him to purchase whatever amount he could. The informant returned and purchased a small amount of cocaine from defendant. After the informant came out of the residence a second time, he advised the police that marijuana plants were growing inside. The police then conducted a search. Defendant was extremely intoxicated. He stated that the trailer was not his and he was only there to take clippings of the plants. The trial court held that the search and seizure were invalid because defendant was unable to give consent to the informant to enter because he was too intoxicated. Therefore, his statements were suppressed. However, the court refused to suppress the evidence found in plain view because the warrantless entry was proper following a sale to an informant. The Fifth District noted that the "consent once removed" doctrine had been applied in only one case in Illinois, *Galdine*. Although the doctrine had been utilized by the federal courts, the facts of those cases were different. In the federal cases, prior to the drug sale, the defendants and the informants had spoken concerning the sale and these conversations were monitored by the agents. In each case, defendant and informant planned the time and place of the sale. Moreover, they agreed upon a predetermined amount and price. In each case, the informant was expressly invited into defendant's dwelling to view the drugs. The defendants knew that the informants would leave to obtain money from their buyers and then return for the drugs. Finally, the informants were in some manner in contact with the agents during the times they were alone with defendants and were able to communicate immediately to the agents that they had established probable cause.[666] In *Finley*, the police recruited the informant immediately prior to the transaction with the defendant; there was no previous connection between the informant and the police. Therefore, the police had no basis to ascertain the reliability of the informant. Moreover, the details of the sale were not established in advance. There was no evidence that defendant specifically invited the informant into the trailer for

---

664. *Id.*

665. 293 Ill. App. 3d 377, 687 N.E.2d 1154 (5th Dist. 1997).

666. *Id.*, 687 N.E.2d at 1160.

the purpose of making a drug sale. There was further no evidence that money ever changed hands. Finally, the record showed that defendant was highly intoxicated at the time, thus, undermining any claim that he had consented to the entry of the informant.[667]

The court further noted that recent Seventh Circuit cases had limited the doctrine. Three elements are necessary, the informant or undercover officer must: "(1) enter[ ] at the express invitation of someone with authority to consent, (2) at that point establish[ ] the existence of probable cause to effectuate an arrest or search, and (3) immediately summon[ ] help from other officers."[668] In *Finley*, the elements were not satisfied. Defendant did not expressly invite informant into the trailer for purposes of transacting a drug buy. Defendant was highly intoxicated at the time and, therefore, unable to consent to entry. Moreover, defendant had no prearrangement with the informant for a drug buy. Further, the informant's initial entry into the trailer did not establish probable cause that cocaine was present. At that time, defendant did not show informant any illegal substances. Finally, at the time of his initial entry, the informant did not make an arrangement for a future sale.[669] Accordingly, defendant's conviction was reversed and remanded for a new trial.

§ 1.44 The Exclusionary Rule

The remedy used to correct Fourth Amendment violations at a criminal trial is the exclusionary rule. The rule provides for the suppression of evidence at a judicial proceeding when the evidence, although probative, has been obtained in violation of a defendant's right to be free from unreasonable searches and seizures.[670] The two purposes of the exclusionary rule are to deter future wrongdoings by police officers by eliminating the use of evidence obtained unlawfully and to assure judicial integrity in that judges would not be tainted by handling the illegal evidence.[671] The rationale for the exclusionary rule has

---

667. *Id.*, 687 N.E.2d at 1161.

668. *Id.*

669. *Id.*

670. Mapp v. Ohio, 367 U.S. 643 (1961); Weeks v. United States, 232 U.S. 383 (1914). *See, e.g.*, People v. Parker, 192 Ill. App. 3d 779, 549 N.E.2d 626 (1st Dist. 1989) (line-up identification and testimony that defendant was driving stolen car at time of arrest both found to be inadmissible as "fruits" of defendant's illegal arrest).

671. People v. Myles, 62 Ill. App. 3d 931, 379 N.E.2d 897 (2d Dist. 1978). *See also* People v. Madison, 121 Ill. 2d 195, 520 N.E.2d 374 ("deterrence" is primary purpose of exclusionary rule), *cert. denied*, 488 U.S. 907 (1988); People v. McCrimmon, 225 Ill. App. 3d 456, 588 N.E.2d 444 (2d Dist. 1992) (defendant's battery of officer before search not subject to suppression because independent

nothing to do with aiding the truth-seeking process but instead seeks to "deter future deprivations of individuals' rights by similar attempts to improperly obtain evidence."[672] Moreover, the rule can be invoked only by one whose rights have been personally violated by the illegal government action.[673]

In *Pennsylvania Board of Probation & Parole v. Scott*,[674] the United States Supreme Court construed the exclusionary rule narrowly, finding that it applies only to criminal trials, and held that it was not applicable to state parole revocation proceedings.[675] Consequently, evidence obtained in violation of a parolee's Fourth Amendment right need not be excluded therein.[676] The Court reiterated that it had repeatedly held that the state's use of evidence that was obtained in violation of the Fourth Amendment does not necessarily violate the constitution.[677] Instead, the exclusionary rule is a judicially created rule for deterrence and, therefore, is not applicable to all proceedings. The Court further reiterated that it has repeatedly refused to apply the exclusionary rule to anything other than criminal trials.[678] The Court declined again to extend the scope of the exclusionary rule. Applying the exclusionary rule to parole revocation proceedings would hinder the functioning of the state parole systems and would alter the traditional flexible nature of parole revocation proceedings. Further, in this context, it possessed only minimal deterrent effect. The cost of excluding reliable evidence at parole revocation proceedings was "particularly high."[679] Parolees are given a limited degree of freedom in exchange for their promise to comply with the terms of their release. The states thus have an overwhelming interest in assuring that parolees comply with the terms of their release. If the Court allowed the exclusion of evidence, as urged in the

---

of the officer's later improper search). *But see* People v. Carter, 284 Ill. App. 3d 745, 672 N.E.2d 1279, 1286 (5th Dist. 1996) (exclusionary rule barred admission of evidence where evidence was obtained subsequent to officer's unlawful entry into defendant's home in violation of Fourth Amendment and independent source rule did not substantiate admission of evidence).

672. People v. Jackson, 67 Ill. App. 3d 24, 384 N.E.2d 591, 593 (4th Dist. 1979) (citing United States v. Calandra, 414 U.S. 338 (1974)).

673. United States v. Payner, 447 U.S. 727 (1980); Alderman v. United States, 394 U.S. 165, 171 (1969).

674. 118 S. Ct. 2014 (1998).

675. *Id.* at 2018.

676. *Id.* at 2022.

677. *Id.* at 2019.

678. *Id.*

679. *Id.*

instant case, it would hinder the states' abilities to administer parole releases effectively.[680]

Additionally, such a rule is incompatible with the nature of revocation proceedings wherein the states have wide latitude to structure the proceedings. Generally, traditional rules of evidence are not applicable, and the proceedings are not entirely adversarial. If the exclusionary rule were applied, it would significantly alter the nature of such proceedings. In particular, application of the exclusionary rule generally requires extensive litigation, and such litigation is inconsistent with parole revocation proceedings.

Finally, the Court found that there would be little deterrent effect. The police generally do not know that a suspect is a parolee and, thus, look for evidence of criminality with an eye towards a trial, not parole revocation. This is the deterrent factor.[681] Even if it is a parole officer, the deterrent effect remains minimal. Parole officers are generally more like supervisors to parolees than adversaries.

It is clear that not all evidence obtained from illegal searches and seizures is automatically suppressible.[682] Although evidence obtained directly from an illegal search or seizure will usually be suppressed, evidence obtained indirectly from such a search can be found admissible if it is determined that circumstances have purged the evidence of any taint associated with the illegal activity.[683]

In *Arizona v. Evans*,[684] the United States Supreme Court held that the exclusionary rule does not require suppression of evidence obtained in violation of the Fourth Amendment, where erroneous information led to an arrest and the erroneous information resulted from clerical errors of court employees.[685] The Court found that exclusion would not sufficiently deter future errors, particularly where the rule was designed to deter police misconduct, not mistakes of court employees.[686] In addition, there was no evidence that exclusion would have a significant effect on court employees who are responsible

---

680. *Id.* at 2020.

681. *Id.* at 2021.

682. Brown v. Illinois, 422 U.S. 590 (1975); People v. Dortch, 109 Ill. App. 3d 761, 441 N.E.2d 100 (1st Dist. 1982) (citing Wong Sun v. United States, 371 U.S. 471 (1963)). *See also* People v. Villarreal, 152 Ill. 2d 368, 604 N.E.2d 923 (1992) (noting that evidence obtained during an unlawful search which related to past or existing criminal activity may be excluded, but evidence of crimes which arise from and are in reaction to an illegal search may not).

683. Wong Sun v. United States, 371 U.S. 471 (1963).

684. 514 U.S. 1 (1995).

685. *Id.* at 4.

686. *Id.* at 13–15.

for informing officers that a warrant had been quashed.[687] These employees
have no stake in the outcome of any particular criminal proceeding and would
not alter their behavior should their errors mandate exclusion.[688] In this case,
the defendant was stopped for a routine traffic violation and after the police
checked the computer file, they arrested him based on an outstanding misdemeanor warrant. After the arrest, the officers searched his car and found a bag
of marijuana. The defendant sought suppression of the marijuana in his trial for
possession because the misdemeanor warrant had been quashed prior to the
police stopping him.[689] The court clerks had failed to correct the computer to
reflect that the warrant was quashed.[690] The Supreme Court refused to suppress
the evidence based upon the above analysis.[691] What remains to be seen is whether
a clerical *police* error would require a different result.[692]

§ 1.45   — Illinois Procedure for Suppressing Evidence

Illinois has codified its procedures for suppressing illegally seized evidence.[693] Section 114-12 of the Illinois Code of Criminal Procedure provides

---

687. *Id.* at 15.

688. *Id.*

689. *Id.* at 4.

690. *Id.* at 5.

691. *Id.* at 4.

692.   In *State v. White*, 660 So. 2d 664 (Fla. 1995), the Florida Supreme Court
held that the exclusionary rule bars use of evidence seized after an arrest
premised on police computer error. *Id.* at 667. In this case, a warrant for
defendant's arrest had been served on him and, therefore, was not, in fact,
outstanding when the police stopped him and arrested him. *Id.* at 666. According
to the court, this error boiled down to police failure to "maintain up-to-date and
accurate computer records" which fit "squarely within the class of governmental
action that the exclusionary rule was designed to deter." *Id.* at 667. In enforcing
such a rule, police will be encouraged to diligently maintain their computer
records. In conclusion, the court stated: "It is repugnant to the principles of a free
society that a person should ever be taken into police custody because of a
computer error precipitated by government carelessness. As automation increasingly invades modern life, the potential for Orwellian mischief grows. Under such
circumstances, the exclusionary rule is a 'cost' we cannot afford to be without".
Id. at 667–68, quoting *State v. Evans*, 866 P.2d 869, 872 (Ariz. 1994), *rev'd*, 514
U.S. 1 (1995). Additionally, the good faith exception did not apply because the
true facts that the warrant was void were within the collective knowledge of
the sheriff department, and the arresting officer was charged with knowledge
of. *White*, 660 So. 2d at 668.

693. 725 ILCS 5/114-12.

that evidence can be suppressed if it was obtained through an illegal warrantless search and seizure.[694] Moreover, the section provides that evidence seized during a search and seizure pursuant to a warrant may be suppressed if: (1) the warrant was insufficient on its face; (2) the evidence seized was not what was described in the warrant; (3) there was no probable cause for the issuance of the warrant; or (4) the warrant was illegally executed.[695]

A motion to suppress the fruits of an illegal search or seizure must be presented to the court in writing[696] and must state facts establishing why the search and seizure was unlawful.[697] The judge may receive evidence on any issue of fact necessary to determine the motion[698] and may resolve conflicts by evaluating the credibility of the witnesses.[699]

The state may urge that the peace officer's conduct was taken in a reasonable and objective good faith belief that the conduct was proper and that the evidence discovered should not be suppressed if otherwise admissible. The court shall not suppress evidence which it determines was seized by a peace officer who acted in good faith.[700] In addition, even if the search warrant is partially invalid, the entire warrant is not necessarily tainted, because courts can simply sever the invalid portion from the rest of the search warrant.[701]

On a motion to quash an arrest and to suppress its fruits, the burden of proving the arrest was illegal by a preponderance of the evidence is on the defendant.[702] However, once the defendant has made a prima facie showing of a lack of probable cause, the burden of going forward with the evidence shifts to the state.[703] Likewise, on a motion to suppress the fruits of a search, the burden of proving the search was illegal by a preponderance of the evidence is

---

694. 725 ILCS 5/114-12(a)(1).

695. 725 ILCS 5/114-12(a)(2).

696. 725 ILCS 5/114-12(b); People v. Foster, 76 Ill. 2d 365, 392 N.E.2d 6 (1979).

697. 725 ILCS 5/114-12(b).

698. *Id.*

699. People v. James, 44 Ill. App. 3d 300, 358 N.E.2d 88 (2d Dist. 1976); People v. Adkins, 28 Ill. App. 3d 342, 328 N.E.2d 633, 635 (5th Dist. 1975).

700. People v. Stewart, 104 Ill. 2d 463, 473 N.E.2d 1227, 1233 (1984), *cert. denied,* 471 U.S. 1120 (1985).

701. People v. McCoy, 135 Ill. App. 3d 1059, 482 N.E.2d 200 (2d Dist. 1985); People v. Hellemeyer, 28 Ill. App. 3d 491, 328 N.E.2d 626 (5th Dist. 1975).

702. 725 ILCS 5/114-12(b); People v. Walls, 87 Ill. App. 3d 256, 408 N.E.2d 1056, 1062–63 (1st Dist. 1980).

703. People v. Jones, 114 Ill. App. 3d 576, 449 N.E.2d 547 (1st Dist. 1983); People v. Garcia, 94 Ill. App. 3d 940, 419 N.E.2d 542 (1st Dist. 1981).

on the defendant.[704] Once he or she establishes a prima facie lack of probable cause, the burden of going forward with evidence to establish the legal justification for the search shifts to the state.[705] In both situations, a ruling on such a motion is not final and can be reversed at any time during the subsequent trial.[706] However, if a suppression order is not appealable under Supreme Court Rule 604(a)(1),[707] and no timely reconsideration is obtained from the judge who entered the order, then the only avenue of relief open to a dissatisfied party is appeal of that order; the propriety of the order cannot be reviewed by another trial judge.[708] The trial court's ultimate ruling on a motion to suppress is given great deference by a reviewing court and will not be disturbed unless found to be manifestly erroneous.[709] Moreover, in reviewing a denial of a motion to suppress, an appellate court may consider trial testimony as well as evidence presented at the hearing on the motion.[710]

In general, motions to suppress must be filed before trial.[711] However, a motion to suppress may be filed and considered during trial if the court determines either that an opportunity did not exist previously or that the defendant was not aware of the grounds for the motion before trial.[712] The judge's ruling on whether to allow the filing of a suppression motion during trial is subject to appellate review.[713] Moreover, a failure to raise a suppression

---

704.　725 ILCS 5/114-12(b); People v. Boston, 73 Ill. App. 3d 107, 391 N.E.2d 503 (1st Dist. 1979).

705.　People v. Boston, 73 Ill. App. 3d 107, 391 N.E.2d 503 (1st Dist. 1979); People v. Jackson, 57 Ill. App. 3d 720, 373 N.E.2d 729, 733 (1st Dist. 1978).

706.　People v. Jones, 114 Ill. App. 3d 576, 449 N.E.2d 547 (1st Dist. 1983); People v. Taylor, 99 Ill. App. 3d 15, 424 N.E.2d 1246 (1st Dist. 1981).

707.　S. Ct. Rule 604(a)(1).

708.　People v. Williams, 138 Ill. 2d 377, 563 N.E.2d 385 (1990); People v. Taylor, 50 Ill. 2d 136, 277 N.E.2d 878 (1971).

709.　People v. Garcia, 97 Ill. 2d 58, 454 N.E.2d 274, 279 (1983), *cert. denied,* 467 U.S. 1260 (1984); People v. Free, 94 Ill. 2d 378, 447 N.E.2d 218, 229, *cert. denied,* 464 U.S. 865 (1983). Review is *de novo* if the facts are undisputed. People v. James, 163 Ill. 2d 302, 645 N.E.2d 195, 199 (1995).

710.　People v. Caballero, 102 Ill. 2d 23, 464 N.E.2d 223, *cert. denied,* 469 U.S. 964 (1984); People v. Conner, 78 Ill. 2d 513, 401 N.E.2d 525 (1979); People v. Braden, 34 Ill. 2d 516, 216 N.E.2d 808 (1966).

711.　725 ILCS 5/114-12(c).

712.　*Id.*

713.　*Compare* People v. Grotti, 112 Ill. App. 3d 718, 445 N.E.2d 946 (5th Dist. 1983) (court's decision to allow defendant to file motion during trial was proper because defendant could not have been aware of grounds before trial) *with* People v. Davidson, 116 Ill. App. 3d 164, 451 N.E.2d 978 (5th Dist. 1983) (no reason why

issue through a proper method at the trial level waives later consideration of the issue.[714]

§ 1.46 — Exceptions

It must be emphasized that the mere fact that evidence is the fruit of an illegal search and seizure does not automatically mean that the evidence will be excluded for all purposes at trial. Both Illinois courts and the United States Supreme Court have refused to apply a "but for" rule in this area.[715] A variety of exceptions to the exclusionary rule have been judicially created.

§ 1.47 — — The Good Faith Exception

The Illinois Supreme Court has announced its intention to follow the United States Supreme Court's decision to recognize a good faith exception to the exclusionary rule.[716] This means that the exclusionary rule may not be used to prevent the use of any evidence in the state's case in chief when that evidence was seized by police officers who reasonably relied on a facially valid warrant. This exception is the result of a balancing test that concluded that when an officer obtains a warrant in good faith and it is reasonable for the officer to rely on its validity, excluding evidence that is found to be tainted would not have a significant deterrent effect on either the police or the magistrate who issued the warrant.[717]

---

motion could not have been filed before trial; error to consider it during trial); People v. Rathgeb, 113 Ill. App. 3d 943, 447 N.E.2d 1351 (4th Dist. 1983) (no error for trial court to refuse to allow defendant to file motion during trial where defendant had received sufficient information by time of preliminary hearing to enable him to file pretrial motion).

714. People v. Nilsson, 44 Ill. 2d 244, 255 N.E.2d 432, *cert. denied,* 398 U.S. 954 (1970).

715. Brown v. Illinois, 422 U.S. 590 (1975); Wong Sun v. United States, 371 U.S. 471 (1963); People v. Price, 76 Ill. App. 3d 613, 394 N.E.2d 1256 (1st Dist. 1979); People v. Washington, 60 Ill. App. 3d 662, 377 N.E.2d 397 (1st Dist. 1978); People v. Faulisi, 51 Ill. App. 3d 529, 366 N.E.2d 1072 (1st Dist. 1977); People v. Pettis, 12 Ill. App. 3d 123, 298 N.E.2d 372 (1st Dist. 1973).

716. People v. Stewart, 104 Ill. 2d 463, 473 N.E.2d 1227, 1233 (1984) (citing United States v. Leon, 468 U.S. 897, 920–21 (1984)). *See* People v. Walensky, 286 Ill. App. 3d 82, 675 N.E.2d 952, 959–61 (1st Dist. 1996) (explaining distinction between *Krueger* and *Leon* good faith exceptions).

717. *Leon,* 468 U.S. at 922. *See* People v. Cooke, 299 Ill. App. 3d 273, 701 N.E.2d 526, 532 (4th Dist. 1998) (officer's good faith reliance on warrant found to be made more reasonable by fact warrant was partially valid).

However, the United States Supreme Court emphasized that the good faith exception would not apply in several situations:[718]

1. if the issuing magistrate or judge was misled by information that the affiant knew was false or would have known was false but for his or her reckless disregard of the truth;[719]

2. if the issuing magistrate wholly abandoned his or her judicial role;[720]

3. if the officer relied on a warrant based on an affidavit "so lacking in indicia of probable cause to render official belief in its existence entirely unreasonable";[721] or

4. if the officer relied on a warrant so facially deficient that the executing officer could not reasonably presume it to be valid.[722]

Although the good faith test has been adopted by the Illinois Supreme Court,[723] at least one Illinois court has had occasion to distinguish it. In *People*

---

718. The Illinois Supreme Court in *People v. Stewart,* 104 Ill. 2d 463, 473 N.E.2d 1227 (1984), had no occasion to discuss these special circumstances.

719. *Leon,* 468 U.S. at 923 (citing Franks v. Delaware, 438 U.S. 154 (1978)); People v. Wehde, 210 Ill. App. 3d 56, 568 N.E.2d 910 (2d Dist. 1991) (court applied *Leon* factors and determined officers acted reasonably in presenting information to obtain warrant and relying on warrant; deficiency due to judge's failure and therefore suppression would not deter police misconduct). *See also* People v. Eagle Books, Inc., 151 Ill. 2d 235, 602 N.E.2d 798, 806 (1992) (noting that neither the United States Supreme Court nor the Illinois Supreme Court has extended the good faith exception to the "constitutionality of a search for materials presumptively protected by the first amendment").

720. *Leon,* 468 U.S. at 923 (citing Lo-Ji Sales v. New York, 442 U.S. 319 (1979)).

721. *Leon,* 468 U.S. at 923 (citing Brown v. Illinois, 422 U.S. 590, 610–11 (1975) (Powell, J., concurring in part)); Illinois v. Gates, 462 U.S. 213 (1983) (White, J., concurring in the judgment).

722. *Leon,* 468 U.S. at 923 (citing Massachusetts v. Sheppard, 468 U.S. 981 (1984)); People v. Lipscomb, 215 Ill. App. 3d 413, 574 N.E. 2d 1345 (4th Dist. 1991) (officers could reasonably rely on warrant not obviously defective); People v. Taylor, 198 Ill. App. 3d 667, 555 N.E.2d 1218 (3d Dist. 1990) ("good faith" exception not applicable to search warrant lacking time and date of issuance and judge's signature).

723. *See* People v. Rehkopf, 153 Ill. App. 3d 819, 506 N.E.2d 435 (2d Dist. 1987) (held *Leon* good faith standard applies to state officers relying on federal search warrant, even though warrant was stale and items found in plain view were not listed in warrant); People v. Porter, 141 Ill. App. 3d 71, 489 N.E.2d 1154 (5th Dist.), *cert. denied,* 479 U.S. 951 (1986).

v. Joseph,[724] a Chicago police officer on patrol spotted an individual he knew, put the individual's name in his mobile computer unit, and was informed that there was a bond forfeiture warrant outstanding against him. During the subsequent arrest, a controlled substance was recovered. It was later learned that the computer erred in not reflecting that the warrant had been quashed. On appeal, the state maintained that the good faith exception should apply because the conduct of the police in making the arrest was objectively reasonable. The appellate court excluded the evidence and distinguished *Leon,* holding that recognizing a good faith exception in this situation would tend to reward police department inefficiency. At least one Illinois court has refused to extend the *Leon* rule to a warrantless situation.[725]

The Illinois Supreme Court in *People v. Krueger*[726] held that it would not follow the United States Supreme Court's decision in *Illinois v. Krull,*[727] that recognized a good faith exception to the exclusionary rule where an officer reasonably relies, in objective good faith, on a statute that is later declared to be unconstitutional. The *Krueger* court held that the *Krull* good faith exception is inconsistent with article 1, section 6 of the Illinois Constitution in that the exclusionary rule has always been understood to bar evidence which is gathered under the authority of an unconstitutional statute and draws no distinction between statutes known to be unconstitutional and those which are later

---

724. 128 Ill. App. 3d 668, 470 N.E.2d 1303 (1st Dist. 1984). *See also* People v. Turnage, 162 Ill. 2d 299, 642 N.E.2d 1235, 1240–41 (1994) (*Leon* inapplicable where prosecutor failed to present facts to show whether those obtaining warrant had objective reasonable belief in warrant's validity; court applied *Whiteley v. Warden,* quashed arrest, and suppressed evidence); People v. Mourecek, 208 Ill. App. 3d 87, 566 N.E.2d 841 (2d Dist. 1991) (no good faith reliance on electronically communicated information that was stale).

725. People v. Vought, 174 Ill. App. 3d 563, 528 N.E.2d 1095 (2d Dist. 1988), *cert. denied,* 492 U.S. 911 (1989). *See also* People v. McGee, 268 Ill. App. 3d 32, 644 N.E.2d 439, 447 (2d Dist. 1994) (finding *Krull* good faith exception incompatible with the state constitutional guarantee against unreasonable invasions of privacy, no good faith exception allowed when officer relied on validity of statute later declared unconstitutional because it permitted unreasonable search and seizure without particularized probable cause necessary under the Illinois Constitution).

726. 175 Ill. 2d 60, 675 N.E.2d 604 (1996), *cert. denied,* 118 S. Ct. 49 (1997). *But see* People v. Nwosu, 284 Ill. App. 3d 538, 672 N.E.2d 366, 368–69 (1st Dist. 1996) (recognizing *Krull* good faith exception exists where police reasonably rely, acting in good faith, on a statute later declared invalid for ambiguity), *vacated and remanded,* 171 Ill. 2d 578, 676 N.E.2d 1284 (1997), *adhered to* 289 Ill. App. 3d 487, 683 N.E.2d 148 (1st Dist. 1997).

727. 480 U.S. 340 (1987).

determined unconstitutional.[728] The *Krueger* court further distinguished *Krull*, finding that the rights of Illinois citizens prevailed over permitting the state a grace period for unconstitutional search and seizure statutes, where such grace period seriously threatened Fourth Amendment jurisprudence.[729] However, the Illinois Supreme Court was careful to note that the *Krueger* decision did not alter Illinois' recognition of the *Leon* good faith exception.[730]

§ 1.48   — — Inevitable Discovery

The United States Supreme Court in *Nix v. Williams*[731] adopted the inevitable discovery exception to the exclusionary rule. This rule holds that illegally obtained evidence is admissible if the state can establish by a preponderance of the evidence that the evidence would have been ultimately discovered by lawful means. The Court balanced deterrence of improper police conduct against the importance of a jury's having all probative evidence of a crime and held that allowing the use of evidence that would have been inevitably discovered places the prosecution in the same position it would have been had no police misconduct occurred.

Illinois has long recognized the inevitable discovery exception.[732]

---

728.   *Krueger*, 175 Ill. 2d 60, 675 N.E.2d at 610.

729.   *Id.*, 675 N.E.2d at 612.

730.   *Id.* The holding of *Krueger* was reaffirmed by the court in *People v. Wright*, 183 Ill. 2d 16, 697 N.E.2d 693, 697 (1998). *See also* People v. Carlson, 185 Ill. 2d 546, 708 N.E.2d 372, 378 (1999) (anticipatory search warrant issued and executed prior to *Ross* admissible based upon *Leon* good faith exception).

731.   467 U.S. 431 (1984).

732.   Courts usually find that:
> evidence inevitably would have been discovered where (1) the condition of the evidence when actually found by lawful means would have been the same as that when improperly obtained; (2) the evidence would have been discovered through an independent line of investigation untainted by the illegal conduct; and (3) the independent investigation was already in progress at the time the evidence was unconstitutionally obtained.

People v. Perez, 258 Ill. App. 3d 133, 630 N.E.2d 158, 162 (2d Dist. 1994) (cocaine improperly removed from defendant's pocket would have inevitably been discovered in a subsequent search incident to arrest); People v. Seawright, 228 Ill. App. 3d 939, 593 N.E.2d 1003 (1st Dist. 1992) (defendant's motion to suppress evidence seized during a warrantless search conducted prior to his giving consent was denied; the evidence seized would have been ultimately discovered after police received consent); People v. Faysom, 131 Ill. App. 3d 517, 475 N.E.2d 945 (1st Dist. 1985) (gun would have been ultimately recovered by police); People v. Cunningham, 130 Ill. App. 3d 254, 473 N.E.2d 506 (1st Dist. 1984)

§ 1.49 — — Independent Source

The independent source exception was first articulated by the United States Supreme Court in 1920 in *Silverthorne Lumber Co. v. United States*[733] and was reaffirmed by the Court in 1984 in *Segura v. United States*.[734] This doctrine holds that even though certain evidence is discovered as the result of an illegal search and seizure, it may still be admissible if the state can establish that it would have been found through independent legal means. For example, in *Segura* the defendant maintained that an illegal entry into an apartment should have resulted in the exclusion of all evidence seen by the police during that entry. Invoking the independent source doctrine, the Supreme Court held that the police knew about the contraband before they entered the apartment. This prior information was an independent source of the information used to obtain a subsequent warrant to seize the contraband. Therefore, the admission of the contraband into evidence was proper. The independent source doctrine is also recognized in Illinois.[735]

(identification would have been inevitably discovered); People v. Farmer, 91 Ill. App. 3d 262, 414 N.E.2d 779 (5th Dist. 1980) (statements were admissible through inevitable discovery exception even though police misconduct preceded discovery of evidence); People v. Williams, 62 Ill. App. 3d 874, 379 N.E.2d 1222 (1st Dist. 1978) (police already possessed defendant's fingerprints and had reason to connect him with crime); People v. Horton, 49 Ill. App. 3d 531, 364 N.E.2d 551 (1st Dist. 1977) (1973 fingerprints not fruit of 1974 illegal arrest, therefore admissible); People v. Stinson, 37 Ill. App. 3d 229, 345 N.E.2d 751 (1st Dist. 1976) (evidence of credit card charges not excluded despite discovery of violation because information was in state's possession and would have been uncovered during state's preparation of case). *But see* People v. Conard, 213 Ill. App. 3d 1068, 572 N.E.2d 1203 (3d Dist. 1991) (coin purse unlawfully seized in *Terry* stop would not have been inevitably discovered under search incident to arrest exception).

733. 251 U.S. 385 (1920).

734. 468 U.S. 796 (1984). *See also* Murray v. United States, 487 U.S. 533 (1988) ("independent source" doctrine even permits introduction of evidence initially discovered during an unlawful search, but later obtained independently from lawful activities untainted by the initial illegality). *But see* People v. Carter, 284 Ill. App. 3d 745, 672 N.E.2d 1279, 1284–85 (5th Dist. 1996) (where officers illegally entered a home and only sought a warrant after residents refused to consent to search, the illegality influenced the decision of the police to seek the warrant; thus the prosecution could not be permitted to profit from illegal activity and independent source rule would not justify admissibility of the evidence).

735. People v. Cunningham, 130 Ill. App. 3d 254, 473 N.E.2d 506 (1st Dist. 1984); People v. Brumfield, 100 Ill. App. 3d 382, 426 N.E.2d 1012 (1st Dist. 1981);

Another area in which the independent source doctrine is involved concerns the problem of whether to consider an in-court identification to be the fruit of an illegal seizure of the defendant. In *United States v. Crews*,[736] the United States Supreme Court held that such an identification is proper if the state can establish that it is supported by an independent basis. Among the factors to consider are the witness's ability to identify the defendant from observations made at the time of the crime, as well as his or her knowledge of and ability to recount significant details about the crime. Illinois courts will not hesitate to admit such an in-court identification if an independent basis is established.[737]

§ 1.50   — — Attenuation

Clearly, evidence that is directly obtained from an illegal search and seizure must be suppressed through the exclusionary rule.[738] This type of evidence could be considered primary evidence. Another type of evidence might be classified as secondary or derivative in character. For example, following an illegal search and seizure, a defendant might give a confession or certain information that might lead to other evidence. An Illinois court will also suppress this kind of evidence unless it finds it to be sufficiently attenuated from the illegal search and seizure. The Illinois Supreme Court has described the inquiry as "whether granting establishment of the primary illegality, the evidence to which instant objection is [being] made has been come at . . . by means sufficiently distinguishable to be purged of the primary taint."[739] First, the burden is on the defendant to establish the primary illegality

---

People v. Williams, 79 Ill. App. 3d 817, 398 N.E.2d 1099 (1st Dist. 1979); People v. Horton, 49 Ill. App. 3d 531, 364 N.E.2d 551 (1st Dist. 1977). *See also* United States v. Clemens, 58 F.3d 318, 329 (7th Cir. 1995) (evidence discovered during warrantless protective sweep of defendant's home did not have to be suppressed if evidence was legitimately rediscovered during a second, valid search; second search was not tainted by first because affidavit for second search, which demonstrated probable cause, contained only information obtained before first illegal entry).

736. 445 U.S. 463 (1980).

737. People v. Payne, 98 Ill. 2d 45, 456 N.E.2d 44 (1983), *cert. denied,* 465 U.S. 1036 (1984); People v. Sanderlin, 105 Ill. App. 3d 811, 434 N.E.2d 1158 (4th Dist. 1982); People v. Glover-El, 102 Ill. App. 3d 535, 430 N.E.2d 147 (1st Dist. 1981), *cert. denied,* 458 U.S. 1110 (1982).

738. Wong Sun v. United States, 371 U.S. 471 (1963); People v. Wilson, 60 Ill. 2d 235, 326 N.E.2d 378 (1975); People v. Walters, 187 Ill. App. 3d 661, 543 N.E.2d 508 (2d Dist. 1989) (evidence should have been suppressed where consent was invalid as fruit of illegal warrant).

739. *Wilson,* 60 Ill. 2d 235, 326 N.E.2d at 380 (quoting *Wong Sun,* 371 U.S. at 488).

and to show a connection between the illegality and what are alleged to be the fruits of the illegality. Then the prosecution has the burden of establishing by clear and convincing evidence that the evidence is sufficiently untainted by the illegality.[740]

Perhaps the most common application of the attenuation doctrine occurs in the area of the admissibility of confessions and admissions following an illegal arrest or stop. The Illinois Supreme Court has identified several factors to consider in deciding whether such a statement has been obtained by exploitation of an illegal arrest or stop: (1) the temporal proximity of the arrest and the confession; (2) the presence or absence of intervening circumstances; (3) the flagrancy of the official misconduct; and (4) whether or not *Miranda* warnings were given.[741] Thus, for example, in *People v. Gabbard*,[742] the Illinois Supreme Court found that the defendant's confession was sufficiently attenuated from his illegal arrest because the arrest was not for the offense to which defendant

---

740. People v. Wilson, 60 Ill. 2d 235, 326 N.E.2d 378 (1975); People v. Martin, 382 Ill. 192, 46 N.E.2d 997 (1942); People v. Nash, 78 Ill. App. 3d 172, 397 N.E.2d 480 (1st Dist. 1979).

741. People v. Gabbard, 78 Ill. 2d 88, 398 N.E.2d 574, 577 (1979) (citing Dunaway v. New York, 442 U.S. 200 (1979)); Brown v. Illinois, 422 U.S. 590 (1975)). *See also* People v. Smith, 232 Ill. App. 3d 121, 596 N.E.2d 789 (1st Dist. 1992) (utilizing similar factors to determine attenuation of a line-up).

742. People v. Gabbard, 78 Ill. 2d 88, 398 N.E.2d 574 (1979). *See* People v. Austin, 293 Ill. App. 3d 784, 688 N.E.2d 740, 745 (1st Dist. 1997) (defendant's confession not purged of taint of illegal arrest where defendant made statement approximately five hours after illegal arrest and no attenuation: statements by two co-defendants not independent intervening circumstances because statements of these two were also tainted—it is improper to use tainted evidence to remove taint from defendant's confession), *cert. denied*, 119 S. Ct. 575 (1998); People v. Agnew, 152 Ill. App. 3d 1037, 504 N.E.2d 1358 (2d Dist. 1987) (lack of attenuation of taint; two and one-half hours between illegal arrest and defendants' confessions held insufficient attenuation of taint despite fact that defendants were given *Miranda* warnings prior to making their statements). *But see* People v. Ornelas, 295 Ill. App. 3d 1037, 693 N.E.2d 1247, 1254 (1st Dist. 1998) (intervening probable cause existed to attenuate defendant's confession from his illegal arrest where statement was made by person illegally arrested with defendant on unrelated charges that implicated defendant in murder; defendant not under arrest for charge of murder at time and police were not aware of murder; neither was arrested for the murder nor for gaining evidence on the unrelated charges); People v. Wright, 294 Ill. App. 3d 606, 691 N.E.2d 94, 99 (1st Dist. 1998) (confession sufficiently attenuated from illegal arrest where confession took place after statements made by defendant's brother, while under lawful arrest, implicated defendant in murder because defendant's statement not made until after brother made statements and defendant was confronted with these statements and given *Miranda* warnings).

confessed, the arrest was not for the purpose of questioning the defendant, the defendant was given *Miranda* warnings, and the interrogating officer was not aware of the illegal arrest. However, in *People v. Townes,*[743] the supreme court suppressed the defendant's voluntary confession when it found that the confession was the result of continuous station house questioning over a twelve-hour period during which no probable cause existed.[744]

In *People v. Jennings,*[745] the court concluded that defendant's confession was not sufficiently attenuated from his illegal arrest and, therefore, had to be suppressed. Fifteen-year-old defendant and three of his friends were walking down an alley in the area where defendant had shot someone several days earlier. Because the group was in a rival gang territory, they had the gun which the defendant had used in the shooting. Another boy, Buffen, was carrying it. As they group was walking, the police approached them, and Buffen removed the gun from his waistband and began to run. The police handcuffed all four and placed them in a squad car. They then retrieved the gun and took the group to the police station. At the station, the police contacted an eyewitness to the shooting and obtained a description of the perpetrator's coat. Buffen was interviewed, and he told the police the gun was the defendant's. The police observed that Buffen's jacket did not match that of the description given to them.[746] The police then sought to interview the defendant. They observed that his jacket was inside out. After removing his jacket and finding that it matched the description, they gave him *Miranda* warnings, and he confessed.

The trial court concluded that defendant's arrest was illegal and suppressed his jacket. However, it declined to suppress his confession, finding that it was sufficiently attenuated from the arrest.[747] The appellate court looked at the four factors outlined in *Brown* and *Gabbard* and observed that the giving of *Miranda* warnings and temporal proximity were of little significance. However, even

---

743. 91 Ill. 2d 32, 435 N.E.2d 103 (1982).

744. People v. Townes, 91 Ill. 2d 32, 435 N.E.2d 103 (1982). *See* People v. Travis, 122 Ill. App. 3d 671, 462 N.E.2d 654 (1st Dist. 1984) (facts found to be "analogous" to *Dunaway;* confession suppressed); People v. Fox, 111 Ill. App. 3d 243, 443 N.E.2d 1179 (3d Dist. 1982) (illegal detention and questioning continued through entire evening; confession suppressed even though *Miranda* warnings were given); People v. Fitzpatrick, 107 Ill. App. 3d 876, 438 N.E.2d 222 (5th Dist. 1982) (police interrogated defendant without telling him he was free to leave; confession suppressed). *See also* People v. Holveck, 171 Ill. App. 3d 38, 524 N.E.2d 1073 (1st Dist. 1988), *aff'd,* 141 Ill. 2d 84, 565 N.E.2d 919 (1990) (incriminating statements suppressed where defendant detained without probable cause and giving of *Miranda* warning was only intervening event).

745. 296 Ill. App. 3d 761, 695 N.E.2d 1303 (1st Dist. 1998).

746. *Id.,* 695 N.E.2d at 1304–05.

747. *Id.,* 695 N.E.2d at 1305.

considering these factors, neither supported attenuation.[748] The court found that the factors of official misconduct and the presence of intervening circumstances were the most relevant. As to official misconduct, it noted that a judge was less likely to find attenuation where the police conduct was flagrant. In other words, "where the police embark upon a course of illegal conduct in the hope that some incriminating evidence . . . might be found," attenuation was not likely to be found.[749] In *Jennings*, the conduct demonstrated purposefulness. The police observed only Buffen carrying the gun. Once they recovered the gun and secured the area, they had reason to hold only Buffen. Further, after they took the boys to the station, they consulted with an eyewitness. This supported a conclusion that defendant's illegal arrest was undertaken to obtain incriminating evidence regarding the murder.[750] Thus, it factored against attenuation.

With regard to intervening circumstances, the court noted that when suspects are confronted with untainted evidence, this is often sufficient to support attenuation.[751] However, here, defendant was confronted with tainted and untainted evidence; a more problematic situation. The court outlined the three potential intervening factors that were present, two of which were untainted (recovery of the gun and Buffen's statement that the gun belonged to the defendant). However, the defendant was also confronted with tainted evidence: his jacket.[752] Based on the fact that the defendant was wearing the jacket inside out, showing that he knew that there was a problem with it, and the fact that he confessed shortly after being confronted with it, the court could not say that the jacket was not a prominent factor in his decision to confess. It refused to conclude that the jacket simply played a *de minimis* role. Accordingly, there were insufficient intervening circumstances to support a finding of attenuation, and the appellate court reversed the conviction and remanded for a new trial without his confession.[753]

Other types of evidence are also subject to the attenuation, or "fruit of the poisonous tree," analysis. Illinois courts have held that pretrial identification can be suppressible fruit of an illegal search and seizure.[754] Likewise,

---

748. *Id.*, 695 N.E.2d at 1306.

749. *Id.*

750. *Id.*

751. *Id.*, 695 N.E.2d at 1307.

752. *Id.*, 695 N.E.2d at 1308.

753. *Id.*

754. People v. Smith, 232 Ill. App. 3d 121, 596 N.E.2d 789 (1st Dist. 1992) (finding that the illegal arrest was a pretext for obtaining a line-up identification and thus line-up was not attenuated from the illegal arrest and was properly suppressed). *But see* People v. Dortch, 109 Ill. App. 3d 761, 441 N.E.2d 100 (1st Dist. 1982) (attenuation found because police conduct was "neither purposeful nor flagrant";

fingerprints may also be excluded as fruit of an illegal arrest.[755] Also, a consent to search may be excluded as the fruit of an illegal arrest.[756]

§ 1.51 — Permissible Trial Uses of Illegally Obtained Evidence

Even if evidence is suppressed as the fruit of an illegal search and seizure, there are situations in which it may still be introduced at trial. For example, if damaging evidence is suppressed as a fruit of an illegal search and the defendant later implies to the jury that the search recovered no evidence, the defendant is deemed to have opened the door to the state's use of the suppressed evidence to correct any misconception.[757] Furthermore, suppressed evidence can be used to impeach the inaccurate testimony of a defendant.[758]

§ 1.52 — Standing

The fact that evidence has been illegally seized does not mean that it will be per se excluded from a criminal trial. The exclusionary rule can be invoked only by the persons whose constitutional rights were directly violated by the gov-

---

confession admissible); People v. Holdman, 51 Ill. App. 3d 484, 366 N.E.2d 993 (1st Dist. 1977), *rev'd,* 73 Ill. 2d 213, 383 N.E.2d 155 (1978) (on-scene identification admissible because police had probable cause to arrest), *cert. denied,* 440 U.S. 938 (1979).

755. People v. Williams, 62 Ill. App. 3d 874, 379 N.E.2d 1222 (1st Dist. 1978); People v. Hinkle, 23 Ill. App. 3d 134, 318 N.E.2d 690 (5th Dist. 1974). *See* Davis v. Mississippi, 394 U.S. 721 (1969).

756. People v. Koniecki, 135 Ill. App. 3d 394, 481 N.E.2d 973 (4th Dist. 1985); People v. Odom, 83 Ill. App. 3d 1022, 404 N.E.2d 997 (3d Dist. 1980). *But see* People v. Tingle, 279 Ill. App. 3d 706, 665 N.E.2d 383, 390 (1st Dist. 1996) (search and seizure determined lawful where illegally arrested individual directed officer's attention to his disabled and double-parked car, and officer's seizure of gun in plain view and subsequent search of rest of vehicle were reasonable since officer did not exploit the illegal arrest, asked no questions, and used no force).

757. People v. Payne, 98 Ill. 2d 45, 456 N.E.2d 44 (1983); People v. George, 49 Ill. 2d 372, 274 N.E.2d 26 (1971) (proper for state to use evidence because defendant brought out such testimony in cross-examination of prosecutor's witness).

758. People v. Brown, 40 Ill. App. 3d 1003, 353 N.E.2d 244 (1st Dist. 1976) (proper to introduce suppressed photograph of defendant wearing hat and holding gun when defendant testified that he owned neither hat nor gun); People v. Hearn, 34 Ill. App. 3d 919, 341 N.E.2d 129 (4th Dist. 1976) (proper to introduce suppressed key when defendant testified that she never owned such key).

ernment's improper actions.[759] This idea has often been referred to as a "standing" issue, but it is more accurately viewed as simply a question of whether the defendant's own constitutional rights have been violated.[760] Illinois has adopted the analysis used by the United States Supreme Court in *Rakas v. Illinois*,[761] *United States v. Salvucci*,[762] and *Rawlings v. Kentucky*.[763] *Rakas* held that the issue of standing involves "two inquiries: first, whether the proponent of a particular legal right has alleged 'injury in fact,' and, second, whether the proponent is asserting his own legal rights and interests rather than basing his claim for relief upon the rights of third parties."[764] In this case the Court found that passengers in a car who asserted no property or possessory interest in either the car or the property seized from it had no privacy interest that could be violated by an unreasonable search. A defendant must show he or she has a "legitimate expectation of privacy in the invaded place" to suppress the evidence seized.[765]

---

759. Alderman v. United States, 394 U.S. 165 (1965); People v. Keller, 93 Ill. 2d 432, 444 N.E.2d 118 (1982).

760. People v. Morrow, 104 Ill. App. 3d 995, 433 N.E.2d 985 (1st Dist. 1982) (citing Rakas v. Illinois, 439 U.S. 128 (1978)). *Compare* People v. Ervin, 269 Ill. App. 3d 141, 645 N.E.2d 355, 360 (1st Dist. 1994) (defendant lacked standing to contest warrantless search and seizure conducted in home of former wife whom he cared for regularly).

761. People v. Morrow, 104 Ill. App. 3d 995, 433 N.E.2d 985 (1st Dist. 1982).

762. 448 U.S. 83 (1980).

763. 448 U.S. 98 (1980). *See* People v. Johnson, 114 Ill. 2d 170, 499 N.E.2d 1355 (1986), *cert. denied*, 480 U.S. 951 (1987).

764. *Rakas*, 439 U.S. at 139. *See also* People v. Barton, 286 Ill. App. 3d 954, 677 N.E.2d 476, 480 (5th Dist. 1997) (defendant did not have standing to contest the voluntariness of three witnesses' statements because it was not the defendant's Fourth Amendment rights that were allegedly violated).

765. *Rakas*, 439 U.S. at 143. *See also* People v. McCoy, 269 Ill. App. 3d 587, 646 N.E.2d 1361, 1364 (4th Dist. 1995) (no standing to challenge search where neither driver nor passengers had driver's license nor paperwork for rental car; therefore, no showing of possessory interest in car, no claim of ownership in items seized, and no legitimate expectation of privacy in engine compartment where cocaine found); People v. Harre, 263 Ill. App. 3d 447, 636 N.E.2d 23, 27 (5th Dist. 1994) (no legitimate expectation of privacy where defendant was on property for limited purpose of cutting weeds and brush and to perform maintenance and clean up).

In *Bond v. United States*, 77 F.3d 1009, *cert. denied*, 519 U.S. 909 (1996), the court held that when defendant denied ownership of a suitcase just prior to police searching it, he had abandoned it and lost any Fourth Amendment protection in the suitcase. By denying ownership, he forfeited his privacy interest in the suitcase and therefore could not challenge the propriety of the search which uncovered $128,000. *Id.* at 1013–14.

The following factors may be considered relevant in determining whether the defendant had a reasonable expectation of privacy in the area searched: "whether a defendant (1) was legitimately present in the area searched, (2) had a possessory interest in the area or property seized, (3) had used the area searched or property seized, (4) had an ability to control or exclude others from using the property, and (5) had a subjective expectation of privacy in the property."[766]

In *United States v. Salvucci,*[767] the Court overruled the so-called "automatic standing" rule. The rule had held that when possession of seized evidence was an essential element of the offense charged, the defendant did not have to show that his or her own constitutional rights had been violated but merely that the evidence had been seized unlawfully.[768] Instead, the Court reemphasized that even in possession cases, the defendant must first establish that his or her own constitutional rights were violated before the court can suppress the evidence.

Rawlings v. Kentucky[769] held that even legal ownership of an item does not always guarantee that one has a protected Fourth Amendment interest. Thus, the Court held that the defendant could not challenge the search of his companion's purse even though he claimed ownership of the drugs seized therein. Only the companion, not the defendant, had a protected expectation of privacy in the purse.

In continuing to require a personal privacy interest invasion, the Supreme Court in *United States v. Padilla,*[770] held that there is no "co-conspirator" exception to the rule regarding who may challenge a search or seizure. Only a defendant who can demonstrate that his or her own Fourth Amendment rights had been violated by the challenged search or seizure has standing.[771] The Court found that co-conspirators have no special standing even though they may be in a supervisory role or have joint control over the place searched.[772]

---

766. People v. Johnson, 237 Ill. App. 3d 860, 605 N.E.2d 98, 102 (3d Dist. 1992) (court found that defendant had a legitimate expectation of privacy in premises where the owner allowed the defendant to store furniture and tools and receive telephone calls there). *But see* People v. Brown, 277 Ill. App. 3d 989, 661 N.E.2d 533, 537–38 (1st Dist. 1996) (where individual was only on the premises for the day, failed to prove any proprietary interest, and never indicated any intent to stay at the premises, individual lacked standing to contest search of third party's apartment).

767. United States v. Salvucci, 448 U.S. 83 (1980).

768. This rule had been established in *Jones v. United States,* 362 U.S. 257 (1960).

769. Rawlings v. Kentucky, 448 U.S. 98 (1980).

770. 508 U.S. 77 (1993).

771. *Id.* at 81.

772. *Id.* at 82.

Using these principles, Illinois courts have found that although the owner of a car has standing to challenge a search of a vehicle,[773] a passenger does not,[774] nor does a nonowner driver even when his or her passenger is the car's owner.[775] The only way a passenger is able to suppress incriminating evidence found in the vehicle is to show that the stop of the vehicle was improper and that the evidence seized was a fruit of the illegal stop.[776] Yet at least one court has found a passenger in a car to have standing to challenge a search of the car's trunk and of containers in the car belonging to the passenger.[777]

However, in *People v. Bower*,[778] the court held that an individual, who convinced a friend to procure a rental car for him after he was turned down by the rental company, had no standing to object to a search of the car even though he had sole possession and control of it. It concluded that he had no reasonable expectation of privacy in the car.[779] Defendant was fully aware that the vehicle's owner (the rental company) had not given authorization or consent for him to possess the car or to use it.[780]

Illinois courts have denied standing to: the lessor of a garage;[781] the lessee of a bedroom in an apartment who tried to suppress evidence found in a storage

---

773. People v. Struhart, 93 Ill. App. 3d 534, 417 N.E.2d 676 (1st Dist. 1981).

774. People v. Gibson, 114 Ill. App. 3d 488, 449 N.E.2d 182 (2d Dist. 1983); People v. Norris, 101 Ill. App. 3d 664, 428 N.E.2d 987 (4th Dist. 1981); People v. Beroukas, 98 Ill. App. 3d 990, 425 N.E.2d 5 (2d Dist. 1981). *See also* People v. McCoy, 269 Ill. App. 3d 587, 646 N.E.2d 1361, 1364 (4th Dist. 1995) (passenger lacks standing to challenge search of another's car unless passenger has legitimate expectation of privacy in place searched); People v. Manikowski, 186 Ill. App. 3d 1007, 542 N.E.2d 1148 (5th Dist. 1989) (even passenger who had paid portion of traveling expenses and had personal items in car had no standing to contest search of left wheel well of car); People v. Coleman, 140 Ill. App. 3d 806, 489 N.E.2d 455 (2d Dist. 1986) (defendant has no standing to contest search of automobile although he was passenger and his mother owned and was operating vehicle).

775. People v. Flowers, 111 Ill. App. 3d 348, 444 N.E.2d 242 (2d Dist. 1982).

776. People v. Lagrone, 124 Ill. App. 3d 301, 464 N.E.2d 712 (1st Dist. 1984); People v. Kunath, 99 Ill. App. 3d 201, 425 N.E.2d 486 (2d Dist. 1981); People v. Fox, 97 Ill. App. 3d 58, 421 N.E.2d 1082 (2d Dist. 1981).

777. People v. Manke, 181 Ill. App. 3d 374, 537 N.E.2d 13 (3d Dist. 1989).

778. 291 Ill. App. 3d 1077, 685 N.E.2d 393 (3d Dist. 1997), *cert. denied*, 524 U.S. 905 (1998).

779. *Id.*, 685 N.E.2d at 396.

780. *Id.*, 685 N.E.2d at 398.

781. People v. Koris, 107 Ill. App. 3d 821, 438 N.E.2d 593 (1st Dist. 1982).

closet in another part of the apartment;[782] the owner of a house who tried to suppress evidence found underneath an open porch when the evidence could be seen from an adjoining yard;[783] and a gunshot victim who argued that the police had no authority to remove his clothes from the hospital where he was being treated.[784] The United States Supreme Court has found that a defendant lacks standing to object to the police's combing through his garbage left in opaque bags outside his house for collection by the trash collector.[785] However, Illinois courts have found the following defendants to have standing to challenge a search: the occupant of a motel room;[786] a defendant who occasionally stayed in another's apartment, kept some clothes there, and paid rent to the tenants;[787] and a part-time employee who challenged the legality of police entry onto his employer's premises.[788] Moreover, a defendant has standing to suppress the fruits of an invalid search based on his or her reasonable expectation of privacy in his or her person and clothing even though he or she denies a

---

782. People v. Devine, 98 Ill. App. 3d 914, 424 N.E.2d 823 (3d Dist. 1981), *cert. denied,* 458 U.S. 1109 (1982). *See* People v. Cohen, 146 Ill. App. 3d 618, 496 N.E.2d 1231 (2d Dist. 1986) (social guest in defendant's home does not have standing to contest search of home).

783. People v. Holt, 91 Ill. 2d 480, 440 N.E.2d 102 (1982).

784. People v. Sutherland, 92 Ill. App. 3d 338, 415 N.E.2d 1267 (1st Dist. 1980).

785. California v. Greenwood, 486 U.S. 35 (1988).

786. People v. Wilson, 86 Ill. App. 3d 637, 408 N.E.2d 988 (2d Dist. 1980). *See also* People v. Kozlowski, 278 Ill. App. 3d 40, 662 N.E.2d 630, 633 (2d Dist. 1996) (defendant had possessory interest in hotel room despite the fact that he was behind in payment, his possessions had been removed, and his room had been cleaned in preparation for re-renting, where prior to search defendant made late payment and was still in possession of key); People v. Carini, 151 Ill. App. 3d 264, 502 N.E.2d 1206 (1st Dist. 1987) (lessee of storage unit, which lessee kept locked, had standing to challenge warrantless search of storage unit).

787. People v. Seybuld, 98 Ill. App. 3d 236, 423 N.E.2d 1132 (2d Dist. 1981) (supplement to opinion on denial of petition for rehearing). *See also* People v. Walters, 187 Ill. App. 3d 661, 543 N.E.2d 508 (2d Dist. 1989) (defendant in mother's apartment); People v. Bolden, 152 Ill. App. 3d 631, 504 N.E.2d 835 (1st Dist. 1986) (defendant living in girlfriend's apartment and using apartment address as his place of residence had standing to challenge search of apartment).

788. People v. Davis, 86 Ill. App. 3d 557, 407 N.E.2d 1109 (2d Dist. 1980). *See also* People v. Rios, 278 Ill. App. 3d 1013, 664 N.E.2d 153 (1st Dist. 1996) (defendants who were allowed access to apartment temporarily to repair it lacked subjective expectation of privacy in apartment even though allowed to store tools there; thus, no standing to challenge search and seizure).

possessory interest in the fruits themselves.[789] In *People v. Alexander*,[790] the Illinois Appellate Court held that defendant had standing to challenge the search of a garage even though the garage was owned by his sister and he did not have a key to it on the date in question.[791] The court based its decision on the fact that defendant regularly used the garage to repair cars, may have operated his business out of the garage, presumably had the ability to control or exclude others from using the garage, exercised ownership rights over some of the items in the garage, and had a subjective expectation of privacy. This expectation was reasonable as to the garage and the items stored in it.[792] Evidence which the police found after illegally searching the garage should have been suppressed because the search was not incident to arrest,[793] and the items were not within plain view.[794]

Generally, the time to raise the issue of lack of standing is at the suppression hearing. If the state does not raise the issue at that time, yet still prevails on the motion, it may raise the standing issue for the first time on appeal.[795] However, if the trial court rules in favor of the defendant and the state failed to raise the standing issue, the state is precluded from raising the issue on appeal.[796]

---

789. People v. Davis, 187 Ill. App. 3d 265, 543 N.E.2d 154 (1st Dist. 1989).

790. 272 Ill. App. 3d 698, 650 N.E.2d 1038 (1st Dist. 1995).

791. *Id.*, 650 N.E.2d at 1043.

792. *Id.*

793. *See* n. 585, *supra.*

794. *See* n. 444, *supra.*

795. People v. Keller, 93 Ill. 2d 432, 444 N.E.2d 118 (1982).

796. People v. Holloway, 86 Ill. 2d 78, 426 N.E.2d 871 (1981).

2

CONFESSIONS

Howard B. Eisenberg/Ralph Ruebner*

---

* Professor Howard E. Eisenberg authored this chapter for the first edition. Professor Ralph Ruebner revised it for the second and third editions.

§ 2.01   Scope and Overview

This chapter concerns the admissibility at trial of statements made by criminal defendants. Such statements will usually be confessions in which the accused admits involvement in the criminal conduct. This chapter also discusses statements that appear neutral or even exculpatory but are ultimately offered against the defendant.[1] Indeed, for *Miranda* purposes, neither exculpatory

---

1. For the purposes of discovery, the Illinois Supreme Court has distinguished between admissions against interest and confessions. People v. Georgev, 38 Ill. Ill. 2d 165, 230 N.E.2d 851, 858 (1967), *cert. denied*, 390 U.S. 998 (1968); People v. Stanton, 16 Ill. 2d 459, 158 N.E.2d 47, 51 (1959). This is not a valid distinction when considering the constitutional admissibility of such a declaration.

statements nor incriminating statements can be offered by the prosecution unless the defendant is informed of his or her constitutional rights and makes an effective waiver.[2]

Because a confession is "the highest type of evidence known to law,"[3] in the majority of cases defendants attempt to keep such evidence from being considered by the trier of fact by filing motions to suppress. This chapter will detail the procedure and grounds for filing suppression motions as well as the related issues involving statements allegedly made by criminal defendants.

A primary constitutional underpinning for the exclusion of incriminating statements made by criminal defendants is the Fifth Amendment to the United States Constitution, which provides: "No person . . . shall be compelled in any criminal case to be a witness against himself . . . ."[4] This provision applies to state prosecutions through the Fourteenth Amendment to the Constitution.[5] Section 10 of Article I of the Illinois Constitution of 1970 similarly provides: "No person shall be compelled in a criminal case to give evidence against himself . . . ."[6] Although the language of the state and federal constitutions is somewhat different, the distinctions have been held to be semantic, and the two provisions have been construed by the courts generally the same way.[7]

Although each of the bases for seeking exclusion of a statement is ultimately grounded in the due process provisions of the Fourteenth Amendment or in the self-incrimination or right-to-counsel provisions of the state and federal constitutions, attacks on confessions will be based on one or more of the following specific theories:

1. Confession not voluntarily made. In these cases efforts are made to ex-clude the confession because the circumstances under which the state-ment was made demonstrate that it was not the product of the defendant's conscious and voluntary desire. Although early cases in this area involved physically abusing the defendant to literally "beat out" a confession, the emphasis has shifted to psychological coercion, the nature of the environment in which the statement was obtained, and the nature of the defendant, as determined by the totality of the circumstances surrounding the confession.

---

2. People v. Hoffman, 84 Ill. 2d 480, 419 N.E.2d 1145, 1147 (1981).

3. People v. Byrd, 21 Ill. 2d 114, 171 N.E.2d 782, 783 (1961).

4. U.S. CONST. amend. V.

5. Malloy v. Hogan, 378 U.S. 1 (1964).

6. ILL. CONST. art. I, § 10.

7. People ex rel. Hanrahan v. Power, 54 Ill. 2d 154, 295 N.E.2d 472, 475 (1973); People v. Schmoll, 77 Ill. App. 3d 762, 396 N.E.2d 634, 636 (2d Dist. 1979), *cert. denied,* 447 U.S. 928 (1980).

2. *Miranda* violations. In *Miranda v. Arizona*[8] the United States Supreme Court declared that before any in-custody interrogation an accused must be informed of various constitutional rights, and that if the defendant is not so admonished and fails to make a voluntary, knowing, and intelligent waiver, the statement cannot be admitted. Although *Miranda* has undergone some erosion, it remains a frequent basis for attack on the admissibility of confessions.

3. Confessions made after an unlawful arrest or detention. If the confession is made after an illegal arrest or unlawful detention, it is subject to suppression, even if the statement was otherwise voluntary and in compliance with *Miranda*.

4. Denial of right to counsel. This basis for attacking the admission of a confession is that the statement was obtained in violation of the defendant's Sixth Amendment right to counsel. This issue arises in the context of a case that has already reached a critical stage at which the right to an attorney has attached. Although not infrequently coupled with a *Miranda* question, the right here is an additional and separate issue.

5. Statements made as part of an examination to determine a defendant's fitness to stand trial may be introduced only if the defendant raises the issue of insanity or intoxication at trial, and even then the statements are admissible only on those issues.[9] However, if the defendant calls the court-appointed psychiatrist, the defendant waives the protection of the statute.[10] Similarly, the United States Supreme Court found, in *Buchanan v. Kentucky*,[11] that once a defendant requested a psychological evaluation or presented psychiatric evidence, the prosecution could introduce evidence obtained as a result of the psychological evaluation without violating the defendant's right to the privilege against self-incrimination or right to counsel. The Court concluded that under *Estelle v. Smith*,[12] once a defendant presented a psychological defense, he or she could anticipate the use of such evidence in rebuttal.

In attacking a statement given by a defendant, the defense counsel will often combine grounds for suppression. Although a "shotgun" approach to advocacy is seldom of value, in seeking to suppress a statement counsel is often faced

---

8. 384 U.S. 436 (1966).

9. 725 ILCS 5/104-14(a).

10. People v. Kashney, 111 Ill. 2d 454, 490 N.E.2d 688, 691–93 (1986).

11. 483 U.S. 402 (1987).

12. 451 U.S. 454 (1981).

with a defendant whose recollection of facts and candor is less than desired. In addition, the information available to counsel often arguably supports more than one basis for attack, particularly when the defendant does not know what the officers who interrogated him or her will testify to at a suppression hearing. These factors often require counsel to advance alternative theories of suppression, which has created factual, legal, and strategic overlaps in the potential areas for suppression. However, if, after a complete discussion with the defendant, there is no colorable basis for attack, the defense counsel should not be obligated to move to suppress a statement, and no motion should be made. If the defendant asserts a set of facts that, if true, would be grounds for suppression, a motion specifying the basis should be made alleging the legal and factual predicate for such relief.

§ 2.02 Proceedings in Which Statements May Be Attacked

Illinois is one of the few states that permits a motion to suppress to be made at the preliminary hearing.[13] Because discovery in Illinois does not occur until after bind-over,[14] often defense counsel will not have adequate information to prepare and present a motion to suppress at the preliminary hearing.[15] In addition, there might be a strategic advantage in allowing the development of a record at the preliminary hearing for future use at trial or in a suppression motion after bind-over.

Counsel will generally limit a preliminary hearing suppression motion to those cases in which the facts are so egregious that suppression appears certain or in which the counsel desires to obtain some strategic advantage through the motion, such as requiring the prosecution to call witnesses in response to the motion who otherwise would not have been called at the preliminary hearing.

Another important consideration is the res judicata effect of a decision on a motion to suppress made at the preliminary hearing. The denial of a motion to suppress made at the preliminary hearing will be res judicata and binding on the trial court, absent exceptional circumstances or additional evidence.[16] An

---

13. 725 ILCS 5/109-3(e).

14. S. Ct. Rule 411.

15. It is possible, however, for defense counsel, before a preliminary hearing but after charging the accused, to subpoena police reports. People ex rel. Fisher v. Carey, 77 Ill. 2d 259, 396 N.E.2d 17 (1979).

16. People v. Holland, 56 Ill. 2d 318, 307 N.E.2d 380, 381 (1974). However, the denial of a motion to suppress may be relitigated by the defendant if the prosecution was dismissed following the denial of the first motion, thereby denying the defendant the ability to obtain appellate review of the original order denying the motion to suppress. People v. Busija, 155 Ill. App. 3d 741, 509 N.E.2d 168 (1st Dist. 1986).

order granting a suppression motion made at the preliminary hearing is res judicata and binding on the trial court, with the prosecution's only remedy an interlocutory appeal.[17] Thus, the defense counsel may be placed in the position of evaluating the forum and selecting the judge before whom the defendant has the best chance of prevailing. Given the natural and understandable reluctance of judges to take the drastic step of suppressing evidence at a preliminary hearing and the lack of complete information in the hands of the defense counsel, in the large majority of cases the motion to suppress will be made in the trial court, not at the preliminary hearing.

In the majority of cases the defense counsel should have all of the available facts at his or her command before filing and pursuing a motion to suppress. Obviously, a careful and complete interview with the defendant is essential, as is discussion with any other available witnesses. Discovery of "any written or recorded statements and the substance of any oral statements made by the accused or by a codefendant, and a list of witnesses to the making and acknowledgement of such statements" as authorized by Illinois Supreme Court Rule 412(a)(ii), and chapter 725, section 5/114-10 of the Illinois Compiled Statutes should be routine in every criminal case unless the counsel is certain no such statements were obtained. If possible, the defense counsel or an investigator should interview the officers who obtained the statements from the defendant so that the most complete picture of the circumstances can be developed before the filing of the motion or hearing on the motion.

A statement or confession might also be attacked in a probation revocation proceeding, but the basis for such an attack is more limited than at trial. Although an attack on a confession as being involuntary is proper,[18] a voluntary confession will not be suppressed in a probation revocation proceeding because of a technical violation of the *Miranda* requirement.[19]

§ 2.03   Basic Requirements for the Suppression Motion

The procedural vehicle used to challenge the admissibility of a confession or statement at trial is a motion to suppress the evidence, as authorized by Illinois Compiled Statues chapter 725, section 5/114-11. Section 114-11(b) requires the motion to suppress to be in writing, and the motion must state

17. People v. Taylor, 50 Ill. 2d 136, 277 N.E.2d 878 (1971).

18. People v. Knight, 75 Ill. 2d 291, 388 N.E.2d 414, 417 (1979); People v. Peterson, 74 Ill. 2d 478, 384 N.E.2d 348, 350–51 (1978).

19. People v. Palmer, 74 Ill. App. 3d 130, 392 N.E.2d 781 (3d Dist. 1979); People v. Diesing, 67 Ill. App. 3d 109, 384 N.E.2d 575 (2d Dist. 1978).

specifically all grounds asserted for suppression of the statement.[20] Frequently circuit courts are relaxed about the requirements of specificity in criminal motion practice, and sometimes attorneys who do a high volume of criminal defense work prepare form motions for submission in every case. Although this might work in some instances, it will almost certainly inure to the defendant's detriment if the case is reviewed by an appellate court.[21]

Although it is sometimes impossible to file a specific motion because the defendant lacks adequate facts to state his basis, as a general rule the more specific and comprehensive the grounds, the better. Thus, although defendant's assertion that the police illegally obtained the statement because "it was not the product of defendant's voluntary will" gives some notice of the basis for the motion, defendant would be more successful to seek suppression by asserting the precise elements which make the confession involuntary. For example, defendant's motion may be more successful if it read:

> The confession was involuntary because it was the product of an eight hour interrogation by three members of the City Police Department in a room in which the temperature was estimated by the defendant to have exceeded eighty degrees and in which there were no windows; during which time Detectives Mary Jane Smith and Harry Legg stated that if the defendant did not confess the Department of Public Aid would remove defendant's children from his home; during which period of time defendant was offered no food or drink and was not allowed to use the rest room; and during which period the defendant became physically ill, and, indeed, vomited in a waste paper basket in the interrogation room.

The latter motion gives the court a better picture of the totality of the situation, informs the state's attorney of the nature of the motion, and colors the pleading in a way favorable to the defendant at the outset.

§ 2.04   Timing for the Suppression Motion

As noted above, a motion to suppress can be made at the preliminary hearing but is usually reserved for the trial court. In the trial court the motion must be made before the trial commences, unless there was no opportunity for the proceedings or the defendant was not aware of the grounds for that motion

---

20. People v. Robinson, 87 Ill. App. 3d 621, 410 N.E.2d 121 (3d Dist. 1980); People v. Fentress, 133 Ill. App. 2d 38, 272 N.E.2d 801 (1st Dist. 1971), *cert. denied,* 405 U.S. 1044 (1972).

21. *Robinson,* 87 Ill. App. 3d 621, 410 N.E.2d at 124; People v. Fentress, 133 Ill. App. 2d 38, 272 N.E.2d 801 (1st Dist. 1971), *cert. denied,* 405 U.S. 1044 (1972).

before the trial.[22] Through appropriate discovery the defendant will usually have notice of any statement in the prosecution's possession and thus will know that a suppression motion is required. Nevertheless, even if the counsel fails to file a timely motion, the trial court has discretion to entertain such a motion after trial has begun.[23]

§ 2.05 Suppression of Confession vs. Weight of Confession

It must be emphasized that a confession or statement obtained in violation of the defendant's constitutional rights for any of the indicated reasons is subject to complete exclusion from evidence. Attorneys sometimes confuse the notion of suppression of the evidence with the weight to be afforded the evidence once admitted. The United States Supreme Court in *Jackson v. Denno*[24] made clear that it is impermissible to allow the same jury that is to consider the defendant's guilt to also consider whether a statement was obtained in a constitutional manner. The Supreme Court feared that no jury could disregard a confession once heard, so it prohibited the jury from hearing the declaration until its admissibility was determined by the court. Indeed, in Illinois a preliminary hearing outside the jury's presence was required to admit a confession even before *Denno*,[25] thus ensuring that suppressed evidence is never heard by the jury that will ultimately try the case.

If the motion to suppress is denied, the defense counsel can still argue to the jury that the statement should be given little or no weight based on the unsuccessful arguments advanced in the suppression motion. Thus, in *Crane v. Kentucky*,[26] the Supreme Court ruled that a defendant was denied due process of law when the state trial court denied his request to challenge the reliability and credibility of the confession at trial, even after the court had ruled the confession voluntary and denied the motion to suppress. The Court found that the defendant had a separate constitutional right to argue to the jury that the confession was not worthy of belief. This obviously is a much less attractive alternative from the defendant's point of view because the damaging evidence

---

22. 725 ILCS 5/114-11(g).

23. People v. Hoffman, 84 Ill. 2d 480, 419 N.E.2d 1145, 1147 (1981). Although the admissibility of a confession can be raised either by a pretrial suppression motion or by a contemporaneous objection, there is no need for a defendant to make an objection if the court has already determined that the confession is admissible in a pretrial motion. People v. Calderon, 101 Ill. App. 3d 469, 428 N.E.2d 571, 576 (1st Dist. 1981).

24. 378 U.S. 368 (1964).

25. People v. Lefler, 38 Ill. 2d 216, 230 N.E.2d 827 (1967); People v. Miller, 13 Ill. 2d 84, 148 N.E.2d 455, 462, *cert. denied,* 357 U.S. 943 (1958).

26. 476 U.S. 683 (1986).

is heard by the jury. A suppression motion is the only way the constitutional admissibility of a statement can be raised. An argument made to the jury at trial that the statement should be disregarded does not preserve the constitutional issue, and if a proper suppression motion is not made the defendant will not obtain appellate review of the question based only on an argument to the jury that the confession was not voluntary. On rare occasions, however, the appellate court will review the admissibility of a confession in the absence of a suppression motion if the trial record unambiguously shows that the confession was illegally obtained.[27]

§ 2.06 Order and Burden of Proof

The burden of going forward with the evidence and the burden of proving a confession was voluntary is on the state.[28] Thus a hearing must be held to determine whether the statement was voluntary,[29] even if the defendant does not request such a hearing.[30] The prosecution has the burden of proving by a preponderance of the evidence that any statement was voluntarily made.[31]

Although *Miranda* itself indicated that the prosecution has a "heavy burden" to prove that the defendant waived his or her constitutional rights, as a technical matter the state must sustain its burden only by a preponderance of the evidence.[32] As with any basic constitutional right in a criminal case, a waiver of the right cannot be presumed from a silent record,[33] and thus in every case the prosecution must prove that the statement was voluntary and that the defendant's Fifth Amendment rights were effectively waived. Because the state has the burden of proof on a suppression motion, the prosecution will initially offer evidence, even though the motion is made by the defendant.

---

27. People v. Parham, 141 Ill. App. 3d 149, 490 N.E.2d 65, 69 (1st Dist. 1986).

28. 725 ILCS 5/114-11(d).

29. In determining whether defendant voluntarily confessed, the trial judge must establish whether the interrogators overcame defendant's will in order to obtain a confession or whether defendant confessed "freely, voluntarily and without compulsion or inducement of any sort." People v. Nodine, 209 Ill. App. 3d 1031, 568 N.E.2d 994, 996 (3d Dist. 1991). *See also* People v. Argo, 133 Ill. App. 3d 421, 478 N.E.2d 873, 879 (3d Dist. 1985) (defendant's confession held voluntary under the totality of the circumstances).

30. People v. Mosley, 100 Ill. App. 2d 361, 241 N.E.2d 476, 478 (1st Dist. 1968).

31. People v. Reid, 136 Ill. 2d 27, 554 N.E.2d 174 (1990), *amended on other grounds,* 221 Ill. App. 3d 695, 583 N.E.2d 1 (1st Dist. 1991).

32. Lego v. Twomey, 404 U.S. 477 (1972).

33. People v. Murrell, 60 Ill. 2d 287, 326 N.E.2d 762, 764 (1975).

In a recent supreme court case, *People v. R.D.,*[34] Illinois repudiated the "material witness" rule which was in effect since 1922. Prior to the Illinois Supreme Court's ruling in *R.D.*, the court had limited the "material witness" rule in *People v. Patterson.*[35] In that case, the court stated that the rule was not a "mechanical" one but rather a "practical" one which earlier courts created to assist them in evaluating the voluntariness of a confession. The purpose of the rule was to safeguard the accused against "improperly induced confessions and not to require an empty exercise."[36] Therefore, if a trial judge, in evaluating the voluntariness of a confession, requires that the state produce all material witnesses, then the prosecutor must do so. On the other hand, if the trial judge can make the decision without the testimony of all the material witnesses, then in the exercise of discretion the judge may rule nonetheless. The court reasoned that "[i]n the final analysis, whether a confession is voluntary or involuntary is a matter of competency of the evidence which should be left to the discretion of the trial court."[37]

In *R.D.*, the "material witness" rule was eliminated entirely based on the court's finding that only a minority of states presently have such a rule, that the current circumstances no longer warrant the rule, particularly the liberal discovery rules, and finally, that the accused is sufficiently protected by both federal and state constitutional and statutory rules.[38] First, the court noted that at the time the rule was created, the accused was not entitled to any pretrial discovery rights. Because of this, the court had placed the burden on the state to produce all the material witnesses to a confession in order to compensate him or her somewhat.[39] However, Illinois currently has very liberal discovery rules, particularly one which requires the state to disclose the identification of every witness to the taking of the confession prior to any suppression hearing. Because of these rules, the defendant is able to prepare a pretrial challenge to the confession, and therefore there is no need for a separate "material witness" rule.[40]

In addition, current statutes and court rules allow the defendant to cross-examine and impeach any witness who he or she calls to the stand. At the time the rule was created, this was not true. Again, because of this, there is no need for a distinct rule.[41]

---

34. People v. R.D., 155 Ill. 2d 122, 613 N.E.2d 706, 714 (1993).
35. 154 Ill. 2d 414, 610 N.E.2d 16 (1992), *cert. denied,* 510 U.S. 879 (1993).
36. *Id.,* 610 N.E.2d at 32.
37. *Id.*
38. *R.D.,* 155 Ill. 2d 122, 613 N.E.2d at 718.
39. *Id.,* 613 N.E.2d at 714.
40. *Id.,* 613 N.E.2d at 715.
41. *Id.*

Finally, there is a wide range of constitutional and statutory protections, both federal and state, which are now available to protect a defendant against coerced self-incrimination and subsequent admissibility of an involuntary confession. Most notable are the *Miranda* admonitions and the right to a pretrial hearing regarding the voluntariness of a confession.[42] Since current constitutional law protects the accused, there is no longer a need to retain an independent rule. Therefore, *R.D.* held that the state is no longer required to call all material witnesses, unless it cannot meet its burden of proving that the confession was voluntary without such witness(es).[43]

In *People v. Braggs*,[44] the court held that the trial court erred in refusing to conduct a hearing on the defendant's motion to suppress where the defendant was found unfit to stand trial and was unable to be present at such a hearing.[45] Section 104-11 clearly authorizes the trial court to resolve such motions even after a defendant has been found unfit.[46] In this case, the defendant's presence was not essential to a fair determination of the issues, and therefore a hearing should have been conducted.[47]

In the typical situation, the prosecution will adduce evidence tending to support the waiver of constitutional rights or the voluntary nature of the statement. The defense will counter with evidence that, if believed, would lead to suppression of the statement. The ultimate determination will be a mixed question of fact and law in which the trial judge is free to believe the prosecution witnesses and disbelieve the defense testimony or vice versa.[48]

Although courts speak of the prosecution bearing a heavy burden in these matters, and although the law demands that the state sustain its burden in proving the admissibility of any statement, as a practical matter a defendant should not rely on the prosecution's failure to carry its burden but should affirmatively adduce evidence that will sustain the defendant's position. If the defendant is to prevail, he or she will have to overcome the natural inclination of judges to presume that the police have acted properly and are testifying truthfully.

---

42. *Id.,* 613 N.E.2d at 716.

43. *Id.,* 613 N.E.2d at 717.

44. 302 Ill. App. 3d 602, 707 N.E.2d 172 (1st Dist. 1998).

45. *Id.,* 707 N.E.2d at 175.

46. 725 ILCS 5/104-11(d).

47. *Braggs,* 302 Ill. App. 3d 602, 707 N.E.2d at 175.

48. People v. Jones, 47 Ill. 2d 135, 265 N.E.2d 125, 126–28 (1970), *overruled on other grounds* by People v. Rehbein, 74 Ill. 2d 435, 386 N.E.2d 39 (1978), *cert. denied,* 442 U.S. 919 (1979).

§ 2.07 Standing to Object

A defendant obviously has the right to object to the admissibility of his or her own statement. However, a more difficult issue is presented when the incriminating statement in question was given by a third party. In *Bruton v. United States*,[49] the Supreme Court held that a co-defendant's confession implicating the defendant is not admissible in evidence where the co-defendant does not take the stand and is not subject to cross-examination, unless the defendant has confessed and the confession "interlocks with and supports the confession of his co-defendant,"[50] because the admission of the evidence would deny the nonconfessing defendant the right to subject his or her confessing co-defendant to cross-examination.

In *Lee v. Illinois*,[51] the Supreme Court considered the admissibility of the confession given by a nontestifying co-defendant, which implicated Lee. The Court found that such confessions are inherently unreliable and violate a criminal defendant's right to confrontation. Such statements may be intended by the co-defendant to shift the blame to the defendant and are, therefore, less credible than usual hearsay.

Henceforth, in order for the confession of a nontestifying co-defendant to be admissible, the prosecution must show particularized guarantees of trust-worthiness. The fact that the co-defendant's confession may still have been voluntary is not dispositive because the co-defendant may have a motivation to place the blame on the defendant. Moreover, even if the confessions interlock,[52] the co-defendant's confession still lacks the indicia of trustworthiness so long as the discrepancies between the co-defendant's statement and that of the defendant are not insignificant.

Following *Lee,* one Illinois court required that the trials of the two defendants be severed in order to utilize the confession of the co-defendant, unless there

---

49. 391 U.S. 123 (1968). In *People v. Lee,* 87 Ill. 2d 182, 429 N.E.2d 461 (1981), the Illinois Supreme Court discussed the procedure for raising the *Bruton* issue, concluding that ordinarily a motion for a separate trial must be made before the trial commences in which the movant demonstrates what prejudice will attach to a joint trial. The court further held that a co-defendant's statement admitted in violation of *Bruton* could be cumulative and thus its admission is harmless error.

50. Parker v. Randolph, 442 U.S. 62 (1979); People v. Davis, 97 Ill. 2d 1, 452 N.E.2d 525, 534–35 (1983).

51. 476 U.S. 530 (1986).

52. Cruz v. New York, 481 U.S. 186 (1987) (Court adapted "indicia of reliability" test to be applied whether or not confessions "interlocked," seemingly abandoning "interlocking confession" doctrine first suggested by plurality in *Parker v. Randolph,* 442 U.S. 62 (1978)).

were independent indicia of reliability produced by the state.[53] Another court found that where the victim's statement corroborated the co-defendant's confession there were independent indicia of reliability to allow for the admission of the confession, even under the *Lee* test.[54] While there remains the possibility of using the co-defendant's confession to attack the credibility of the defendant, and not as substantive evidence, where the prosecutor has relied on the co-defendant's confession in argument, the use will be considered substantive and the admission of the confession considered error.[55]

However, in *Richardson v. Marsh*,[56] the Supreme Court decided that the admission of a confession that has been redacted to remove all reference to the nonconfessing defendant was not forbidden by *Bruton*, even if the defendant is linked to the confession by other evidence, so long as the jury has been instructed not to consider the confession against the defendant. The majority of the Court found that the jury would follow the instructions not to consider the evidence against the nonconfessing defendant.

In *Gray v. Maryland*,[57] the Court limited the holding of *Richardson*. In *Gray*, the co-defendant's confession was redacted by substituting defendant's name with a blank space or the word "deleted." The Court held *Bruton* applied.[58] It distinguished *Richardson* where co-defendant's confession had been redacted to omit all references to the defendant being involved in the offense.[59] In *Gray*, the state deleted defendant's (nonconfessing) name. However, the co-defendant's confession still directly referenced the existence of a co-defendant.[60] The Court held that *Bruton* applies where a redaction "replaces a defendant's name with an obvious indication of deletion, such as a blank space, the word 'deleted,' or a similar symbol."[61] To do so leaves a situation so close to that found offensive in *Bruton* that the same concerns applied. The jury was likely to link

---

53. People v. Lincoln, 157 Ill. App. 3d 700, 510 N.E.2d 1026, 1029–30 (1st Dist. 1987) (citing Cruz v. New York, 481 U.S. 186 (1987)).

54. People v. Gibson, 156 Ill. App. 3d 459, 509 N.E.2d 563, 566 (1st Dist. 1987) (noting that in *Lee* victim had been murdered and thus was not available to corroborate suspect's confession).

55. People v. Johnson, 116 Ill. 2d 13, 506 N.E.2d 563 (1987); People v. Bennett, 162 Ill. App. 3d 36, 515 N.E.2d 840 (1st Dist. 1987). *See also* People v. Fort, 147 Ill. App. 3d 14, 497 N.E.2d 416, 422 (1st Dist. 1986).

56. 481 U.S. 200 (1987).

57. 523 U.S. 185 (1998).

58. *Id.* at 192–95.

59. *Id.* at 194.

60. *Id.* at 196.

61. *Id.* at 194.

the omission to the defendant.[62] Further, the omission was likely to draw the jury's attention to it and overemphasize it.[63] Finally, the statement would nonetheless be directly accusatory.[64]

As a general rule a defendant lacks standing to object to and seek suppression of the statements made by third parties and thus is left to argue the weight to be afforded such a confession by the jury.[65] The prosecution is under no obligation to prove that the third-party statements were voluntary or obtained under constitutional conditions.[66] Moreover, a defendant cannot move to suppress a statement given by a third party by asserting that the statement violated *Miranda*.[67]

The only exception to this general rule is for cases in which the conduct of the police in obtaining the third-party statement was so offensive that courts will exclude the statement on the basic theory that it is a violation of due process to rely on a confession that was beaten out of anyone.[68]

§ 2.08　Fruit of an Illegal Confession

If the court grants the motion to suppress, the statement obviously cannot be used by the state in its case-in-chief. An involuntary statement may not be used to impeach a defendant, whereas a technical violation of *Miranda*

---

62. *Id.* at 193.

63. *Id.*

64. *Id.*

65. People v. Houston, 36 Ill. App. 3d 695, 344 N.E.2d 641 (1st Dist. 1976), *cert. denied,* 429 U.S. 1109 (1977). *See also* People v. Govea, 299 Ill. App. 3d 76, 701 N.E.2d 76, 86 (1st Dist. 1998) (defendant lacked standing to contest admissibility of his own confession as tainted fruit of an unlawful arrest as well as confession of his sister because challenge based on alleged violation of another person's constitutional rights).

66. People v. Sickles, 55 Ill. App. 3d 35, 370 N.E.2d 660, 663 (3d Dist. 1977).

67. People v. Joyner, 50 Ill. 2d 302, 278 N.E.2d 756, 762 (1972), *overruled on other grounds* by People v. Dawson, 60 Ill. 2d 278, 326 N.E.2d 755, *cert. denied,* 423 U.S. 835 (1975).

68. LaFrance v. Bohlinger, 499 F.2d 29 (1st Cir.), *cert. denied,* 419 U.S. 1080 (1974); Bradford v. Johnson, 476 F.2d 66 (6th Cir. 1973), *aff'g,* 354 F. Supp. 1331 (E.D. Mich. 1972). These are extremely unusual cases with aggravated facts. There are no Illinois cases in which such an attack on a third-party confession has been made. *But see* People v. Bates, 25 Ill. App. 3d 748, 324 N.E.2d 88, 90 (1st Dist. 1975). Courts are quite reluctant to extend the right of a defendant to attack third-party statements. *See, e.g.,* Harris v. White, 745 F.2d 523 (8th Cir. 1984).

does not foreclose the use of a confession.[69] In addition, other information gained as a result of the confession may also be subject to suppression as fruit of the unconstitutional interrogation.[70] In determining whether the fruit of a statement obtained in violation of the *Miranda* requirements may be admitted, the court will attempt to determine whether further suppression will deter police misconduct. If not, the fruit of the confession will not be suppressed.[71] In *Oregon v. Elstad*,[72] the Court upheld the admissibility of a statement made after proper *Miranda* warnings had been administered even though the police had obtained an earlier statement that was not admissible because of the failure to follow the *Miranda* procedures. The Supreme Court distinguished the fruit of a voluntary statement obtained in violation of the technical requirements of *Miranda* from the fruit of an involuntary statement. Justice O'Connor, writing for the six-justice majority, concluded that if the initial statement is voluntary, even while violating the technical requirements of *Miranda*, the subsequent statement given after *Miranda* warnings is not inherently tainted.

The Court explained that a statement given in the absence of *Miranda* warnings is presumptively violative of a defendant's privilege against selfincrimination, but such a statement is not inherently coerced or involuntary. The Court found that the subsequent administration of *Miranda* warnings cured the condition that rendered the original statement inadmissible. Under such circumstances the defendant's privilege against self-incrimination was not violated by the second statement and that statement could be properly admitted. Justices Brennan, Marshall and Stevens dissented.

In cases involving the fruit of involuntary statements, the courts will attempt to determine whether the unconstitutional statement tainted the later, validly obtained evidence. Thus the prosecution must prove not only that the second statement was admissible but that it was also "sufficiently an act of free will to purge the primary taint."[73] In *Brown v. Illinois,* the Court suggested that factors such as "[t]he temporal proximity of the arrest and the confession, the presence of intervening circumstances . . . and, particularly, the purpose and flagrancy

---

69. Harris v. New York, 401 U.S. 222 (1971); People v. Peterson, 74 Ill. 2d 478, 384 N.E.2d 348, 350 (1978).

70. Wong Sun v. United States, 371 U.S. 471 (1963). *See also* People v. Wilson, 60 Ill. 2d 235, 326 N.E.2d 378 (1975).

71. Michigan v. Tucker, 417 U.S. 433 (1974); People v. Bell, 105 Ill. App. 3d 208, 434 N.E.2d 35 (2d Dist. 1982), *cert. denied,* 459 U.S. 1213 (1983).

72. Oregon v. Elstad, 470 U.S. 298 (1985); In re T.S., 151 Ill. App. 3d 344, 502 N.E.2d 761 (4th Dist. 1986) (written statement given after proper warnings not admissible when it was mere reiteration of oral statement obtained prior to admonitions under circumstances court found to be coercive).

73. Brown v. Illinois, 422 U.S. 590, 602 (1975) (citing *Wong Sun,* 371 U.S. at 486).

of the official misconduct are all relevant" to determining if the fruits of the initial illegality should be suppressed,[74] assuming that the final statement was voluntary.[75] This is also the test applied when determining whether the administration of *Miranda* warnings attenuates the taint of an illegal arrest.

§ 2.09   Waiver by Failure to Seek Suppression

Generally, where an accused fails to object to the introduction into evidence of an admission or confession, its reception into evidence without preliminary proof of voluntariness is proper and not open to review.[76] There may be cases in which the record so blatantly suggests that the confession was not voluntary that a trial court is obligated to hold a suppression hearing sua sponte,[77] but in the vast majority of cases the failure to file a motion to suppress will constitute a waiver of an attack on the admissibility of the confession.[78] Thus, when a motion to suppress is not made, the issue is forever lost to a defendant, and he or she cannot obtain relief on this issue except by demonstrating that the failure of his or her trial attorney denied him or her effective representation. Then the attention will shift from the admissibility of the confession to the reason the counsel failed to seek suppression of the statement. Although reviewing courts will seldom find the failure to file a motion to suppress to be evidence of constitutionally ineffective representation, in many cases the failure to file such a motion is inexplicable.[79]

Some attorneys respond to this problem by simply filing a form motion to suppress in every case in which there is a confession and argue that this is the

---

74. *Brown,* 422 U.S. at 603–04.

75. People v. Pierce, 88 Ill. App. 3d 1095, 411 N.E.2d 295, 300–307 (5th Dist. 1980).

76. People v. Hicks, 44 Ill. 2d 550, 256 N.E.2d 823, 825, *cert. denied,* 400 U.S. 845 (1970). In *People v. Strader,* 38 Ill. 2d 93, 230 N.E.2d 569 (1967), the supreme court held that a defendant convicted in 1957 was entitled to raise the claim of a coerced confession in a postconviction petition filed in 1962, not withstanding the fact that no preliminary motion to suppress was made before the original trial. The court relied on the fact that the United States Supreme Court had held *Jackson v. Denno,* 378 U.S. 368 (1964), to be retroactive. Whether the same result would occur today is questionable.

77. People v. Friedman, 79 Ill. 2d 341, 403 N.E.2d 229, 236 (1980); People v. Ortiz, 22 Ill. App. 3d 788, 317 N.E.2d 763, 769 (1st Dist. 1974).

78. People v. Gacy, 103 Ill. 2d 1, 468 N.E.2d 1171, 1181 (1984), *cert. denied,* 470 U.S. 1037 (1985); People v. Terrell, 62 Ill. 2d 60, 338 N.E.2d 383, 384 (1975); People v. Conley, 118 Ill. App. 3d 122, 454 N.E.2d 1107, 1114 (1st Dist. 1983); People v. Scott, 106 Ill. App. 2d 98, 245 N.E.2d 490, 494–95 (1st Dist. 1969).

79. *Conley,* 118 Ill. App. 3d 122, 454 N.E.2d at 1114–15; People v. Henry, 103 Ill. App. 3d 1143, 432 N.E.2d 359, 361 (3d Dist. 1982).

proper strategy. Nevertheless there are other ways for an attorney to protect himself or herself from after-the-fact attacks on the failure to file such a motion. These alternatives include careful detailing of strategic decisions in the case file and candid discussions with the client that are then reflected in the file.

§ 2.10 Waiver of Issue by Pleading Guilty

A properly entered plea of guilty constitutes a waiver of all nonjurisdictional defects.[80] Thus, by entering a plea of guilty a defendant waives the right to object to the admissibility of any statement or confession that might be introduced against him or her, even if a motion to suppress was made before the plea and even if there appears to be a valid constitutional claim.[81]

Although some states do allow for appeals from the denial of motions to suppress, even after pleas of guilty,[82] Illinois does not, and thus a plea of guilty will constitute a waiver of the suppression issue. The issue can be preserved only by proceeding to trial.

§ 2.11 Appellate Review of Decisions on Motions to Suppress

If the circuit court grants a motion to suppress, the proceedings on this issue will then terminate, unless the prosecution files a written notice that it will not take an interlocutory appeal from the order suppressing the confession.[83] Obviously, if the prosecution is to obtain appellate review, it must take such an interlocutory appeal, as appeal following acquittal is barred by the double jeopardy provisions of the state and federal constitutions. As a practical matter, if the state's attorney fails to file a notice of appeal the trial will proceed even without the formal written waiver by the prosecutor. If the motion to suppress is denied no interlocutory appeal is allowed. The defendant can only appeal the decision after conviction.

Even after a motion to suppress is denied, the objection to the admissibility of the confession must be renewed by a written motion for new trial following conviction. The failure to renew such issue in a posttrial motion may constitute waiver of the issue for appeal, although in death penalty cases the Illinois court has indicated that it will review confession issues, even without a properly

---

80. People v. Ondrey, 65 Ill. 2d 360, 357 N.E.2d 1160, 1162 (1976).

81. People v. Brown, 41 Ill. 2d 503, 244 N.E.2d 159, 160 (1969); People v. Jones, 7 Ill. App. 3d 146, 287 N.E.2d 227, 228 (1st Dist. 1972).

82. See, e.g., WIS. STAT. § 971.31(10); See also Lefkowitz v. Newsome, 420 U.S. 283 (1975).

83. 725 ILCS 5/114-11(g).

preserved posttrial motion, if the matter was raised at trial because it is a constitutional claim which could be raised by postconviction petition.[84]

The Illinois Appellate Court has viewed questions on suppression motions as primarily factual determinations that will not be reversed on appeal unless "manifestly erroneous"[85] or against the manifest weight of the evidence,[86] with questions of credibility clearly to be resolved by the trial court.[87]

As a strategic matter, counsel will seldom want to base an appeal on an assertion that the factual determination of the trial court was so clearly erroneous as to warrant reversal. Rather, the counsel seeking reversal will usually attempt to take the case outside the realm of a factual issue and will argue that the circuit court misapplied the law to the facts at hand.[88] Even when a trial court determination is reversed as being contrary to the manifest weight of the evidence, often that will be accompanied by some aspect of misconduct on the part of law enforcement,[89] although trial courts will be reversed if they simply ignore unrefuted evidence.[90] In situations where there is arguably sufficient evidence to sustain the trial court's determination, it may be wise for an appellant to present the issue as a mixed question of fact and law. In such circumstances one need not directly attack the fact finding that requires a demonstration that the conclusion was clearly incorrect but may still seek reversal on the legal question. The appellate court will afford the legal question de novo review and not the higher standard required to overturn a factual question.[91]

Even if the appellate court determines that the confession was erroneously admitted at trial, the court may still uphold the conviction if it concludes that

---

84. People v. Enoch, 122 Ill. 2d 176, 522 N.E.2d 1124, 1132, *cert. denied*, 488 U.S. 917 (1988).

85. People v. Brooks, 51 Ill. 2d 156, 281 N.E.2d 326, 332 (1972).

86. People v. Mallett, 45 Ill. 2d 388, 259 N.E.2d 241, 245 (1970). *See* People v. Dinwiddie, 299 Ill. App. 3d 636, 702 N.E.2d 181, 185 (1st Dist. 1998) (applying "manifest weight of the evidence" test to juvenile confession).

87. People v. Davis, 97 Ill. 2d 1, 452 N.E.2d 525, 534 (1983).

88. People v. Weinstein, 46 Ill. 2d 222, 263 N.E.2d 62 (1970) (incorrect retroactive application of *Miranda*); People v. Lumpp, 113 Ill. App. 3d 694, 447 N.E.2d 963 (1st Dist. 1983) (court misapplied "material witness rule"); People v. Baine, 82 Ill. App. 3d 604, 403 N.E.2d 57 (5th Dist. 1980) (trial court applied "incorrect test for determining voluntariness").

89. People v. Payton, 122 Ill. App. 3d 1030, 462 N.E.2d 543 (5th Dist. 1984).

90. People v. Rhoads, 73 Ill. App. 3d 288, 391 N.E.2d 512, 526–27 (1st Dist. 1979).

91. LaVallee v. Delle Rose, 410 U.S. 690, 698–99 (1973) (Marshall, J., dissenting). *See also* People v. Lippert, 89 Ill. 2d 171, 432 N.E.2d 605, 607–08, *cert. denied*, 459 U.S. 841 (1982).

the admission of the confession was harmless beyond a reasonable doubt[92] because its admission would not have affected the outcome of the trial.[93] Prejudice has been found when the prosecution relied on the improperly admitted statements in its cross-examination of the defendant;[94] in its argument to the jury;[95] when other evidence failed to support conviction;[96] and where the improperly admitted confession was so devastating that a new trial had to follow despite ample additional evidence of the defendant's guilt.[97] On the question of the prejudicial nature of the admission of an illegally obtained confession, the United States Supreme Court long ago observed:

> [t]he prosecution cannot on the one hand offer evidence to prove guilt, and which by the very offer is vouched for as tending to that end, and on the other hand for the purpose of avoiding the consequences of the error, caused by its wrongful admission, be heard to assert that the matter offered as a confession was not prejudicial because it did not tend to prove guilt.[98]

In many cases, however, the courts have found the improper admission of evidence to be harmless beyond a reasonable doubt when the properly admitted evidence of guilt was "overwhelming,"[99] when the confession was merely corroborative of properly admitted evidence,[100] or when the improperly admitted evidence was not emphasized or was not a major part of the prosecution's case.[101]

§ 2.12   Involuntary Confessions: Definition

A confession given by a defendant will not be admissible if it is involuntary, meaning that the accused's will was overborne at the time he or she confessed

---

92. Chapman v. California, 386 U.S. 18 (1967); People v. Riszowski, 22 Ill. App. 3d 741, 318 N.E.2d 10, 17 (1st Dist. 1974).

93. People v. King, 61 Ill. 2d 326, 335 N.E.2d 417, 418 (1975).

94. People v. Smith, 93 Ill. 2d 179, 442 N.E.2d 1325, 1330 (1982), *cert. denied,* 461 U.S. 937 (1983).

95. People v. Feagans, 118 Ill. App. 3d 991, 455 N.E.2d 871, 874–75 (4th Dist. 1983).

96. People v. Washington, 68 Ill. 2d 186, 369 N.E.2d 57, 60–61 (1977), *cert denied,* 435 U.S. 981 (1978).

97. People v. Hill, 78 Ill. 2d 465, 401 N.E.2d 517, 521 (1980).

98. Bram v. United States, 168 U.S. 532, 541 (1897).

99. People v. Douglas, 58 Ill. App. 3d 149, 373 N.E.2d 1385, 1388 (4th Dist. 1978).

100. People v. Merrero, 121 Ill. App. 3d 716, 459 N.E.2d 1158, 1163 (2d Dist. 1984).

101. People v. Rehbein, 54 Ill. App. 3d 393, 369 N.E.2d 190, 195 (1st Dist. 1977), *aff'd,* 74 Ill. 2d 435, 386 N.E.2d 39 (1978).

so the statement cannot be deemed the product of a rational intellect and a free will.[102] The test is whether the confession has been made freely, voluntarily, and without compulsion or inducements of any sort.[103] This issue is separate from whether the defendant was informed of his or her constitutional rights or was afforded counsel and will be determined on the "totality of all the relevant circumstances."[104] The judge makes his or her determination based on all the circumstances encompassing the making of the statement, "including the existence of any threats, promises, or physical coercion, the length and intensity of the interrogation, and the age, intelligence, experience, and physical condition of the defendant."[105] However, the United States Supreme Court has indicated that the admission of an involuntary statement is mere "trial error," and thus it may be evaluated in the context of other evidence to determine whether the admission of the involuntary statement is harmless, beyond a reasonable doubt.[106]

---

102. People v. Kincaid, 87 Ill. 2d 107, 429 N.E.2d 508, 511 (1981), *cert. denied,* 455 U.S. 1024 (1982).

103. People v. Argo, 133 Ill. App. 3d 421, 478 N.E.2d 873, 879 (3d Dist. 1985).

104. People v. Johnson, 44 Ill. 2d 463, 256 N.E.2d 343, 347, *cert. denied,* 400 U.S. 958 (1970).

105. People v. Green, 179 Ill. App. 3d 1, 535 N.E.2d 413, 421 (1st Dist. 1988). *See also* People v. Gilliam, 172 Ill. 2d 484, 670 N.E.2d 606, 613–16 (1996) (defendant's signed statement was determined voluntary despite the fact that he was questioned from 1:30 p.m. to 5:30 a.m. and claimed that he was not properly fed or allowed to use the washroom; the credibility of the witnesses who refuted these claims was properly determined by the trial court), *cert. denied,* 520 U.S. 1105 (1997).

106. Arizona v. Fulminante, 499 U.S. 279, 288 (1991) (defendant's confession to informant was coerced because he was motivated to confess by fear of violence; error was not harmless). In this case, the defendant was incarcerated in a federal correctional institution for possession of a firearm by a felon. *Id.* at 282. He became friends with an informant for the FBI. *Id.* at 282–83. The informant heard rumors that the defendant was suspected of murdering a child in Arizona and began questioning him about the killing. *Id.* at 283. The informant later learned that the defendant was getting tough treatment from fellow inmates because of the rumor and offered to protect him in exchange for the truth about the murder. *Id.* The defendant confessed to the crime and was later convicted with the confession. *Id.* at 284. In determining that the confession was coerced, the Court stated that there was a "credible threat of physical violence unless the defendant confessed" to the crime. *Id.* at 287. Coercion does not depend on actual violence by a government agent. *Id.* at 287. Fear of physical violence may suffice. *Id.* at 287–88. The fear of physical violence from fellow inmates, in absence of protection from his friend, motivated the defendant in this case to confess. *Id.* at 288. Defendant's will was thus overborne so as to render the confession the product of coercion. *Id.* Five Justices stated that the harmless error doctrine

Although courts occasionally are faced with an allegation that the confession was obtained through torture or physical abuse, the assertions are usually of more subtle forms of coercion and focus on any duress, fear, or threats utilized to obtain confessions; on deception used by the law enforcement officials; and on the vulnerable nature of the defendant. When the issue of the voluntariness of a confession is raised the court will review the totality of the circumstances to determine first if the way the confession was obtained was proper and second, whether the nature of the defendant is relevant to determining whether the confession was voluntary.[107] This means that in the case of a juvenile or a defendant with below average mentality an otherwise voluntary confession might be found inadmissible, and circumstances that would be found impermissible for an average defendant will not result in the suppression of a statement given by a sophisticated, streetwise suspect.

§ 2.13 Confessions Obtained After Physical Abuse

A confession obtained by force or brutality is not voluntary and is not admissible. When an accused suffers injuries while in police custody, clear and convincing proof is required to establish that the injuries were not the result of police brutality.[108]

The decision of whether the confession resulted from a fear of physical abuse is a factual determination to be made by the trial court based on the totality of the circumstances and will not be reversed unless contrary to the manifest weight of the evidence.[109] In reaching such a determination the physical

---

applied to the admission of an involuntary confession, but in this case it was not harmless beyond a reasonable doubt. *Id*. at 295–96.

107. People v. Turner, 56 Ill. 2d 201, 306 N.E.2d 27 (1973); People v. Berry, 123 Ill. App. 3d 1042, 463 N.E.2d 1044 (4th Dist. 1984); People v. Stone, 61 Ill. App. 3d 654, 378 N.E.2d 263 (5th Dist. 1978).

108. People v. Davis, 35 Ill. 2d 202, 220 N.E.2d 222, 224–25 (1966); People v. Alexander, 96 Ill. App. 2d 113, 238 N.E.2d 168, 172 (1st Dist. 1968). *See also* People v. Wilson, 116 Ill. 2d 29, 506 N.E.2d 571, 576 (1987) (admission of confession not harmless error where state failed to produce evidence explaining all of defendant's injuries, prosecution failed to sustain its burden, and confession was inadmissible); People v. Clark, 114 Ill. 2d 450, 501 N.E.2d 123, 127 (1986) (without any evidence that defendant's injuries occurred while he was in custody, state not required to explain injuries to defendant when they were noticed while he was in police custody). *But see* Arizona v. Fulminante, 499 U.S. 279 (1991) (admission of involuntary statement is subject to harmless error analysis).

109. People v. Hubbard, 222 Ill. App. 3d 605, 584 N.E.2d 285, 289 (1st Dist. 1991); People v. Lewis, 75 Ill. App. 3d 259, 393 N.E.2d 1098, 1113 (1st Dist. 1979). *See, e.g.*, People v. Taylor, 269 Ill. App. 3d 772, 646 N.E.2d 1280, 1287 (1st Dist.

mistreatment of the defendant is but one circumstance to consider, albeit a significant factor.[110] In *People v. O'Leary,*[111] the Illinois Supreme Court, finding that all of the circumstances required suppression, overturned the admission of a confession obtained half an hour after the defendant had been sprayed in the face with tear gas and placed in "the hole."

In contrast, in *People v. Brown,*[112] the court found defendant's statement was voluntary even though he claimed the police repeatedly beat him and that he told the police he desired counsel.[113] Defendant was twenty years old, had prior experience with the criminal justice system, had earned his GED in jail, and had been advised of his *Miranda* rights before each interrogation.[114] Although the evidence concerning mistreatment was conflicting, defendant's testimony was undercut by the paramedic's report which stated that the defendant had no health complaints and by his court-reported statement in which he denied any complaints of mistreatment. The length of time between the arrest and the statement also did not render the confession involuntary. Much of the time was spent in transport between different police stations, and the stay at the first station was caused by the defendant who provided a false name and age to the police upon his arrest. In addition, the defendant was only subjected to two short interrogations before confessing to the crime charged in this case.[115] He was given food and drink, allowed to use the bathroom, and allowed to use the phone.[116] Finally, there was no credible evidence that the defendant requested counsel at any time during the interrogations.[117]

1995) (trial court's decision finding no physical coercion in obtaining defendant's statement not against manifest weight of evidence where record contained no photograph illustrating alleged beatings, although jury viewed photograph and weighed it with all the other evidence and doctor's testimony inconclusive that defendant suffered injury while in custody).

110. Reck v. Pate, 367 U.S. 433, 440 (1961).

111. 45 Ill. 2d 122, 257 N.E.2d 112 (1970).

112. 169 Ill. 2d 132, 661 N.E.2d 287 (1996).

113. *Id.*, 661 N.E.2d at 294.

114. *Id.*

115. *Id.*

116. *Id.*, 661 N.E.2d at 295.

117. *Id. But* see People v. Bounds, 171 Ill. 2d 1, 662 N.E.2d 1168, 1180 (1995) (medical evidence contradicted defendant's claim that he had been physically abused where the medical technician testified that he saw no bruises, cuts, sores, swellings, or bandages on the defendant), *cert. denied*, 519 U.S. 876 (1996).

Although the prosecution has the burden to establish the voluntariness of any confession by a preponderance of the evidence,[118] there will often be a factual dispute over whether there was any physical force used on the defendant. The cases demonstrate that a defendant is most likely to prevail on this factual determination if the assertion is supported by independent or police evidence and not simply the testimony of the defendant.[119] Where there is evidence that the defendant was injured while in police custody, or if the defendant suffers "unexplained injuries" while in police custody,[120] the prosecution bears the burden of proving by clear and convincing evidence that the confession was not the result of physical abuse.[121] The state must demonstrate more than mere denial by the police of coercion or abuse.[122]

§ 2.14 Confessions Obtained by Threats of Physical Abuse

A confession made as the result of fear is not admissible.[123] Indeed, early on the Illinois Supreme Court made clear that it would not tolerate the "sweating" of an accused or the use of the "third degree" to coerce a

---

118. People v. Clark, 114 Ill. 2d 450, 501 N.E.2d 123, 126 (1986); People v. McGuire, 35 Ill. 2d 219, 220 N.E.2d 447 (1966); People v. Lewis, 75 Ill. App. 3d 259, 393 N.E.2d 1098 (1st Dist. 1979).

119. *Compare* People v. Davis, 35 Ill. 2d 202, 220 N.E.2d 222 (1966) and People v. Alexander, 96 Ill. App. 2d 113, 238 N.E.2d 168 (1st Dist. 1968) *with* People v. Lewis, 75 Ill. App. 3d 259, 393 N.E.2d 1098 (1st Dist. 1979) and People v. Hester, 39 Ill. 2d 489, 237 N.E.2d 466, 473 (1968), *cert. dismissed,* 397 U.S. 660 (1970), *overruled on other grounds* by People v. Anderson, 113 Ill. 2d 1, 497 N.E.2d 485, *cert. denied,* 479 U.S. 1012 (1986). *See also* People v. Cannon, 293 Ill. App. 3d 634, 688 N.E.2d 693, 697 (1st Dist. 1997) (defendant entitled to hearing on motion to suppress confession where new evidence presented regarding tortured prisoners at same place defendant alleged to have been tortured).

120. People v. Woods, 184 Ill. 2d 130, 703 N.E.2d 35, 43–44 (1998).

121. People v. Wilson, 116 Ill. 2d 29, 506 N.E.2d 571, 575 (1987) (citing People v. La Frana, 4 Ill. 2d 261, 122 N.E.2d 583, 586 (1954)). *But see* People v. Kidd, 175 Ill. 2d 1, 675 N.E.2d 910, 923 (1996) (defendant's confession was determined voluntary and not a product of police abuse where although there was evidence defendant had a mark on his forehead after his confession, he presented no evidence that the injury occurred while he was in custody or that he did not have it before he was taken into custody), *cert. denied,* 520 U.S. 1269 (1997).

122. *Wilson,* 116 Ill. 2d 29, 506 N.E.2d at 575. *See also La Frana,* 4 Ill. 2d 261, 122 N.E.2d at 586 (under circumstances where physical coercion is alleged, the burden of establishing that the police did not administer the injuries in order to obtain the confession can only be met by clear and convincing testimony as to the manner of their occurrence).

123. People v. Davis, 399 Ill. 265, 77 N.E.2d 703, 706 (1948).

confession, either with or without actual physical abuse.[124] Although the Illinois Supreme Court has made clear that "an involuntary confession obtained by brutality or coercion is wholly unreliable and is the most flagrant violation of the principles of freedom and justice,"[125] the question still is regarded as a factual determination by the trial court that will not be set aside except if contrary to the manifest weight of the evidence.[126] The mere assertion that a confession was obtained by duress does not mandate its exclusion. Rather, the issue becomes one of fact for the trial court to resolve.[127] In *People v. McGuire*,[128] the Illinois Supreme Court remanded a case for a full evidentiary hearing and declined to grant a new trial or suppress the statement, even in the face of evidence that a police officer said he would have liked to have killed the defendant before the confession was made. In evaluating whether police conduct is coercive, the trial judge assesses the witnesses' credibility.[129]

§ 2.15   Other Types of Threats or Promises

In *Bram v. United States,* the United States Supreme Court declared that "a confession, in order to be admissible, must be free and voluntary; that is, must not be extracted by any sort of threats or violence, nor obtained by any direct or implied promises, however slight, nor by the exertion of any improper influence . . . ."[130] Applying this rule, the United States Supreme Court set aside

---

124. People v. Holick, 337 Ill. 333, 168 N.E. 169, 172 (1929); People v. Rogers, 303 Ill. 578, 136 N.E. 470, 474–75 (1922), *overruled on other grounds* by People v. R.D., 155 Ill. 2d 122, 613 N.E.2d 706 (1993). *See* People v. Clemon, 259 Ill. App. 3d 5, 630 N.E.2d 1120, 1124 (1st Dist. 1994) (defendant's statement resulted from "horrendously coercive" environment where 11 suspects held and questioned, witness heard suspects screaming, witness saw officer hit one suspect and witness heard defendant scream for 15 minutes when three or four officers were in room with him with door shut).

125. People v. Hall, 413 Ill. 615, 110 N.E.2d 249, 254 (1953).

126. People v. Joe, 31 Ill. 2d 220, 201 N.E.2d 416, 418 (1964). *See also* People v. King, 109 Ill. 2d 514, 488 N.E.2d 949, 955–56 (trial court's determination that confession was not result of physical abuse sustained as not against manifest weight of evidence, notwithstanding defendant's testimony that he was beaten with baseball bat to extract confession), *cert. denied,* 479 U.S. 872 (1986).

127. People v. Byrd, 21 Ill. 2d 114, 171 N.E.2d 782, 783 (1961).

128. 35 Ill. 2d 219, 220 N.E.2d 447 (1966).

129. People v. Dodds, 190 Ill. App. 3d 1083, 547 N.E.2d 523, 531 (1st Dist. 1989). *See also* People v. Jones, 184 Ill. App. 3d 412, 541 N.E.2d 132, 140 (1st Dist. 1989) (where only the defendant testifies that there was police coercion, the best person to assess credibility is the trial judge).

130. 168 U.S. 532, 542–43 (1897).

an Illinois conviction for the sale and possession of marijuana that was based, at least in part, on a confession made by the defendant after the police told her that state financial aid for her infant children would be cut off if she did not cooperate.[131]

When medical treatment was withheld for nine hours while the suspect was interrogated, the trial court's determination that the confession was involuntary was supported by the evidence where the defendant may have believed that medical treatment was dependent upon his statement.[132] However, in *People v. Williams*,[133] the court held that defendant's confession was voluntary even though at the time he made it he was suffering from gunshot wounds. Defendant shot a police officer and in response was shot himself. On the way to the hospital, the paramedic, out of curiosity, asked him why he had shot the officer.

---

131. Lynumn v. Illinois, 372 U.S. 528 (1963), *rev'g*, 21 Ill. 2d 63, 171 N.E.2d 17, 20 (1961) (wherein Illinois Supreme Court found admission of confession to be nonprejudicial). *See also* People v. Gilliam, 172 Ill. 2d 484, 670 N.E.2d 606, 619–20 (1996) (defendant's statement was determined voluntary despite his claim that it was induced by threats of arresting his girlfriend and taking his infant daughter to the DCFS; testimony of the defendant's psychologist that defendant was especially susceptible to police pressures and thus subjected to a form of psychological compulsion to confess was inadmissible because whether a defendant falsely confessed to protect his family is not a concept beyond the understanding of ordinary citizens as required for admission of expert testimony), *cert. denied*, 520 U.S. 1105 (1997); People v. Bounds, 171 Ill. 2d 1, 662 N.E.2d 1168, 1180 (1995) (defendant was unable to show that his will was overcome where officers threatened to release the name of defendant's girlfriend to the news media as this conduct was aimed at the girlfriend, was not communicated to defendant, and was not made to elicit information from the defendant), *cert. denied*, 519 U.S. 876 (1996); People v. Robinson, 286 Ill. App. 3d 903, 676 N.E.2d 1368, 1370–71 (4th Dist. 1997) (defendant's confession determined not involuntary due to alleged promise of leniency towards girlfriend where defendant expressed willingness to make statement; it was defendant himself who initiated and controlled bargaining, and there were no other factors indicative of involuntariness).

132. People v. Strickland, 129 Ill. 2d 550, 544 N.E.2d 758 (1989). *But see* People v. Hornsby, 277 Ill. App. 3d 227, 660 N.E.2d 110, 113–14 (1st Dist. 1995) (defendant's confession voluntary even though he claimed he was deprived of insulin and was in insulin reaction from imbalanced diet at time he confessed, where he received insulin on the morning before taken to police station, gave statement shortly after arriving at station, was twice given food, had good color and skin was warm and dry when he was taken to the hospital, and defendant discharged in good condition 10 minutes after an insulin shot); People v. Poole, 222 Ill. App. 3d 689, 584 N.E.2d 368, 374 (1st Dist. 1991) (defendant's confession voluntary even though defendant alleged he was promised pain medication).

133. 181 Ill. 2d 297, 692 N.E.2d 1109, *cert. denied*, 119 S. Ct. 192 (1998).

The defendant stated that he shot him because he did not want to go to jail. The trial court denied defendant's motion to suppress. Defendant appealed, contending that his confession was not voluntary pursuant to *Strickland* and *Mincey* due to the nature of his injuries. The court stated that although defendant was suffering from gunshot wounds, the facts of his case were clearly distinguishable from the facts of cases wherein confessions were suppressed. When the paramedics arrived at the scene, defendant was uncooperative and abusive. Further, he was stable and did not appear to be in shock. His wound appeared to have stopped bleeding and he was not medicated. Instead, he was coherent and able to give personal information.[134] The testimony provided by the paramedics was corroborated by police testimony. Although defendant complained to the police of pain, he was coherent and able to answer questions. Further, when the defendant arrived at the hospital, he was alert and able to consent to surgery. Finally, the tenor of defendant's statement was inconsistent with one whose will was overborne. Accordingly, the trial court properly found that the statement was voluntary under a totality of the circumstances analysis.[135]

In Illinois the promise of leniency in a charge or anticipated sentence does not necessarily mean that the statement is inadmissible. Rather, the promise will be considered as one of the various factors in the totality.[136] Even when the confession is made after a promise for a significant reduction in charge or sentence, it is the subjective belief of the defendant about the validity of the promise that is dispositive. It does not matter if the promise is made by someone who actually lacked the authority to fulfill the commitment, as long as all of the circumstances show that it was a product of the defendant's free will.[137] In

---

134. *Id.*, 692 N.E.2d at 1117.

135. *Id.*, 692 N.E.2d at 1118.

136. This will sometimes result in the suppression of the confession. People v. Ruegger, 32 Ill. App. 3d 765, 336 N.E.2d 50 (4th Dist. 1975); People v. Peck, 18 Ill. App. 3d 112, 309 N.E.2d 346 (1st Dist. 1974). Often it will result in the admission of the confession as being voluntary. People v. Noe, 96 Ill. App. 3d 762, 408 N.E.2d 483 (3d Dist. 1980); People v. Dozier, 67 Ill. App. 3d 611, 385 N.E.2d 155 (4th Dist. 1979) (defendant told "it would be in his favor, his benefit to tell the truth").

137. People v. Sickley, 114 Ill. App. 3d 167, 448 N.E.2d 612 (3d Dist. 1983). *See also* People v. Oaks, 169 Ill. 2d 409, 662 N.E.2d 1328, 1345–47 (trial judge did not err in denying motion to suppress defendant's confession on alleged false and misleading promises made by interrogators, where comments conveyed to defendant to tell truth; judge would look unfavorably upon him if he did not, and advised defendant that evidence of victim's injuries contradicted his story; nature of comments were not promises of help in exchange for statement), *cert. denied,* 519 U.S. 873 (1996); People v. Johnson, 285 Ill. App. 3d 802, 674 N.E.2d 844, 848–49 (1st Dist. 1996) (defendant's confession not induced by promises where

other jurisdictions confessions made after a promise of leniency in charging or sentencing have been declared to be invalid. Thus, the Georgia Supreme Court struck down a conviction based on a confession obtained after the prosecutor promised to seek a greatly reduced sentence,[138] and both the California and Florida Supreme Courts have ruled confessions inadmissible when made in exchange for promises not to seek the death penalty in murder cases.[139]

The Illinois Supreme Court, in a case raising the issue of an agreement not to seek the death penalty if the suspect confessed, declared that when a confession was made after the state's attorney promised not to seek the death penalty, the confession was admissible, but the defendant was entitled to specific performance of the promise made before the confession so that the imposition of the death penalty was not permissible.[140]

In *People v. Rhoads,* the appellate court excluded a confession made after a police officer said to the defendant: "Well, you need help and if you talk to us we'll see that you get some help . . . . We think that you're sick."[141] Similarly, when a drug addict was promised entry into a treatment program if he confessed, the statement was found to be involuntary under the totality of the circumstances.[142]

Illinois has declined to adopt a per se rule invalidating confessions made after some type of promise. The courts will apply the totality of circumstances test and decide on a case-by-case basis. For example, a statement was not voluntary when it was motivated by the defendant's fear of physical violence, absent protection from an undercover agent posing as a prison inmate, who promised to protect defendant from other inmates.[143] First, the court will have to find that the promise was actually made, and second, determine that the defendant's will was overborne by the promise. If both are proven the statement should not be admitted. The *Brownell*[144] case in which the Illinois Supreme Court ordered specific performance of a promise not to seek the death penalty in a murder case in exchange for a statement must be considered in light of the fact that it arose after the death penalty had already been imposed and was first

---

statements made to him conveyed the import of telling the truth and informed him that if he did not, the trial judge might look upon him unfavorably).

138. Johnson v. Georgia, 238 Ga. 27, 230 S.E.2d 849 (1976).

139. People v. Johnson, 70 Cal. 2d 469, 74 Cal. Rptr. 889, 450 P.2d 265 (1969); Brewster v. State, 386 So. 2d 232 (Fla. 1980).

140. People v. Brownell, 79 Ill. 2d 508, 404 N.E.2d 181, 186–88, *cert. denied,* 448 U.S. 811 (1980).

141. 73 Ill. App. 3d 288, 391 N.E.2d 512, 526 (1st Dist. 1979).

142. People v. Koesterer, 44 Ill. App. 3d 468, 358 N.E.2d 295 (5th Dist. 1976).

143. Arizona v. Fulminante, 499 U.S. 279, 288 (1991).

144. People v. Brownell, 79 Ill. 2d 508, 404 N.E.2d 181 (1980).

raised on a postconviction motion after the conviction and confession had been upheld on direct appeal.

§ 2.16 Confessions Claimed to Be Based on Other Exhortations Made to the Accused

Often, a defendant will claim that the confession was improperly induced by law enforcement officials who urged him or her to "tell the truth." The law is "firmly established that, in the absence of a suggestion of benefit to the defendant, mere exhortation to tell the truth does not render inadmissible a subsequent confession."[145] However, it has been held that "the statement that it is better to tell the truth may be made under such circumstances as to make a confession afterwards incompetent."[146] This is a factual question to be resolved by the trial court and will not be reversed on appeal unless it is against the manifest weight of the evidence.[147]

Absent unusual circumstances or a defendant who lacks normal capacity, a confession will be found valid if made after the defendant is told by the police that the prosecutor will be informed of his or her cooperation if he or she confesses;[148] that it would be "easier" on the defendant if he or she confessed;[149] that "it would be better" to confess;[150] that the defendant should confess "to make peace with yourself, your God, and your children;"[151] or that the defendant would get a "fair trial" if he or she confessed.[152] In each of these situations the courts viewed such words of encouragement in the totality of the circumstances and have not, absent significant additional factors, found statements made after such exhortations to have been involuntarily obtained.

---

145. People v. Wipfler, 68 Ill. 2d 158, 368 N.E.2d 870, 876 (1977).

146. People v. Klyczek, 307 Ill. 150, 138 N.E. 275, 277 (1923).

147. People v. Taylor, 58 Ill. 2d 69, 317 N.E.2d 97, 101–02 (1974).

148. People v. Hubbard, 55 Ill. 2d 142, 302 N.E.2d 609, 614 (1973).

149. People v. Hartgraves, 31 Ill. 2d 375, 202 N.E.2d 33, 36 (1964), *cert. denied,* 380 U.S. 961 (1965).

150. People v. McGuire, 39 Ill. 2d 244, 234 N.E.2d 772, 774, *cert. denied,* 393 U.S. 884 (1968).

151. People v. Bowen, 87 Ill. App. 3d 221, 408 N.E.2d 993, 997 (1st Dist. 1980).

152. People v. Makes, 103 Ill. App. 3d 232, 431 N.E.2d 20, 23 (2d Dist. 1981).

§ 2.17 Deception Utilized to Obtain Confession

Police not infrequently resort to some type of deception when questioning a suspect.[153] In an early case the Illinois Supreme Court excluded a confession obtained from the defendant who was interrogated while strapped involuntarily to an inoperative polygraph after requesting, but being denied, counsel. The court found the use of the polygraph to be "illegal" and that it "influenced, if it did not induce" the confession.[154] In subsequent cases the Illinois courts have viewed police deception more leniently and have found such practices objectionable only to the extent that they involve "affirmative acts of fraud or deceit." Thus, in *People v. Smith*,[155] the court admitted a statement made when the police failed to disclose that the victim had died, although the defendant had not inquired about the victim's condition, while in *People v. Groleau*,[156] the trial court's suppression of a confession was affirmed when the police affirmatively misrepresented the condition of the victim.[157]

It now appears that even if the police knowingly misrepresent the nature of the evidence against the defendant and subsequently obtain a confession,[158] the confession will be admissible unless the deceit is "of a nature likely to produce

---

153. *See generally* White, *Police Trickery in Inducing Confessions,* 127 U. PA. L. REV. 581 (1979).

154. People v. Sims, 395 Ill. 69, 69 N.E.2d 336, 338 (1946).

155. 108 Ill. App. 2d 172, 246 N.E.2d 689, 692 (2d Dist. 1969), *cert. denied,* 397 U.S. 1001 (1970). *See* People v. Brown, 301 Ill. App. 3d 995, 705 N.E.2d 162, 168 (2d Dist. 1998) (where police informed a juvenile and his mother that he was to be questioned concerning garbage can fires and police deliberately failed to mention that an infant had died in the fire, defendant's subsequent statement was admissible because "criminal suspects do not have the right to be informed of the specific criminal offenses or potential criminal offenses for which they may be charged when questioned by police"; further, "officers were under no affirmative duty to disclose the entire scope of their investigation to defendant and his mother").

156. 44 Ill. App. 3d 807, 358 N.E.2d 1192 (1st Dist. 1976).

157. People v. Groleau, 44 Ill. App. 3d 807, 358 N.E.2d 1192 (1st Dist. 1976); People v. Smith, 108 Ill. App. 2d 172, 246 N.E.2d 689 (2d Dist. 1969).

158. In *People v. Martin,* 102 Ill. 2d 412, 466 N.E.2d 228, 234, *cert. denied,* 469 U.S. 935 (1984), the majority of the Illinois Supreme Court held:

> It is undisputed that the police and assistant State's Attorney falsely informed the defendant that [his co-defendant] had given a statement naming him as the "triggerman." The deception, however, does not invalidate the confession as a matter of law. The circumstance, while relevant, is but one factor to consider when making a determination of voluntariness [citations omitted]. Other factors to be considered include the age, education, and intelligence of the accused, the duration of

an untrustworthy confession" or was "so reprehensible as to be offensive to basic notions of fairness."[159] Thus, in *People v. Boerckel* and *People v. Pritchet,* the court upheld confessions made after the defendants had been told incorrectly that their fingerprints were found at the crime scene,[160] and in *People v. Houston* the court upheld a confession made after the defendant had been falsely informed that he had been implicated by another person in the robbery.[161] Also, in *People v. Torry,*[162] the court upheld defendant's confession made after police incorrectly informed him that the victim's blood had been found on his clothing.[163] The Illinois Supreme Court has held that police misrepresentation by itself is not enough to invalidate a knowing waiver of defendant's constitutional rights or a later voluntary statement.[164] Instead, police deception is only one of the relevant elements a trial judge contemplates in evaluating voluntariness.[165] However, in *People v. Payton,* the court reversed a conviction based on a confession obtained after the defendant was falsely told both that the victim of the crime had identified him and that his fingerprints were found at the scene of the crime.[166] The law is clear that there is nothing impermissible about using properly obtained evidence as a device to encourage a defendant to confess.[167]

The emphasis on determining whether the deception was likely to produce a false statement has been criticized as inconsistent with the basic rules for

---

questioning, and whether he received his constitutional rights or was subjected to any physical punishment [citations omitted].

159. People v. Boerckel, 68 Ill. App. 3d 103, 384 N.E.2d 815, 822 (5th Dist.), *cert. denied,* 447 U.S. 911 (1979).

160. *Id.*; People v. Kashney, 111 Ill. 2d 454, 490 N.E.2d 688, 693 (1986); People v. Pritchett, 23 Ill. App. 3d 368, 319 N.E.2d 101 (2d Dist. 1974) (abstract).

161. 36 Ill. App. 3d 695, 344 N.E.2d 641, 646–47 (1st Dist. 1976), *cert. denied,* 429 U.S. 1109 (1977).

162. 212 Ill. App. 3d 759, 571 N.E.2d 827 (1st Dist. 1991).

163. *Id.,* 571 N.E.2d at 833.

164. *Id. See also* People v. Holland, 121 Ill. 2d 6, 520 N.E.2d 270, 288 (1987) (defendant was told witness identified his vehicle at scene of crime), *aff'd,* 493 U.S. 474 (1990).

165. *Torry,* 212 Ill. App. 3d 759, 571 N.E.2d at 833. *See also* People v. Kashney, 111 Ill. 2d 454, 490 N.E.2d 688, 693 (1986) (defendant falsely told fingerprint found at scene); People v. Martin, 102 Ill. 2d 412, 466 N.E.2d 228, 234 (defendant falsely told accomplice gave statement naming him as triggerman), *cert. denied,* 469 U.S. 935 (1984).

166. People v. Payton, 122 Ill. App. 3d 1030, 462 N.E.2d 543 (5th Dist. 1984).

167. People v. McKinley, 69 Ill. 2d 145, 370 N.E.2d 1040 (1977), *cert. denied,* 435 U.S. 975 (1978); People v. Weinstein, 46 Ill. 2d 222, 263 N.E.2d 62 (1970); People v. Smith, 93 Ill. App. 3d 1133, 418 N.E.2d 172 (1st Dist. 1981).

determining whether a confession is voluntary,[168] but increasingly courts have applied this test in reviewing confessions obtained by deceit.

Another form of deceit is for the police to appear sympathetic to the defendant so as to encourage him or her to confess. Although there are cases in which this "false friend" technique has resulted in the exclusion of confessions,[169] as a general proposition the false friendship or sympathy will be viewed only as one factor in the totality of circumstances surrounding the confession.[170]

Police misconduct is not, however, limited to affirmative acts. In *People v. Harbach*,[171] the court held that the failure of police to inform the defendant that his father had posted bail and that he was free to go was a "major factor" in finding the defendant's inculpatory statements inadmissible.[172]

As in the preceding sections, the issue here is to be resolved considering the totality of the circumstances. If police use affirmative deception under circumstances that make a false confession likely, the statement must be suppressed. Short of that, it would appear that the deception is simply another factor to be considered.

§ 2.18 The Nature and Duration of the Interrogation as Relevant to the Admissibility of the Confession

As is apparent from the foregoing discussion, any decision to admit or exclude a confession attacked as being involuntary will turn on a combination of factors. Primary among those factors will be the nature of the interrogation itself: where it took place, its length, the physical surroundings, and the people present.

The United States Supreme Court has adopted the so-called *McNabb-Mallory* rule, based on its decisions in *McNabb v. United States*[173] and *Mallory v. United States*.[174] It provides that if a confession is obtained after an unnecessary delay between arrest and initial appearance, it must be excluded from

---

168. 2 RINGEL, SEARCHES & SEIZURES, ARRESTS & CONFESSIONS 25—15 to 25—16 (release no. 6, June 1984).

169. Leyra v. Denno, 347 U.S. 556 (1954).

170. People v. Tanser, 75 Ill. App. 3d 482, 394 N.E.2d 616, 619 (2d Dist. 1979).

171. 298 Ill. App. 3d 111, 698 N.E.2d 281 (2d Dist. 1998).

172. *Id.*, 698 N.E.2d at 285–86.

173. 318 U.S. 332 (1943).

174. 354 U.S. 449 (1957), *superseded by statute as stated in* United States v. Manuel, 706 F.2d 908, 912 (9th Cir. 1983).

evidence in a federal criminal prosecution.[175] This rule does not apply to state prosecutions,[176] and the Supreme Court of Illinois has consistently declined to adopt *McNabb-Mallory* as a matter of Illinois law.[177]

In Illinois the length of the interrogation or the length of detention are simply factors to be considered in the totality.[178] Illinois case law indicates that a judge will not suppress a confession even if made after a lengthy period of detention and before the defendant appears in court as long as the confesssion was voluntary and did not otherwise violate defendant's constitutional rights.[179] Thus, a confession obtained after the defendant had been confined for forty-four hours was admitted on a finding that the statement was voluntary and that *McNabb-Mallory* did not apply.[180] A confession given by a fifteen-year-old defendant after a thirty-four-hour period of confinement was found proper,[181] and a sixteen-year-old defendant's statement given after a twenty-six-hour detention was found admissible by a divided Illinois Supreme Court.[182]

Thus, in *People v. House*,[183] the Illinois Supreme Court admitted a statement obtained after the defendant was held forty-nine hours in a

---

175. In title 18, section 3501(c) of the United States Code, Congress attempted to codify *McNabb-Mallory* by declaring that confessions obtained within six hours of arrest that were otherwise voluntary are admissible. If the confession is obtained beyond the six-hour period, the statement is not per se inadmissible, and the delay is but one factor to be considered in light of the surrounding circumstances. United States v. Edwards, 539 F.2d 689, 691 (9th Cir.), *cert. denied*, 429 U.S. 984 (1976).

176. Gallegos v. Nebraska, 342 U.S. 55, 63–64 (1951).

177. People v. Howell, 60 Ill. 2d 117, 324 N.E.2d 403, 405 (1975), *superseded by statute as stated* in People v. Bartee, 177 Ill. App. 3d 937, 532 N.E.2d 997, 998 (2d Dist. 1988); People v. Jackson, 23 Ill. 2d 274, 178 N.E.2d 299, 301 (1961).

178. People v. Earl, 34 Ill. 2d 11, 213 N.E.2d 556 (1966).

179. People v. Mendoza, 208 Ill. App. 3d 183, 567 N.E.2d 23, 36 (2d Dist. 1991) (citing People v. Dodds, 190 Ill. App. 3d 1083, 547 N.E.2d 523, 529 (1st Dist. 1989)). *See also* In re Lamb, 61 Ill. 2d 383, 336 N.E.2d 753, 756 (1975) (26 hours), *cert. denied*, 425 U.S. 938 (1976); People v. Nicholls, 42 Ill. 2d 91, 245 N.E.2d 771, 778 (1969) (34 hours), *cert. denied*, 396 U.S. 1016 (1970); People v. Taylor, 40 Ill. 2d 569, 241 N.E.2d 409, 412 (1968) (50 hours); People v. Reader, 26 Ill. 2d 210, 186 N.E.2d 298, 302 (1962) (44 hours).

180. *Reader*, 26 Ill. 2d 210, 186 N.E.2d at 302.

181. People v. Richardson, 32 Ill. 2d 472, 207 N.E.2d 478 (1965), *cert. denied*, 384 U.S. 1021 (1966).

182. In re Lamb, 61 Ill. 2d 383, 336 N.E.2d 753 (1975), *cert. denied*, 425 U.S. 938 (1976), *overruled on other grounds* by People v. R.D., 155 Ill. 2d 122, 613 N.E.2d 706 (1993).

183. 141 Ill. 2d 323, 566 N.E.2d 259 (1990).

windowless interview cell furnished only with a table and two chairs.[184] Defendant was interviewed intermittently for twenty-five hours.[185] He made an inculpatory statement after twenty-five hours and confessed fully twelve hours later.[186] The court found the circumstances of confinement not sufficient to overcome the defendant's free will but condemned police "brinkmanship."[187] Similarly, the appellate court held that a confession obtained after the defendant had been held for fifty-seven hours before being brought before a judge was voluntary.[188] The court found that there was nothing inherently coercive under the circumstances.[189] In another instance, a confession obtained after the defendant had been held for thirty hours and denied personal needs was found voluntary.[190] Finally, a confession given by a fifteen-year-old after a thirty-four-hour period of confinement was found proper.[191]

The length of delay when combined with other factors, however, has resulted in the suppression of confessions.[192] In *People v. Davis*[193] a one-week delay was found excessive, and in *People v. Harper*[194] a twenty-one-day delay was found to require suppression. But each case also involved a defendant who was either beaten or otherwise in need of medical care during his lengthy period of

---

184. *Id.,* 566 N.E.2d at 285.

185. *Id.,* 566 N.E. 2d at 281.

186. *Id.*

187. *Id.,* 566 N.E. 2d at 283.

188. People v. Mendoza, 208 Ill. App. 3d 183, 567 N.E.2d 23, 35 (2d Dist. 1991).

189. *Id.*

190. People v. Dodds, 190 Ill. App. 3d 1083, 547 N.E.2d 523, 531–32 (1st Dist. 1989).

191. People v. Richardson, 32 Ill. 2d 472, 207 N.E.2d 478, 480 (1965), *cert. denied,* 384 U.S. 1021 (1966). *But see* In re L.L., 295 Ill. App. 3d 594, 693 N.E.2d 908, 915 (2d Dist. 1998) (confession of a 13-year-old who attended special education classes, had limited mental abilities, was taken from his home in the middle of the night, was deprived of sleep, interrogated for three hours during middle of night without presence of parents, was involuntary where police were evasive in their conduct and frustrated parents' attempts to confer with son); People v. McGhee, 154 Ill. App. 3d 232, 507 N.E.2d 33, 38 (1st Dist. 1987) (totality of circumstances including age (16), length of detention, authorities' failure to notify parents or juvenile officers as required by statute, lack of sleep, refusal to allow mother to see defendant, and lack of probable cause to arrest renders confession involuntary).

192. *See* 1 W. LAFAVE & J. ISRAEL, CRIMINAL PROCEDURE § 6.2(c) at 445 (1985) (instructing that courts typically exclude confessions when defendant shows he or she was especially susceptible to coercion).

193. 35 Ill. 2d 202, 220 N.E.2d 222 (1966).

194. 36 Ill. 2d 398, 223 N.E.2d 841 (1967).

detention and interrogation. In *People v. Duncan*,[195] a confession obtained after the defendant had been "in the hole" in the house of corrections for eighteen days was found to be involuntary because the Illinois Supreme Court concluded that the defendant had been denied "the rudimentary necessities of life," which, taken in conjunction with all of the other factors in the case, warranted suppression of the statement.

Other factors such as the time of day of the interrogation, the suspect's ability to sleep, the physical surroundings, the availability of food and drink, the use of the rest room, and the suspect's ability to confer with someone other than the police will all be viewed as relevant to the ultimate determination of whether the confession was voluntary. Thus, the length of the detention and interrogation, the nature of the defendant, and the totality of the circumstances surrounding the interrogation will be viewed together to determine whether the confession was voluntary.[196]

§ 2.19   The Age, Intelligence, Emotional Stability, and Sophistication of the Suspect as Relevant to the Admissibility of the Confession

In *Colorado v. Connelly*,[197] the United States Supreme Court rejected the contention that a confession was involuntary because the suspect suffered from a mental illness that made it impossible for him to exercise his free will. The majority of the Court concluded that the constitutional test for voluntariness relates only to what happens to statements obtained as the result of official misconduct. While the mental status of the defendant may render it worthy of little weight, the Court found that it was nevertheless voluntary in a constitutional sense because it was not obtained as the result of coercive government misconduct.

Connelly certainly brings into question the long line of Illinois cases that have considered the suspect's mental condition and intelligence level a valid consideration when determining the constitutional validity of a confession.

It is frequently asserted that the confession was not voluntary because of the age, mental capacity, or emotional state of the defendant. Although the Illinois courts have frequently looked to the age and intellect of the suspect when determining whether a statement was voluntary, these factors alone have not resulted in the suppression of statements. In *People v. Scott*,[198] the Illinois

---

195. 40 Ill. 2d 105, 238 N.E.2d 595 (1968).

196. *See, e.g.*, People v. Mrozek, 52 Ill. App. 3d 500, 367 N.E.2d 783, 787 (3d Dist. 1977).

197. 479 U.S. 157 (1987).

198. 148 Ill. 2d 479, 594 N.E.2d 217, 229 (1992), *cert. denied*, 507 U.S. 989 (1993).

Supreme Court admitted the confession given by a mentally ill person with an IQ of 75 who had a history of mental illness. In *People v. Hester,*[199] the Illinois Supreme Court admitted the confession given by a fourteen-year-old boy with the intellectual capability of an eleven-year-old (an IQ of 75) given after more than twelve hours of incommunicado custody. The court, in an extended discussion, determined that the totality of the circumstances warranted admission of the statement.[200] In *In re Lamb,*[201] the Illinois Supreme Court admitted a sixteen-year-old boy's statement made after an extended period of detention, finding that "[d]espite his youth, respondent was not a stranger to the criminal justice system."[202] In *People v. Richardson,*[203] the Illinois Supreme Court admitted the statement of a fifteen-year-old, finding no evidence of coercion.

Although the Appellate Court in Illinois has indicated that the admission of a child's confession "is a sensitive concern"[204] and is subject to careful review to determine whether the statements are voluntary,[205] the ultimate question in a juvenile case remains the totality of the circumstances.[206] A suppression hearing judge must carefully scrutinize a juvenile's confession to ensure that it is "voluntary and not coerced, suggested or the product of juvenile's ignorance of rights, his adolescent fantasy, fright or despair."[207] Under the totality of the circumstances, he or she must have confessed "freely, without compulsion or inducement of any sort." In evaluating the confession, the judge must consider the accused's characteristics and the details of the interrogation.[208] Similarly,

---

199. 39 Ill. 2d 489, 237 N.E.2d 466 (1968), *cert. dismissed,* 397 U.S. 660 (1970), *overruled on other grounds* by People v. Anderson, 113 Ill. 2d 1, 495 N.E.2d 485, *cert. denied,* 479 U.S. 1012 (1986).

200. *But see* People v. Robinson, 301 Ill. App. 3d 634, 704 N.E.2d 968, 973–74 (2d Dist. 1998) (juvenile's confession involuntary due to police interference with parents' presence at questioning, lack of juvenile officer, and, most importantly, his age (14), and his mental capacity, mental retardation with a third- or fourth-grade reading level).

201. 61 Ill. 2d 383, 336 N.E.2d 753 (1975), *cert. denied,* 425 U.S. 938 (1976), *overruled on other grounds* by People v. R.D., 155 Ill. 2d 122, 613 N.E.2d 706 (1993).

202. *Lamb,* 61 Ill. 2d 383, 336 N.E.2d at 756.

203. 32 Ill. 2d 472, 207 N.E.2d 478 (1965), *cert. denied,* 384 U.S. 1021 (1966).

204. People v. Prude, 66 Ill. 2d 470, 363 N.E.2d 371, 373, *cert. denied,* 434 U.S. 930 (1977).

205. People v. Avery, 88 Ill. App. 3d 771, 410 N.E.2d 1093, 1097 (1st Dist. 1980).

206. In re N.E.R., 159 Ill. App. 3d 320, 512 N.E.2d 132 (4th Dist. 1987); In re J. S., 121 Ill. App. 3d 927, 460 N.E.2d 412, 416–17 (1st Dist. 1984).

207. People v. R.B., 232 Ill. App. 3d 583, 597 N.E.2d 879, 885 (1st Dist. 1992).

208. *Id.*

the defendant's age, experience with the criminal system, timing of the arrest, presence or absence of parents, familiarity with English, food or lack of food, and the length of detention are also relevant factors.[209] Thus, even though the Illinois cases require that a juvenile's confession be subjected to "special care" before its admission, in the large majority of cases the confessions of juveniles have been admitted, even when combined with evidence of below normal intelligence.[210] In *People v. Stone*,[211] the court overturned the admission of a seventeen-year-old boy's confession to indecent liberties with a child, finding that the age of the suspect, "his somewhat less than average IQ," and his emotional immaturity, combined with the pressure the suspect's juvenile probation officer applied to him indicated that the defendant's will was overborne and that the confession was not voluntary. Indeed, *Stone* might properly be read to stand for the proposition that the encouragement of the probation officer in light of the emotional vulnerability of the defendant, not the age of

---

209. *Id.*, 597 N.E.2d at 885–86. *See also* In re J.O., 231 Ill. App. 3d 853, 596 N.E.2d 1285, 1287 (3d Dist. 1992) (age, timing, and availability to parents proper factors); People v. Holcomb, 192 Ill. App. 3d 158, 548 N.E.2d 613, 623 (1st Dist. 1989) (youth and length of detention proper factors).

210. People v. Hester, 39 Ill. 2d 489, 237 N.E.2d 466 (1968), *cert. dismissed,* 397 U.S. 660 (1970), *overruled on other grounds* by People v. Anderson, 113 Ill. 2d 1, 495 N.E.2d 485, *cert. denied,* 479 U.S. 1012 (1986); People v. Avery, 88 Ill. App. 3d 771, 410 N.E.2d 1093 (1st Dist. 1980). *See also* People v. Jett, 294 Ill. App. 3d 822, 691 N.E.2d 145, 151 (5th Dist. 1998) (special care used to scrutinize record in determining whether juvenile confession voluntary under a totality of circumstances; defendant's confession admissible even though he attended special education classes where he confessed because he did not want to get in trouble, and record, including videotape of confession, demonstrated it was voluntary); In re W.C., 167 Ill. 2d 307, 657 N.E.2d 908, 923 (1995) (trial judge *must* take into account mental capacity of defendant age 13; defendant's waiver valid even though moderately mentally retarded and may possibly not have had ability to understand words and terms contained in *Miranda* warnings, where defendant's mom stopped questioner and asked for explanation after which defendant did not indicate he did not understand; in addition, assistant state's attorney gave simplified explanation); People v. Nilsson, 230 Ill. App. 3d 1051, 595 N.E.2d 1304, 1309 (1st Dist. 1992) (defendant's waiver of *Miranda* rights was held valid despite fact he had a learning disability and warnings were given by sign language); In re J.S., 121 Ill. App. 3d 927, 460 N.E.2d 412, 418 (1st Dist. 1984) (defendant's waiver valid even though Hispanic, 14, and he claimed not to comprehend the English language where he conversed during questioning in English). *But see* In re T.S., 151 Ill. App. 3d 344, 502 N.E.2d 761 (4th Dist. 1986) (15-year-old who attended alternative school did not voluntarily confess after police falsely told him that there was evidence linking him to crime and that he would be free to go if he confessed).

211. 61 Ill. App. 3d 654, 378 N.E.2d 263 (5th Dist. 1978).

the suspect, was the primary factor leading to suppression of the statement. Similarly, in *People v. Berry,*[212] the court suppressed a confession given by a seventeen-year-old of subnormal intelligence when the police conduct "border[ed] on deception." In *People v. Johnson,*[213] a seventeen-year-old's confession was found involuntary where he had been in special education classes and was questioned in a small, windowless office outside the presence of his grandmother and without benefit of *Miranda* warnings.

"[E]vidence of limited intellectual capacity does not, itself, indicate a defendant is incapable of waiving his constitutional rights and making a confession. That is but one issue to be considered in the totality of the circumstances under which the confession was made."[214] Applying this test the Illinois courts have upheld the admission of confessions given by persons of below normal intelligence.[215] In *People v. Turner,*[216] however, the Illinois Supreme Court reversed the conviction of a retarded adult, finding that he had invoked his right to counsel under *Miranda.* Although it noted that the mental capacity of the suspect is one of the factors to be considered in passing on the

---

212. 123 Ill. App. 3d 1042, 463 N.E.2d 1044, 1048 (4th Dist. 1984).

213. 221 Ill. App. 3d 588, 584 N.E.2d 165, 170 (3d Dist. 1991). *See also* In re L.L., 295 Ill. App. 3d 594, 693 N.E.2d 908, 915 (2d Dist. 1998) (confession of a 13-year-old who attended special education classes, had limited mental abilities, was taken from his home in the middle of the night, was deprived of sleep, interrogated for three hours during middle of night without presence of parents, was involuntary where police were evasive in their conduct and frustrated parents' attempts to confer with son).

214. People v. Murphy, 72 Ill. 2d 421, 381 N.E.2d 677, 686 (1978).

215. People v. Mallett, 45 Ill. 2d 388, 259 N.E.2d 241 (1970); People v. Hester, 39 Ill. 2d 489, 237 N.E.2d 466 (1968); People v. Gore, 116 Ill. App. 3d 780, 452 N.E.2d 583 (3d Dist. 1983); People v. Avery, 88 Ill. App. 3d 771, 410 N.E.2d 1093 (1st Dist. 1980). *See also* People v. Phillips, 226 Ill. App. 3d 878, 589 N.E.2d 1107, 1111 and 1114 (2d Dist. 1992) (defendant's statement admissible even though he was 18 with a mental age of nine and had an IQ of between 65–70, particularly where he had prior experience with the justice system); People v. Nergon, 220 Ill. App. 3d 754, 580 N.E.2d 1301, 1310 (1st Dist. 1991) (defendant's statement admissible even though he was of low intelligence, educably mentally handicapped, and had poor oral and written comprehension); People v. Long, 217 Ill. App. 3d 940, 578 N.E.2d 26, 33 (1st Dist. 1991) (defendant's statement admissible even though he was mildly mentally retarded, had an IQ of 67 and no prior experience, in light of fact he lived with his wife and three children with no other adult supervision); People v. Kokoraleis, 149 Ill. App. 3d 1000, 501 N.E.2d 207, 215 (2d Dist. 1986) (defendant's statement admissible even though he had an IQ of 75, was borderline mentally retarded, was of low intelligence, and had poor verbal skills), *cert. denied,* 498 U.S. 944 (1990).

216. 56 Ill. 2d 201, 306 N.E.2d 27 (1973).

voluntary nature of the confession, the Illinois Supreme Court did not resolve the issue on the basis of voluntariness but on the *Miranda* question. In *People v. Redmon*,[217] the appellate court suppressed a statement given by a seventeen-year-old boy of limited mental capacity who was "obviously confused" regarding his rights.

Similarly, the argument that a defendant who is emotionally upset cannot voluntarily confess has been rejected in favor of reviewing all of the circumstances surrounding the confession.[218] Likewise, alcohol and its effects on an individual may be a relevant factor in assessing the voluntariness of a confession.[219]

One factor the courts have considered supportive of the admission of a confession, particularly a statement by a young suspect or a person of borderline mentality, is that person's experience with the criminal justice system. In several cases the Illinois courts have viewed the defendant's prior experience with the police as indicative of the voluntariness of the confession and waiver of constitutional rights.[220]

Finally, Illinois courts have looked to the availability of an interested adult for the juvenile before a confession was made. If the trial judge finds that the state did not take appropriate steps in ensuring a conference with the adult, the judge will often suppress the confession.[221] In *People v. R.B.*,[222] the Illinois Appellate Court held that the trial judge should have granted defendant's

---

217. 127 Ill. App. 3d 342, 468 N.E.2d 1310 (1st Dist. 1984).

218. People v. Merkel, 23 Ill. App. 3d 298, 319 N.E.2d 77, 81 (2d Dist. 1974).

219. People v. Foster, 168 Ill. 2d 465, 660 N.E.2d 951 (1995), *cert. denied,* 519 U.S. 831 (1996). However, in *Foster*, the court found that defendant's alcohol use and its alleged ability to cause blackouts, memory loss, and loss of consciousness due to his diabetic condition did not render defendant's confession involuntary. *Id.,* 660 N.E.2d at 957. The facts showed that 8½ hours passed from the time defendant was taken into custody until the time he confessed. Three police officers testified he did not appear intoxicated, they did not believe he was under the influence of alcohol or drugs, and he was not visibly suffering from any physical problems. In addition, the assistant state's attorney testified he saw no physical problems and defendant spoke coherently and answered questions in a logical fashion. *Id.*

220. In re Lamb, 61 Ill. 2d 383, 336 N.E.2d 753 (1975), *cert. denied,* 425 U.S. 938 (1976), *overruled on other grounds* by People v. R.D., 155 Ill. 2d 122, 613 N.E.2d 706 (1993); People v. Nemke, 46 Ill. 2d 49, 263 N.E.2d 97 (1970), *cert. denied,* 402 U.S. 924 (1971); People v. Hill, 39 Ill. 2d 125, 233 N.E.2d 367, 372, *cert. denied,* 392 U.S. 936 (1968); People v. Clemens, 9 Ill. App. 3d 312, 292 N.E.2d 232, 235 (1st Dist. 1972).

221. People v. Knox, 186 Ill. App. 3d 808, 542 N.E.2d 910, 913 (1st Dist. 1989).

222. 232 Ill. App. 3d 583, 597 N.E.2d 879 (1st Dist. 1992).

motion to suppress his confession where the totality of the circumstances surrounding the custodial interrogation demonstrated that the confession was coerced and involuntary. The court found that the interrogating police officers failed to ensure that defendant conferred with an adult interested in his welfare prior to the time he made an incriminating statement. Likewise, the police repeatedly questioned the defendant, isolated him from his family and friends, and withheld food for more than fifteen hours.[223]

The Seventh Circuit, addressing the opposite of youth, held that no special standard is mandated for advanced age in determining whether a confession is voluntarily given.[224]

§ 2.20 Background and Decision in *Miranda v. Arizona*

Miranda has its roots in an Illinois case, *Escobedo v. Illinois*.[225] In *Escobedo*, the United States Supreme Court declared that a confession obtained from a

---

223. *Id.,* 597 N.E.2d at 886–87. *See also* In re L.L., 295 Ill. App. 3d 594, 693 N.E.2d 908, 915 (2d Dist. 1998) (confession of a 13-year-old who attended special education classes, had limited mental abilities, was taken from his home in the middle of the night, was deprived of sleep, interrogated for three hours during middle of night without presence of parents, was involuntary where police were evasive in their conduct and frustrated parents' attempts to confer with son); People v. Montanez, 273 Ill. App. 3d 844, 652 N.E.2d 1271, 1278 (1st Dist. 1995) (15-year-old defendant's confession involuntary where interrogated without being afforded opportunity to confer with concerned adult and interrogated throughout the night as part of police conduct designed to elicit confession and obstruct parental counselling), *cert. denied,* 517 U.S. 1251 (1996). *But see* People v. McNeal, 298 Ill. App. 3d 379, 698 N.E.2d 652, 661–62 (1st Dist. 1998) (statements of two juveniles admissible despite lack of parental or adult consultation because defendants were streetwise, had prior experience with the legal system, and stated they understood their constitutional rights); People v. Fuller, 292 Ill. App. 3d 651, 686 N.E.2d 6, 18 (1st Dist. 1997) (murder confession of emotionally disturbed 14-year-old, given without presence of interested adult, inadmissible; however, confession given later in presence of juvenile officer while parents were in next room voluntary and admissible); People v. Rhonda F., 289 Ill. App. 3d 148, 682 N.E.2d 225, 230–31 (1st Dist. 1997) (15-year-old's murder confession voluntary where brought in for questioning as a witness, not under arrest, during middle of the day, questioned for only 30 to 45 minutes, police attempted to contact youth officer, girl did not want to see father, was not allowed to see grandmother whom police believed would injure her and was not person legally responsible for her care, and confession was about the death of her mother; as soon as defendant made statements inconsistent with other evidence, police gave *Miranda* warnings and sought a youth officer).

224. United States v. Sablotny, 21 F.3d 747, 751 (7th Cir. 1994).

225. 378 U.S. 478 (1964), *overruled by* Miranda v. Arizona, 384 U.S. 436 (1966).

defendant who had repeatedly requested counsel, while the attorney was in the police station requesting to see his client, was obtained in violation of the Sixth Amendment right to counsel. The Court's decision turned on the conclusion that the process had shifted from the investigatory stage to the accusatory stage, that the defendant was in custody while he was interrogated, and that he had invoked his right to counsel. The Illinois Supreme Court had determined the confession voluntary under the totality of the circumstances test and that there was no right to counsel at the interrogation, even though both the suspect and the attorney had made such a request.[226] *Escobedo* is important because the United States Supreme Court departed from the traditional analysis of reviewing all of the circumstances surrounding the confession to determine whether it was lawful. Here the confession was neither beaten out of the defendant, nor coerced, nor the product of deception, and it would have been admissible except for the denial of requested counsel.

Escobedo, as *Miranda* after it, created tremendous controversy. The facts of the case were extreme, involving a defendant who had demanded an attorney and an attorney who had demanded access to his client. These facts would distinguish *Escobedo* from virtually all other cases.[227] Indeed, in *People v. Hartgraves,*[228] the Illinois Supreme Court affirmatively found that *Escobedo* did not require any affirmative action on the part of police to caution defendants about their constitutional rights and applied only in the rare case in which the defendant had requested counsel.

Miranda v. Arizona clarified the Supreme Court's intent in *Escobedo* and found specifically that the right to counsel is incident to the Fifth Amendment, while *Escobedo* was based on the Sixth Amendment's right to counsel. In *Miranda,* the Court reviewed cases from Arizona, New York, and California and a federal prosecution from Kansas City. In each case the defendant, while in custody, had given an incriminating statement without first being informed of the constitutional right to remain silent and right to the assistance of counsel. Chief Justice Warren, speaking for the five-justice majority, outlined the nature of police interrogation generally and concluded that although the statements in the cases before the Court might "not have been involuntary in traditional terms . . . in none of [the] cases did the officers undertake to afford appropriate

---

226. People v. Escobedo, 28 Ill. 2d 41, 190 N.E.2d 825 (1963).

227. Nevertheless, *Escobedo* still remains viable after *Miranda.* Thus, in 1982 the Illinois Supreme Court found that if the police deny an attorney access to a client, there can be no valid waiver by the defendant if the suspect has not been informed that the attorney was present and seeking to consult with him or her. People v. Smith, 93 Ill. 2d 179, 442 N.E.2d 1325, 1329 (1982), *cert. denied,* 461 U.S. 937 (1983).

228. 31 Ill. 2d 375, 202 N.E.2d 33, 36 (1964), *cert. denied,* 380 U.S. 961 (1965).

safeguards at the outset of the interrogation to insure that the statements were truly the product of free choice."[229]

To overcome the inherently coercive nature of police interrogation, the Supreme Court in *Miranda* specified that before any statement obtained from a suspect who was in custody could be admitted, the police first had to inform the suspect of the right to remain silent and the right to counsel and obtain a valid waiver of those rights. The waiver could not be assumed from silence and the prosecution had the "heavy burden" of proving the waiver.[230] The chief justice summarized the Court's conclusion:

> [W]hen an individual is taken into custody or otherwise deprived of his freedom by the authorities in any significant way and is subjected to questioning, the privilege against self-incrimination is jeopardized. Procedural safeguards must be employed to protect the privilege, and unless other fully effective means are adopted to notify the person of his right of silence and to assure that the exercise of the right will be scrupulously honored, the following measures are required. He must be warned prior to any questioning that he has the right to remain silent, that anything he says can be used against him in a court of law, that he has the right to the presence of an attorney, and that if he cannot afford an attorney one will be appointed for him prior to any questioning if he so desires. Opportunity to exercise these rights must be afforded him throughout the interrogation. After such warnings have been given, and such opportunity afforded him, the individual may knowingly and intelligently waive these rights and agree to answer questions or make a statement. But unless and until such warnings and waiver are demonstrated by the prosecution at trial, no evidence obtained as a result of interrogation can be used against him.[231]

Miranda has probably engendered more controversy and litigation, emphasizing every aspect of the decision, than any other case decided by the United States Supreme Court. It is important to note that as the years have passed and the Burger Supreme Court has become firmly established, the Supreme Court has come to view *Miranda* primarily as a prophylactic vehicle for controlling police misconduct and not a means of protecting the Fifth and Sixth Amendment rights of arrestees. As such, the Court, although reaffirming the basic validity of the decision, has refused to expand *Miranda,* and in some instances

---

229. Miranda v. Arizona, 384 U.S. 436, 457 (1966).

230. *Id.* at 475.

231. *Id.* at 479–80.

it has clearly restricted its application.[232] The following outlines the primary contexts in which *Miranda* questions arise.

§ 2.21 Proceedings in Which *Miranda* Applies

In *Berkemer v. McCarty*,[233] the United States Supreme Court clarified the types of criminal proceedings in which *Miranda* applies. A unanimous Court determined that "a person subjected to custodial interrogation is entitled to the benefit of the procedural safeguards enunciated in *Miranda* regardless of the severity of the offense of which he is suspected or for which he was arrested."[234] The Court went on, however, and excluded routine roadside traffic stops from the *Miranda* requirements, finding the interrogation incident to a traffic stop "quite different from stationhouse interrogation" because the motorist is not "at the mercy of the police."[235]

In addition to criminal proceedings,[236] *Miranda* applies to juvenile proceedings where the charge of delinquency is based on the commission of a criminal offense and the proceedings may result in the minor's loss of freedom.[237]

There are several types of proceedings in which *Miranda* does not apply. First, a grand jury witness need not be given *Miranda* warnings before testifying, and the testimony may still be used against the witness in subsequent criminal proceedings.[238] In a probation or parole revocation proceeding in which a confession has been obtained in violation of *Miranda*, the statement will be admitted if voluntary under the totality of circumstances.[239]

---

232. New York v. Quarles, 467 U.S. 649 (1984) (creation of a public safety exception to *Miranda* requirement); Minnesota v. Murphy, 465 U.S. 420 (1984) (refusal to extend *Miranda* requirements to interviews with probation officers); Fare v. Michael C., 442 U.S. 707 (1979) (refusal to equate request to see probation officer with request to see lawyer for *Miranda* purposes); Beckwith v. United States, 425 U.S. 341 (1976) (refusal to extend *Miranda* to noncustodial questioning).

233. 468 U.S. 420 (1984).

234. *Id.* at 434.

235. *Id.* at 438. *Accord* People v. Nunes, 143 Ill. App. 3d 1072, 494 N.E.2d 202 (2d Dist. 1986).

236. *Miranda* applies only to cases in which the original trial began after the date of the decision, which was June 13, 1966. Johnson v. New Jersey, 384 U.S. 719 (1966); People v. Cook, 78 Ill. App. 2d 219, 222 N.E.2d 13, 14–15 (1st Dist. 1966).

237. In re McMillan, 51 Ill. App. 3d 940, 367 N.E.2d 494, 496 (1977), *vacated*, 74 Ill. 2d 478, 384 N.E.2d 348 (1978); People v. Horton, 126 Ill. App. 2d 401, 261 N.E.2d 693 (1st Dist. 1970).

238. United States v. Mandujano, 425 U.S. 564 (1976).

239. People v. Peterson, 74 Ill. 2d 478, 384 N.E.2d 348, 351 (1978).

The warnings are not required before the admission of a statement in a prison disciplinary hearing.[240]

Finally, the United States Supreme Court has stated in explicit dicta that *Miranda* does not apply to "civil" deportation hearings.[241] This is consistent with the great weight of authority holding that *Miranda* does not apply to civil proceedings for mental health commitment,[242] license revocation, or employment termination.[243]

In Illinois, a school dean is not required to give *Miranda* warnings before interviewing a student.[244]

§ 2.22   Custody Requirement of *Miranda*

Miranda applies only to confessions obtained while the defendant is in custody or is otherwise deprived of freedom in some significant way.[245] Thus, if a suspect is free to leave the scene of the interrogation, he or she is not in custody for *Miranda* purposes.[246] Moreover, *Miranda* does not apply even if the criminal investigation has advanced to the accusatory stage and has focused on the person interrogated, as long as the questioning remains noncustodial.[247]

Miranda was not intended to cover the "[g]eneral on-the-scene questioning as to facts surrounding a crime or other general questioning of citizens in the

---

240. Baxter v. Palmigiano, 425 U.S. 308 (1976).

241. Immigration & Naturalization Serv. v. Lopez-Mendoza, 468 U.S. 1032 (1984).

242. In re Ottolini, 73 Ill. App. 3d 971, 392 N.E.2d 736 (5th Dist. 1979); Massachusetts v. Gomes, 355 Mass. 479, 245 N.E.2d 429 (1969). In Illinois, proceedings under the Sexually Dangerous Persons Act, although technically civil in nature, still require that the defendant be given *Miranda* warnings if in custody. People v. Pettit, 97 Ill. App. 3d 692, 423 N.E.2d 513, 518 (2d Dist. 1981). *Contra* People v. Potter, 85 Ill. App. 2d 151, 228 N.E.2d 238 (4th Dist. 1967). Neither the Fifth nor the Fourteenth Amendment protects a person in a court-ordered psychiatric examination under the Sexually Dangerous Persons Act. Allen v. Illinois, 478 U.S. 364 (1986).

243. Distaola v. Department of Registration & Educ., 72 Ill. App. 3d 977, 391 N.E.2d 489 (1st Dist. 1979) (barber license); Douglas v. Daniels, 64 Ill. App. 3d 1022, 382 N.E.2d 90 (1st Dist. 1978) (discharge as police officer); Church v. Powell, 40 N.C. App. 254, 252 S.E.2d 229 (1979) (driver's license revocations); Brewer v. Department of Motor Vehicles, 23 Wash. App. 412, 595 P.2d 949 (1979).

244. People v. E.M., 262 Ill. App. 3d 302, 634 N.E.2d 395, 400 (2d Dist. 1994).

245. Miranda v. Arizona, 384 U.S. 436, 444 (1966).

246. Oregon v. Mathiason, 429 U.S. 492, 495 (1977).

247. Beckwith v. United States, 425 U.S. 341 (1976).

fact-finding process."[248] In *Stansbury v. California*,[249] the United States Supreme Court delineated the rule for determining when a person is "in custody" and therefore entitled to *Miranda* warnings. The Court reaffirmed that "a police officer's subjective view that the individual under questioning is a suspect, if undisclosed, does not bear upon the question whether the individual is in custody for purposes of *Miranda*."[250] It found that the same principle applies even when the interrogator does not believe that the individual being questioned is not a suspect. The Court pointed out:

> Save as they are communicated or otherwise manifested to the person being questioned, an officer's evolving but unarticulated suspicions do not affect the objective circumstances of an interrogation or interview, and thus cannot affect the *Miranda* custody inquiry.[251]

An officer's beliefs or thoughts may only bear upon the custody issue if they are conveyed in some manner to the person being questioned, and then they are only relevant to the extent that they would affect how a reasonable person would assess those beliefs or thoughts under all the circumstances.[252]

In Illinois a determination of whether the defendant was in custody will turn on a two-pronged analysis depending on both the intent of the officer and the understanding of the arrestee. The understanding of the suspect will not be based on the subjective thought of the individual arrestee, but on "what a reasonable man, innocent of any crime, would have thought had he been in the defendant's shoes."[253] This is an objective test of whether a reasonable person would believe that under the circumstances he or she was free to leave the scene

---

248. *Miranda*, 384 U.S. at 477; People v. Hoffman, 84 Ill. 2d 480, 419 N.E.2d 1145, 1148 (1981); People v. Parks, 48 Ill. 2d 232, 269 N.E.2d 484 (1971), *cert. denied*, 404 U.S. 1020 (1972); People v. Maiden, 210 Ill. App. 3d 390, 569 N.E.2d 120, 123 (1st Dist. 1991); People v. Clark, 84 Ill. App. 3d 637, 405 N.E.2d 1192, 1194 (1st Dist. 1980).

249. 511 U.S. 318 (1994).

250. *Id.* at 324.

251. *Id.*

252. *Id.* at 325.

253. People v. Wipfler, 68 Ill. 2d 158, 368 N.E.2d 870, 873 (1977). Thus in *In re N.E.R.*, 159 Ill. App. 3d 320, 512 N.E.2d 132 (4th Dist. 1987), the court found that a 15-year-old suspect was "in custody" when he was interviewed by police in a closed (perhaps locked) police car under circumstances in which it was not clear whether he could leave and when the investigation had already focused on him.

of the interrogation or whether he or she had been deprived of freedom in some significant way.[254]

The question of whether a suspect is "in custody" depends on a review of the totality of the circumstances, including: the location, length, mood, and mode of interrogation; the number of police officers present; any indicia of formal restraint or arrest; the intention of the officers; and the extent of the knowledge of the officers.[255] The judge must determine whether, under all of these circumstances, a reasonable person would believe that he or she was in custody.[256] An assertion at the end of an interview that interviewee was "free to leave" may imply that the interviewee was not free to leave up to that time.[257]

In making this objective determination, Illinois courts have considered several factors, including: (1) "location, length, mood and mode of the interrogation"; (2) "the number of police officers present"; (3) "any evidence of restraint"; and (4) "the intentions of the officers and focus of their investigation."[258] Under this objective test, the defendant may be found to be in custody

---

254. People v. Clark, 225 Ill. App. 3d 636, 587 N.E.2d 1050 (3d Dist. 1992); People v. Anderson, 84 Ill. App. 3d 637, 405 N.E.2d 1192, 1194 (1st Dist. 1980).

255. People v. Brown, 136 Ill. 2d 116, 554 N.E.2d 216, 220 (1990).

256. *Id.*

257. *Id.,* 554 N.E.2d at 221.

258. People v. Patterson, 146 Ill. 2d 445, 588 N.E.2d 1175, 1180, *cert. denied,* 506 U.S. 838 (1992). *See* People v. Fair, 159 Ill. 2d 51, 636 N.E.2d 455, 465 (defendant not in custody and *Miranda* warnings not required where defendant voluntarily entered police station, search conducted was precautionary measure, defendant was not handcuffed or fingerprinted, defendant was never told under arrest, freedom of movement was not restrained by either a show of authority or physical force, defendant was never told he could not leave, and he never asked to leave), *cert. denied,* 513 U.S. 1020 (1994); People v. Williams, 272 Ill. App. 3d 868, 651 N.E.2d 532, 539 (1st Dist. 1995) (where defendant voluntarily accompanied police to station not under arrest); People v. Holmes, 255 Ill. App. 3d 271, 626 N.E.2d 412, 413 (5th Dist. 1994) (defendant not in custody for purposes of *Miranda* where voluntarily went to sheriff's office; officers did not tell him he was under arrest, nor did they induce him against his will to accompany them; defendant was not handcuffed or otherwise restrained; was only questioned on two occasions for 45 minutes, and there was no indication that formal arrest procedures were forthcoming; defendant was allowed to move about freely, given food and drink, and allowed to speak with girlfriend), *overruled in part by* People v. Goyer, 265 Ill. App. 3d 160, 638 N.E.2d 390 (4th Dist. 1994). *But see* People v. Wheeler, 281 Ill. App. 3d 447, 667 N.E.2d 158, 164–65 (2d Dist. 1996) (defendant was in custody as of 5:30 p.m. because a reasonable person in defendant's position would perceive that questioning was custodial considering all factors: defendant was questioned in a small, windowless room located in a secured section of a hospital from 6:00 a.m. to noon; while at the hospital,

for *Miranda* purposes even when the officers assert he or she is free to leave, if the nonverbal conduct indicates the contrary is true.[259] Conversely, the fact that a suspect is given *Miranda* warnings does not necessarily mean the person is "in custody."[260] Several courts have also suggested that the absence of probable cause for arrest is evidence that the suspect was not in custody.[261]

In a recent Fourth District case, the Illinois Appellate Court stated that before the state assumes its burden of proving that a reasonable person would believe he or she was in custody, the defendant must, as a threshold matter, introduce some evidence that he or she subjectively believed he or she was in custody.[262] Absent some affirmative evidence of defendant's subjective belief, the "trial court need not consider what a reasonable person in the same position would have believed and can simply deny the motion to suppress."[263] The court concluded that requiring the defendant to go forward on the issue would not interfere with the right against self-incrimination because the state is not allowed to use defendant's testimony from pre-trial hearing substantively at his or her subsequent trial.[264]

Although the location of the interrogation is often a major factor in determining whether a defendant is in custody, it is not controlling. In both *Oregon*

---

defendant could not visit her aunt and uncle; defendant was driven to the police station by a detective; defendant was questioned again from 1:00 p.m. to 6:15 p.m. at the police station; the questioning became adversarial at 5:30 p.m. when defendant was confronted with evidence and the results of an earlier polygraph test as well as the fact that a pathologist felt she was not telling the truth; and by this time, defendant had not slept for 34 hours and was informed by the police that she was the focus of the investigation).

259. People v. Berry, 123 Ill. App. 3d 1042, 463 N.E.2d 1044, 1048 (4th Dist. 1984); People v. Hentz, 75 Ill. App. 3d 526, 394 N.E.2d 586 (1st Dist. 1979). *See* In re C.A.G., 259 Ill. App. 3d 595, 631 N.E.2d 473, 475 (3d Dist. 1994) (*Miranda* warnings required where 15-year-old taken from school in unmarked police car and given polygraph by state police even though told he could leave; reasonable person would believe in custody based on circumstances of polygraph examination, age, and statement to defendant by police that he was going to be arrested anyway so he might as well confess), *overruled in part by* People v. Goyer, 265 Ill. App. 3d 160, 638 N.E.2d (4th Dist. 1994).

260. People v. Lucas, 132 Ill. 2d 399, 548 N.E.2d 1003 (1989).

261. Washington v. Hilliard, 89 Wash. 2d. 430, 573 P.2d 22 (1977) (en banc); United States v. Warren, 578 F.2d 1058 (5th Cir. 1978) (en banc), *cert. denied,* 446 U.S. 956 (1980); Louisiana v. Johnson, 393 So. 2d 1255 (La. 1981).

262. People v. Goyer, 265 Ill. App. 3d 160, 638 N.E.2d 390, 393 (4th Dist. 1994).

263 *Id.*

264. *Id.*, 638 N.E.2d at 394.

v. Mathiason[265] and *California v. Beheler,*[266] the United States Supreme Court ruled that *Miranda* did not apply to police station questioning in which the suspect was free to leave, and in *People v. Burris,*[267] the Supreme Court of Illinois held that when a suspect voluntarily accompanied the police to the station house for interrogation, he was not in their custody for *Miranda* purposes. However, the application of *Miranda* is not limited to station house questioning.[268] It has often been held that an interrogation in the arrestee's own home can fall within the purview of *Miranda*.[269] However, in other cases the questioning of a suspect at home has been found to be noncustodial for *Miranda* purposes because the circumstances indicated the suspect was not restrained.[270]

Questioning that occurs at more neutral, third-party locations, such as places of employment, stores, or hospitals, have generally been considered noncustodial unless the suspect was under arrest or otherwise under the control of law enforcement authorities.[271] Thus, Illinois courts have determined that prison inmates are in custody, within the meaning of the Fifth Amendment, and therefore they are entitled to *Miranda* warnings before being questioned.[272]

---

265. 429 U.S. 492 (1977).

266. 463 U.S. 1121 (1983).

267. 49 Ill. 2d 98, 273 N.E.2d 605, 608–09 (1971).

268. New York v. Quarles, 467 U.S. 649, 654 n.4 (1984). *See also* United States v. Murray, 89 F.3d 459, 461–62 (7th Cir. 1996) (defendant not in custody for *Miranda* purposes where defendant, while seated in the back of a squad car following a traffic violation stop, was questioned about a gun that had been found in defendant's vehicle, as there was no evidence that defendant's freedom was in some significant way deprived). *But see* In re N.E.R., 159 Ill. App. 3d 320, 512 N.E.2d 132 (4th Dist. 1987) (court applied *Miranda* to interrogation that took place in closed police car).

269. Orozco v. Texas, 394 U.S. 324 (1969) (defendant's bedroom); People v. Hoffman, 81 Ill. App. 3d 304, 401 N.E.2d 323 (4th Dist. 1980) (defendant's trailer), *vacated on other grounds,* 84 Ill. 2d 480, 419 N.E.2d 1145 (1981); People v. Hentz, 75 Ill. App. 3d 526, 394 N.E.2d 586 (1st Dist. 1979) (defendant's home).

270. People v. Johnson, 96 Ill. App. 3d 763, 422 N.E.2d 50 (1st Dist. 1981).

271. People v. Reeder, 2 Ill. App. 3d 471, 276 N.E.2d 768, 770–71 (2d Dist. 1971) (hospital). *See generally* 2 RINGEL, SEARCHES & SEIZURES, ARRESTS & CONFESSIONS 27—15 and 27—16 (release no. 6, June 1984). *See* People v. Anderson, 225 Ill. App. 3d 636, 587 N.E.2d 1050 (3d Dist. 1992) (search in clothing store).

272. People v. Easley, 148 Ill. 2d 281, 592 N.E.2d 1036, 1042 (1992), *cert. denied,* 506 U.S. 1082 (1993). *But see* People v. Patterson, 146 Ill. 2d 445, 588 N.E.2d 1175, 1181 (*Miranda* warnings not necessary under peculiar circumstances of the case because purpose of interrogation was to safeguard defendant from other inmates, environment was not coercive, and there was no pressure on defendant), *cert. denied,* 506 U.S. 838 (1992).

The custody requirement obviously leads to the conclusion that a confession given to a private individual need not be preceded by *Miranda* warnings.[273] Moreover, a parole or probation officer need not admonish a client who is not in custody, even if the client is legally compelled to appear before the probation officer and discuss matters affecting his or her supervision.[274] *Murphy* is a clear indication that the present United States Supreme Court has retreated from the notion that a coercive atmosphere triggers a finding of custody to a more mechanical definition of the concept based on the defendant's freedom to terminate the interrogation and leave the premises.

When the suspect does not know that the person to whom he is speaking is a police officer, *Miranda* does not apply, even if a custodial interrogation takes place. Thus, in *Illinois v. Perkins,*[275] where a police officer posed as a jail inmate, the agent was not required to give *Miranda* warnings to a jailed suspect before asking questions regarding an uncharged crime.[276] Such a situation lacked the inherent coercion which underlies *Miranda* and was not a police dominated atmosphere.[277] No Sixth Amendment right to counsel was implicated because the suspect had not yet been charged with the offense.[278]

In another decision clearly expanding the exceptions to the *Miranda* rule, the United States Supreme Court said that no *Miranda* admonitions were

---

273. People v. Hawkins, 53 Ill. 2d 181, 290 N.E.2d 231, 233 (1972); 2 RINGEL, SEARCHES & SEIZURES, ARRESTS & CONFESSIONS 26—17 and 26—18 (release no. 6, June 1984). However, a statement given to private individuals might still be subject to suppression if involuntary. People v. Cooper, 96 Ill. App. 3d 607, 421 N.E.2d 934 (5th Dist. 1981). *See also* People v. Lucas, 132 Ill. 2d 399, 548 N.E.2d 1003 (1989) (family members are not acting as agents for police when they urge suspect to confess, unless police officers have incited or coached family members to prompt confession); People v. Dove, 147 Ill. App. 3d 659, 498 N.E.2d 279 (4th Dist. 1986) (statement given to private individual might still require warnings if individual was acting as police informant, but warnings would not be required if former informant obtained statements from defendant on his own).

274. Minnesota v. Murphy, 465 U.S. 420 (1984); People v. Pettit, 97 Ill. App. 3d 692, 423 N.E.2d 513, 518 (2d Dist. 1981).

275. 496 U.S. 292 (1990).

276. *Id.* at 300. *Accord* People v. Latona, 218 Ill. App. 3d 1093, 579 N.E.2d 394, 397 (2d Dist. 1991) (defendant's visit with undercover officer in large open visitation area and questions regarding whether defendant wanted to hire officer to kill defendant's daughter's boyfriend admissible). *But see* People v. Easley, 148 Ill. 2d 281, 592 N.E.2d 1036, 1052 (1992) (statement elicited by police agent pretending to gather information for defendant's attorney obtained in violation of the due process clause of the Fourteenth Amendment), *cert. denied,* 506 U.S. 1082 (1993).

277. *Perkins,* 496 U.S. at 297.

278. *Id.* at 300.

required when public safety required obtaining information. In *New York v. Quarles*,[279] the Court emphasized the need to balance the prophylactic nature of the *Miranda* requirements against the need for public safety. Thus, when the officer asked a suspect who had just been arrested "where the gun was," the majority of the Supreme Court found that the need to protect the officers obviated the need to give immediate *Miranda* warnings, even though the suspect was in handcuffs, was surrounded by at least four officers, and had been found to be unarmed. Although this appears to be a new, major exception to *Miranda*, it is too early to determine its impact.[280] Without question, however, this decision demonstrates the current emphasis given the *Miranda* decision by the United States Supreme Court—that is, the case is viewed primarily, if not exclusively, as a prophylactic vehicle to curtail police misconduct and not as a rule designed to protect a suspect's Fifth Amendment rights.

§ 2.23 Interrogation Requirement of *Miranda*

The second requirement of *Miranda* is that the confession must come as the result of an interrogation as opposed to a volunteered statement by the suspect.[281] Additionally, *Miranda* applies only to "testimonial" evidence obtained from the suspect.[282] The leading case on the meaning of interrogation for *Miranda* purposes is *Rhode Island v. Innis*.[283] In that case the Court declared that *Miranda* applies to "either express questioning or its functional equivalent . . . any words or actions on the part of the police (other than those normally attendant to arrest and custody) that the police should know are reasonably likely to elicit an incriminating response . . . ."[284] In *Innis*, the issue was whether a statement made by the defendant as a result of a conversation between two officers in the suspect's presence was the result of an interrogation. The

---

279. 467 U.S. 649 (1984).

280. In *People v. Williams*, 173 Ill. 2d 48, 670 N.E.2d 638 (1996), *cert. denied*, 520 U.S. 1122 (1997), the court held that the defendant's statement and gun were admissible in a murder case pursuant to the public safety exception to *Miranda* where the arresting officer asked the defendant if he had any weapons on his person and the defendant told the arresting officer, while in custody but before the officer read him his *Miranda* rights, that he was keeping a loaded gun in the attic of a house occupied by two families. *Id.*, 670 N.E.2d at 652–53.

281. Miranda v. Arizona, 384 U.S. 436, 478 (1966).

282. Pennsylvania v. Muniz, 496 U.S. 582 (1990) (no warnings required to observe defendant's slurred speech or lack of muscular coordination; videotapes of drunk driving defendant showing such conditions could be admitted without *Miranda* warnings being given).

283. 446 U.S. 291 (1980).

284. *Id.* at 301.

Supreme Court first decided that the statement was not the result of a direct interrogation and second that "it cannot be said . . . that [the officers] should have known that their conversation was reasonably likely to elicit an incriminating response from the [suspect]."[285] Summarizing, Justice Stewart stated that "the case thus boils down to whether . . . the officers should have known that the respondent would suddenly be moved to make a self-incriminating response."[286] It is important to note that in *Innis* the Court drew a fine distinction between what constitutes an interrogation for *Miranda* purposes under the Fifth and Fourteenth Amendments to the Constitution and what constitutes an interrogation for Sixth Amendment purposes as raised in *Brewer v. Williams.*[287] Justice Stewart makes clear in *Innis* that the definitions are not interchangeable.[288]

The *Innis* test requires a court to look at the facts and determine whether it was the officer's intention to elicit a statement and whether a defendant would reasonably have believed he or she was being subjected to an interrogation. Thus the admission "I'm drunk, I'll admit it" made by a person charged with driving while intoxicated during the officer's explanation of the breath analysis procedure was not the product of an interrogation.[289] Nor was a statement made by a defendant after being confronted, at his own request, by the victim of an assault.[290] As in *Innis,* the Illinois Appellate Court found a statement made by an arrestee in response to a conversation between two officers who did not address any question to him was not the product of an interrogation.[291] A statement given by a suspect after the police had asked him to give a statement without his attorney present, arranged for the defendant to meet with his wife, and attempted to involve the suspect's priest in the process, was still not considered an interrogation because no question was actually put to the defendant, nor were the circumstances such that the officers could have reasonably expected the defendant to have made an incriminating statement.[292] Finally, the Illinois Appellate Court held that a

---

285. *Id.* at 303.

286. *Id.*

287. 430 U.S. 387 (1977). See § 2.32.

288. *Innis,* 446 U.S. at 300 n.4.

289. People v. Reed, 92 Ill. App. 3d 1115, 416 N.E.2d 694 (4th Dist. 1981).

290. People v. Nunn, 101 Ill. App. 3d 983, 428 N.E.2d 1158 (1st Dist. 1981).

291. People v. Jumper, 113 Ill. App. 3d 346, 447 N.E.2d 531 (4th Dist. 1983).

292. People v. Brownell, 123 Ill. App. 3d 307, 462 N.E.2d 936 (2d Dist. 1984). *See* People v. Childs, 272 Ill. App. 3d 787, 651 N.E.2d 252, 257 (4th Dist. 1995) (defendant not entitled to *Miranda* warnings where police asked him where a suspect was and defendant replied he did not know who the suspect was, even though statement later used to prosecute defendant for obstruction of justice, because there was no evidence defendant was involved in crime for which suspect was sought and the question did not involve past conduct of defendant; even if

police request to an individual in custody to consent to a search after the individual had been given *Miranda* warnings and he had requested counsel, did not constitute an interrogation for purposes of *Miranda*. Such a request, the court concluded, is not reasonably likely to elicit an incriminating response and does not violate a defendant's Fifth Amendment right against self-incrimination.[293]

The factual equivalent of an interrogation has been found when an officer stated to a person charged with driving after revocation, "You know better than to drive that car,"[294] and when a suspect charged with battery was informed that "the victim may die."[295] Illinois courts also concluded that confronting a suspect with the discrepancies in his or her story[296] or with the fact that accomplices had given statements and there was a strong case against the suspect[297] was so likely to elicit a response that it constituted an interrogation for *Miranda* purposes. The determination of this question does not turn on whether the defendant initiated the statement but on what the officers might have reasonably anticipated. Thus, even when the defendant sought out the officers, *Miranda*

Miranda warnings were required, the statement need not be suppressed because of exigent circumstances), *cert. denied*, 516 U.S. 1134 (1996).

293. People v. Alvarado, 268 Ill. App. 3d 459, 644 N.E.2d 783, 788–89 (4th Dist. 1994). *See also* United States v. LaGrone, 43 F.3d 332, 339 (7th Cir. 1994) (defendant's request to seek counsel's guidance on police request to consent to search of business did not invoke *Miranda* rights; in order for *Miranda* to apply, police must be conducting an interrogation or an interrogation must be imminent).

294. People v. Burson, 90 Ill. App. 3d 206, 412 N.E.2d 1160 (3d Dist. 1980). *See also* Pennsylvania v. Muniz, 496 U.S. 582 (1990) (instructions to drunk driving suspects on how to perform sobriety and breath tests not likely to be perceived as calling for any verbal response and thus did not constitute custodial interrogation).

295. People v. Rodriguez, 96 Ill. App. 3d 431, 421 N.E.2d 323 (1st Dist. 1981).

296. People v. Savory, 113 Ill. App. 3d 346, 447 N.E.2d 531 (4th Dist. 1983).

297. People v. Sanders, 55 Ill. App. 3d 178, 370 N.E.2d 1213 (2d Dist. 1977). In *People v. Enoch*, 122 Ill. 2d 176, 522 N.E.2d 1124, *cert. denied*, 488 U.S. 917 (1988), the suspect requested that counsel be provided prior to the inter rogation, and the questioning was stopped. The defendant then asked the booking officer the name of the murder victim, and the officer said, "Kay Burns." The defendant responded, "Oh no, not Kay Burns" and told the officer that he had seen her the previous evening and had walked to within a block of her home with her. This statement was admitted at trial over defendant's objections. The court found it to be the defendant's voluntary statement and not the product of police interrogation because the officer's statement was not reasonably likely to elicit an incriminating response from the suspect. Informing the defendant that he was being booked for the murder of Kay Burns was clearly a police action normally attendant to arrest and custody.

warnings were still required if the officers could have reasonably anticipated that an incriminating statement was about to be made.[298]

In *People v. Pierce*,[299] the court held that the trial judge properly suppressed defendant's statements where they were made while in custody and without *Miranda* warnings. In this case, defendant pulled a motorcycle into a private drive and the police stopped him and asked to see his license and registration. When defendant became belligerent, the officer arrested him and placed him in the back of the squad car. When defendant expressed concern over impoundment of the bike, the officer stated he would not impound it if defendant answered whether the bike belonged to him, whether it was registered to him, whether it was insured, and whether it had valid plates.[300] The court found this to be interrogation requiring *Miranda* warnings because the questions were reasonably likely to evoke an incriminating response that could have led to the filing of charges against defendant.[301]

The routine booking procedure is not an interrogation for *Miranda* purposes because it is not intended to elicit incriminating admissions.[302] This is true even if that information is subsequently used to obtain a search warrant of the defendant's apartment[303] or if the routine booking information (the defendant's age) is itself an element of the offense (indecent liberties).[304]

Once the suspect begins a spontaneous unsolicited statement that is not the result of an interrogation, the police are under no obligation to interrupt the suspect to administer the *Miranda* warnings.[305] This rule also applies to an on-the-scene investigation in which the police ask a general question such as "why are you here?" and the respondent gives an incriminating statement.[306]

---

298. People v. Levendoski, 100 Ill. App. 3d 755, 426 N.E.2d 1241 (3d Dist. 1981).

299. 285 Ill. App. 3d 5, 673 N.E.2d 750 (3d Dist. 1996).

300. *Id.*, 673 N.E.2d at 751.

301. *Id.*, 673 N.E.2d at 752.

302. People v. Fognini, 47 Ill. 2d 150, 265 N.E.2d 133 (1970), *cert. denied*, 402 U.S. 911 (1971). *See* Pennsylvania v. Muniz, 496 U.S. 582 (1990) (*Miranda* warnings need not be administered if questions are asked as part of routine booking procedure).

303. People v. Davis, 103 Ill. App. 3d 792, 431 N.E.2d 1210 (1st Dist. 1981).

304. People v. Dalton, 91 Ill. 2d 22, 434 N.E.2d 1127 (1982).

305. In re Orr, 38 Ill. 2d 417, 231 N.E.2d 424, 427 (1967), *cert. denied*, 391 U.S. 924 (1968); People v. Baer, 19 Ill. App. 3d 346, 311 N.E.2d 418, 420 (4th Dist. 1974).

306. People v. Cart, 102 Ill. App. 3d 173, 429 N.E.2d 553, 563 (2d Dist. 1981), *cert. denied*, 459 U.S. 942 (1982).

§ 2.24   Specific Nature of the *Miranda* Warnings

The Supreme Court in the *Miranda* decision itself was unusually precise in describing the required admonitions. The Court declared in two separate sections of its opinion that before any questioning the suspect has to be informed of the right to remain silent, of the fact that any statement given might be used against him or her as evidence, and of the right to retained or publicly assigned counsel before any questioning.[307] It is not necessary for the authorities to inform a suspect of the nature of the interrogation, and once a valid waiver of rights has been obtained, it is valid regardless of the subject matter of the interrogation.[308] Nevertheless the admonitions need not follow the precise language of the *Miranda* decision, as long as the suspect is informed of the rights governed by the decision.[309] In *California v. Prysock,* the Supreme Court upheld a conviction in which the defendant was informed of his right to have counsel present during the interrogation and the right to have an attorney appointed at no expense, but not the right to have an attorney appointed before and during the interrogation. The majority of the Supreme Court concluded that the warning given adequately conveyed to the defendant his right to have counsel present before and during the interrogation.

A decade earlier virtually the same question was similarly resolved by the Illinois Supreme Court in *People v. Prim:* "*Miranda* does not specify the precise language to be used in conveying the warnings. Certainly the holding of that case does not contemplate a ritualistic recital of meaningless words. Rather it requires an intelligent conveying to the individual involved of the rights set forth in that decision."[310]

Although the issue of the precise admonitions relating to the right to counsel has been litigated with some frequency, the warnings have been upheld as long as the notion that an attorney can be made available to the suspect before any questioning begins is conveyed.[311] The admonitions are not adequate, however, if they merely ask the defendant if he or she wants a lawyer rather than informing him or her of the right to counsel.[312] Nor was the confession admissible when the defendant requested to see a named public defender only to be told that "no public defender was available in the police station and if he

---

307. Miranda v. Arizona, 384 U.S. 436, 444, 467–73 (1966).

308. Colorado v. Spring, 479 U.S. 564 (1987).

309. California v. Prysock, 453 U.S. 355 (1981).

310. 53 Ill. 2d 62, 289 N.E.2d 601, 604 (1972), *cert. denied,* 412 U.S. 918 (1973), *overruled on other grounds* by People v. King, 66 Ill. 2d 551, 363 N.E.2d 838 (1977).

311. People v. Bunting, 18 Ill. App. 3d 99, 309 N.E.2d 316 (1st Dist. 1974).

312. Smith v. Lane, 426 F.2d 767 (7th Cir.), *cert. denied,* 400 U.S. 874 (1970).

wanted to keep his mouth shut he could talk to one when he came to court."[313] Foreign language instructions that vary from the precise language of *Miranda* have been upheld if they convey the general right to remain silent and to counsel.[314] No additional admonitions are required because of the suspect's youth.[315]

In *Duckworth v. Eagan,*[316] the suspect was given standard *Miranda* warnings, but the police then said: "We have no way of giving you a lawyer, but one will be appointed for you, if you wish, if and when you go to court."[317] Following *Prysock,* Eagan argued that the warnings conditioned his right to counsel on a future occurrence: his appearance in court. Five members of the Supreme Court disagreed. The Court noted that the initial warnings "touched all of the bases required by *Miranda*" and specifically informed the defendant of his right to have counsel present during questioning, even if he could not afford one.[318] The additional information merely described Indiana procedure. The Court noted that *Miranda* does not require that attorneys be producible on call, only that the police inform suspects of their right to counsel.[319] Since that was done, Eagan's statement was admissible.

Although the preferred practice is to give a suspect both written and oral warnings, it is not essential that the warnings required by *Miranda* be given in oral rather than written form.[320] Although many confessions have been upheld in cases in which only written admonitions were afforded the suspect,[321] the government's burden is more difficult when only written warnings are given because the prosecution must then prove that the suspect could read and understand the admonitions.[322]

All suspects are entitled to the same warnings. Thus, a young offender is entitled to no additional admonitions,[323] and an attorney suspect has the right

---

313. People v. MacNab, 163 Ill. App. 3d 153, 516 N.E.2d 547 (1st Dist. 1987).

314. People v. Merrero, 121 Ill. App. 3d 716, 459 N.E.2d 1158 (2d Dist. 1984).

315. People v. Prude, 66 Ill. 2d 470, 363 N.E.2d 371, 373, *cert. denied,* 434 U.S. 930 (1977).

316. 492 U.S. 195 (1989).

317. *Id.* at 198.

318. *Id.* at 203.

319. *Id.*

320. United States v. Sledge, 546 F.2d 1120, 1121 (4th Cir.), *cert. denied,* 430 U.S. 910 (1977). *See also* North Carolina v. Butler, 441 U.S. 369 (1979) (waiver of written warnings upheld despite refusal to sign waiver form).

321. United States v. Comiskey, 460 F.2d 1293 (7th Cir. 1972).

322. United States v. Sledge, 546 F.2d 1120 (4th Cir.), *cert. denied,* 430 U.S. 910 (1977).

323. People v. Prude, 66 Ill. 2d 470, 363 N.E.2d 371, 373 (1977).

to the full set of warnings.[324] In *Miranda,* the Court noted that if the police know that the suspect has an attorney or adequate funds to retain counsel, the warnings relating to the rights of indigent need not be given,[325] but that doubt should be resolved in favor of the warnings. In most instances, the presence of counsel will obviate the need for warnings relating to the right to an attorney.[326]

§ 2.25   Timing of *Miranda* Warnings

The *Miranda* warnings must precede any interrogation, although preliminary or clerical questions may be asked a suspect who is in custody without warnings.[327]

The warning must be given freshly, that is, given reasonably close to the time of the waiver of the rights and the actual interrogation. The freshness requirement generally excludes confessions given days or weeks after the warnings.[328] In Illinois no statement has ever been excluded because the *Miranda* warnings were stale; confessions given the day after the warnings have been admitted,[329] as well as statements given several hours after the defendant was informed of his or her rights.[330] In *People v. Garcia,*[331] the Illinois Supreme Court, in what it believed had never directly been addressed before, looked at the issue of staleness. In this case, defendant was given *Miranda* warnings at 10:30 P.M., waived them, and gave a written statement. Two and one-half hours later, while being fingerprinted, an officer asked her why she was shaking so much. She stated it was because she had just shot her husband. The officer then asked her what kind of gun she used and where she had gotten it, and she

---

324. New Jersey v. Stein, 70 N.J. 369, 360 A.2d 347 (1976); Pennsylvania v. Cohen, 221 Pa. Super. 244, 289 A.2d 96, *cert. denied,* 409 U.S. 981 (1972).

325. Miranda v. Arizona, 384 U.S. 436, 473 n.43 (1966).

326. United States v. Brown, 569 F.2d 236 (5th Cir. 1978) (*en banc*); United States v. Stribling, 437 F.2d 765 (6th Cir.), *cert. denied,* 402 U.S. 973 (1971); United States v. Jackson, 390 F.2d 317 (2d Cir.), *cert. denied,* 392 U.S. 935 (1968); Frohmann v. United States, 380 F.2d 832 (8th Cir.), *cert. denied,* 389 U.S. 976 (1967).

327. People v. Morrissey, 49 Ill. App. 3d 622, 364 N.E.2d 454, 457–58 (1st Dist. 1977).

328. Freeman v. Alabama, 342 So. 2d 435 (Ala. App. 1977) (26 days); Scott v. Arkansas, 251 Ark. 918, 475 S.W.2d 699 (1972) (three months); People v. Quirk, 58 Cal. App. 3d 230, 129 Cal. Rptr. 679 (1976).

329. People v. Padilla, 70 Ill. App. 3d 406, 387 N.E.2d 985, 989 (1st Dist. 1979), *cert. denied,* 445 U.S. 961 (1980); People v. Henne, 23 Ill. App. 3d 567, 319 N.E.2d 596, 600 (2d Dist. 1974).

330. People v. Hill, 39 Ill. 2d 125, 233 N.E.2d 367, *cert. denied,* 392 U.S. 936 (1968); People v. Rosario, 4 Ill. App. 3d 642, 281 N.E.2d 714 (1st Dist. 1972).

331. 165 Ill. 2d 409, 651 N.E.2d 100 (1995).

responded.[332] The court found that the officer's first question was not interrogation as it was not directed at her crime.[333] However, it did find that the subsequent questions constituted interrogation. The question before the court was whether the *Miranda* warnings given at 10:30 P.M. were still in effect at the time of processing. The court answered affirmatively and found that the prior warnings had not become stale. The court adopted a totality of the circumstances test and held that under a totality of the circumstances present in this case, defendant was still aware of her constitutional rights during processing. Specifically, she had been given warnings for a second time just two and one-half hours before, and she had given a second statement which was consistent with her first statement. Finally, defendant had vast experience with the criminal justice system.[334]

In *People v. Wilson*,[335] the Illinois Supreme Court held that the reading of *Miranda* warnings following a voluntary but unwarned statement cured admissibility problems. A subsequent statement which is voluntary and preceded by *Miranda* warnings and a knowing and intelligent waiver will be admissible against the defendant. Once a suspect has been warned of his or her rights, he or she is free to exercise his or her own decision whether to make a second statement.[336] In this case, the defendant only became a suspect and was entitled to *Miranda* warnings after he told the officers that he was supposed to receive $500 for acting as the lookout during the robbery. Although he made a first written statement without the benefit of warnings, he was subsequently given warnings and made a voluntary statement which was admissible against him. There was no evidence that the second statement was preceded by interrogation, force, threats or harassment. Moreover, defendant was not continually questioned about the crimes after the first statement. Finally, he was not coerced or forced into making the first statement; he made it voluntarily.[337]

§ 2.26   Waiver of Constitutional Rights

Even if the *Miranda* warnings are properly administered, the prosecution still bears the burden of proving that the defendant waived his or her constitutional rights before the admission of any confession. In *Miranda,* the Supreme Court adopted the test for waiver, first articulated in *Johnson v. Zerbst*,[338] that

---

332.   *Id.*, 651 N.E.2d at 104.

333.   *Id.*, 651 N.E.2d at 108.

334.   *Id.*, 651 N.E.2d at 108–09.

335.   164 Ill. 2d 436, 647 N.E.2d 910 (1994), *cert. denied*, 516 U.S. 876 (1995).

336.   *Id.*, 647 N.E.2d at 918.

337.   *Id.*

338.   304 U.S. 458, 464 (1938).

it must be "knowing and intelligent."[339] A knowing waiver requires both an uncoerced choice and a sufficient level of comprehension to make a knowing and voluntary waiver. In a *Miranda* situation, the suspect makes a voluntary and knowing waiver when he or she understands the words of the warnings, knows what rights are encompassed in the warnings, and comprehends the consequences which result from the waiver.[340] Absent sufficient evidence to show a waiver of the constitutional rights, courts will presume that the defendant did not waive the rights.[341] The prosecution must sustain its burden only by a preponderance of the evidence;[342] the trial court need not be convinced beyond a reasonable doubt. The finding of the trial court will not be disturbed unless it is contrary to the manifest weight of the evidence.[343]

The Illinois Supreme Court explained the matter of waiver in this way:

> The purpose of advising an accused of his rights is to enable him to make an intelligent decision, and to understand the consequences of that decision, and the fact that the advice was iterated and reiterated, and that he said he understood it, is of little consequence unless the defendant was possessed of the intelligence to understand the admonition.[344]

Although *Miranda* itself speaks of the waiver being "specifically made after the warnings,"[345] an express written or oral waiver is not required. The Supreme Court in *North Carolina v. Butler* determined that in "at least some cases waiver can be clearly inferred from the actions and words of the person interrogated," even if he or she refuses to make an explicit waiver.[346] "The test is that there be a showing of a knowing intent to speak without counsel."[347]

The question of whether the defendant waived his or her rights before making a statement will be determined from all of the circumstances

---

339. Edwards v. Arizona, 451 U.S. 477, 482 (1981); People v. Turner, 56 Ill. 2d 201, 306 N.E.2d 27, 30 (1973).

340. People v. Bernasco, 138 Ill. 2d 349, 562 N.E.2d 958 (1990), *cert. denied*, 500 U.S. 932 (1991).

341. Tague v. Louisiana, 444 U.S. 469 (1980).

342. Lego v. Twomey, 404 U.S. 477 (1972).

343. People v. Prim, 53 Ill. 2d 62, 289 N.E.2d 601, 606 (1972), *cert. denied*, 412 U.S. 918 (1973).

344. People v. Turner, 56 Ill. 2d 201, 306 N.E.2d 27, 30 (1973).

345. Miranda v. Arizona, 384 U.S. 436, 470 (1966).

346. 441 U.S. 369, 373 (1979).

347. People v. Brooks, 51 Ill. 2d 156, 281 N.E.2d 326, 332 (1972).

surrounding the confession.[348] In reaching that conclusion, the courts will look to the age, familiarity with English, and mental capacity of the suspect.[349] Language barriers may in some instances impair an individual's ability to waive his or her rights in a knowing manner.[350] Courts will exercise "special care . . . [in] evaluating the confessions of youthful or mentally deficient individuals."[351] Applying this test, the appellate court in *People v. Gonzales* upheld the admission of a confession given by a fifteen-year-old boy with an IQ of 70. In *In re Potts,* the appellate court found a confession by a twelve-year-old boy to be admissible, while in *Gonzalez*[352] an oral statement in English of a person who could neither read nor write English was admitted when the warnings were given in both English and Spanish and the appellate court viewed a videotape of the interrogation conducted in English. A confession obtained from an

---

348. In re Potts, 58 Ill. App. 3d 550, 374 N.E.2d 891 (1st Dist. 1978). *See also* People v. Batac, 259 Ill. App. 3d 415, 631 N.E.2d 373, 381 (2d Dist. 1994) (defendant, under totality of circumstances, knowingly and voluntarily waived his previously invoked right to counsel; about 15 minutes into interview, defendant indicated he wanted an attorney, officer told defendant he had that right and interview would terminate; within 30 seconds after termination defendant stated he would like to go ahead and talk, defendant initiated conversation after one officer again explained interview was terminated and that they could not talk to him because he had requested an attorney).

349. People v. Baker, 9 Ill. App. 3d 654, 292 N.E.2d 760 (4th Dist. 1973). *See also* People v. Matney, 293 Ill. App. 3d 139, 686 N.E.2d 1239, 1244 (2d Dist. 1997) (defendant knowingly and intelligently waived his *Miranda* rights even though he contended to be intoxicated, had organic brain damage, and low intelligence where trial court heard audiotape statements and police and psychological testimony).

350. United States v. Heredia-Fernandez, 756 F.2d 1412, 1415 (9th Cir.), *cert. denied,* 474 U.S. 836 (1985). *See also* People v. Teran-Cruz, 272 Ill. App. 3d 573, 650 N.E.2d 663, 667 (1st Dist. 1995) (defendant knowingly and intelligently waived rights where evidence showed defendant was fully advised that counsel speaking with him was assistant state's attorney who was working against him; defendant was no stranger to the criminal justice system; defendant had previous dealings with public defenders, was given *Miranda* in Spanish both orally and in writing; and translation of "abogado para el estado" is attorney *for* the State, not attorney *from* the state); Perri v. Director, Dep't of Corrections, 817 F.2d 448, 452 (7th Cir.) (where defendant given rights in Italian and stated in English that he understood those rights, waiver was knowing and intelligent), *cert. denied,* 484 U.S. 843 (1987).

351. People v. Redmon, 127 Ill. App. 3d 342, 468 N.E.2d 1310, 1314 (1st Dist. 1984).

352. 22 Ill. App. 3d 83, 316 N.E.2d 800 (2d Dist. 1974).

intoxicated suspect, however, may be excluded,[353] as was the confession given by an arrestee who was coming out of a coma resulting from a drug overdose.[354] Mere evidence of intoxication or drug influence is insufficient reason to suppress a confession.[355] The trial judge will suppress a statement on the grounds of intoxication or drug use only if the declarant was "so grossly intoxicated as to be incapacitated" at the time the statement was made.[356] Any degree short of this standard goes to the weight to be given to the confession but it does not affect its admissibility. However, the continuing viability of this line of cases is placed in doubt by the United States Supreme Court decision in *Colorado v. Connelly,*[357] wherein it was held that the mental status of the defendant is irrelevant to a determination of whether the waiver of constitutional rights was valid, so long as no coercive police conduct or overreaching was involved.

---

353. People v. Roy, 49 Ill. 2d 113, 273 N.E.2d 363 (1971). *But see* People v. Sleboda, 166 Ill. App. 3d 42, 519 N.E.2d 512, 518 (2d Dist. 1988) (defendant's statement admissible even though a breathalyzer test indicated a blood alcohol level of over .22 because testimony established that defendant was able to stand and walk unassisted, that he was responsive to questions, was able to follow directions, and did not have slurred speech).

354. People v. Markiewicz, 38 Ill. App. 3d 495, 348 N.E.2d 240 (1st Dist. 1976). *But see* People v. Glass, 232 Ill. App. 3d 136, 597 N.E.2d 660, 669 (1st Dist. 1992) (defendant's waiver knowing and intelligent even though he was passed out at time of arrest and had to be awakened where first statement made three hours later and subsequent statements given more than 24 hours later).

355. People v. Kincaid, 87 Ill. 2d 107, 429 N.E.2d 508, 518 (1981), *cert. denied,* 455 U.S. 1024 (1982); People v. Santiago, 222 Ill. App. 3d 255, 582 N.E.2d 1304, 1312 (1st Dist. 1991).

356. People v. Matthews, 205 Ill. App. 3d 371, 562 N.E.2d 1113, 1135 (1st Dist. 1990). *See also* People v. Johnson, 285 Ill. App. 3d 802, 674 N.E.2d 844, 851 (1st Dist. 1996) (defendant's substance abuse was determined insufficient to render him incapable of waiving his rights where evidence demonstrated that defendant was responsive during questioning, provided a detailed description of the events, vividly recollected verbatim conversations, was lucid and alert, and where his statement showed numerous manipulative and clever acts); People v. Silas, 278 Ill. App. 3d 400, 663 N.E.2d 443, 447–48 (2d Dist. 1996) (defendant knowingly and intelligently waived his *Miranda* rights before making inculpatory statements; although defendant had smoked crack cocaine approximately five hours before the police interview, defendant responded accurately to the detective's questions, provided a coherent account of the events before and during the crime in question, and later gave testimony that did not clearly indicate he was grossly intoxicated or lacked the capacity to knowingly waive his rights despite his testimony that he was still feeling the effects of the cocaine during the interview).

357. 479 U.S. 157 (1987).

In addition to considering the intelligence, understanding, and capacity of the suspect, courts will also review the conduct of the police to determine whether there was an effective waiver of the defendant's constitutional rights. It is well established that physical abuse by the police during interrogation will affect the voluntariness of the confession.[358] The state bears the burden of proving by clear and convincing evidence that no abuse occurred when the defendant is injured while in custody.[359] In *Miranda,* the Court stated that "any evidence that the accused was threatened, tricked, or cajoled into a waiver will, of course, show that the defendant did not voluntarily waive his privilege."[360] In Illinois no such trick or threat will be found unless there is some fraud or deceit on the part of the police.[361] Thus a confession given to a police officer who was a "trusted friend" of the suspect was not considered improper,[362] while a statement given after the suspect was falsely told that his fingerprints were found at the crime scene and that he had been identified by the victim of the burglary was found inadmissible, even after a waiver of the *Miranda* rights.[363] Often, courts combine the issue of whether a waiver of the rights was effective with an analysis of whether the confession was voluntary.[364] It thus is likely that if the waiver is found ineffective for *Miranda* purposes, the statement will also be found inadmissible as involuntary.[365]

§ 2.27　Renewal of Questioning After Assertion of Rights

A recurring problem in the area of waiver is what happens after a suspect refuses to waive his or her rights. Specifically, under what circumstances can a statement be validly obtained after a suspect invokes the right to remain silent or have counsel present? In *Miranda,* the Court ruled that once the suspect indicates a desire to remain silent, the interrogation must cease.[366] Generally,

---

358. People v. Wilson, 116 Ill. 2d 29, 506 N.E.2d 571, 576 (1987).

359. *Id.,* 506 N.E.2d at 575.

360. Miranda v. Arizona, 384 U.S. 436, 476 (1966).

361. People v. Smith, 108 Ill. App. 2d 172, 246 N.E.2d 689 (2d Dist. 1969), *cert. denied,* 397 U.S. 1001 (1970).

362. People v. Coddington, 123 Ill. App. 2d 351, 259 N.E.2d 382 (5th Dist. 1970).

363. People v. Payton, 122 Ill. App. 3d 1030, 462 N.E.2d 543 (5th Dist. 1984).

364. See footnotes 102–224 and accompanying text in this chapter.

365. People v. Berry, 123 Ill. App. 3d 1042, 463 N.E.2d 1044, 1048 (4th Dist. 1984); People v. Stone, 61 Ill. App. 3d 654, 378 N.E.2d 263 (5th Dist. 1978). *See generally* 2 RINGEL, SEARCHES & SEIZURES, ARRESTS & CONFESSIONS 28—19 (release no. 6, June 1984).

366. Miranda v. Arizona, 384 U.S. 436, 473 (1966). *But see* People v. Shaw, 278 Ill. App. 3d 939, 664 N.E.2d 97, 103 (1st Dist. 1996) (court would not infer defendant

even an equivocal invocation of the right to remain silent is sufficient to require the police to cut off questioning.[367]

However, in *Davis v. United States*,[368] the United States Supreme Court held that when a suspect ambiguously or equivocally makes a reference to an attorney during interrogation and a reasonable officer in light of all the circumstances can not tell whether the suspect is invoking his or her right to counsel, the officer is not required to immediately cease questioning.[369] Although the Court noted that it would be "good police practice" for interrogators to clarify the suspect's statement and ask questions to determine whether he or she actually desires counsel's presence, it declined to adopt such a mandate.[370]

In this case, at some point during interrogation, defendant stated "Maybe I should talk to a lawyer."[371] The Court found this reference to be ambiguous. It further believed that the officers acted properly in attempting to clarify this statement; however, the officers were not required to clarify the statement nor

---

invoked Fifth Amendment right to remain silent where he pretended to be unable to communicate with officers as "the fifth amendment affords no protection to those who play manipulative games because they are angry with the police.").

367. Christopher v. Florida, 824 F.2d 836, 841 (11th Cir. 1987), *cert. denied*, 484 U.S. 1077 (1988); Martin v. Wainwright, 770 F.2d 918, 924 n.6 (11th Cir. 1985), *cert. denied*, 479 U.S. 909 (1986); State v. Bey, 548 A.2d 846, 856 (N.J. Super. Ct. 1988). *See also* People v. Burnfield, 295 Ill. App. 3d 256, 692 N.E.2d 412, 417 (5th Dist. 1998) (statement to police "maybe I should talk to an attorney" after which police ceased questioning but defendant began talking again sufficiently equivocal, and therefore did not invoke right to counsel; even if sufficient to invoke right to counsel, defendant's confession harmless error because evidence of guilt overwhelming). *But see* People v. Smith, 152 Ill. 2d 229, 604 N.E.2d 858, 869 (1992) (defendant's statement "[l]eave me alone" in response to questioning did not invoke Fifth Amendment privilege), *cert. denied*, 507 U.S. 1040 (1993).

368. 512 U.S. 452 (1994).

369. *Id.* at 458–61.

370. *Id.* at 461. *See* People v. Allen, 272 Ill. App. 3d 394, 650 N.E.2d 250, 257–58 (1st Dist. 1995) (*Miranda* rights honored where assistant state's attorney asked defendant "Understanding these rights, do you wish to talk to us now?" after defendant responded to question, "Understanding these rights do you wish to talk to us now?" with "No," because defendant was not prodded to give an affirmative answer and defendant immediately evidenced intent to continue questioning; assistant state's attorney merely followed defendant's answer with question insuring defendant understood rights and defendant immediately and unequivocally stated he wished to continue talking).

371. *Davis*, 512 U.S. 455. *See also* People v. Oaks, 169 Ill. 2d 409, 662 N.E.2d 1328, 1347 (defendant's Fifth Amendment right to counsel not violated where stated "Should I see a lawyer"; not an unambiguous or unequivocal request for attorney), *cert. denied*, 519 U.S. 873 (1996).

to cease questioning. When a suspect invokes the *Miranda* right to counsel, he or she is "require[d], at a minimum, [to make] some statement that can reasonably be construed as an expression of a desire for the assistance of counsel."[372] Thus, although a suspect is not required to "speak with the discrimination of an Oxford don," he or she must "unambiguously" request counsel in a manner sufficiently clear for reasonable officers to understand that the suspect desires an attorney.[373]

In *People v. McDaniel*,[374] the Illinois Supreme Court held that defendant failed to invoke his right to counsel when questioned at the hospital because his request was equivocal at best.[375] Therefore, the incriminating statement which he later made, prior to being taken into custody, was admissible.[376] In this case, defendant had apparently been advised of his *Miranda* rights but continued to talk to police officers. At some point, he spoke with his father, and his father allegedly told the police that the defendant no longer wished to speak with them until he had an attorney present.[377] Defendant testified at the suppression hearing, that he in fact had previously made this request and made it again after hearing his father's statement to the police. Defendant did not attempt to locate an attorney until approximately two and one-half hours later at the sheriff's office at which time he was in custody.[378] The supreme court found that the trial court's finding that defendant had not invoked his right of counsel until he was at the sheriff's station was not against the manifest weight of the evidence.[379] As a side note, defendant was an educated individual and had previously been a police officer. Although the supreme court agreed that the defendant had not sufficiently requested an attorney at the hospital prior to being placed in custody, implicit in the court's decision is that a person may invoke his or her *Miranda* right to counsel without first being advised of the *Miranda* warnings and that custody is not necessary.

Although that aspect is clear, the issues have arisen over the circumstances under which the interrogation may recommence after it had ceased. The appellate court in *People v. Pendleton*[380] found that once a suspect had indicated a desire not to make a statement, it was improper for the officer to ask the

---

372. *Davis*, 512 U.S. at 459.

373. *Id.*

374. 164 Ill. 2d 173, 647 N.E.2d 266 (1995).

375. *Id.*, 647 N.E.2d at 271.

376. *Id.*, 647 N.E.2d at 270.

377. *Id.*, 647 N.E.2d at 271.

378. *Id.*, 647 N.E.2d at 270.

379. *Id.*

380. 24 Ill. App. 3d 385, 321 N.E.2d 433 (1st Dist. 1974).

suspect "if he had any questions concerning the case" or to respond to a question from the suspect by asking a crucial question.[381] The court found this to be a form of interrogation. In *Michigan v. Mosley,*[382] the United States Supreme Court was confronted with a defendant who had been arrested in connection with some robberies. After being informed of his *Miranda* rights he declined to make any statement, and the interrogation terminated. Two hours later another detective interviewed Mosley at another location about an unrelated murder. Mosley gave an incriminating statement that was admitted at trial. In finding the ultimate confession admissible, the Court determined that it was absurd to conclude that *Miranda* be read either to prohibit any further questioning after the invocation of rights or to allow resumed interrogation after only a "momentary respite."[383] The Court concluded that the issue was whether the defendant's right to terminate the interrogation was "scrupulously honored."[384] The *Mosley* Court resolved the question by pointing out that the police had honored the defendant's initial refusal to give a statement and that the statement was given to a different officer, after a two-hour break and after fresh admonitions were administered, all in relation to a different offense. Therefore the confession was admissible.

In *Edwards v. Arizona,*[385] the United States Supreme Court ruled that a confession should have been suppressed when the defendant, after first invoking his right to counsel, gave a statement the next day without seeing a lawyer and after the police initiated a new interrogation and once again advised him of his *Miranda* rights. The Court ruled that once a defendant invokes his right to counsel he cannot be subjected to police-initiated interrogation. This is true even if the ultimate statement is voluntary.[386] The Supreme Court stated specifically that once a defendant indicates a desire to deal with police only through counsel, he or she "is not subject to further interrogation by the authorities until counsel has been made available to him, unless [he]

---

381. *But see* People v. Wright, 272 Ill. App. 3d 1033, 651 N.E.2d 758, 764 (1st Dist. 1995) (act of advising defendant of expected arrival of assistant state's attorney and function she would perform was statement designed to apprise defendant of anticipated custodial events and did not constitute reinitiation of conversation by officers), *cert. denied*, 516 U.S. 1133 (1996).

382. 423 U.S. 96 (1975).

383. *Id.*

384. *Id.* at 104.

385. 451 U.S. 477 (1981).

386. *Id.* at 483. *See* People v. Sullivan, 209 Ill. App. 3d 1096, 568 N.E.2d 447, 450–51 (4th Dist. 1991) (defendant's custodial statements suppressed where the police initiated interrogation without counsel after defendant had invoked right to counsel).

himself initiates further communications, exchanges, or conversations with the police."[387]

The United States Supreme Court expanded the rule of *Edwards* in *Arizona v. Roberson*.[388] The Court held that the rule applies to bar police-initiated interrogation in the context of an interrogation concerning a separate crime.[389] In this case, the defendant was arrested at the scene of a burglary, and after police advised him of his rights under *Miranda,* he said that he "wanted a lawyer before answering *any* questions."[390] The police officer recorded this fact in the written report of the incident. Three days later and while the defendant was still in custody, a different officer interrogated the defendant about an unrelated burglary after advising him of his rights. This officer was unaware of the previous request for counsel.[391]

The United States Supreme Court held that the police were barred from initiating any questioning because the defendant unambiguously expressed his desire to deal with the police only through counsel.[392] The Court distinguished this case from *Mosley* by stating that *Mosley* itself noted that a suspect's decision to cut off questioning does not raise the presumption that he is unable to proceed without a lawyer's advice. However, a request for counsel, on the other hand, raises such a presumption.[393] Consequently, *any* police-initiated interrogation following a suspect's request for counsel, whether it concerns the same or a different offense, or whether the same or different law enforcement officials are involved, is presumptively coercive.[394] Therefore, statements taken from that interrogation must be suppressed.

---

387. *Edwards,* 451 U.S. at 484–85. *See also* People v. Wright, 272 Ill. App. 3d 1033, 651 N.E.2d 758, 764 (1st Dist. 1995) (defendant reinitiated conversation with police after invoking right to counsel where after police advised defendant of procedures that were going to be followed including arrival of assistant state's attorney, defendant then asked date of murder), *cert. denied,* 516 U.S. 1133 (1996).

388. 486 U.S. 675 (1988).

389. *Id.* at 682.

390. *Id.* at 683.

391. *Id.*

392. *Id.* at 686.

393. *Id.* at 683.

394. *Id.* at 687. *But see* People v. Hicks, 132 Ill. 2d 488, 548 N.E.2d 1042, 1045 (1989) (defendant waived his Sixth Amendment right to counsel and the Fifth Amendment right to counsel concerning a different offense, where the defendant volunteered information concerning the first offense).

But in *People v. Whitehead,*[395] the confession was admitted notwithstanding the fact that the suspect had initially requested to see counsel. After being visited by his sister-in-law, the defendant initiated discussions with police and ultimately gave an inculpatory statement. The Illinois Supreme Court found that the police did nothing to encourage the sister-in-law to suggest that the defendant confess nor was there any misconduct or trickery involved.

A similar result was reached by the United States Supreme Court in *Arizona v. Mauro.*[396] In *Mauro,* the defendant invoked his right to counsel after being afforded *Miranda* warnings. Later, the defendant's wife insisted on seeing him, and the conversation was openly tape recorded. In the conversation with his wife, the defendant made statements that were later introduced to rebut his claim of insanity. The Court found that the conversation between the defendant and his wife was not the functional equivalent of an interrogation and that no psychological ploys had been used by the police to induce the statement. The statements were thus properly admitted.

Edwards thus stands for the proposition that once a defendant invokes the right to have counsel present, he or she can not be questioned without seeing an attorney, as long as he or she remains silent and does not initiate further contact with the police.[397] Once suspects indicate clearly that they do not want to continue the interrogation in the absence of counsel, the questioning must stop. The police cannot ask suspects additional questions that require them to clarify or reiterate their request for counsel. In *People v. St. Pierre,*[398] the defendant first said he wanted counsel prior to any interrogation, but upon further questioning by police, he responded ambiguously to questions about counsel and ultimately said he did not desire counsel present. The Illinois Supreme Court suppressed his confession because it was obtained after a clear request for counsel, which the police did not honor. Once the suspect said he wanted counsel, the questioning should have ended, and thus his subsequent ambiguous responses or change of mind was irrelevant. Although the *Miranda* right to counsel is not offense specific, its assertion can not be inferred by the invocation of the Sixth Amendment right to counsel vis-a-vis an unrelated

---

395. 116 Ill. 2d 425, 508 N.E.2d 687, 691–92, *cert. denied,* 484 U.S. 933 (1987).

396. 481 U.S. 520 (1987).

397. People v. Washington, 68 Ill. 2d 186, 369 N.E.2d 57 (1977), *cert. denied,* 435 U.S. 981 (1978); People v. Spivey, 209 Ill. App. 3d 584, 568 N.E.2d 327, 332 (1st Dist. 1991); People v. Hammock, 121 Ill. App. 3d 874, 460 N.E.2d 378 (1st Dist. 1984), *cert. denied,* 470 U.S. 1003 (1985); People v. James, 100 Ill. App. 3d 986, 427 N.E.2d 606 (4th Dist. 1981); People v. Sluder, 97 Ill. App. 3d 459, 423 N.E.2d 268 (3d Dist. 1981).

398. 122 Ill. 2d 95, 522 N.E.2d 61 (1988), *cert. denied,* 506 U.S. 942 (1992).

charged offense.[399] If the defendant does not respond to *Miranda* warnings, the interrogation may continue. However, any statement made by the defendant would be inadmissible unless the state offers adequate proof that the defendant understood the right to remain silent and had waived the right.[400] The defendant's request for counsel must be clear, however, and absent such clarity the

---

399. McNeil v. Wisconsin, 501 U.S. 171 (1988) (defendant charged with armed robbery in West Allis, Wisconsin; public defender appointed at initial appearance before court commissioner to represent him; while in jail, he was questioned three times about unrelated murder, attempted murder and armed robbery that occurred in Calendonia, Wisconsin; defendant advised of his *Miranda* rights each time; he waived them properly and gave incriminating statements about Calendonia crimes; subsequently, defendant charged with Calendonia crimes, trial court refused to suppress statements, and defendant was convicted; supreme court held that accused's invocation of right to counsel concerning West Allis crime did not cover Calendonia crimes and that police were not precluded from further questioning on unrelated and yet uncharged crimes; United States Supreme Court affirmed Wisconsin Supreme Court decision holding that although *Miranda* is nonspecific offense right, one cannot infer it from accused having used his Sixth Amendment right to counsel on unrelated charge). *Accord* People v. Perry, 147 Ill. 2d 430, 590 N.E.2d 454, 456 (1992) (invocation of the Sixth Amendment right to counsel for a robbery did not constitute in vocation of the Fifth Amendment right to counsel as to unrelated and uncharged offenses); People v. Fayne, 283 Ill. App. 3d 382, 669 N.E.2d 1172, 1178–79 (5th Dist. 1996) (defendant's invocation of Sixth Amendment right to counsel for one offense did not constitute invocation of Fifth Amendment right to counsel for unrelated and uncharged offenses due to critical distinctions: while the Sixth Amendment right to counsel attaches at or after the initiation of adversary judicial proceedings, the Fifth Amendment right to counsel only applies to interrogations taking place while the defendant is in custody regardless of the initiation of any formal judicial proceedings; the purpose of the Sixth Amendment is "to protect an unaided layman at critical confrontations with law enforcement officials who are expert adversaries, after the adverse positions of these parties have been solidified with respect to a particular alleged crime," while the purpose of the Fifth Amendment is to protect "the suspect's desire to deal with the police only through counsel"; whereas the Sixth Amendment is offense-specific and cannot be invoked for all future prosecutions, the Fifth Amendment, once asserted, prohibits any further interrogation for any offense in the absence of counsel); People v. Maust, 216 Ill. App. 3d 173, 576 N.E.2d 965, 970 (1st Dist. 1991) (defendant who had not previously invoked his right to counsel at custodial interrogation, and who accepted assistance of an attorney at arraignment, did not presumptively invoke his Fifth Amendment right to counsel during subsequent custodial interrogation regarding unrelated criminal activity for which the accused had not yet been charged).

400. People v. Stack, 112 Ill. 2d 301, 493 N.E.2d 339, 341 (defendant can end interogation only by making an overt response), *cert. denied*, 479 U.S. 870 (1986).

police may reinitiate or continue the interrogation.[401] If the defendant reinitiates the conversation, the interrogation may continue even after the defendant previously requested counsel.[402] The appellate court in one case decided that if the defendant had requested counsel and had actually spoken with the lawyer, the police could later reinitiate the interrogation, *Edwards* notwithstanding.[403]

Similarly, in *People v. Winsett*,[404] the Illinois Supreme Court allowed evidence obtained after police officers reinitiated questioning of a defendant who had invoked his *Miranda* right to counsel. The court was called upon to ascertain the application of the fruit of the poisonous tree doctrine to *Miranda*, an issue unresolved by the United States Supreme Court.[405] In *Winsett*, defendant invoked his right to counsel both at the time of arrest and during custodial interrogation. Nonetheless, the police continued to question him for two to two-and-a-half hours. By virtue of this interrogation, the police obtained a statement from the defendant which implicated an accomplice. Ultimately, a statement was also obtained from the accomplice implicating the defendant. The trial court suppressed the defendant's confession because it violated his *Miranda* rights but did find that the confession was voluntary. However, the trial court rejected defendant's argument that the accomplice's statement was the fruit of the poisonous tree.[406]

---

401. People v. Smith, 102 Ill. 2d 365, 466 N.E.2d 236, *rev'd,* 469 U.S. 91 (1984). In reversing the decision of the Illinois Supreme Court, the United States Supreme Court found that the defendant's initial request for counsel was not ambiguous and that any ambiguity was created only by subsequent questioning after the initial invocation of the right to counsel. In *People v. Evans,* 125 Ill. 2d 50, 530 N.E.2d 1360 (1988), *cert. denied,* 490 U.S. 1113 (1989), after being informed of his right to counsel, the suspect asked police: "You mean, I can have a PD [public defender] in here, or do you mean I have to wait?" After being told of his right to have counsel present, the defendant asked how long it would take and was told: "It will take a little while. I'll stop the questioning, and we will call for a public defender." Defendant then said: "No, go ahead" and gave an incriminating statement. The court concluded that Evans's questions about counsel were not requests to have counsel present. Here, defendant merely made an inquiry which referred to an attorney, and "not every reference to an attorney, no matter how vague, indecisive or ambiguous, should constitute an invocation of the right to counsel." *Id.,* 530 N.E.2d at 1371. Thus, the statement was admissible.

402. People v. Aldridge, 79 Ill. 2d 87, 402 N.E.2d 176 (1980); People v. Morgan, 67 Ill. 2d 1, 364 N.E.2d 56, 58–59, *cert. denied,* 434 U.S. 927 (1977); People v Brownell, 123 Ill. App. 3d 307, 462 N.E.2d 936, 944 (2d Dist. 1984).

403. People v. Denby, 102 Ill. App. 3d 1141, 430 N.E.2d 507, 513 (5th Dist. 1981).

404. 153 Ill. 2d 335, 606 N.E.2d 1186 (1992), *cert. denied,* 510 U.S. 831 (1993).

405. *Id.,* 606 N.E.2d at 1201.

406. *Id.,* 606 N.E.2d at 1190–91.

In addressing whether that was a correct ruling, the supreme court reviewed both *Miranda* and *Edwards,* noting that under *Miranda* if a defendant invokes his or her right to counsel, interrogation must cease. However, *Edwards* refined this ruling and held that questioning could not be reinitiated by the police without counsel being present. Any statement taken in violation of *Edwards* would be inadmissible in the state's case-in-chief under the Fifth Amendment exclusionary rule.[407] On the other hand, a statement would be admissible if the defendant initiated the interrogation and his or her statement was voluntary.[408] Moreover, under the Fourth Amendment's exclusionary rule and the fruit of the poisonous tree doctrine, any physical or testimonial evidence obtained in violation of defendant's *Miranda* rights is admissible. The court pointed out that the exclusionary rules under the Fourth and Fifth Amendments are different.[409] When police violate *Miranda's* right to counsel but the confession is nonetheless voluntary, the fruit of the poisonous tree doctrine is not applicable.[410] Thus, the state may use a voluntary statement obtained in violation of *Miranda* for impeachment purposes.[411]

The question presented to the court in *Winsett* was whether police interrogation after defendant invoked his right to counsel was a *Miranda* violation or a constitutional violation. If it was a *Miranda* violation, the accomplice's statement would be admissible. If, however, the renewed interrogation was a constitutional violation, the accomplice's statement would not be admissible. The supreme court found this police conduct to be a mere *Miranda* violation.[412] It reasoned that the right to counsel established in *Miranda* was not a constitutional right but instead a prophylactic device fashioned to safeguard a defendant's right against compelled self-incrimination.[413] It follows that a statement obtained in violation of the *Miranda* right to counsel is inadmissible in the state's case-in-chief. However, if the evidence is used for any other purpose,

---

407. *Id.,* 606 N.E.2d at 1194.

408. *Id.,* 606 N.E.2d at 1195.

409. *Id.,* 606 N.E.2d at 1196.

410. *Id.*

411. *Id.,* 606 N.E.2d at 1198.

412. *Id.,* 606 N.E.2d at 1199.

413. *Id.,* 606 N.E.2d at 1196, 1201. The Illinois Supreme Court's interpretation was approved in *United States ex rel. Winsett v. Washington* by the Northern District of Illinois in addressing a petition for a writ of habeas corpus. 860 F. Supp. 479 (N.D. Ill. 1994). It too agreed that the fruit of the poisonous tree doctrine does not apply when police fail to cease interrogating an individual after that individual had requested counsel because no constitutional right is implicated. *Id.* at 484. However, it did believe that the balance of evils present under such circumstances should warrant a finding that any evidence obtained in violation of one's right to counsel, including a third person's testimony, should be inadmissible. *Id.* at 485.

the trial judge must analyze it under a voluntariness test. If the defendant's statement is voluntary, any derivative evidence obtained from it will be admissible.[414]

In this case, although defendant's *Miranda* rights were violated, the trial court held that the statement was voluntary. Therefore, the identity of the accomplice and his subsequent statements were not the fruits of the poisonous tree and thus were admissible.[415]

The issue of what constitutes the initiation of further communication with the police after an invocation of the right to counsel was discussed by the United States Supreme Court in *Oregon v. Bradshaw*.[416] In this case a plurality of the Court identified a two-step analysis to determine whether a statement could be admitted after a suspect initially stated a desire to consult with counsel. The voluntariness of a later statement is determined by examining the totality of the circumstances. The relevant circumstances include: whether significant time elapsed between the exercise of rights and the second interrogation; whether new *Miranda* warnings were given before the police resumed questioning; whether different officers conducted the second interrogation; and, whether there was an explanation for the defendant's reconsideration of his right to remain silent.[417] The first step is to determine whether the suspect initiated the conversation after asking for counsel. The question of who initiated the new interrogation after a request for counsel had been made is a factual determination to be made by the trial judge, and this determination will be set aside only if it is manifestly erroneous.[418] *Bradshaw* makes apparent that virtually any type of communication between the suspect and the police related to the offense is sufficient to constitute reinitiation. For the second step, the court will ascertain whether there was then a knowing and intelligent waiver of the right to counsel and to remain silent, based on a totality of the circumstances. *Bradshaw* strongly suggests that if a defendant initiates conversation with the police about the offense and is then reinformed of the *Miranda* rights, the statement will be admitted, *Edwards* notwithstanding. However, the Illinois Supreme Court in *People v. Edwards*,[419] held that police officers may not reinitiate interrogation once the defendant requests counsel, and even if the suspect "waives" counsel after renewed interrogation, the confession is inadmissible.[420]

---

414. *Winsett,* 153 Ill. 2d 335, 606 N.E.2d at 1200.

415. *Id.,* 606 N.E.2d at 1201.

416. 462 U.S. 1039 (1983).

417. People v. Reyes, 181 Ill. App. 3d 246, 536 N.E.2d 990, 996 (1st Dist. 1989).

418. Minnick v. Mississippi, 498 U.S. 146 (1990).

419. 144 Ill. 2d 108, 579 N.E.2d 336 (1991), *cert. denied,* 504 U.S. 942 (1992).

420. *Id.,* 579 N.E.2d at 348. *See* People v. Olivera, 164 Ill. 2d 382, 647 N.E.2d 926, 931 (defendant's rights were violated when following line-up, defendant asked

In *People v. Trotter*,[421] the court held that when officers questioned the defendant about making a possible statement and why his attorney was not present, they violated the *Edwards* rule. The court found that the detective's statement implicitly introduced the subject of further questioning by initiating a discussion concerning the matter of representation. Moreover, the court found that defendant had not initiated a conversation about the investigation. The defendant's request to speak with the detective about matters unrelated to the investigation was not an *Edwards* inquiry because it did not evince a desire to open up a more generalized discussion relating directly or indirectly to the investigation.[422] In *People v. Woolley*,[423] the court held that defendant's right to counsel was not violated where he reinitiated conversation with police. The defendant was taken into custody for questioning. Approximately two and one-half hours later, the police told him his wife had implicated him in the shootings in question. At this point, according to the police: "[The defendant] kind of sat straight up into his chair and basically said that he wanted an attorney. He then said that I killed them. Yeah. I killed them."[424] Apparently, the police then told him that he had only this one chance to speak to them but that if he wanted to do so, he would have to recant his request for an attorney. He then told the police he wanted to speak without an attorney. He confessed and later provided a tape-recorded statement that was transcribed and signed by him. Both officers testified at defendant's motion to suppress that they believed that he had reinitiated the interrogation with them by saying "I killed

---

"What happened?", officer responded defendant was "positively identified", defendant asked what happens next, officer allegedly advised him of his rights and subsequently defendant made an incriminating statement; where statement to officer immediately following line-up did not evince a willingness to discuss the investigation and officer did not respond with warnings but instead answered defendant's question, officer's response was designed to, and in fact did, elicit further comment by defendant which culminated in incriminating statement), *cert. denied*, 516 U.S. 863 (1995); People v. Ravellette, 263 Ill. App. 3d 906, 636 N.E.2d 105, 110–11 (1st Dist. 1994) (defendants' *Edwards* rights violated when police did not cease interrogation after defendants had invoked right to counsel; statement to first defendant "Why do you want to do this? You're doing so well?" constituted continued interrogation whose purpose was to elicit incriminating response where defendant never initiated conversations with police; allowing third defendant to talk to second defendant violated rule of *Edwards* because only reason for encounter was to get second defendant to waive right to counsel, cooperate with police, and make an incriminating statement).

421. 254 Ill. App. 3d 514, 626 N.E.2d 1104 (1st Dist. 1993).

422. *Id.*, 626 N.E.2d at 1111.

423. 178 Ill. 2d 175, 687 N.E.2d 979 (1997), *cert. denied*, 524 U.S. 955 (1998).

424. *Id.*, 687 N.E.2d at 989.

them." Defendant denied making this statement and testified that after he stated to the police that he wanted an attorney he also stated that he did not commit the crimes.

Under *Edwards* there is a two-point inquiry: (1) whether the accused rather than the police initiated further conversation and, if so, (2) whether the subsequent waiver of the right to counsel was knowing and intelligent.[425] Here, there was no question that the defendant had invoked his right to counsel and that the police subsequently interrogated him. The court concluded, however, that the evidence supported the trial court's finding that the defendant himself reinitiated the conversation after he had requested counsel. According to the court, an accused need not explicitly state that he wishes to resume interrogation. Whether the defendant said that he had he committed the crime or said he did not commit the crime was not important. The important factor was that by making any statement following his request for counsel, the defendant evinced a willingness to continue a generalized discussion about the crime.[426] The court rejected the defense argument that simply because the statement followed immediately after his request for counsel it was part of it. First, the two interrogating officers did not interpret the statement as being part of his request for counsel. Further, defendant did not himself claim that his statement was part of his request for counsel. There is nothing in *Edwards*, concluded the court, that holds that the reinitation cannot come immediately after a request for counsel.[427]

In cases in which the suspect has invoked the right to remain silent, rather than the right to counsel, the courts do not apply an outright prohibition on renewed interrogation. Following *Mosley,* the courts will look to whether the initial desire to remain silent was "scrupulously honored" and at the circumstances surrounding the resumed interrogation. If there is a significant lapse of time between the first and subsequent interrogation, and if fresh *Miranda* warnings are administered, courts have been inclined to admit the statement made after the resumed questioning,[428] particularly in cases in which a different officer conducts the subsequent questioning and when the subsequent questioning is about a different offense than the first questioning.[429] Absent a significant time lapse and renewed warnings, the subsequent confession is not admissible.[430]

---

425. *Id.,* 687 N.E.2d at 990.

426. *Id.,* 687 N.E.2d at 991.

427. *Id.,* 687 N.E.2d at 992.

428. People v. Fleming, 103 Ill. App. 3d 194, 431 N.E.2d 16 (2d Dist. 1981).

429. People v. Young, 115 Ill. App. 3d 455, 450 N.E.2d 947 (2d Dist. 1983).

430. People v. Faison, 78 Ill. App. 3d 911, 397 N.E.2d 1233 (3d Dist. 1979). *See* People v. Batac, 259 Ill. App. 3d 415, 631 N.E.2d 373, 381 (2d Dist. 1994)

In *People v. Morrow*,[431] the appellate court was faced with such a question and found that the trial judge properly denied defendant's motion to suppress.[432] In this case, the defendant was arrested at 1:25 a.m. by Officer Dudley and given his *Miranda* warnings. Defendant stated he understood them and did not wish to speak at this time; he did not request counsel.[433] At 2:00 a.m., Officer Sheetz took defendant to an interview room and was admonished. Defendant stated he understood his rights and did not request counsel.[434] At 2:30 a.m., Officer McCoy joined defendant and Sheetz and again read defendant his rights. Defendant did not request counsel, agreed to speak with officers, and signed a waiver.[435] A break was taken at 3:30 a.m. during which the police obtained evidence that defendant was at the scene of the crime. At 3:51 a.m., the interrogation resumed; defendant was admonished, and he agreed to speak with the officers. At 4:00 a.m., another break was taken and interrogation resumed at 4:36 a.m. At this time, defendant was admonished; he agreed to speak with officer and signed a consent form. He did not request an attorney or remain silent. During this interrogation, defendant made a written statement.[436] A break was taken at 5:20 a.m., and at 6:20 a.m. a videotape of defendant's statement was made after he agreed to do so.[437] The court held that defendant's rights were "scrupulously honored." It reasoned that at 1:25 a.m. and 2:00 a.m., the defendant was admonished and was not asked any questions other than if he understood his rights. This was not custodial interrogation. The first custodial interrogation occurred at 2:30 a.m., at which time defendant chose not to remain silent. Defendant agreed to speak with the officers and signed a consent form.[438] The court further explained that the result would have been the same even if it found defendant had invoked his right to remain silent at 1:25 a.m. There was sufficient time between 1:25 a.m. and 2:00 a.m. to satisfy the requirements of "significant time lapse."[439] Two different police officers were involved: at 1:25

(renewed questioning of defendant proper under *Mosley* where police ceased questioning immediately after defendant invoked right to silence and did not reinitiate interrogation until 45 minutes later when defendant was given new *Miranda* warnings and not repeatedly "badgered" by police).

431. 269 Ill. App. 3d 1045, 647 N.E.2d 1100 (5th Dist. 1995).

432. *Id.*, 647 N.E.2d at 1107.

433. *Id.*, 647 N.E.2d at 1103.

434. *Id.*

435. *Id.*, 647 N.E.2d at 1104.

436. *Id.*

437. *Id.*

438. *Id.*

439. *Id.*, 647 N.E.2d at 1105.

a.m. it was Officer Dudley and at 2:00 a.m. it was Officer McCoy. Defendant was given fresh *Miranda* warnings each time, and although the interrogation concerned the same offense there was no evidence that the officers were deliberately coercive or were using improper tactics. According to the court, the officers took every precautionary measure to assure that defendant's rights were protected.[440]

In *People v. Cole*,[441] the court held that defendant's statement to FBI agents, "I don't want to talk to you guys," was not a general invocation of the right to remain silent. The reference to "you guys" referred only to the FBI agents, and therefore state authorities properly spoke to defendant and obtained an incriminating statement from him.[442]

It is significant to remember that the Fifth Amendment right against self-incrimination is distinct and exclusive of *Miranda* warnings. Therefore, courts do not require that a defendant be subjected to custodial interrogation before he or she may invoke the Fifth Amendment privilege.[443] Moreover, *Edwards* established that the right to have counsel present during interrogation is so important and fundamental that a defendant may invoke the right whether or not an arrest had taken place. Accordingly, in *People v. Spivey*, the court suppressed defendant's statements where the police failed to honor his pre-arrest invocation of his right to remain silent and right to counsel. In addition, the court found that the coercive environment created by the police in which the defendant was subjected to incommunicado "incarceration" supported suppression.[444]

§2.28 Use of Statement That Violates *Miranda* for Purposes of Impeachment

A statement that violates *Miranda* cannot be used by the prosecution in its case-in-chief. But in *Harris v. New York*,[445] the United States Supreme Court held that an otherwise voluntary statement that violated *Miranda* could be used to impeach a defendant. Otherwise, Chief Justice Burger suggested, the protections of *Miranda* would "be perverted into a

---

440. *Id.*, 647 N.E.2d at 1107.

441. *See, e.g.*, People v. Bounds, 171 Ill. 2d 1, 662 N.E.2d 1168, 1180–81 (1995) (eight hours is not an unreasonably long period of custody and will not nullify the voluntariness of a subsequent statement), *cert. denied*, 519 U.S. 876 (1996).

442. *Id.*, 665 N.E.2d at 1280.

443. People v. Young, 201 Ill. App. 3d 521, 558 N.E.2d 1287, 1290 (1st Dist. 1990), *aff'd*, 153 Ill. 2d 383, 607 N.E.2d 123 (1992), *cert. denied*, 510 U.S. 829 (1993).

444. People v. Spivey, 209 Ill. App. 3d 584, 568 N.E.2d 327, 333 (1st Dist. 1991).

445. 401 U.S. 222 (1971).

license to use perjury."[446] Confessions that are involuntary, whether or not they violate *Miranda,* cannot be used for impeachment purposes, however.[447] The rule allowing statements that violate *Miranda* to be used for impeachment is in addition to the usual rule that "[i]f a defendant procures, invites or acquiesces in the admission of evidence, even though it be improper, he cannot complain."[448] Thus, if the defendant opens the door to illegally obtained evidence, he or she cannot then object to references by the prosecution to that evidence.[449] On further appeal, the Illinois Supreme Court held that a defendant's previously suppressed statement may be introduced to impeach a witness other than the defendant.[450] However, in *James v. Illinois,*[451] the United States Supreme Court held that the rule allowing for the impeachment of a defendant by illegal evidence would not be extended to impeach the testimony of other defense witnesses.[452]

§ 2.29   Use of Silence for Purposes of Impeachment

In *Doyle v. Ohio,*[453] the United States Supreme Court held that a defendant was denied due process when the prosecutor sought to impeach his exculpatory testimony at trial by questioning him about his silence after being arrested and informed of his *Miranda* rights. This prohibition extends to comments made by the prosecutor in a closing argument and has been the rule in Illinois since at least 1914.[454] A comment on the defendant's silence invites the jury to draw

---

446. *Id.* at 256.

447. People v. Peterson, 74 Ill. 2d 478, 384 N.E.2d 348, 350 (1978); People v. James, 153 Ill. App. 3d 131, 505 N.E.2d 1118, 1121 (1st Dist. 1987) (appellate court determined that when confession was obtained after illegal arrest, in violation of defendant's Fourth Amendment rights, statement could not be used even for impeachment because court concluded that admission of such statement would not deter police misconduct), *rev'd,* 123 Ill. 2d 523, 528 N.E.2d 723 (1988), *rev'd,* 493 U.S. 307 (1990).

448. People v. Burage, 23 Ill. 2d 280, 178 N.E.2d 389, 391 (1961), *cert. denied,* 369 U.S. 808 (1962).

449. People v. Payne, 98 Ill. 2d 45, 456 N.E.2d 44, 46 (1983), *cert. denied,* 465 U.S. 1036 (1984).

450. People v. James, 123 Ill. 2d 523, 528 N.E.2d 723 (1988), *rev'd,* 493 U.S. 307 (1990).

451. 493 U.S. 307.

452. *Id.* at 320.

453. 426 U.S. 610 (1976).

454. People v. Pfanschmidt, 262 Ill. 411, 104 N.E. 804, 819 (1914). *See also* People v. Herrett, 137 Ill. 2d 195, 561 N.E.2d 1 (1990); People v. Green, 74 Ill. 2d 444, 386 N.E.2d 272, 275 (1979).

an adverse inference from the suspect's silence, in derogation of the privilege against self-incrimination. This rule does not apply, however, if the defendant testifies that he or she had given the police an exculpatory statement after arrest but the police deny the statement was given,[455] or if the prosecutor cross-examines the defendant on why he or she gave the police a different story than he or she testified to at trial.[456] Both the United States Supreme Court and the Illinois Supreme Court upheld convictions in which the prosecution adduced evidence that showed that each defendant gave an oral statement but then refused to reduce his confession to writing. In *Connecticut v. Barrett*,[457] the Court concluded that even if the defendant did not understand the legal implications of giving the oral statement, the statement was still admissible even if the suspect requested counsel before making a written statement. Once the defendant made the decision to give a statement, the police were not required "to ignore the tenor or sense of a defendant's response" to the *Miranda* warnings. The Illinois court reasoned, in *People v. Christensen*,[458] that once the defendant decided to give an oral confession, he had waived any Fifth Amendment right, and that the evidence regarding his refusal to give a written statement was not an impermissible reference to his silence. Indeed, it had no Fifth Amendment implications whatsoever. Such a cross-examination is not considered a comment on the defendant's silence but rather is proper cross-examination based on inconsistent statements, even if the "inconsistent descriptions of events may be said to involve 'silence' insofar as it omits facts included in the other version."[459] In *People v. Nolan*,[460] the court rejected a tacit admission exception to the *Doyle* rule. In *Nolan*, the defendant claimed at trial that the shooting of his wife was an accident. Over objection, the prosecution was allowed to introduce testimony that the defendant made no reference to the shooting being an accident when he reported the event to the police or when he told his brother-in-law that he had killed his wife. The court found such evidence to be an impermissible comment on the defendant's silence, which required a new trial.

---

455. People v. Queen, 56 Ill. 2d 560, 310 N.E.2d 166 (1974).

456. Anderson v. Charles, 447 U.S. 404 (1980); People v. Rehbein, 74 Ill. 2d 435, 386 N.E.2d 39 (1978), *cert. denied,* 442 U.S. 919 (1979).

457. 479 U.S. 523 (1987).

458. 116 Ill. 2d 96, 506 N.E.2d 1253, 1262–63, *cert. denied,* 484 U.S. 873 (1987).

459. *Anderson,* 447 U.S. at 409.

460. 152 Ill. App. 3d 260, 504 N.E.2d 205, 210–11 (2d Dist. 1987).

The United States Supreme Court has held that the rule of *Doyle* does not apply to pre-arrest silence[461] or to silence before the administration of the *Miranda* warnings.[462] On this question, however, the Illinois Supreme Court has so far applied a stricter test and applies *Doyle* to situations in which the *Miranda* warnings were not given.[463] This conflict has been noted but not resolved by the Illinois Supreme Court.[464]

The cases above suggest that in order for a defendant to claim the advantage of *Doyle* or its Illinois counterparts, a defendant must have made no statement and may not subsequently assert that he or she did make a statement. If the defendant makes a statement or claims at trial that he or she did, the court might well find that the prosecutor's cross-examination or comment is not a comment on the defendant's silence but on his or her inconsistent testimony.[465] It should also be noted that although Illinois applies *Doyle* to non-*Miranda* situations, the Illinois Supreme Court has never explicitly resolved the conflict or decided to apply a stricter test than the United States Supreme Court, though the court could certainly follow that course.

An impermissible comment on the defendant's silence can still be harmless error if the evidence of the defendant's guilt is so strong or if his or her testimony is thoroughly discredited by evidence other than the impeaching evidence.[466] The state may not utilize the defendant's silence or invocation of the privilege against self-incrimination at the time of his arrest to rebut a claim of insanity. The courts have found such evidence, used for rebuttal but not

---

461. Jenkins v. Anderson, 447 U.S. 231 (1980). *But see* People v. Shaw, 278 Ill. App. 3d 939, 664 N.E.2d 97 (1st Dist. 1996) (defendant not denied fair trial where prosecutor elicited testimony and argued in closing that defendant feigned inability to hear or communicate when originally questioned; issue waived and even if not, defendant did not invoke Fifth Amendment right to silence by feigning inability to communicate; there is no constitutional invocation when defendant's silence simply raises question of ability to communicate, not unwillingness to communicate).

462. Fletcher v. Weir, 455 U.S. 603 (1982).

463. People v. Beller, 74 Ill. 2d 514, 386 N.E.2d 857 (1979).

464. People v. Miller, 96 Ill. 2d 385, 450 N.E.2d 322, 326 (1983). *See also* People v. Krogh, 123 Ill. App. 3d 220, 462 N.E.2d 790 (1st Dist. 1984).

465. People v. Pegram, 124 Ill. 2d 166, 529 N.E.2d 506 (1988) (improper for prosecutor to argue to jury members that they should not believe defendant's trial testimony because he had not previously informed authorities of his version of facts; improper comment on defendant's pre-trial silence).

466. People v. Beller, 74 Ill. 2d 514, 386 N.E.2d 857 (1979); People v. Green, 74 Ill. 2d 444, 386 N.E.2d 272 (1979).

impeachment, both an impermissible comment on the defendant's silence and a violation of *Miranda*.[467]

§ 2.30 Confessions Obtained Through Illegal Arrest

It has long been the law in Illinois that a confession obtained as the result of an unlawful arrest or search is not admissible against the defendant.[468] Thus, when a person is arrested without probable cause, any statement made as a result of that arrest is subject to suppression, even if *Miranda* warnings are given.[469] "To hold otherwise would permit the police to be free to arrest without probable cause, secure in the knowledge that the mere giving of the *Miranda* warnings might result in their obtaining a confession which would be admissible at trial."[470]

Not every confession obtained after an illegal arrest is subject to suppression, however. The test is not that a confession is excluded if it would not have been obtained "but for" the illegal arrest. Rather, the test is whether the confession "has been come at by exploitation of [the illegal arrest] or instead by means sufficiently distinguishable to be purged of the primary taint."[471] The prosecution must prove by clear and convincing evidence that

---

467. People v. Anderson, 113 Ill. 2d 1, 495 N.E.2d 485, 487, *cert. denied,* 479 U.S. 1012 (1986); People v. Stack, 112 Ill. 2d 301, 493 N.E.2d 339, 341–42, *cert. denied,* 479 U.S. 870 (1986); People v. Murphy, 157 Ill. App. 3d 115, 509 N.E.2d 1323, 1327 (1st Dist. 1987).

468. People v. DeLuca, 343 Ill. 269, 175 N.E. 370 (1931); People v. Fox, 111 Ill. App. 3d 243, 443 N.E.2d 1179, 1182 (3d Dist. 1982).

469. Brown v. Illinois, 422 U.S. 590, 601–03 (1975); People v. Creach, 69 Ill. App. 3d 874, 387 N.E.2d 762, 775–77 (1st Dist. 1979), *aff'd in part, rev'd on other grounds in part,* 79 Ill. 2d 96, 402 N.E.2d 228, *cert. denied,* 449 U.S. 1010 (1980). If there is probable cause to arrest suspects on one charge, the police may interrogate them about a second, more serious offense. Thus, in *People v. Evans,* 125 Ill. 2d 50, 530 N.E.2d 1360 (1988), *cert. denied,* 490 U.S. 1113 (1989), the Illinois Supreme Court rejected a murder defendant's argument that his arrest for a misdemeanor was a pretext for questioning him about the murder. The court reviewed the question solely to consider whether there was probable cause for the misdemeanor arrest. Finding such probable cause ended the court's inquiry. "Merely because defendant was in custody for one charge does not preclude the police from investigating other unrelated charges concerning the defendant." *Id.,* 530 N.E.2d at 1369.

470. People v. Riszowski, 22 Ill. App. 3d 741, 318 N.E.2d 10, 16 (1st Dist. 1974).

471. Wong Sun v. United States, 371 U.S. 471, 488 (1963).

the confession is attenuated—that is, not tainted by the illegal arrest.[472] The United States Supreme Court in *Brown v. Illinois*[473] developed an attenuation analysis and suggested several factors that would be considered in determining whether the confession was the result of an exploitation of the illegal arrest or, in the words of *Wong Sun,* was "sufficiently an act of free will to purge the primary taint of the unlawful invasion."[474] These factors include whether *Miranda* warnings were given, the temporal proximity of the arrest and the confession, the presence of intervening circumstances, and "particularly, the purpose and flagrancy of the official misconduct."[475] Applying these criteria, the United States Supreme Court in *Dunaway v. New York*[476] ruled inadmissible a confession obtained two hours after an unlawful arrest where "there was no intervening event of any significance whatsoever."[477] Similarly, in *Taylor v. Alabama*[478] the United States Supreme Court excluded a confession obtained after a six-hour interval following arrest during which the defendant was three times advised of his *Miranda* rights and an ex parte arrest warrant was issued.

The Illinois Appellate Court has considered several circumstances under which a confession was the product of an illegal arrest. In *People v. Franklin,*[479] the police picked up the defendant when he failed to appear for a polygraph examination. The police informed Franklin of his *Miranda* rights and interrogated him before leaving him overnight in the interrogation room. The next morning he took the polygraph examination. After being informed that the results revealed deception, the defendant confessed. The court ruled that the statement was improperly admitted even though it was obtained after proper *Miranda* warnings and was conceded to be "voluntary." The court concluded that the taint of the unlawful arrest was not cured either by the *Miranda* warnings or by the intervening fact that the defendant flunked the polygraph. The court pointed out that the polygraph itself was the result of the illegal detention and thus could not be considered a valid intervening factor. A similar result was reached by the First District of the Appellate Court, which

---

472. People v. Wilson, 60 Ill. 2d 235, 326 N.E.2d 378, 380 (1975); People v. Young, 206 Ill. App. 3d 789, 564 N.E.2d 1254 (1st Dist. 1990).

473. 422 U.S. 590, 601–03 (1975); *Creach,* 69 Ill. App. 3d 874, 387 N.E.2d at 775–77.

474. *Wong Sun,* 371 U.S. at 486.

475. *Brown,* 422 U.S. at 603–04.

476. 442 U.S. 200 (1979).

477. *Id.* at 218. *See also* People v. Wallace, 299 Ill. App. 3d 9, 701 N.E.2d 87, 94 (1st Dist. 1998) (considering added time in which voluntary attendance at police station turned into involuntary seizure prior to formal arrest).

478. 457 U.S. 687 (1982).

479. 115 Ill. 2d 328, 504 N.E.2d 80 (1987).

found that a confession obtained after the defendant had been illegally arrested was improperly admitted, notwithstanding the fact that while the defendant was in custody another suspect supplied information that normally would have constituted probable cause to arrest the first suspect.[480] These cases underscore the proposition that whether a confession is "attenuated" from the illegal arrest is a factual question depending on a "totality of circumstances," including the length of the illegal detention, the circumstances of the detention, and whether—and when—*Miranda* warning was given.[481]

Similarly, when a suspect was arrested without probable cause, taken to the police station, informed of his *Miranda* rights, and interrogated for only ten minutes before he confessed, the Illinois Supreme Court found that the statement was the product of the illegal arrest which was not purged by the administration of *Miranda* warnings.[482]

In *Rawlings v. Kentucky*,[483] the United States Supreme Court upheld the admission of a statement obtained after 45 minutes in the "congenial atmosphere" of a living room. Justice Rehnquist, writing for the majority in *Rawlings,* noted that the defendant was given *Miranda* warnings, that the statement was spontaneous and voluntary, and that there was no suggestion of police misconduct. It is important to note that the majority in *Rawlings* placed particular emphasis on the voluntary nature of the confession and not on the temporal relationship between the illegal arrest and the statement. The emphasis on the administration of *Miranda* warnings and the spontaneous nature of the statement suggests a greater emphasis on such considerations than suggested in *Brown* and *Dunaway.*

The Illinois Supreme Court in *People v. Gabbard*[484] admitted a statement given by a defendant who was improperly arrested for a different offense, given *Miranda* warnings, shown a composite sketch that resembled him, and then identified in a line-up. These factors led the court to conclude that the confession was the result of intervening factors and not the illegal arrest. In *People v. Matthews,*[485] the court held that the length of time between defendant's initial custody and his incriminating statement, along with other intervening events and circumstances of significance, established the attenuation established in *Brown.* Therefore, the taint which would render the statement

---

480. People v. McGhee, 154 Ill. App. 3d 232, 507 N.E.2d 33 (1st Dist. 1987).

481. *E.g.,* People v. Ealy, 146 Ill. App. 3d 557, 497 N.E.2d 101 (1st Dist. 1986), *cert. denied,* 479 U.S. 1066 (1987).

482. People v. Holveck, 141 Ill. 2d 84, 565 N.E.2d 919 (1990).

483. 448 U.S. 98 (1980).

484. 78 Ill. 2d 88, 398 N.E.2d 574 (1979).

485. 205 Ill. App. 3d 371, 562 N.E.2d 1113 (1st Dist. 1990).

inadmissible was removed.[486] Similarly, it has been held that an intervening circumstance includes the confrontation of the arrestee with untainted evidence that produces a voluntary desire to confess.[487] In *People v. Townes*,[488] the Illinois Supreme Court placed particular emphasis on the language in *Brown* and *Dunaway*, which concludes that a confession obtained after an illegal arrest should be suppressed if the arrest had an improper "quality of purposefulness," in that it appears to have been an "expedition for evidence." Similarly, the court suggested that the detention of the defendant "resembled a traditional arrest."

Although the Illinois Supreme Court in *Towne* made no reference to the decision in *Rawlings v. Kentucky,* there is a consistent theme. In *Rawlings* the Court upheld a confession given voluntarily in an atmosphere that was informal and noncoercive, while in *Towne* the court found that a statement given after thirteen hours of intense interrogation was subject to suppression. These cases do suggest that primary emphasis should be placed on the motivation and intent of the police. If they have no intent to obtain a statement from the defendant, are interviewing him or her on unrelated charges, or detain him or her in a less oppressive atmosphere, the statement may well be admitted. If, however, the detention is manifestly designed to obtain information about the offense charged, if the interrogation is prolonged, and if the interrogation appears to be a typical arrest-interrogation situation, the statement may be suppressed.

Although the time interval between arrest and confession is the most frequently mentioned factor in these cases, Justice Stevens' observation in *Dunaway* warrants consideration:

> The temporal relationship between the arrest and the confession may be an ambiguous factor. If there are no relevant intervening circumstances, a prolonged detention may well be a more serious exploitation of an illegal arrest than a short one. Conversely, even an immediate confession may have been motivated by a prearrest event such as a visit with a minister.[489]

These cases indicate that if the confession is obtained after an illegal arrest, the fact that the statement was voluntary under the totality of the circumstances or that the defendant was informed of the *Miranda* rights will not automatically render the statement admissible. However, under

---

486. *Id.,* 562 N.E.2d at 1134–35.

487. People v. Lekas, 155 Ill. App. 3d 391, 508 N.E.2d 221, 237 (1st Dist. 1987), *cert. denied,* 485 U.S. 942 (1988); In re R. S., 93 Ill. App. 3d 941, 418 N.E.2d 195, 199–200 (3d Dist. 1981).

488. 91 Ill. 2d 32, 435 N.E.2d 103, 105, *cert. denied,* 459 U.S. 878 (1982).

489. Dunaway v. New York, 442 U.S. 200, 220 (1979) (Stevens, J., concurring).

such circumstances the illegal taint of the improper arrest may be shown to be attenuated from the ultimate confession and the causal connection between the arrest and statement broken. Absent the prosecution's ability to show that the taint was attenuated under the factors stated in *Brown v. Illinois* and its progeny, the statement must be suppressed.[490] In *People v. Jennings*,[491] the court concluded that the defendant's confession was not sufficiently attenuated from his illegal arrest and, therefore, had to be suppressed. The fifteen-year-old defendant and three of his friends were walking down an alley in the area where the defendant had shot someone several days earlier. Because the group was in a rival gang's territory, they had the gun that the defendant had used in the shooting. Another boy, Buffen, was carrying it. As they were walking, the police approached them, and Buffen removed the gun from his waistband and began to run. The police handcuffed all four and placed them in a squad car. They then retrieved the gun and took the group to the police station. At the station, the police contacted an eyewitness to the shooting and obtained a description of the perpetrator's coat. Buffen was interviewed, and he told the police that the gun was the defendant's. The police observed that Buffen's jacket did not match that of the description given to them.[492] The police then sought to interview the defendant. They observed that his jacket was inside out. After removing his jacket and finding that it matched the description, they gave him *Miranda* warnings, and he confessed.

The trial judge concluded that the defendant's arrest was illegal and suppressed his jacket. However, it declined to suppress his confession, finding that it was sufficiently attenuated from the arrest.[493] The appellate court noted the four factors outlined in *Brown* and *Gabbard* and observed that the giving of *Miranda* warnings and temporal proximity were of little significance. However, even considering these factors, neither supported attenuation.[494] The court found that the factors of official misconduct and the presence of intervening circumstances were the most relevant. As to official misconduct, it noted that a judge was less likely to find attenuation where the police conduct was flagrant.

---

490. People v. Thomas, 123 Ill. App. 3d 857, 463 N.E.2d 832, 837–38 (1st Dist. 1984). *See* People v. Gonzalez, 268 Ill. App. 3d 224, 643 N.E.2d 1295, 1300 (1st Dist. 1994) (trial judge erred in denying defendant's motion in limine excluding witness' testimony where testimony was discovered through defendant's illegal arrest; testimony tainted by illegal arrest); People v. Bates, 267 Ill. App. 3d 503, 642 N.E.2d 774, 777 (1st Dist. 1994) (statement obtained from co-defendant's coerced confession may not serve to attenuate taint of defendant's illegal arrest and his confession must be suppressed).

491. 296 Ill. App. 3d 761, 695 N.E.2d 1303 (1st Dist. 1998).

492. *Id.*, 695 N.E.2d at 1304–05.

493. *Id.*, 695 N.E.2d at 1305.

494. *Id.*, 695 N.E.2d at 1306.

In other words, "where the police embark upon a course of illegal conduct in the hope that some incriminating evidence . . . might be found," attenuation was not likely to be found.[495] In *Jennings*, the conduct demonstrated purposefulness. The police observed only Buffen carrying the gun. Once they recovered the gun and secured the area, they had reason to hold only Buffen. Further, after they took the boys to the station, they consulted with an eyewitness. This supported a conclusion that the defendant's illegal arrest was undertaken to obtain incriminating evidence regarding the murder.[496] Thus, it factored against attenuation.

With regard to intervening circumstances, the court noted that when a suspect is confronted with untainted evidence, this is often sufficient to support attenuation.[497] However, here, the defendant was confronted with tainted and untainted evidence; a more problematic situation. The court outlined the three potential intervening factors that were present, two of which were untainted (recovery of the gun and Buffen's statement that the gun belonged to the defendant). However, the defendant was also confronted with tainted evidence: his jacket.[498] Based on the fact that the defendant was wearing the jacket inside out, showing that he knew that there was a problem with it, and the fact he confessed shortly after being confronted with it, the court could not say that the jacket was not a prominent factor in his decision to confess. It refused to conclude that the jacket simply played a *de minimis* role. Accordingly, there were insufficient intervening circumstances to support a finding of attenuation, and the appellate court reversed the conviction and remanded for a new trial without his confession.[499]

In *James v. Illinois*,[500] the defendant's statement was suppressed as being the fruit of an unlawful arrest.[501] At trial, a defense witness (not the defendant) testified that defendant had black hair on the day of the murder.[502] The state was allowed to introduce part of the previously excluded statement in which the defendant had said his hair was reddish on the day of the offense.[503] This was consistent with the testimony of the prosecution's witness.[504] The jury was

---

495. *Id.*

496. *Id.*

497. *Id.*, 695 N.E.2d at 1307.

498. *Id.*, 695 N.E.2d at 1308.

499. *Id.*

500. 493 U.S. 307 (1990).

501. *Id.* at 309–10.

502. *Id.* at 310.

503. *Id.*

504. *Id.*

instructed to consider the statement only for the purpose of impeachment and not as substantive evidence.[505] The defendant did not testify at all.[506]

The Illinois Supreme Court reversed the suppression order,[507] finding that the defendant could not hide behind the perjury of a defense witness.[508] On certiorari, the United States Supreme Court reversed the Illinois Supreme Court and ordered the statement suppressed.[509] The five-justice majority concluded that the policy warranting the admission of an illegal statement to impeach the defendant did not apply to the impeachment of a defense witness.[510] The Court reasoned that a witness is more likely to be deterred by the threat of a perjury prosecution than is a defendant and that an expansion of the rule allowing for admission of illegally obtained statements would deter defendants from calling witnesses.[511] Finally, the majority (which included Justices Brennan and Marshall) feared that expansion of the rule allowing for the admission of illegally obtained evidence would undermine the deterrent purpose of the exclusionary rule.[512]

§ 2.31 Confessions Obtained After Unreasonable Period of Detention

The United States Supreme Court has adopted the so-called *McNabb-Mallory* rule based on its decisions in *McNabb v. United States*[513] and *Mallory v. United States*.[514] The rule provides that if a confession is obtained after an unnecessary delay between arrest and initial appearance, it must be excluded from evidence in a federal criminal prosecution.[515] This rule does not apply to

---

505. *Id.*

506. *Id.*

507. People v. James, 123 Ill. 2d 523, 528 N.E.2d 723 (1988).

508. *Id.,* 528 N.E.2d at 729.

509. *James,* 493 U.S. at 320.

510. *Id.* at 313–14.

511. *Id.* at 314–15.

512. *Id.* at 317.

513. 318 U.S. 332 (1943).

514. 354 U.S. 449 (1957).

515. In title 18, section 3501(c) of the United States Code, Congress attempted to codify *McNabb-Mallory* by declaring that confessions obtained within six hours of arrest that were otherwise voluntary were admissible. If the confession is ob tained beyond the six-hour period, the statement is not per se inadmissible, and delay is but one factor to be considered in light of the surrounding circumstances. United States v. Edwards, 539 F.2d 689, 691 (9th Cir.), *cert. denied,* 429 U.S. 984 (1976).

state prosecutions,[516] and the Supreme Court of Illinois has consistently declined to adopt *McNabb-Mallory* as a matter of Illinois law.[517]

Thus, in Illinois the fact that a defendant has been held an unreasonable time before initial presentment may be a fact demonstrating that the confession was not voluntary, but the lengthy delay is not, in and of itself, grounds for suppression. This issue is discussed in greater detail in the section on voluntary confessions.[518]

§ 2.32   Statements Obtained in Violation of the Right to Counsel

A separate issue from the questions of whether the confession was voluntary and whether the requirements of *Miranda* were complied with is whether the statement was obtained from the defendant in violation of his or her right to counsel, which is guaranteed by the Sixth Amendment to the United States Constitution. This issue arises from the United States Supreme Court's decisions in *Massiah v. United States*[519] and *Brewer v. Williams.*[520]

In *Massiah,* an already indicted defendant who was not in custody made incriminating statements to a co-defendant who agreed to become a government agent. The Supreme Court excluded the statements from evidence at trial, deciding that because the right to counsel had already attached, the government could not interrogate the defendant in the absence of counsel. Such an interrogation violated the defendant's right to counsel guaranteed by the Sixth Amendment.

---

516. Gallegos v. Nebraska, 342 U.S. 55, 63–64 (1951).

517. People v. Howell, 60 Ill. 2d 117, 324 N.E.2d 403, 405 (1975), *superseded by statute as stated in* People v. Clarke, 231 Ill. App. 3d 504, 596 N.E.2d 872 (5th Dist. 1992); People v. Jackson, 23 Ill. 2d 274, 178 N.E.2d 299, 301 (1961). *See, e.g.,* People v. Bounds, 171 Ill. 2d 1, 662 N.E.2d 1168, 1180–81 (1995) (eight hours is not an unreasonably long period of custody and will not nullify the voluntariness of a subsequent statement), *cert. denied,* 519 U.S. 876 (1996); People v. Groves, 294 Ill. App. 3d 570, 691 N.E.2d 86, 92–93 (1st Dist. 1998) (statement voluntary in spite of four-day detention prior to making it, even though defendant only 19 years old, he did not sleep much, and there were many interrogations late in evening or early in morning).

518. See notes 173–196 and accompanying text in this chapter.

519. 377 U.S. 201 (1964), made applicable to the states through the Fourteenth Amendment in *McLeod v. Ohio,* 381 U.S. 356 (1965).

520. 430 U.S. 387 (1977).

Although some courts felt that *Miranda* had superseded *Massiah*,[521] in *Brewer* the United States Supreme Court again in 1977 relied on the Sixth Amendment right to counsel to find that a statement given by an already charged defendant was inadmissible when the defendant's attorney had obtained an agreement from the police not to question the defendant but the police engaged in conduct that the Supreme Court found to be an interrogation.

There are several apparent distinctions between the *Massiah-Brewer* situation and that dealt with in *Miranda*. First, in order for *Massiah* and *Brewer* to apply, the right to counsel must already have attached. This means the adversary proceedings have already commenced against the defendant in the form of a formal charge, preliminary hearing, indictment, or information.[522]

However, acceptance of counsel at an extradition hearing does not trigger a Sixth Amendment right to counsel for all future proceedings even though his Sixth Amendment right to counsel had already attached at the extradition hearing.[523] The rule does not apply before the constitutional right to counsel has attached, even if the defendant has retained an attorney known to the police.[524] Moreover, if the right to counsel has attached on a charge unrelated to that which the defendant is being interrogated about, the Sixth Amendment does not prohibit an interrogation in the absence of the attorney who is representing the defendant on the other case.[525]

The Sixth Amendment right to counsel, which does not attach until the initiation of adversarial judical proceedings, is offense specific, and thus the

---

521. United States v. Mandley, 502 F.2d 1103 (9th Cir. 1974); Moore v. Wolff, 495 F.2d 35 (8th Cir. 1974); United States v. Dority, 487 F.2d 846 (6th Cir. 1973).

522. Kirby v. Illinois, 406 U.S. 682, 689 (1972); People v. Kavinsky, 91 Ill. App. 3d 784, 414 N.E.2d 1206, 1213 (1st Dist. 1980). *See also* People v. Thompkins, 121 Ill. 2d 401, 521 N.E.2d 38, 50–51 (supreme court determined that Sixth Amendment right to counsel had not attached when only complaint for preliminary examination charging defendant with murder had been issued and when he had been neither indicted nor arraigned; defendant gave statement while he was awaiting his initial court appearance and after he had talked on telephone to attorney whom his wife had contacted; attorney instructed defendant to make no statement to police; inasmuch as defendant properly waived his *Miranda* rights, statement was properly admissible without violating his Sixth Amendment right to counsel), *cert. denied*, 488 U.S. 871 (1988); People v. Chambers, 261 Ill. App. 3d 123, 633 N.E.2d 123, 128 (4th Dist. 1994) (defendant did not invoke Sixth Amendment right to counsel at police board hearing because at that time no formal charges, indictment, or information had been filed against him), *cert. denied*, 513 U.S. 1194 (1995).

523. People v. Makiel, 263 Ill. App. 3d 54, 635 N.E.2d 941, 952 (1st Dist. 1994).

524. People v. Woollums, 93 Ill. App. 3d 144, 416 N.E.2d 725, 728 (4th Dist. 1981).

525. People v. Martin, 102 Ill. 2d 412, 466 N.E.2d 228, 232, *cert. denied*, 469 U.S. 935 (1984).

police could interrogate a jailed defendant about uncharged offenses, even after the right to counsel had attached on the charged but unrelated crime.[526]

When the new charge is closely related to the original charge, the right to counsel may apply. In *People v. Clankie*,[527] the defendant had been convicted of two burglaries but was granted a new trial. Between the first and second trials, a police informant obtained a statement from the defendant that covered both the original offenses and a different burglary of the same premises. Following *Maine v. Moulton*,[528] the Illinois Supreme Court found that the informant's statement violated the defendant's constitutional right to counsel not only for the original offense, but for the new offense as well. The court noted that the original and new burglaries were "extemely closely related" and that the right to counsel for the original charges could not "constitutionally be isolated from the right to counsel for the uncharged offense."[529] In *People v. Wahl*,[530] the court expanded upon and further defined the "closely related offenses" exception. It first noted that the purpose of the exception was "to prevent the State from interrogating a defendant about a distinct course of criminal conduct—one capable of supporting a new charge—outside of the presence of the defendant's attorney, when the fruits of a successful interrogation will be admissible as substantive proof of the charges upon which adversarial judicial criminal proceedings have commenced. Put another way, [the second interrogation] functions as a continuation of the investigation of the factual transaction forming the basis of the previously charged offense."[531] In determining whether the exception applies, the court stated that three factors should be evaluated: (1) whether the victim or targets are the same (the most important factor); (2) the amount of time between the acts (the shorter the period, the greater likelihood they are the same); and (3) whether a different police authority or sovereign conducted the second interrogation.[532] In this case, prior to interrogation on March 11, 1991, the defendant had been charged with aggravated criminal sexual abuse against R.F. and K.W. Subsequent to the March 11 interrogation, the defendant was charged with aggravated criminal sexual abuse against four other children. He argued that the latter charges were so closely related to the prior charges that the police violated his Sixth Amendment right to counsel. The court disagreed. The latter charges were against different individuals; the time span between the acts amounted to

---

526. McNeil v. Wisconsin, 501 U.S. 171, 175 (1991).

527. 124 Ill. 2d 456, 530 N.E.2d 448 (1988).

528. 474 U.S. 159 (1985).

529. *Clankie*, 124 Ill. 2d 456, 530 N.E.2d at 451.

530. 285 Ill. App. 3d 288, 674 N.E.2d 454 (2d Dist. 1996).

531. *Id.*, 674 N.E.2d at 462.

532. *Id.*

approximately a nine-month period, were not continuous, and were "interspersed among the ordinary acts of life;" and finally, the defendant was not interrogated by a different law enforcement agency.[533]

Miranda, however, may apply before the time the Sixth Amendment right to counsel has attached, as long as the defendant is in custody.[534] *Massiah* and *Brewer* apply even if the defendant is not in custody, as the facts in *Massiah* demonstrate. Under *Massiah* and *Brewer,* once the right to counsel attaches the police may not engage in any conduct deliberately designed to elicit incriminatory information from the defendant.[535] This places the defendant for whom the right to counsel has attached in very much the same position as a defendant who has invoked the right to counsel under *Miranda:* the police cannot thereafter initiate an interrogation.[536]

In *Innis v. Rhode Island,*[537] the United States Supreme Court suggested that there is a difference in the nature of interrogation for *Miranda* and Sixth Amendment purposes, and thus there is a split of authority in Illinois on the question of whether an interrogation under *Miranda* is the same as an interrogation for *Massiah* and *Brewer* purposes.[538] Nevertheless a close reading of the cited footnote in *Innis* reveals that the United States Supreme Court was concerned with pointing out that custody is not required for an interrogation under *Massiah and Brewer,* although it is under *Miranda,* and that in one situation the Fifth Amendment is implicated, while in the other the issue arises from the Sixth Amendment. There is no suggestion in *Innis* that the nature of the police conduct is different in the two situations, and thus the Illinois Supreme Court in *People v. Aldridge*[539] considered an interrogation to be the same from both *Miranda* and Sixth Amendment purposes when focusing on the conduct of the police and the defendant. Unless the police deliberately

---

533. *Id.,* 674 N.E.2d at 463.

534. See footnotes 173–196 and accompanying text in this chapter.

535. United States v. Henry, 447 U.S. 264 (1980); Massiah v. United States, 377 U.S. 201, 206 (1964); People v. Kavinsky, 91 Ill. App. 3d 784, 414 N.E.2d 1206, 1213 (1st Dist. 1980). For a discussion of the interrogation requirement of *Miranda,* see footnotes 281–306 and accompanying text in this chapter.

536. *See* Minnick v. Mississippi, 498 U.S. 146 (1990).

537. 446 U.S. 291, 300 n.4 (1980).

538. *Compare* Kavinsky, 91 Ill. App. 3d 784, 414 N.E.2d at 1213 n.7 (suggesting that definition of *interrogation* is different for Sixth Amendment than for *Miranda* purposes) *with* People v. Jumper, 113 Ill. App. 3d 346, 447 N.E.2d 531, 534 (4th Dist. 1983) (concluding that meaning of interrogation is same for both situations).

539. 79 Ill. 2d 87, 402 N.E.2d 176, 179 (1980).

intended to elicit the information, it may be admitted.[540] Moreover, if the defendant initiates the contact with the police, even after the right to counsel has attached, a statement may still be taken by the police in the absence of counsel as long as there is a knowing and intentional waiver and the statement is voluntary, applying a standard similar to that of *Miranda* situations.[541]

In *People v. Hicks*,[542] the Illinois Supreme Court held that by initiating conversation with a deputy, the defendant voluntarily waived his right to have counsel present during interrogations concerning a charged offense and a separate offense.[543] In this case, after arraignment and after appointment of counsel, a detective transferred defendant to a different correctional facility.[544] Defendant volunteered some statements regarding the burglary with which he was charged. The detective informed defendant that he could not discuss the matter because he had an attorney. The defendant continued to discuss the

---

540. In both *Aldridge* and *Kavinsky* the courts found that the interrogation occurred only after the conversation was initiated by the defendant. *See also* Kuhlman v. Wilson, 477 U.S. 436 (1986) (in order to suppress statement given to jailhouse informant, defendant must show "that the police and their informant took some action, beyond merely listening, that was designed deliberately to elicit incriminating remarks"; absent such showing, there was no constitutional violation when police informant was placed in cell with defendant and told simply to "keep his ears open" for names of other persons who committed offense; finding no "secret interrogation" of defendant by informant, majority of Court upheld admission of statement); People v. Dove, 147 Ill. App. 3d 659, 498 N.E.2d 279 (4th Dist. 1986) (court first excluded state ment made by defendant to police informant who was wired with listening device, in violation of defendant's Sixth Amendment right to counsel, but admitted later confession given to same person, who was then operating "on his own" and not as an informant).

541. *Aldridge,* 79 Ill. 2d 87, 402 N.E.2d at 180; People v. Johnson, 96 Ill. App. 3d 763, 422 N.E.2d 50, 57 (1st Dist. 1981). *See also* People v. Kidd, 129 Ill. 2d 432, 544 N.E.2d 704, 713–14 (1989) (defendant's waiver of Sixth Amendment right to counsel invalid where represented by counsel). The explanation of rights for a defendant who has a Sixth Amendment right to counsel is identical to that afforded under *Miranda;* no more explicit or detailed admonitions are required. People v. Thomas, 116 Ill. 2d 290, 507 N.E.2d 843, 846, *aff'd,* Patterson v. Illinois, 487 U.S. 285 (1988); People v. Owens, 102 Ill. 2d 88, 464 N.E.2d 261, 267, *cert. denied,* 469 U.S. 963 (1984).

542. 132 Ill. 2d 488, 548 N.E.2d 1042 (1989).

543. *Id.,* 548 N.E.2d at 1046. *But see* People v. Navarroli, 121 Ill. 2d 516, 521 N.E.2d 891, 895 (1988) (defendant's Sixth Amendment right to counsel not violated when subject to postindictment questioning outside the presence of counsel regarding criminal activity which the defendant merely witnessed but did not participate in because Sixth Amendment right to counsel had not attached).

544. *Hicks,* 132 Ill. 2d 488, 548 N.E.2d at 1044.

matter. Later, as the vehicle passed the site of a different burglary, the detective "jokingly" asked defendant whether he had any knowledge concerning that particular burglary. Defendant incriminated himself in response to this questioning.

The court determined that defendant's waiver was knowingly and intelligently made and was not limited by the Sixth Amendment right to counsel.[545] The court reasoned that a defendant's invocation of his right to counsel shows that an accused is not able to deal with custodial interrogation unless counsel is present. If the accused waives his right to counsel, it indicates that he believes he is able to deal with the interrogation without counsel's presence. Because the defendant did not limit his waiver to the Sixth Amendment and he freely chose to speak, the confession was voluntary and admissible.[546]

The United States Supreme Court, in *Moran v. Burbine*,[547] held that so long as the suspect validly waived his right to counsel, the police were under no obligation to tell the suspect that an attorney had sought to consult with him. The Illinois Supreme Court, in *People v. Holland*,[548] adopted *Burbine* and distinguished it from its 1982 decision in *People v. Smith*.[549] In *Smith*, the court determined that the defendant had been denied his right to counsel when he had already seen the lawyer and had retained him as counsel, and when a partner of the retained counsel went to the jail to see the suspect. In *Burbine* and *Holland* a relative secured counsel, the suspect was unaware that counsel had been retained, and all conversations between the police or prosecutor and the attorney were by telephone.

Since *Burbine* was decided, several states have found that the failure or refusal of police to inform a suspect of an attorney's attempt to provide counsel to the suspect rendered invalid a waiver of the suspect's rights under their own state constitutions.[550] The Illinois Supreme Court, in *People v. Griggs*,[551] distinguished this case from *Holland* and *Burbine* factually. The court held that

---

545. *Id.,* 548 N.E.2d at 1045.

546. *Id.,* 548 N.E.2d at 1045–46.

547. 475 U.S. 625 (1986).

548. 121 Ill. 2d 136, 520 N.E.2d 270 (1987), *aff'd,* 493 U.S. 474 (1990).

549. 93 Ill. 2d 179, 442 N.E.2d 1325 (1982), *cert. denied,* 461 U.S. 937 (1983).

550. State v. Stoddard, 206 Conn. 157, 537 A.2d 446, 457 (1988) (suppression of statements required where state did not prove that officer's failure to properly communicate to defendant his attorney's efforts to reach him would not have altered defendant's appraisal and understanding of circumstances); Bryan v. State, 571 A.2d 170 (Del. 1990) (reaffirming pre-*Burbine* ruling in *Weber v. State*, 457 A.2d 674 (Del. 1983)); Roeder v. State, 768 S.W.2d 745 (Tex. Crim. App. 1988) (reaffirming pre-*Burbine* ruling in *Dunn v. State*, 696 S.W.2d 561 (Tex. Crim. App. 1985)).

551. 152 Ill. 2d 1, 604 N.E.2d 257, 269 (1992).

a suspect who knows that an attorney had been retained for him or her cannot validly waive the Fifth Amendment right to counsel if the police refuse or fail to inform the suspect that the attorney has made efforts to reach or counsel him or her. However, in order for this rule to apply, the attorney must be present at the place of interrogation.

The Illinois Supreme Court has now rejected *Burbine*'s holding and analysis pursuant to state constitutional law.[552] In *People v. McCauley*, the court held that the police, either prior to or during custodial interrogation, cannot refuse an appointed or retained counsel access to his or her client. This is true whether the suspect has knowledge of the attorney's appointment or retention or not.[553] According to the court, under the Illinois Constitution, when the suspect is not informed that an attorney is present and seeking to consult with him or her, there can be no knowing or intelligent waiver of the right to counsel. The court relied on *Smith*, rejected the factual distinction made in *Holland* because the *Burbine* analysis cannot depend on factual variations, and followed *Griggs*.[554] The court found that *Griggs* was grounded in state law and expressly affirmed *Smith*. A suspect's awareness of his attorney's appointment or retention is not decisive of *Smith*'s application.[555] That case held for the proposition that "where a suspect is not informed that his attorney is present, unsuccessfully seeking access to him," he or she is denied the right to counsel which violates the Illinois Constitution.[556] In conclusion, the court found that "*Holland* preserved the *Smith* rule . . . [and that] *Griggs* then expressly reaffirmed and relied on *Smith's* rationale as a matter of state constitutional law to reject *Burbine's* Federal constitutional analysis."[557]

McCauley does not apply when the defendant is merely "on the threshold" of having an attorney.[558] In *Johnson*, the defendant was in a holding cell waiting to appear at a preliminary hearing on a rape charge. The defendant was to have counsel appointed at that hearing. Before he appeared, detectives removed him to police headquarters to question him about an unrelated murder investigation. After waiving his *Miranda* rights, the defendant confessed to the murder. On

---

552. People v. McCauley, 163 Ill. 2d 414, 645 N.E.2d 923 (1994). *See also* People v. Albrecht, 271 Ill. App. 3d 629, 649 N.E.2d 57, 62 (1st Dist. 1995) (no valid waiver of right to counsel where police not inform defendant that attorney retained by family present and requesting to speak with him).

553. *McCauley*, 163 Ill. 2d 414, 645 N.E.2d at 929.

554. *Id.*, 645 N.E.2d at 929–36.

555. *Id.*, 645 N.E.2d at 936.

556. *Id.*, 645 N.E.2d at 935.

557. *Id.*, 645 N.E.2d at 936.

558. People v. Johnson, 182 Ill. 2d 96, 695 N.E.2d 435, 440, *cert. denied*, 119 S. Ct. 451 (1998).

appeal, the court refused to suppress the confession. Unlike *McCauley*, the police in *Johnson* "neither interfered with defendant's access to a readily available attorney nor failed to inform defendant of an attempted contact by that attorney."[559] Absent deliberate "deceitful acts" or "egregious conduct" by the police in preventing the defendant from having the assistance of counsel, the statement was admissible.[560]

The court in *People v. Milestone*[561] held that the means by which the authorities are informed of an attorney's representation of the defendant is irrelevant. The defendant's right to counsel does not hinge on the attorney making his or her representation known in person at the police station.[562] In *Milestone*, an attorney was denied access to the defendant when he tried to reach him by telephone. The defendant did not know the attorney, and the police did not tell the defendant that the attorney was trying to contact him.[563] The court held that the defendant's right against self-incrimination under the Illinois Constitution had been denied because the police denied him access to his attorney. Whether a person in custody is denied his or her rights does not turn on whether the attorney was physically present at the police station or whether he or she informed the police on the telephone rather than in person that he or she represents the defendant. The deciding factor is whether the attorney reasonably informed the police that he or she represents the defendant and not the manner in which the police are informed.[564]

However, a defendant's right to counsel under *Miranda* is not invoked where an attorney for the defendant relates to a federal law enforcement officer that the defendant was not to be questioned pertaining to any matter while the attorney was representing the defendant on unrelated charges.[565] Accordingly, ensuing custodial interrogation about the instant charges did not have to be suppressed as no unambiguous request for counsel had been made by the defendant as to the instant charges.[566]

In *Michigan v. Jackson*,[567] the Court extended the rule of *Edwards v. Arizona*,[568] which held that once a suspect invokes his right to counsel under

---

559. *Id.*

560. *Id.*, 695 N.E.2d at 441.

561. 283 Ill. App. 3d 682, 671 N.E.2d 51 (3d Dist. 1996).

562. *Id.*, 671 N.E.2d at 54.

563. *Id.*, 671 N.E.2d at 53.

564. *Id.*, 671 N.E.2d at 54.

565. United States v. McKinley, 84 F.3d 904, 908–09 (7th Cir. 1996).

566. *Id.* at 910.

567. 475 U.S. 625 (1986).

568. 451 U.S. 477 (1981).

Miranda, the police cannot thereafter initiate an interrogation of the suspect. In *Jackson* the Court adopted a similar rule to Sixth Amendment cases, finding that once a defendant had invoked his right to counsel at arraignment or similar proceedings, the police could not initiate an interrogation of the defendant without counsel being present.

Thus the Sixth Amendment provides an additional safeguard for a person who already has the right to counsel, whether or not he or she is in custody. Under such circumstances he or she cannot be interrogated in the absence of counsel unless he or she initiates the contact with police and then voluntarily and knowingly waives the right to counsel. *Brewer* demonstrates that once the right to counsel has attached the police may not initiate an interrogation, even if there is subsequently a waiver of counsel. Before the attachment of the right to counsel, however, under *Miranda* the police may initiate an interrogation and obtain incriminating information after a valid waiver. The difference is that under *Miranda* the police can seek to interrogate the defendant, as long as he or she does not invoke the right to counsel, while under *Massiah* and *Brewer* such conduct is prohibited. Once the defendant initiates contact, however, the defendant is in precisely the same situation under either *Miranda* or *Massiah* and *Brewer.* At that point, he or she can waive counsel and be interrogated. The defendant's statement will be admitted if the waiver is found to be proper.

In *Michigan v. Harvey,*[569] the United States Supreme Court concluded that a statement obtained in violation of a defendant's Sixth Amendment right to counsel could be used for impeachment.[570] In *Harvey,* the Court viewed the exclusionary rule established by *Michigan v. Jackson*[571] as a "prophylactic rule," similar to that created by *Miranda.*[572] The Court thus extended the rule of *Harris v. New York,*[573] which allows the impeachment of a defendant with a voluntary statement but which nonetheless violates *Miranda.*[574]

In *People v. Young,*[575] the Illinois Supreme Court held that in regard to an accused's invocation of his Fifth and Sixth Amendment rights, a police officer's knowledge of the invocation will be imputed to other law enforcement authorities within the State of Illinois.[576] However, Illinois courts refuse to extend this

---

569.   494 U.S. 344 (1990).

570.   *Id.* at 348.

571.   475 U.S. 625 (1986).

572.   *Harvey,* 494 U.S. at 350.

573.   *See* footnote 445.

574.   401 U.S. 222, 226 (1971).

575.   People v. Young, 153 Ill. 2d 383, 607 N.E.2d 123 (1992), *cert. denied,* 510 U.S. 829 (1993).

576.   *Id.,* 607 N.E.2d at 126 (court refused to hold defendant's invocation of his Fifth and Sixth Amendment rights in Wisconsin should be imputed to Illinois authorities).

rule to another state's knowledge of defendant's invocation.[577] Thus, if another state knows of the accused's invocation of his rights, Illinois courts will not impute this knowledge to Illinois authorities who later interrogate the suspect where the purposes for imputing knowledge are not present.[578] Moreover, the *Young* court held that Illinois authorities have no duty to inquire of authorities outside the State of Illinois when there is no reason to believe those authorities questioned the defendant and where there is no reasonable procedure to direct such an inquiry.[579]

---

577. *Id.*, 607 N.E.2d at 128. One purpose for imputing knowledge between authorities is to prevent law enforcement officials from circumventing an ac cused's request for counsel by transferring the accused to another officer. The second purpose is to give effect to *Edwards. Id.*, 607 N.E.2d at 126.

578. *Id.*, 607 N.E.2d at 129–30.

579. *Id.*

3

CHARGING

The Honorable Kenneth L. Gillis
Mr. Iain D. Johnston

---

§ 3.01   Introduction

The initiation of a criminal prosecution is a step of great significance. The prosecution, on behalf of the community, signals its intent to designate the defendant as a criminal, as an "enemy of the people," as Ibsen put it. If that could be accomplished, punishment would surely follow.

The initiation of prosecution has an enormous personal impact on the defendant, who finds himself or herself pitted against all of the "People of the State of Illinois." Emotional distress, physical deterioration, and financial hardship are foreseeable consequences of just being prosecuted.

The forms and procedures within the charging stage play a distinct role in the final outcome of the case. Although we have thankfully retreated from the ancient world where form reigned high over substance, the form of the charge and the method of charging become significant as the case is later tried to verdict or finding.

Fairness in the charging phase (always the obligation of government "for the people"), discovery, the right to a speedy trial, and the right to counsel all begin within the charging stage and have reverberating effects throughout the criminal proceedings. The charging stage is, for the prosecution, an exercise in sound discretion, fairness, and conscientious attention to details. For the defense it requires vigilance to see that a client's rights are respected and bracing for the battle that will soon begin.

§ 3.02   Initiating Prosecution

There are three ways in which a prosecution may be commenced: by complaint, by information, or by indictment. Failure to use one of these methods of formal charging will be fatal to any conviction.[1]

If an offense is a felony, meaning it is punishable by a term of imprisonment in a penitentiary,[2] it must be initiated either by indictment or information. Illinois Compiled Statutes chapter 725, section 5/111-2 states: "All prosecutions of felonies shall be by information or by indictment. No prosecution may be pursued by information unless a preliminary hearing has been held or waived . . . and at that hearing probable cause . . . found."[3]

---

1. 725 ILCS 5/111-1.

2. People v. Jarrett, 57 Ill. App. 2d 169, 206 N.E.2d 835 (1st Dist. 1965).

3. 725 ILCS 5/111-2(a). There is, however, no right to be indicted by a grand jury in a state criminal proceeding as this aspect of the Fifth Amendment is not

Prosecution of offenses that are misdemeanors,[4] which might be punished by fine or incarceration time in an institution that is not a penitentiary (a county jail, for example), is initiated by complaint.[5] Of course, there is nothing prohibiting a prosecutor from bringing a misdemeanor charge by indictment or information.

An indictment is an accusation by the grand jury; an information is an accusation brought by the state's attorney.[6] Illinois Compiled Statutes chapter 725, sections 5/102-11 and 5/102-12 define these terms: " 'Indictment' means a written statement, presented by the Grand Jury to a court, which charges the commission of an offense."[7] " 'Information' means a verified written statement signed by the State's Attorney, and presented to a court, which charges the commission of an offense."[8]

A complaint is an accusation initiated by a private citizen or a police officer: " 'Complaint' means a verified written statement other than an information or an indictment, presented to a court, which charges the commission of an offense."[9]

All three methods of initiating a prosecution must charge the defendant in such a way that he or she will know the nature and elements of the offense charged.[10] These directory principles, thought to have little force, have recently been employed to decide serious substantive issues. In *People v. Pankey*,[11] a defendant was chargeable with traffic offenses and aggravated battery on the arresting officer. The officer filed a charge of aggravated battery against the defendant on a uniform citation for traffic offense form. Later in the day the defendant appeared in court, without a state's attorney present, and entered a plea of guilty to the aggravated battery charge. He was fined 50 dollars and costs. The next day the state's attorney filed an information charging aggravated battery. The defendant appeared and moved to dismiss because of double

---

applicable to the states. People v. Easley, 288 Ill. App. 3d 487, 680 N.E.2d 776, 781 (3d Dist. 1997).

4. 720 ILCS 5/2-11.

5. 725 ILCS 5/111-2(b).

6. 725 ILCS 5/102-11, 5/102-12. People v. Moore, 199 Ill. App. 3d 747, 557 N.E.2d 537, 549 (1st Dist. 1990) (rules of criminal proceedings instituted by indictment apply to proceedings instituted by information), *cert. denied*, 498 U.S. 1032 (1991).

7. 725 ILCS 5/102-1.

8. 725 ILCS 5/102-12.

9. 725 ILCS 5/102-9.

10. People v. Edge, 406 Ill. 490, 94 N.E.2d 359 (1950); People v. Alvarado, 301 Ill. App. 3d 1017, 704 N.E.2d 937 (2d Dist. 1998).

11. 94 Ill. 2d 12, 445 N.E.2d 284 (1983).

jeopardy. The state's attorney contended that the first "prosecution" was invalid because it occurred without his knowledge or consent and urged that the subsequent charge be prosecuted. The Illinois Supreme Court agreed with the state's attorney. It held that the first guilty plea was invalid because the state's attorney was not present and did not acquiesce to the procedure. The court reasoned that the police officer was without authority to prosecute the charge of aggravated battery because "only the State's Attorney has the authority to file a felony charge."[12]

It may be questionable for a court to rely on cases decided for one purpose and apply them to situations in different settings, but that was done in *People v. Racanelli*.[13] In this case, the issue was when adversary proceedings began in order for the Sixth Amendment right to counsel to become viable. The defense contended that it was early in the course of the investigation, when the police had obtained a warrant for the arrest of the defendant. To get the arrest warrant, a police officer signed a complaint alleging that the defendant had committed murder. The state, however, argued that murder, a felony, could not lawfully be prosecuted by complaint and thus attachment happened much later, when the defendant was indicted by the grand jury for murder. The appellate court agreed with the state.

> Illinois law provides that felony prosecutions must be commenced by indictment or information and not by complaint . . . . Further, only the State's Attorney has the authority to file a felony charge, and a police officer is without that authority to prosecute such a charge . . . . Thus, the State cannot be said to have filed a formal charge committing itself to the prosecution of Racanelli simply with the filing of a complaint by a police officer.[14]

The majority in *Racanelli* went on to decide that because a valid prosecution had not begun until the later date, the defendant's right to counsel was postponed to the later date as well.[15]

---

12. *Id.*, 445 N.E.2d at 288.

13. 132 Ill. App. 3d 124, 476 N.E.2d 1179 (1st Dist. 1985).

14. *Id.*, 476 N.E.2d at 1183.

15. *Id.* Note that Justice Pincham dissented. He cited section 111-2(a), which reads: "No prosecution may be pursued by information unless a preliminary hearing his been held or waived . . . and at that hearing probable cause to believe the defendant committed an offense was found, and the provisions of section 109-3.1 of this Code have been complied with." *Id.*, 476 N.E.2d at 1201. Justice Pincham did not elaborate. Did he mean that a complaint for preliminary hearing could become a valid initial phase of a prosecution if a preliminary hearing occurs and then an information is issued by the state's attorney? And if a complaint for

One line of cases, including *Racanelli,* has held that an arrest warrant by itself does not formally charge the defendant with a crime.[16] Some of these cases bring in an additional factor—the absence of prosecutorial involvement.[17] But even slight prosecutorial conduct may be of consequence. In *People v. Jones,*[18] the victim testified that prior to the line-up he was shown the stocking used as a mask in the crime while he was "talking to the State's Attorney."[19] In holding that adversary judicial criminal proceeding had been initiated and the right to counsel had attached, the *Jones* court stated: "There being nothing in the record negating the fact that the State's Attorney was involved at that time and since the stocking bore no relation of any kind to the lineup, it follows that it was shown to [the victim] in the preparation of the prosecutor's case."[20]

While there is a split of authority, the larger body of case law holds that the right to counsel automatically attaches with the filing of a criminal complaint.[21]

The Illinois Supreme Court has touched on this issue in *People v. Wilson.*[22] The court found that a complaint for an arrest warrant presented by a police officer (not by an Assistant State's Attorney) to a judge *ex parte* did not trigger the right to counsel, since "adversary proceedings" had not yet begun. Similarly, in *People v. Young,*[23] a prosecutor initiated a fugitive warrant to another state to extradite the defendant back to Illinois. Neither that conduct nor the

---

preliminary hearing could become valid, isn't it in fact valid at the time that it issues?

16. *See, e.g.,* People v. Mitchell, 116 Ill. App. 3d 44, 451 N.E.2d 934, 936 (5th Dist. 1983), *modified on other grounds,* 105 Ill. 2d 1, 473 N.E.2d 1250, *cert. denied,* 470 U.S. 1089 (1985); People v. Dockery, 72 Ill. App. 2d 345, 355, 219 N.E.2d 687, 692 (1st Dist. 1966).

17. People v. Boswell, 111 Ill. 2d 571, 488 N.E.2d 273 (1986); People v. Jones, 148 Ill. App. 3d 133, 498 N.E.2d 772 (1st Dist. 1986).

18. 148 Ill. App. 3d 133, 498 N.E.2d 772 (1st Dist. 1986).

19. *Id.,* 498 N.E.2d at 777.

20. *Id.*

21. People v. Dove, 147 Ill. App. 3d 659, 498 N.E.2d 279 (4th Dist. 1986); People v. Fleming, 134 Ill. App. 3d 562, 480 N.E.2d 1221 (1st Dist. 1985); People v. Jumper, 113 Ill. App. 3d 346, 447 N.E.2d 531 (4th Dist. 1983); People v. Faulkner, 86 Ill. App. 3d 136, 407 N.E.2d 126 (1st Dist. 1980); People v. Giovanetti, 70 Ill. App. 3d 275, 387 N.E.2d 1071 (1st Dist. 1979).

22. 116 Ill. 2d 29, 506 N.E.2d 571, 580–81 (1987).

23. 153 Ill. 2d 383, 607 N.E.2d 123 (1992), *cert. denied,* 510 U.S. 829 (1993).

appointment of a public defender in the other state had been enough to signal the start of the adversary phase.[24]

The issue was also reached in *People v. Kidd*,[25] where the Illinois Supreme Court cited with approval the United States Supreme Court case of *Maine v. Moulton*.[26] In *Moulton*, two defendants, represented by counsel, had been indicted. However, the co-defendant began to cooperate with the police, wearing a secret listening device and speaking with Moulton about the pending charges, as well as other matters. The information so gathered by the co-defendant (a police agent) was held to be in violation of *Kirby v. Illinois*,[27] and Moulton's uncounseled statements were barred because they violated his Sixth Amendment right to counsel. The Illinois Supreme Court in *Kidd* reached this same conclusion. There, the defendant had been arraigned, but because of withdrawal of counsel, there was no lawyer technically representing him at the time of the interrogation. The "adversary judicial criminal proceedings" had begun.[28]

§ 3.03   Form of the Charge

There are six requirements for a valid charging document,[29] five of which are routine. These five are that the charge must be in writing,[30]

---

24. *Id.*, 607 N.E.2d at 132–33.

25. 129 Ill. 2d 432, 544 N.E.2d 704 (1989).

26. 474 U.S. 159, 170 (1985).

27. 406 U.S. 682, 689 (1972).

28. *Kidd*, 129 Ill. 2d 432, 544 N.E.2d at 711–12.

29. 725 ILCS 5/111-3; People v. Dunskus, 282 Ill. App. 3d 912, 668 N.E.2d 1138, 1141–42 (1st Dist. 1996) (traffic citation charging defendant with driving under the influence that did not originally specify "of alcohol" or cite to statutory provision was determined to be sufficient; defendant was aware that charge involved consumption of alcohol and not drugs because he had the accident report, the alcohol influence report, and medical records prior to the trial); People v. Weber, 264 Ill. App. 3d 310, 636 N.E.2d 902, 905–06 (1st Dist. 1994) (indictment valid where compliance with statutory requirements); People v. Moore, 119 Ill. App. 3d 747, 557 N.E.2d 537, 549 (1st Dist. 1990) (information or indictment valid on its face sufficient to require a trial of the charge), *cert. denied*, 498 U.S. 1032 (1991). *But see* People v. Moulton, 282 Ill. App. 3d 102, 668 N.E.2d 1078, 1082 (3d Dist. 1996) (home invasion charge properly dismissed because it failed to state offense; co-owner of a home does not fall within the scope of the home invasion statute).

30. *People v. Wotchko*, 74 Ill. App. 2d 151, 219 N.E.2d 371 (5th Dist. 1966), is a case where the defendants were brought to court by the sheriff and then orally advised by the judge of the charges made against them. No complaint, indictment,

state the name of the offense,[31] state the statutory provision by number,[32] state the date and the county of the offense,[33] and state the name of the accused.[34] If an offense alleged in an information is based on a series of acts, and the information fails to allege that any of the acts took place within the statute of limitations, the statute will be tolled when there are sufficient specific facts in the information to enable the defendant to prepare his or her defense and to apprise the accused that the last act occurred within the limitations period.[35] Similarly, a charging instrument which alleges violations of a not yet effective statute, and which is based on a series of acts, is sufficient if the instrument alleges that some

---

or information had been filed. The appellate court held that the convictions could not stand.

31. 725 ILCS 5/111-3(a)(1).

32. 725 ILCS 5/111-3(a)(2).

33. The importance of the date of the offense charged is one of limitation. The date signals the time within which the prosecution can bring the charge. For example, if the offense of robbery (a felony) is said to have occurred on April 29, 1983, the state has three years to bring that charge under Chapter 720, section 5/3-5. The date charged need not be proven precisely. People v. Alexander, 99 Ill. App. 3d 810, 425 N.E.2d 1386 (3d Dist. 1981), aff'd, 93 Ill. 2d 73, 442 N.E.2d 887 (1982). But see People v. Barlow, 188 Ill. App. 3d 393, 544 N.E.2d 947, 953 (1st Dist. 1989) (date of the offense is not an essential element of the offense). In People v. Berg, 277 Ill. App. 3d 549, 660 N.E.2d 1003 (2d Dist. 1996), the court held that aggravated arson was not included under section 2-5(a) which allows for prosecution at any time. Instead, a prosecution for aggravated arson must occur within three years of the crime. The language of the section was clear and unambiguous (id., 660 N.E.2d at 1004), and the court would not read offenses into it that were not there. Id., 606 N.E.2d at 1005. Although the legislature had recently amended this section and added concealment of a homicidal death and aggravated arson, the amendment was not retroactive because it was clear the legislature, by amending the provision, did not previously intend to include these crimes within the provision. Id., 660 N.E.2d at 1005–06. See People v. Holmes, 292 Ill. App. 3d 855, 686 N.E.2d 1209, 1212–14 (2d Dist. 1997) (statutory amendment eliminating venue as an element of criminal offense (5-6(a) and 5/114-1(d-5)) did not apply retroactively because it was not a clarification of prior law and involved substantive matters, not procedural ones).

34. 725 ILCS 5/111-3(a)(5). If the name of the accused is not known, the accused is to be identified by any name or description "with reasonable certainty." People v. Alexander, 190 Ill. App. 3d 192, 546 N.E.2d 1032, 1035 (3d Dist. 1989) (victim's name need not be alleged in charging instrument).

35. People v. Thingvold, 191 Ill. App. 3d 144, 547 N.E.2d 657, 659 (2d Dist. 1989), aff'd, 145 Ill. 2d 441, 584 N.E.2d 89 (1991).

of the acts occurred after the statute's effective date.[36] The sixth condition is more knotty. It requires that the "nature and elements" of the offense be set forth. There are two general ways of complying with this requirement: the crime may be charged in the language of the statute, or facts that constitute a crime may be set out in the charging document.

Dozens of Illinois cases have approved the charging of an offense by using the language of the statute. As was stated in *People v. Isaacs,*[37] "where the language of the statute defining an offense so far particularizes such offense that by its use alone the accused is notified with reasonable certainty of the precise offense with which he is charged, an indictment drawn substantially in the language of the statute is sufficient."[38]

---

36. People v. Streit, 193 Ill. App. 3d 443, 550 N.E.2d 244, 246 (3d Dist. 1990), *rev'd on other grounds,* 142 Ill. 2d 13, 566 N.E.2d 1351 (1991).

37. 37 Ill. 2d 205, 226 N.E.2d 38 (1967).

38. *Id.,* 226 N.E.2d at 42. *See also* People v. Evans, 125 Ill. 2d 50, 530 N.E.2d 1360 (1988), *cert. denied,* 490 U.S. 1113 (1989); People v. Joyce, 210 Ill. App. 3d 1059, 569 N.E.2d 1189 (2d Dist. 1991); People v. Foley, 206 Ill. App. 3d 709, 565 N.E.2d 39 (1st Dist. 1990). In *People v. Smith,* 259 Ill. App. 3d 492, 631 N.E.2d 738, 741 (4th Dist. 1994), the court upheld the sufficiency of a charge alleging forgery by delivery. The court noted that the prosecutor is not required to plead evidentiary details. Since a charge is a preliminary matter, it need only contain a cursory statement of the facts. Similarly, in *People v. Selby,* 298 Ill. App. 3d 605, 698 N.E.2d 1102, 1108 (4th Dist. 1998), the court upheld the sufficiency of an indictment charging employees of the Department of Corrections with official misconduct. At the indictment stage, the state must simply allege the elements of the charge, not prove them. Though due process requires that the indictment be sufficient enough to provide the defendant with fair and adequate notice, the indictment does not need to be specifically detailed. As long as the regulation or statute upon which the indictment is drawn has some valid application, the indictment is sufficient. *But see* People v. Alvarado, 301 Ill. App. 3d 1017, 704 N.E.2d 937, 941 (2d Dist. 1998) (informations charging defendants with attempting to obstruct justice by furnishing false information, in language of statute, were insufficient where statute only defined crime in general terms; in such case, information must present facts comprising charges so that defendants may adequately prepare defense); People v. Wilkinson, 285 Ill. App. 3d 727, 674 N.E.2d 794, 798 (3d Dist. 1996) (indictment charging defendant with official misconduct cannot be simply in the language of the statute because the indictment needs to state what the act was that was in excess of lawful authority); People v. Scott, 285 Ill. App. 3d 95, 673 N.E.2d 1152, 1155 (2d Dist. 1996) (the disorderly conduct complaint was insufficient because it failed to specify the subsection defining the particular conduct that constituted an offense and it failed to specify the nature and elements of the offense with particularity; the disorderly conduct statute is broad and general in nature and therefore a charge under the statute must contain facts that defendant's conduct was "knowing and unreasonable"

Of course, it is not necessary that the charge be in the precise language of the statute if the nature and elements of the charge are adequately identified.[39] In *United States v. Fern*,[40] the court stated that an indictment would be found to be sufficient, even though it "does not track" the statutory language, if there is enough of the statutory language within the indictment to adequately inform the defendant of the charges against him. The goal, obviously, is that the defendant know precisely what charge is being made against him or her so that he or she may prepare a defense[41] and avoid being put in jeopardy twice for the same offense.[42] Also, the count in the indictment must support the conviction. In *People v. Melmuka*,[43] the defendant was charged by an indictment with the offense of attempted burglary. The court found the defendant not guilty of attempted burglary but guilty of attempted theft. The appellate court stated that attempted theft was not a lesser included offense of attempted burglary; thus, the defendant could not be convicted of an offense with which he was not charged.[44]

---

and minimally state some connection between the conduct and how it creates disorder); People v. Meras, 284 Ill. App. 3d 157, 671 N.E.2d 746, 751 (1st Dist. 1996) (the means of killing is not an essential element of first degree murder and need not be stated in the indictment, therefore the state's inclusion of "with a blunt object" could have been omitted as surplusage); People v. Foxall, 283 Ill. App. 3d 724, 670 N.E.2d 1175, 1177 (3d Dist. 1996) (information charging defendant with disorderly conduct for knowingly transmitting a false report to DCFS was insufficient because it failed to state exactly what in the report was allegedly false; pleading such a charge in language of the statute alone was insufficient).

39. People v. Harvey, 53 Ill. 2d 585, 294 N.E.2d 269 (1973).

40. 155 F.3d 1318 (11th Cir. 1998).

41. People v. Blanchett, 33 Ill. 2d 527, 212 N.E.2d 97 (1965); People v. Alvarado, 301 Ill. App. 3d 1017, 704 N.E.2d 937, 941 (2d Dist. 1998); People v. Weber, 264 Ill. App. 3d 310, 636 N.E.2d 902, 905 (1st Dist. 1994); People v. Podhrasky, 197 Ill. App. 3d 349, 554 N.E.2d 578 (5th Dist. 1990); People v. Wilkinson, 194 Ill. App. 3d 660, 551 N.E.2d 327 (1st Dist. 1990); People v. Pisani, 180 Ill. App. 3d 812, 536 N.E.2d 247 (2d Dist. 1989).

42. People v. Flynn, 375 Ill. 366, 31 N.E.2d 591 (1940); People v. Selby, 298 Ill. App. 3d 605, 698 N.E.2d 1102, 1108 (4th Dist. 1998); People v. Hall, 291 Ill. App. 3d 411, 683 N.E.2d 1274, 1278 (1st Dist. 1997); People v. Parsons, 284 Ill. App. 3d 1049, 673 N.E.2d 347, 352–53 (1st Dist. 1996).

43. 173 Ill. App. 3d 735, 527 N.E.2d 982 (1st Dist. 1988).

44. *Id.*, 527 N.E.2d at 983.

It is mandatory, not merely directory, that the charging document set forth the nature and elements of the offense.[45] Without those essentials, it is said that the trial court is without jurisdiction because the charging document "fails to charge an offense."[46] Generally, it is sufficient if the charging document states the offense in the language of the statute, because the statute contains the essential elements that must be pleaded.[47] If a prosecutor pleads the whole statute, obviously all of the elements of the offense would be included and this procedure would meet constitutional standards, except where the statute itself does not describe the proscribed act sufficiently. An offense is properly charged if all material parts of the statute are pleaded. For example, the offense of battery may be committed in two different ways: by a touching that is "insulting or provoking" or by a touching that causes bodily harm. To plead that a defendant knowingly made physical contact with another alleges neither an insulting or provoking physical contact nor a contact that causes bodily harm. Therefore, such a charge is fatally defective.[48]

The allegations of a charging document must also be consistent with the statute. For example, an assault is defined as placing another in reasonable apprehension of receiving a battery. It might be called "attempted battery."

---

45. People v. Pujoue, 61 Ill. 2d 335, 335 N.E.2d 437 (1975). *See* People v. Morris, 135 Ill. 2d 540, 544 N.E.2d 150, 152 (1990) (where there are multiple counts in indictment, indictment should be read as whole so that elements missing from one count could be supplied by another count). *See also* People v. Villareal, 114 Ill. App. 3d 389, 449 N.E.2d 198 (2d Dist. 1983) (amended complaint lacked necessary elements; thus, defect was fatal). *But see* People v. Oaks, 169 Ill. 2d 409, 662 N.E.2d 1328, 1343 (murder and aggravated battery indictments not duplicitous or void; language "creating a situation" referred to means of committing crime and not integral to offense and therefore need not be included; also not duplicitous because charged single offense in the alternative, it did not join more than one offense), *cert. denied*, 519 U.S. 873 (1996).

46. People v. Wallace, 57 Ill. 2d 285, 312 N.E.2d 263 (1974); People v. Alvarado, 301 Ill. App. 3d 1017, 704 N.E.2d 937, 941 (2d Dist. 1998) (stating that a charging instrument is insufficient if the state fails to allege an element of the charged offense, or if the facts alleged fail to constitute an offense). *But see* People v. Gilmore, 63 Ill. 2d 23, 344 N.E.2d 456 (1976); People v. McClurg, 195 Ill. App. 3d 381, 552 N.E.2d 290 (4th Dist. 1990). *See also* People v. Moton, 277 Ill. App. 3d 1010, 661 N.E.2d 1176, 1178 (3d Dist. 1996) (where indictment charging defendant with unlawful use of weapon by a felony included one name for defendant and two aliases, there could be no presumption he was same person allegedly convicted of felony in Tennessee; without benefit of presumption and lacking any evidence defendant was person referred to in Tennessee conviction, underlying history in felony not proved).

47. People v. Banks, 75 Ill. 2d 383, 388 N.E.2d 1244 (1979).

48. People v. Abrams, 48 Ill. 2d 446, 271 N.E.2d 37, 46 (1971).

Therefore, an assault complaint is fatally defective if it alleges a "touching," which is an element of battery.[49]

Special care must be given to a charge when the statute is of a general nature, as nouveau regulatory measures sometimes are and traditional statutes can be. Consider the pleading of a defendant charged with reckless conduct. A charge that the defendant did "perform recklessly certain acts" is such a vague description as to leave an accused person without notice of what he or she is being charged. The charge lacks particularity—that is, it covers a wide range of possible conduct. The charge would make it difficult to defend the accused.[50]

---

49. *Id.*, 271 N.E.2d at 45.

50. People v. Beard, 191 Ill. App. 3d 371, 547 N.E.2d 1041 (3d Dist.1989); People v. Hayes, 75 Ill. App. 3d 822, 394 N.E.2d 80 (2d Dist. 1979). *See* People v. Selby, 298 Ill. App. 3d 605, 698 N.E.2d 1102, 1108 (4th Dist. 1998) (indictment of correctional officers for official misconduct consisting of "socializing" with inmates was not defective; though court could find no decision interpreting term *socializing* or *socialize*, it assigned words their commonly understood meanings and accordingly held that defendants were sufficiently informed to prepare defense); People v. Richmond, 278 Ill. App. 3d 1042, 663 N.E.2d 1090, 1092 (3d Dist. 1996) (an indictment for aggravated criminal sexual abuse was not fatally defective because the charge lacked descriptions of "sexual penetration" and "sexual conduct" where the indictment allowed adequate preparation of defense, and where the indictment and the record of the proceedings was sufficient to bar subsequent prosecution for the same conduct); People v. Bergeson, 255 Ill. App. 3d 601, 627 N.E.2d 408, 409 (2d Dist. 1994) (charge of disorderly conduct specific enough to allow defendant to prepare defense and bar subsequent prosecution); People v. Ikpoh, 242 Ill. App. 3d 365, 609 N.E.2d 1025, 1037 (2d Dist. 1993) (in dictment for aggravated criminal sexual abuse sufficient where it merely alleged "sexual conduct," indictment need not state defendant's specific sexual conduct in order to apprise him with reasonable certainty of accused offense), *cert. denied*, 511 U.S. 1089 (1994); People v. Krause, 241 Ill. App. 3d 394, 609 N.E.2d 980, 982, 983 (2d Dist. 1993) (if statutory language does not particularize offense, indictment must specify act defendant committed; defendant sufficiently apprised of charge in indictment for official misconduct by stating personal advantage was "facilita tion of prostitution in which defendant intended to engage"). *But see* People v. Alvarado, 301 Ill. App. 3d 1017, 704 N.E.2d 937, 941 (2d Dist. 1998) (informations charging defendants with obstruction of justice were insufficient because no "identifiable or potentially chargeable offense" was named; providing false birthdate to peace officer alone does not violate obstructing justice statute); People v. Wilkinson, 285 Ill. App. 3d 727, 674 N.E.2d 794, 798 (3d Dist. 1996) (an indictment charging defendant with official misconduct cannot simply be in language of statute but needs to state what the act was that was in excess of lawful authority; indictment was insufficient in this case); People v. Foxall, 283 Ill. App. 3d 724, 670 N.E.2d 1175, 1177 (3d Dist. 1996) (indictment charging disorderly conduct for knowingly transmit-

The charging document must also stand as a bar to double jeopardy if the defendant were to be reprosecuted. Consider *People v. Peters*,[51] where the pleading was that the defendant "not then and there . . . regularly licensed to practice law . . . did then and there . . . willfully represent himself as authorized to practice law . . . ." The court found the charging document to be fatally defective, observing that it failed to allege what representations were made and whether they were made verbally or in writing, directly or indirectly. "It is essential that a criminal pleading be sufficiently specific," the court held.[52] In *People v. Panagiotis*,[53] a forgery case involving airline tickets, the two theft counts in the indictment described the quantity of tickets as "over 2 or more."[54] The court felt that the descriptions were too vague and failed to adequately describe the alleged stolen property, so the court vacated the conviction of theft.[55] Contrast, however, *People v. Wisslead*,[56] a case involving the rather general unlawful restraint statute.[57] Wisslead was charged with unlawful restraint in that he knowingly and without legal authority detained Nancy Rutlege Wisslead. The charge paralleled the language of the statute, but that did not "leave room for wide speculation as to the nature of the conduct alleged," the supreme court stated, upholding the charge and the conviction.[58] The supreme court concluded: "So long as the statutory language used describes specific

---

ting a false report to DCFS which alleged sexual misconduct was vague because sexual misconduct can include a myriad of possible acts); People v. Davis, 281 Ill. App. 3d 984, 668 N.E.2d 119, 124 (1st Dist. 1996) (an indictment charging official misconduct in words of the statute alone was insufficient; inclusion of additional allegations was insufficient to inform defendant of "nature and elements of charges against him"); People v. Janowski, 279 Ill. App. 3d 634, 665 N.E.2d 531, 533 (4th Dist. 1996) (information charging violation of Fish and Aquatic Life Code was insufficient to specify which provision defendant violated by possessing snakes and turtles).

51. 10 Ill. 2d 577, 141 N.E.2d 9, 10 (1957); *Selby*, 298 Ill. App. 3d 605, 698 N.E.2d at 1109; People v. Podhrasky, 197 Ill. App. 3d 349, 554 N.E.2d 578 (5th Dist.1990).

52. *Peters*, 10 Ill. 2d 577, 141 N.E.2d at 11.

53. 162 Ill. App. 3d 866, 516 N.E.2d 280 (1st Dist. 1987).

54. *Id.*, 516 N.E.2d at 283.

55. *Id.*

56. 108 Ill. 2d 389, 484 N.E.2d 1081 (1985).

57. 720 ILCS 5/10-3(a).

58. *Wisslead*, 108 Ill. 2d 389, 484 N.E.2d at 1084.

conduct then there is no need for the charge to specify the exact means by which the conduct was carried out."[59]

Similarly, in *People v. Mehelic*,[60] the defendant was charged with official misconduct under section 33-3(c).[61] The information alleged that "(1) defendant was Nameoki Township Highway Commissioner; (2) while he was in this capacity he 'directed' township employees to perform 'maintenance work' on his personal automobile; (3) such a directive was in excess of his lawful authority as defined by statute; and (4) this directive was given by defendant with the intent to obtain personal advantage."[62] The court found that the information substantially complied with section 111-3. The court stated that "[w]hile the information does not precisely state what is meant by 'obtaining pecuniary benefit for himself,' one reasonably can surmise from the information's language that the 'pecuniary benefit' defendant allegedly sought to obtain was the performance of 'maintenance work' upon his personal automobile without charge."[63] The court also stated that "[a]lthough the term 'lawful authority' derives its meaning from a set of rules not contained in the official-misconduct statute, the phrase 'in excess of his lawful authority' is sufficiently definite to enable public officials and their employees to determine the propriety of their actions."[64] In *People v. Bartlett*,[65] the defendant was charged by a six-count indictment with violating the Securities Act based on an illegal pyramid scheme. Counts I and II alleged that the defendant had knowingly engaged in a course of business in connection with the sale of securities that tended to work a fraud and deceit upon the buyers. The trial court dismissed these counts, finding that the state failed to allege that anyone relied on the alleged false statements. Counts III and IV alleged that defendant had circulated a statement in an illegal scheme with reasonable grounds to know that certain material representations

---

59. *Id.* In *People v. Hinton*, 259 Ill. App. 3d 484, 631 N.E.2d 773, 776 (4th Dist. 1994), the court stated that in determining the sufficiency of an indictment as it relates to subsequent prosecutions, the court must look to the entire record on appeal. *See also* People v. Santiago, 279 Ill. App. 3d 749, 665 N.E.2d 380, 382 (1st Dist. 1996) (naming of wrong victim in armed robbery information did not invalidate conviction because defendant was not prejudiced in preparation of defense).

60. 152 Ill. App. 3d 843, 504 N.E.2d 1310 (5th Dist. 1987).

61. 720 ILCS 5/33-3(c).

62. *Mehelic*, 152 Ill. App. 3d 843, 504 N.E.2d at 1314.

63. *Id.*, 504 N.E.2d at 1314–15. *See also* People v. Selby, 298 Ill. App. 3d 605, 698 N.E.2d 1102, 1110 (4th Dist. 1998) (holding that although indictment of official misconduct under section 33-3(c) could have specifically set forth personal or pecuniary advantage defendant allegedly received, indictment was nevertheless sufficient for notice and fair warning).

64. *Id.*, 504 N.E.2d at 1315.

65. 294 Ill. App. 3d 435, 690 N.E.2d 154 (2d Dist. 1998).

therein were false. The trial court dismissed these counts, finding that the state failed to allege that the statements were "required by any provision of this Act."

With regard to counts I and II, the appellate court reversed. The indictment tracked the language of the statute and added specific factual allegations to support the charges. The statute does not specifically require that anyone had relied on the statement. Nonetheless, the court did agree with the state that the element of reliance is inherent in the allegation that defendant's conduct tended to work a fraud and deceit.[66] According to the court, the term *fraud* has an accepted legal definition. Based on this, the legislature is presumed to have intended to incorporate the element of reliance into the statutory language. Consequently, the trial court erred in dismissing counts I and II.[67]

With regard to counts III and IV, the provision relied upon by the state provided: "It shall be a violation of the provisions of this Act for any person: . . . [t]o sign or circulate any statement, prospectus, or other paper or document required by any provision of this Act knowing or having reasonable grounds to know any material representation therein contained to be false or untrue."[68] The trial court agreed with defendant that the phrase *required by any provision of this Act* modified statement, prospectus, other paper, and document. Therefore, the trial judge concluded that the indictment failed to allege that the statement was one required by the Act and failed to charge an offense. The appellate court disagreed. Interpretation of the statute in this manner would render the term *statement* meaningless. There would be no difference between a statement and "other paper or document."[69] The trial court's interpretation would not comport with the broad purpose of the Act to protect the public from unscrupulous securities dealers.[70] Based on the last antecedent rule, in part, the court concluded that "required by any provision of this Act" modified only the word *documents*. Accordingly, the trial court erred in dismissing counts III and IV of the indictment.[71]

When an indictment is challenged for the first time on appeal, the standard used to measure its sufficiency is whether "it apprised the accused of the precise offense charged with sufficient specificity to prepare his [or her] defense and allow pleading a resulting conviction as a bar to future prosecution arising from the same conduct."[72] The standard of review for sufficiency at the trial court

---

66. *Id.*, 690 N.E.2d at 156.

67. *Id.*

68. 815 ILCS 5/12(H).

69. *Bartlett*, 294 Ill. App. 3d at 435, 690 N.E.2d at 156.

70. *Id.*, 690 N.E.2d at 157.

71. *Id.*

72. People v. Yarbrough, 128 Ill. 2d 460, 539 N.E.2d 1228, 1233 (1989); People v. Selby, 298 Ill. App.3d 605, 698 N.E.2d 1102, 1109 (4th Dist. 1998); People v.

level is more stringent than the standard at the appellate level.[73] At the trial level, the charging document must give notice of all of the essential elements of the offense to withstand defendant's motion to dismiss.[74]

Where a statute contains a monetary, weight, or age limit, the limit must be pleaded. For example, a dollar limit such as in theft or criminal damage to property, a weight limit such as in controlled substances offenses, or an age limit such as in sex offenses must be pleaded and proven. Consider *People v. Clutts,*[75] where the defendant was charged with a Class I offense of delivery of over 200 grams of amphetamine tablets. The charging document, however, read that the defendant delivered "50,000 amphetamine tablets." The charge was silent about the weight of the controlled substance. The trial judge found the defendant guilty of the lesser Class 4 offense, which had no weight limit. The appellate court affirmed, not

---

Alvarado, 301 Ill. App. 3d 1017, 704 N.E.2d 937, 941 (2d Dist. 1998); People v. Scott, 285 Ill. App. 3d 95, 673 N.E.2d 1152, 1154 (2d Dist. 1996); People v. Parsons, 284 Ill. App. 3d 1049, 673 N.E.2d 347, 352 (1st Dist. 1996); People v. Goebel, 284 Ill. App. 3d 618, 672 N.E.2d 837, 842 (2d Dist. 1996); People v. Libbra, 268 Ill. App. 3d 194, 643 N.E.2d 845, 847 (5th Dist. 1994); People v. Smith, 264 Ill. App. 3d 82, 637 N.E.2d 1128, 1132 (3d Dist. 1994); People v. Gwinn, 255 Ill. App. 3d 628, 627 N.E.2d 699, 701 (2d Dist. 1994); People v. Bergeson, 255 Ill. App. 3d 601, 627 N.E.2d 408, 409 (2d Dist. 1994); People v. Krause, 241 Ill. App. 3d 394, 609 N.E.2d 980, 982 (2d Dist. 1993); People v. Grogan, 197 Ill. App. 3d 18, 554 N.E.2d 665 (1st Dist. 1990); People v. Alexander, 190 Ill. App. 3d 192, 546 N.E.2d 1032 (3d Dist. 1989); People v. Wendt, 183 Ill. App. 3d 389, 539 N.E.2d 768 (2d Dist. 1989); People v. Mortenson, 178 Ill. App. 3d 871, 533 N.E.2d 1134 (2d Dist. 1989).

73. People v. Davis, 281 Ill. App. 3d 984, 668 N.E.2d 119, 122 (1st Dist. 1996); *Libbra,* 268 Ill. App. 3d 194, 643 N.E.2d at 847; People v. Escalante, 256 Ill. App. 3d 239, 627 N.E.2d 1222, 1226 (2d Dist. 1994); People v. King, 253 Ill. App. 3d 705, 625 N.E.2d 453, 454 (3d Dist. 1993); People v. Penn, 177 Ill. App. 3d 179, 533 N.E.2d 383, 385 (5th Dist. 1988). *See also* Timothy P. O'Neill, *Beating a Charge Requires Beating the Clock,* Chicago Daily Law Bulletin, March 14, 1997, at 5. When a defendant challenges the sufficiency of a charge on a motion to withdraw guilty plea, the court must use the standard set forth in section 116-2 of the code, rather than the standard in section 111-3. *See* People v. Carroll, 258 Ill. App. 3d 371, 630 N.E.2d 1337, 1340 (4th Dist. 1994).

74. People v. Doneski, 288 Ill. App. 3d 1, 679 N.E.2d 462, 466 (1st Dist. 1997); *Penn,* 177 Ill. App. 3d 179, 533 N.E.2d at 385; People v. Thingvold, 191 Ill. App. 3d 144, 547 N.E.2d 657, 659 (2d Dist. 1989), *aff'd,* 145 Ill. 2d 441, 584 N.E.2d 89 (1991). *See also* People v. Meyers, 158 Ill. 2d 46, 630 N.E.2d 811, 815 (1994) (essential elements of crime charged must appear in complaint); People v. Weber, 264 Ill. App. 3d 310, 636 N.E.2d 902, 905 (1st Dist. 1994) (at trial level standard of review is whether the indictment states the nature of the offense and adequately sets forth each of the elements of that offense).

75. 43 Ill. App. 3d 366, 356 N.E.2d 1367 (5th Dist. 1976).

because the weight of over 200 grams had not been proven (it had been proven), but because that weight had not been alleged in the charging document.[76] The defendant had not been placed on trial for a Class 1 offense.

Where intent is a statutory element of the offense—for example, "intent to defraud" or "with intent to facilitate a prisoner's escape"—that element must be pleaded.[77] Similarly, if a particular mental state is an element of the offense—for example, "to permanently deprive" the victim—a charging document would be fatally defective if it omitted that element.[78] "However, where a particular mental state is not a part of the definition of an offense, it is possible that the charging instrument need not allege a specific mental state . . . . Also, where the mental state of knowledge is implicit from the specific allegation of defendant's act as set forth in the charging instrument, it is beyond serious contention that defendant [is] sufficiently apprised of the crime charged."[79]

---

76. *Id.*, 356 N.E.2d at 1370.

77. People v. Vraniak, 5 Ill. 2d 384, 125 N.E.2d 513, *cert. denied*, 349 U.S. 1963 (1955); People v. Greene, 92 Ill. App. 2d 201, 235 N.E.2d 295 (1st Dist. 1968). *See* People v. Rivers, 194 Ill. App. 3d 193, 550 N.E.2d 1179 (1st Dist. 1990) (failure to expressly allege specific intent not fatal). *But see* People v. Scott, 285 Ill. App. 3d 95, 673 N.E.2d 1152, 1155 (2d Dist. 1996) (a disorderly conduct complaint must contain facts to show that a particular conduct is "knowing and unreasonable").

　　A good example of an information held deficient for failing to allege a mental state is *People v. Langford,* 195 Ill. App. 3d 366, 552 N.E.2d 274 (4th Dist. 1990). In *Langford,* the defendant was charged by information with a violation of the Timber Buyers Licensing Act. *Id.*, 525 N.E.2d at 275. The defendant pleaded guilty but subsequently moved to withdraw. *Id.* Both the act and the information failed to designate a mental state, but the trial judge construed the charge as an absolute liability offense. *Id.*, 525 N.E.2d at 276. In reversing, the appellate court held that the charge required a knowing mental state. *Id.* However, if an offense is a general intent crime, the indictment need not allege a mental state. People v. Boland, 205 Ill. App. 3d 1009, 563 N.E.2d 963, 970 (1st Dist. 1990). Similarly, where the statute is silent as to intent, no intent needs to be charged. People v. Nibbio, 180 Ill. App. 3d 513, 536 N.E.2d 113, 118 (5th Dist. 1989). *See, e.g.,* People v. Soteras, 295 Ill. App. 3d 610, 693 N.E.2d 400, 405 (2d Dist. 1998) (murder indictment upheld even though it lacked allegation of intent, where it contained the word *murder* and referred to murder statute; murder is general intent crime); People v. Lee, 294 Ill. App. 3d 738, 691 N.E.2d 117, 120–21 (3d Dist. 1998) (armed robbery indictment upheld even though it failed to allege a mental state because robbery is a general intent crime).

78. People v. Hayn, 116 Ill. App. 2d 241, 253 N.E.2d 575 (3d Dist. 1969).

79. People v. Blackwood, 131 Ill. App. 3d 1018, 476 N.E.2d 742, 744 (3d Dist. 1985). *See, e.g.*, People v. Bofman, 283 Ill. App. 3d 546, 670 N.E.2d 796, 799 (1st Dist. 1996) ("[A]n indictment charging an accused is not defective for failure to allege

In an official misconduct case charged under 725 ILCS 5/33-3(b) or (c), the issue is whether an act performed in one's official capacity was done to exploit one's official position. In *People v. Selby*,[80] a correctional officer was charged with engaging in sexual intercourse with prison inmates. Selby claimed, on a motion to dismiss the indictment, that the allegations failed to demonstrate that his conduct resulted from an exploitation of his official position, apparently arguing that his uniform and his conduct may have been unconnected. The appellate court rejected this argument, stating that the indictments "sufficiently apprise[d] Selby [that] he used his employment position to engage in proscribed activity."[81]

Selby argued, alternatively, that the indictments were insufficient because sexual activity with prison inmates is not a "personal advantage" as contemplated by the law, which requires an official act performed with "intent to obtain a personal advantage for himself or another."[82] Most reported official misconduct cases involve wrongdoing with a pecuniary goal in mind. But the appellate court stated that the misconduct here could have been done for some unknown "personal advantage," and if the defendant were curious about what the particular advantage was underpinning these charges he could move for a bill of particulars.[83]

In *People v. Schultz*,[84] a case involving section 11-401 of the vehicle code, the defendant was issued a traffic ticket for leaving the scene of an accident. The defendant argued that the complaint failed to allege the requisite mental state. In affirming the conviction, the appellate court followed *People v. Tammen*.[85] The court stated that "[o]rdinarily, the failure to allege the requisite mental state fatally flaws a criminal prosecution."[86] But because uniform traffic

---

a mental state where the statute defining the offense charged does not include a mental state"). *See* People v. Soteras, 295 Ill. App. 3d 610, 693 N.E.2d 400, 405 (2d Dist. 1998) (murder indictment upheld even though it lacked allegation of intent, where it contained the word *murder* and referred to murder statute; murder is general intent crime); People v. Lee, 294 Ill. App. 3d 738, 691 N.E.2d 117, 120–21 (3d Dist. 1998) (armed robbery indictment upheld even though it failed to allege a mental state because robbery is a general intent crime).

80. 298 Ill. App. 3d 605, 698 N.E.2d 1102, 1109–10 (4th Dist. 1998).

81. *Id.*, 698 N.E.2d at 1110.

82. *Id., citing* 720 ILCS 5/33-3(c); People v. Mehelic, 152 Ill. App. 3d 843, 504 N.E.2d 1310, 1314 (5th Dist. 1987).

83. *Selby,* 298 Ill. App. 3d 605, 698 N.E.2d at 110.

84. 173 Ill. App. 3d 738, 527 N.E.2d 984 (1st Dist. 1988).

85. 40 Ill. 2d 76, 237 N.E.2d 517 (1968).

86. *Schultz,* 173 Ill. App. 3d 738, 527 N.E.2d at 987.

tickets are only used for misdemeanors, naming the offense and citing it is sufficient. The court determined that "the instant complaint was sufficiently specific for it to be generally understood."[87] The court also observed that "the ticket supplied enough particular details to enable defendant to prepare his defense."[88]

Another important "vagueness" decision came in *People v. Larson,*[89] where the appellate court found a uniform traffic ticket void because it lacked "necessary certainty." The court said that:

> Generally, a criminal complaint that lacks the necessary certainty to charge an offense is void and may be attacked at any time. . . . A charging instrument must set forth the nature and elements of the offense charged. 725 ILCS 5/111-3(a)(3). . . . In the reckless driving context, a complaint must set forth the particular act or acts that comprised the offense. *People v. Griffin,* 36 Ill. 2d 430, 433 (1967); . . . . The complaint here does not do so.[90]

Larson is also important for distinguishing between a complaint, indictment, or information on the one hand and a uniform traffic ticket on the other; an issue addressed by the Illinois Supreme Court in the *Tammen*[91] case. *Tammen* applied to uniform traffic tickets, as distinguished from the long form complaint used in *Larson.* A traffic ticket written by a police officer on the scene is clearly a different creature than a complaint written by a State's Attorney. The *Larson* court found the difference to be significant, signaling a higher responsibility for State's Attorneys, even when charging misdemeanors by long form complaints.[92]

Inchoate offenses, such as attempt, need not plead the elements of the intended offense[93] but must plead the specific intent to commit the principal offense.[94] If a statute proscribes certain conduct in alternative ways, a charging document based on that statute must not plead in the alternative because that

---

87. *Id.,* 527 N.E.2d at 988.

88. *Id.*

89. 296 Ill. App. 3d 647, 695 N.E.2d 524, 525 (2d Dist. 1998).

90. *Id.,* 695 N.E.2d at 525.

91. *Id.,* 695 N.E.2d at 526 (citing People v. Tammen, 40 Ill. 2d 76, 237 N.E.2d 517, 518–19 (1968)).

92. *Larson,* 296 Ill. App. 3d 647, 695 N.E.2d at 526.

93. People v. Lonzo, 59 Ill. 2d 115, 319 N.E.2d 481 (1974). *See also* People v. Woodward, 55 Ill. 2d 134, 302 N.E.2d 62 (1973).

94. *Lonzo,* 59 Ill. 2d 115, 319 N.E.2d at 483. *See also* People v. Evans, 125 Ill. 2d 50, 530 N.E.2d 1360, 1381 (1988) (charge for attempt does not have to be set out

would present a nonspecific charge. Where a pleading contains the disjunctive "or," care must be taken that the charge is not uncertain.[95]

In *People v. Capitol News, Inc.*,[96] the Illinois Supreme Court addressed the issue of a disjunctive indictment. A charge tracking the language of the statute defining the crime which uses the disjunctive "or" is a sufficient charge under some circumstances.[97] However, it will not be sufficient if the statute names disparate and alternative acts, any one of which will constitute an offense.[98] In *Capitol News*, the statute provided that if a person intentionally or recklessly sells, delivers, or provides or offers or agrees to sell, deliver, or provide any obscene writing he or she commits a crime.[99] The court stated that because the statute describes disparate and alternative acts, the performance of any one of which constitutes an offense, the indictments were void.[100]

In *People v. Sheehan*,[101] the Illinois Supreme Court held that prior DUI offenses which had resulted in supervision could be used to enhance a subsequent DUI charge from a misdemeanor to a felony.[102] The court rejected defendant's argument that only those DUI charges which had resulted in

---

as fully or specifically as is required for charging the completed offense), *cert. denied*, 490 U.S. 1113 (1989).

95. People v. Heard, 47 Ill. 2d 501, 266 N.E.2d 340 (1970). *See also* People v. Meyers, 158 Ill. 2d 46, 630 N.E.2d 811, 815–16 (1994) (statement of legal status in disjunctive in complaint for tax sale fraud not render legally insufficient; defendants were not required to defend as both owners and agents); People v. Lewis, 147 Ill. App. 3d 249, 498 N.E.2d 1169, 1172 (1st Dist. 1986) (indictment essentially tracked language of statute but court stated that "[t]he fact that the word 'or' is used several times in the statutory definition does not, in an of itself, render the term 'sexual conduct' imprecise"), *cert. denied*, 482 U.S. 907 (1987).

96. 137 Ill. 2d 162, 560 N.E.2d 303 (1990), *cert. denied*, 498 U.S. 1121 (1991).

97 *Heard*, 47 Ill. 2d 501, 266 N.E.2d at 342. *See* People v. Weber, 264 Ill. App. 3d 310, 636 N.E.2d 902, 906 (1st Dist. 1994) (indictment language stating defendant strangled and knifed victim to death proper to charge first degree murder); People v. Brown, 259 Ill. App. 3d 579, 630 N.E.2d 1334, 1334 (3d Dist. 1994) (instrument not void where stated "(1) actual possession 'on or about his person' and (2) constructive possession 'on his own land or in his own abode or fixed place of business' "); People v. King, 253 Ill. App. 3d 705, 625 N.E.2d 453, 454 (3d Dist. 1993) ("entering or remaining" sufficient charge).

98. *Capitol News, Inc.*, 137 Ill. 2d 162, 560 N.E.2d at 308 (citing People v. Heard, 47 Ill. 2d 501, 266 N.E.2d 340 (1970)).

99. *Capitol News, Inc.*, 137 Ill. 2d 162, 560 N.E.2d at 308.

100. *Id.*

101. 168 Ill. 2d 298, 659 N.E.2d 1339 (1995).

102. *Id.*, 659 N.E.2d at 1343.

conviction could be used for enhancement.[103] The statute used the term "committed" as opposed to "convicted."[104] The court looked to the plain language of the statute and also to other provisions of the code in which the legislature had used "committed" and "convicted" in the same sentence or where it had used "convicted" alone. Based on this, the court reasoned the legislature knew the difference and had it intended to include only those DUI charges which resulted in convictions to be used for enhancement, it would have expressly done so through appropriate language.[105] Because defendant's prior DUI charges which had resulted in supervision could be used to enhance his subsequent DUI charge, the complaints in this case were improperly dismissed.[106]

In *People v. Karraker*,[107] the appellate court held that defendant was prejudiced where he was tried on several charges, brought in a single indictment, before the same jury.[108] The three charges contained in the indictment, unlawful possession of a weapon by a felon, unlawful use of a weapon, and theft, were unrelated and not part of the same comprehensive transaction.[109]

§ 3.04   Amending the Charge

Illinois Compiled Statutes chapter 725, section 5/111-5 states that an indictment, information, or complaint "may be amended on motion by the State's Attorney . . . at any time because of formal defects."[110] In the leading case of

---

103. *Id.*, 659 N.E.2d at 1342.

104. *Id.*

105. *Id.*, 659 N.E.2d at 1343.

106. *Id.*, 659 N.E.2d at 1344–45.

107. 261 Ill. App. 3d 942, 633 N.E.2d 1250 (3d Dist. 1994).

108. *Id.*, 633 N.E.2d at 1256.

109. *Id.*

110. 725 ILCS 5/111-5. *See generally Indictments—Amendment or Variance,* Annot., 85 L.Ed.2d 878 (1987).

The case of *People v. House,* 202 Ill. App. 3d 893, 560 N.E.2d 1224, 1232 (4th Dist. 1990), contains a good restatement of the law on this issue:

> If the amendment does not involve a material change in the averments of the original information, the original information is not abandoned and trial may be had on it as amended without a new plea. [citation omitted] However, when the amendment seeks to change the nature of the offense with which the defendant is charged, the amendment is not technical. [citation omitted] An error in the citation of a statutory provision is a formal rather than substantive defect, when the amendment does not affect the substance of the charge. The finding that the matter is a formal defect is strengthened when the defendant is not surprised by the amendment. [citation omitted]

People v. Kincaid,[111] the Illinois Supreme Court pointed out that section 111-5 was not exclusive and that in the case of a nonformal but fundamental defect, there also exists a right to amend, just as there was at common law.[112] *Kincaid* negated the holding in *People v. Clark,*[113] that an amendment to an information that fails to state a crime is an abandonment of the original.[114] A recent case adeptly explains the law on this point. In *People v. McCoy,*[115] the defendant was originally charged with possession of cocaine. Four months before trial, the trial judge permitted the prosecution to amend the information to read "heroin" instead of "cocaine." The state argued that the word *cocaine* was merely a "miswriting." The appellate court affirmed, stating:

> Section 111-5 of the Criminal Code permits a charging instrument to be amended to correct formal defects, including a miswriting. . . . The amendment is permissible if the change is not material or does not alter the nature and elements of the offense charged. . . . A formal amendment is warranted especially where there is no resulting surprise or prejudice to the defendant or where the record shows that he was otherwise aware of the actual charge. . . . If an amendment to an information corrected a formal defect, no reverification is required.[116]

See also People v. Kimbrough, 163 Ill. 2d 231, 644 N.E.2d 1137, 1145 (1994) ("A formal defect in an indictment may be corrected at any time upon motion by either party"; citation to incorrect statutory provision (distribution rather than possession) was a typographical error or formal defect which could be amended). *See, e.g.,* People v. Dunskus, 282 Ill. App. 3d 912, 668 N.E.2d 1138, 1142 (1st Dist. 1996) (the court determined it was proper to allow state to amend a traffic citation to include "of alcohol" and to cite the statutory provision; the addition of a statutory citation is a correction of a formal defect and the addition of "of alcohol" was a correction of miswriting); People v. Nathan, 282 Ill. App. 3d 608, 668 N.E.2d 648, 650 (4th Dist. 1996) (the addition of "asphyxiated deceased with bedsheet or blanket" was a narrative on how the crime was committed and not an essential element of the offense).

111. 87 Ill. 2d 107, 429 N.E.2d 508 (1981), *cert. denied,* 455 U.S. 1024 (1982).

112. *Id.,* 429 N.E.2d at 515–16.

113. 407 Ill. 353, 9 N.E.2d 425 (1950).

114. People v. Spencer, 160 Ill. App. 3d 509, 513 N.E.2d 514, 516 (4th Dist. 1987) (forgery conviction affirmed in which state amended information to attach document that was allegedly forged).

115. 295 Ill. App. 3d 988, 692 N.E.2d 1244, 1247–48 (1st Dist. 1998).

116. *Id.,* 692 N.E.2d at 1248.

Amending an indictment for nonformal but fundamental defects is a sticky point. Indictments, thought of as the "work of the grand jury," have historically been treated in a manner different from informations, which originate with the state's attorney.[117] The 1887 case of *Ex Parte Bain*[118] sets forth the rule of nonamendability of indictments,[119] and the modern United States Supreme Court case of *Stirone v. United States*[120] reaffirmed that rule, at least as far as it prohibits the broadening of the indictment to add what amounts to an additional charge. Justice Black wrote, reversing the conviction, that "[Stirone] was convicted on a charge the grand jury never made against him."[121]

This occurred again in *People v. Smith.*[122] Here, the armed defendant entered an automotive repair shop and took money from the cash register. Smith then went down to the basement where there was a safe. Upon encountering two employees in the basement, the defendant's gun went off, killing one employee.

---

117. *Kincaid,* 87 Ill. 2d 107, 429 N.E.2d at 515.

118. 121 U.S. 1 (1887), *overruled by* Russell v. United States, 369 U.S. 749 (1962), *as stated in* United States v. Cina, 699 F.2d 853, 857 (7th Cir.) (amendment or variance allowed to stand if it does not change an "essential" or "material" element of charge so as to prejudice defendant), *cert. denied,* 464 U.S. 991 (1983); People v. Meras, 284 Ill. App. 3d 157, 671 N.E.2d 746, 751 (1st Dist. 1996) ("A variance between the facts alleged and the proof is not fatal if the facts in question are not essential elements of the offense charged"). *But see* United States v. Miller, 471 U.S. 130, 144 (1985) ("To the extent *Bain* stands for the proposition that it constitutes an unconstitutional amendment to drop from an indictment those allegations that are unnecessary to an offense that is clearly contained within it, that case has simply not survived. To avoid further confusion, we now explicitly reject that proposition.").

119. *Bain,* 121 U.S. at 6 (citing Lord Mansfield in Rex v. Wilkes, 4 Burr. 2527 ("There is a great difference between amending indictments and amending informations")).

120. 361 U.S. 212 (1960).

121. *Id.* at 219. In *People v. Patterson,* 267 Ill. App. 3d 933, 642 N.E.2d 866, 869 (1st Dist. 1994), the appellate court held that the trial court erred in allowing the prosecutor to amend a charge. The appellate court found that amending the charge as to the weight of a controlled substance is not a formal defect but rather a material amendment. The weight of the controlled substance is an element of the offense. *See also* People v. Tellez-Valencia, 295 Ill. App. 3d 122, 692 N.E.2d 407, 409 (2d Dist.) (indictment for predatory criminal sexual assault of child defective because it failed to state an offense where later declared invalid, state could not amend indictment to charge different crime, i.e., aggravated criminal sexual assault, particularly where it attempted to do so on appeal because defendant had already been tried and convicted of predatory criminal sexual assault of child; indictment could only be amended by grand jury), *appeal granted,* 179 Ill. 2d 612 (1998).

122. 183 Ill. 2d 425, 701 N.E.2d 1097 (1998).

Smith then ran away. The state charged Smith by indictment with felony-murder predicated on armed robbery, and a separate charge of armed robbery.[123] However, the state failed to specifically charge Smith with attempted armed robbery of the safe.[124] Smith was convicted on both charges and appealed, arguing that the indictment did not specify which armed robbery was the basis for the felony-murder charge. The state argued that the attempted armed robbery of the safe could be substituted for the armed robbery of the cash register as the predicate offense for felony-murder. The court, however, agreed with Smith, holding that the state's philosophy of "substituting" a charge that was never made for one stated in the indictment denied the defendant his due process.[125]

Thus, even today, courts are still very careful to scrutinize the amendment of an indictment to ensure that the defendant can fairly prepare his defense. Explicit amendments made against the rule of nonamendability are not the only ones that may later cause the reversal of a conviction. For example, recent federal cases have described a "constructive amendment" error as either (1) when the prosecutor, during the presentation of evidence, or in closing argument, widens the bases for conviction beyond those set forth in the indictment; or (2) when the trial judge, through instructions, broadens the possible bases for conviction beyond those intended by the grand jury. Each of these forms of "constructive amendment" is prohibited and can result in reversal of a conviction.[126]

Section 111-5 states some of the correctable defects by amendment:

> (a) Any miswriting, misspelling or grammatical error; (b) Any misjoinder of the parties defendant; (c) Any misjoinder of the offense charged; (d) The presence of any unnecessary allegation; (e) The failure to negative any exception, any excuse or proviso contained in the statute defining the offense; or (f) The use of alternative or disjunctive allegations as to the acts, means, intents or results charged.[127]

---

123. *Id.*, 701 N.E.2d at 1098.

124. *Id.*, 701 N.E.2d at 1100.

125. *Id.*

126. Two cases set out the doctrine: the recent case of *United States v. Cusimano,* 148 F.3d 824, 829 (7th Cir. 1998), where the defendant raised the issue around "other crimes" evidence but the court rejected the argument, as contrasted with the better defense scenario in *United States v. Floresca,* 38 F.3d 706, 710 (4th Cir. 1994), where the trial judge gave an instruction on a subsection of a statute upon which the grand jury did not indict the defendant.

127. 725 ILCS 5/111-5.

In *People v. Benitez*,[128] the court reiterated that a returned grand jury indictment may not be amended by the state's attorney except as authorized by statute.[129] The grand jury returned an indictment which failed to charge defendant with murder. Upon realizing the error, the state's attorney had a secretary prepare a second indictment which named defendant, two additional defendants, and changed the name of the victim.[130] The state's attorney never filed a motion to amend nor presented the second indictment to the grand jury.[131] The court stated that it could not "sanction such a practice" and that the state's attorney "do[es] not have the authority to amend grand jury indictments at will." Based on the fact the first indictment failed to charge defendant, and the second indictment was not valid, defendant's conviction was reversed.[132] As was made clear in *Kincaid,* this section does not attempt to state when a charging document may not be amended. It merely sets out a nonexclusive list of situations when it can be amended.[133] For example, in *People v. Jones*[134] the name of the victim of an armed robbery was shown in the indictment as Charles Mundy, when it should have been Delbert Mundy. (Delbert was the father of Charles.) Over defense objection, the trial court permitted the amendment, and the appellate court agreed. Although amending the misnomer of a victim is not enumerated in section 111-5, "the victim's name is not an essential element of the crime charged," and the amendment was a "mere formality."[135]

---

128. 169 Ill. 2d 245, 661 N.E.2d 344 (1996).

129. *Id.*, 661 N.E.2d at 348.

130. *Id.*

131. *Id.*

132. *Id.*, 661 N.E.2d at 349.

133. People v. Kincaid, 87 Ill. 2d 107, 429 N.E.2d 508, 514 (1981); People v. Montefolka, 287 Ill. App. 3d 199, 678 N.E.2d 1049, 1054–55 (1st Dist.) (challenge to home invasion charge in preamendment form insufficient because amendment made one year before trial and, therefore, no prejudice to defendant; charge prior to amendment alleged that defendant committed offense by "entering" home knowing someone was inside; charge subsequent to amendment alleged defendant committed offense by "remaining" in home knowing someone one inside), *cert. denied*, 522 U.S. 916 (1997); People v. Nathan, 282 Ill. App. 3d 608, 668 N.E.2d 648, 650 (4th Dist. 1996) (allowing state to amend indictment to further specify the manner in which defendant committed aggravated battery against a correctional officer at the close of all evidence proper); People v. Priola, 203 Ill. App. 3d 401, 561 N.E.2d 82, 91 (2d Dist. 1990) (disregarding "surplusage" in indictment not improper amendment).

134. 53 Ill. 2d 460, 292 N.E.2d 361 (1973).

135. *Id.*, 292 N.E.2d at 363; People v. Bae, 176 Ill. App. 3d 1065, 531 N.E.2d 931, 939 (1st Dist. 1988) (amending name of owner of building in arson charge was

The ancient art of technical pleading is a lost one, thank goodness, and reviewing courts often permit amendments to avoid an extremely technical outcome.[136] The case of *People v. Coleman*[137] illustrates. In *Coleman,* the defendant was charged in an indictment with murder by stabbing, but during the trial the state moved to amend the indictment to charge murder by asphyxiation. The appellate court held that this was permissible because the means used to commit the murder did not charge a different crime, and the means used to kill "was not essential but a formal part of the indictment which could be amended pursuant to 111-5 . . . . "[138] After the trial court permitted the amendment, the defense did not move for a continuance or postponement of proceedings and showed no prejudice because of the amendment. Thus, by evaluating the fairness of the total trial, the appellate court was able to determine that the amendment did not take the defense by surprise or in any way deprive the defendant of a fair trial.[139]

---

formal defect). *See also* People v. Todd, 178 Ill. 2d 297, 687 N.E.2d 998, 1012 (1997) (substituting "created" for "committed" merely a formal defect that could be amended without materially changing the count), *cert. denied*, 119 S. Ct. 77 (1998); People v. McCoy, 295 Ill. App. 3d 988, 692 N.E.2d 1244, 1248 (1st Dist. 1998) (amendment of information charging defendant with possession of "white heroin" rather than cocaine appropriate because it did not alter material nature or elements of crime and was mere formal defect); People v. Barlow, 188 Ill. App. 3d 393, 544 N.E.2d 947, 953 (1st Dist. 1989) (amending date is formal defect); People v. Fountain, 179 Ill. App. 3d 986, 534 N.E.2d 1303, 1309 (1st Dist. 1989) (amending the weapon used from "bottle" to "piece of wood" is a formal defect).

136. "Great niceties and strictness of pleading should only be countenanced and supported when it is apparent that the defendant may be surprised on the trial, or unable to meet the charge or make preparations for his defense . . . ." People v. Cohen, 303 Ill. 523, 135 N.E. 731, 731 (1922). *Cohen* was cited with approval in *People v. Coleman,* 49 Ill. 2d 565, 276 N.E.2d 721, 723 (1971).

137. 49 Ill. 2d 565, 276 N.E.2d 721 (1971).

138. *Id.,* 276 N.E.2d at 724.

139. *Id.* When a defendant is neither surprised or prejudiced by an amendment to the charge, the amendment will generally be upheld. *See* People v. Hester, 271 Ill. App. 3d 954, 649 N.E.2d 1351, 1354 (4th Dist. 1995); People v. Spreyne, 256 Ill. App. 3d 505, 628 N.E.2d 251, 255 (1st Dist. 1993). *See, e.g.,* People v. Montefolka, 287 Ill. App. 3d 199, 678 N.E.2d 1049, 1054–55 (1st Dist.) (challenge to charge of home invasion in its preamendment form insufficient because amendment made one year before trial and no prejudice to defendant; charge prior to amendment alleged that defendant committed offense by "entering" home knowing someone was inside; charge subsequent to amendment alleged defendant committed offense by "remaining" in home knowing someone one inside), *cert. denied*, 522 U.S. 916 (1997).

Section 111-5 magnanimously, but perhaps too broadly, states that a charging document may be amended at any time.[140] But that provision likely means "at any time before conviction." The situation of guilt vel non, and to what offense, would seem to be frozen at that moment.[141] An information may be amended. However, after a material change in an information, which is a charge sworn to originally by the state's attorney, the amended version should be reverified, and the failure to do so could pose a prosecutor trouble.[142] The problem in amending an indictment is whether a reviewing court will find the change as formal. *People v. Betts*[143] presents an example of an improper, nonformal amendment to an indictment. The indictment first read that the defendant delivered Dexedrine, "which is a narcotic." The state, over objection, moved to amend the indictment to read Dexedrine, "which is not a narcotic." The amendment changed, among other things, the class of felony from Class 2 to Class 3, apparently to the benefit of the defendant. But a majority of the appellate court held it was no benefit because the issue of whether Dexedrine was narcotic may have been important to the grand jury. "[P]erhaps the grand jurors agreed, that trafficking in narcotics is far more serious an affair . . .," the majority speculated, reversing the conviction.[144]

In contrast, *People v. Berg*[145] is an example of a formal amendment to an indictment. Count II originally alleged that the defendant "willfully caused the health of such child to be injured in that prompt medical treatment was not obtained for the child's injuries."[146] On the first day of trial, Count II was amended, and the word *endangered* was substituted for the word *injured*.[147] The defendant claimed the amendment was a fundamental change; the state

---

140. 725 ILCS 5/111-5; People v. Wallace, 210 Ill. App. 3d 325, 568 N.E.2d 1332, 1338 (1st Dist. 1991) (prosecutor allowed to amend armed robbery indictment on second day of trial to change names of victims); People v. Harris, 205 Ill. App. 2d 873, 563 N.E.2d 874, 875 (1st Dist. 1990) (state allowed to amend complaint after prosecution rested); People v. Bae, 176 Ill. App. 3d 1065, 531 N.E.2d 931, 939 (1st Dist. 1988) (prior to selecting jury, state allowed to amend arson and murder indictment to reflect the correct building owner). *But see* People v. Arbo, 213 Ill. App. 3d 828, 572 N.E.2d 417, 420 (3d Dist. 1991) (felony theft conviction vacated because trial judge allowed state to amend indictment on second day of trial).

141. *See* People v. Allen, 8 Ill. App. 3d 176, 289 N.E.2d 467 (3d Dist. 1972) (appellate court refused to permit state's attorney to amend a charge on appeal).

142. People v. Troutt, 51 Ill. App. 3d 656, 366 N.E.2d 370 (5th Dist. 1977).

143. 78 Ill. App. 3d 200, 397 N.E.2d 106 (1st Dist. 1979).

144. *Id.,* 397 N.E.2d at 109.

145. 171 Ill. App. 3d 316, 525 N.E.2d 573 (3d Dist. 1988).

146. *Id.,* 525 N.E.2d at 575.

147. *Id.*

claimed it was not. The court held that it was only formal because (1) when the defendant filed a motion for a bill of particulars, he neither raised an objection to the language used nor did he claim that he did not understand the charge;[148] (2) "the common everyday meanings of the two words would not constitute a fundamental change in the charge when read in the context of the statute."[149]

§ 3.05 Historical Functions of the Grand Jury

Surrounded by a surprisingly good image, the grand jury, which is a body of 16 citizens usually without special training or education, has almost limitless power to search out crime and charge those thought to be criminals. It is, as one United States Supreme Court decision described it, a "body with powers of investigation and inquisition, the scope of whose inquiries is not to be limited

---

148. *Id.*

149. *See also* People v. Jones, 162 Ill. App. 3d 487, 515 N.E.2d 471, 474 (4th Dist. 1987) (court affirmed conviction in which state amended indictment to include necessary element of offense because no objection was made in circuit court and charge was sufficient to establish double jeopardy defense to another charge in same offense); People v. Doss, 161 Ill. App. 3d 258, 514 N.E.2d 502, 506 (4th Dist. 1987) ("A formal defect is one which does not affect the nature and elements of the offense.").

In *People v. Taylor,* 153 Ill. App. 3d 710, 506 N.E.2d 321, 331–32 (4th Dist. 1987), the original charge against the defendant was made by indictment. Four days prior to the beginning of trial, the state filed additional counts by way of information. These counts were the only ones charging the defendant with the felony of aggravated criminal sexual abuse. The court stated:

> Section 111-2(a) of the Code of Criminal Procedure [citation omitted] requires that felony charges be brought by information only after a preliminary hearing at which probable cause has been found. No probable cause hearing was held in regard to those charges nor was such a hearing waived. The State contends that any infirmity in those amended charges was cured by section 111-2(f) of the Code of Criminal Procedure [citation omitted] which states that when charges are brought by information or complaint after a preliminary hearing or waiver thereof, "such prosecution may be for all offenses arising from the same transaction or conduct of a defendant." [citation omitted].

> Had the State initiated the instant prosecution by information or complaint, section 111-2(f) would have cured any problem and permitted the subsequent amendments made here. However, the Code of Criminal Procedure of 1963 makes no similar provision to allow amendments to indictments without either a further indictment or a preliminary hearing. Allowing an indictment which arises from a finding of probable cause by a grand jury to be amended in the same way as complaints or informations filed after a court has found probable cause would be supported by logic. It is not supported by the express wording of the statutes.

narrowly by questions of propriety or forecasts of the probable result of the investigation, or by doubts whether any particular individual will be found properly subject to an accusation of crime."[150] The leading case, *United States v. Calandra*,[151] held that "[a] grand jury proceeding is not an adversary hearing in which guilt or innocence of the accused is adjudicated. Rather it is an *ex parte* investigation to determine whether a crime has been committed and whether criminal proceedings should be instituted against any person."[152] The grand jury has broad investigative powers. "When the grand jury is performing its investigatory function into a general problem area . . . society's interest is best served by a thorough and extensive investigation . . . ."[153] Another uplifting statement of the grand jury's role can be found in *United States v. Alred*,[154] where the court of appeals said that the role of a grand jury was to perform its public responsibility having a "broad investigative authority in determining whether a crime has been committed and in identifying perpetrators . . . . A grand jury investigation is not complete until all clues have been exhausted and every witness examined."[155] The grand jury enjoys a special role in ensuring fair and effective law enforcement.[156]

The power to compel a person to appear before a grand jury has been firmly established.[157] When a grand jury subpoena or subpoena duces tecum for documents or things is issued to a person or a corporation, a duty falls on that person to obey the subpoena and appear before the grand jury.[158] The

---

150. Blair v. United States, 250 U.S. 273, 282 (1919); People v. DeLaire, 240 Ill. App. 3d 1012, 610 N.E.2d 1277, 1282 (2d Dist. 1993) (grand jury can investigate merely on suspicion); People v. Fassler, 213 Ill. App. 3d 43, 571 N.E.2d 749, 750 (5th Dist.) (presence of person unauthorized by statute warrants dismissal), *rev'd on other grounds,* 153 Ill. 2d 49, 605 N.E.2d 576 (1992).

151. 414 U.S. 338 (1974).

152. *Id.* at 343–44.

153. Wood v. Georgia, 370 U.S. 375, 392 (1962).

154 144 F.3d 1405, 1413 (11th Cir. 1998).

155. *Id.*

156. *Calandra,* 414 U.S. at 343; People v. Hayes, 139 Ill. 2d 89, 564 N.E.2d 803, 815 (1990) (purpose of grand jury's investigative power is not only to charge the guilty but also to protect the innocent from unfounded criminal prosecution), *cert. denied,* 499 U.S. 967 (1991). *See also* In re October 1985 Grand Jury, 124 Ill. 2d 466, 530 N.E.2d 453, 456 (1988).

157. Kastigar v. United States, 406 U.S. 441 (1972).

158. See *Branzburg v. Hayes,* 408 U.S. 665, 688 (1972), where reporters were subpoenaed before grand juries. The reporters resisted the subpoenas, basically relying on the First Amendment. A majority of five justices held against the reporters, saying, "[T]he grand jury's authority to subpoena witnesses is not only historic . . . , but essential to its task."

English common law recognized that the public had a right to every person's evidence.[159] Today "full disclosure" is said to require a person to talk to the grand jury.[160] No matter seems too small or evanescent for a grand jury's attention. Once the Cook County state's attorney sought a special grand jury to investigate a toxic cloud. As the landmark case of *Hale v. Henkel*[161] stated:

> So valuable is inquisitorial power of the grand jury that, in States where felonies may be prosecuted by information as well as indictment, the power is ordinarily reserved to courts of impaneling grand juries for investigation of riots, frauds and nuisances, and other cases where it is impracticable to ascertain in advance the names of the persons implicated.[162]

Like all ancient and powerful things, the grand jury has its share of myths, or if not myths, then truths rendered less truthful by the passage of time. Consider the proposition in all high school civics books that the "grand jury stands between the accuser and the accused."[163] That simply is not true. The prosecutor meets the grand jury on his or her first day of service or when beginning some special investigation. The prosecutor works side by side with the sixteen persons day by day. He or she brings forth witnesses, explains the law, and becomes a co-worker. In short, the prosecutor helps the grand jury. It

---

159. Countess of Shrewsbury's Case, 2 How. St. Tr. 769, 778 (1612). *See Kastigar,* 406 U.S. at 443.

160. Blair v. United States, 250 U.S. 273, 281 (1919).

161. 201 U.S. 43 (1906), *overruled on other grounds* by Murphy v. Waterfront Comm'n of New York Harbor, 378 U.S. 52 (1964).

162. *Hale,* 201 U.S. at 65.

163. In *Wood v. Georgia,* 370 U.S. 375, 390 (1962), a free speech case, Chief Justice Earl Warren wrote:

> Historically, this body [the grand jury] has been regarded as a primary security to the innocent against hasty, malicious and oppressive persecution; it serves the invaluable function in our society of standing between the accuser and the accused, whether the latter be an individual, minority group, or other, to determine whether a charge is founded upon reason or was dictated by an intimidating power or by malice and personal ill will.

He cited *Hale v. Henkel,* 201 U.S. 43, 59 (1906), where Justice Henry Billings Brown, just before his retirement, wrote about the grand jury "standing be tween the accuser and the accused." Justice Brown cited no authority for his statement. *See* People v. Fassler, 213 Ill. App. 3d 43, 571 N.E.2d 749, 751 (5th Dist. 1991) (grand jury today is a powerful tool for prosecutor), *rev'd on other grounds,* 153 Ill. 2d 49, 605 N.E.2d 576 (1992); People v. Coleman, 205 Ill. App. 3d 567, 563 N.E.2d 1010, 1014 (4th Dist. 1990) (role and function of state's attorney); People v. Nash, 183 Ill. App. 3d 924, 539 N.E.2d 822, 825 (4th Dist. 1989).

would not be uncommon for the seventeen people to celebrate birthdays and share other private aspects of life. It would take a very unusual case, or an unusually insensitive prosecutor, to bring a grand jury between the accused and the wishes of the prosecutor. Another myth is that the grand jury "protects citizens from unfounded allegations."[164] The theory here, and I remember this from high school, is that if you are truly innocent the grand jury will secretly look into the matter and then vote a "no bill," and your neighbors will not be the wiser. This may be true for some lesser crimes or nonprominent citizens, but for a major offense or a prominent citizen today, everyone will know. Everyone finds out the work of the grand jury through the media. Of course, the actual testimony heard inside the grand jury room remains secret and is seldom revealed. But by piecing together a notice of an investigation, the identity of witnesses who may appear, and comments of witnesses or their attorneys after leaving the grand jury, the media can easily project the task of the grand jury.[165] Some observers speculate that an unscrupulous prosecutor might even purposely leak information to the media to frighten other potential witnesses into telling the grand jury the truth. The grand jury system has had its critics.[166] What is surprising is that it has not had more. The grand jury is English in origin, secret in its work, and managed by one attorney without input from the accused. American society, on the other hand, prides itself in being inventive, open, and evenhanded. The relatively high position of the grand jury in American society can only be attributed, then, to the quality of the work done by the citizens and attorneys who become the persona behind the legal form. Only careful, controlled, and conscientious actions would keep this institution as popular as it is.

---

164. Anyone who has ever been around a modern courthouse knows that the short distance between the press room and the grand jury waiting chamber means a story. Reporters quickly learn to identify the prosecutors working with the grand jury and the foreman, who makes returns of indictments to the judge, and would easily recognize any prominent citizens, politicians, and so forth.

165. There may be other documents to help the media. There could be defense motions to quash subpoenas filed with the judge or arguments of defense attorneys, who may be more anxious to be found in the media spotlight than to keep a client out of it. And, of course, there can be intentional or unintentional leaks from the prosecutor's office, where numerous secretaries, investigators, administrators, and attorneys know of the "secret" inquiry.

166. 4 *Works of Jeremy Bentham* 320 (1983); Calkins, *Abolition of the Grand Jury in Illinois,* 1966 U. ILL. L.F. 423.

§ 3.06 Formation of the Grand Jury

Section 112-2 of the Illinois Code of Criminal Procedure sets out the rules for impaneling a grand jury.[167] It provides that a grand jury will consist of 16 persons, 12 of whom will constitute a quorum.[168] Section 112-3 provides for the length of time a grand jury may sit (its "life") and for the number of grand juries that populous or less populous counties may have. In populous counties more than six may sit at the same time; less populous counties may have just one at any given time.[169] Two laws govern how grand jurors are selected. Some may find the laws in conflict, but there is no case law on the subject. Section 112-1 states that the grand jurors will be summoned and selected "according to law."[170] Section 309/15 of chapter 705 ("Jurors"), however, states: "The judge of the circuit court may order a special venire to be issued for a grand jury at any time when he is of the opinion that public justice requires it."[171] The latter provision, thought to permit empaneling a blue-ribbon grand jury, was given passing approval in *People v. Sears*.[172]

Section 112-4[173] provides that 12 jurors must concur "that the evidence before them constitutes probable cause that a person has committed an offense," and in that case the state's attorney is instructed to "prepare a bill of indictment." If there is a vote of 12 or more for indictment, it is said that the grand jury has voted a "true bill"; otherwise it votes a "no bill."[174]

The Illinois law is that an indictment returned by a legally constituted grand jury is valid and sufficient to justify a trial on the charge, and technical, but insubstantial, breaches in any procedure will not likely undo the indictment.[175]

Regarding technical or procedural flaws in the grand jury process, the Illinois Supreme Court has held that there exists a "presumption that an indictment returned by a legally constituted grand jury is valid, and it is sufficient to justify

---

167. 725 ILCS 5/112-2.When in doubt about any procedures, a prosecutor is well advised to seek an order from the circuit court judge with authority over the grand jury to gain court approval. This would apply to extending the life of a grand jury and other procedural problems.

168. 705 ILCS 305/16.

169. 705 ILCS 5/112-3.

170. 705 ILCS 5/112-1.

171. 705 ILCS 305/19.

172. 49 Ill. 2d 14, 273 N.E.2d 380 (1971).

173. 725 ILCS 5/112-4(d).

174. 705 ILCS 305/17.

175. People v. Whitlow, 89 Ill. 2d 322, 433 N.E.2d 629, *cert. denied,* 459 U.S. 830 (1982).

a trial of the charge on the merits."[176] Dismissal of an indictment as a remedy for procedural errors within the process will not be considered "unless defendant demonstrates that he was substantially prejudiced by the form of the indictment."[177] *People v. Curoe,*[178] an appellate court case, displays the distinction vividly. In this case the reviewing court considered chapter 705, section 305/17,[179] which requires the grand jury foreman to sign his name as foreman at the foot of said endorsement and shall "note thereon the name or names of the witness or witnesses upon whose evidence the [indictment] shall have been found."[180] Curoe was indicted by a grand jury that heard only an unsworn prosecutor summarize or read from a transcript of testimony of four witnesses heard earlier by another grand jury. The endorsement of the grand jury witnesses included the names of the four witnesses but not that of the prosecutor. The appellate court refused to dismiss the indictment, observing that the object of the statute was to give notice to the accused and that the defendant did not claim the erroneous endorsement prevented him from learning the names of the persons who appeared before the grand jury or in any way impeded his defense.[181] But the court took a sharply different view of unsworn testimony resting as the basis for an indictment. In *Curoe,* the court pointed to section 112-4(c),[182] which requires that the foreman "shall preside over all hearings and swear all witnesses" and that complaints and informations have to be sworn to and thus verified. The appellate court held: "[I]t would be anomalous if an

---

176. *Id.*, 433 N.E.2d at 632.

177. People v. Curoe, 97 Ill. App. 3d 258, 422 N.E.2d 931, 937 (1st Dist. 1981). *See also* People v. Wilkey, 202 Ill. App. 3d 756, 559 N.E.2d 1178, 1179 (3d Dist. 1990) (delays in charging may be grounds for dismissal of charge where due process violation occurs, but violation must be serious); People v. Valenzuela, 180 Ill. App. 3d 671, 536 N.E.2d 160, 163 (2d Dist. 1989) (defendant's motion to dismiss indictment because of preindictment delay must show actual and substantial prejudice). As the court stated in *People v. Valenzuela:*

> In the context of preindictment delay, a defendant must first make a clear showing of actual and substantial prejudice. [citation omitted] If he [or she] does so, the burden then shifts to the State to show the reasonableness, if not the necessity, of the delay. [citation omitted] Finally, if this two-step process ascertains both substantial prejudice and reasonableness of the delay, then the court must balance the interests of the defendant and the public in determining whether to dismiss the charge.

Id.

178. *Curoe,* 97 Ill. App. 3d 258, 422 N.E.2d at 937.

179. 705 ILCS 305/17.

180. *Curoe,* 97 Ill. App. 3d 258, 422 N.E.2d at 937.

181. *Id.*

182. 725 ILCS 5/112-4(c).

indictment could be returned solely upon the unsworn representations of a witness appearing before the grand jury. To sanction such a practice would open a veritable Pandora's box of possible evils. No citizen would be immune from indignities . . . ."[183]

Other cases involving procedural flaws have also followed the substantial prejudice rule. In *People v. Haag,*[184] it was alleged that the prosecutor failed to inform the grand jury, as required by section 112-4(b), that it had a right to subpoena the prospective defendant.[185] Despite the factual question of whether the grand jury was so advised, the appellate court held that "[e]ven were we to determine the grand jury was not advised of its power to subpoena defendant . . . the indictment was not subject to dismissal on that ground."[186] The *Haag* court relied on section 114-1(a)(5), which provides that an indictment may be dismissed if "a Grand Jury . . . acted contrary to Article 112 . . . which results in substantial injustice to the defendant."[187] The burden is on the defendant, the appellate court held, to show that "actual and substantial prejudice" befell him or her.[188]

Issues of preindictment delay have seldom been raised in Illinois, and when raised, are sometimes shaped in terms of speedy trial violations.[189]

In *People v. Lawson,*[190] the Illinois Supreme Court held that preindictment delay may be construed as a violation of due process. In *Lawson,* three defendants were indicted for delivery and possession of a controlled substance. The alleged violations occurred nearly one year before the indictment. The trial court dismissed the charges on the grounds that the delay denied the defendants due process. The supreme court affirmed the trial court's power to dismiss under the theory, but reversed as applied to the individual defendants. In order

---

183. *Curoe,* 97 Ill. App. 3d 258, 422 N.E.2d at 939. *Cf.* People v. Bissonnette, 20 Ill. App. 2d 970, 313 N.E.2d 646, 649 (2d Dist. 1974) (improper for sworn prosecutor to read entire transcript to grand jury). *But see* United States v. Hodge, 496 F.2d 87, 99 (5th Cir. 1974).

184. 80 Ill. App. 3d 135, 399 N.E.2d 284 (2d Dist. 1979).

185. 725 ILCS 5/112-4(b).

186. *Haag,* 80 Ill. App. 3d 135, 399 N.E.2d at 287.

187. 725 ILCS 5/114-1(a)(5).

188. *Haag,* 80 Ill. App. 3d 135, 399 N.E.2d at 288.

189. *See, e.g.,* People v. Prevo, 302 Ill. App. 3d 1038, 706 N.E.2d 505 (4th Dist. 1999). *See also* People v. McDuffee, 299 Ill. App. 3d 283, 701 N.E.2d 532, 535 (4th Dist. 1998) (recounting how defendant motioned to dismiss on speedy trial grounds and court denied this, holding that defendant was responsible for delay due to his previous motion for substitution of judge and continuance; accordingly, speedy trial requirement was tolled), *appeal granted,* 182 Ill. 2d 562, 707 N.E.2d 1243 (1999).

190. 67 Ill. 2d 449, 367 N.E.2d 1244 (1977).

to establish such a violation, the defendant must make a "clear showing of actual and substantial prejudice."[191] Such a showing shifts the burden to the state which must "show the reasonableness, if not the necessity, of the delay."[192]

In the federal context, the issue can be found in *United States v. Lovasco*,[193] where the Supreme Court stated that preindictment delay could amount to a violation of Fifth Amendment due process rights, often argued in terms of whether the defendant showed that there was tactical prosecutorial misconduct. Some circuits have gone further in foreclosing the issue, stating that even if there is intentional misconduct, it does not necessarily mean that prejudice befell the defendant.[194] The recent case of *United States v. Castillo*[195] sets forth the issue. Prejudice can be proven by showing, among other things, the loss of a key defense witness or waiting until the defendant reaches an age when he can be tried as an adult, rather than as a juvenile."

§ 3.07　The Fifth Amendment and the Grand Jury Witness

It is axiomatic that the Fifth Amendment to the United States Constitution grants to a person a privilege against being compelled to give self-incriminating evidence. That privilege is in force before a grand jury, whether federal or state, and at a trial.[196] Typically, a witness expresses the desire to refuse to give testimony because of his or her fear of self-incrimination. The witness may remain silent unless protected by immunity against the use of his or her answers or of evidence derived from the answers.[197] In practice, the Fifth Amendment stands strong as a protection against the awesome investigative powers of the grand jury. The early case of *Counselman v. Hitchcock*[198] illustrates. In this

---

191.　*Id.*, 367 N.E.2d at 1248.

192.　*Id.*

193.　431 U.S. 783, 795 (1977).

194.　United States v. Valentine, 783 F.2d 1413, 1416 (9th Cir. 1986).

195.　140 F.3d 874 (10th Cir. 1998).

196.　United States v. Washington, 431 U.S. 181 (1977); People v. Billups, 301 Ill. App. 3d 812, 705 N.E.2d 119, 121 (5th Dist. 1998) (state is required to advise defendant of his Fifth Amendments rights before testifying at grand jury hearing once it is clear that he has become target of indictment; merely asking him whether he would like to remain silent fails to adequately explain his rights); People v. Gaines, 188 Ill. App. 3d 451, 544 N.E.2d 974 (1st Dist. 1989) (distinction between transactional immunity and use and derivative use immunity and protection afforded federal grand jury witness when charged in state court).

197.　Malloy v. Hogan, 378 U.S. 1, 11 (1964).

198.　142 U.S. 547 (1892), *overruled on other grounds by* Kastigar v. United States, 406 U.S. 441 (1972) (Fifth Amendment applies but can be overcome by immunity).

case, the grand jury was investigating certain railroad rates under an act to regulate commerce. Charles Counselman was called before the grand jury, and in response to a question he said,"I decline to answer, Mr. Milchrist, on the ground that it might tend to criminate [sic] me."[199] The government contended that the witness was not entitled to plead the "privilege of silence," except in a criminal case. The United States Supreme Court stated simply: "[B]ut such is not the language of the Constitution. Its provision is that no person shall be compelled in any criminal case to be a witness against himself."[200] The Court held that the case before the grand jury was a criminal case.[201]

The government need not sit still for the Fifth Amendment plea. It has alternatives. It may compel the testimony after a grant of immunity. In *Kastigar v. United States*,[202] the witnesses had been given immunity from prosecution. The district court ordered the witnesses to testify. When they refused they were brought before the judge, who then found them in contempt of court and committed them to jail until they answered or until the term of the grand jury had expired. Justice Powell, writing for the Court, stated that "[t]he power of government to compel persons to testify in court or before grand juries and other governmental agencies is firmly established in Anglo-American jurisprudence." However, "the power to compel testimony is not absolute. There are a number of exceptions from the testimonial duty, the most important of which is the Fifth Amendment against compulsory self-incrimination."[203] The Fifth Amendment, said Powell, "marks an important advance in the development of our liberty." But immunity statutes are not incompatible with the values fostered by the Fifth Amendment.[204] The Court in *Kastigar* upheld the contempt convictions, holding that the witnesses were protected as much by the immunity

---

199. *Hitchcock*, 142 U.S. at 549.

200. *Id.* at 562.

201. *Id.*

202. 406 U.S. 441 (1972).

203. *Id.* at 443.

204. *Id.* at 451. The Illinois immunity provision is found in chapter 725, sections 5/106-1 and 5/106-2. In *People v. Giokaris*, 243 Ill. App. 3d 37, 611 N.E.2d 571 (2d Dist. 1993), the Illinois Appellate Court held that the immunity afforded by these provisions is transactional, not use immunity. *Id.*, 611 N.E.2d at 573. When the state grants transactional immunity to an individual under the statute, it cannot prosecute that individual for the offense to which the compelled testimony relates. Thus, the individual is given *full* immunity. Moreover, transaction immunity provides broader protection than either derivative use immunity (immunity from use of testimony only) or the Fifth Amendment privilege against self-incrimination. The court found that the state must strictly comply with the statute and that the trial judge does not have discretion to decrease the level of immunity granted an individual. *Id.*, 611 N.E.2d at 574–75. The court made this finding relying on *People ex rel. Cruz v.*

as they would have been by the Fifth Amendment. "The immunity therefore is coextensive with the privilege and suffices to supplant it," the Court said.[205]

But what of other damage to the person, other than criminal prosecution? Cases of the United States Supreme Court have held that a state "may not impose substantial penalties because a witness elects to exercise his fifth amendment right not to give incriminating testimony against himself."[206] In *Gardner v. Broderick*,[207] a police officer was called before a grand jury investigating police corruption. He was threatened with the loss of his job if he did not testify without a grant of immunity. When he refused, his employment was terminated, but the Court held that the officer could not be discharged solely for refusing to give up a right that is guaranteed him by the Constitution. "[T]he mandate of the great privilege against self-incrimination does not tolerate the attempt, regardless of the ultimate effectiveness, to coerce a waiver of the immunity it confers on penalty of the loss of employment."[208]

The same relief was granted in *Lefkowitz v. Cunningham*,[209] where a New York political party official was divested of his party office. A New York law had prohibited the holding of party or public office if an official refused to testify or declined to waive immunity from the later use of his or her testimony

---

Fitzgerald, 66 Ill. 2d 546, 363 N.E.2d 835, 837 (1977), and rejecting *In re January 1986 Grand Jury No. 217*, 155 Ill. App. 3d 445, 508 N.E.2d 277, 287 (1st Dist. 1987). *Giokaris,* 243 Ill. App. 3d 37, 611 N.E.2d at 575.

In 1993, pursuant to the Illinois Constitution, Art. IV, sec. 10, the legislature enacted section 106-2.5, giving judges the authority to grant witnesses use immunity. The statute states in pertinent part:

> (b) In lieu of the immunity provided in Section 106-2 of this Code, in any investigation before a Grand Jury, or trial in any court, the court on motion of the state shall order that a witness be granted immunity from prosecution in a criminal case as to any information directly or indirectly derived from the production of evidence from the witness if the witness has refused or is likely to refuse to produce the evidence on the basis of his or her privilege against self-incrimination.

> (c) The production of evidence so compelled under the order, and any information directly or indirectly derived from it, may not be used against the witness in a criminal case, except in a prosecution for perjury, false swearing, or an offense otherwise involving a failure to comply with the order. An order of immunity granted under this Section does not bar prosecution of the witness, except as specifically provided in this Section.

725 ILCS 5/106-2.5.

205.　*Kastigar,* 406 U.S. at 462.

206.　Gardner v. Broderick, 392 U.S. 273 (1968).

207.　392 U.S. 273 (1968).

208.　*Id.* at 279.

209.　431 U.S. 801 (1977).

against him or her. Answering the point that government officials should be in a different position regarding their official duties, the Court said: "Government has compelling interests in maintaining an honest police force and civil service, but this Court did not permit those interests to justify infringement of Fifth Amendment rights in [other cases], where alternative methods of promoting state aims were no more apparent than here."[210]

In *Conn v. Gabbert,*[211] the United States Supreme Court addressed a complaint of damages made not by a witness at a grand jury proceeding, but by the attorney of a witness called to testify. In this case,[212] prosecutors subpoenaed the witness to testify and produce any correspondence she had received from one of the defendants. The witness told prosecutors she had turned over all her letters from that defendant to her attorney, Gabbert. When the witness appeared to testify before the grand jury accompanied by Gabbert, prosecutors, believing Gabbert had the letters on his person, had Gabbert taken to a private room and searched. At the same time, prosecutors called the witness to testify, and began questioning her without Gabbert present in or outside the grand jury room. Gabbert brought suit, claiming his right to practice his profession was violated by the unreasonable governmental interference of executing a search warrant on him while his client was testifying before the grand jury.[213] Upon review, the Supreme Court disagreed, holding that Gabbert had not been damaged. Although he has a due process right to choose his field of employment, that right is still subject to government regulation. This was just an "inevitable interruption of [his] daily routine" that we all may experience at times.[214]

One challenge to a grand jury subpoena is that the government has not established the relevancy of the testimony. In *In re Grand Jury Proceedings,*[215] the grand jury had called an attorney to testify regarding the authenticity of the client's signature and photograph on an Immigration and Naturalization Service document. The attorney argued that the subpoena compelling her testimony must be quashed because the government failed to make a preliminary showing, by affidavit, of legitimate need and rele-

---

210. *Id.* at 808.

211. 119 S. Ct. 1292 (1999).

212. This case arose from the infamous California "Menendez Brothers" murder trial of Erik and Lyle Menendez, accused of killing their parents. Paul Gabbert was the attorney for Traci Baker, former girlfriend of defendant Lyle Menendez. Prosecutors had reason to believe Menendez had written a letter to Baker telling her to lie at trial. In fact, the first Menendez trial ended in a hung jury. The incident described here occurred during the grand jury proceedings for the retrial of the Menendez brothers.

232 *Conn,* 119 S. Ct. at 1294.

214 *Id.* at 1296.

215. 791 F.2d 663 (8th Cir. 1986).

vance of her testimony. The attorney argued that she could not be compelled to testify absent such an affidavit.[216]

The court, without discussion, refused to adopt the attorney's argument and stated that "[t]he Government amply demonstrated the relevancy of the [attorney's] testimony and the purpose for which it seeks the information during these proceedings. We see no reason to require that the Government file an affidavit reiterating these legitimate purposes."[217] The court went on to conclude that the burden was on the attorney to establish that the information sought fell within the attorney-client privilege. Having failed that burden, the attorney cannot then assert the requirement of a statement of need and relevancy.[218]

§ 3.08   Equality in Composition of Grand Jury

Like petit juries, grand juries must be composed of people from all groups, classes, and races within the community. Discrimination against any group, class, or race is a constitutional impropriety striking at "the fundamental values of our judicial system and our society as a whole."[219] The case of *Rose v. Mitchell*,[220] a modern United States Supreme Court decision, shows the power of the philosophy that co-exists with the realities of proof. Mitchell, a black man, was indicted by a grand jury in Tipton County, Tennessee. He sought to have the indictment dismissed on the grounds that the array and the foreman had been selected in a racially discriminatory manner. Relief was denied in the Tennessee courts and the federal district court, but the court of appeals

---

216. *Id.* at 665.

217. *Id. See also* In re Grand Jury Subpoena Served Upon Doe, 781 F.2d 238 (2d Cir. 1985) (en banc) (government not required to make preliminary showing of need prior to enforcement of grand jury subpoena served on attorney whose client is target of grand jury investigation), *cert. denied,* 475 U.S. 1108 (1986). *Cf.* In re Grand Jury Proceedings, 507 F.2d 963 (3d Cir.), *cert. denied,* 421 U.S. 1015 (1975); In re Grand Jury Proceedings, 486 F.2d 85 (3d Cir. 1973), *cert. denied,* 421 U.S. 1015 (1975).

218. *In re Grand Jury,* 791 F.2d at 666.

219. Rose v. Mitchell, 443 U.S. 545, 556 (1979). *See also* Castaneda v. Partida, 430 U.S. 482, 493 (1977); Neal v. Delaware, 103 U.S. 370, 394 (1881); Strauder v. West Virginia, 100 U.S. 303 (1880). In *Hill v. Texas,* 316 U.S. 400, 406 (1942), the Court found that although 8,000 blacks paid poll taxes in the county in question, no black had ever served on the county grand jury in 16 years. Chief Justice Stone stated: "Equal protection of the laws is something more than an abstract right. It is a command which the State must respect, the benefits of which every person may demand."

220. 443 U.S. 545 (1979).

reversed,[221] finding error in the method of selecting the grand jury foreman. The United States Supreme Court reaffirmed its stand on principles of equality. "Discrimination on the basis of race, odious in all aspects, is especially pernicious in the administration of justice."[222] It tied that philosophy to the grand jury, stating that a "defendant's right to equal protection of the laws has been denied when he is indicted by a grand jury from which members of a racial group purposefully have been excluded."[223] But the Court insisted that claims of discrimination must be proven.

> The first step is to establish that the group is one that is a recognizable, distinct class, singled out for different treatment . . . . Next, the degree of underrepresentation must be proved, by comparing the proportion of the group in the total population to the proportion called to serve as [foreman], over a significant period of time . . . . Finally, . . . a selection procedure that is susceptible of abuse or is not racially neutral supports the presumption of discrimination . . . ."[224]

And in Mitchell's case, the Court found the statistics to be inadequate. "Inasmuch as there is no evidence in the record of the number of foremen appointed, it is not possible to perform the calculations and comparisons needed to permit a court to conclude that a statistical case of discrimination had been made out . . . ," the Court held.[225]

In *Campbell v. Louisiana*,[226] the United States Supreme Court held that a Louisiana white defendant has standing to challenge the exclusion of black jurors on a grand jury. The defendant sought only to challenge the appointment of the grand jury foreman because in over seventeen years no black had served as a foreman in a system that appoints the foreman before the grand jury itself had been chosen. The Court treated defendant's challenge as one alleging discrimination in the selection of the grand jurors.[227] The court noted that the *Powers* rationale was as applicable to grand jurors as it was to petit jurors.[228]

---

221. Mitchell v. Rose, 570 F.2d 129 (6th Cir. 1978), *rev'd*, 443 U.S. 545 (1979) (*see* textual discussion).

222. *Mitchell*, 443 U.S. at 555.

223. *Id.* at 556.

224. *Id.* at 565.

225. *Id.* at 571. In *Castaneda*, by contrast, 39 percent of the grand jurors had Spanish surnames, but the county's population was 79.1 percent Mexican-American. The Court found sufficient evidence of purposeful discrimination.

226. 118 S. Ct. 1419 (1998).

227. *Id.* at 1422.

228. *Id.* at 1423.

Regardless of the defendant's race, he or she suffers significant injury when the grand jury is tainted by race discrimination. The grand jury is a vital and central component of the judicial process. Its integrity depends on the integrity of its formation. If the grand jury's formation is tainted by race discrimination, the fairness of the grand jury is called into question.[229] Further, there is no reason why a white defendant should not be an advocate for the grand jury than he or she would be for the petit jury. Either type of juror has the same lack of incentive to bring a challenge on their own.[230] "We find [defendant], like any other white defendant, has standing to raise an equal protection challenge to discrimination against black persons in the selection of his grand jury."[231] The Court did confine its decision to the standing issue and declined to address the extent and nature of a due process claim based on an allegation of discrimination in the selection of the grand jury.[232]

The Court further found that the Louisiana Supreme Court had erred in its interpretation of *Hobby v. United States*.[233] According to the Court, the relevant assumption of *Hobby* was that a defendant has standing to litigate whether a conviction was procured by means of procedures that contravene due process.[234] *Hobby* did not hold that such standing was lacking, as the Louisiana Supreme Court found. Moreover, *Hobby* involved selection of the foreperson prior to the selection of the grand jury. It did not involve selection of the foreperson before the balance of the grand jury had been chosen as was Louisiana's practice. Thus, the question of discrimination in jury selection was not at issue.[235]

The Court further declined to address whether defendant had standing to raise a fair cross section challenge, because the issue was not addressed by either the state appellate or supreme court.[236]

§ 3.09   Prosecutorial Conduct Before the Grand Jury

In a modern and complex world, the grand jury could not work without the assistance of the prosecutor. The prosecutor brings forth witnesses and stands as a legal advisor to the grand jury.[237] But the work of the prosecutor is

---

229. *Id.*

230. *Id.* at 1424.

231. *Id.*

232. *Id.*

233. 468 U.S. 339 (1984).

234. *Campbell*, 118 S. Ct. at 1425.

235. *Id.*

236. *Id.*

237. People v. DiVencenzo, 183 Ill. 2d 239, 700 N.E.2d 981, 989 (1998).

circumscribed. He or she must always work within the bounds of propriety. For all its independence, the grand jury is still an integral part of the trial court, and that court, in its inherent supervisory power over the grand jury, has the authority to order and examine transcripts of grand jury proceedings to determine if there have been any instances of prosecutorial misconduct.[238] The burden of proof is on the defendant to show any irregularity, and mere speculation on that subject is not sufficient to sustain the burden.[239] The case of *People v. Linzy*[240] is a good example of the latitude the prosecution enjoys when working with the grand jury. In *Linzy,* the prosecutor presented evidence that the defendant, Darlene Linzy, had shot and killed two women in a tavern altercation. There was some evidence that one of the women had approached the defendant and slapped her before the shooting. A grand juror asked the prosecutor if the slapping of the defendant by the victim could have amounted to provocation. The prosecutor replied negatively, stating that "a slap or hot words would not be considered serious provocation."[241] The supreme court found no abuse of power, holding that the prosecutor's statement was made "in the exercise of the prosecutor's function as advisor to the grand jury."[242] It is

---

238. People v. Sears, 49 Ill. 2d 14, 273 N.E.2d 380 (1971); People v. Fassler, 153 Ill. 2d 49, 605 N.E.2d 576 (1992) (defendant must prove substantial injustice to procure a dismissal of an indictment based on a violation of section 112-6(a); defendant did not prove that the victim's mother's presence in court without permission prejudiced him).

239. People v. Easter, 102 Ill. App. 3d 974, 430 N.E.2d 612 (1st Dist. 1981). Even if the defendant can prove prosecutorial misconduct, the defendant must also show how the conduct prejudiced him or her. In *People v. Hayes,* 139 Ill. 2d 89, 564 N.E.2d 803 (1990), *cert. denied,* 499 U.S. 967 (1991), the Illinois Supreme Court agreed that the prosecutor had acted improperly in calling a witness to testify before the grand jury after the indictment against the defendant was returned; however, the court concluded, "[W]e fail to see how the defendant was prejudiced." *Id.,* 564 N.E.2d at 816. *See also DiVincenzo,* 183 Ill. 2d 239, 700 N.E.2d at 991 (stating that, though prosecutor's conduct of asking grand jury to reconsider was improper, defendant failed to show how this violated his due process rights); People v. Arrington, 297 Ill. App. 3d 1, 696 N.E.2d 1229, 1231 (2d. Dist. 1998) (demonstrating clearly that burden is on defendant to prove not only irregularity, but that irregularity caused him to suffer actual or substantial ment of special prosecutor was denied when he failed to prove this prejudice; mere fact that prosecutor's cousin owned store defendant attempted to rob was not sufficient proof to sustain defendant's burden).

240. 78 Ill. 2d 106, 398 N.E.2d 1 (1979).

241. *Id.,* 398 N.E.2d at 2.

242. *Id.*

clear that a prosecutor has a legitimate role as legal advisor to the grand jury,[243] and Illinois courts have given that office considerable latitude in the exercise of that role.[244] Generally speaking, only intentional and outrageous prosecutorial misconduct has been held to require dismissal of the indictment.[245] Moreover, the defendant must prove that the conduct prejudiced him or her.[246] In addition to prejudice to the defendant, courts can consider the nature of the prosecutorial misconduct. In *People v. Meccia*,[247] the trial court dismissed the indictment against defendant for prosecutorial misconduct before the grand jury.[248] It specifically found that defendant's Fourth, Fifth, and Sixth Amendment rights had been violated.[249] The state did not contest this finding but argued that the charges against the defendant should not have been dismissed because he could not show prejudice.[250] The appellate court looked beyond the prejudice aspect and analyzed the seriousness of the misconduct.[251] The trial court found, and the appellate court agreed, that this case was a "very serious, outlandish example of overreaching by the State and the Chicago Police Department and the State's Attorney's Office."[252] Based upon the state's

---

243. Hughes v. Kiley, 67 Ill. 2d 261, 367 N.E.2d 700 (1977); People v. Davis, 205 Ill. App. 3d 865, 563 N.E.2d 869, 871 (1st Dist. 1990) (convictions will not be reversed because of misstatement of law by the prosecutor before grand jury).

244. People v. Johnson, 97 Ill. App. 3d 1055, 423 N.E.2d 1206 (1st Dist. 1981), *cert. denied*, 455 U.S. 951 (1982). *See* People v. Seehausen, 193 Ill. App. 3d 754, 550 N.E.2d 702, 705 (2d Dist. 1990).

245. *See* United States v. Roth, 777 F.2d 1200 (7th Cir. 1985); United States v. Hogan, 712 F.2d 757 (2d Cir. 1983); United States v. Chanen, 549 F.2d 1306 (9th Cir.), *cert. denied,* 434 U.S. 825 (1977); United States v. Estepa, 471 F.2d 1132 (2d Cir. 1972); In re D.T., 141 Ill. App. 3d 1036, 490 N.E.2d 1361 (1st Dist. 1986). *See* People v. DiVincenzo, 183 Ill. 2d 239, 700 N.E.2d at 991 (providing examples of intentional or outrageous conduct: if prosecutor deliberately misleads grand jury, uses false testimony, presents deceptive evidence, pressures or coerces grand jury); People v. Torres, 245 Ill. App. 3d 297, 613 N.E.2d 338, 340–41 (2d Dist. 1993) (prosecutorial misconduct warrants dismissal of indictment only when defendant's due process rights are violated "such that his right to a fair trial is prejudiced" or where the conduct "in some way undermines the integrity of the judicial process").

246. Bank of Nova Scotia v. United States, 487 U.S. 250, 254 (1988); *DiVincenzo,* 183 Ill. 2d 239, 700 N.E.2d at 991.

247. 275 Ill. App. 3d 123, 655 N.E.2d 1113 (1st Dist. 1995).

248. *Id.*, 655 N.E.2d at 1115.

249. *Id.*

250. *Id.*

251. *Id.*, 655 N.E.2d at 1116.

252. *Id.*

flagrant disregard for defendant's constitutional rights, the appellate court upheld the dismissal.[253]

However, courts may not invoke their supervisory power to circumvent the harmless error rule.[254] In other words, the harmless error doctrine applies to grand jury indictments. In evaluating whether a trial judge should dismiss an indictment before the conclusion of a trial, the type of violation which is alleged controls the standard of prejudice required. When defendant seeks a dismissal for a nonconstitutional error, the judge can only dismiss the indictment if actual prejudice is proven, *i.e.*, " 'if it is established that the violation substantially influenced the grand jury's decision to indict,' or if there is 'grave doubt' that the decision to indict was free from the substantial influence of such violations."[255] On the other hand, when the "structural protections of the grand jury have been so compromised as to render the proceedings fundamentally unfair," the judge will apply the presumption of prejudice standard.[256]

Where a grand jury votes a "no bill," may prosecutors ask the grand jury to reconsider its finding of "no probable cause"? A key case that shapes the beginning of the inquiry, but does not reflect its end, is the Illinois Supreme Court's *People v. DiVincenzo*.[257] In *DiVincenzo*, a transcript of a morning session of the grand jury showed that the grand jury had rejected a charge of first-degree murder. Later in the day, after prosecutors learned of the vote, one prosecutor made an additional presentation to the grand jury to "remind" the jurors of the "pertinent law." He told the grand jury in the afternoon that "he was concerned that they might not have a clear understanding of the law."[258] However, the prosecutors "left cases and statutory definitions for the grand jury."[259]

The supreme court held that "[t]o warrant dismissal of the indictment, the defendant must . . . show that the prosecutors prevented the grand jury from returning a meaningful indictment by misleading or coercing it."[260] The court determined that merely asking the grand jury to reconsider was "not sufficient, by itself, to warrant dismissal of the indictment."[261] The court added that "[a]

---

253. *Id.*

254. *Nova Scotia,* 487 U.S. at 254.

255. *Id.* at 256 (quoting United States v. Mechanik, 475 U.S. 66, 78 (1986)).

256. *Nova Scotia,* 487 U.S. at 257.

257. 183 Ill. 2d 239, 700 N.E.2d 981 (1998).

258. *Id.,* 700 N.E.2d at 990.

259. *Id.*

260. *Id.,* 700 N.E.2d at 991.

261. *Id.*

determination of no probable cause carries no preclusive effect," and that "[n]o doctrine limits a grand jury to one vote on a proposed indictment."[262]

The court found that "[s]tanding alone, the prosecutors' request for reconsideration does not show that the will of the grand jury was overborne by the prosecutors."[263] Hence, where the prosecutors cannot be said to be misleading or coercive, and where the grand jury exhibits that it is operating independently from the prosecutors, a second request for a true bill may be permissible. The parameters of the issue have been set. Future cases will determine whether the admonitions in *DiVincenzo* turn into teeth to bar a second request where there is evidence of improper conduct that prejudices the defendant's right to a fair hearing before the grand jury.

How far can any search for prosecutorial wrongdoing go? That question was answered by *People ex rel. Sears v. Romiti*.[264] In this case attorneys for potential defendants moved to stop a grand jury investigation, arguing that the special prosecutor was exhorting the grand jurors to indict and engaging in other misconduct. The supreme court drew the line at any investigation that would go beyond the record.[265] It would not permit the interrogation of grand jurors as to activities dehors the record.[266]

In *People v. Benitez*,[267] an unusual set of facts produced significant law regulating the way prosecutors may create indictments. Benitez was convicted of murder. Throughout the trial, and on appeal, Benitez contended that he was "never properly charged" with any offense. The charging process began smoothly as the state presented evidence to the grand jury showing that Benitez and two others committed a murder. After the evidence was presented, a prosecutor asked the grand jury for a "true bill," and after deliberations the foreperson of the grand jury announced "true bill." But there was a problem. When the indictment was produced, only one defendant appeared on the indictment, and that person was not the defendant, Benitez. That indictment was signed by the foreperson of the grand jury. That day, the 31st of the month, was the last day that the grand jury sat.

Nevertheless, the State's Attorney's Office notified Benitez that he had been indicted, and some time later Benitez and his lawyer appeared for arraignment. Counsel was given a copy of the charges, which—somehow—did reflect the

---

262. *Id.*

263. *Id.*

264. 50 Ill. 2d 51, 277 N.E.2d 705, 707 (1971), *cert. denied*, 406 U.S. 921 (1972).

265. *See also DiVincenzo*, 183 Ill. 2d 239, 700 N.E.2d at 990 (stating that courts reviewing indictments generally limit their review to grand jury proceeding transcript).

266. *Sears*, 50 Ill. 2d 51, 277 N.E.2d at 709.

267. 169 Ill. 2d 245, 661 N.E.2d 344 (1996).

name of the defendant, as well as the other two men charged. The grand jury that heard the evidence originally had not been reconvened, and no later grand jury heard the evidence again. Yet the indictment given on arraignment tracked the evidence presented to the grand jury.

During trial, thirteen months later, apparently a copy of the first indictment surfaced, and the defense attorney raised the issue with the trial judge hearing the bench trial. After some investigation by defense counsel, the trial judge ruled that the "second" indictment was "valid." Benitez was convicted of murder.

At a posttrial evidentiary hearing, the defendant brought proof of the procedures of the Cook County grand jury. In particular, the defendant presented a volume of the "Clerk's Journal" that showed Benitez's name had been on the indictment for murder on the day of the true bill and that one of the grand jurors had personally made the entry in the Journal. However, a search of all other records failed to provide any documentation of a true bill naming Benitez. It was proven that secretaries in the grand jury unit prepared the second indictment, the one that named Benitez, but that the indictment had never been signed by the grand jury foreperson.

The state argued that there "simply had been a mistake in the paper work."[268] In particular, the prosecutor argued at the trial level, "[t]he paper work occurs, the State's Attorney's Office prepares the [i]ndictment charging one person, then they prepare a piece of paper work charging three people with [m]urder two months later. . . . Who cares that the wrong person was charged in the document that we didn't proceed on."[269] On appeal, with more tact, the state argued that the "first indictment" was a "mistyped document" that should be considered "superfluous," and that the "second indictment" was "independently valid."[270]

The Illinois Supreme Court, after a review of the legal history and Illinois law, noted that "[t]he grand jury had not been reconvened between" the erroneous indictment and the second (corrected) indictment.[271] The court stated that it could not "condone" the casual approach of the prosecutor's office when dealing with a critical stage of the charging process, and the state should not have "arrogated for itself the power to amend the indictment as it saw fit."[272] The court ruled that Benitez was "never properly charged with any offense."[273] Lastly, the court ruled that double jeopardy principles were not

---

268. *Id.*, 661 N.E.2d at 347.

269. *Id.*

270. *Id.*

271. *Id.*, 661 N.E.2d at 348.

272. *Id.*, 661 N.E.2d at 349.

273. *Id.*

involved, and that the state could bring proceedings "anew with a proper charging instrument."[274]

Must a prosecutor correct perjury or false testimony if it is brought to the grand jury? Obviously, during a trial a prosecutor has a constitutional duty to correct false testimony when heard by a jury or judge.[275] Does a similar duty fall on a prosecutor before a grand jury? In an opinion in chambers by Justice Rehnquist, the question was answered negatively. He stated: "The grand jury does not sit to determine the truth of the charges brought against a defendant, but only to determine whether there is probable cause to believe them true, so as to require him to stand his trial."[276] In this regard it may consider hearsay as well as evidence that had been obtained in violation of the Fourth Amendment.[277] Justice Rehnquist concluded that "[w]hile the presentation of inadmissible evidence at trial may pose a substantial threat to the integrity of that fact finding process, its introduction before the grand jury poses no such threat."[278] No one, it is supposed, who has been through the emotional and financial rigors of a criminal prosecution would agree with the justice.

Another question is whether the prosecutor has a duty to present exculpatory evidence to the grand jury. Although this question does not appear to have been raised in the Illinois courts, several federal courts have addressed the issue. These courts have developed two theories regarding the prosecutor's duty. The first is that the prosecutor has no duty to present exculpatory evidence to the grand jury.[279] The second approach appears to utilize a compromise to either

---

274. *Id.,* 661 N.E.2d at 351.

275. Napue v. Illinois, 360 U.S. 264 (1959).

276. Bracy v. United States, 435 U.S. 1301, 1302 (1978).

277. *Id.* People v. Rivera, 176 Ill. App. 3d 781, 531 N.E.2d 372, 378 (3d Dist. 1988) (indictment not dismissed where evidence presented to grand jury was not intentionally false or misleading), *cert. denied,* 480 U.S. 1046 (1989). *See also* People v. Bryant, 241 Ill. App. 3d 1007, 609 N.E.2d 910, 920 (1st Dist. 1993) (indictment not dismissed where state used evidence against two individuals and it applied to only one, where confusion cleared up by later testimony); People v. DeLaire, 240 Ill. App. 3d 1012, 610 N.E.2d 1277, 1283 (2d Dist. 1993) (exclusionary rule does not bar use of illegally obtained evidence by grand jury and its use does not require dismissal of an indictment).

278. *Bracy,* 435 U.S. at 1302 (1978); People v. J.H., 136 Ill. 2d 1, 554 N.E.2d 961 (exclusionary rule does not bar grand jury's consideration of illegally obtained evidence since suppression of evidence at trial is readily available remedy to prosecutorial misconduct), *cert. denied,* 498 U.S. 942 (1990).

279. United States v. Busher, 817 F.2d 1409 (9th Cir. 1987); United States v. Adamo, 742 F.2d 927 (6th Cir. 1984), *cert. denied,* 469 U.S. 1193 (1985); United States v. Sears, Roebuck and Co., 719 F.2d 1386 (9th Cir. 1983), *cert. denied,* 465 U.S. 1079 (1984).

an affirmative-duty or a no-duty stance and has been adopted by three of the United States Courts of Appeals. In *United States v. Page*,[280] the court stated:

> The Second and Seventh Circuits have suggested that, although a prosecutor need not present all conceivably exculpatory evidence to the grand jury, it must present evidence that clearly negates guilt. [citations omitted] This is the better and more balanced rule, which we adopt. Under this standard the prosecutor is not obliged to ferret out and present every bit of potentially exculpatory evidence. But when *substantial* exculpatory evidence is discovered in the course of an investigation, it must be revealed to the grand jury. This promotes judicial economy. If a fully informed grand jury cannot find probable cause to indict, there is little chance the prosecution could have proved guilt beyond a reasonable doubt to a fully informed petit jury.[281]

However, the Supreme Court of the United States has recently addressed this issue and resolved the conflict in the federal courts. In *United States v. Williams*,[282] the Supreme Court held that the district court judge cannot dismiss an otherwise valid indictment merely because the government failed to disclose "substantial exculpatory evidence" to the grand jury.[283] The Court set forth several reasons for reaching this decision. First, the Court looked to the historic function of the grand jury and its established independence from the judiciary in both its power to investigate and the manner in which it exercises that power.[284] Particularly, the Court noted the fact that the grand jury requires no authorization from the district court to initiate an investigation. The only limit placed on the grand jury's power of investigation is that the grand jury cannot override the constitutional rights of witnesses. Short of this, the grand jury "act[s] independently of either prosecuting attorney *or judge*."[285] The Court further noted that in the past, it has held steadfast to its reluctancy to allow judicial supervisory power to prescribe the grand jury's manner of investigation, instead allowing it virtual independence.[286] Perhaps most importantly, the Court found that if it required the prosecutor to present such evidence to the

---

280. United States v. Page, 808 F.2d 723 (10th Cir.), *cert. denied,* 482 U.S. 918 (1987).

281. *Id.* at 727–28. *See also* United States v. Flomenhoft, 714 F.2d 708, 712 (7th Cir. 1983), *cert. denied,* 465 U.S. 1068 (1984); United States v. Ciambrone, 601 F.2d 616, 622–23 (2d Cir. 1979).

282. 504 U.S. 36 (1992).

283. *Id.* at 55.

284. *Id.* at 48.

285. *Id.* at 49.

286. *Id.* at 49–50.

grand jury, the Court would be altering the grand jury's historical role and "transforming it from an accusatory to an adjudicatory body."[287] Historically, only the prosecutor presents evidence and generally his or her side only; the target is awarded no opportunity to offer a defense or evidence.[288] Therefore, it would be contradictory to require a prosecutor to present such exculpatory evidence when the suspect himself or herself is not required, or even allowed, to present such evidence.[289] Moreover, because the grand jury has no obligation to consider all "substantial exculpatory" evidence, there is no basis to require the prosecutor to present all exculpatory evidence. Finally, since district court judges cannot review the evidence supporting the grand jury's decision to indict, there is no logic in requiring them to review the sufficiency of the evidence which the prosecutor failed to present to the grand jury.[290] In conclusion, the Supreme Court held that "courts have no authority to prescribe such a duty [to present exculpatory evidence] pursuant to their inherent supervisory authority over their own proceedings."[291]

Similarly, the Illinois Appellate Court addressed the issue of exculpatory evidence and adhered to the United States Supreme Court's ruling. In *People v. Torres*,[292] the court held that the state has "no general [on-going] duty to present exculpatory evidence to the grand jury."[293] However, prosecutors may have a duty to divulge information if by intentionally withholding such information, the prosecutor would deny defendant his or her due process rights. In this case, the defendant's due process rights were not violated. During a grand jury investigation of a car passenger, the prosecutor failed to advise the grand jury that the driver of the automobile claimed ownership of the drugs and guns found in the car. Moreover, the passenger was unaware that these items were present in the car. Because there was no evidence presented that this alleged exculpatory evidence would be admissible at trial or that if the grand jury knew of the evidence it would not have indicted the passenger, the defendant's due process rights were not violated. In addition, defendant failed to show "actual and substantial prejudice" which is required before an indictment may be dismissed.[294]

Even though a prosecutor has wide tactical latitude before a grand jury, he or she must not mislead the jury that it is hearing direct evidence when in fact

287. *Id.* at 51.

288. *Id.* at 51–52 (citing numerous authorities from England and the United States).

289. *Id.* at 52.

290. *Id.* at 53.

291. *Id.* at 55.

292. 245 Ill. App. 3d 397, 613 N.E.2d 338 (2d Dist. 1993).

293. *Id.,* 613 N.E.2d at 341.

294. *Id.*

it is hearing hearsay. A prosecutor, however, has no affirmative obligation to tell the jury in haec verba that it is listening to hearsay.[295] A prosecutor has no duty to disclose all that he or she knows,[296] and he or she need not "inform the grand jury of the existence of additional or more direct evidence."[297] A prosecutor must perform all statutory duties, such as informing the grand jury in accordance with Illinois Compiled Statutes chapter 725, section 5/112-4(b) that it may subpoena anyone against whom the state might seek an indictment.[298] A prosecutor must inform the grand jury that a judge had previously found no probable cause on the same evidence.[299]

In *People v. Benitez*,[300] the appellate court found that the failure of the foreperson and assistant state's attorney to sign the indictment did not require reversal of the conviction.[301] The foreperson's signature is for the information of the court only. It does not affect the substantive rights of an accused.[302] The prosecutor's signature is also not required.[303]

§ 3.10   Quantum of Evidence to Indict by Grand Jury

The landmark case of *United States v. Calandra*[304] held that the validity of an indictment is not affected by the character of the evidence considered by the grand jury. The indictment may be based on pure hearsay.[305] Challenges to the

---

295. United States v. Estepa, 471 F.2d 1132 (2d Cir. 1972).

296. *Id.* at 1136.

297. United States v. Basurto, 497 F.2d 781 (9th Cir. 1974).

298. 725 ILCS 5/112-4(b).

299. *Id.*

300. 269 Ill. App. 3d 182, 645 N.E.2d 478 (1st Dist. 1994), *rev'd on other grounds*, 169 Ill. 2d 245, 661 N.E.2d 344 (1996) (although reversed on improper amendment of indictment grounds). See text § 3.04.

301. *Id.,* 645 N.E.2d at 480.

302. *Id.*

303. *Id.,* 645 N.E.2d at 481.

304. 414 U.S. 338 (1974). Calandra was asked questions by the grand jury based on evidence that had been seized by government agents in violation of the Fourth Amendment. Nevertheless, a majority of the United States Supreme Court held that a witness could not refuse to answer questions on the ground that they were based on illegally obtained evidence.

305. Costello v. United States, 350 U.S. 359, 361 (1956); People v. Hopkins, 53 Ill. 2d 452, 292 N.E.2d 418 (1973); People v. Myers, 46 Ill. 2d 270, 263 N.E.2d 113 (1970); People v. Jones, 19 Ill. 2d 37, 166 N.E.2d 1 (1960); People v. Moore, 199 Ill. App. 3d 747, 557 N.E.2d 537 (1st Dist. 1990), *cert. denied,* 498 U.S. 1032 (1991).

quality of the evidence heard by the grand jury are regularly rejected to avoid a "kind of preliminary trial to determine the competency and adequacy of the evidence before the grand jury."[306] In *People v. Rodgers*,[307] the Illinois Supreme Court determined that a trial court has the power to review the grand jury transcripts to determine if there was some evidence before the grand jury of the charge brought against the defendant. It stated: "To return a true bill where there is absolutely no evidence connecting the accused to the offense charged would be an abdication of the important responsibility with which the grand jury has been entrusted."[308] Thus in *Rodgers* the Illinois Supreme Court made it clear that the same type of judicial review of grand jury transcripts that is used when there is a claim of prosecutorial misconduct is to be employed where there is a claim of a total lack of evidence. But an indictment, which is valid on its face, is not subject to challenge on the ground that the grand jury acted on inadequate evidence,[309] or as the court in *Rodgers* put it, "[n]or will it be necessary to determine whether any evidence was presented as to each element of the offense. We require only that there be some evidence relative to the charge."[310] It is important to remember that when challenges are made to the nature of the evidence heard before the grand jury, grand jury transcripts should be made a part of the trial record for appellate review.[311] Many Illinois cases hold that an indictment should not be dismissed, unless all of the evidence heard by the

---

306. *Costello*, 350 U.S. at 362.

307. 92 Ill. 2d 283, 442 N.E.2d 240 (1982).

308. *Id.*, 442 N.E.2d at 243.

309. The law on this point is fundamental. In *Holt v. United States*, 218 U.S. 245 (1910), the Court refused to quash the indictment even though it found that aside from incompetent evidence, "there was very little evidence against the accused." *See* People v. Gill, 264 Ill. App. 3d 451, 637 N.E.2d 1030, 1034 (1st Dist. 1992) ("[I]t has been repeatedly held that a defendant cannot properly challenge the sufficiency of the evidence presented to the grand jury.").

310. *Rodgers*, 92 Ill. 2d 283, 442 N.E.2d at 244; People v. J.H., 136 Ill. 2d 1, 554 N.E.2d 961, 968 (some evidence), *cert. denied*, 498 U.S. 942 (1990); People v. Finley, 209 Ill. App. 3d 968, 568 N.E.2d 412, 416 (3d Dist. 1991) (same). *See also* People v. Edwards, 243 Ill. App. 3d 280, 611 N.E.2d 1196, 1200 (1st Dist. 1993) (evidence connecting defendant may be direct or circumstantial from which an inference can be drawn, therefore, *some* evidence is sufficient; police officer's minimal testimony to grand jury was "some evidence" which "tended to connect" defendant), *cert. denied*, 511 U.S. 1071 (1994).

311. *Rodgers*, 92 Ill. 2d 283, 442 N.E.2d at 244; People v. Davis, 205 Ill. App. 3d 865, 563 N.E.2d 869 (1st Dist. 1990) (defendant must provide transcript in appellate record).

grand jury was incompetent,[312] and that hearsay testimony is not incompetent evidence for purposes of this rule.[313]

A good restatement of the law in Illinois is found in the case of *In re D.T.*[314] In that case, the minor-defendant moved to dismiss the indictment on the basis that the state had made reference to the defendant's juvenile record in violation of the protective confidentiality provisions of the Juvenile Court Act.[315] Holding that section 2-10 of the act[316] does not specifically mention grand jury proceedings and that the confidentiality provisions do not amount to an absolute prohibition against disclosure, the court stated:

> It is well established that grand jury proceedings are generally unrestrained by the technical, procedural, and evidentiary rules which govern the conduct of criminal trials. [citations omitted] The rationale behind the broad scope given to the grand jury is that the indictment is a formal charge, not a trial on the merits. Thus, the proceedings do not require the degree and quality of proof necessary for a conviction. [citations omitted] In addition, the validity of an indictment is not affected by the character of the evidence considered. As long as there is some evidence in support of the charges [citations omitted], and the indictment is valid on its face, it is not subject to challenge on the ground that the grand jury acted on the basis of inadequate or incompetent evidence. [citations omitted] Moreover, the court will not dismiss a charge based upon allegations of prosecutorial misconduct unless the conduct results in actual and substantial prejudice to [the] defendant. [citation omitted][317]

---

312. People v. Orr, 10 Ill. 2d 95, 139 N.E.2d 212 (1956), *cert. denied,* 353 U.S. 987 (1957); People v. Wheeler, 403 Ill. 78, 84 N.E.2d 832 (1949); People v. Meisenhelter, 317 Ill. App. 511, 47 N.E.2d 108 (1943). *See* People v. Bryant, 241 Ill. App. 3d 1007, 609 N.E.2d 910, 920 (1st Dist. 1993) (officer's testimony, which was conclusory in form, sufficiently based on facts obtained through investigation, therefore, not knowingly false or in reckless disregard of the truth).

313. People v. Creque, 72 Ill. 2d 515, 382 N.E.2d 793 (1978), *cert. denied,* 441 U.S. 912 (1979). It should also be mentioned at this point that the prosecution is not required to inform the grand jury that hearsay evidence is being heard instead of actual eyewitness testimony.

314. 141 Ill. App. 3d 1036, 490 N.E.2d 1361 (1st Dist. 1986).

315. 705 ILCS 405/1-1.

316. 705 ILCS 405/1-8.

317. *D.T.,* 141 Ill. App. 3d 1036, 490 N.E.2d at 1364. *See also* United States v. Busher, 817 F.2d 1409 (9th Cir. 1987) (defendant challenging indictment carries heavy burden; must demonstrate that prosecutor engaged in flagrant conduct that deceived grand jury or significantly impaired its ability to exercise independent judgment); People v. DiVincenzo, 183 Ill. 2d 239, 700 N.E.2d 981, 989 (1998)

The defendant also contended that the indictment was improper because the prosecutor misinformed the jury as to the legal standards for murder. The court held that although the prosecutor did not quote the statute verbatim in response to a query as to why the state sought an indictment for murder, the court held that the substance of the response was accurate and that it did not present false or misleading evidence.[318]

§ 3.11   Independence and Court Supervision of the Grand Jury

The independence of the grand jury has been honored and protected in Illinois either because of history or a sense that an independent grand jury may be useful in the future. Only a great confidence in the 16 people—citizens without any prior experience or expertise—could justify this faith. An unusual case at an unusual time illustrates some restraints on the independence of the grand jury and presents some judicial controls over the grand jury. The case is *People v. Sears.*[319] Barnabas F. Sears, a leading member of the bar, was appointed as a special prosecutor by chief criminal court judge Joseph A. Power after a federal grand jury had raised serious questions about the deaths of Fred Hampton and Mark Clark during a raid on an apartment on West Monroe Street in Chicago on December 4, 1969. Hampton and Clark were members of the highly publicized Black Panther Party. The raid was conducted by police officers assigned to the state's attorney's office, which was then headed by Edward V. Hanrahan. Judge Joseph Power lived in the 11th ward of Chicago, as did Mayor Richard J. Daley, and the two had been friends and political allies. Chicago had been the site of the 1968 Democratic Convention, where antiwar demonstrators and the Chicago police department had violent confrontations. 1969 was a year of unrest. Students against the Vietnam War, blacks seeking political rights and leadership, avowed leftist groups such as Students For A Democratic Society, were all active, all scrutinizing the government, and all seeking answers to their questions and solace for their doubts. In this climate, a number of individuals filed petitions in the circuit court requesting a special grand jury to investigate the occurrence. Finally, a full six months after the raid, Judge Power appointed Sears as a special prosecutor. Sears was also ordered to examine the report of the federal grand jury and to take necessary steps to determine if there were any violations of state law. Finally, on December 7, 1970, one year and three days after the raid, a special grand jury was impaneled.

(noting that defendants may only challenge validity of grand jury's indictment and then only if they can demonstrate obvious prosecutorial misconduct).

318. *D.T.*, 141 Ill. App. 3d 1036, 490 N.E.2d at 1365.

319. 49 Ill. 2d 14, 273 N.E.2d 380 (1971).

Late in 1970 and in the first months of 1971, the grand jury heard witnesses
"without undue incident," as the supreme court phrased it.[320] But on April 22,
1971, Judge Power summoned Sears and the grand jury to his courtroom. After
some dialogue Judge Power instructed Sears that every witness who had
testified before the federal grand jury was to be called before the special grand
jury. The federal grand jury had not indicted anyone. Four days later, Sears and
the grand jury again appeared before Judge Power. After extensive colloquy,
Sears refused to obey Power's order of April 22. Judge Power then found Sears
in contempt of court for his failure to subpoena every witness who had testified
before the federal grand jury. Sears was fined 50 dollars per hour until the time
subpoenas were issued. In a related matter, a Chicago police officer named
Meade, an alleged target of the grand jury, filed a petition with Judge Power
claiming that media coverage of the grand jury's work would confuse and
frustrate its deliberations. Meade asked that the grand jury be discharged. A
mandamus petition was filed by the Chicago Bar Association and the Chicago
Council of Lawyers with the Illinois Supreme Court, apparently to get the
matter away from Judge Power. It requested that Judge Power be ordered to
expunge certain orders that had threatened the grand jury's work. One of those
orders entered by Judge Power had granted Meade standing to seek relief. Judge
Power met further with Sears, the foreman of the grand jury, and a court reporter
and stated that he would permit members of the grand jury to communicate
with him privately at any time, provided that the juror was sworn and a court
reporter was present. The bar associations and others requested the Illinois
Supreme Court to issue a writ of prohibition to Judge Power to prohibit him
from holding in camera conferences with individual grand jurors. These issues
came before the Illinois Supreme Court.

On the question of whether a state's attorney can be ordered to subpoena
certain witnesses before the grand jury, Sears argued that "[t]he grand jury is
independent of the court, beyond judicial control, and has the power to hear
such evidence as it desires and indict whom it chooses."[321] The supreme court
responded:

> We have reviewed the authorities cited in Sears's brief and they appear to
> support his contentions that the circuit court cannot limit the scope of the
> grand jury's investigation and that the grand jury may make presentments
> of its own knowledge without instructions or authority of the court. These
> authorities, however, are not relevant to the issues presented . . . .[322]

---

320. *Id.*, 273 N.E.2d at 383.
321. *Id.*, 273 N.E.2d at 385.
322. *Id.*, 273 N.E.2d at 386.

After six pages, including a passing reference to *Levine v. United States,*[323] which stated that "[t]he grand jury is an arm of the court and its in camera proceedings constitute a 'judicial inquiry,' "[324] the Illinois Supreme Court gave its holding on this issue, stating:

> [T]o adopt the rule for which Sears contends would vest in the State's Attorney the nonreviewable discretion as to what evidence is to be presented to the grand jury. This in our opinion could lead to abuse of process, purpose and function of the grand jury and is inconsistent with its historic place in our system of justice.[325]

The court further held that:

> there may be circumstances under which the circuit court will have jurisdiction to direct that witnesses be subpoenaed to appear before a grand jury. The preservation of historic independence of the grand jury, however, requires that such supervisory power be exercised only when failure to do so will effect a deprivation of due process or result in a miscarriage of justice.[326]

Having expressed a broad rule of grand jury independence with a small exception, the court found that the "circumstances shown here do not furnish a sufficient basis for the action" by Judge Power, and Sears' contempt finding was reversed.[327] The court then went on to consider whether targets of grand jury investigations have standing to question the ongoing work of the grand jury. Sears argued that although his conduct before the grand jury was "not above judicial scrutiny, such scrutiny may be invoked only after indictment and 'is justified only where . . . a clear and positive showing is made of gross and

---

323. Levine v. United States, 362 U.S. 610, 617 (1960). Levine was granted full immunity by the prosecution and then was ordered by the judge to answer certain questions before the grand jury. Levine refused. The judge cleared his courtroom of spectators and in effect turned his courtroom into the grand jury and again ordered Levine to answer each question. Levine was found in contempt. For the United States Supreme Court the case raised the issue of the public's right to be present in a courtroom. The Court affirmed the trial judge's procedure with Justices Black, Douglas, and Brennan and Chief Justice Warren dissenting.

324. *Id.* at 617.

325. *Sears,* 49 Ill. 2d 14, 273 N.E.2d at 389.

326. *Id.*

327. *Id.*

prejudicial irregularity influencing the grand jury in returning indictments.' "[328]
Judge Power argued that he had general supervisory power over a grand jury
while in session. The court avoided the issue of standing and agreed with Judge
Power that the circuit court "may act prior to indictment to prevent injustice
and abuse of process . . . ."[329] A wrongful indictment inflicts substantial harm
to a defendant that is not entirely remedied by an acquittal, the court said. It
held that "[t]he grand jury is an integral part of the court and not the tool of the
prosecutor and neither the prosecutor nor the grand jury is vested with power
to proceed without regard to due process."[330] With regard to the question of
whether a judge could meet with grand jurors who wished to communicate with
him or her privately, the court stated: "[I]t is our opinion that such procedure
is not desirable and presents the possibility of infringement upon the historic
independence of the grand jury and its proceedings. We hold that the court has
jurisdiction to meet *in camera* with the grand jury."[331]

But as to meetings with individual grand jurors, the court granted the writ
of prohibition and banned that practice.[332]

§ 3.12 Grand Jury Reports

Part of the grand jury's common law powers, still possible in the federal
court system, is the issuing of a grand jury report without indictment. It was a
federal grand jury's report about the deaths of Black Panther leaders Fred
Hampton and Mark Clark that moved Cook County authorities to investigate
the matter.[333]

Illinois law seems to be against the practice, evidently because of the fear
that a report would compromise the secrecy of the grand jury should the

---

328. *Id.,* 273 N.E.2d at 391.

329. *Id.,* 273 N.E.2d at 392.

330. *Id.* The Illinois Supreme Court again reasserted the circuit court's authority over
a grand jury in *In re October 1985 Grand Jury,* 124 Ill. 2d 466, 530 N.E.2d 453,
455 (1988), stating:
> This court, however, has previously recognized a circuit court's authori-
> ty to enforce or set aside a grand jury subpoena as being within its
> inherent supervisory powers over the grand jury process [citation omit-
> ted]. If a witness fails to appear before a grand jury upon service of
> process, the power to compel his attendance is within the court's
> supervisory power over the grand jury process.

331. *Sears,* 49 Ill. 2d 14, 273 N.E.2d at 392. *See also* In re Antitrust Grand Jury, 805
F.2d 155, 161 (6th Cir. 1986) (citing to federal cases where in camera inspection
of grand jury testimony has been approved).

332. *Sears,* 49 Ill. 2d 14, 273 N.E.2d at 392.

333. People v. Sears, 49 Ill. 2d 14, 273 N.E.2d 380 (1971).

evidence heard and the conclusions drawn by the grand jury be made public. In *In Re Report of the Grand Jury*,[334] the court held that "no statute authorizes a grand jury in this State to file a general report," and so "[a] grand jury does not have a license to file as circuit court records general reports of social ills."[335]

If possible, a grand jury report would be a powerful communicative device and may, if drawn carefully, breach secrecy no more than an indictment.

§ 3.13   Grand Jury Secrecy and Interests of Justice Exception

In Illinois there is a statutory escape valve from the concept of grand jury secrecy found in Illinois Compiled Statutes chapter 725, section 5/112-6(b); "Matters other than the deliberations and vote of any grand juror shall not be disclosed by the State's Attorney, except as otherwise provided for in subsection (c). The court may direct that a Bill of Indictment be kept secret until the defendant is in custody or has given bail and in either event the clerk shall seal the Bill of Indictment and no person shall disclose the finding of the Bill of Indictment except when necessary for the issuance and execution of a warrant."[336] There are similar provisions under the federal rules and in most jurisdictions.

---

334. 108 Ill. App. 3d 232, 438 N.E.2d 1316 (3d Dist. 1982).

335. *Id.,* 438 N.E.2d at 1319.

336. 725 ILCS 5/112-6(b). P.A. 85-690 (1987) amends section 112-6(b), Secrecy of Grand Jury Proceedings, to provide that matters other than the deliberations and vote of any grand juror "shall not be disclosed by the State's Attorney, except as otherwise provided in subsection (c)." New subsection (c) provides:

> (1) Disclosure otherwise prohibited by this Section of matters occurring before the Grand Jury, other than its deliberations and the vote of any grand juror, may be made to:
>
> a. a State's Attorney for use in the performance of such State's Attorney's duty; and
>
> b. such government personnel as are deemed necessary by the State's Attorney in the performance of such State's Attorney's duty to enforce State criminal law.
>
> (2) Any person to whom matters are disclosed under paragraph (1) of this subsection (c) shall not use the Grand Jury material for any purpose other than assisting the State's Attorney in the performance of such State's Attorney's duty to enforce State criminal law. The State's Attorney shall promptly provide the court, before which was impaneled the Grand Jury whose material has been disclosed, with the names of the persons to whom such disclosure has been made.
>
> (3) Disclosure otherwise prohibited by this Section of matters occurring before the Grand Jury may also be made when the court, preliminary

The Illinois Supreme Court in *People v. Fassler*[337] set out the test for improper conduct before the grand jury. In *Fassler,* the state was seeking a true bill for aggravated criminal sexual assault upon a thirteen-year-old female. At the trial level, the judge dismissed the indictment because the young victim's mother was present with her daughter in the grand jury room when her daughter testified. The mother was not authorized by any judge to be present before the grand jury, yet the only thing she said during the proceedings was "calm down" when the girl was visibly upset.[338] The indictment was dismissed under the authority of paragraph 114-1(a)(5), as an indictment "returned by a Grand Jury which acted contrary to Article 112 of this Code and which results in substantial injustice to the defendant."[339]

The Illinois Supreme Court agreed that having unauthorized people in attendance was not proper, but not an impropriety in this case to justify dismissal of the indictment.[340] The court stated "[i]f the legislature had intended that a violation of section 112-6(a) should result in dismissal of an indictment without a showing of injustice, it could have omitted that requirement."[341] The court held that Fassler had failed to make a convincing case of "substantial injustice."[342]

Requests for grand jury transcripts often come when civil litigation arises from a criminal investigation before the grand jury, or where the grand jury investigates one aspect of an event or one person's conduct during an event and later indicts for a different aspect or a different person.

If a court is considering disclosure of grand jury transcripts, what standard should be used? As was stated in *Douglas Oil Co. v. Petrol Stops Northwest,*[343] "[d]isclosure is appropriate only in those cases where the need for it outweighs the public interest in secrecy, and that the burden of demonstrating this balance rests upon the private party seeking disclosure."[344] The test is easier to posit than to apply. The Court went on to state that "as the considerations justifying

---

to or in connection with a judicial proceeding, directs such in the interests of justice or when a law so directs.

725 ILCS 5/112-6(b), (c).

337. 153 Ill. 2d 49, 605 N.E.2d 576 (1992).

338. *Id.,* 605 N.E.2d at 578.

339. *Id., citing* ILL. REV. STAT. 1989, ch. 38, ¶ 114-1(a)(5).

340. When dealing with the young witness before the grand jury, a prosecutor would be well advised to seek the permission of a judge to have any caregiver present in the grand jury as the witness testifies.

341. *Fassler,* 753 Ill. 2d 49, 605 N.E.2d at 579.

342 *Id.*

343. 441 U.S. 211 (1979).

344. *Id.* at 223.

secrecy become less relevant, a party asserting a need for grand jury transcripts will have a lesser burden in showing justification."[345] That rule might be restated as "the less you need them, the easier they are to get."

Situations involving the civil branch of a prosecutor's office present further complications. In *United States v. Sells Engineering, Inc.*,[346] a federal grand jury was convened to investigate charges of fraud on the navy, and certain documents were subpoenaed from Sells. After indictment, a plea bargain ended the criminal proceedings, but then the government moved for disclosure of all grand jury materials to attorneys in the justice department's civil division for use in a possible civil suit against Sells. The Supreme Court rejected the government's position that all attorneys with the justice department qualified for automatic disclosure of grand jury materials and held that automatic access to grand jury materials was limited to "those attorneys who conduct the criminal matters" and that other government attorneys must obtain an order from a judge to gain disclosure.[347]

Another secrecy issue is displayed by *Illinois v. Abbott & Associates, Inc.*[348] In this case the Attorney General of Illinois sought from the United States Attorney General transcripts, documents, and other materials gathered by two federal grand juries that had been investigating violations of the federal antitrust laws. A provision of the Clayton Act states that the attorney general must make available to the state attorney general materials relevant to any potential cause of action under the act. Neither party sought to use Rule 6(e) of the Federal Rules of Criminal Procedure, which provides for secrecy of federal grand jury matters but does permit narrowly focused requests showing "particularized needs."[349] The United States Supreme Court affirmed the district court's refusal to disclose the grand jury materials and stated that the rule of secrecy was "so important, and so deeply rooted in our traditions" that disclosure could only come through the strict test of rule 6(e).[350]

Using federal case law interpreting rule 6(e) of the Federal Rules of Criminal Procedure, the Illinois Appellate Court for the Second District interpreted section 112-6(b). In *Board of Education v. Verisario,*[351] an earlier grand jury investigation had been conducted, apparently seeking evidence of criminal wrongdoing, concerning a school teacher accused of unethical, immoral, and unprofessional conduct. The matter was the subject of a board of education

---

345. *Id.*

346. 463 U.S. 418 (1983).

347. *Id.* at 427.

348. 460 U.S. 557 (1982).

349. *Id.* at 567.

350. *Id.* at 572.

351. 143 Ill. App. 3d 1000, 493 N.E.2d 355 (2d Dist. 1986).

administrative hearing seeking the teacher's dismissal from the school system. A hearing officer issued a subpoena to the police department for documents, including documents originally obtained by the police pursuant to a grand jury subpoena. Verisario sought a protective order under section 112-6(b). The state's attorney argued that he was acting "in the performance of his duties" and that, therefore, such disclosure was permitted by section 112-6(b). Citing *United States v. Sells Engineering, Inc.,*[352] the *Verisario* court decided that the "in the performance of his duties" language contained in the statute was limited to enforcement of criminal law. The court stated that

> to permit a State's Attorney to disclose grand jury matters in response to any civil or administrative subpoena would be contrary to the basic policy of grand jury secrecy behind section 112-6(b). We hold, therefore, that the disclosure of grand jury materials by a State's Attorney for use in a civil or administrative proceeding is not in the performance of his duties under section 112-6(b).[353]

The second issue raised in *Verisario* concerned the disclosure of handwriting exemplars allegedly disclosed publicly at Verisario's earlier forgery trial. The court noted that section 112-6(b) permits disclosure by a state's attorney in the performance of his duties, by a court order in the interests of justice, or when disclosure is directed by a law. While acknowledging a factual dispute as to whether the earlier disclosure had actually taken place, the court stated that the statute does not permit disclosure on the basis that grand jury material had been disclosed at a criminal trial. The court concluded, "While such disclosure may be relevant in determining whether a court should order disclosure in the interests of justice, public disclosure does not, by itself, justify the disclosure as claimed here by appellant."[354]

Obviously, the appellate court was correct in conditioning disclosure on the decision of the court rather than mere prior disclosure. If the latter test were the law, an unscrupulous state's attorney could merely introduce the grand jury documents in any minor criminal proceeding, proclaim them as "disclosed," and hence render them fully disclosable at any later date. The *Verisario* court wisely used a plain-meaning interpretation of section 112-6(b) and left the decision with the courts.

---

352. 463 U.S. 418 (1983).

353. Board of Education v. Verisario, 143 Ill. App. 3d 1000, 493 N.E.2d 355, 358 (2d Dist. 1986).

354. *Id.*, 493 N.E.2d at 358.

The state's attorney also argued that disclosure was permitted because the subpoena was a direction by a law. The court easily dispensed with this argument when it held that a subpoena is not a "law."[355]

While the preceding three issues would seem to ultimately preclude any disclosure of material once utilized by a grand jury, the court determined that certain documents were susceptible to disclosure if they were sought for their own sake, for their intrinsic value in the course of a lawful investigation, rather than to learn what took place before the grand jury. If the disclosure would not seriously compromise the secrecy of the grand jury investigation, disclosure is permissible. In ruling that disclosure of certain telephone records was not prohibited, the court stated:

> In shielding only matters occurring before the grand jury, section 112-6(b) was designed to protect from disclosure only the essence of what takes place in the grand jury room, in order to preserve the freedom and integrity of the deliberative process. [citation omitted] This serves to protect the identity of witnesses or jurors, the substance of the testimony, the strategy or direction of the investigation, the deliberations or questions of jurors, and the like. [citation omitted] The mere fact that a particular document is reviewed by a grand jury does not convert it into a matter occurring before the grand jury within the meaning of section 112-6(b). [citation omitted][356]

It is interesting to speculate whether *Verisario* would have been decided differently in light of the later decision in *United States v. John Doe, Inc. I.*[357] Although it can be argued that *Doe* is distinguishable on the basis of its unique facts, the United States Supreme Court determined that rule 6(e) does not require a government attorney involved in a grand jury investigation to obtain a court order before making continued use of grand jury materials in a civil proceeding.

In *Doe,* the government attorneys who conducted the grand jury investigations were from the antitrust division of the Department of Justice. They also prepared the civil litigation, though consulting with lawyers from the civil division before initiating the civil suit. The Court stated that it was relying on a plain reading of rule 6(e) and, therefore, did not address the parties' arguments that continued use of grand jury material would threaten the values of grand jury privacy as enunciated in *United States v. Sells Engineering, Inc.*[358]

---

355. *Id.*

356. *Id.,* 493 N.E.2d at 359.

357. 481 U.S. 102 (1987).

358. 463 U.S. 418 (1983).

Writing for the five-person majority, Justice Stevens stated that rule 6(e) prohibits disclosure of information about the workings of a grand jury to persons not authorized to have access to it. But an attorney who was involved in a grand jury investigation may later review that material in a manner that does not involve further disclosure to others. Therefore, under the facts of this case, there was no disclosure.

Justice Brennan, writing in dissent, said that a civil attorney "lacks both the prosecutor's special role in supporting the grand jury, and the prosecutor's own crucial need to know what occurs before the grand jury."[359] Putting in perspective the status of grand jury materials, Justice Brennan stated:

> The exceptional powers [of the grand jury] are wielded not on behalf of the prosecutor, but in aid of the grand jury as an "arm of the court." [citation omitted] They are employed to permit the grand jury to fulfill its "invaluable function in our society of standing between the accuser and the accused . . . to determine whether a charge is found upon reason." [citation omitted] Thus, the information generated by the grand jury's inquiry is "not the property of the Government's attorneys, agents or investigators, nor are they entitled to possession of them in such a case. Instead, those documents are records of the court." [citations omitted][360]

The recent principal case citing section 112-6(b) is *People v. DiVincenzo*.[361] The citation to the statute is merely in passing. The Illinois Supreme Court stated, "[p]ursuant to statute, the grand jury proceedings are conducted in secrecy. See 725 ILCS 5/112-6 (West 1994). The State's Attorney's office plays a substantial role in the grand jury proceedings and serves as advisor to the grand jury."[362]

§ 3.14   Subpoena Power of the Grand Jury

When a grand jury issues a subpoena duces tecum for records, checks, or other documents, what is the subpoena recipient's position? In most cases the recipient cooperates, of course, but in some circumstances other interests arise. In some situations the recipient contends that he or she is protected by the Fourth Amendment right against unreasonable searches, the Fifth Amendment protection against self-incrimination, or a statutory privilege that protects certain

---

359. *John Doe,* 481 U.S. at 119.

360. *Id.*

361. 183 Ill. 2d 239, 700 N.E.2d 981, 989 (1998). The case is discussed more fully in § 3.09 of this chapter.

362. *Id.,* 700 N.E.2d at 989.

privacy interests.[363] The government, on behalf of the grand jury, may respond that the recipient of the subpoena does not have legitimate privacy interests under the Fourth Amendment, is an entity outside the personal protections of the Fifth Amendment, or is an entity required by law to keep and provide records that is not protected by the Fifth Amendment. The Fifth Amendment protects an individual and the business records of a sole proprietor from compulsory disclosure to a grand jury,[364] but persons who hold documents in a representative capacity or corporations, pure and simple, are not protected by the Constitution. The case of *Bellis v. United States*[365] presented difficult questions on this issue. Bellis was a senior partner of a law firm, and his secretary-bookkeeper kept control of the books and records. Bellis, after being served with a subpoena duces tecum for "all partnership records" for certain years, refused to produce the records, claiming that the Fifth Amendment did not require him to do so lest he might incriminate himself. The United States Supreme Court stated that "[i]t has long been established . . . that the Fifth Amendment privilege against compulsory self-incrimination protects an individual from compelled production of his personal papers and effects as well as compelled oral testimony."[366] This privilege applies not only to an individual but also to the sole proprietor of a business or the sole law practitioner. The Fifth Amendment is not limited strictly to documents of "more intimate information," the Court said. On the other hand (sad words for many a lawyer), the Court stated: "[A]n equally long line of cases has established that an individual cannot rely upon the privilege to avoid producing the records of a collective entity which are in his possession in a representative capacity, even if these records might incriminate him personally."[367] A corporation cannot claim the Fifth Amendment privilege, and the same principle applies to Bellis, who was acting "on behalf of

---

363. In *People v. Feldmeier*, 286 Ill. App. 3d 602, 676 N.E.2d 723 (2d Dist. 1997), the court held that the state's attorney abused its subpoena power in obtaining defendant's financial and bank records by issuing a grand jury subpoena returnable to the state's attorney's office. *Id.*, 676 N.E.2d at 724. By not making the records returnable to the court, the prosecutor could obtain constitutionally protected private matters. *Id.*

364. Boyd v. United States, 116 U.S. 616 (1886). The privilege is "personal." "It adheres basically to the person . . . ," the Supreme Court said in *Couch v. United States*, 409 U.S. 322, 328 (1973). Ms. Couch made the mistake of transferring the records of her sole proprietorship to her accountant. "[The accountant], not the taxpayer, is the only one compelled to do anything," the Court said, ruling that the subpoena duces tecum on the accountant was valid. *Id.* at 329.

365. 417 U.S. 85 (1974).

366. *Id.* at 87.

367. *Id.* at 88.

theorganization."[368] The Court concluded: "We think it is similarly clear that partnerships may and frequently do represent organized institutional activity so as to preclude any claim of Fifth Amendment."[369] Leaving aside the question of the small family partnership, which obviously has elements of privacy, the Court held that Bellis could not properly assert the privilege against self-incrimination. *United States v. Doe*[370] has enormously restricted the holding in both *Boyd* and *Bellis.*

> The Court's most recent pronouncements in *United States v. Doe* [citation omitted], clearly imply that there is little left of the *Boyd* doctrine. In expressly rejecting the suggestion in *Bellis* that contents of business records of a sole proprietorship are protected by the fifth amendment [citation omitted], the Court emphasized that the amendment "protects the person asserting the privilege only from *compelled* self-incrimination." [citation omitted] (emphasis in original)[371]

Records held in a "representative capacity" are not private and not protected by the Fifth Amendment.[372] Similarly, bank records are not likely to be accorded constitutional protection. In *United States v. Miller,*[373] the issue involved the government's subpoenas duces tecum for the defendant's bank records. The government became interested in the defendant after an unfortunate fire disclosed a 7,500-gallon distillery operating without the formalities of the government's taxing regulations. The United States Supreme Court held that the documents subpoenaed were not the defendant's private papers and that no Fourth Amendment interests were involved. Even though the defendant contended that he had a legitimate expectation of privacy, the Court said that "[t]he depositor takes the risk, in revealing his affairs to another, that the information will be conveyed by that person to the Government."[374] On the privacy side, the Fifth Amendment does protect the business records of a sole proprietor from compulsory disclosure to a grand jury, just as it does an individual.[375] If an individual is required by law to keep certain records, the required records exception may arise. The required records exception applies to records with public aspects that are ordinarily kept and where the government has a legitimate regulatory purpose, such as where a person does business with

---

368. *Id.* at 93.

369. *Id.*

370. 465 U.S. 605 (1983).

371. In re Steinberg, 837 F.2d 527, 529 (1st Cir. 1988).

372. United States v. White, 322 U.S. 694 (1944).

373. 425 U.S. 435 (1976).

374. *Id.* at 443.

375. Boyd v. United States, 116 U.S. 616, 616 (1886).

the government or gets money from the government. In *People v. Bickham*,[376] a grand jury issued a subpoena duces tecum for the Medicaid records of a doctor. The doctor contended that he was protected by the Fifth Amendment and that the doctor-patient privilege also protected the secrecy of the documents. The state's attorney responded that the records were required under the law. The Illinois Supreme Court held that the doctor could assert the physician-patient privilege. There had been no consent for disclosure of the medical records by any of the patients, and the statutory exceptions to the privilege were not applicable because it was not a case involving a criminal action relating to malpractice or abortion.[377]

In the case of *In re October 1985 Grand Jury No. 746*,[378] while investigating the accountant's client for alleged underpayment of taxes, the grand jury issued the accountant a subpoena calling for the production of, among other things, the client's tax returns. The Illinois Supreme Court affirmed the appellate court's decision to allow the grand jury to subpoena an accountant's records.[379] The court held that the tax returns were not confidential,[380] despite 225 ILCS 450/27: "A public accountant shall not be required . . . to divulge information or evidence which has been obtained by him in his confidential capacity as a public accountant."

The required records exception was considered and applied in *In re January 1986 Grand Jury No. 217*.[381] In that case, the grand jury was investigating certain nonpayment of retailer occupation taxes. It issued a subpoena duces tecum for the appellants' records. They declined to give up the records, and were found to be in contempt of court. The appellants were granted immunity pursuant to the Illinois immunity provision,[382] but claimed that it was insufficient to protect their Fifth Amendment rights and refused to give up the records.

On appeal, the state argued that the records sought came under the required records doctrine because they are required by statute. The court considered the various records, finding that the inventory records and invoices, which were kept by all business owners, fell within the required records doctrine. Citing

---

376. 89 Ill. 2d 1, 431 N.E.2d 365 (1982).

377. *Id.*, 431 N.E.2d at 368.

378. 124 Ill. 2d 466, 530 N.E.2d 453 (1988).

379. *Id.*, 530 N.E.2d at 454.

380. *Id.*, 530 N.E.2d at 459.

381. 155 Ill. App. 3d 445, 508 N.E.2d 277 (1st Dist. 1987), *cert. denied*, 484 U.S. 1064 (1988). *See also* In re October 1985 Grand Jury No. 746, 154 Ill. App. 3d 288, 507 N.E.2d 6 (1st Dist. 1987) (accountant's privilege), *vacated on other grounds*, 124 Ill. 2d 46, 530 N.E.2d 453 (1988) (information provided by a client to accountant is not confidential and thus not privileged).

382. 225 ILCS 450/27.

Doe,[383] the court held that the required records doctrine does not violate the Fifth Amendment, which guards only against a defendant's compelled testimonial communication. In *In re October 1985 Grand Jury,*[384] the Illinois Supreme Court held that the state must file a petition for writ of mandamus if the state wishes appellate court review of a trial court's order quashing a subpoena.[385]

With regard to private documents, the court tests the subpoena by balancing the reasonableness of the intrusion against the validity of the subpoena.[386] The reasonableness is tested by determining: "(1) whether the document is relevant to the inquiry; and (2) whether the specification of the document to be produced is adequate but not excessive for the purpose of the relevant inquiry."[387]

Finally, the Illinois Supreme Court has set parameters on the grand jury's right to subpoena evidence other than documents in *In re May 1991 Will County Grand Jury.*[388] The court first noted that section 112-4 gives the grand jury power to subpoena witnesses as well as the right to demand evidence from the witnesses, within constitutional bounds.[389] The court set forth different levels of proof for assorted types of evidence which the grand jury may seek to obtain. First, before demanding a voice[390] or handwriting exemplar,[391] the grand jury does not have to make a preliminary showing that the invasion is reasonable. As precedent establishes, these types of intrusions are reasonable under the Fourth Amendment. On the other hand, turning to more intrusive invasions, the court first declared that the Illinois Constitution provides more protection against privacy invasions than the United States Constitution.[392] It further found that an individual's privacy interest in his or her physical person must be protected.[393] Therefore, once a privacy interest is established, the court must determine the reasonableness of the search and seizure by balancing the need

---

383. 465 U.S. 604, 611 (1984).

384. 124 Ill. 2d 466, 530 N.E.2d 453 (1988).

385. *Id.,* 530 N.E.2d at 456 (client's tax returns not privileged under section 27 of Illinois Public Accounting Act, 225 ILCS 450/27).

386. People v. DeLaire, 240 Ill. App. 3d 1012, 610 N.E.2d 1277, 1283 (2d Dist. 1993) (relying on In re May 1991 Will County Grand Jury, 152 Ill. 2d 381, 604 N.E.2d 929, 935 (1992)).

387. *DeLaire,* 240 Ill. App. 3d 1012, 610 N.E.2d at 1283.

388. 152 Ill. 2d 381, 604 N.E.2d 929 (1992).

389. *Id.,* 604 N.E.2d at 933.

390. *Id.,* 604 N.E.2d at 934 (citing United States v. Dionisio, 410 U.S. 1, 14 (1973)).

391. *Will County,* 152 Ill. 2d 381, 604 N.E.2d at 934 (citing People ex rel. Hanrahan v. Power, 54 Ill. 2d 154, 295 N.E.2d 472, 475 (1973)).

392. *Id.*

393. *Id.,* 604 N.E.2d at 935.

for the intrusion against the protected interest of the person.[394] Thus, some "quantum of relevance must also be established before a subpoena is issued for physical evidence."[395]

With regard to physical evidence of a noninvasive nature, such as line-ups and fingerprinting, the grand jury must make "some showing of individualized suspicion as well as relevance.[396] This may be done by using a state's attorney's affidavit. Moreover, in order to obtain hair samples, including pubic and head

---

394. *Id.*

395. *Id.*

396. *Id.*, 604 N.E.2d at 935–36. In *In re Rende*, 262 Ill. App. 3d 464, 633 N.E.2d 746 (1st Dist. 1993), the appellate court found that although the grand jury had subpoena power to compel a person to appear for a line-up, the order compelling enforcement of the subpoena was error because the subpoena was unsworn, factually insufficient, and not brought to the court's attention. *Id.*, 633 N.E.2d at 750. There was an insufficient showing that the line-up was relevant and supported by individualized suspicion. *Id.*, 633 N.E.2d at 749. The prosecutor's statement made to the grand jury was not sworn and was unreliable because it did not identify the source of the information. The statement did not positively assert that defendant was a target. *Id.* Finally, the trial judge did not examine or was guided by the statement. *Id.*, 633 N.E.2d at 750. The subpoena was addressed to the grand jury and not the court and the court did not examine the statement for relevancy and individualized suspicion which is the duty of the court.

In *January 1996 Term Grand Jury, Subpoena Duces Tecum v. Williams*, 283 Ill. App.3d 883, 671 N.E.2d 1134 (4th Dist. 1996), the trial court's denial of the defendant's motion to quash a grand jury subpoena duces tecum was affirmed where an Illinois state police officer's testimony before the grand jury clearly demonstrated individualized suspicion and relevance of obtaining the defendant's lineup photo, handwriting samples, and fingerprints for the grand jury. *Id.*, 671 N.E.2d at 1138. The appellate court concluded that the officer did not misuse the grand jury's powers and was not engaged in an "independent investigation" by suggesting to the grand jury that it obtain the materials stated in the subpoena duces tecum. *Id.*, 671 N.E.2d at 1141.

In *People v. Payne*, 282 Ill. App.3d 307, 667 N.E.2d 643 (1st Dist. 1996), the court held that relevance and individualized suspicion, but not probable cause, are necessary for the grand jury to compel production of dental impressions. *Id.*, 667 N.E.2d at 646. The court analogized the taking of dental impressions to the noninvasive physical evidence of lineups, fingerprints, palm prints, and voice and handwriting exemplars and distinguished the taking of dental impressions from the taking of blood or hair samples, stating that the making of dental impressions does not involve an actual taking or removal of evidence from the body, and, thus, does not violate an individual's bodily integrity and privacy rights. *Id.* The court held that the grand jury subpoena was proper in this case because the demand for the defendant's dental impressions was supported by both relevance and individualized suspicion. *Id.*

hair, the grand jury must show probable cause before a subpoena for the evidence will be issued.[397]

§ 3.15   The Grand Jury and the Right to Financial Privacy Act of 1978

The Right to Financial Privacy Act of 1978[398] has been used in the issuance of grand jury subpoenas for bank records. The act purports to require that financial records of a bank customer "shall be returned and actually presented to the grand jury." Invoking a lenient interpretation of the language, the United States Court of Appeals for the Seventh Circuit, in *United States v. A Residence Located at 218 3rd Street*,[399] ruled that the requirements of the act do not mandate personal delivery of the subpoenaed records by the financial institution. The court concluded that the statute was worded passively, and only states to whom the records must be delivered—not who must actually present them. Two of the latest cases attempting to use the protections of the act are *United States v. U.S. Bancorp*[400] and *Taylor v. Air Force*.[401]

§ 3.16   News Media and Grand Jury Subpoenas

An issue addressed by the United States Circuit Court of Appeals for the Sixth Circuit was whether a television reporter can withhold videotapes from a grand jury on the basis of a First Amendment privilege. In *In re Grand Jury Proceedings*,[402] a television reporter received a subpoena duces tecum for certain video tapes. The tapes had been made while the reporter was filming a feature on Detroit's street gangs. The police had gained information that the assailants of a murdered police officer may have been present when the reporter was filming and were pictured in the film. The reporter refused to give up the tape and was found in contempt.

In declining to read the First Amendment in a way that hampers "fair and effective law enforcement," the court stated:

> [C]ourts should, as did the Michigan state courts, follow the admonition of the majority in Branzburg to make certain that the proper balance is struck between freeedom of the press and the obligation of all citizens to

---

397.   *Will County,* 152 Ill. 2d. 381, 604 N.E.2d at 937, 939.

398.   12 U.S.C. § 3420.

399.   805 F.2d 256 (7th Cir. 1986).

400.   12 F. Supp. 2d 982 (D. Minn. 1998).

401.   18 F. Supp. 2d 1184 (D. Colo. 1998).

402.   810 F.2d 580 (6th Cir. 1987).

give relevant testimony, by determining whether the reporter is being harrassed in order to disrupt his relationship with confidential news sources, whether the grand jury's investigation is being conducted in good faith, whether the information sought bears more than a remote and tenuous relationship to the subject of the investigation, and whether a legitimate law enforcement need will be served by forced disclosure of the confidential source relationship.[403]

The reporter argued that the court should adopt a "qualified privilege," as put forth by the dissenters in *Branzburg v. Hayes*.[404] The court declined. Other circuits have, in certain situations, placed a greater burden on the government when seeking grand jury information from a reporter.[405] The Sixth Circuit concluded that the proper balance is struck when the freedom of the press and the obligation of all citizens to give relevant testimony are considered, along with what disruption of a reporter's relationship with confidential news sources will result, whether the grand jury investigation is being conducted in good faith, and whether a legitimate law enforcement need will be served by the forced disclosure. A concurring judge reiterated the importance of this balancing test.[406]

Another factor to consider in this balancing test, however, is the media's current strength and predominance in society. For example, *Cukier v. American Medical Association*[407] called attention to the Illinois Reporter's Privilege Act.[408] The appellate court in that case stated "[t]he reporter's privilege has evolved from a common law recognition that the compelled disclosure of a reporter's sources could compromise the news media's first amendment right to freely gather and disseminate information."[409] The balance test, therefore, is not as easy as it may seem.

---

403. *Id.* at 586.

404. 408 U.S. 665 (1972).

405. *See* United States v. Burke, 700 F.2d 70, 77 (2d Cir.), *cert. denied,* 464 U.S. 816 (1983); Zerilli v. Smith, 656 F.2d 705, 713 (D.C. Cir. 1981); United States v. Cuthbertson, 630 F.2d 139, 147 (3d Cir. 1980), *rev'd on other grounds,* 651 F.2d 189 (3d Cir.) (only way to overcome media's privilege is to demonstrate that information can only be practicably obtained from media), *cert. denied,* 454 U.S. 1056 (1981).

406. In re Grand Jury Proceedings, 810 F.2d 580, 588–89 (6th Cir. 1987) (Guy, J. concurring).

407. 259 Ill. App. 3d 159, 630 N.E.2d 1198 (1st Dist. 1994).

408. 735 ILCS 5/8-901.

409. *Cukier,* 259 Ill. App. 3d 159, 630 N.E.2d at 1200, *citing* In re Special Grand Jury Investigation of Alleged Violation of Juvenile Court Act (1984), 104 Ill. 2d 419, 472 N.E.2d 450, 452 (1984).

§ 3.17 The Preliminary Hearing

Illinois Compiled Statutes chapter 725, section 5/109-1(a)[410] sets out the rights of an arrested person. Whether the person is arrested with or without a warrant, the statute commands that the arrestee be brought before a judge "without unnecessary delay."[411] Section 109-1(b)[412] sets out the duties of the judge. It requires the judge to inform the defendant of the charge against him or her and to provide the defendant with a copy of the charge. It also requires that the defendant be told of the right to counsel, and if indigent, of the appointment of a public defender or other attorney to represent him or her. Section 109-1(b) sets out two other important rights: the right to a preliminary hearing and the right to bail.[413] Section 109-3 refers to a preliminary hearing as a preliminary examination,[414] and Article 110 sets forth the rules of bail. Section 109-3 establishes the standard of proof applicable at a preliminary hearing. Section 109-3(a) states a "judge shall hold the defendant to answer" the charges made against him or her "if from the evidence it appears there is probable cause to believe an offense has been committed by the defendant . . . ."[415]

Section 109-3.1(b), enacted into law in 1983, ensures a prompt determination of probable cause either by a preliminary hearing or an indictment by the grand jury within 30 days from the date of custody.[416] The section has a parallel provision for persons "on bail or recognizance," and in those situations the law states that the defendant must receive the probable cause determination within 60 days from the date arrested.[417] Section 109-3.1(b) and (c) has some commonsense exceptions—for example, delay occasioned by the defendant.[418]

In Illinois the preliminary hearing is a critical stage during which the defendant has a right to counsel.[419] A preliminary hearing is not a mini-trial. It

---

410. 725 ILCS 5/109-1(a).

411. People v. Dove, 147 Ill. App. 3d 659, 498 N.E.2d 279 (4th Dist. 1986); People v. Durham, 142 Ill. App. 3d 473, 491 N.E.2d 832 (4th Dist. 1986).

412. 725 ILCS 5/109-1(b)(1), (2).

413. 725 ILCS 5/109-1(b)(3), (4).

414. 725 ILCS 5/109-3.

415. 725 ILCS 5/109-3(a).

416. 725 ILCS 5/109-3.1(b). See *People v. Bartee*, 177 Ill. App. 3d 937, 532 N.E.2d 997 (2d Dist. 1988), for a good discussion of the history of the right, both statutory and constitutional, to a prompt probable cause determination in Illinois.

417. 725 ILCS 5/109-3.1(b).

418. 725 ILCS 5/109-3.1(b)(1)–(6), 5/109-3.1(c).

419. People v. Adams, 46 Ill. 2d 200, 263 N.E.2d 490 (1970), *aff'd,* 405 U.S. 278 (1972).

has been described as a "much less searching exploration into the merits of a case than a trial, simply because its function is the more limited one of determining whether probable cause exists to hold the accused for trial."[420] The Illinois Supreme Court has described the ambit of a preliminary hearing as limited to its purpose of determining whether there is probable cause to hold the defendant for trial.[421] A preliminary hearing is not designed to be a discovery proceeding for the defense,[422] and the court may terminate the proceeding once probable cause has been found.[423] Hearsay evidence is admissible at the preliminary hearing.[424] For example, in one case the court held that a charge should not have been dismissed by the trial court where the prosecutor failed to bring two eyewitnesses to the preliminary hearing to testify.[425]

By the express language of Illinois Supreme Court Rule 411, the discovery rules within this rule are not applicable before or during a preliminary hearing.[426] The rule provides that its ambit begins following an indictment or information. However, in *People ex rel. Fisher v. Carey,*[427] the Illinois Supreme Court approved a system for obtaining at least partial discovery during the critical preliminary examination: the defense can subpoena documents or police reports. The Illinois Supreme Court observed that the subpoena power, just as the power to compel witnesses to testify in person, is constitutional. The use of a subpoena duces tecum for records or reports is likewise protected. The power of a subpoena is not dependent on discovery rules, stated the Illinois Supreme Court, citing *United States v. Nixon.*[428] "We decline to hold that the public defender [the defense attorney in the case] may not subpoena police reports prior to a preliminary hearing."[429]

---

420. Barber v. Page, 390 U.S. 719, 725 (1968).

421. People v. Horton, 65 Ill. 2d 413, 358 N.E.2d 1121 (1976). *See also* People v. Riddle, 141 Ill. App. 3d 97, 489 N.E.2d 1176, 1179 (5th Dist. 1986) ("The purpose of a preliminary hearing is to ensure that a criminal defendant is not held without a prompt showing of probable cause").

422. *Horton,* 65 Ill. 2d 413, 358 N.E.2d at 1124.

423. People v. Bonner, 37 Ill. 2d 553, 229 N.E.2d 527 (1967), *cert. denied,* 392 U.S. 910 (1968); People v. Marshall, 50 Ill. App. 3d 615, 365 N.E.2d 1122 (1st Dist. 1977).

424. People v. Jones, 75 Ill. App. 2d 332, 221 N.E.2d 29 (1st Dist. 1966).

425. People v. Blackman, 91 Ill. App. 3d 130, 414 N.E.2d 246 (2d Dist. 1980).

426. S. Ct. Rule 411.

427. 77 Ill. 2d 259, 396 N.E.2d 17 (1979).

428. 418 U.S. 683 (1974), *superseded by statute on other grounds as stated in* Bourjaily v. United States, 483 U.S. 171, 177–78 (1987).

429. *Carey,* 77 Ill. 2d 259, 396 N.E.2d at 20.

The defense attorney must file a subpoena to receive police reports. A court has no authority to hold a state's attorney in contempt for refusing to obey an order to produce photocopies of a police report when the defense attorney does not make a formal request. In *People v. Huntley*,[430] the appellate court held that the trial court abused its discretion when it ordered the state to produce police reports before a preliminary hearing. The court cited *People ex rel. Fisher v. Carey*[431] and stated that issuance of a subpoena duces tecum is conditioned upon the defense attorney's formal request.[432]

The preliminary hearing must be prompt. The Constitution of 1970 requires a prompt preliminary hearing,[433] and section 109-3.1(b) sets time limits.[434] In *Gerstein v. Pugh*,[435] the United States Supreme Court held that the Fourth Amendment requires a prompt judicial determination of probable cause as a prerequisite to an extended pretrial detention following a warrantless arrest.[436] In *County of Riverside v. McLaughlin*,[437] the Supreme Court determined what was "prompt."[438] In *McLaughlin*, the county combined probable cause hearing with arraignment procedures and required that a hearing must be conducted within two days, excluding weekends and holidays.[439] McLaughlin brought a class action under section 1983.[440] While incarcerated in Riverside County Jail, McLaughlin filed a complaint in the United States District Court for the Central District of California seeking injunctive and declaratory relief.[441] The complaint alleged that he had not yet received a probable cause determination.[442] The District Court granted relief and the Ninth Circuit affirmed.[443] The Supreme Court heard the case to resolve a conflict among the circuits.[444]

In holding that probable cause hearings held within 48 hours of a warrantless arrest generally comply with the Fourth Amendment, the United

---

430.   144 Ill. App. 3d 64, 493 N.E.2d 1193 (5th Dist. 1986).

431.   77 Ill. 2d 259, 396 N.E.2d 17 (1979).

432.   *Huntley,* 144 Ill. App. 3d 64, 493 N.E.2d at 1196.

433.   Ill. Const. art. I, § 7.

434.   725 ILCS 5/109-3.1(b).

435.   420 U.S. 103 (1975).

436   *Id.* at 126.

437.   500 U.S. 44 (1991).

438.   *Id.* at 47.

439.   *Id.*

440.   42 U.S.C. § 1981 (1988).

441.   *McLaughlin,* 500 U.S. at 48.

442.   *Id.*

443.   *Id.* at 49.

444.   *Id.* at 50.

States Supreme Court emphasized the need for flexibility in determining whether a person receives a prompt probable cause hearing.[445] The Court stated, "[t]aking into account the competing interests articulated in *Gerstein,* we believe that a jurisdiction that provides judicial determinations of probable cause within 48 hours of arrest will, as a general matter, comply with the promptness requirement of *Gerstein.*"[446] The Court warned, however, that it was announcing only a general rule and that a probable cause determination within 48 hours may, under some circumstances, violate the promptness requirement.[447]

In dissent, Justice Scalia found that the Court's approach of balancing the interests of the police against the individual, a reasonableness test, was improper in light of the history of the promptness requirement.[448] Scalia concludes that a probable cause determination is sufficiently prompt if it occurs no more than 24 hours after arrest because that time period is all that is necessary to complete the administrative steps incident to an arrest.[449]

What happens if the hearing is untimely? In 1973, the Illinois Supreme Court decided *People v. Hendrix,*[450] in which the defendant was indicted without a preliminary hearing after having fled the state. The defendant was arrested in Tennessee, waived extradition, and was returned to Illinois. He was promptly indicted and then he rejected a proffered preliminary hearing. The defendant moved to have the case dismissed on the ground that no preliminary hearing for probable cause was held before the indictment. The motion was granted by the trial court, but the reviewing court reversed, holding that total immunity from any prosecution was too high a price for the failure to ensure the right to a preliminary hearing and that that remedy would not be granted.[451]

The state may refile charges against a defendant, under section 114-1(e),[452] even after dismissal of the original charges based on the untimeliness of a probable cause determination. The court in *People v. Bartee*[453] found that the dismissal should be without prejudice because the legislature permits the state, after a dismissal based on untimeliness, to file new charges or return a new indictment.[454]

---

445. *Id.* at 53–55.

446. *Id.* at 56.

457. *Id.*

448. *Id.* at 65–66. (Scalia, J., dissenting).

449. *Id.* at 68 (Scalia, J., dissenting).

450. 54 Ill. 2d 165, 295 N.E.2d 724 (1973).

451. *Id.,* 295 N.E.2d at 725.

452. 725 ILCS 5/114-1(e).

453. 177 Ill. App. 3d 937, 532 N.E.2d 997 (2d Dist. 1988).

454. *Id.,* 532 N.E.2d at 999.

Two years later the supreme court decided *People v. Howell*.[455] Howell was held in jail for 65 days without a preliminary hearing, but the court ruled that that did not violate his right to a fair trial. The court first considered suppressing statements as a possible remedy, akin to the federal *McNabb-Mallory* rule, but declined that concept. The court stated: "We have heretofore considered delay in presenting a defendant to a judge following his arrest only as a circumstance to be considered by the court in determining the voluntariness of any statement given by the defendant during this delay."[456]

The court in *Howell*, in what might be viewed as the Wizard of Oz sending little Dorothy to get the magical shoes of the Wicked Witch, then urged the legislature to consider implementation of the preliminary hearing requirement.[457] The legislature still has not been able to do that. One appellate court case stands as a kind of high water mark for delay of a preliminary hearing. In *People v. Kirkley*,[458] the Third District of the Appellate Court found a 176-day delay from arrest to preliminary hearing. It recognized that there were no legislative guidelines or sanctions but stated that in the absence of such "we feel compelled to provide a remedy for the defendants who have suffered an unjustifiable denial of a basic constitutional right."[459] The court then imposed the following sanction:

> It would be senseless to reverse the defendants' conviction, and remand this case so that they could be subjected to a reindictment. (*People v. Hendrix* (1973), 54 Ill. 2d 165, 295 N.E.2d 724.) To grant the defendants a probable cause hearing after their constitutional rights have already been violated would be ludicrous. The only sanction or remedy available in the instant case is a reversal of the judgments of convictions entered against the defendants by the trial court. We do not mean to indicate in any way that the conclusion reached in this case is to be interpreted that we are fixing a determinate number of days which must transpire before a section 7 violation is to be deemed to have occurred. Each case must be considered in light of its facts and circumstances. We are hopeful that our General

---

455. 60 Ill. 2d 117, 324 N.E.2d 403 (1975), *superseded by statute as stated in* People v. Clarke, 231 Ill. App. 3d 504, 596 N.E.2d 872, 873 (5th Dist. 1992) (section 114-1(a)(11) now provides measures for delay in preliminary hearings).

456. *Howell*, 60 Ill. 2d 117, 324 N.E.2d at 405.

457. *Id.*, 324 N.E.2d at 406.

458. 60 Ill. App. 3d 746, 377 N.E.2d 540 (3d Dist. 1978), *superseded by statute as stated in* People v. Roby, 200 Ill. App. 3d 1063, 558 N.E.2d 729, 732 (5th Dist. 1990) (because of section 114-1(e), dismissal without prejudice is no longer available as a sanction for failing to provide a prompt preliminary hearing).

459. *Kirkley*, 60 Ill. App. 3d 746, 377 N.E.2d at 543.

Assembly will soon implement the constitutional provision, to-wit, section 7, article I, of the 1970 Illinois Constitution.[460]

All other appellate court decisions seem to adhere to the *Hendrix-Howell* line.[461] Another Illinois Supreme Court decision stands firm on the issue. In *People v. Dees*,[462] the defendant had been held in custody for 14 days without a preliminary hearing, but there was also a parole violation "hold" to prevent his release on bond. The court held that it was the defendant's obligation to demonstrate that the delay in his appearance before a judicial officer in some way actually prejudiced him. "In the absence of such proof of prejudice, the motion to dismiss the criminal charges . . . should [be] denied."[463]

Similarly, in *People v. Riddle*,[464] the defendant was charged by information on February 14, 1983. On May 5, 1983, the defendant moved to dismiss the information for failure to provide a prompt preliminary hearing. Eventually, a preliminary hearing was held 84 days after the information was filed. The court noted that Article I, section 7 of the Illinois Constitution was unquestionably violated but stated: "Nevertheless, dismissal with prejudice is not available to a defendant as a sanction for such a violation."[465] The court then went on to compare the case to *Kirkley*,[466] and stated:

> Here, by contrast, the delay was less than half as long. Although even this delay cannot be condoned, we have previously declined to follow *Kirkley* where much greater periods of time have been involved. [citation omitted]. Moreover, defendant here posted bond when arrested, he was not incarcerated when his asserted constitutional right was violated, and the delay did not hinder preparation of his defense. [citation omitted]. Under these circumstances, the trial court did not err in refusing to dismiss the charge against the defendant with prejudice.[467]

---

460. *Id.*

461. *See, e.g.,* People v. Anderson, 92 Ill. App. 3d 849, 416 N.E.2d 78 (2d Dist. 1981), *superseded by statute as stated in* People v. Bartee, 177 Ill. App. 3d 937, 532 N.E.2d 997, 999 (2d Dist. 1988) (dismissal not appropriate remedy for failure to give defendant a prompt preliminary hearing).

462. 85 Ill. 2d 233, 422 N.E.2d 616 (1981).

463. *Id.,* 422 N.E.2d at 620.

464. 141 Ill. App. 3d 97, 489 N.E.2d 1176 (5th Dist. 1986).

465. *Id.,* 489 N.E.2d at 1178.

466. 60 Ill. App. 3d 746, 377 N.E.2d 540 (3d Dist. 1978).

467. *Riddle,* 141 Ill. App. 3d 97, 489 N.E.2d at 1178.

Where the state moves to amend or add charges after an initial information or preliminary hearing, the issue arises whether the defendant should be afforded a new preliminary hearing. Section 109-3.1(b)(2) states that no new preliminary hearing is needed if the second set of charges "arose out of the same transaction or conduct" as the earlier charges. However, the state cannot add charges to a grand jury's indictment.

For example, in *People v. Kelly,*[468] the defendant was originally indicted for two hate crimes, committed on October 24th and November 23rd. After the case was set for trial, the state moved to dismiss that two-count indictment and file instead a seven-count information. The state argued, under 109-3.1(b)(2), there need not be a new preliminary hearing because the new charges "arose out of " the old charges.[469] The defendant argued that the seven new charges were substantially different and that he was entitled to a preliminary hearing.[470] Two of the new counts were the same as the old counts, except that the October 24th date was changed to October 23rd. Three of the new charges were not hate crimes. Two other counts had augmented pleadings. Ultimately, the defendant was convicted of three of the new counts. The appellate court reversed, holding that the defendant was entitled to a preliminary hearing. The new charges were not barred from prosecution but could proceed only after a preliminary hearing.

The court noted that an information may be amended to charge additional offenses arising out of the same transaction. But section 111-2(f), which permits this amendment, applies to informations, not indictments. There is no similar statutory provision permitting the state to alter the substance of an indictment.[471] Where the defendant is charged with an indictment, the only alterations permitted are to cure formal defects, not matters of substance.[472] If the changes are of substance, there must be a new indictment from the grand jury or a preliminary hearing. In *Kelly,* the court ruled that the amendments "resulted in a substantial alteration of the indictment"; therefore, the defendant was entitled to a new preliminary hearing.[473]

---

468. 299 Ill. App. 3d 222, 701 N.E.2d 114, 116 (3d Dist. 1998).

469. *Id.*

470. *Id.,* 701 N.E.2d at 115.

471. *Id.,* 701 N.E.2d at 117. *See* People v. Taylor, 153 Ill. App. 3d 710, 506 N.E.2d 321 (4th Dist. 1987).

472. *Kelly,* 299 Ill. App. 3d 222, 701 N.E.2d at 117.

473. *Id.*

§ 3.18 The Arraignment: Starting Point of the Trial

The stage of arraignment is directed by section 113-1 of the Illinois Code of Criminal Procedure. It states: "Before any person is tried for the commission of an offense he shall be called into open court, informed of the charge against him, and called upon to plead thereto."[474]

This first step of a criminal trial[475] has three purposes. It fixes the identity of the defendant and matches him or her to the charges. It formally informs the defendant of the charges against him or her by either handing him or her a copy of the charges or reading the charges to him or her. Lastly, it gives the defendant an opportunity to be heard.

The United States Supreme Court in *Hamilton v. Alabama*[476] described arraignment as a "critical stage in a criminal proceeding" and held that the right to counsel was imperative to guarantee an intelligent plea.[477] The Court, however, noted that the situation might have been different in other states.

> Arraignment has differing consequences in the various jurisdictions. Under federal law an arraignment is a *sine qua non* to the trial itself—the preliminary stage where the accused is informed of the indictment and pleads to it, thereby formulating the issue to be tried. [citation omitted] That view has led some States to hold that arraignment is the first step in a trial (at least in case of felonies) at which time the accused is entitled to an attorney. [citation omitted] In other States arraignment is not "a part of the trial" but "a mere formal preliminary step to an answer or plea."[478]

An arraignment normally affords an opportunity for the accused to plead as a condition to a trial.[479] In Illinois, arraignment is a critical stage, but if it is omitted, the error is waived unless the defendant makes a timely objection.[480] Immunity from prosecution will not be imposed as a sanction for the omission of an arraignment.[481] The arraignment is generally a clear beginning of the

---

474. 725 ILCS 5/113-1.

475. People v. Kurant, 331 Ill. 470, 163 N.E. 411 (1928), *overruled on other grounds by* People v. Hill, 17 Ill. 2d 112, 160 N.E.2d 779, 782 (1959).

476. 368 U.S. 52 (1961).

477. *Id.* at 55.

478. *Id.* at 54 n.4.

479. *Id.*

480. People v. O'Hara, 332 Ill. 2d 436, 163 N.E. 804 (1928); People v. Hahn, 82 Ill. App. 3d 173, 402 N.E.2d 895 (3d Dist. 1980).

481. People v. Hendrix, 54 Ill. 2d 165, 295 N.E.2d 724 (1973); People v. Foley, 162 Ill. App. 3d 282, 515 N.E.2d 351, 355–56 (2d Dist. 1987) (listing cases in which

adversary process.[482] At arraignment, key rights are conveyed to the accused, but may be waived knowingly and intelligently.[483]

§ 3.19 A Practical Problem for Prosecutors in Charging

An interesting example dealing with the problems accompanying proper charging of a defendant is the felony-murder case of *People v. Dekens*.[484] Here, defendant Dekens and a co-felon planned to rob an undercover police officer from whom they had arranged to buy drugs. During the transaction and robbery, the officer shot and killed the co-felon. Dekens was charged with felony-murder but challenged his indictment by arguing that the act causing the co-felon's death "was not done in furtherance of the common design to commit the felony."[485]

This case reached the Illinois Supreme Court, which finally resolved the issue by holding that the indictment was proper. Illinois, the court said, is unlike other jurisdictions in that it follows the "proximate cause" theory of liability for felony-murder,[486] not the agency theory.[487] In Illinois, therefore, a defendant is liable for *any* death "proximately related to the defendant's criminal conduct."[488] The test is whether the resulting death was a direct and proximate

---

courts have refused to set aside convictions obtained without formal plea when defendant failed to object to lack of arraignment).

482. *But see* Matteo v. Superintendent, 171 F.3d 877 (3d Cir.), *cert. denied*, 68 U.S.L.W. 3223 (1999).

483. *See* Boyd v. Dutton, 405 U.S. 1 (1972), describing many of the rights that attach at arraignment. Boyd pled guilty, without the assistance of counsel, and was sentenced to twenty-eight years in prison for forgery. The United States Supreme Court vacated the conviction and remanded the matter for a hearing on whether Boyd understood his waiver of counsel and the consequences of that waiver.

484. 182 Ill. 2d 247, 695 N.E.2d 474 (1998).

485. *Id.*, 695 N.E.2d at 475.

486. *Id.* Under this theory of liability, the defendant committing the felony is liable for any death that was the proximate result of his crime, even if a victim of the crime did the killing. *See* People v. Lowery, 178 Ill. 2d 462, 687 N.E.2d 973, 975–76 (1997).

487. *Dekens*, 182 Ill. 2d 247, 695 N.E.2d at 475. Under this theory of liability, followed by the majority of jurisdictions, the felony-murder doctrine does not apply if the killing can be directly attributed to someone other than the defendant. *See Lowery*, 178 Ill. 2d 462, 687 N.E.2d at 976.

488. *Dekens*, 182 Ill. 2d 247, 695 N.E.2d at 477. Illinois has developed this rule from a line of cases, including: *People v. Pane*, 359 Ill. 246, 194 N.E. 539 (1935) (robbers attacked two brothers, one brother was shot but it could not be determined by whom; defendant robber was charged and convicted of felony-murder);

cause of the defendant's felony, not the identity of the one who actually killed the decedent nor the guilt or innocence of the decedent himself. Accordingly, Dekens was properly charged under the felony-murder doctrine, even though the intended victim (the officer) shot and killed Dekens's co-felon.

Three justices, however, dissented. Justices Bilandic and McMorrow agreed that Illinois should continue to follow the proximate cause theory but disagreed with the majority in the application of the felony-murder doctrine in general.[489] To them, there is a clear distinction between "a third party killing an innocent party and a third party killing a participant in the felony. . . . It is illogical to conclude that the same degree of guilt should attach" to the defendant."[490]

In a separate and more sweeping dissent, Justice Heiple called for a complete abandonment of the proximate cause theory of liability in felony-murder cases. This is the only type of first-degree murder in which the state does not have to prove the defendant's intent. Thus, Justice Heiple read the felony-murder statute to place a burden on the state to prove, at the very least, that the defendant *performed* the acts that actually *caused* the death.[491] If the death was caused by the actions of someone other than the defendant (as here, the police officer who actually shot the co-felon), the felony-murder doctrine should not apply.

People v. Allen, 56 Ill. 2d 536, 309 N.E.2d 544 (1974) (conspirator charged and convicted under felony-murder doctrine for death of police officer killed by another officer during attempted robbery); *People v. Hickman,* 59 Ill. 2d 89, 319 N.E.2d 511 (1974) (defendants charged and convicted under felony-murder doctrine when one officer mistakenly killed another during pursuit after defendants' burglary); *People v. Lowery,* 178 Ill. 2d 462, 687 N.E.2d 973 (1997) (defendant charged and convicted under felony-murder doctrine when intended victim of armed robbery shot at defendants but struck and killed innocent bystander).

Illinois also bases it proximate cause theory on the Committee Comments to Section 9-1, which states, "[i]t is immaterial whether the killing in such a case is intentional or accidental, or is committed by a confederate without the connivance of the defendant . . . or even by a third person trying to prevent the commission of the felony." 720 ILCS § 5/9-1, Committee Comments-1961, at 12–13 (Smith-Hurd 1993). *See Dekens,* 182 Ill. 2d 247, 695 N.E.2d at 476, 478.

489. *Dekens,* 182 Ill. 2d 247, 695 N.E.2d at 478. Justices Bilandic and McMorrow read the same legislation the majority cited as being silent with regard to the identity of the decedent. Accordingly, in their view, neither the legislation nor its comments addressed the issue in this case: whether felony-murder applies when the decedent is a co-felon killed by a third party.

490. *Dekens,* 182 Ill. 2d 247, 695 N.E.2d at 479. These dissenters also pointed out that none of the precedent cases cited by the majority address the issue here. *Payne, Allen, Hickman,* and *Lowery* all involved the killing of an innocent bystander or victim, not a co-felon. *Id.*

491. *Id.,* 695 N.E.2d at 481.

§ 3.20 Judicial Powers

In *People v. Chatman,*[492] the defendant was indicted for possession of cocaine, upon the mere evidence that she delivered a baby addicted to cocaine. The prosecutor candidly admitted that "our evidence would [be] solely that this woman had a cocaine baby . . . . That would be the People's position, and that we would have no other evidence to indicate . . . some of the factual elements [we] have to actually establish at trial."[493] The prosecutor contended that there was enough evidence for the finder of fact to infer that the defendant possessed cocaine. The trial court dismissed the indictment, and the state appealed. The appellate court reversed and remanded the matter, finding that the trial court exceeded its authority by the pretrial inquiry into the sufficiency of the state's evidence. A trial court may only dismiss an indictment for the reasons set out in section 114-1(a), or where there has been a clear violation of due process rights.[494]

The appellate court stated, "[h]ere, even if the trial court had reason to believe that the state's evidence was insufficient as a matter of law, that conclusion cannot support the court's action."[495] The appellate court was wary of encouraging a "sort of preliminary trial on the merits," something the entire court system has forever tried to prevent.

After a trial judge has granted a motion to dismiss criminal charges under section 114-1, a second, and more complex, question arises: can the state properly reindict the defendant? This question was answered, in part, in *People v. Hunter.*[496] In *Hunter*, the trial judge had earlier dismissed a 1995 indictment based on allegedly perjured testimony before the grand jury by one Tellone. Though the judge was not explicit on the grounds for dismissal, the appellate court scoured the record to glean that the dismissal sprung from due process violations. The appellate court found that the "trial court's conclusion was manifestly supported in the record."[497]

After the state reindicted Hunter, the question arose: was the new indictment permitted under the law? Section 114-1(e) states, "[d]ismissal of the charge upon the grounds set forth in subsection (a)(4) through (a)(11) of this section shall not prevent the return of a new indictment." Did a dismissal for due process violations fall within section (a)(4) through (a)(11)? Clearly not. But, the appellate court stated, the ability to cure a violation of the defendant's due

---

492. 297 Ill. App. 3d 57, 60, 696 N.E.2d 1159 (2d Dist. 1998).

493. *Id.,* 696 N.E.2d at 1161.

494. *Id.,* 696 N.E.2d at 1162.

495. *Id.,* 696 N.E.2d at 1163.

496. 298 Ill. App. 3d 126, 698 N.E.2d (2d Dist. 1998).

497. *Id.,* 698 N.E.2d at 232.

process rights was "part of the trial court's inherent authority to guarantee the defendant a fair trial."[498]

The appellate court enunciated what was certainly implied, at least, in section 114-1(e), that the state would be permitted to again indict in "some, but not all" of the situations set forth in section 114-1(a).[499] The appellate court made it clear that "[t]hus, the legislature expressly limited the circumstances under which the State may seek to again indict a defendant following the dismissal of criminal charges [on a pretrial motion]."[500] The appellate court related that the State may bring a new indictment where the previous indictment suffered from a technical error. However, the state is "prohibited from bringing a new indictment [when] a defendant's constitutional right to be free from multiple prosecutions for the same crime, a constitutional and statutory right to a speedy trial, or a contractual right to immunity [is involved]," the situations reflected in section 114-1(a)(1) through (a)(3).[501]

The appellate court candidly admitted that a dismissal for "due process" violations was not covered in section 114-1(a)(1) through (a)(3), but the essence was clear: there exists a "public policy of protecting the public against the overreaching and oppression of the [s]tate," and that deterrents to this improper conduct must be found.[502] The court stated, "[a]s the guardians of the laws, police officers are expected to act with integrity, honesty, and trustworthiness."[503] "This admonition applies with equal force to the prosecution."[504] It was held that the trial court acted properly in dismissing the subsequent indictment, where the first indictment was dismissed for due process violations.

---

498. *Id.*

499. *Id.*

500. *Id.*

501. *Id.*, at 232.

502. *Id.*, 698 N.E.2d at 233.

503. *Id.*, *citing* Sindermann v. Civil Service Comm'n, 275 Ill. App. 3d 917, 657 N.E.2d 41 (2d Dist. 1996).

504. *Hunter*, 298 Ill. App. 3d 126, 698 N.E.2d at 233.

4

PRETRIAL PROCEDURES AND PRACTICES

Richard S. Kling

Pretrial Procedures and Practices

319

§ 4.01 Introduction

Other than one's skill, experience, and creativity, the pretrial motion is perhaps the most important tool available to the criminal defense practitioner for protecting the constitutional and statutory rights of the accused. Through the use of the pretrial motion, the defendant is assured that he or she will be represented by counsel;[1] is afforded the opportunity to be enlarged on bail pending trial;[2] can obtain the service of investigators[3] and experts;[4] can learn what evidence and witnesses the state will seek to introduce against him or her;[5] can learn what evidence and witnesses that the state can use;[6] and can compel witnesses in his or her own behalf to appear in court.[7] If the

---

1. 725 ILCS 5/103-3, 5/103-4, 5/109-1, 5/112-4.1, 5/113-3, 5/113-3.1.

2. 725 ILCS art. 5/110.

3. 725 ILCS 5/113-3.

4. 725 ILCS 5/104-1, 5/104-13, 5/113-3.

5. S. Ct. Rules 411–415.

6. 725 ILCS 5/114-2, 5/114-9, 5/114-10.

7. 725 ILCS 5/115-17. This provision provides:

> It is the duty of the clerk of the court to issue subpoenas, either on the part of the people or of the accused, directed to the sheriff or coroner of any county of this State. A witness who is duly subpoenaed who

defendant suffers from mental illness, it is the pretrial motion that may keep him or her from going to trial until he or she recovers;[8] allows him or her to be tried under special circumstances;[9] provides him or her with a complete defense to the charge;[10] or at least lays the groundwork for mitigation of a death sentence[11] if he or she is found guilty.

So powerful and important is the pretrial motion that not only will it have a significant impact on what will occur at the trial, if there is one, as discussed above, but also on where the trial will be held,[12] when,[13] with what other defendants,[14] on what charges,[15] and before what judge.[16] And in the appropriate case, it is the pretrial motion that will determine whether the defendant will have to go to trial at all.[17]

This chapter discusses many of the motions made available to the criminal defense practitioner implicitly by federal and state constitutional rights enjoyed by the accused, or explicitly by statute and Supreme Court Rules as interpreted by the courts. The motions dealt with in this chapter should, however, not be taken as exhaustive. It is my firm belief that the total list of pretrial motions that might be filed is limited only by the practitioner's creativity and desire to protect the rights of the client.

§ 4.02 Statutory Right to Counsel

Several provisions of Illinois Compiled Statutes chapter 725 provide for the accused's right to counsel in a criminal prosecution. These provisions both overlap and expand the constitutional right to counsel arising from the Fifth and Sixth Amendments to the United States Constitution as applied to the states by the

---

> neglects or refuses to attend any court, under the requisitions of the subpoena, shall be proceeded against and punished for contempt of the court. Attachments against witnesses who live in a different county from that where the subpoena is returnable may be served in the same manner as warrants are directed to be served out of the county from which they issue.

8. 725 ILCS 5/104-10 through 5/104-31.

9. *Id.*

10. 730 ILCS 5/5-2-4, 5/5-3-2.

11. 720 ILCS 5/9-1(c).

12. 725 ILCS 5/114-6.

13. 725 ILCS 5/103-5.

14. 725 ILCS 5/114-7.

15. 725 ILCS 5/114-1, 5/114-7.

16. 725 ILCS 5/114-5.

17. 725 ILCS 5/114-1.

Fourteenth Amendment. Although the provisions vary in importance for the purpose of pretrial motions, the defense counsel should be aware of the encompassing character of the right to counsel in Illinois and the possible opportunities presented thereby. The assistance of counsel in some form is available to the accused virtually from the point of arrest or other restraint on liberty.

§ 4.03 — Chapter 725, Section 5/103-3

Chapter 725, section 5/103-3(a) establishes the right of "[p]ersons who are arrested . . . to communicate with an attorney of their choice and a member of their family. . . . within a reasonable time after arrival at the first place of custody." This basic due process provision[18] allows the arrested person to notify family members concerning his or her whereabouts and the nature of the charges against him or her and to begin the process of securing representation to protect his or her rights.[19] One court has read the "spirit of the rule" to even permit the accused to contact a friend for these purposes,[20] although in my experience, it is difficult enough for defendants to try to call their lawyers.

The statute provides for this communication "within a reasonable time," but the time framework is quite flexible and often anything but reasonable. In a case in which the accused was arrested one day, counsel was appointed the next day, and a motion for change of venue was filed two days later, the court was "unable to discern any substantial prejudice resulting from the alleged inability

---

18. ILL. COMP. STAT. ANN. 725 ILCS 5/5-103-3, Committee Comments (Smith-Hurd 1992).

19. People v. Prim, 53 Ill. 2d 62, 289 N.E.2d 601, 606 (1972) (no violation when defendant was arrested at mother's house and mother knew where he was being held), *cert. denied,* 412 U.S. 918 (1973), *overruled on other grounds* by People v. King, 66 Ill. 2d 551, 363 N.E.2d 838, 843 (1977):

> The purpose of the statute is to permit a person held in custody to notify his family of his whereabouts and to notify them of the nature of the offense with which he is charged so that arrangements may be made for bail, representation by counsel and other procedural safeguards that the defendant cannot accomplish for himself while in custody.

See People v. Hattery, 183 Ill. App. 3d 785, 539 N.E.2d 368, 395 (1st Dist. 1989) (this section does not give defendant the right to family visits other than during normal visiting hours nor the right to have a family member present during interrogation).

20. People v. Lopez, 93 Ill. App. 2d 426, 235 N.E.2d 652, 654 (3d Dist. 1968) (no reversible error because violation was harmless):

> The literal wording of the Illinois rule requires the police to permit an accused person to contact a lawyer and a member of the family. We are of the opinion that the spirit of the rule would include a friend and the police should have permitted him to make his contact.

to communicate with counsel to such an extent as to constitute a clear denial of due process."[21] Even a period of five days may not constitute reversible error when the accused makes no incriminating statements.[22] "Section 103-3 is not a *per se* rule of exclusion or reversal, and absent the substantive right to counsel, the making of incriminating statements in custodial interrogation, or evidence of abuse of police procedures, a defendants' [sic] conviction will not be reversed because of a violation of this section."[23]

Thus, although section 103-3 articulates what would appear to be a basic due process right of the accused, given the frequent breach and unwillingness of the courts to enforce it by sanctions, the most the defense bar can hope is that it might encourage proper police procedure and that sometimes it is a vehicle by which the accused can begin the process of release and defense.

§ 4.04 — Chapter 725, Section 5/103-4

Chapter 725, section 5/103-4 fleshes out the right to the assistance of counsel by providing that "[a]ny person committed, imprisoned or restrained of his liberty for any cause whatever" will "be allowed to consult with any licensed attorney at law of this State . . . as many times and for such period each time as is reasonable."[24] Thus, the initial right merely to communicate becomes the full-blown right to consult. The importance of this provision for pretrial motions is clear in that the accused has the statutory right "to consult with counsel at any time after being taken into custody," "whether or not such person is charged with a crime."[25]

Most right-to-counsel issues arise, however, under the statute that is intended to supplement the basic right herein afforded, section 113-3.[26] The cases that do invoke section 103-4 generally involve *Miranda*[27] issues concerning the

---

21. People v. Dimond, 54 Ill. App. 3d 439, 369 N.E.2d 593, 596 (3d Dist. 1977).

22. People v. Ishman, 44 Ill. 2d 61, 254 N.E.2d 482 (1969).

23. People v. Martin, 121 Ill. App. 3d 196, 459 N.E.2d 279, 289–90 (2d Dist. 1984). *See also* People v. Donalson, 50 Ill. App. 3d 678, 365 N.E.2d 658 (1st Dist. 1977).

24. 725 ILCS 5/103-4. *See also* People v. Golden, 117 Ill. App. 3d 150, 453 N.E.2d 15, 20 (5th Dist. 1983) (constitutional right to counsel limited to criminal proceedings which result in actual imprisonment; statutory right is similarly limited).

25. ILL. COMP. STAT. ANN. 725 ILCS 5/103-4, Committee Comments (Smith-Hurd 1992). *But see* People v. Cadwell, 160 Ill. App. 3d 495, 513 N.E.2d 539, 541 (4th Dist. 1987) (an individual does not have right to speak to counsel before submitting to breath test in DUI proceeding).

26. 725 ILCS 5/113-3.

27. Miranda v. Arizona, 384 U.S. 436 (1966).

right to an attorney during custodial interrogation and the waiver of that right.[28] In *People v. Smith*,[29] the court found reversible error when the police refused to allow an attorney to see his client and did not inform the client that the attorney had attempted to see him. "We hold that when police, prior to or during custodial interrogation, refuse an attorney appointed or retained to assist a suspect access to the suspect, there can be no knowing waiver of the right to counsel if the suspect has not been informed that the attorney was present and seeking to consult with him."[30] The court relied on both the Fifth and Sixth Amendment grounds articulated in *Miranda*.

In *Moran v. Burbine*,[31] the United States Supreme Court dealt with an attorney who called the police station and advised the police that if they wanted to question the defendant, she would appear. Police informed the attorney that the defendant would not be questioned, but then proceeded to interview the defendant within an hour.[32] The Supreme Court held that the defendant's Fifth Amendment rights did not turn on police misrepresentation to his attorney since he (the defendant) did not know of his attorney's attempt.[33]

The Illinois Supreme Court, however, disagrees: "The day is long past in Illinois . . . where attorneys must shout legal advice to their clients, held in custody, through the jail house door."[34] Article 1, section 10 of the Illinois Constitution "simply does not permit police to delude custodial suspects, exposed to interrogation, into falsely believing they are without immediately available legal counsel and also prevent counsel from accessing and assisting their client during the interrogation."[35]

---

28. People v. Smith, 93 Ill. 2d 179, 442 N.E.2d 1325 (1982), *cert. denied,* 461 U.S. 937 (1983).

29. 93 Ill. 2d 179, 442 N.E.2d 1325 (1982).

30. *Id.,* 442 N.E.2d at 1329. *See also* People v. Krueger, 82 Ill. 2d 305, 412 N.E.2d 537 (1980), *cert. denied,* 451 U.S. 1019 (1981); People v. Hammock, 121 Ill. App. 3d 874, 460 N.E.2d 378 (1st Dist. 1984), *cert. denied,* 470 U.S. 1003 (1985); People v. Amft, 109 Ill. App. 3d 619, 440 N.E.2d 924 (1st Dist. 1982); People v. Sluder, 97 Ill. App. 3d 459, 423 N.E.2d 268 (3d Dist. 1981); People v. Rafac, 51 Ill. App. 3d, 1, 364 N.E.2d 991 (3d Dist. 1977). Note: The suppression of statements because of *Miranda* violations is covered elsewhere in this volume. See also *United States ex rel. Sanders v. Rowe,* 460 F. Supp. 1128 (N.D. Ill. 1978), for an extensive discussion of *Miranda* and its progeny in relation to Illinois law.

31. 475 U.S. 412, 417 (1986).

32. *Id.*

33. *Id.* at 421.

34. People v. McCauley, 163 Ill. 2d 414, 645 N.E.2d 923, 929 (1994).

35. *Moran,* 475 U.S. at 423.

Apart from *Miranda* issues, however, counsel should be aware of the extent to which this provision enables consultation with any person in custody.[36] Section 103-4 provides an attorney with the opportunity to consult promptly, privately, and extensively with his or her client to assure protection of the client's rights and begin the defense. Any intentional violation of this right of the accused by a peace officer may subject the officer to prosecution for official misconduct under section 103-8.[37]

§ 4.05 — Chapter 725, Section 5/109-1(b)(2)

Chapter 725, section 5/109-1 provides the procedure to be followed when a person is arrested, including that the arrested person must be brought before a judge and advised of the right to counsel, and if indigent, have counsel appointed for him or her in accord with section 113-3. This informs the "accused at an early stage of certain fundamental rights which would seem desirable in any system of justice,"[38] including the right "to prompt presentment to a judicial officer for a determination of the probable cause for detention."[39]

A main issue arising under this provision is one of timing, because the arrested person must be taken before a judge, informed of the charges, advised

---

36. Of historical note is the scope of this statute in its previous form (ILL. REV. STAT. ch. 38, § 736(b), (c) (1961)). In *People v. Escobedo,* 28 Ill. 2d 41, 190 N.E.2d 825, 831 (1963), the Illinois Supreme Court stated:

> These statutes show a legislative policy against the police or other public officers insulating a person from his attorney, but it does not follow that the legislature intended that the statutes operate to insulate the person from the police or other public officials . . . . Having given due weight to the various considerations involved, we are of the opinion that the right of a person in custody to see and consult with his attorney does not deprive the police of their right to a reasonable opportunity to interrogate outside the presence of counsel.

Obviously, the assessment of the statute is no longer entirely accurate in light of *Escobedo v. Illinois,* 378 U.S. 478 (1964), *Miranda,* and the plethora of ensuing cases.

37. Section 103/8. Mandatory Duty Of Officers. Any peace officer who intentionally prevents the exercise by an accused of any right conferred by this Article or who intentionally fails to perform any act required of him by this Article shall be guilty of official misconduct and may be punished in accordance with Section 33-3 of the "Criminal Code of 1961" approved July 28, 1961, as heretofore and hereafter amended [720 ILCS 5/33-3].

725 ILCS 5/103-8.

38. ILL. COMP. STAT. ANN. 725 ILCS 5/109-1, Committee Comments (Smith-Hurd 1992).

39. People v. Goree, 115 Ill. App. 3d 157, 450 N.E.2d 342, 344 (5th Dist. 1983).

of the right to counsel, and have bail set "without unnecessary delay."[40] Presumably, in light of *Miranda,* at least if police attempt to secure a statement, an arrested person has already been informed of the right to counsel by reason of the Fifth Amendment. Furthermore, as discussed above, under sections 103-3 and 103-4 an arrested person has the statutory right to communicate and consult with an attorney before his or her initial appearance before a judge, although this may be a right in form only if the person is unaware of it before his or her court appearance. Thus, the issue of delay normally arises from the state's failure to conduct the overall procedure without unnecessary delay.

Delay itself is not sufficient for the dismissal of charges or the exclusion of incriminating statements.[41] Rather, the accused must show "substantial and actual prejudice" occasioned by the delay in presentment to a judicial officer.[42] Once the defendant has met his or her burden, the state has the burden to show the reasonableness or necessity of the delay.[43] A delay of 36 hours between a late night arrest and the appearance before a judge, during which time the defendant appeared in line-ups, was held to be "minimal" and "reasonable considering the time necessary to perform the administrative steps incident to arrest."[44] The facts and circumstances of each case determine what constitutes an unreasonable or unnecessary delay.[45]

---

40. 725 ILCS 5/109-1.

41. Delay in bringing a detainee before a judge is only one factor in determining voluntariness; it does not render a statement inadmissible by itself. People v. House, 141 Ill. 2d 323, 566 N.E.2d 259, 284 (1990); People v. Seawright, 228 Ill. App. 3d 939, 593 N.E.2d 1003, 1020 (1st Dist. 1992).

42. People v. Dees, 85 Ill. 2d 233, 422 N.E.2d 616, 618 (1981). *See also* People v. Williams, 230 Ill. App. 3d 761, 595 N.E.2d 1115, 1128 (1st Dist. 1992) (63 hour delay did not violate right to a prompt determination of probable cause where the defendant failed to show prejudice).

43. People v. Littleton, 175 Ill. App. 3d 105, 529 N.E.2d 700, 703 (1st Dist. 1988).

44. People v. Martin, 121 Ill. App. 3d 196, 459 N.E.2d 279, 288–89 (2d Dist. 1984). *See also* People v. House, 141 Ill. 2d 323, 566 N.E.2d 259, 284 (1990) (legislative directives of paragraph (a) do not mean police forsake all duties to comply or that police do not have reasonable latitude to fully investigate crime; noncompliance with provisions does not necessarily vitiate a conviction nor render otherwise voluntary confession inadmissible); People v. Smith, 222 Ill. App. 3d 473, 584 N.E.2d 211, 217 (1st Dist. 1991) (holding a defendant beyond court call to conduct a lineup did not violate his rights where police had probable cause to detain him).

45. *Martin,* 459 N.E.2d at 288. *See also* People v. Mallett, 45 Ill. 2d 388, 259 N.E.2d 241 (1970); People v. Jackson, 23 Ill. 2d 274, 178 N.E.2d 299 (1961).

§ 4.06 — Chapter 725, Section 5/113-3

Chapter 725, section 5/113-3[46] provides that "[e]very person charged with an offense shall be allowed counsel before pleading to the charge." This is the right to counsel at the point from which the adversary criminal proceedings has most clearly begun. If the accused at the time of arraignment has not yet retained counsel, he or she will be given time to do so.[47] If the accused is indigent, the court must appoint either the public defender or other counsel to represent him or her.[48] This is the statutory recognition that the accused's right to "counsel under the sixth amendment cannot be dependent upon ability to pay for an attorney's services."[49] Most issues arising under this section concern the determination of indigency, whether the defendant qualifies for the appointment of counsel, and the granting of continuances for the accused to retain counsel of his or her choice.

"The obvious purpose of our statute is to protect the rights of an accused from being impaired by the absence of legal counsel."[50] The failure to advise the accused of the right to counsel at arraignment and to provide counsel if needed is reversible error. "It is by now well established that arraignment is a 'critical stage' in a felony case and that the right to counsel attaches automatically before any plea is made or accepted."[51] However, a technical violation

---

46.   Sec. 113-3. (a) Every person charged with an offense shall be al lowed counsel before pleading to the charge. If the defendant desires counsel and has been unable to obtain same before arraignment the court shall recess court or continue the cause for a reasonable time to permit defendant to obtain counsel and consult with him before pleading to the charge . . . .

   725 ILCS 5/113-3(a).

47. 725 ILCS 5/113-3(a).

48. 725 ILCS 5/113-3(b).

49. People v. Cook, 81 Ill. 2d 176, 407 N.E.2d 56, 58 (1980). *See* People v. Matthews, 297 Ill. App. 3d 772, 697 N.E.2d 925 (3d Dist. 1998) (order to reimburse county for defense costs without conducting hearing of defendant's finances is plain error).

50. People v. Rebenstorf, 37 Ill. 2d 572, 229 N.E.2d 483, 485 (1967), *cert. denied,* 390 U.S. 924 (1968).

51. People v. Hessenauer, 45 Ill. 2d 63, 256 N.E.2d 791, 794 (1970). See Kirby v. Illinois, 406 U.S. 682 (1972); Hamilton v. Alabama, 368 U.S. 52 (1961).

   "Critical stage" analysis has also been used to establish the constitutional right to counsel at the preliminary hearing under section 109-3. *See* People v. Adams, 46 Ill. 2d 200, 263 N.E.2d 490 (1970), *aff'd,* 405 U.S. 278 (1972) (determining that the holding in *Coleman v. Alabama,* 399 U.S. 1 (1970), applies to preliminary hearings in Illinois).

of the statute that does not result in actual prejudice to the accused is harmless error.[52] Thus, when the accused stated he would obtain his own counsel within a week but the judge appointed the public defender, who entered a plea of not guilty, there was no reversible error because the plea could be withdrawn and other counsel substituted later. "The action by the court here in appointing an attorney for the defendant served to insure the protection of his rights and the entry of the not-guilty plea in no way disadvantaged him."[53]

The right to counsel under the Sixth and Fourteenth Amendments to the United States Constitution and section 5/113-3 "includes the right to be represented by counsel of one's own choice,"[54] at least for the nonindigent accused.[55] However, although a request for a continuance at the time of the arraignment

---

However, a lineup conducted before the formal charge is not considered to be a critical stage or part of the adversarial criminal proceeding. Therefore, the accused has no right to counsel at such lineups. People v. Burbank, 53 Ill. 2d 261, 291 N.E.2d 161 (1972), *cert. denied,* 412 U.S. 951 (1973); People v. Martin, 121 Ill. App. 3d 196, 459 N.E.2d 279 (2d Dist. 1984). This was so even when the accused's attorney stated he intended to be present and a delay was requested. People v. Lamacki, 121 Ill. App. 3d 403, 459 N.E.2d 1142 (1st Dist.), *cert. denied,* 469 U.S. 885 (1984). *See also* People v. Garrett, 179 Ill. 2d 239, 688 N.E.2d 614, 619 (1997) (defendant not denied counsel at lineup held one month after arrest and initial appearance in court; adversarial process had not initiated, because no formal charges against defendant nor significant prosecutorial involvement by the prosecutor at that time). Furthermore, a pretrial hypnotic session is not a critical stage affording the accused the right to presence of counsel. People v. Gibson, 117 Ill. App. 3d 270, 452 N.E.2d 1368 (4th Dist. 1983).

52. People v. Nash, 183 Ill. App. 3d 924, 539 N.E.2d 822, 828 (4th Dist. 1989) (substantial compliance with section is sufficient).

53. *Rebenstorf,* 37 Ill. 2d 572, 229 N.E.2d at 485.

54. People v. Green, 42 Ill. 2d 555, 248 N.E.2d 116, 117 (1969); 725 ILCS 5/113-3(a). *See* People v. Bodoh, 200 Ill. App. 3d 415, 558 N.E.2d 178, 184 (1st Dist. 1990) (the right to counsel includes the right to be represented by counsel of choice; this right is not absolute since the right must be balanced against public need for efficient and effective administration of justice). *See* People v. Holmes, 141 Ill. 2d 204, 565 N.E.2d 950, 951 (1990).

55. People v. Cox, 22 Ill. 2d 534, 177 N.E.2d 211, 213 (1961), *cert. denied,* 374 U.S. 855 (1963):

> Thus, while the legislature and this court have given indigent defendants the right to be represented by competent counsel, it does not follow that they have the right to choose such appointed counsel . . . . We hold therefore that an indigent defendant does not have the right to choose his court-appointed counsel.

See also People v. Adams, 195 Ill. App. 3d 870, 553 N.E.2d 3, 4 (5th Dist. 1990) (indigent defendant has no right to pick appointed counsel).

to obtain counsel of choice is mandated by section 113-3(a), a delay will not be allowed to "unduly prejudice the other party or interfere with the administration of justice."[56] Assuming a legitimate request for reasonable time for privately retained counsel to appear, the courts support enforcement of the defendant's right to counsel of his or her choice.[57] Thus, where the accused indicated that he had private counsel who he wished to represent him but who was out of town, and the court refused to undertake "any inquiry into the truth of the circumstances," reversible error was committed in forcing the accused to trial with the public defender.[58] Similarly, when private counsel's appearance was on file and the accused wanted to be represented by him, the court improperly coerced the accused into representation by the public defender.[59] The determination of when the accused's right to counsel of his or her choice "unreasonably interferes with the orderly process of judicial administration" will be made on the facts and circumstances of each case.[60]

---

56. People v. Mueller, 2 Ill. 2d 311, 118 N.E.2d 1, 4 (1954). *See* People v. Burrell, 228 Ill. App. 3d 133, 592 N.E.2d 453, 459 (1st Dist. 1992) (in balancing judicial interest of due diligence and a defendant's right to counsel of choice, the judge must address the actual request to determine whether it is being used merely as a delay tactic; factors to consider are whether the defendant has been continuously in custody, whether defendant has informed the court of efforts to obtain counsel, and whether defendant has cooperated with appointed counsel even though dissatisfied with him or her).

57. People v. Hardin, 299 Ill. App. 3d 33, 700 N.E.2d 1057, 1064 (1st Dist. 1998) (trial court violated defendant's right to counsel of choice by not allowing his present attorney to withdraw when defendant hired new attorney who indicated readiness to proceed).

58. *Green,* 42 Ill. 2d 555, 248 N.E.2d at 117.

59. People v. Payne, 46 Ill. 2d 585, 264 N.E.2d 167, 169 (1970):

> The coercive tactic used here of securing ostensible assent by threat of immediate incarceration or increase of bond was, to say the least, questionable judicial practice. In practical effect the result was the same as in *Green*—a summary denial of defendant's request for a continuance to enable him to be represented by counsel of his choice.

60. People v. Spurlark, 67 Ill. App. 3d 186, 384 N.E.2d 767, 774 (1st Dist. 1978). *See* People v. Burson, 11 Ill. 2d 360, 143 N.E.2d 239 (1957) ("spiritual ward" is not type of counsel contemplated by right to assistance of counsel); People v. Langdon, 73 Ill. App. 3d 881, 392 N.E.2d 142 (1st Dist. 1979). *See also* People v. Childress, 276 Ill. App. 3d 402, 657 N.E.2d 1180, 1188 (1st Dist. 1995) (defendant's right to speedy trial violated where defendant requested continuance for private counsel to file his appearance on day of trial and to prepare because counsel was not aware trial was scheduled for that day; there was no evidence defendant's conduct was dilatory or a move to thwart justice).

Note must be taken that an accused is also entitled to represent himself or herself in a criminal prosecution. In addition to having the right to counsel, "[t]he right of a defendant to represent himself, when his choice is intelligently made, is as basic and fundamental as his right to be represented by counsel."[61] Yet, by choosing to represent himself or herself an accused does not necessarily preclude the assistance of counsel; rather, the trial court has discretion "to decide whether defendant may have an attorney to assist and advise him."[62] However, if an accused does proceed pro se, the role of the attorney is one of assistance only. It is not a relationship of co-counsel "because a defendant has no right to both self-representation and the assistance of counsel."[63]

§ 4.07 — Chapter 725, Section 5/113-3(b)

Chapter 725, section 5/113-3(b) establishes the process by which the indigent accused is to be provided counsel.[64] Although an indigent's constitutional

---

61. People v. Sinko, 21 Ill. 2d 23, 171 N.E.2d 9, 10 (1960), *cert. denied,* 365 U.S. 855 (1961). *See* Faretta v. California, 422 U.S. 806 (1975). *But see* People v. Terry, 177 Ill. App. 3d 185, 532 N.E.2d 568, 573 (4th Dist. 1988) (where defendant never clearly and unequivocally expressed desire to proceed pro se, the judge is not required to admonish the defendant of the right to self-representation and absence of admonishment is not error).

62. People v. Bryant, 115 Ill. App. 3d 215, 450 N.E.2d 744, 748 (1st Dist. 1983). *See also* People v. Allen, 37 Ill. 2d 167, 226 N.E.2d 1, *cert. denied,* 389 U.S. 907 (1967); People v. Graves, 134 Ill. App. 3d 473, 480 N.E.2d 1142 (1st Dist. 1984); People v. Lindsey, 17 Ill. App. 3d 137, 308 N.E.2d 111 (1st Dist. 1974). *See, e.g.,* People v. Redd, 173 Ill. 2d 1, 670 N.E.2d 583, 601 (1996) ("The right of self-representation does not carry with it a corresponding right to legal assistance; one choosing to represent himself must be prepared to do just that."), *cert. denied,* 519 U.S. 1063 (1997).

63. People v. Williams, 97 Ill. 2d 252, 454 N.E.2d 220, 227 (1983), *cert. denied,* 466 U.S. 981 (1984), *denial of postconviction relief,* Williams v. Chrans, 50 F.3d 1356 (7th Dist. 1995). *See also* People v. Ephraim, 411 Ill. 118, 103 N.E.2d 363, *cert. denied,* 343 U.S. 930 (1952).

64.   (b) In all cases, except where the penalty is a fine only, if the court determines that the defendant is indigent and desires counsel, the Public Defender shall be appointed as counsel. If there is no Public Defender in the county or if the defendant requests counsel other than the Public Defender and the court finds that the rights of the defendant will be prejudiced by the appointment of the Public Defender, the court shall appoint as counsel a licensed attorney at law of this State, except that in a county having a population of 1,000,000 or more the Public Defender shall be appointed as counsel in all misdemeanor cases where the defendant is indigent and desires counsel unless the case involves multiple defendants, in which case the court may appoint counsel other

right to have appointed counsel in a felony case was recognized in *Gideon v. Wainwright*,[65] it was unclear whether the holding applied to nonfelonies. *Argersinger v. Hamlin*[66] clarified this issue by establishing the right to the assistance of counsel at the prosecution of any offense where imprisonment is the actual penalty.[67] In *Scott v. Illinois*,[68] however, the Supreme Court declined to automatically extend the constitutional protection of appointed counsel to state criminal prosecutions in which imprisonment is an authorized but not ultimately imposed penalty:

> [W]e believe that the central premise of *Argersinger*—that actual imprisonment is a penalty different in kind from fines or the mere threat of imprisonment—is eminently sound and warrants adoption of actual imprisonment as the line defining the constitutional right to appointment of counsel . . . . We therefore hold that the Sixth and Fourteenth Amendments . . . require only that no indigent criminal defendant be sentenced to a term of imprisonment unless the State has afforded him the right to assistance of appointed counsel in his defense.[69]

---

than the Public Defender for the additional defendants. The court shall require an affidavit signed by any defendant who requests court-appointed counsel. Such affidavit shall be in the form established by the Supreme Court containing sufficient information to ascertain the assets and liabilities of that defendant. The Court may direct the Clerk of the Circuit Court to assist the defendant in the completion of the affidavit. Any person who knowingly files such affidavit containing false information concerning his assets and liabilities shall be liable to the county where the case, in which such false affidavit is filed, is pending for the reasonable value of the services rendered by the public defender or other court-appointed counsel in the case to the extent that such services were unjustly or falsely procured.

725 ILCS 5/113-3(b).

65. 372 U.S. 335, 344. "[R]eason and reflection require us to recognize that in our adversary system of criminal justice, any person haled into court, who is too poor to hire a lawyer, cannot be assured a fair trial unless counsel is provided for him."

66. 407 U.S. 25 (1972).

67. *Id.* at 37. "We hold, therefore, that absent a knowing and intelligent waiver, no person may be imprisoned for any offense, whether classified as petty, misdemeanor, or felony, unless he was represented by counsel at his trial." *See* People v. Coleman, 52 Ill. 2d 470, 288 N.E.2d 396 (1972); People v. Morrissey, 52 Ill. 2d 418, 288 N.E.2d 397 (1972).

68. 440 U.S. 367 (1979).

69. *Id.* at 373–74. *See also* People v. Anderson, 73 Ill. App. 3d 948, 392 N.E.2d 174, 175 (5th Dist. 1979):

The obvious problem with *Argersinger* and *Scott* is that the constitutional protection, as interpreted, appears to require the trial judge to determine before trial if a sentence of imprisonment will be imposed if the accused is found guilty, because that determination triggers the defendant's right to counsel.

The statutory right under chapter 725, section 5/113-3(b) affords a somewhat different and more expansive protection because the statute provides for the assistance of counsel "in all cases, except where the penalty is a fine only."[70] Thus, probation would seem to be included in the Illinois statutory protection but not in the federal constitutional one. "[T]he plain meaning of this statutory provision . . . is that a trial court is precluded from imposing a penalty other than a fine on an indigent criminal defendant unless he has . . . appointed counsel or has waived that right."[71]

Since the defendant was not sentenced to a term of imprisonment, the State had no obligation to afford him counsel. It is not, as the defendant argues, the possibility of imprisonment upon conviction that determines when counsel must be provided or knowingly and understandingly waived by the defendant; rather, it is when a defendant is imprisoned that the court must have afforded him this right.

70. 725 ILCS 5/113-3(b). *See* People v. Dass, 226 Ill. App. 3d 562, 589 N.E.2d 1065, 1067 (2d Dist. 1992) (statutory right to counsel in criminal cases is broader than constitutional right).

71. People v. Morgese, 94 Ill. App. 3d 638, 418 N.E.2d 1124, 1127 (2d Dist. 1981): "[D]efendant herein, who was sentenced to a period of probation, was statutorily entitled to court-appointed counsel since she received a penalty other than a fine only." *Id. See also* People v. Sebag, 110 Ill. App. 3d 821, 443 N.E.2d 25 (2d Dist. 1982).

The First District disagrees with the reading of the statute. In *People v. Guice*, 83 Ill. App. 3d 914, 404 N.E.2d 261, 263 (1st Dist. 1979), *cert. denied,* 450 U.S. 968 (1981), the court interpreted *People v. Scott*, 68 Ill. 2d 269, 369 N.E.2d 881 (1977), *aff'd,* 440 U.S. 367 (1979), to hold that "unless the penalty imposed is imprisonment," counsel need not be afforded the indigent defendant. This seems to be a misreading of *Scott*, which stated: "Where the court imposes a penalty of a fine only, a defendant is not statutorily entitled to appointed counsel." *Scott*, 68 Ill. 2d 269, 369 N.E.2d at 883. *Scott* unlike the apparently plain wording of the statute, did not deal with the issue of counsel for a defendant sentenced to probation. *See* People v. Dass, 226 Ill. App. 3d 562, 589 N.E.2d 1065, 1067 (2d Dist. 1992) (no distinction is made under this section between a defendant who receives supervision and a defendant sentenced to probation or conditional discharge); People v. Kosyla, 143 Ill. App. 3d 937, 494 N.E.2d 945, 950 (2d Dist. 1986) (where one defendant is sentenced to one year conditional discharge and ordered to perform community service and co-defendant is sentenced to one year conditional discharge, required to attend correctional training institute, and pay a fine, both are entitled to court appointed counsel).

The determination of indigency is a frequent problem arising under section 113-3(b). The accused must be given a chance to establish his or her indigency, in part by the filing of an affidavit.[72] The failure of a trial court "to make an inquiry into the defendant's financial status before refusing to appoint counsel is a fatal flaw which requires reversal,"[73] though if the accused clearly declines the assistance of counsel, the court does not have to make a determination about indigency.[74] To establish indigency the accused need not be totally devoid of funds,[75] but he or she must lack "the financial resources on a practical basis to retain counsel."[76] Furthermore, the accused's ability to make bail does not relieve the trial court of determining through a hearing whether the accused is indigent.[77] Even the posting of large amounts of bond is insufficient to automatically prove that the accused can retain counsel; there must be an inquiry by the court.[78]

Once indigency is determined, the court will normally appoint the public defender, "whenever that course is feasible and not manifestly unfair to the defendant and would not lead to an undue delay in trial."[79] As noted above, the accused does not have a right to choose his or her counsel, except in the limited situation where the court has appointed counsel and then attempted to remove

---

72. *Sebag,* 110 Ill. App. 3d 821, 443 N.E.2d at 29. *But see* People v. Sims, 244 Ill. App. 3d 966, 612 N.E.2d 1011, 1025 (5th Dist. 1993) (where the defendant failed to file an affidavit listing assets and liabilities, employed private counsel, and posted cash bail of $40,000, the claim of indigency is negated and the defendant is not entitled to county assistance).

73. People v. Miller, 113 Ill. App. 3d 845, 447 N.E.2d 1060, 1061 (4th Dist. 1983). *See also Dass,* 226 Ill. App. 3d 562, 589 N.E.2d at 1067 (judge is required to investigate a defendant's financial situation when the defendant, who is to be sentenced to a penalty other than fine only, requests appointment of counsel).

74. People v. Anthony, 42 Ill. App. 3d 102, 355 N.E.2d 680 (1st Dist. 1976).

75. People v. Miller, 23 Ill. App. 3d 149, 318 N.E.2d 739, 741 (5th Dist. 1974).

76. People v. Morrison, 114 Ill. App. 3d 828, 449 N.E.2d 859, 861 (3d Dist. 1983), *superseded by statute on other grounds as stated in* People v. Whitfield, 146 Ill. App. 3d 322, 496 N.E.2d 743, 745–46 (2d Dist. 1986).

77. People ex rel. Baker v. Power, 60 Ill. 2d 151, 330 N.E.2d 857 (1975). *See also* People v. Cook, 81 Ill. 2d 176, 407 N.E.2d 56 (1980); People v. Eggers, 27 Ill. 2d 85, 188 N.E.2d 30 (1963).

78. People v. Wood, 91 Ill. App. 3d 414, 414 N.E.2d 759, 763 (5th Dist. 1980) (although making of bail did not indicate accused was ineligible for appointed counsel, gratuitous transfer of several parcels of land did so indicate), *cert. denied,* 454 U.S. 847 (1981).

79. People v. Kinion, 97 Ill. 2d 322, 454 N.E.2d 625, 628 (1983).

that counsel over the accused's objection.[80] However, there may be situations in which the accused's interests can be protected only through the appointment of counsel other than the public defender.[81] A potential conflict of interest caused by a public defender representing co-defendants may necessitate appointment of private counsel,[82] although the courts have taken a conservative approach to automatically finding a conflict of interest merely because antagonistic co-defendants are represented by assistant public defenders from the same office.[83] Dissatisfaction with the public defender's representation is not sufficient cause for the appointment of other counsel,[84] nor is any allegation that the client does not get to see the attorney often enough.[85] Rather, in all instances the accused must be able to demonstrate that his or her rights would

---

80. *People v. Davis*, 114 Ill. App. 3d 537, 449 N.E.2d 237 (1st Dist. 1983), presented an unusual situation. The accused first retained counsel. When his funds ran out, the court appointed the previously retained counsel. Disagreement between the appointed counsel and the court led to the counsel's removal and the declaration of a mistrial. When the case came up for retrial, the court refused the request of the accused to reappoint the removed attorney. The appellate court disagreed. "[F]or purposes of removal by the trial court, a court-appointed attorney may not be treated differently than privately retained counsel." *Id.*, 449 N.E.2d at 241. Thus, when the accused chooses to keep counsel that the court has appointed for him or her, he or she does have the limited right to the counsel of his or her choice.

81. People v. Adams, 195 Ill. App. 3d 870, 553 N.E.2d 3, 4 (5th Dist. 1990) (showing of prejudice is required before the court can appoint another counsel). *See* People v. Slaughter, 84 Ill. App. 3d 88, 404 N.E.2d 1058 (3d Dist. 1980) (attorney other than public defender can be appointed but only when prejudice to defendant shown, not at discretion of trial judge), *superseded by statute as stated in* People v. Hall, 114 Ill. 2d 376, 499 N.E.2d 1335, 1343 (1986); People v. Drew, 36 Ill. App. 3d 807, 345 N.E.2d 45 (1st Dist. 1976) (same), *superseded by statute as stated in* People v. Clark, 108 Ill. App. 3d 1071, 440 N.E.2d 387, 392 (1st Dist. 1982).

82. People v. White, 96 Ill. App. 3d 228, 421 N.E.2d 379, 380 (3d Dist. 1981).

83. *See* People v. Spicer, 79 Ill. 2d 173, 402 N.E.2d 169, 175 (1979), *cert. denied*, 446 U.S. 940 (1980), *superseded by statute on other grounds as stated in* People v. Young, 170 Ill. App. 3d 969, 524 N.E.2d 982, 988 (1st Dist. 1988); People v. Robinson, 79 Ill. 2d 147, 402 N.E.2d 157, 169 (1979). *See, e.g., In re* A.P., 277 Ill. App. 3d 593, 660 N.E.2d 1006 (4th Dist. 1996) (because of professional responsibility of attorneys under Rules of Professional Conduct, there is no per se conflict with appointing one assistant public defender to represent mother and another to represent children).

84. People v. Fitzpatrick, 124 Ill. App. 3d 1079, 465 N.E.2d 166, 168 (3d Dist. 1984); People v. Smith, 111 Ill. App. 3d 494, 444 N.E.2d 565, 568 (1st Dist. 1982).

85. People v. Spice, 120 Ill. App. 3d 103, 457 N.E.2d 1055, 1058 (4th Dist. 1983).

be prejudiced by representation by the public defender.[86] In no case will the indigent accused be permitted to use the right to appointed counsel to delay trial or impede the administration of justice.[87]

§4.08 — Payment of Appointed Counsel

Appointed counsel can expect to receive reasonable compensation for representing an indigent. In *People v. Johnson,* the Illinois Supreme Court definitively addressed the matter of "reasonable compensation" under section 113-3(c), at least with respect to counties other than Cook County:

> The formula for reasonable compensation should be the hourly fee normally charged for comparable trial court services, less an amount adequate to satisfy the *pro bono* factor. In determining what constitutes a reasonable fee, the trial court must consider a number of factors, including, but not limited to, time spent and services rendered, the attorney's skill and experience, complexity of the case, overhead costs, and expenses of trial. Another consideration is local conditions, which refers to the number of attorneys, in a given location, who could be called upon to perform *pro bono* work.[88]

To effect this formula the attorney is required to keep an itemized log of his or her services and the services of others on the case.[89] One court, in applying the *Johnson* formula, determined that an attorney's communications with the news media was not an activity "sufficiently related to the defense of the charges . . . to justify compensation," notwithstanding that the communications may have

---

86. *See* People v. Carlson, 79 Ill. 2d 564, 404 N.E.2d 233 (1980); People v. Greer, 79 Ill. 2d 103, 402 N.E.2d 203 (1980); People v. Speed, 106 Ill. App. 3d 890, 436 N.E.2d 712 (2d Dist. 1982), *superseded by statute on other grounds as stated in* People v. Pickens, 226 Ill. App. 3d 1001, 590 N.E.2d 535, 538 (4th Dist. 1992).

87. People v. Taylor, 101 Ill. 2d 508, 463 N.E.2d 705, 713, *cert. denied,* 469 U.S. 866 (1984); People v. Johnson, 45 Ill. 2d 38, 257 N.E.2d 3, 6 (1970).

88. People v. Johnson, 87 Ill. 2d 98, 429 N.E.2d 497, 500 (1981). The basis for providing reasonable compensation for appointed attorneys is the "need for increased representation," and "[t]he need for more effective representation," and "the inequitable burden of representation . . . in counties where there are few capable criminal defense attorneys willing to accept appointment." *Id.,* 429 N.E.2d at 499. *See also* People v. Johnson, 109 Ill. App. 3d 1135, 441 N.E.2d 946 (4th Dist. 1982) (same case as *People v. Johnson,* 87 Ill. 2d 98, 429 N.E.2d 497 (1981), on appeal from removal to circuit court, purports to explain Illinois Supreme Court's formula); *In re* Petition for Fees, 148 Ill. App. 3d 453, 499 N.E.2d. 624, 626 (1986).

89. *Johnson,* 87 Ill. 2d 98, 429 N.E.2d at 500.

335

been in the defendant's best interests.[90] "In counties with a population greater than 2,000,000" (Cook County, Illinois for example), appointed counsel is still apparently limited to the statutorily articulated hourly fee amounts.[91] Even privately retained counsel may be entitled to compensation by the county.[92]

In *People v. Love*,[93] the Illinois Supreme Court held that section 113-3.1 mandates that the trial judge conduct a hearing to determine the defendant's financial circumstances and ability to pay reimbursement for appointed counsel. That inquiry is required even where a cash bail bond had been posted for the defendant. The hearing must address the "foreseeable ability

---

90. People v. Wilson, 117 Ill. App. 3d 744, 453 N.E.2d 949, 953 (4th Dist. 1983). *But see Wilson*, 117 Ill. App. 3d 744, 453 N.E.2d at 954 (considering the complexity of the case, the fact that the defendant proceeded pro se, and in need of various items of lengthy record, photocopying expenses were properly awarded to the attorney).

91.   (c) . . . In counties with a population greater than 2,000,000, the court shall order the county treasurer of the county of trial to pay counsel other than the Public Defender a reasonable fee stated in the order and based upon a rate of compensation of not more than $40 for each hour spent while court is in session and not more than $30 for each hour otherwise spent representing a defendant, and such compensation shall not exceed $150 for each defendant represented in misdemeanor cases and $1250 in felony cases, in addition to expenses reasonably incurred as hereinafter in this Section provided, except that, in extraordinary circumstances, payment in excess of the limits herein stated may be made if the trial court certifies that such payment is necessary to provide fair compensation for protracted representation. A trial court may entertain the filing of this verified statement before the termination of the cause, and may order the provisional payment of sums during the pendency of the cause.

     725 ILCS 5/113-3(c). *But see* People v. Ashford, 162 Ill. App. 3d 212, 514 N.E.2d 1213, 1215 (5th Dist. 1987) (ceilings of $40 and $30 are not intended to be caps in counties having less than 2,000,000 population; judge did not abuse discretion in awarding an hourly rate of $35); People v. Brown, 154 Ill. App. 3d 692, 506 N.E.2d 1059, 1061–62 (4th Dist. 1987) (in determining reasonableness, a judge may consider the affidavit of the defendant, his financial resources, and monetary amounts in the statute); People v. Jones, 148 Ill. App. 3d 453, 499 N.E.2d 624, 626 (5th Dist. 1986) (hourly limits are not binding, but they must be given consideration on reasonableness).

92. People v. Camden, 206 Ill. App. 3d 1, 563 N.E.2d 1161, 1163 (5th Dist. 1990) (where private counsel represented a defendant with court's approval and an actual finding of the defendant's indigency did not appear on record, there was sufficient evidence to infer the defendant's unfortunate economic situation, so that private counsel was entitled to the same compensation as court-appointed counsel).

93. 177 Ill. 2d 550, 687 N.E.2d 32 (1997).

of the defendant to pay reimbursement as well as the costs of the representation provided."[94] At issue was the procedure for ordering defendant to pay reimbursement for legal services by appointed counsel. In *Love*, the trial court ordered defendant to pay for his legal services out of a bond that had been provided by a third party without holding a hearing on the issue of defendant's ability to pay reimbursement. The appellate court found that the trial court's decision ordering reimbursement was improper because a hearing was mandated by section 113-3.1. The supreme court agreed.

First, the court rejected the state's contention that the section simply permits the trial court to conduct such a hearing when it deems a hearing necessary. According to the court, the language of the statute clearly is mandatory. It plainly requires the trial judge to conduct a hearing on defendant's ability to pay reimbursement. Had the court interpreted the statute as the state urged, absurd results would occur. The statute would compel the trial judge to consider specific factors if it conducted a hearing, yet, would not compel a hearing in the first place. Thus, the trial court could avoid considering defendant's financial ability to pay for reimbursement by simply deeming a hearing unnecessary.[95] This, of course, would be illogical.

Further, the state's interpretation was quickly dispelled by the legislative history of the reimbursement provision. The prior version did not require any consideration of defendant's financial ability to pay. It was found unconstitutional in *People v. Cook*.[96] The *Love* court concluded that the *Cook* court "established that due process requires a hearing into a defendant's ability to pay reimbursement as a precondition to ordering such reimbursement."[97] Consequently, the legislative intent in enacting the current provision was to correct the constitutional violation of the predecessor statute and require, not merely allow, a hearing on defendant's financial ability to pay reimbursement. Moreover, the court found that the state could point to no case that supported its position. Conversely, the appellate court had consistently held that a hearing is required.[98]

The court further rejected the state's contention that the hearing could be dispensed with when a bond was posted because the bond "conclusively establishe[s] defendant's ability to pay reimbursement."[99] Again, *Cook* mandated a contrary result. One ground upon which the prior statute was found unconstitutional was its different treatment of defendants who had posted bond

---

94. *Id.*, 687 N.E.2d at 38.

95. *Id.*, 687 N.E.2d at 35.

96. 81 Ill. 2d 176, 407 N.E.2d 56 (1980).

97. *Love*, 177 Ill. 2d 550, 687 N.E.2d at 36.

98. *Id.*, 687 N.E.2d at 36–37.

99. *Id.*, 687 N.E.2d at 37.

and those who had not.[100] There was nothing in the language of the statute that demonstrated different treatment was the intent. Whether defendant posts a bond or not has nothing to do with his or her ability to pay reimbursement, particulary in light of the fact that often the bond is posted by a third person, a factor the trial court is expected to take into consideration when assessing defendant's ability to pay.[101]

§ 4.09 — Expert Witness Fees

The Sixth Amendment right to effective assistance of counsel for indigents means little if counsel is unable to secure expert witnesses in appropriate cases. Accordingly, chapter 725, section 5/113-3(d) provides for the payment of expert witness fees, as long as they do not exceed $250 in capital cases and $50 in other cases.[102] On the basis of constitutional requirements for a fair trial for indigents as well as nonindigents, however, the Illinois Supreme Court has relaxed the statutory amount. Where an expert "might be necessary to establish a defense" in a noncapital felony case, the accused is "entitled to a reasonable fee" to pay for the expert's services.[103] Recognizing the high cost of expert witness fees, the supreme court cautioned:

> We therefore interpret the $250 limitation set forth in section 113-3(d) . . . not as a rigid upper boundary but as a general caution to trial courts that expert fees in excess of that amount are frequently not reasonably required to establish points necessary to a client's defense and as a warning that any excess which is requested should be scrutinized for abuse with special care.[104]

---

100. *Id.*

101. *Id.*, 687 N.E.2d 37–38.

102.   (d) In capital cases, in addition to counsel, if the court determines that the defendant is indigent the court may, upon the filing with the court of a verified statement of services rendered, order the county treasurer of the county of trial to pay necessary expert witnesses for defendant reasonable compensation stated in the order not to exceed $250 for each defendant.

725 ILCS 5/113-3(d).

103. People v. Lawson, 163 Ill. 2d 187, 644 N.E.2d 1172 (1994); People v. Watson, 36 Ill. 2d 228, 221 N.E.2d 645, 649 (1966); People v. Evans, 271 Ill. App. 3d 495, 648 N.E.2d 964 (1st Dist. 1995); People v. Dickerson, 239 Ill. App. 3d 951, 606 N.E.2d 762 (4th Dist. 1992).

104. People v. Kinion, 97 Ill. 2d 322, 454 N.E.2d 625, 631 (1983). A concern of the court was the elimination of the distinction between the expert services available to the public defender and those available to private counsel. In some instances, the appointment of private counsel might serve as a windfall to the county if the

The importance of *Kinion,* in addition to recognizing the need for money amounts that exceed the statutory amount, is the admonition that the court expects appointed counsel to petition for the fees before, rather than after, expending the money.

> We agree . . . that the best practice . . . is, where feasible, to require appointed attorneys to petition the trial court for any amount anticipated to be in excess of $250 before they spend it, and that attorneys who spend any excess which the court does not authorize should run the substantial risk of not receiving compensation for it.[105]

In *People v. Lawson,*[106] the Illinois Supreme Court reaffirmed *Kinion's* suggested procedure for obtaining funds. However the court reiterated that if an indigent accused demonstrates his "constitutional entitlement" for expert testimony, the fact that the request for funds does not identify the particular expert or give an estimate of costs is no bar to authorization for funds to be expended.[107]

To obtain the services of an expert the defense must show that the services are "necessary to prove a crucial issue in the case" and that the defense will be prejudiced without the expert's services.[108] Thus, fees for a psychiatrist were denied where the doctor indicated he would not be testifying about the accused's mental condition at the time of the killing,[109] and in a case where the court authorized fees for a weapons expert, it denied fees for a physician because the testimony was "not shown to have been sufficiently related to the defendant's theory of defense."[110]

The court has emphasized, however, that funds for experts will be authorized only where the testimony "goes to the heart of the defense."[111] "The touch-

---

$250 limit remained in effect, because it would cost the county less to pay the $250 maximum in these cases where a public defender would reasonably have spent more on expert witnesses.

105. People v. Kinion, 97 Ill. 2d 322, 454 N.E.2d 625 (1983).

106. 163 Ill. 2d 187, 644 N.E.2d 1172, 1192 (1994).

107. *Id.*

108. People v. Glover, 49 Ill. 2d 78, 273 N.E.2d 367, 370 (1971). In *Evans,* an expert on battered woman's syndrome was "necessary" for the defendant to establish a defense. People v. Evans, 271 Ill. App. 3d 495, 648 N.E.2d 964, 970 (1st Dist. 1995).

109. People v. Vines, 43 Ill. App. 3d 986, 358 N.E.2d 72, 74–75 (4th Dist. 1976).

110. People *ex rel.* Walker v. Pate, 53 Ill. 2d 485, 292 N.E.2d 387, 393 (1973).

111. People v. Keene, 169 Ill. 2d 1, 660 N.E.2d 901, 905 (1995), *cert. denied,* 519 U.S. 828 (1996).

stone," wrote the court, "is not with what is useful, helpful, valuable, or even important to the defense, but what is 'crucial' to it."[112]

Finally, although the statute does not provide for investigator's fees, some courts have reasoned that money for such services must be provided when an investigator is necessary to prove a crucial issue.[113] As in so many other instances, creative lawyering may determine what experts the court will permit the defense to secure, at whose expense, and how much they will be paid.

In addition to section 113-3(d), there are a number of other provisions in the criminal code dealing with the procuring and payment of experts in behalf of the defense. These include appointment of experts to determine in a pretrial setting if a bona fide doubt of fitness of the defendant exists,[114] or if the defendant is mentally fit to stand trial,[115] physically fit to stand trial,[116] sexually dangerous,[117] insane,[118] or for any other "necessary" purpose.[119]

The issue of the appointment of a psychiatrist for an indigent defendant arose in *Ake v. Oklahoma*,[120] in which the United States Supreme Court found that when a defendant makes a preliminary showing that his or her mental condition at the time of the offense is likely to be a significant factor at trial, constitutionally the state must provide the defense access to a psychiatrist at its expense if the defendant cannot afford one.[121] Illinois cases have extended the *Ake* rule to nonpsychiatric expert witnesses as well.[122]

---

112. *Id.,* 660 N.E.2d at 905.

113. People v. Wilson, 117 Ill. App. 3d 744, 453 N.E.2d 949, 954 (4th Dist. 1983). *See also* People v. Veal, 110 Ill. App. 3d 919, 443 N.E.2d 605 (1st Dist. 1982).

114. 725 ILCS 5/104-11(b).

115. 725 ILCS 5/104-13(a), (e).

116. 725 ILCS 5/104-13(b), (e).

117. 725 ILCS 205/4, 205/4.02.

118. 725 ILCS 5/115-6.

119. 725 ILCS 5/113-3.1(d), (e).

120. 470 U.S. 68 (1985).

121. *Id.* at 74. *See* People v. Evans, 271 Ill. App. 3d 495, 648 N.E.2d 964, 970 (1st Dist. 1995) (trial court erred in denying defendant's request for a fee for an expert witness on battered woman syndrome even though the expert did not testify at trial because the defendant pled guilty; the testimony was necessary to defendant's defense and there is no requirement that a witness must actually testify to be paid).

122. *See* People v. Lawson, 163 Ill. 2d 187, 644 N.E.2d 1172, 1189–90 (1994) (trial court abused discretion in denying a defendant's motion for funds for an expert in fingerprinting and shoeprinting where the expert testimony was necessary to defend; the defendant is not required to supply the court with the name of the expert he or she wishes to employ and an estimate of fee when making a request

§ 4.10 Bail: Generally

Almost thirty-five years ago, one leading commentator characterized the American bail system as scandalous. "It typifies what is worst and most cynical about our system of justice. It discriminates against the poor . . . [and] is to a great degree a socially countenanced ransom of people . . . [which] . . . affects millions directly each year."[123] He observed that "[w]hen the defendant who cannot afford bail goes to jail before trial [he is not only deprived of his freedom, but] loses his present earning capacity, and often his job, [and] his family suffers."[124] He concluded that "[d]efendants who can afford bail are convicted less frequently, and receive lesser sentences when they are convicted[125] . . . [because] . . . a defendant who is released before his trial and is able to maintain his family life and job would be likely to receive more favorable consideration for probation by virtue of his accomplishments on pre-trial release."[126]

---

for funds); People v. Kegley, 175 Ill. App. 3d 335, 529 N.E.2d 1118, 1122–23 (2d Dist. 1988) (defendant denied due process when trial court failed to appoint psychiatrist to determine defendant's mental condition at time offense occurred where defendant was indigent and made preliminary showing that he suffered mental problems). *But see* People v. Finkle, 214 Ill. App. 3d 290, 573 N.E.2d 381, 385 (2d Dist. 1991) (defendant not denied due process when trial judge denied request for appointment of psychiatrist to assist him at recovery hearing where court found treating physicians at institution where defendant was committed to be objective and fair in assisting him); People v. Clankie, 180 Ill. App. 3d 726, 536 N.E.2d 176, 179–80 (2d Dist. 1989) (trial court's denial of defendant's request for appointment of handwriting expert not error because of untimeliness of defendant's motion along with his failure to seek a ruling on the motion at hearing).

In *People v. Keene*, 169 Ill. 2d 1, 660 N.E.2d 901 (1995), *cert. denied*, 519 U.S. 828 (1996), the court found no error in denying defendant's request for appointment of a pathologist to counter evidence that a left-handed person murdered the victim, because the state's case did not turn on proof that the act could only have been done by a left-handed person. *Id.*, 660 N.E.2d at 906. Thus, the expert was not crucial to defendant's case. Moreover, the state's expert did not definitively state that only a left-handed person could have committed the crime. In this case, the primary evidence against defendant was the state's witness' testimony that defendant admitted to committing the crime. This testimony could not be countered by any testimony from a defense pathologist. *Id.*

123. R. GOLDFARB, RANSOM: A CRITIQUE OF THE AMERICAN BAIL SYSTEM, 4–5 (1965).

124. GOLDFARB at 32.

125. GOLDFARB at 33.

126. GOLDFARB at 39.

> The jailed defendant [suffers because he] is able to work with his attorneys, investigators, and witnesses only in limited ways and at limited times . . . . He cannot help seek out evidence, witnesses, and generally aid his own defense. He is locked up in depressing jails with the dregs of society. His property is taken . . . . [A] defendant who is brought into court from an adjacent cell, who has spent a long time in jail, who has not been as able to participate in his defense prior to trial, and who is publicly escorted . . . by a guard, bears some stigma before the court and jury which is not the case with a defendant who casually enters the courtroom, well-groomed, and accompanied by his family and attorney. And most important of all these disadvantages . . . [is] the basic, spiritual loss to the imprisoned defendant.[127]

It is obvious that the effects of an order of no bail or excessively high bail set for the presumptively innocent accused are devastating to the person who remains jailed. A motion to reduce bail is of paramount importance and should be filed as soon as it is practicable to secure the release of the defendant on bail. This will also serve other legitimate purposes, namely as a vehicle for discovery, a method of perpetuating testimony of witnesses, and a sounding out of the prosecution and the judge about the strength of the prosecution and possibly the fairness of the judge.

Thirty-five years since Goldfarb's observation, the law of bail has undergone radical changes in Illinois. By virtue of the passage of a public referendum in November 1986, authorizing amendment of the state constitution, Illinois joined the federal government and increasing number of states in allowing the detention of some criminal defendants without bond when it appears to the court that pretrial release would pose a danger to the community.[128] The constitutional mandate has been implemented by acts defining which offenses may be nonbailable,[129] considerations that should affect the judge's decision on release or nonrelease,[130] the nature of the hearing that must be held to afford due process rights in the bail decision,[131] and the admissibility of statements from the alleged victim.[132]

Article I, section 9 of the Illinois Constitution provides, inter alia, that all persons charged with the commission of an offense

---

127. GOLDFARB at 41–42.

128. ILL. CONST. art. I, § 9.

129. 725 ILCS 5/110-4.

130. 725 ILCS 5/110-6.1(d).

131. 725 ILCS 5/110-6.1(c).

132. 725 ILCS 5/110-5.

shall be bailable by sufficient sureties, except for the following offenses where the proof is evident or the presumption great: capital offenses; offenses for which a sentence of life imprisonment may be imposed as a consequence of conviction; and felony offenses for which a sentence of imprisonment, without conditional and revocable release, shall be imposed by law as a consequence of conviction, when the court, after a hearing, determines that the release of the offender would pose a real and present threat to the physical safety of any person.[133]

For determining whether pretrial bail is to be set, and how much, cases can be broken down into eight categories:

1. potential capital cases;[134]

2. crimes for which life imprisonment is a possibility;[135]

3. felonies which carry with them mandatory prison sentences upon conviction and when the court has determined that the defendant poses a "real and present threat to the physical safety of any person";[136]

4. felonies which carry with them mandatory prison sentences upon conviction but no physical safety threat determination has been made;[137]

5. stalking or aggravated stalking cases when the court has made a physical safety threat determination regarding the alleged victim;[138]

6. certain drug offenses;[139]

7. certain traffic and conservation offenses, ordinance violations and petty offenses, and certain misdemeanors;[140] and

8. all other misdemeanors and felonies.[141]

In all instances, regardless of the type of offense, the police must inform, even if it is by the posting of rights in the station, the arrestees of their rights relative

---

133. ILL. CONST. art. I, § 9.

134. 725 ILCS 5/110-4(a).

135. Id.

136. Id., 5/110-5, 5/110-6.1.

137. 725 ILCS 5/110-4(a).

138. Id., 5/110-5, 5-110-6.3.

139. 725 ILCS 5/110-4(a), 5/110-5.

140. 725 ILCS 5/110-4(a), 5/110-5(c) and (d).

141. 725 ILCS 5/110-4(a).

to bail.[142] Intentional or knowing failure to post the required rights information subjects the offending officer to criminal prosecution.[143] What, then, are the applicable provisions?

When an individual is charged with a capital offense, or an offense punishable by life imprisonment, or an offense for which there is mandatory incarceration on conviction, there is no automatic right to bail. Rather, with respect to offenses for which the defendant could receive the death penalty or life imprisonment, the defendant has the burden of establishing his or her right to bail[144] by demonstrating to the court that there is neither evident proof nor a great presumption of guilt based on the evidence that will be elicited at trial.[145] Assuming that the defendant sustains this burden, the remaining statutory provisions, which are discussed below, govern the amount of bail and any conditions attached thereto.[146] If the defendant fails to meet his burden, both statutorily and constitutionally, he will be incarcerated subject to an order of no bail.[147]

In addition to those defendants who are subject of an order of no bail in connection with capital offenses are those defendants who are charged with "felony offenses for which a sentence of imprisonment, without conditional and revocable release shall be imposed by law as a consequence of conviction . . . ."[148] Legislation has also included stalking and aggravated stalking in this category of nonbailable offenses.[149] An order of "no bail" will be imposed if the following conditions are met:

1.   The state must file a verified petition in which it alleges that the defendant is charged with a felony offense for which a sentence of imprisonment, without probation, periodic imprisonment, or conditional discharge is required by law on conviction, and that "the defendant's admission to bail poses a real and present threat to the physical safety of any person or persons."[150]

---

142. 725 ILCS 5/103-7; People v. Seymour, 80 Ill. App. 3d 221, 398 N.E.2d 1191, 1196 (1st Dist. 1979), *rev'd on other grounds,* 84 Ill. 2d 24, 416 N.E.2d 1070, 1077 (1981).

143. 725 ILCS 5/103-8.

144. 725 ILCS 5/110-4(b).

145. *Id.*

146. 725 ILCS 5/110-5.

147. Ill. Const. art. I, § 9; 725 ILCS 5/110-4.

148. 725 ILCS 5/110-4.

149. 725 ILCS 5/110-6.3.

150. 725 ILCS 5/110-6.1(a). *See also* 725 ILCS 5/110-6.3(a) (stalking and aggravated stalking).

2. The court must conduct a hearing.[151]

3. The court, after the hearing, must determine that "the proof is evident or the presumption great that the defendant has committed" the type of felony that requires mandatory incarceration on conviction.[152]

4. The court must determine that the defendant poses a "real and present threat to the physical safety of any person or persons."[153]

5. The court must determine that "no condition or combination of conditions set forth in Subsection (b) Section 110-10 of this Article can reasonably assure the physical safety of any other person or persons."[154]

Under the statute, the state has the burden of establishing that the defendant "presents a real and present threat to the physical safety of any person or persons."[155] Unlike the specific provision with respect to capital or life imprisonment sentences, however, the statute is silent as to who has the burden of proving either the presence or absence of evident proof or great presumption that the defendant is guilty of the offense. The statute being silent, and the state being the movant, it would seem that the state has the burden of establishing that the proof is evident and the presumption great, as well as the burden of establishing the dangerousness of the person involved.

The balance of the statute, which should be closely scrutinized by counsel, establishes the procedures that the court must follow,[156] and provides the defendant with some *minimal* rights. The defendant has the right to counsel, the right to testify and present witnesses in his own behalf, and the right to cross-examine any witnesses that the state *might* call. The court, *in its discretion,* may "compel the appearance of a complaining witness," although the witness may not be called for the purpose of impeaching his or her credibility. The rules of discovery do not apply. The traditional rules of evidence do not apply. However, the defendant is entitled to get a copy of any statements relied on by the state in its petition. Any statements made at the hearing, while not

---

151. 725 ILCS 5/110-6.1(a)(2). *See also* 725 ILCS 5/110-6.3(b) (stalking and aggravated stalking).

152. 725 ILCS 5/110-6.1(b)(1). *See also* 725 ILCS 5/110-6.3(b)(1) (stalking and aggravated stalking).

153. 725 ILCS 5/110-6.1(b)(2). *See also* 725 ILCS 5/110-6.3(b)(2) (stalking and aggravated stalking).

154. 725 ILCS 5/110-6.1(b)(3). *See also* 725 ILCS 5/110-6.3(b)(4) (stalking and aggravated stalking).

155. 725 ILCS 5/110-4(c).

156. 725 ILCS 5/110-6.1(c). *See also* 725 ILCS 5/110-6.3(c) (stalking and aggravated stalking).

admissible in the state's case-in-chief, are admissible for purposes of impeachment or perjury prosecutions. Finally, even if evidence (including a confession) was illegally seized and would be subject to a motion to suppress, that issue cannot be considered by the court in connection with the bail determination.[157]

Counsel should also note statutory provisions dealing with bail violations which include:

> When a defendant is at liberty on bail or his own recognizance on a felony charge and fails to appear in court as directed, the court shall issue a warrant for the arrest of such person . . . . with a directive to . . . hold such person without bail and to deliver such person before the court for further proceedings. A defendant who is arrested or surrenders within (30) days of the issuance of such warrant shall not be bailable in the case in question unless he shows by the preponderance of the evidence that his failure to appear was not intentional.[158]

The court, in considering the amount of bail to set (if the court is going to set any bail at all), should take into consideration a number of factors, including

> whether the . . . [offense charged involved the] use of or threatened use of violence[;] . . . whether the offense involved corruption of public officials or employees[;] whether there was physical harm or threats of physical harm to any public official, public employee, judge, prosecutor, juror or witness, senior citizen, child or handicapped person[;] whether evidence shows that during the offense or during the arrest the defendant possessed or used a firearm [or other described weaponry][;] whether the evidence shows that the offense committed was related to or in furtherance of the criminal activities of an organized gang or was motivated by defendant's membership in or allegiance to an organized gang[;] the condition of the victim[;] any written statement submitted by the victim or proffer or representation by the State regarding the impact which the alleged criminal conduct has had on the victim and the victim's concern, if any with further contact with the defendant if release on bail[;] whether the offense was based on racial, religious, sexual orientation or ethnic hatred[;] . . . the likelihood of conviction, the sentence applicable upon conviction[;] . . . whether there exists motivation or ability to flee[;] whether there is verification as to prior residence, education, . . . the consent of the defendant to periodic drug testing in accordance with Section 110-6.5[; extradition status][;] . . . whether . . . the defendant is engaged in significant

---

157. 725 ILCS 5/110-6.1(c)(1)(A). *See also* 725 ILCS 5/110-6.3(c)(1)(A) (stalking and aggravated stalking).

158. 725 ILCS 5/110-3.

possession, manufacture, or delivery of a controlled substance or cannabis, either individually or in consort with others[;] whether at the time of the offense charged he was on bond or pre-trial release pending trial, probation, periodic imprisonment or conditional discharge . . . .[159]

There are a multitude of other factors that defense counsel should study.[160] Additionally there are significant changes with respect to the bailability of defendants who are charged with offenses while on bond in connection with other cases,[161] including the fact that when there is a motion to revoke or increase bail information used by the court in its finding or offered in connection with hearings for increase or revocation of bail may be by way of proffer based upon reliable information offered by the state or defendant. All evidence shall be admissible if it is relevant and reliable regardless of whether it would be admissible under the rules of evidence applicable at criminal trials.[162]

With respect to traffic and conservation offenses, ordinance violations, and some misdemeanors the Illinois Supreme Court has promulgated specific rules[163] in recognizing that some offenses warrant release of the alleged offender without undue delay when, "because of the hour or the circumstances, it is not practicable to bring the accused before a judge."[164] Offenses that fall within these rules are governed by specific schedules of amounts of bail (or the posting of "bond cards" or driver's licenses in lieu of money amounts), as are procedures by which bail may be posted, revoked, increased, decreased, forfeited, or returned.[165] These rules do not apply if the alleged offender is actually brought before a judge,[166] nor do they preclude the officer from issuing a

---

159. 725 ILCS 5/110-5.

160. 725 ILCS 5/110-5. The statute also includes as factors a defendant's consent to periodic drug testing and whether the offense was gang related. *See, e.g.*, People v. Brooks, 251 Ill. App. 3d 927, 623 N.E.2d 1380, 1383 (4th Dist. 1993) (conviction for home invasion and aggravated battery of a disabled 68-year-old stroke victim and the defendant's five previous felony convictions were valid reasons for denial of bail).

161. 725 ILCS 5/110-6.

162. 725 ILCS 5/110-6(e)(2).

163. S. Ct. Rule 501 *et seq.*

164. ILL. COMP. STAT. ANN. ILCS S. Ct. Rules 526–28, Note to Rules (Smith-Hurd 1992).

165. S. Ct. Rules 501-56.

166. ILL. COMP. STAT. ANN. ILCS S. Ct. Rules 526-28, Note to Rules (Smith-Hurd 1992).

"Notice to Appear in an appropriate case [citation omitted]."[167] The rules also do not preclude counsel from causing the matter to be heard by a judge with a view toward reducing the rule-scheduled bond amount. In most cases[168] where the scheduled amount of bail is $750 or more, the 10 percent provisions of section 5/110-7[169] apply.[170]

With respect to felonies, including capital offenses for which the defendant has met the burden of demonstrating a right to bail and misdemeanors not specifically articulated in the Supreme Court Rules,[171] the court, in setting bail, should consider a multitude of factors set forth in section 110-5, which include:

1. The existence of doubt about the defendant's guilt;[172]

2. The likelihood that the defendant will appear in court as required;[173]

3. The character of the defendant;[174]

4. The nature of the offense charged;[175]

5. The defendant's past criminal acts and conduct;[176]

6. The financial ability of the defendant;[177]

7. Consent of defendant to periodic drug testing;[178] and

8. Whether the offense committed was related to or in furtherance of criminal activities or an organized gang or motivated by defendant's membership or allegiance to an organized gang.

---

167. ILL. COMP. STAT. ANN. ILCS S. Ct. Rules 526-28, Note to Rules (Smith-Hurd 1992).

168. Not covered are certain truck violations.

169. 725 ILCS 5/110-7.

170. S. Ct. Rule 530.

171. S. Ct. Rules 501-56.

172. People v. Ealy, 49 Ill. App. 3d 922, 365 N.E.2d 149, 157 (1st Dist. 1977).

173. *Id.*

174. *Id.*

175. 725 ILCS 5/110-5(a); People v. Saunders, 122 Ill. App. 3d 922, 461 N.E.2d 1006 (2d Dist. 1984).

176. 725 ILCS 5/110-5(a); People v. Ealy, 49 Ill. App. 3d 922, 365 N.E.2d 149 (1st Dist. 1977).

177. 725 ILCS 5/110-5(a); People v. Saunders, 122 Ill. App. 3d 922, 461 N.E.2d 1006 (2d Dist. 1984).

178. 725 ILCS 5/110-6.5.

In cases involving the possession or delivery of cannabis or controlled substances,[179] the street value of the drugs must also be considered.[180]

In all cases the amount of bail should be sufficient to assure compliance with the bail-bond conditions[181] and commensurate with the nature of the offense charged,[182] but it must not be oppressive.[183] Although excessive bail may not be imposed to prevent an accused from being released on bail,[184] what is excessive or oppressive will be determined on the facts of each individual case.[185] In cases where a fine is the only possible penalty, however, the amount of bail set cannot be more than double the potential assessment.[186]

In addition to setting the amount of bail, courts are granted broad authority in the setting of specific terms and conditions of bail. These include requiring the accused to appear in court[187] and to seek court permission to leave the jurisdiction.[188] Also provided are the procedures by which bail may be increased, decreased, or revoked,[189] assuming with rare exception[190] that the movant has given the opposing side reasonable notice.[191]

---

179. Controlled substance is defined in the Cannabis Control Act, as amended, in 720 ILCS 550/1, or the Illinois Controlled Substances Act, as amended, in 720 ILCS 570/100.

180. 725 ILCS 5/110-5(b)(4). Street value is determined by the court on the basis of police testimony and any other testimony needed.

181. Section 5/110-10 provides bail bond conditions. *See* 725 ILCS 5/110-10. *See, e.g.,* People v. Olson, 241 Ill. App. 3d 488, 608 N.E.2d 913, 917 (4th Dist. 1993) (in delivery of controlled substance prosecution, defendant's current drug use relevant to bond consideration).

182. 725 ILCS 5/110-5(b).

183. 725 ILCS 5/110-5(b)(2).

184. People v. Ealy, 49 Ill. App. 3d 922, 365 N.E.2d 149, 158 (1st Dist. 1977).

185. In *People v. Ealy,* the court held that a $50,000 bail set for an unfit defendant charged with robbery was excessive and obviously set solely to detain the defendant. However, in *People v. Freeman,* 130 Ill. App. 2d 722, 265 N.E.2d 394 (4th Dist. 1970), the court held that a $5,000 bail bond was not excessive where the defendant and five others were arrested and charged with a theft over $150.

186. 725 ILCS 5/110-5(c).

187. 725 ILCS 5/110-10(a)(1).

188. 725 ILCS 5/110-10(a)(3).

189. 725 ILCS 5/110-6.

190. If the state, by verified application for a warrant, alleges "facts or circumstances constituting a violation or threatened violation of any of the conditions of the bail bond," the reasonable notice requirement is dispensed with. 725 ILCS 5/110-6(d), (e).

191. 725 ILCS 5/110-6(d).

The Illinois bail provisions[192] have five other sections that need special consideration by defense counsel: (1) the 10 percent provision;[193] (2) section 5/110-2,[194] which allows a defendant to be released without having to post any cash amount as bail; (3) section 5/110-8[195] by which a defendant can post certain types of property as security for bail; (4) sections dealing with return of the posted money upon completion of the case;[196] and (5) forfeiture provisions.[197]

In drafting Article 110, the legislative committee considered three fundamental premises as underlying the setting of bail:

> (1) Factual studies prove that the greater majority of persons released on bail have no intention of violating bail and will appear for trial.

> (2) To the extent that pecuniary loss is a deterrent, such financial loss should be minimized in the case of the person who appears for trial.

> (3) A person who will jump bail is not deterred by the prospect of pecuniary loss to himself or anyone else so that other deterrents are required.[198]

The five sections given special consideration in the remainder of this chapter are the legislative embodiment of those three premises.

Section 110-7[199] allows a defendant to post as bail, instead of the actual cash amount set by the court, 10 percent of that cash amount, and in any event, no less than 25 dollars.[200] An obvious caveat is that the client and his or her family must be advised that they do not need to post the amount of money they heard the judge set from the bench, but rather only 10 percent of that amount.

In some circumstances the cash bail amount set by the court may be so high that even the "financially better off" accused may be unable to quickly obtain

---

192. 725 ILCS 5/110-1; S. Ct. Rule 501 *et seq.*

193. 725 ILCS 5/110-7(a).

194. 725 ILCS 5/110-2.

195. 725 ILCS 5/110-8.

196. 725 ILCS 5/110-7(f).

197. 725 ILCS 5/110-7(g), (h).

198. ILL. COMP. STAT. ANN. 725 ILCS 5/110-2, Committee Comments (Smith-Hurd 1992).

199. 725 ILCS 5/110-7.

200. 725 ILCS 5/110-7(a).

the necessary funds. Such a defendant may wish to avail himself or herself of section 110-8[201] where stocks, bonds, and real estate documents may be deposited with the clerk of the court in lieu of the cash amount set. One problem with the deposit of such property is the rapid assessment of actual value that must be provided to the clerk.[202] Of perhaps greater significance are the potential consequences that attach to noncompliance with the bail bond conditions, including actual loss of the property.[203] A client with substantial property might be well advised to secure a conventional loan on the property which will upon bail revocation or forfeiture admittedly subject the defendant or his or her family to loss of the money posted but not to loss of the property itself.

A third area of special concern to the defense practitioner is the procedures by which the money posted as bail may be returned, either to the client or to the attorney as part or all of his or her fee.[204] Upon completion of the case, or

---

201. 725 ILCS 5/110-8.

202. 725 ILCS 5/110-8.

203. 725 ILCS 5/110-8(h).

204. 725 ILCS 5/110-7(f). *See* People v. Mompier, 276 Ill. App. 3d 393, 657 N.E.2d 1190, 1195 (1st Dist. 1995) (Illinois Department of Revenue's lien against defendant's bail was invalid because it was posted by a third party); People v. Balaj, 265 Ill. App. 3d 1070, 638 N.E.2d 377, 383 (1st Dist. 1994) (judge did not abuse discretion in awarding a refund to the defendant's trial counsel; the record corroborated the attorney's claim that those who posted bond and paid the retainer planned to pay the fee from their refund and the defendant knew of this agreement); People v. Pino, 230 Ill. App. 3d 802, 596 N.E.2d 36, 37 (1st Dist. 1992) (where bail is forfeited, the judge is not obligated to award an attorney the full amount of bail deposit, less court costs, as a fee for representation).

Bail posted under this provision can also be used to pay fines and court costs. *See* People v. Dale, 112 Ill. 2d 460, 493 N.E.2d 1060, 1061 (1986) (an attorney with the right to bail deposit can only receive the amount repayable to the defendant, however, the amount is first subject to court costs and fines); People v. Hans, 221 Ill. App. 3d 82, 581 N.E.2d 712, 714 (5th Dist. 1991) (judge did not err in ordering the bond applied to outstanding court costs in the defendant's other criminal cases); People v. Markovich, 195 Ill. App. 3d 999, 552 N.E.2d 1232, 1236 (5th Dist. 1990) (bail posted under 10% provision is presumed to be posted by the defendant and can be used to pay fines despite a third-party claim on the funds); People v. Owens, 174 Ill. App. 3d 156, 528 N.E.2d 446, 448–49 (4th Dist. 1988) (where the defendant is ordered to pay a fine, a petition to revoke periodic imprisonment is filed, and bond at issue is posted in the same case, there is no separate cause, merely an extension of the case in which the fine is ordered; therefore, no error exists in the judge's order directing bond to be applied to court costs and the fine previously levied against defendant); People v. Foreman, 153 Ill. App. 3d 346, 505 N.E.2d 731, 739 (2d Dist.) (judge properly refused to return

at least when the defendant is discharged from any obligations of bail,[205] 90 percent of the money posted, "unless the court orders otherwise will be returned to the accused or the defendant's designee by an assignment executed at the time the bail amount is deposited."[206] Note that although the court may refund to the accused an amount greater than 90 percent (but in my experience the request is seldom made by the defense counsel), "in no event shall the amount retained by the clerk as . . . costs be less than $25."[207]

The final significant statutory provision that relates to releasing a defendant on bail pending disposition of his or her case is section 110-2.[208] It allows the accused to be released on his or her own recognizance (that is, his or her signature with a money amount stated but no money or property actually having to be posted) "[w]hen from all the circumstances the court is of the opinion that the defendant will appear as required."[209] Counsel, in moving the court for release of the accused on his or her own recognizance, should emphasize that the recognizance provisions "shall be liberally construed to effectuate the purpose of relying upon contempt of court proceedings or criminal sanctions instead of financial loss to assure the appearance of the defendant."[210] Other than not having to post cash or property as security for his or her appearance, an accused released on his or her own recognizance is subject to all of the terms, conditions, and obligations set forth in the bail statute.

Of final concern to the defendant, whether released on recognizance or on money or property posted, is what happens if he or she fails to comply with the bail conditions. The possibilities are numerous. The amount of bail actually posted may be forfeited,[211] and a civil judgment for the full amount of bail set is entered.[212]

---

bail provided by the defendant's uncle, applying it instead to court costs and $100,000 fine levied against the defendant), *cert. denied,* 484 U.S. 854 (1987).

205. The amount posted at trial may be posted by the defendant as bail on appeal, if the court so orders. 725 ILCS 5/110-7(d).

206. 725 ILCS 5/110-7(f).

207. 725 ILCS 5/110-7(f); People v. Groleau, 156 Ill. App. 3d 742, 509 N.E.2d 1337, 1344 (2d Dist. 1987) (judge has discretion to return more than 90% of the posted bond); People v. Fox, 130 Ill. App. 3d 795, 475 N.E.2d 1, 2 (1st Dist. 1985) (same).

208. 725 ILCS 5/110-2.

209. 725 ILCS 5/110-2.

210. 725 ILCS 5/110-2.

211. 725 ILCS 5/110-7(g). *But see* People v. Denny, 238 Ill. App. 3d 819, 605 N.E.2d 600, 603 (4th Dist. 1992) (paragraph (g) not self-executing, court required to take action).

212. 725 ILCS 5/110-7(g). *See, e.g.,* People v. Chaney, 257 Ill. App. 3d 247, 628 N.E.2d 944, 948 (1st Dist. 1993) (defendant's mother's hardship in having to

Thus, a defendant who has posted $1,000 in cash (10 percent of a $10,000 bond) not only loses the cash actually deposited but suffers a civil judgment of $10,000. A defendant released on his or her own recognizance is also subject to a judgment in the full amount of the bond set by the court.[213] The defendant who has posted stocks, bonds, or real estate as security under section 110-8[214] suffers the same potential judgment liability, with the judgment satisfied out of forced sale of the property.[215] Moreover, all defendants are subject, if they fail to comply with bail conditions, to an increase in bail[216] or possible revocation of bail altogether,[217] as well as criminal sanctions depending on the nature of the breach.[218] Because so much is at stake—money, property, loss of freedom pending trial, inability to aid in investigation and preparation of the case, and the subconscious, if not conscious, effect on the court that still must rule on motions, proof of guilt, and sentencing—the accused's compliance with bail conditions cannot too often or too strenuously be stressed.

Finally, there are several provisions dealing with appeal aspects of bail, whether set too high or denied. Under some circumstances the state is specifically given the right to appeal;[219] in others, the defendant is granted that right.[220] And under some provisions the right to appellate review is accorded to both the state and the defense.[221] Because bail appeals by defendants are made by

---

repay borrowed funds to post bail did not ameliorate the risk of forfeiture she knowingly assumed and the state had a right to judgment after the defendant's noncompliance with the bail conditions).

213. 725 ILCS 5/110-2.

214. 725 ILCS 5/110-8.

215. 725 ILCS 5/110-8(g), (h).

216. 725 ILCS 5/110-6(b).

217. 725 ILCS 5/110-6.

218. 720 ILCS 5/32-10.

219. "The State may appeal any order permitting release on personal recognizance." 725 ILCS 5/110-2. "The State may appeal any order where the court has increased or reduced the amount of bail or altered the conditions of the bail bond or granted bail where it has previously been revoked." 725 ILCS 5/110-6(g). "The state may appeal any order granting bail or setting a given amount of bail." 725 ILCS 5/110-5(d). The state's right to appeal under sections 2 and 6 has been held void. People v. Heim, 182 Ill. App. 3d 1075, 538 N.E.2d 1259, 1262 (2d Dist. 1989). However, no decision has found the state's right to appeal under sections 5, 6.1, and 6.3 unconstitutional.

220. S. Ct. Rule 604(c) (sets forth requirements for bail appeals by defendants before conviction).

221. "After entry of an order by the trial court allowing or denying bail pending appeal either party" may appeal. 725 ILCS 5/110-7(e).

motion[222] and without briefs[223] or oral argument,[224] in my experience such motions are usually heard within days, or at the most a couple of weeks, of the time they are filed.

§ 4.11 Bail and the Material Witness

Although I have been unable to find a case dealing with the subject, of more than passing interest in an appropriate case are the Illinois provisions that authorize the preliminary hearing court, after a finding of probable cause, to "require any material witness for the State or defendant to enter into a written undertaking to appear at the trial."[225] The court may also order the witness to execute a recognizance bond with provisions "for the forfeiture of a sum certain in the event the witness does not appear at the trial," and may order the sheriff to take into and keep in custody any "witness who refuses to execute a recognizance."[226] Finally, a witness who violates the terms of a recognizance bond is subject to being charged with the offense of bail jumping, being held in contempt of court, or both.[227] In my twenty-eight years of practice, I have seen these provisions utilized twice: once by me and once by the state.

§ 4.12 Introduction to Discovery Rules

The rules of the Supreme Court of Illinois regulating discovery in criminal cases[228] divide the materials the defense is entitled to into a number of broad categories. These include:

1. names and addresses of witnesses that the state intends to call, along with their statements;[229]

---

222. The defendant must file a verified motion in the appellate court together with "a verified copy of the motion to answer filed in the trial court." S. Ct. Rule 604(c)(2).

223. *Id.*

224. S. Ct. Rule 604(c)(5).

225. 725 ILCS 5/109-3(d).

226. *Id.*

227. 720 ILCS 5/32-10, 725 ILCS 5/109-3(d).

228. S. Ct. Rules 411-15. Note that rule 411 applies the discovery rules only to felony charges. People *ex rel.* Daley v. Fitzgerald, 123 Ill. 2d 175, 526 N.E.2d 131, 134 (1988) (rules limited to felony proceedings). *But see* People v. Olinger, 176 Ill. 2d 326, 680 N.E.2d 321, 343 (1997) (circuit court has inherent discretionary authority to order discovery in postconviction proceedings).

229. S. Ct. Rule 412(a)(i). *Cf.* 725 ILCS 5/114-9 (motion for list of witnesses).

2.   statements by the accused or a co-defendant, and witnesses to those statements;[230]

3.   grand jury transcripts of testimony of the accused and of witnesses the state intends to call;[231]

4.   experts' reports and "a statement of qualifications of the expert";[232]

5.   various types of physical objects that the prosecutor either intends to use or that were obtained from or belong to the accused;[233]

6.   impeachable prior convictions of state witnesses;[234]

7.   information on electronic surveillance;[235]

8.   evidence favorable to the accused;[236] and

9.   any other relevant material reasonably requested by the defense.[237]

This section discusses each of the broad general categories of discovery contained in rule 412, a number of "rules within the rule," and several discovery-applicable provisions covered by other rules of the supreme court or established case law. With the rules as the starting point, what actually is discoverable in any criminal case is limited only by the imagination, creativity, and perseverance of the criminal defense practitioner and his or her willingness to vigorously represent the accused.

---

230. S. Ct. Rule 412(a)(ii). Compliance with this section is mandatory. People v. Siefke, 195 Ill. App. 3d 135, 551 N.E.2d 1361, 1365 (2d Dist. 1990); People v. Robinson, 189 Ill. App. 3d 323, 545 N.E.2d 268, 273 (1st Dist. 1989). *See* People v. Jones, 245 Ill. App. 3d 674, 615 N.E.2d 373, 376 (2d Dist. 1993) (discovery violation occurs when state fails to tender statement of defendant made to civilian even though name of witness was listed in state's answer as probable witness).

231. S. Ct. Rule 412(a)(iii).

232. S. Ct. Rule 412(a)(iv).

233. S. Ct. Rule 412(a)(v).

234. S. Ct. Rule 412(a)(vi).

235. S. Ct. Rule 412(b).

236. S. Ct. Rule 412(c).

237. S. Ct. Rule 412(h).

§ 4.13   Discovery of Witnesses' Names, Addresses, and Statements

Supreme Court Rule 412(a)(i) provides that "upon written motion of defense counsel,"[238] the state must tender to the defense "the names and last known addresses of persons whom the state intends to call as witnesses, together with their relevant written or recorded statements, memoranda containing substantially verbatim reports of their oral statements, and a list or memoranda reporting or summarizing their oral statements."[239]

Analytically, the rule provides for five distinguishable sets of information to which the defense is entitled: (1) names of witnesses[240] the state intends to call; (2) their last-known addresses;[241] (3) their written or recorded statements;[242] (4) memoranda containing substantially verbatim reports of their

---

238. All materials subject to rule 412 disclosure must be provided by the state only when the defense has filed a written request.

239. S. Ct. Rule 412(a)(i). *See* People v. Holmes, 141 Ill. 2d 204, 565 N.E.2d 950, 961 (1990) (defendant is entitled to statements in the state's possession if they are relevant and not privileged); People v. Williams, 220 Ill. App. 3d 297, 581 N.E.2d 228, 233 (1st Dist. 1991) (no violation exists where the substance of a victim's statement is contained in a police report, grand jury testimony, or discoverable in pretrial examination of the victim).

240. People v. Schutz, 201 Ill. App. 3d 154, 559 N.E.2d 289 (4th Dist. 1990). *But see* People v. Fauntleroy, 224 Ill. App. 3d 140, 586 N.E.2d 292, 306 (1st Dist. 1991) (until the state decides to call a witness, no disclosure is required, because the state does not know if the witness will be called in rebuttal until it hears the defense evidence); People v. Maldonado, 193 Ill. App. 3d 1062, 550 N.E.2d 1011, 1015 (1st Dist. 1989) (disclosure may be denied where substantial risk of harm, intimidation, bribery, economic reprisal, or unnecessary annoyance or embarrassment to witness exists). *But see* People v. Perez, 209 Ill. App. 3d 457, 568 N.E.2d 250, 257 (1st Dist. 1991) (where an informant plays an active role in a criminal act, it is reasonable to conclude that the state intends to call the witness in rebuttal); People v. Washington, 182 Ill. App. 3d 168, 537 N.E.2d 1354, 1358 (1st Dist. 1989) (rebuttal witnesses must be disclosed when the state forms the intent to call).

241. *But see* People v. Shockley, 195 Ill. App. 3d 148, 551 N.E.2d 1370, 1378 (2d Dist. 1990) (disclosure of a rape victim's new address is not required where the substantial risk of unnecessary annoyance or embarrassment exists, particularly when the defendant's wife called the victim and tried to convince her to drop the charges).

242. *But see* People v. Hanks, 210 Ill. App. 3d 817, 569 N.E.2d 205, 207 (5th Dist. 1991) (the state has no duty to procure a witness' statements where tapes are in the possession of secret service agents in another state).

oral statements;[243] and (5) a list of memoranda that report or summarize their oral statements.[244] In my experience, counsel may expect to routinely receive the names of anyone and everyone who ever had anything to do with the case and who might be called by the prosecution, rather than only those persons that the state intends to call. Occasionally, counsel will receive the names of witnesses who might be of help to the defense.[245] Counsel may also expect to routinely receive the last-known addresses of the witnesses, though the passage of time from the incident to the trial should encourage defense counsel to move periodically for an amended list.[246] The state also tenders, usually automatically upon a defense request, written or recorded witness statements.

The problem most often encountered by the defense concerns the obligation of the state to tender "memoranda containing substantially verbatim reports" of the witness's oral statements,[247] and a list of the memoranda.[248] A defense request for such material is usually met by one of two responses from the state: either no such memoranda exist,[249] or the writings that do exist are the work product of the prosecutor and are not subject to disclosure.[250] Regardless of the

---

243. *But see* People v. Mahaffey, 128 Ill. 2d 388, 539 N.E.2d 1172, 1186 (where a witness's statement is not memorialized, the rule does not appear to require disclosure), *cert. denied,* 493 U.S. 873 (1989); People v. Thompkins, 121 Ill. 2d 401, 521 N.E.2d 38, 48 (where notes are from a witness interview taken by Alabama officials, the state has no obligation to procure and produce them), *cert. denied,* 488 U.S. 871 (1988).

244. *But see* People v. Allen, 272 Ill. App. 3d 394, 650 N.E.2d 250 (1st Dist. 1995); People v. Wielgos, 220 Ill. App. 3d 812, 581 N.E.2d 298, 301 (1st Dist. 1991) (disclosure of oral statements made by a defendant is required, but the rule does not require a verbatim transcript of the statements), *cert. denied,* 506 U.S. 844 (1992); People v. Uselding, 217 Ill. App. 3d 1063, 578 N.E.2d 100, 107 (1st Dist. 1991) (the state's failure to disclose an interview with a potential witness does not warrant a new trial where the defendant knew of the witness' existence, knew what she might testify to, and the testimony was cumulative).

245. *See* the discussion of the state's obligation to tender the names and addresses of witnesses favorable to the accused in § 4.22.

246. This is so despite the "continuing duty to disclose" imposed on buth the state and the defense by Supreme Court Rule 415(b).

247. S. Ct. Rule 412(a)(i).

248. S. Ct. Rule 412(a)(i).

249. Counsel must be suspicious, to say the least, especially in multiwitness cases where the state maintains that no memoranda embodied by the rule exist.

250. Matters not subject to disclosure.

  (i) *Work product.* Disclosure under this rule and Rule 413 shall not be required of legal research or of records, correspondence, reports or

response, there is recourse. Upon written motion of defense counsel, the court must conduct an in camera inspection of the sought-after memoranda, and if it is found to be within the rule's framework, the court must order the state to give the material to the defense.[251] "The court is not to consider whether the prior statements [reflected in the memoranda] would in fact be useful . . . only the defense should be permitted to make that determination."[252] All the court is obliged to determine is if the materials examined are "properly producible."[253]

The court has wide discretion in determining what items are "properly producible," especially because the state must "produce a list of all memoranda reporting or summarizing oral statements *whether or not the memorandum appears to the State to be substantially verbatim reports of such statements.*"[254] In exercising their discretion, courts have ordered disclosure of items ranging from the state's "preparation sheets"[255] to rough notes,[256] and have even ordered the state to "reconstitute" destroyed notes for the purposes of in camera inspection.[257] "[W]hile the discovery rules do not require the State to reduce all its witnesses' statements to writing, when the failure to preserve a state-

---

memoranda to the extent that they contain the opinions, theories or conclusions of the State or members of its legal or investigative staffs, or of defense counsel or his staff.

S. Ct. Rule 412(j)(i). *See* People v. Elzey, 203 Ill. App. 3d 153, 560 N.E.2d 1107, 1112 (1st Dist. 1990) (rule does not require disclosure of legal research, reports, or memos which contain conclusions, opinions, or theories; logs describing another crime and reasons why no charges should be brought against the defendant for it are not discoverable because they are conclusions); People v. Mack, 128 Ill. 2d 231, 538 N.E.2d 1107, 1115 (1989) (the state's notes from jury selection which contain opinions, theories, and conclusions are protected from disclosure), *cert. denied,* 493 U.S. 1093 (1990).

251. S. Ct. Rule 412(a)(i); People v. Szabo, 94 Ill. 2d 327, 447 N.E.2d 193 (1983). *But see* People v. Young, 128 Ill. 2d 1, 538 N.E.2d 453, 475 (1989) (denying *in camera* inspection of the state's notes of a pretrial interview with a state's witness does not deny a defendant the opportunity to effectively cross-examine the witness or deny the defendant the right to confront the witness).

252. *Szabo,* 94 Ill. 2d 327, 447 N.E.2d at 201.

253. *Id.*; People v. Allen, 47 Ill. 2d 57, 264 N.E.2d 184 (1970).

254. Committee Comment to Rule 412(a)(i). *See Szabo,* 94 Ill. 2d 327, 447 N.E.2d at 201 (emphasis added by court).

255. People v. Robinson, 46 Ill. 2d 229, 263 N.E.2d 57 (1970).

256. *Szabo,* 94 Ill. 2d 327, 447 N.E.2d at 202.

257. *Id.,* 447 N.E.2d at 204.

ment . . . amounts to an intentional tactic to prevent disclosure . . . it will not be condoned."[258]

§ 4.14   Discovery of Statements by the Defendant

Supreme Court Rule 412(a)(ii) requires the state to tender "any written or recorded statements and the substance of any oral statements made by the accused or by a codefendant, and a list of witnesses to the making and acknowledgement of such statements."[259] "The rule encompasses not only formal statements made to the authorities but also statements made *to anyone* that might have a bearing on the defendant's guilt or innocence."[260] The duty of the state to disclose such statements "is a continuing duty which is violated whether the State's neglect was inadvertent or purposeful."[261] "Compliance with [the] rule . . . is only excused [where the prosecution is] unaware of the

---

258. *Id.,* 447 N.E.2d at 203. Here, the defendant's conviction was reversed and the case remanded to the trial court for the state to reconstruct destroyed notes and to submit them to the court for the rule 412(a)(i) *in camera* inspection.

259. S. Ct. Rule 412(a)(ii). *But see* People v. Nettnin, 216 Ill. App. 3d 794, 576 N.E.2d 417, 421 (2d Dist. 1991) (the state's failure to provide the reverse side of two pages of a police report containing the defendant's statement to the arresting officer does not deny him a fair trial where his statements are not strong enough to have an effect on the weight of the evidence against the defendant).

260. People v. Eliason, 117 Ill. App. 3d 683, 453 N.E.2d 908, 913 (2d Dist. 1983). *See also* People v. Weaver, 92 Ill. 2d 545, 442 N.E.2d 255, 260 (1982). *See* People v. Siefke, 195 Ill. App. 3d 135, 551 N.E.2d 1361 (2d Dist. 1990). *See also* People v. Wright, 186 Ill. App. 3d 159, 542 N.E.2d 367, 370 (1st Dist. 1989) (rule includes all of the defendant's statements regardless of when or where made; no exception for innocent or inadvertent suppression by the state). *See, e.g.,* People v. Allen, 272 Ill. App. 3d 394, 650 N.E.2d 250, 255–56 (1st Dist. 1995) (state's failure to disclose the contents of defendant's oral confession to police warranted the reversal of the conviction); People v. Furlong, 217 Ill. App. 3d 1047, 578 N.E.2d 77, 81 (1st Dist. 1991) (defendant's drug conviction reversed because state failed to disclose defendant's inculpatory statement as to his source of cocaine and damaging defense). *See also* People v. Matthews, 299 Ill. App. 3d 914, 702 N.E.2d 291 (1st Dist. 1998); People v. Brandon, 283 Ill. App. 3d 358, 669 N.E.2d 1253 (4th Dist. 1996); People v. Tripp, 271 Ill. App. 3d 194, 648 N.E.2d 241 (1st Dist. 1995).

261. *Eliason,* 117 Ill. App. 3d 683, 453 N.E.2d at 913; People v. Varela, 194 Ill. App. 3d 364, 551 N.E.2d 323 (3d Dist. 1990). *See also* People v. Harris, 123 Ill. 2d 113, 526 N.E.2d 335, 351 (state's deliberate failure to disclose supplemental information undercut defendant's attempt to impeach witness and denied fair trial), *cert. denied,* 488 U.S. 902 (1988).

existence of the statement prior to trial and could not have become aware of it in the exercise of due diligence."[262]

The Illinois Supreme Court in *People v. Weaver*[263] found that the prosecutor's failure to provide the defense with discovery of the defendant's alleged admission to her mother-in-law required a new trial. Pursuant to rule 412(a)(ii), the prosecutor supplied defense counsel with a copy of the grand jury transcript which supposedly contained all the statements of the defendant in the state's possession.[264] On the ninth day of trial, however, the state called the victim's sister to the stand.[265] She testified that the defendant had told her that she was having an affair with the athletic director at the high school.[266] The state's attorney had known of the statement for about three weeks but had "inadvertently" failed to inform the defense.[267] The court found that the state's failure to inform the defense was a violation of rule 412(a)(ii), which requires the prosecutor to disclose upon written motion *any* written or recorded statements made by the accused and a list of witnesses to its making.[268] The rule, said the court, encompasses not only formal statements made to the authorities but also statements made to *anyone* where such statements might have a bearing on the defendant's guilt or innocence.[269] The fact that the prosecutor did not learn of the alleged admission until three weeks before trial, concluded the court, in no way negated the duty to disclose.[270] The court found that the discovery violation had occurred whether or not the state's neglect was inadvertent.[271]

---

262. People v. Brown, 106 Ill. App. 3d 1087, 436 N.E.2d 696, 700 (1st Dist. 1982). *See* People v. Robinson, 226 Ill. App. 3d 649, 589 N.E.2d 1093, 1099 (3d Dist. 1992) (where the state is not aware of the existence of a statement prior to trial, no discovery violation exists), *aff'd,* 157 Ill. 2d 68, 623 N.E.2d 352, 361 (1993). *See also In re* C.J., 166 Ill. 2d 264, 652 N.E.2d 315, *cert. denied,* 516 U.S. 993 (1995). Note that in *People v. Bounds,* the supreme court repeated its admonition that failure of defense counsel to avail himself of a continuance upon learning of a discovery violation waives the claim on appeal. 171 Ill. 2d 1, 662 N.E.2d 1168, 1189 (1995), *cert. denied,* 519 U.S. 876 (1996).

263. 92 Ill. 2d 545, 442 N.E.2d 255 (1982).

264. *Id.,* 442 N.E.2d at 259.

265. *Id.*

266. *Id.*

267. *Id.,* 442 N.E.2d at 260.

268. *Id.*

269. *Id.*

270. *Id.*

271. *Id. See also* People v. Tripp, 271 Ill. App. 3d 194, 648 N.E.2d 241, 248 (1st Dist. 1995); People v. Williams, 220 Ill App. 3d 297, 581 N.E.2d 228, 232–34 (1st Dist. 1991); People v. Furlong, 217 Ill. App. 3d 1047, 578 N.E.2d 77, 79–80 (1st

Sanctions for discovery violations are wide ranging. The court may require additional discovery, bar use of the evidence by the offending party, or grant a continuance.[272] When evidence is not disclosed, prejudice to the defendant warranting some sanction is ascertained by evaluating "(1) the strength of the undisclosed evidence, (2) the likelihood that prior notice could have helped the defense discredit the [non-disclosed] evidence, (3) the feasability of a continuance [or relief] rather than a more drastic sanction, and (4) the wilfulness of the state in failing to disclose."[273]

A final note on production of the defendant's statement concerns when the request for production should be made. Obviously, the sooner counsel knows all the evidence in the case, whether inculpatory or exculpatory, the more effective the investigation and representation will be. Although the Supreme Court Rule requirement for statement disclosure is applicable only after an indictment or information is filed,[274] counsel, before indictment or information, might make a request for production under Illinois Compiled Statutes chapter 725, section 5/114-10.[275] And, although the information the defense is entitled to under section 114-10 is not as expansive as that under Supreme Court Rule 412(a)(ii),[276] receipt of the material the defense is entitled to under the statute at least enables counsel to begin preparing his or her client's defense days or even weeks earlier, instead of waiting for the indictment or information to be filed.

§ 4.15 Discovery of Grand Jury Transcripts

The defense, upon written motion, is also entitled to receive from the state "a transcript of those portions of grand jury minutes containing testimony of

---

Dist. 1991); People v. Robinson, 189 Ill. App. 3d 323, 545 N.E.2d 268, 272–74 (1st Dist. 1989).

272. People v. Clemons, 277 Ill. App. 3d 911, 661 N.E.2d 476, 481 (1st Dist. 1996).

273. People v. Allen, 272 Ill. App. 3d 394, 650 N.E.2d 250, 256 (1st Dist. 1995).

274. S. Ct. Rule 411.

275. Sec. 114-10. Motion to Produce Confession. (a) On motion of a defendant in any criminal case made prior to trial the court shall order the State to furnish the defendant with a copy of any written confession made to any law enforcement officer of this State or any other State and a list of the witnesses to its making and acknowledgement. If the defendant has made an oral confession a list of the witnesses to its making shall be furnished.

725 ILCS 5/114-10.

276. Only written confessions and a list of witnesses are discoverable under 725 ILCS 5/114-10. Under rule 412(a)(ii) statements of the defendant, as well as confessions, are discoverable, as are statements of co-defendants.

the accused and relevant testimony of persons whom the prosecuting attorney intends to call as witnesses."[277] The transcribed testimony is usually routinely tendered upon a defense request. However, counsel, before or even at trial, might consider in an appropriate case asking witnesses if they testified on a prior occasion.

§ 4.16   Discovery of Experts' Statements, Reports, and Physical Objects

The provisions of Illinois Supreme Court Rule 412(a)(iv) and (v) are a further specification of the types of material and information available to defense counsel upon written motion. Preliminarily, it must be noted that the production of most material and information under these provisions is not automatic.[278] The "burden rests squarely upon the defendant . . . to pursue and ascertain any relevant information in the preparation of his defense."[279] Although a court may occasionally enter a form discovery motion on its own when the accused fails to do so,[280] the rule requires the discovery request to be upon written motion.[281]

Although some material discoverable under these provisions is exculpatory and thus must be provided by the prosecution under rule 412(c), whether the defense requests it or not,[282] defense counsel must be as specific as possible in requesting the material sought. For example, a defense request for the "results" of a physical examination of the complainant may be insufficient to require mandatory disclosure of the fact that the examination occurred.[283] Failure to request under rule 412(a) specific information about a lineup resulted in the proper withholding by the state of the fact that a witness had selected two

---

277. S. Ct. Rule 412(a)(iii). *But see* People v. Perry, 226 Ill. App. 3d 326, 589 N.E.2d 776, 785 (1st Dist. 1992) (defendant is not surprised or deprived of time to prepare even though a grand jury testimony is first presented during the trial).

278. ILL. COMP. STAT. ANN., Committee Comments (Smith-Hurd 1992).

279. People v. Borawski, 61 Ill. App. 3d 774, 378 N.E.2d 255, 258 (5th Dist. 1978).

280. People v. Son, 111 Ill. App. 3d 273, 443 N.E.2d 1115, 1119 (2d Dist. 1982).

281. S. Ct. Rule 412(a).

282. Brady v. Maryland, 373 U.S. 83 (1963); People v. Newbury, 53 Ill. 2d 228, 290 N.E.2d 592, 597 (1972).

283. People v. Visgar, 120 Ill. App. 3d 584, 457 N.E.2d 1343, 1349 (2d Dist. 1983) (The information regarding the mere fact of whether a physical examination was conducted was never requested and, unless accompanied by the results of that examination, was not subject to mandatory disclosure.).

photographs of different men displaying features similar to those of the armed robber.[284]

In addition, the rule requires that the material and information requested under these provisions must be within the "possession or control" of the prosecution, including the "various investigative personnel."[285] Thus, there was no failure to disclose relevant medical reports where the reports were in the possession of the Chicago Transit Authority medical director and unknown to the prosecution.[286] Nor was nondisclosure improper when the prosecutor did not have possession or control of a burned automobile that the accused alleged was material to his defense against a charge of burning a house.[287] However, the reports of a lab analysis done by a police department crime laboratory are considered to be in the possession and control of the prosecution and thus are subject to discovery requests.[288]

The material and information provision included in rules 412(a)(iv) and 412(a)(v) breaks down into three basic categories, with certain characteristics unique to each.

§ 4.17 — Rule 412(a)(iv)—Experts' Statements

Rule 412(a)(iv) covers the reports and statements of experts "made in connection with the particular case."[289] These include the results of physical and mental examinations, scientific tests, experiments, and comparisons. The area encompassed by this provision is quite broad, apparently limited only by the requirement that experts' reports or statements be connected to the particular case. Thus, it is not the relevancy of the material or its inculpatory or exculpatory character that is crucial under this provision. It is the actual connection of the material to the case.[290]

---

284. People v. Abner, 113 Ill. App. 3d 434, 447 N.E.2d 541, 543 (3d Dist. 1983).

285. S. Ct. Rule 412(a), (e), (f).

286. People v. Sakalas, 85 Ill. App. 3d 59, 405 N.E.2d 1121, 1132 (1st Dist. 1980).

287. People v. Schabatka, 18 Ill. App. 3d 635, 310 N.E.2d 192, 197 (3d Dist. 1974), *cert. denied,* 420 U.S. 928 (1975). *Accord Visgar,* 120 Ill. App. 3d 584, 457 N.E.2d at 1349; People v. Molsby, 66 Ill. App. 3d 647, 383 N.E.2d 1336 (1st Dist. 1978); People v. Gaitor, 49 Ill. App. 3d 449, 364 N.E.2d 484 (1st Dist. 1977).

288. People v. Curtis, 48 Ill. App. 3d 375, 362 N.E.2d 1319, 1324–25 (1st Dist. 1977).

289. It states: "(a)(iv): any reports or statements of experts, made in connection with the particular case, including results of physical or mental examinations and of scientific tests, experiments, or comparisons, and a statement of qualifications of the expert." S. Ct. Rule 412(a)(iv).

290. Ill. Comp. Stat. Ann. ILCS S. Ct. Rule 412, Committee Comments (Smith-Hurd 1992).

Included among discoverable reports and statements are ballistics tests,[291] the results of a physical examination of the complainant,[292] a firearms use report,[293] a police crime laboratory's analysis of physical evidence,[294] and the report of a polygraph technician who examined a key witness.[295] For practical purposes, all information and material related to an expert's participation in a particular case is discoverable by the defense.

The prosecution's failure to produce the information and material included in rule 412(a)(iv) or its untimely production of the information and material may be reversible error, especially when considered in conjunction with rule 412(c), which embodies the constitutional requirements of *Brady v. Maryland*.[296] This provision, unlike rule 412(a), requires the prosecution to disclose favorable evidence whether or not it is requested.[297] And, though often in retrospect, it is not up to the prosecutor to determine what evidence is favorable to the accused. That determination is made by the defense.[298]

Thus, in *People v. Bass*,[299] it was reversible error for the prosecution to withhold a polygraph examiner's report of the examination of the only eyewitness to the murder when the defense discovery motion had included a request for "any written or recorded statements" by witnesses and "any reports and results of any and all scientific tests, experiments and examinations made by

---

291. People v. Taylor, 107 Ill. App. 3d 1019, 438 N.E.2d 565, 568 (1st Dist. 1982); People v. Baxtrom, 61 Ill. App. 3d 546, 378 N.E.2d 182, 190 (5th Dist. 1978).

292. People v. Visgar, 120 Ill. App. 3d 584, 457 N.E.2d 1343, 1349 (2d Dist. 1983).

293. People v. Cannon, 62 Ill. App. 3d 556, 378 N.E.2d 1339, 1343 (1st Dist. 1978).

294. People v. Curtis, 48 Ill. App. 3d 375, 362 N.E.2d 1319, 1324–25 (1st Dist. 1977).

295. People v. Smith, 122 Ill. App. 3d 609, 461 N.E.2d 534, 539 (3d Dist. 1984); People v. Bass, 84 Ill. App. 3d 624, 405 N.E.2d 1182, 1186–87 (1st Dist. 1980).

> (c) Except as is otherwise provided in these rules as to protective orders, the State shall disclose to defense counsel any material or information within its posses sion or control which tends to negate the guilt of the accused as to the offense charged or would tend to reduce his punishment therefor.

S. Ct. Rule 412(c).

296. 373 U.S. 83, 87 (1963). "We now hold that the suppression by the prosecution of evidence favorable to an accused upon request violates due process where the evidence is material either to guilt or to punishment, irrespective of the good faith or bad faith of the prosecution."

297. People v. Newbury, 53 Ill. 2d 228, 290 N.E.2d 592, 597 (1972).

298. People v. Trolia, 69 Ill. App. 3d 439, 388 N.E.2d 35, 42–43 (1st Dist.), *cert. denied*, 444 U.S. 911 (1979); People v. Dixon, 19 Ill. App. 3d 683, 312 N.E.2d 390, 394–95 (1st Dist. 1974).

299. 84 Ill. App. 3d 624, 405 N.E.2d 1182 (1st Dist. 1980).

experts or others."[300] Insofar as the witness's credibility had been placed before the jury and was "pivotal" in the case, "any efforts to reduce the efficacy of his testimony were therefore relevant and material, if not crucial."[301] The report might have contained information or led to information affecting defense strategy and trial preparation.[302]

Moreover, the defense is entitled to a legible copy of any expert's report. Without a legible report, the accused cannot be put on notice "as to the possible uses which it might have for his defense."[303] Especially when the report might have tended to negate guilt, "the reviewing court will not speculate as to what use the defense could or would have put the evidence in question."[304] Although the accused in *People v. Keith* retained some responsibility to seek a legible copy, when the prosecution answered that it had no information tending to negate the accused's guilt, "[t]he State, in effect, led the defendant to the erroneous belief that the illegible report could not be helpful in his defense."[305]

In spite of, or perhaps in light of *Brady,* if the material discoverable under rule 412(a)(iv) is not produced by the state or is produced in an untimely fashion, it is not per se reversible error if the material turns out to be nonexculpatory or it has not prejudiced the defense.[306] When such evidence is untimely produced, "[t]he court may, in its discretion, order a continuance, mandate disclosure of these materials and permit their use at trial."[307] With *Brady* in mind, the state's failure to disclose a polygraph examiner's report of an examination of the complainant until after trial was not reversible error, because the report was not favorable to the accused.[308]

§ 4.18 — Rule 412(a)(iv)—Qualifications of Experts

Rule 412(a)(iv) requires the prosecution to produce "a statement of qualifications of the expert" who makes any reports or statements discov-

---

300. *Id.,* 405 N.E.2d at 1187; People v. Smith, 122 Ill. App. 3d 609, 461 N.E.2d 534, 538–39 (3d Dist. 1984).

301. *Bass,* 84 Ill. App. 3d 624, 405 N.E.2d at 1187.

302. *Id.*

303. People v. Keith, 66 Ill. App. 93, 383 N.E.2d 655, 660 (5th Dist. 1978).

304. *Id.,* 383 N.E.2d at 658.

305. *Id.,* 383 N.E.2d at 661.

306. People v. Cannon, 62 Ill. App. 3d 556, 378 N.E.2d 1339, 1342 (1st Dist. 1978) (production during trial of firearm's use report and its admission by trial judge was not error, absent showing of surprise or prejudice).

307. People v. Curtis, 48 Ill. App. 3d 375, 362 N.E.2d 1319, 1325 (1st Dist. 1977).

308. People v. Hutchison, 55 Ill. App. 3d 716, 371 N.E.2d 201, 204 (3d Dist. 1977).

erableunderthisprovision.[309] Although it does not deal specifically with this provision, *People v. Cornille*[310] highlights the potential importance of Supreme Court Rule 412(a)(iv). In *Cornille,* the court granted postconviction relief after it was established that the state's key expert witness in an arson trial was in fact an imposter. The court commented: "[I]t is obvious that every party, including the State, has an obligation to verify the credentials of its expert witnesses. It is only on the basis of these credentials that experts are permitted to offer their professional opinions concerning the factual issues disputed in the criminal proceeding."[311] If the expert's qualifications determine whether he or she can testify at trial, pretrial examination of the qualifications of an expert who makes a report may be critical to the defense. Only by examining the qualifications of the expert, as well as his or her findings, can the defense fully assess the character of the evidence and develop theories to attack the weight of the evidence, if not its admissibility.

§ 4.19 — Rule 412(a)(v)—Documentary Evidence and Tangible Objects

Rule 412(a)(v) encompasses books, papers, documents, photographs, and tangible objects that the prosecutor "intends to use in the hearing or trial" or "which were obtained from or belong to the accused."[312] The disjunctive character of the two clauses indicates a discovery limitation on material not obtained from the accused. The accused is entitled to the items listed in this provision if (1) the items were obtained from or belong to him or her; (2) the prosecution intends to use the items at trial; or (3) the items are favorable to the defense.[313]

Thus, on one hand, the prosecution's failure to turn over composite drawings and photographs used in a pretrial show-up was not violative of the accused's right to discovery.[314] Even if the prosecution later uses tangible evidence at

---

309. S. Ct. Rule 412(a)(iv).

310. 95 Ill. 2d 497, 448 N.E.2d 857 (1983).

311. *Id.,* 448 N.E.2d at 865–66.

312. "[A]ny books, papers, documents, photographs or tangible objects which the prosecuting attorney intends to use in the hearing or trial or which were obtained from or belong to the accused . . . ." S. Ct. Rule 412(a)(v).

313. People v. Newbury, 53 Ill. 2d 228, 290 N.E.2d 592, 598 (1972) ("Unless photographs are favorable to the defense, and there is no such contention, they are not automatically discoverable by the defendant unless the prosecution intends to use them at trial or unless they were obtained from the defendant. *See* Rule 412(a)(v), 50 Ill. 2d R.412(a)(v) . . . .").

314. People v. Son, 111 Ill. App. 3d 273, 443 N.E.2d 1115, 1119–20 (2d Dist. 1982).

trial, such as a photograph, to respond to an issue unexpectedly raised by the defense, there is no violation of discovery insofar as the prosecution had no intention to use the tangible object.[315]

On the other hand, the *Brady* provision (rule 412(c)) and the provision for the discovery of physical material overlap. The prosecution may not withhold physical objects by disclaiming their use at trial when the objects are potentially exculpatory. When the accused made a timely motion for the production of physical evidence and specifically requested in court that the state produce a shoe found at the crime scene that was mentioned in a crime laboratory report, the prosecution's failure to produce the shoe was reversible error in light of the defense presented.[316] As a warning to defense counsel, the court noted that the "demands for the shoe's production could have been more forcefully asserted when the prosecution did not comply with the court's directions."[317] Counsel should have made a specific motion for the court to compel production once the prosecution failed to voluntarily produce the requested item.

Furthermore, it was reversible error for the prosecution not to produce the torn sweatshirt of an accused when the defense made a proper motion for material evidence and a specific request for the item. Because the accused claimed self-defense, "[t]he sweatshirt's materiality . . . is beyond question . . . . Defendant was the sole eyewitness to testify for the defense, and the sweatshirt could have provided corroboration of her testimony. Since we find that a specific request was made by defendant for material evidence, the State's failure to produce is reversible error."[318] Additionally, the prosecution cannot fail to produce an item of physical evidence and then comment at trial on the absence of that evidence to assail the credibility of the accused's story.[319]

---

315. People v. Malone, 67 Ill. App. 3d 150, 385 N.E.2d 12, 14–15 (1st Dist. 1978) (no error when prosecution used but did not produce before trial photograph of accused with particular hairstyle; photograph was taken on day of his arrest on other charges; prosecution had no intention to use photograph and was unaware of its relevancy until accused put on his witness), *rev'd on other grounds*, 78 Ill. 2d 34, 397 N.E.2d 1377 (1979). *Accord* People v. Molsby, 66 Ill. App. 3d 647, 383 N.E.2d 1336, 1342 (1st Dist. 1978) (when prosecution did not produce photographs in response to discovery motion but later used them at trial, there was no discovery violation even though photos placed accused at scene of crime before his arrest there; prosecution had not intended to use photographs and did so only to impeach witness).

316. People v. Nichols, 63 Ill. 2d 443, 349 N.E.2d 40, 43 (1976).

317. *Id.*, 349 N.E.2d at 43.

318. People v. Bennett, 82 Ill. App. 3d 225, 402 N.E.2d 650, 654–55 (1st Dist. 1980).

319. People v. Wisniewski, 8 Ill. App. 3d 768, 290 N.E.2d 414, 416–17 (5th Dist. 1972) (state failed to produce piece of water pipe found at scene in case where

The finding of error in withholding material evidence properly requested "is not dependent upon an affirmative showing by the defendant that he was prejudiced in fact."[320] That the production of withheld evidence may have resulted in a revision of defense strategy can be sufficient to show error.[321]

The defense must be as specific as possible in requesting the production of physical evidence under rule 412(a)(v). Some courts have found that a request for any physical evidence is not specific enough to produce photographs of the crime scene, because "[p]hysical evidence generally refers to items taken from the crime scene."[322] Where an object was not in fact regarded as evidence by the prosecution and the defense never made a specific request for it despite the opportunity to do so, it was not error for the prosecution to dispose of that item, because on review it could be seen that the object's production would not have created reasonable doubt about the accused's guilt.[323] Again, however, defense counsel should in limine vigorously argue that it is only the defendant, not the prosecutor, who can and should determine what is evidence within the purview of this rule and *Brady*.[324]

Finally, the defense counsel has the obligation under rule 412(e) to inspect material and information made available by the state in its answer to a defense discovery motion. When a piece of paper on which the accused had written, known as the "list," was available for inspection under rule 412(e), the accused could not claim a discovery violation when the prosecution did not specify the "list" in response to the discovery motion or point out its significance but merely mentioned "paper" in its answer.[325] Similarly, the prosecution's answer to a discovery motion listing "miscellaneous papers" was sufficient to notify the accused of certain checks, when the defense had other reasons to know of their existence.[326]

In summary, the provisions of rule 412(a)(iv) and (v) in conjunction with rule 412(c) are all designed to protect the rights of the accused as well as to

---

    accused argued that victim had attacked him with piece of pipe; difference in pipe found at scene and one described by accused was not controlling).

320. People v. Loftis, 55 Ill. App. 3d 456, 370 N.E.2d 1160, 1169 (1st Dist. 1977).

321. *Id.* (failure to produce panties worn by alleged rape victim was reversible error when victim testified that panties had been torn in struggle but in fact panties showed no such tear).

322. People v. Elbus, 116 Ill. App. 3d 104, 451 N.E.2d 603, 606 (4th Dist. 1983).

323. People v. Ruffalo, 69 Ill. App. 3d 532, 388 N.E.2d 114, 117 (1st Dist. 1979).

324. People v. Dixon, 19 Ill. App. 3d 683, 312 N.E.2d 390, 394–95 (1st Dist. 1974).

325. People v. Anthony, 38 Ill. App. 3d 190, 347 N.E.2d 179, 182–84 (4th Dist. 1976).

326. People v. Britt, 22 Ill. App. 3d 695, 318 N.E.2d 138, 143 (1st Dist. 1974) ("The defense apparently made no further effort to have these items particularized nor to inspect them despite an offer by the State to permit inspection").

facilitate the criminal prosecution process. They aim at justice by providing for a criminal prosecution process that is fair as well as truth-seeking. The court in *Ruffalo* articulately summarized this due process character of the discovery rules in light of *Brady* and *Agurs*.[327]

> Where evidence is withheld from the defense either in spite of a defense request for it or when it is of such a character as to be of obvious importance to the defense, the prosecution has abused its position so that its conduct amounts to a "suppression" and a denial of due process has occurred; where, however, there has been no defense request for the particular evidence in question and that evidence is not of apparent importance to the defense, there has been no "suppression" and no denial of due process has occurred unless that evidence had demonstrable exculpatory potential.[328]

The caveat is that if you think the evidence might exist, ask for it as specifically as possible (obviously, without violating the client's privilege). If you fail to make a specific request, your client bears the chance of conviction, with your failure having aided the issue. Whether your client will successfully argue your incompetency is another issue entirely.

§ 4.20   Discovery of Prior Convictions of State's Witnesses

Upon written motion of defense counsel, the state must disclose "any record of prior criminal convictions, which may be used for impeachment, of persons whom the State intends to call as witnesses at the hearing or trial."[329] The prosecutor must also disclose the prior adjudications of his or her witnesses for impeachment purposes pursuant to the Juvenile Court

---

327. Brady v. Maryland, 373 U.S. 83 (1963); United States v. Agurs, 427 U.S. 97 (1976); People v. Newberry, 166 Ill. 2d 310, 652 N.E.2d 288 (1995).

328. People v. Ruffalo, 69 Ill. App. 3d 532, 388 N.E.2d 114, 117 (1st Dist. 1979).

329.   (a) Except as is otherwise provided in these rules as to matters not subject to disclosure and protective orders, the State shall, upon written motion of defense counsel, disclose to defense counsel the following material and information within its possession or control:

                                        * * *

     (vi) any record of prior criminal convictions, which may be used for impeachment, of persons whom the State intends to call as witnesses at the hearing or trial.

     S. Ct. Rule 412(a)(vi). *See also* People v. Godina, 223 Ill. App. 3d 205, 584 N.E.2d 523, 526 (3d Dist. 1991) (pending felony charge against a material state witness is subject to disclosure under *Brady*).

Act.[330] Although the Supreme Court Rule is applicable only to felony prosecutions,[331] disclosure of prior convictions of state witnesses is mandated under *Brady v. Maryland*. Note, however, that while some "information may be so significant that the State's duty to disclose is not dependent upon the defendant's request,"[332] the rule does require that the motion be in writing, and defense counsel is well advised to comply with the letter of the rule to avoid possible waiver.

The rule imposes an obligation on the state to not merely provide what information it has in the file, but to obtain criminal histories of its potential witnesses and to disclose any records of prior convictions that may be used for impeachment purposes at trial to the defense counsel on request.[333] Noncompliance with the state's continuing duty to disclose its witnesses' criminal records is excused "only where, through the exercise of due diligence, the prosecutor did not know and could not have known of the existence of the record."[334] Defense counsel need not condition the request by providing information such as the date of birth or social security number of the witness to make

---

330. 705 ILCS 405/1-10(c). See further discussion in § 4.28, *infra*.

331. People v. Elbus, 116 Ill. App. 3d 104, 451 N.E.2d 603 (4th Dist. 1983). *See* S. Ct. Rule 411.

332. People v. Veal, 58 Ill. App. 3d 938, 374 N.E.2d 963, 981 (1st Dist. 1978), *cert. denied,* 441 U.S. 908 (1979). Of interest is that this decision appears to go beyond the constitutional requirement of *Brady v. Maryland,* 373 U.S. 83 (1963), which conditions discovery disclosure on the defendant's actual request. *Cf.* People v. Ruffalo, 69 Ill. App. 3d 532, 388 N.E.2d 114 (1st Dist. 1979).

333. People v. Higgins, 71 Ill. App. 3d 912, 390 N.E.2d 340 (1st Dist. 1979); People v. Elston, 46 Ill. App. 3d 103, 360 N.E.2d 518 (4th Dist. 1977). Note also Illinois Supreme Court Rule 412(f) and (g), which provides:

> (f) The State should ensure that a flow of information is maintained between the various investigative personnel and its office sufficient to place within its possession or control all material and information relevant to the accused and the offense charged.

> (g) Upon defense counsel's request and designation of material or information which would be discoverable if in the possession or control of the State, and which is in the possession or control of other governmental personnel, the State shall use diligent good faith efforts to cause such materials to be made available to defense counsel; and if the State's efforts are unsuccessful and such material or other governmental personnel are subject to the jurisdiction of the court, the court shall issue suitable subpoenas or orders to cause such material to be made available to defense counsel.

S. Ct. Rule 412(f), (g).

334. People v. Tonkin, 142 Ill. App. 3d 802, 492 N.E.2d 596, 598 (3d Dist. 1986).

a valid request.[335] However, where a timely written request is made by defense counsel and the state answers that it has no such material, the noncompliance will be excused if neither the state nor its agents actually possess the material sought.[336]

Regulation of discovery and sanctions for discovery violations are within the sound discretion of the trial courts.[337] Therefore, reviewing courts are reluctant to grant new trials based on the state's failure to disclose the criminal records of witnesses even where appropriate requests were made.[338] The tendency of the courts is to weigh the "necessity" of the information and its effect on the outcome of the proceedings to determine whether the defendant was unfairly prejudiced.[339] Moreover, a claim of prejudice must be founded on more than mere conjecture;[340] where there is sufficient evidence to sustain a conviction, courts will usually hold the error harmless.[341] It is obvious, thus, that counsel must establish a record at trial to reflect not only what information is sought but why the information is critical to the defense—that is, how the defendant will be prejudiced if the information is not provided.

§ 4.21 Discovery of Electronic Surveillance

The rule further provides that the "State shall inform defense counsel if there has been any electronic surveillance (including wiretapping) of conversations to which the accused was a party, or of his premises."[342]

---

335. People v. Molsby, 66 Ill. App. 3d 647, 383 N.E.2d 1336 (1st Dist. 1978).

336. *Id.*, 383 N.E.2d at 1342.

337. People v. Morgan, 112 Ill. 2d 111, 492 N.E.2d 1303 (1986), *cert. denied*, 479 U.S. 1101 (1987); People v. Weaver, 92 Ill. 2d 545, 442 N.E.2d 255 (1982); People v. Matthews, 299 Ill. App. 3d 914, 702 N.E.2d 291 (1st Dist. 1998); People v. Dahl, 110 Ill. App. 3d 295, 442 N.E.2d 321 (4th Dist. 1982).

338. People v. Veal, 58 Ill. App. 3d 938, 374 N.E.2d 963 (1st Dist. 1978), *cert. denied*, 441 U.S. 908 (1979).

339. People v. Dunklin, 104 Ill. App. 3d 685, 432 N.E.2d 1323 (1st Dist. 1982).

340. People v. Lewis, 60 Ill. 2d 152, 330 N.E.2d 857 (1975); People v. Simpson, 272 Ill. App. 3d 63, 650 N.E.2d 265 (4th Dist. 1995).

341. People v. Veal, 58 Ill. App. 3d 938, 374 N.E.2d 963 (1st Dist. 1978), *cert. denied*, 441 U.S. 908 (1979). *See also* People v. Pearson, 102 Ill. App. 3d 732, 430 N.E.2d 304 (1st Dist. 1981) (state failed to turn over records of four occurrence witnesses, but none had possible felonies; therefore, court held that there was no error). *But see* People v. Galloway, 59 Ill. 2d 158, 319 N.E.2d 498 (1974) (witness, who was drug addict and former prostitute, made undercover buy from defendant; court held that failure to turn over witness's record demanded reversal).

342. S. Ct. Rule 412(b).

The need for this information is obvious insofar as preparation of a defense, pretrial motions, and trial and/or possible plea negotiations are concerned. In arguing the right to this information, counsel should consider, in addition to rule 412(b), whether the electronically monitored conversations are statements of witnesses to which the defense is entitled discovery under rule 412(a)(i),[343] statements of the accused or co-defendant to which the defense is entitled discovery under rule 412(a)(ii),[344] evidence favorable to the accused,[345] or evidence subject to the court's discretionary powers of disclosure.[346] Counsel might also consider, in making a rule 412(b) request or in receiving rule 412(b) material, a number of other relevant provisions, including the substantive law of electronic eavesdropping as an offense,[347] judicial supervision of eavesdropping,[348] motions to suppress eavesdropped conversations,[349] and specific alternative provisions by which discovery of eavesdropped conversations might be received.[350]

§ 4.22   Discovery of Evidence Favorable to the Accused

In 1963 the United States Supreme Court first declared that the state has an obligation to tender to the accused any evidence that is favorable to the accused insofar as it tends to negate guilt or potentially lessen the punishment. "[S]uppression by the prosecution of . . . [such evidence] upon request violates due process . . . irrespective of the good faith or bad faith of the prosecution."[351]

---

343. Rule 412(a)(i) statements are discussed in § 4.13.

344. Discussed in § 4.14.

345. To which the defendant is entitled under rule 412(c) and *Brady*, which are discussed in § 4.17.

346. "Upon a showing of materiality to the preparation of the defense, and if the request is reasonable, the court in its discretion may require disclosure to defense counsel of relevant material and information not covered by this rule." S. Ct. Rule 412(h).

347. 720 ILCS 5/14-1.

348. 725 ILCS 5/108A-1 through 5/108A-11.

349. 725 ILCS 5/108A-9.

350. 725 ILCS 5/108A-9 provides, inter alia:

> (b) . . . Upon the filing of . . . [a motion to suppress the contents of an eavesdropped conversation] . . . the judge may in his discre tion make available to the moving party or his attorney such portions of the recorded conversation or evidence derived therefrom as the judge determines to be in the interests of justice.

351. Brady v. Maryland, 373 U.S. 83, 87 (1963).

In *Kyles v. Whitley*,[352] the United States Supreme Court reiterated the rule that the state has an obligation under *Brady* to disclose any evidence which is favorable to the defendant.[353] The Court held that the prosecutor "has a duty to learn of any favorable evidence known to the others acting on the government's behalf . . . including the police" and then "gauge the likely net effect of all such evidence and make disclosure when the point of 'reasonable probability' is reached."[354] In this case, the Court found that the state had failed to disclose evidence which was favorable to the defendant,[355] which denied him a fair trial.[356] The evidence withheld was vast and the Court found that its disclosure may very well have made a difference in the jury's result.[357] The evidence withheld would have demonstrated that the "eyewitnesses were not consistent in describing the killer, that two out of the four eyewitnesses testifying were unreliable, that the most damning physical evidence was subject to suspicion, that the investigation that produced it was insufficiently probing, and that the principal police witness was insufficiently informed or candid."[358] The Court went through each item of evidence extensively and analyzed the effect it would have had on defendant's case.[359] The Court, in summation, found that based on the cumulative nature of the suppressed evidence, it did not have confidence that the jury's verdict would have been the same.[360]

Illinois Supreme Court Rule 412(c) is essentially an embodiment of the *Brady* decision, although unlike *Brady*, the rule requires the prosecutor to turn over the favorable material whether or not the defense makes a request: "[T]he State shall disclose to defense counsel any material or information within its

---

352. 514 U.S. 419 (1995); People v. Hobley, 182 Ill. 2d 404, 696 N.E.2d 313, 328 (1998) (reiterating that "the prosecution cannot escape its duty under *Brady* by contending that the suppressed evidence was known only to police investigators and not to the prosecution"). *See also* People v. Segoviano, 297 Ill. App. 3d 860, 697 N.E.2d 792 (1st Dist.), *appeal granted,* 181 Ill. 2d 586, 706 N.E.2d 502 (1998); People v. Diaz, 297 Ill. App. 3d 362, 696 N.E.2d 819 (1st Dist. 1998); People v. Moore, 279 Ill. App. 3d 152, 663 N.E.2d 490 (5th Dist. 1996).

353. *Kyles,* 514 U.S. at 421.

354. *Id.* at 437.

355. *Id.* at 428–29.

356. *Id.* at 441.

357. *Id.* at 441–45.

358. *Id.* at 454.

359. *Id.* at 441–51.

360. *Id.* at 453–54.

possession or control[361] which tends to negate the guilt of the accused as to the offense charged or would tend to reduce his punishment therefor."[362]

The state must be held to its responsibility to produce exculpatory or mitigating evidence. "A prosecution that withholds evidence on demand of an accused which, if made available, would tend to exculpate him or reduce the penalty helps shape a trial that bears heavily on the defendant. That casts the prosecution in the role of an architect of a proceeding that does not comport with the standards of justice . . . ."[363] It should also be noted that whether the prosecutor acted in good or bad faith is *not* relevant.

What evidence tends to negate the guilt of the accused or to reduce the punishment is governed only by the creativity of counsel tempered by the facts of each case. Such evidence may include the confidential psychiatric records of a state witness,[364] exculpatory statements of the defendant,[365] material for impeachment,[366] physical evidence corroborative of the

---

361. *See* discussion of the obligation of the state to get material and information into its possession in § 4.25 in this chapter.

362. S. Ct. Rule 412(c). This rule codifies *Brady*. People v. Velez, 123 Ill. App. 3d 210, 462 N.E.2d 746, 752 (1st Dist. 1984). *But see* People v. Clemons, 277 Ill. App. 3d 911, 661 N.E.2d 476, 481 (1st Dist. 1996) (state does not have duty to voluntarily disclose defendant's statement to police where not exculpatory or supporting a claim of innocence).

363. People v. Gennardo, 184 Ill. App. 3d 287, 539 N.E.2d 400, 409 (1st Dist. 1989).

364. People v. Di Maso, 100 Ill. App. 3d 338, 426 N.E.2d 972 (1st Dist. 1981); People v. Phipps, 98 Ill. App. 3d 413, 424 N.E.2d 727 (4th Dist. 1981).

365. People v. Abendroth, 52 Ill. App. 3d 359, 367 N.E.2d 571 (4th Dist. 1977) (tape recordings of conversation authorized by defendant); People v. Cauthen, 51 Ill. App. 3d 516, 366 N.E.2d 1037 (1st Dist. 1977).

366. United States v. Esposito, 523 F.2d 242 (7th Cir. 1975), *cert. denied,* 425 U.S. 916 (1976). *But see* People v. Pecoraro, 175 Ill. 2d 294, 677 N.E.2d 875, 883, 885–86 (state did not violate *Brady* where it failed to disclose certain impeachment evidence that the wife of the victim was arrested for soliciting the murder of her husband because the arrest was simple and was not a conviction; therefore, this evidence could not be used for impeachment purposes; since this evidence was inadmissible, it would not have affected the outcome of defendant's trial; state also did not violate *Brady* by failing to disclose to defendant that two of its witnesses had failed a polygraph test because defendant's argument regarding the ability of such information to aid his defense was speculative), *cert. denied,* 118 S. Ct. 193 (1997).

defense,[367] police reports that contain favorable evidence,[368] promises of leniency to a state witness,[369] payments of money,[370] and even reports reflecting the interview of witnesses made by another attorney (not the defense or prosecuting attorney in the case at bar) to which the state's attorney prosecuting the present case was privy.[371]

---

367. *Pecoraro,* 175 Ill. 2d 294, 677 N.E.2d at 886–87 (no violation of *Brady* where police failed to preserve evidence of defendant's mental and physical condition at time he confessed since no evidence such preservation would have produced exculpatory evidence); People v. Nichols, 63 Ill. 2d 443, 349 N.E.2d 40 (1976) (shoe found outside burgled premises that defendant argued would suggest that someone other than he was offender); People v. Bennett, 82 Ill. App. 3d 225, 402 N.E.2d 650 (1st Dist. 1980) (defendant's torn sweatshirt that supported his theory of self-defense).

368. People v. Cagle, 41 Ill. 2d 528, 244 N.E.2d 200 (1969), *superseded by statute on other grounds as stated in* People v. Perry, 52 Ill. 2d 156, 287 N.E.2d 129, 129 (1972). *But see Pecoraro,* 175 Ill. 2d 294, 677 N.E.2d at 881–82 (no violation of *Brady* occurred where state failed to disclose a statement made by a witness in which he confessed to the murder for which the defendant was on trial because the statement was inadmissible hearsay and no evidence of sufficient indicia of reliability existed to warrant admission, thus, there was no reasonable probability that disclosure would alter the outcome of defendant's trial); People v. Brooks, 214 Ill. App. 3d 531, 573 N.E.2d 1306, 1313 (1st Dist. 1991) (no violation exists where the state failed to produce an inconclusive gunshot residue test which may have helped the defendant); People v. Lann, 194 Ill. App. 3d 623, 551 N.E.2d 276, 282 (1st Dist. 1990) (failure to disclose a report showing one set of fingerprints not the defendant's is not grounds for reversing a conviction, where the report has little probative value and evidence of the defendant's guilt is overwhelming).

369. Giglio v. United States, 405 U.S. 150 (1972); De Marco v. United States, 415 U.S. 449 (1974). *But see Pecoraro,* 175 Ill. 2d 294, 677 N.E.2d at 884–85 (no violation of *Brady* occurred where state failed to disclose alleged agreement with a witness that if she assisted in the prosecution of defendant, she would not be prosecuted for solicitation of murder for hire); People v. Diaz, 297 Ill. App. 3d 362, 696 N.E.2d 819, 826–29 (1st Dist. 1998) (state violated *Brady* where it withheld evidence that its prime witness received a greatly reduced sentence in exchange for testimony, particularly where the sentence was illegal and state failed to correct the witness's perjured testimony that he did not receive a deal for testifying; state compounded this perjury by arguing in closing argument that there was no such deal; based on this "outrageous" conduct the court could not find that the deal did not contribute to defendant's conviction, particularly because the witness was crucial to the state's case and concluded that defendant was denied a fair trial by the fact that the "integrity of our criminal justice system has been tainted").

370. People v. Gennardo, 184 Ill. App. 3d 287, 539 N.E.2d 400, 411 (1st Dist. 1989).

371. People v. DeStefano, 30 Ill. App. 3d 935, 332 N.E.2d 626, 630 (1st Dist. 1975) ("The rule is well-established . . . that the prosecution, upon request must furnish

Finally, as an indication of the potential scope of "evidence favorable to the accused" that the state must tender to the defense, but by no means indicative of an exhaustive list, when the "reliability of a given witness may well be determinative of guilt or innocence," evidence affecting credibility falls within the rule requiring disclosure by the prosecution.[372] Thus, because the courts have concluded that narcotics addiction affects one's credibility as a witness and is the proper subject of cross-examination,[373] the prosecution would have

---

to the defense statements containing favorable information or material within their possession or control"). *But see* Wood v. Bartholomew, 516 U.S. 1, 5–7 (1995) (although the prosecution did not disclose to the defense that a witness had failed a polygraph test, the evidence was not "material" under *Brady*, and thus did not justify setting aside a conviction because there was no reasonable probability that the disclosure of the evidence would have resulted in a different result at trial, where the polygraph evidence was not admissible under Washington state law and where defendant's counsel admitted that disclosure would not have affected the scope of his cross-examination of the witness).

372. *Giglio,* 405 U.S. at 154 (citing Napue v. Illinois, 360 U.S. 264, 269 (1959)). *But see* People v. Alduino, 260 Ill. App. 3d 665, 633 N.E.2d 106, 110 (2d Dist. 1994) (trial court did not err in refusing to grant a mistrial, where the state failed to disclose that two of its witnesses had been shown a photo array and lineup and did not identify anyone, as the evidence was not material in a constitutional sense because the defendant's picture was not included in the array, and the defendant did not participate in the lineup). *Compare* People v. Coleman, 183 Ill. 2d 366, 701 N.E.2d 1063 (1998). Here, the defendant (postconviction petitioner) convicted of murder, etc., alleged (with a supporting affidavit) that the state failed to disclose the fact that a witness "told police that defendant did not have the same complexion as the gunman . . . and . . . that the gunman was someone she had recognized from the neighborhood and that she had never seen the defendant in the neighborhood." *Id.,* 701 N.E.2d at 1075. That witness, at trial, made a "tentative" identification of the defendant. *Id.,* 701 N.E.2d at 1067. The court agreed that such evidence is indeed *Brady* material. *Id.,*701 N.E.2d at 1077. Where the state presents evidence at trial that they know is false (here, that the defendant "could have been the gunman"), "the failure to disclose is 'part and parcel of the presentation of false evidence' . . . and therefore 'corrupts . . . the truth-seeking function of the trial process.'" *Id.,* 701 N.E.2d at 1078 (citing United States v. Vozzella, 124 F.3d 389, 392 (2d Cir. 1997), and United States v. Agurs, 427 U.S. 97, 103 (1976)).

373. People v. Galloway, 59 Ill. 2d 158, 319 N.E.2d 498, 501 (1974); People v. Strother, 53 Ill. 2d 95, 290 N.E.2d 201 (1972); People v. Lewis, 25 Ill. 2d 396, 185 N.E.2d 168 (1962). In *People v. Armstrong,* the court reaffirmed a defendant's right to cross-examination on narcotics addiction, though a jury instruction is not required. 183 Ill. 2d 130, 700 N.E.2d 960 (1998), *cert. denied,* 119 S. Ct. 1150 (1999).

an obligation under *Brady* and the rule[374] to tender arrest records as well as information regarding "provable" convictions.[375] Note that the "same *Brady* rules apply even where suppressed evidence was known only to police investigators and not to the prosecutor."[376] However, the state's attorney cannot be imputed with the responsibility for evidence destroyed by the Department of Children and Family Services and the destruction provides no basis for dismissal of defendant's petition.[377]

§ 4.23 Misdemeanor Discovery

Although the Illinois Supreme Court Rules providing for discovery in criminal cases apply only to felonies,[378] a defendant charged with a misdemeanor does have some discovery rights to obtain some materials. On motion, the defendant is entitled to (1) a list of the state's witnesses,[379] (2) any confession made by the defendant,[380] (3) evidence that negates the defendant's guilt,[381] (4) results of Breathalyzer tests,[382] and (5) statements and reports of

---

374. S. Ct. Rule 412(c).

375. People v. Galloway, 59 Ill. 2d 158, 319 N.E.2d 498 (1974). *See* People v. Sharrod, 271 Ill. App. 3d 684, 648 N.E.2d 1141, 1145 (1st Dist. 1995) (a new trial was granted where the state failed to disclose that the identification witness was on juvenile supervision at the time of the initial identification of the defendant, since the evidence goes to the question of bias based on the witness's hope or expectation of leniency from the state).

376. People v. Hobley, 182 Ill. 2d 404, 696 N.E.2d 313, 331 (1998).

377. *In re* C. J., 166 Ill. 2d 264, 652 N.E.2d 315, 318, *cert. denied*, 516 U.S. 993 (1995).

378. S. Ct. Rule 411; People v. Schmidt, 56 Ill. 2d 572, 309 N.E.2d 557 (1974); People v. Elbus, 116 Ill. App. 3d 104, 451 N.E.2d 603 (4th Dist. 1983); People v. Narducy, 23 Ill. App. 3d 805, 320 N.E.2d 235 (1st Dist. 1974).

379. 725 ILCS 5/114-9; *Schmidt,* 56 Ill. 2d 572, 309 N.E.2d at 558. *But see* People v. Hunter, 124 Ill. App. 3d 516, 464 N.E.2d 659, 675 (1st Dist. 1984) (section exempts rebuttal witnesses from disclosure).

380. 725 ILCS 5/114-10; *Schmidt,* 56 Ill. 2d 572, 309 N.E.2d at 558. *See, e.g.,* People v. Agyei, 232 Ill. App. 3d 546, 597 N.E.2d 696, 701 (1st Dist. 1992) (use of defendant's statement in violation of discovery rules requires a new trial only where the defendant has been prejudiced and the judge failed to eliminate the prejudice; the court must consider the strength of the undisclosed evidence, the likelihood that prior notice could help the defense discredit evidence, the feasibility of continuance, and the wilfulness of the state in failing to disclose).

381. Brady v. Maryland, 373 U.S. 83 (1962); *Schmidt,* 56 Ill. 2d 572, 309 N.E.2d at 558.

382. *Schmidt,* 56 Ill. 2d 572, 309 N.E.2d at 558.

prosecution witnesses that the defense may use for impeachment.[383] Note that although a license recission hearing is a civil proceeding, even there *Schmidt* discovery is available.[384]

In addition, an indispensible means of securing information and witnesses is the subpoena,[385] which is one aspect of the accused's Sixth Amendment right of compulsory process.[386] That right, and consequently the right to subpoena, applies to all criminal cases, including misdemeanors.[387]

§ 4.24 Bill of Particulars

When a defendant is charged with the commission of an offense, but the indictment, information, or complaint is not specific enough for the defendant to prepare a defense, the defendant is entitled to a bill of particulars.[388] The purpose of a bill of particulars is to notify the defendant, in greater detail, of the specific charges against him or her and to inform the defendant of the particular transaction that is the basis of that charge so that he or she can adequately prepare a defense to the allegations.[389] Note that regardless of the granting of a motion for a bill of particulars, the indictment, information, or complaint must be sufficient on its face.[390] A bill of particulars is only a supplement to the formal charge and cannot cure a defective charge.[391]

The defendant must move for a bill of particulars in writing[392] before arraignment or within a reasonable time thereafter.[393] The motion must specify

---

383. *Id.*

384. *See* People v. Brummett, 279 Ill. App. 3d 421, 664 N.E.2d 1074, 1078 (4th Dist. 1996); People v. Teller, 207 Ill. App. 3d 346, 565 N.E.2d 1046, 1049 (2d Dist. 1991); People v. Finley, 21 Ill. App. 3d 335, 315 N.E.2d 229, 234 (3d Dist. 1974).

385. For a full discussion of the use of subpoenas, see § 4.26.

386. "In all criminal prosecutions, the accused shall enjoy the right to . . . have compulsory process for obtaining witnesses in his favor . . . ." U.S. Const. amend. VI; People ex rel. Fisher v. Carey, 77 Ill. 2d 259, 396 N.E.2d 17 (1979).

387. People v. Harris, 91 Ill. App. 3d 1, 413 N.E.2d 1369 (4th Dist. 1980).

388. 725 ILCS 5/111-6.

389. Ill. Comp. Stat. Ann. 725 ILCS 5/111-6, Committee Comments (Smith-Hurd 1992)). *See also* People v. Lee, 57 Ill. App. 3d 927, 373 N.E.2d 744 (2d Dist. 1978); People v. Honn, 47 Ill. App. 3d 378, 362 N.E.2d 90 (4th Dist. 1977).

390. A defendant must be charged in accordance with 725 ILCS 5/111-3.

391. Ill. Comp. Stat. Ann. 725 ILCS 5/111-6, Committee Comments (Smith-Hurd 1992); People v. Lee, 57 Ill. App. 3d 927, 373 N.E.2d 744 (1978); People v. Kite, 10 Ill. App. 3d 620, 295 N.E.2d 100 (1st Dist. 1973).

392. 725 ILCS 5/111-6; Ill. Comp. Stat. Ann. 725 ILCS 5/114-2, Committee Comments (Smith-Hurd 1992).

393. 725 ILCS 5/114-2.

which particulars of the offense are necessary for the defendant to prepare a defense[394]—for example, the date,[395] time,[396] and address[397] of the alleged offense. However, courts have consistently held that the elements of time and place are "subsidiary matters which are separate and distinct from the substantive matter of stating the nature and elements of the offense charged."[398] Note that a bill of particulars cannot cure a void charge.[399] If the defendant is not satisfied with the particulars provided, he or she may move for a more specific bill or an additional bill.[400] The trial court is vested with the discretion to grant a motion for a bill of particulars,[401] a denial of which is reversible error only if that discretion was abused.[402] Any bill provided may be amended by the state "at any time before trial subject to such conditions as justice may require."[403]

In addition to providing the defendant with necessary information, another important function of a bill of particulars is that at trial, the state's evidence is limited to the transaction set out in the bill of particulars,[404] although a variance between the bill of particulars and the evidence is fatal only if the inconsistency is so substantial that it misled the defendant in the preparation of the defense.[405]

---

394. See ILL. COMP. STAT. ANN. 725 ILCS 5/111-6, Committee Comments (Smith-Hurd 1992).

395. People v. Adams, 109 Ill. App. 2d 385, 248 N.E.2d 748 (1st Dist. 1969).

396. People v. Patrick, 75 Ill. App. 2d 93, 220 N.E.2d 243 (3d Dist. 1966), aff'd, 38 Ill. 2d 255, 230 N.E.2d 843 (1967).

397. People v. Blanchett, 33 Ill. 2d 527, 212 N.E.2d 97, on remand, 73 Ill. App. 2d 91, 218 N.E.2d 491 (4th Dist. 1965).

398. Village of Huntley v. Oltmann, 242 Ill. App. 3d 725, 611 N.E.2d 632, 635 (2d Dist. 1993).

399. People v. Meyers, 158 Ill. 2d 46, 630 N.E.2d 811, 815 (1994).

400. People v. Bain, 359 Ill. 455, 195 N.E. 42 (1935).

401. People v. Lanzotti, 61 Ill. App. 3d 451, 378 N.E.2d 369 (4th Dist. 1978).

402. ILL. COMP. STAT. ANN. 725 ILCS 5/111-6, Committee Comments (Smith-Hurd 1992).

403. 725 ILCS 5/114-2(b).

404. 725 ILCS 5/111-6.

405. People v. Long, 65 Ill. App. 3d 21, 382 N.E.2d 327 (1st Dist. 1978). See also People v. Steele, 124 Ill. App. 3d 761, 464 N.E.2d 788, 792 (2d Dist. 1984) (a bill of particulars limits evidence the state may introduce, but a date specified in the bill does not preclude the state from offering proof that the offense charged was in fact committed on a different date).

§ 4.25 Motion for Preservation of Evidence

Although a defendant may be entitled to receive evidence and reports about evidence pursuant to the discovery rules,[406] *Brady v. Maryland,*[407] or the subpoena power,[408] request for the evidence is obviously meaningless if the evidence no longer exists. The vehicle by which evidence is preserved is a motion for preservation (or an order of protection) of the evidence involved.

The motion should be specific in delineating what evidence the defense seeks to preserve and why. The "what" aspect is limited only by counsel's knowledge of the case and his or her creativity. Counsel might consider not only substantive evidence that the state is expected to introduce against the defendant[409] but also informational evidence.[410]

Why the evidence should be preserved is somewhat more problematic. Arguably, if evidence is destroyed and a defendant is thus unable to analyze or examine it, some type of due process or confrontational problem may exist.[411] Yet, there has been a marked erosion of the rule, especially when the destruction is unintentional,[412] unavoidable, or interpreted by the courts as harmless to the defendant, who can still rely on the state's analysis.[413]

---

406. *See* the discussion in §§ 4.12–4.23.

407. 373 U.S. 83 (1963).

408. *See* the discussion in § 4.26.

409. For example, fingerprints in a burglary, blood in a homicide or sex offense, or narcotics in a controlled substances case.

410. Police or other emergency agency telephone tapes; records that businesses routinely destroy; computer disks that are erased.

411. People v. Dodsworth, 60 Ill. App. 3d 207, 376 N.E.2d 449 (4th Dist. 1978) (where state destroyed all of controlled substance that was subject of prosecution, defendant's due process rights were violated; note that state could have used only one-third of destroyed sample and intentionally and needlessly destroyed the rest). *See also* People v. Watson, 36 Ill. 2d 228, 221 N.E.2d 645 (1966); People v. Taylor, 54 Ill. App. 3d 454, 369 N.E.2d 573 (5th Dist. 1977).

412. People v. Jordan, 103 Ill. 2d 192, 469 N.E.2d 569 (1984) (deceased's remains were released to next of kin).

413. People v. Flatt, 75 Ill. App. 3d 930, 394 N.E.2d 1049 (3d Dist. 1979) (destruction of glass on which fingerprint was found not harmful to defendant who could rely on state's report and photographs), *vacated on other grounds,* 82 Ill. 2d 250, 412 N.E.2d 509 (1980).

In fact, the First District has overruled *Dodsworth* and *Taylor*[414] in *People v. Tsombanidis*[415] in light of *Arizona v. Youngblood*,[416] where the United States Supreme Court held that "unless a criminal defendant can show bad faith on the part of police, failure to preserve potentially useful evidence does not constitute a denial of due process of law."[417]

Note, however, that the facts are determinative of the issue. The Second District held that *Tsombanidis*' reliance on *Youngblood* was "legally flawed due to the nature of the evidence that was destroyed."[418] The supreme court agreed.[418.1]

For example, the Supreme Court has held that the due process clause of the Fourteenth Amendment does not require law enforcement officials to preserve breath samples in a DUI prosecution.[419] To successfully assert a due process violation, the defense must establish: (1) the destroyed evidence "possess[es] an exculpatory value that was apparent before the evidence was destroyed"; and (2) the evidence is "of such a nature that the defendant would be unable to obtain comparable evidence by other available means."[420]

In *People v. Newberry*,[421] the Illinois Supreme Court held that charges against defendant must be dismissed for a due process violation where the state destroyed the substance in a prosecution for unlawful possession of a look-alike substance after defendant made a discovery request for it.[422] The court also found dismissal proper as a discovery violation sanction pursuant to Rule 415(g)(i). The court distinguished *Youngblood* and found that here the evidence was essential to the outcome of the case.[423] Defendant had no alternative means to show that he was not guilty of the crime charged.[424] The court made this

---

414. *Dodsworth,* 60 Ill. App. 3d 207, 376 N.E.2d 449; *Taylor,* 54 Ill. App. 3d 454, 369 N.E.2d 573.

415. 235 Ill. App. 3d 823, 601 N.E.2d 1124, 1131 (1st Dist. 1992). *But see* People v. Newberry, 265 Ill. App. 3d 688, 638 N.E.2d 1196 (2d Dist. 1994), *aff'd,* 166 Ill. 2d 310, 652 N.E.2d 288 (1995).

416. 488 U.S. 51, 58 (1988).

417. *Id.*

418. Newberry, 265 Ill. App. 3d 688, 638 N.E.2d at 1199.

418.1. See discussion below.

419. California v. Trombetta, 467 U.S. 479, 485–91 (1984).

420. *Id.* at 488.

421. 166 Ill. 2d 310, 652 N.E.2d 288 (1995).

422. *Id.,* 652 N.E.2d at 289.

423. *Id.,* 652 N.E.2d at 291.

424. *Id.*

ruling even though the state may have destroyed the evidence inadvertently. There is no need to show bad faith according to this court.[425]

Regardless of the judicial trend, counsel should consider a preservation or protection motion for a number of reasons: if the motion is not granted and evidence sought is destroyed, the issue has been preserved for review,[426] and if the motion is sustained, evidence that is preserved pursuant to the motion may provide invaluable information or, through defense analysis or testimony, lead to conclusions contrary to those reached by the state's experts. At the very least, evidence that has been preserved and is thus available to the defense for independent analysis, especially if that analysis yields the same conclusions as those reached by the state, may encourage changes in the defense strategy or even in plea negotiations.

§ 4.26 Subpoenas

The use of a subpoena[427] and subpoena duces tecum[428] is essential to the investigation and preparation of almost every criminal case. Subpoenas are used to secure the presence of witnesses in court and to procure documentary evidence. Their scope is limited only by considerations of whether:

1) . . . the documents are evidentiary and relevant;

2) . . . [the documents] are not otherwise procurable reasonably in advance of trial by exercise of due diligence;

3) . . . the party cannot properly prepare for trial without such production and inspection in advance of trial and that the failure to obtain such inspection may tend to unreasonably delay the trial; and

4) . . . the application is made in good faith and is not intended as a general "fishing expedition."[429]

---

425. *Id.*, 652 N.E.2d at 292.

426. When evidence has been destroyed, the appropriate motion is a spoliation motion. Also worth considering, if the indictment is not dismissed, is a motion to bar the state from introducing testimony about the results or analysis of the destroyed evidence (motion to exclude).

427. From the Latin *sub* (under) and *poena* (penalty), requiring the presence of a person.

428. Requires the production of documents.

429. United States v. Nixon, 418 U.S. 683, 699–700 (1974), *overruled on other grounds* by Bourjaily v. United States, 483 U.S. 171 (1987).

The authority for the issuance of subpoenas in Illinois is found in the Supreme Court Rules,[430] Code of Civil Procedure,[431] and a variety of statutory provisions.[432] It may be used to procure reports or witnesses beyond those discoverable under the Supreme Court Rules on discovery, either where the

---

430.　　(a) Service of Subpoenas. Any witness shall respond to any lawful subpoena of which he or she has actual knowledge, if payment of the fee and mileage has been tendered. Service of a subpoena by mail may be proved prima facie by a return receipt showing delivery to the witness or his or her authorized agent by certified or registered mail at least seven days before the date on which appearance is required and an affidavit showing that the mailing was prepaid and was addressed to the witness, restricted delivery, with a check or money order for the fee and mileage enclosed.

　　S. Ct. Rule 237(a).

　　(g) Upon defense counsel's request and designation of material or information which would be discoverable if in the possession or control of the State, and which is in the possession or control of other governmental personnel, the State shall use diligent good faith efforts to cause such material to be made available to defense counsel; and if the State's efforts are unsuccessful and such material or other governmental personnel are subject to the jurisdiction of the court, the court shall issue suitable subpoenas or orders to cause such material to be made available to defense counsel.

　　S. Ct. Rule 412(g).

431.　　The clerk of any court in which an action is pending shall, from time to time, issue subpoenas for those witnesses and to those counties in the State as may be required by either party. Every clerk who shall refuse so to do shall be guilty of a petty offense and fined any sum not to exceed $100. An order of court is not required to obtain the issuance by the clerk of a subpoena duces tecum. For good cause shown, the court on motion may quash or modify any subpoena or, in the case of a subpoena duces tecum, condition the denial of the motion upon payment in advance by the person in whose behalf the subpoena is issued of the reasonable expense of producing any item therein specified.

　　735 ILCS 5/2-1101.

432.　　It is the duty of the clerk of the court to issue subpoenas, either on the part of the people or of the accused, directed to the sheriff or coroner of any county of this State. A witness who is duly subpoenaed who neglects or refuses to attend any court, under the requisitions of the subpoena, shall be proceeded against and punished for contempt of the court. Attachments against witnesses who live in a different county from that where the subpoena is returnable may be served in the same manner as warrants are directed to be served out of the county from which they issue.

　　725 ILCS 5/115-17.

rules are not applicable to the type of case involved[433] or where what is requested is not ordinarily discoverable under the rules.[434]

The seminal case in Illinois related to the scope and authority for the issuance of subpoenas is *People ex rel. Fisher v. Carey.*[435] In *Fisher,* an assistant public defender served subpoenas duces tecum on the Chicago Police Department requesting production of police reports at the preliminary hearing. The state's attorney's office intercepted the subpoenaed material on two theories: (1) because the police department is the investigative body of the office of the state's attorney, the state's attorney has the "right to review the subpoenaed records . . . before the court or the defendant gets them"; and (2) under the discovery rules, admittedly not applicable in the preindictment stage, subpoenas may be issued by the defense only if the "State's efforts" to secure reports in the possession of "other 'governmental personnel' . . . are unsuccessful."[436] The Illinois Supreme Court, however, disagreed with both propositions.[437]

In ruling that the defense does have the right to issue subpoenas before the filing of an information or return of an indictment, separate from the discovery rules, the court recognized that for a defendant "[t]he use of subpoenas or 'to have compulsory process for obtaining witnesses in his favor' in 'all criminal prosecutions' " is guaranteed by the Sixth Amendment to the Federal

---

433. Supreme Court Rule 411 limits the discovery to felony charges "following indictment or information." Thus, misdemeanors and ordinance violations as well as preindictment or preinformation felony charges are not covered by the rules.

434. For a discussion of what is discoverable under the rules, *see* §§ 4.12–4.23. *But see* Lannert v. Ramirez, 214 Ill. App. 3d 1102, 574 N.E.2d 238, 240 (5th Dist. 1991) (purpose of this rule is to furnish parties with an efficient method of obtaining witnesses and objects at trial and should not be substitute for discovery; it is preferable to use discovery rules during the discovery phase and this rule for production at trial).

435. 77 Ill. 2d 259, 396 N.E.2d 17 (1979).

436. *Id.,* 396 N.E.2d at 19.

437. In *People v. Nohren,* 283 Ill. App. 3d 753, 670 N.E.2d 1208 (4th Dist. 1996), the court held that the state may use a subpoena duces tecum to investigate a crime for which the defendant has not yet been charged. *Id.,* 670 N.E.2d at 1211. In this case, it was proper for the state to issue a subpoena to the hospital where the defendant was taken after he was involved in a one car accident for results of blood alcohol tests. *Id.,* 670 N.E.2d at 1212. The court rejected defendant's contention that the state was on a "fishing expedition" when it sought the results, finding that when the state issued the subpoena it had probable cause to believe the defendant was intoxicated on the night in question. *Id.,* 670 N.E.2d at 1212–13.

Constitution and applicable to state criminal proceedings.[438] This guarantee encompasses the production of documentary evidence by subpoena duces tecum.[439]

Moreover, "[t]he use of subpoenas is a judicial process, constitutionally and statutorily independent of the discovery rules,"[440] especially because the courts possess the "inherent discretionary authority . . . of seeing that the criminal trial process is fair and achieves its goal of ascertaining the truth."[441]

In addition to recognizing a defendant's right to issue subpoenas apart from the discovery rules, the Fisher court also emphasized that "the subpoena is a *judicial process or court writ*"[442] for which the office of the state's attorney may not be the conduit. "Subpoenaed material should be sent directly to the court, . . . [which] then determines the relevance and materiality of the materials, and whether they are privileged [citations omitted], as well as whether the subpoena is unreasonable or oppressive."[443]

The significance of *Fisher* cannot be overstated. The decision affirms a defendant's constitutionally protected and statutorily articulated right to have subpoenas issued apart from the discovery rules, and it is to the court, not to the office of the prosecutor, that subpoenaed materials and witnesses must be returned. Thus, subpoenas may be issued in misdemeanors,[444] which are not

---

438. *Carey,* 77 Ill. 2d 259, 396 N.E.2d at 20 (citing Washington v. Texas, 388 U.S. 14, 23 (1967)).

439. *Carey,* 77 Ill. 2d 259, 396 N.E.2d at 20. *See also* People v. Shukovsky, 128 Ill. 2d 210, 538 N.E.2d 444 (1988). *See, e.g.,* People v. Chengary, 301 Ill. App. 3d 895, 704 N.E.2d 727 (1st Dist. 1998) (reversing denial to obtain defendant's medical records that could establish that defendant had blood-alcohol level of .24).

440. People v. Harris, 91 Ill. App. 3d 1, 413 N.E.2d 1369, 1370 (4th Dist. 1980).

441. *Id.,* 413 N.E.2d at 1370.

442. *Carey,* 77 Ill. 2d 259, 396 N.E.2d at 19 (emphasis added).

443. *Id.,* 396 N.E.2d at 19–20. Subpoenas issued by the state must command defendant to produce the requested items to the court, not to the state's attorney. If the subpoena demands production to the state's attorney, it is an abuse of subpoena power and the trial court will quash the subpoena. People v. Walley, 215 Ill. App. 3d 971, 575 N.E.2d 596 (2d Dist. 1991); People v. Hart, 194 Ill. App. 3d 997, 552 N.E.2d 1 (2d Dist. 1990). In *People v. Smith,* 259 Ill. App. 3d 492, 631 N.E.2d 738, 745 (4th Dist. 1994), the appellate court held that the trial court did not err in suppressing evidence defendant supplied to the state's attorney under a subpoena which directed production to the state's attorney and not to the court because defendant lacked the opportunity to challenge the validity of the subpoena before turning the evidence over. *See* People v. Mitchell, 297 Ill. App. 3d 206, 696 N.E.2d 849 (5th Dist. 1989).

444. People v. Harris, 91 Ill. App. 3d 1, 413 N.E.2d 1369 (4th Dist. 1980). *See* further discussion in § 4.23.

subject to the discovery rules, and in felonies before the time that the discovery rules become applicable[445] with the assurance that if the prosecutor has an objection to the scope or use of a subpoena, it will be the judge, not the prosecutor, who decides the issue.[446] Thus, the state's attorney may no longer determine what the defense is entitled to by filtering out or keeping what the prosecutor perceives to be objectionable.[447]

§ 4.27 Motion for Evidence Deposition

Supreme Court Rule 414 provides, inter alia, that if it is substantially possible that a witness with relevant testimony will be unavailable at a hearing or trial, "upon motion and notice to both parties and their counsel" the court may order that witness to submit to an evidence deposition.[448] The deposition is taken under the rules applicable to civil cases,[449] though this notice requirement would seem to be premised on federal constitutional grounds[450] not of concern in litigation. Although the substantial possibility of unavailability of the proposed deponent coupled with the relevant testimony requirement of the rule might equal good cause for taking the deposition,[451] because a defendant enjoys a Sixth Amendment constitutional right of confrontation and cross-examination,[452] it is only on a showing of extraordinary circumstances that a deposition taken in accordance with the rule can be introduced against the accused at trial.[453] This rule is available equally to the state or defense, though obviously Sixth Amendment considerations do not apply when it is the defendant who is moving for an evidence deposition of a state witness.

---

445. People ex rel. Fisher v. Carey, 77 Ill. 2d 259, 396 N.E.2d 17 (1979). *See* People v. Mitchell, 297 Ill. App. 3d 206, 696 N.E.2d 849 (5th Dist. 1998) (affirming grant of defendant's subpoena *duces tecum* to obtain all police communications, written or recorded statements, etc. related to apprehension, arrest, and interrogation of defendant).

446. *Harris,* 91 Ill. App. 3d 1, 413 N.E.2d at 1370.

447. People ex rel. Fisher v. Carey, 77 Ill. 2d 259, 396 N.E.2d 17 (1979); People v. Harris, 91 Ill. App. 3d 1, 413 N.E.2d 1369 (1980).

448. S. Ct. Rule 414.

449. S. Ct. Rules 206, 210.

450. Due process right to confront and cross-examine any witness whose deposition is taken. S. Ct. Rule 414(e).

451. People v. Zehr, 110 Ill. App. 3d 458, 442 N.E.2d 581 (3d Dist. 1982), *aff'd,* 103 Ill. 2d 472, 469 N.E.2d 1062 (1984).

452. Ohio v. Roberts, 448 U.S. 56 (1980); People v. Payne, 30 Ill. App. 3d 624, 332 N.E.2d 745, 749–50 (1st Dist. 1975).

453. *Zehr,* 103 Ill. 2d 472, 469 N.E.2d at 1065–66.

A motion for the taking of an evidence deposition might be considered by defense counsel under any one of a number of circumstances, but especially when the proposed deponent is extremely old or ill, a professional (for example, a psychiatrist or firearms expert) who because of other trial or professional commitments is probably not going to be available at trial, or even a rival gang member who, because of his or her "avocation," will likely be unavailable at trial.[454]

Although Supreme Court Rule 414 does not define the unavailability of a witness, Rule 804 of the Federal Rules of Evidence provides generally accepted criteria to which Illinois courts might look for guidance.[455]

Finally, one example of how Illinois addresses evidence depositions. In *People v. Johnson,*[456] the defendant was charged with sexually assaulting a

---

454. *But see* People v. Hayes, 139 Ill. 2d 89, 564 N.E.2d 803, 816 (1990) (the taking of a deposition is not appropriate where the defense counsel is unable to persuade a state's witness to speak or give a sworn statement), *cert. denied,* 499 U.S. 967 (1991).

455. Rule 804 of the Federal Rules of Evidence states:

> (a) Definition of unavailability.—"Unavailability as a witness" includes situations in which the declarant—

> (1) is exempted by ruling of the court on the ground of privilege from testifying concerning the subject matter of his statement; or

> (2) persists in refusing to testify concerning the subject matter of his statement despite an order of the court to do so; or

> (3) testifies to a lack of memory of the subject matter of his statement; or

> (4) is unable to be present or to testify at the hearing because of death or then existing physical or mental illness or infirmity; or

> (5) is absent from the hearing and the proponent of his statement has been unable to procure his attendance (or in the case of a hearsay exception under subdivision (b)(2), (3), or (4), his attendance or testimony) by process or other reasonable means.

> A declarant is not unavailable as a witness if his exemption, refusal, claim of lack of memory, inability, or absence is due to the procurement or wrongdoing of the proponent of his statement for the purpose of preventing the witness from attending or testifying.

> *See also* Naylor v. Gronkowski, 9 Ill. App. 3d 302, 292 N.E.2d 227 (1st Dist. 1972) (witness is considered unavailable if exercising Fifth Amendment privilege or is unable to remember relevant facts). *See* People v. Gore, 6 Ill. App. 3d 51, 284 N.E.2d 333, 336 (1st Dist. 1972), *cert. denied,* 411 U.S. 907 (1973). *But see* People v. Rocha, 191 Ill. App. 3d 529, 547 N.E.2d 1335, 1341–42 (2d Dist. 1989), where the Second District held that a child who was unable "to testify because of fear, unable to communicate in the courtroom setting or incompetence," is "unavailable."

456. People v. Johnson, 118 Ill. 2d 501, 517 N.E.2d 1070 (1987).

child.[457] At trial, the testimony of the five-year-old complaining witness and her seven-year-old brother was recorded on videotape for presentation to the jury.[458] The defendant was not allowed in the courtroom when the complaining witness's testimony was recorded.[459] The defendant was convicted as charged.[460] The defendant challenged the use of videotaped testimony, and the court found it improper under rule 414.[461]

The court held that although videotaped depositions are permissible in Illinois and are within a trial judge's discretion, under rule 414, the judge must first find the deponent to be unavailable for trial testimony.[462] In this case a concern that a child might be fearful of testifying did not render the youngster unavailable under the rule.[463] Note that the "[t]estimony taken outside the presence of the jury for later admission at trial, even if taken in a courtroom with a judge presiding, is an evidence deposition that must comply with Supreme Court Rule 414."[464]

§ 4.28   Obtaining Juvenile Records

The use at trial of juvenile records to impeach a prosecution witness may provide a reasonable doubt necessary to avoid a conviction, especially when the impeached witness provides a "crucial link in the [prosecution's] proof."[465] Under some circumstances the right to use the fact of a juvenile adjudication, or at least the consequences that flow from an adjudication, is of constitutional magnitude.[466] Understandably, then, the prosecution, on the articulable rationale of protecting the confidentiality of juvenile offenders, almost invariably will object to any defense efforts to secure production of juvenile court records.

The Juvenile Court Act[467] does contain a number of separate and distinct provisions that directly relate to the confidentiality of juvenile records and proceedings. Only certain designated persons are entitled to be present at

---

457. *Id.,* 517 N.E.2d at 1070.

458. *Id.*

459. *Id.*

460. *Id.*

461. *Id.*

462. *Id.,* 517 N.E.2d at 1073.

463. *Id. But see* People v. Rocha, 191 Ill. App. 3d 529, 547 N.E.2d 1335 (2d Dist. 1989).

464. People v. Spain, 285 Ill. App. 3d 228, 673 N.E.2d 414, 423 (1st Dist. 1996).

465. Douglas v. Alabama, 380 U.S. 415, 419 (1965).

466. Davis v. Alaska, 415 U.S. 308 (1974).

467. 705 ILCS 405.

hearings or proceedings under the act, and the court may even, "for the minor's protection and for good cause shown, prohibit any person or agency present in court from further disclosing the minor's identity."[468] The act narrowly restricts law enforcement agencies from disclosing their records relating to minors[469] and establishes detailed criteria under which juvenile court records themselves must be kept confidential, with only limited access.[470] Finally, the act purports to provide the manner and circumstances under which juvenile court records may be admissible in other proceedings,[471] as well as the method for expungement in appropriate cases.[472]

The fact that the state has a legitimate interest in protecting the anonymity of juvenile offenders does not require, however, a hard and fast "juvenile-records-may-never-be-used-for-any-purpose" rule. *Davis v. Alaska,*[473] incorporated in Illinois Compiled Statutes chapter 705, section 405/1-10(c),[474] provides a case in point.

In *Davis,* the defense sought to cross-examine the state's key witness, a juvenile who was on probation, about his possible bias against the defendant because of his "vulnerable status as a probationer."[475] The defense argued that the juvenile probationer might be subject to undue pressure by the state to testify against the defendant because it was the state that conceivably could proceed against the juvenile on a violation of probation if he refused to cooperate. On the rationale of juvenile offender confidentiality, that cross-examination was not allowed.

In reversing Davis's conviction, the United States Supreme Court held that the Sixth Amendment to the Constitution guarantees the right of an accused in a criminal prosecution "to be confronted with the witness against him."[476] That right includes the right of meaningful cross-examination "by which the believability of a witness and the truth of his testimony are tested."[477] "[C]ross-examination [which is] directed toward revealing possible biases, prejudices,

---

468. 705 ILCS 405/1-5.

469. 705 ILCS 405/1-7.

470. 705 ILCS 405/1-8.

471. 705 ILCS 405/1-10.

472. 705 ILCS 405/1-9.

473. 415 U.S. 308 (1974).

474. "[I]n proceedings under this Act or in criminal proceedings in which anyone who has been adjudicated delinquent under Section 5-3 is to be a witness, and then only for purposes of impeachment and pursuant to the rules of evidence for criminal trials." 705 ILCS 405/1-10(c).

475. *Davis,* 415 U.S. at 318.

476. *Id.* at 315.

477. *Id.* at 316.

or ulterior motives of the witness"[478] is one of the key ways in which the credibility of a witness is properly attacked. In balancing the state's policy of juvenile offender confidentiality against the defendant's right to effective cross-examination, which is protected by the Sixth Amendment's confrontation clause, the Court opted for ensuring the defendant's constitutionally guaranteed right.[479]

It is obviously incumbent upon the defense attorney seeking juvenile records to develop a theory that justifies disclosure of the juvenile offender's records. Assuming that that theory comports with the *Davis* articulated constitutional mandate, appropriate, creative use of such material at trial may determine the outcome, and denial of access by the trial court may be the basis of a reversal on appeal.

§ 4.29 Production of Informants

The usual rule on disclosure of the identity of informants is that disclosure is not required unless the informant will be a witness at the trial or at a pretrial hearing, or where nondisclosure would violate the defendant's constitutional rights.[480] The articulated rationale for the rule is that citizens are encouraged to report crime if their anonymity is assured. Informants are protected from what might befall them if their identity were disclosed, and the public interest in effective law enforcement is furthered.[481]

---

478. *Id.*

479. *Id.* at 320. For Illinois decisions following *Davis*, see *People v. Norwood*, 54 Ill. 2d 253, 296 N.E.2d 852 (1973); *People v. McClendon,* 146 Ill. App. 3d 1004, 497 N.E.2d 849, 854 (4th Dist. 1986); *People v. Holsey,* 30 Ill. App. 3d 716, 332 N.E.2d 699 (1st Dist. 1975). Note that the Fourth District, in *People v Kerns*, held that while witnesses other than the defendant are subjected to juvenile adjudication impeachment, the rule does not allow juvenile adjudications to be used to impeach the defendant. 229 Ill App. 3d 938, 595 N.E.2d 207, 208–209 (4th Dist. 1992). In *People v Triplett*, 108 Ill. 2d 463, 485 N.E.2d 9, 19 (1985), the supreme court reaffirmed the holding of *Norwood* and *McClendon.*

480. S. Ct. Rule 412(j)(ii):

> (ii) *Informants.* Disclosure of an informant's identity shall not be required where his identity is a prosecution secret and a failure to disclose will not infringe the constitutional rights of the accused. Disclosure shall not be denied hereunder of the identity of witnesses to be produced at a hearing or trial.

481. Roviaro v. United States, 353 U.S. 53 (1957); People v. Pearson, 210 Ill. App. 3d 1079, 569 N.E.2d 1334, 1337 (2d Dist. 1991) (the rationale underlying this rule concerning the production of informants is stated).

If the state intends to call the informant as a witness, his or her identity must be disclosed.[482] There is no fixed rule, however, for disclosure of the identity of an informant who will not be called by the state.[483] Under such circumstances, where disclosure is sought by the defense, the court must balance the public interest in effective law enforcement against the defendant's constitutional right to confront witnesses, prepare a defense, and be tried fairly.[484] Disclosure will be required when the identity of the informant is relevant and helpful to the defense of the accused or is necessary to ensure fairness.[485] The burden, however, is on the defendant to show a need for disclosure that will override the privilege of nondisclosure.[486] Whether a court will order disclosure depends on "the particular circumstances of each case, taking into consideration the crime charged, the possible defenses, the possible significance of the informer's testimony, and other relevant factors."[487]

---

482. S. Ct. Rule 412(j)(ii).

483. Roviaro v. United States, 353 U.S. 53 (1957).

484. *Id.* at 62; People v. Woods, 139 Ill. 2d 369, 565 N.E.2d 643, 651 (1990) (an informant's testimony is material to the defendant's entrapment defense, because the informant introduced defendant to the undercover officer and encouraged him to sell drugs to the officer; the judge erred in not ordering disclosure). *See* People v. Bufford, 277 Ill. App. 3d 862, 661 N.E.2d 357 (1st Dist. 1995).

485. *Roviaro,* 353 U.S. at 62. What is "relevant" and "helpful" is subject to a case-by-case balancing test and counsel's creativity in formulating a theory of the defense. *See* People v. Herron, 218 Ill. App. 3d 561, 578 N.E.2d 1310, 1319 (2d Dist. 1991) (defendant has the burden of demonstrating necessity).

486. People v. Duncan, 104 Ill. App. 3d 701, 432 N.E.2d 1328 (1st Dist. 1982). *See* People v. Torres, 189 Ill. App. 3d 494, 545 N.E.2d 387, 391 (1st Dist. 1989) (before the state is required to produce an informant, the defendant needs to show materiality and relevance).

487. Roviaro v. United States, 353 U.S. 53 (1957). *See* People v. Woods, 139 Ill. 2d 369, 565 N.E.2d 643, 649 (1990) (privilege may be overcome where an informant participated in, witnessed, or helped set up crime); People v. Witherspoon, 216 Ill. App. 3d 323, 576 N.E.2d 1030, 1036 (1st Dist. 1991) (disclosure is not required and defendant did not meet burden of establishing need, where an officer testified that he relied on an informant two times in last three months, the informant led to the seizure of drugs in both cases, and the officer verified the informant's address); People v. Perez, 209 Ill. App. 3d 457, 568 N.E.2d 250, 257 (1st Dist. 1991) (factors relevant to disclosure include whether the informant played active role by participating in or witnessing in the criminal activity and whether the informant assisted in setting up its commission beyond being a mere tipster); People v. Torres, 189 Ill. App. 3d 494, 545 N.E.2d 387, 391 (1st Dist. 1989) (factors include the crime charged, possible defenses, and possible significance of the informant's testimony).

§ 4.30 — Piercing the Privilege

Because the state might label someone an informant who is not legally defined as such to avoid disclosure, an understanding of what an informant is becomes paramount. An informant is:

> [A]n undisclosed person who confidentially volunteers material informa-
> tion of violations of the law to officers charged with enforcement of that
> law. As we understand the term, persons who supply information only after
> being interviewed by police officers, or who give information as witnesses
> during the course of an investigation, are not informers . . . . [also,] a
> participant in the transaction upon which the charge against the accused is
> based often is not treated as an informer.[488]

Where the informant was an actual participant in or a witness to the crime, disclosure is required,[489] because in both situations the informant is a material witness in the case whose disclosure is required for the defendant to adequately prepare a defense.[490] At the very least, defense counsel will be allowed to

---

488. Gordon v. United States, 438 F.2d 858, 875 (5th Cir.), *cert. denied,* 404 U.S. 828 (1971).

489. Roviaro v. United States, 353 U.S. 53 (1957); United States v. Conforti, 200 F.2d 365 (7th Cir. 1952), *cert. denied,* 345 U.S. 925 (1953); People v. Lewis, 57 Ill. 2d 232, 311 N.E.2d 685 (1974); People v. Coleman, 124 Ill. App. 3d 597, 464 N.E.2d 827 (3d Dist. 1984); People v. Chaney, 27 Ill. App. 3d 366, 326 N.E.2d 491 (1st Dist. 1975), *aff'd,* 63 Ill. 2d 216, 347 N.E.2d 138 (1976); People v. Perez, 25 Ill. App. 3d 371, 323 N.E.2d 399 (1st Dist. 1974). *See Woods,* 139 Ill. 2d 369, 565 N.E.2d at 649 (if an informant participated or assisted and disclosure would not endanger him or her, disclosure is required); *Perez,* 209 Ill. App. 3d 457, 568 N.E.2d at 257 (disclosure is required for a material witness because the witness had an active role in the crime). *But see* People v. Deveaux, 204 Ill. App. 3d 392, 561 N.E.2d 1259, 1263 (1st Dist. 1990) (disclosure is not required where the informant is not witness to the crime charged, even though the informant provided information regarding another illegal act of defendant's).

490. People v. Coleman, 124 Ill. App. 3d 597, 464 N.E.2d 827 (1984). *See* People v. Bufford, 277 Ill. App. 3d 862, 661 N.E.2d 357, 360 (1st Dist. 1995) (defendant denied right to present defense in prosecution for constructive possession of narcotics where state failed to disclose informant, when defendant's defense was that another individual owned the narcotics; informant was part of transaction which led to defendant, and thus his testimony was critical to defendant's defense; state also failed to show disclosure would have endangered informant).

interview the informant to determine if he or she wants to call the informer as a witness.[491]

When an informant merely reported a crime, however, the courts are less prone to order disclosure on the rationale that the informant is not a crucial witness whose identity is necessary to a constitutionally sound defense.[492] If the informant is not a material witness whose testimony is essential to the guilt or innocence of the defendant or would be helpful to the defense, disclosure is unnecessary.[493] It is apparent that the accused must convince the court that only the defense can intelligently determine if the informant's testimony is helpful to the defendant.[494]

§ 4.31 — Entrapment as a Defense

When the accused raises the defense of entrapment and the informant's testimony is crucial to rebut the defendant's testimony, the informant must be called to testify.[495] Although some courts have held that the failure to rebut the defendant's testimony of entrapment leaves only an inference against the state,[496] counsel must argue that the informant's testimony is so crucial to the

---

491. Roviaro v. United States, 353 U.S. 53 (1957); People v. Lewis, 57 Ill. 2d 232, 311 N.E.2d 685 (1974); People v. Perez, 25 Ill. App. 3d 371, 323 N.E.2d 399 (1974). *See* People v. Torres, 189 Ill. App. 3d 494, 545 N.E.2d 387, 391 (1st Dist. 1989) (defendant is entitled, at the least, to interview an informant where the defendant is the only witness in position to amplify or contradict state's witness' testimony).

492. People v. McCray, 33 Ill. 2d 66, 210 N.E.2d 161 (1965), *aff'd,* 386 U.S. 300 (1967); People v. Mack, 12 Ill. 2d 151, 145 N.E.2d 609 (1957).

493. People v. Mack, 12 Ill. 2d 151, 145 N.E.2d 609 (1957). *See also* People v. Durr, 28 Ill. 2d 308, 192 N.E.2d 379 (1963), *cert. denied,* 376 U.S. 973 (1964); People v. Gonzalez, 87 Ill. App. 3d 610, 410 N.E.2d 146 (1st Dist. 1980). *See* People v. Velez, 123 Ill. App. 3d 210, 462 N.E.2d 746, 753 (1st Dist. 1984) (disclosure is not required where an informant could not testify to facts bearing on a case against the defendant).

494. *See* further discussion in §§ 4.12–4.23.

495. People v. Jones, 73 Ill. App. 2d 55, 219 N.E.2d 12 (1st Dist. 1966). *See also* People v. Taylor, 269 Ill. App. 3d 772, 646 N.E.2d 1280 (1st Dist. 1995); People v. Raess, 146 Ill. App. 3d 384, 496 N.E.2d 1186 (1st Dist. 1986).

496. People v. Strong, 21 Ill. 2d 320, 172 N.E.2d 765 (1961) (no per se rule regarding criminal disposition when government provides defendant with narcotics), *overruled in part, on other grounds* by People v. Cross, 77 Ill. 2d 396, 396 N.E.2d 812, 816 (1979); People v. Dillard, 68 Ill. App. 3d 897, 386 N.E.2d 920 (2d Dist. 1979); People v. Stutzel, 13 Ill. App. 3d 406, 300 N.E.2d 642 (2d Dist. 1973).

defense that failure to call the informant is reversible error.[497] As a practical matter, however, if the state fails to rebut the defendant's testimony regarding entrapment, either by the informant's testimony or by other evidence, the conviction could not stand because the defense evidence stands unrebutted and uncontradicted.

In all cases where disclosure is sought, the state will invariably argue for nondisclosure on the claim that disclosure will result in harm to the inform-ant.[498] Although the argument may have merit and certainly finds support in the statute and case law, the state, in urging nondisclosure, has the burden of proving that the risk of harm to the informant is real and that it outweighs the defendant's right to disclosure.[499] A mere unsupported assertion by the state is not sufficient to prevent disclosure of the informant's identity.[500]

The balancing test of *Roviaro v. United States* does not apply to preliminary hearings, motions to suppress, or other pretrial proceedings, where disclosure is always required if an informant is going to be a witness.[501] Even if the informant is not expected to testify, the court has discretion to order disclosure.[502]

If the judge has the slightest doubt about the credibility of the testifying police officer at a motion to suppress hearing, production of the informant may be ordered.[503] Moreover, an informer who participates in the crime charged must be disclosed at a motion to suppress hearing (based on lack of probable cause to search or arrest) if other evidence does not establish the requisite probable cause.[504] In *People v. Wolfe*, failure to order disclosure was error

---

497. People v. Spahr, 56 Ill. App. 3d 434, 371 N.E.2d 1261 (4th Dist. 1978); People v. Jones, 73 Ill. App. 2d 55, 219 N.E.2d 12 (1st Dist. 1966).

498. S. Ct. Rule 412(i):

> (i) Denial of Disclosure. The court may deny disclosure authorized by this rule and Rule 413 if it finds that there is substantial risk to any person of physical harm, intimidation, bribery, economic reprisals, or unnecessary annoyance or embarrassment resulting from such disclo-sure which outweighs any usefulness of the disclosure to counsel.

499. People v. Lewis, 57 Ill. 2d 232, 311 N.E.2d 685 (1974). *See also* People v. Kliner, 185 Ill. 2d 81, 705 N.E.2d 850 (1998), *cert. denied,* 68 U.S.L.W. 3224 (1999); People v. Glenn, 63 Ill. App. 3d 344, 380 N.E.2d 390 (5th Dist. 1978); People v. Gibson, 54 Ill. App. 3d 898, 370 N.E.2d 262 (4th Dist. 1977).

500. People v. Gibson, 54 Ill. App. 3d 898, 370 N.E.2d 262 (1977).

501. S. Ct. Rule 412(j)(ii).

502. People v. McCray, 33 Ill. 2d 66, 210 N.E.2d 161 (1965).

503. People v. Clifton, 42 Ill. 2d 526, 250 N.E.2d 649 (1969). *See* People v. Friend, 177 Ill. App. 3d 1002, 533 N.E.2d 409, 415 (2d Dist. 1988).

504. *Cf.* People v. Wolfe, 73 Ill. App. 2d 274, 219 N.E.2d 634 (1st Dist. 1966); People v. Clifton, 42 Ill. 2d 526, 250 N.E.2d 649 (1969); People v. Durr, 28 Ill. 2d 308, 192 N.E.2d 379 (1963), *cert. denied,* 376 U.S. 973 (1964).

because a material witness was not produced at the hearing and therefore the defendant was for all practical purposes denied a true hearing on the motion.[505] The fact that the informant later testified at trial did not cure the error.[506]

The scope of the informant's privilege is only as broad as its purpose. When the disclosure of a conversation with a privileged informant will not reveal his or her identity, the conversation is not privileged.[507] When the defendant already knows the identity of the informant, the privilege is no longer applicable.[508]

§ 4.32 Remedies for Discovery Violations

If the court finds that disclosure is required under any of the foregoing discovery theories, the state must comply with discovery orders or suffer statutory sanctions.[509] These can include permitting full discovery, granting a continuance,[510] excluding the evidence offered,[511] dismissing the charge

---

505. People v. Wolfe, 73 Ill. App. 2d 274, 219 N.E.2d 634 (1st Dist. 1966).

506. *Id.*, 219 N.E.2d at 638.

507. Roviaro v. United States, 353 U.S. 53 (1957).

508. *Id.* at 60; People v. Pearson, 210 Ill. App. 3d 1079, 569 N.E.2d 1334, 1337 (2d Dist. 1991). *See also* People v. Woods, 139 Ill. 2d 369, 565 N.E.2d 643, 650–51 (1990) (if informant's identity known to defense, no reason to shield from disclosure where defendant needed formal disclosure to present defense).

509. (i) If at any time during the course of the proceedings it is brought to the attention of the court that a party has failed to comply with an applicable discovery rule or an order issued pursuant thereto, the court may order such party to permit the discovery of material and information not previously disclosed, grant a continuance, exclude such evidence, or enter such other order as it deems just under the circumstances.

(ii) Wilful violation by counsel of an applicable discovery rule or an order issued pursuant thereto may subject counsel to appropriate sanctions by the court.

S. Ct. Rule 415(g).

510. *See, e.g.*, People v. Smith, 220 Ill. App. 3d 76, 580 N.E.2d 918, 920 (3d Dist. 1991) (where the state waited until minutes before trial to inform the defendant of a rebuttal witness' statement contradicting a prior statement, the court should have granted the defendant's request for continuance; the judge abused discretion in allowing the state to use the second statement); People v. Robinson, 189 Ill. App. 3d 323, 545 N.E.2d 268, 273 (1st Dist. 1989) (right to continuance is automatic if the defendant did not learn of an undisclosed statement until the jury hears it). *See* People v. Ward, 301 Ill. App. 3d 862, 704 N.E.2d 777 (1st Dist. 1998).

511. People v. Elworthy, 214 Ill. App. 3d 914, 574 N.E.2d 727, 736 (1st Dist. 1991) (exclusion is proper where a party wilfully violates discovery to obtain a tactical advantage, which may minimize the effectiveness of cross-examination and the

against the defendant,[512] a contempt citation against the offending attorney,[513] or any sanction that is "just under the circumstances."[514] What is just under the circumstances, however, requires the sanction imposed to be proportionate to the magnitude of the discovery violation.[515] The ultimate sanction, which is dismissal of the charge, is appropriate only where failure to disclose an informant's identity results in substantial prejudice to the defendant.[516]

---

ability to adduce rebuttal evidence); People v. Shiflet, 125 Ill. App. 3d 161, 465 N.E.2d 942, 955 (2d Dist. 1984) (exclusion of evidence is proper but sanction harsh). *See* People v. Wydra, 265 Ill. App. 3d 597, 637 N.E.2d 741 (1st. Dist. 1994); People v. Trice, 217 Ill. App. 3d 967, 577 N.E.2d 1197 (1st Dist. 1991).

512. People v. Lawson, 67 Ill. 2d 449, 367 N.E.2d 1244 (1977). *See* People v. Newberry, 166 Ill. 2d 310, 652 N.E.2d 288, 292 (1995) (trial judge justified in dismissing charges against defendant after state destroyed controlled substance or look-alike subsequent to defendant's motion for discovery); People v. Raess, 146 Ill. App. 3d 384, 496 N.E.2d 1186, 1192 (1st Dist. 1986) (dismissal is warranted where the state refused to comply with discovery, made no argument against dismissal, and offered no alternative sanction). *See also* People v. Burrows, 148 Ill. 2d 196, 592 N.E.2d 997 (1992), *cert. denied,* 506 U.S. 1055 (1993); People v. Heinzmann, 232 Ill. App. 3d 557, 597 N.E.2d 942 (5th Dist. 1992).

513. S. Ct. Rule 415(g)(ii). *See* People v. Huntley, 144 Ill. App. 3d 64, 493 N.E.2d 1193, 1196 (5th Dist. 1986) (contempt is the proper means to enforce court orders).

514. S. Ct. Rule 415(g)(i). *See* People v. Preatty, 256 Ill. App. 3d 579, 627 N.E.2d 1199 (2d Dist. 1994) (failure to disclose that state's main witness had pending felony charge required reversal); People v. Furlong, 217 Ill. App. 3d 1047, 578 N.E.2d 77 (1st Dist. 1991) (state's failure to disclose defendant's inculpatory statement introduced at trial required reversal); People v. Lipscomb, 215 Ill. App. 3d 413, 574 N.E.2d 1345, 1360 (4th Dist. 1991) (factors to determine whether a new trial is warranted include closeness of evidence, strength of undisclosed evidence, and likelihood that prior notice would help defendant discredit evidence); People v. Gutirrez, 205 Ill. App. 3d 231, 564 N.E.2d 850, 866 (1st Dist. 1990) (new trial warranted only when undisclosed evidence is material in a constitutional sense, *e.g.,* would affect the jury verdict); People v. Landgham, 182 Ill. App. 3d 148, 537 N.E.2d 981, 987 (1st Dist. 1989) (denying a mistrial not disturbed where the state failed to tender the defendant's statement in response to a discovery request); People v. Eliason, 117 Ill. App. 3d 683, 453 N.E.2d 908, 914 (2d Dist. 1983) (relevant factors include strength of undisclosed evidence, likelihood prior notice would help defendant discredit, feasibility of continuance, and wilfullness of the state's failure to disclose). *See, e.g.,* People v. Holmes, 141 Ill. 2d 204, 565 N.E.2d 950, 961 (1990) (court may delete material unrelated to the defendant's case before turning over the state's documents to the defendant).

515. People v. Lawson, 67 Ill. 2d 449, 367 N.E.2d 1244 (1977).

516. *Id.,* 367 N.E.2d at 1247.

People v. Matthews[517] illustrates where a discovery violation by the state resulted in a reversal and remand for a new trial. After being identified in a lineup as the "shooter," Matthews responded that he was identified only because the witness was a member of a rival gang.[518] This statement was not disclosed by the state to defense counsel.[519] At trial, Matthews testified and denied his gang affiliation.[520] On cross-examination, the judge allowed introduction of the statement for impeachment.[521] On appeal, the court considered the following four factors to determine if the discovery violation required a new trial: "the closeness of the evidence, the strength of the undisclosed evidence, the likelihood that prior notice would have helped the defense discredit the evidence, and the willfulness of the state in failing to disclose the new evidence."[522] The court determined the use of the undisclosed statement resulted in undue prejudice to the defendant and remanded for a new trial.[523]

§ 4.33 State's Discovery Right

The state's discovery rights are broad, limited only by constitutional protections enjoyed by the defendant.[524] It is applicable in felony prosecutions following indictment or information;[525] it is not available in misdemeanor cases.[526] Illinois Supreme Court Rule 413[527] details what the accused must disclose to the prosecution. For example, the state is entitled to receive notice and details of a proposed alibi defense but only if it provides

---

517. 299 Ill. App. 3d 914, 702 N.E.2d 291, 296 (1st Dist. 1998).

518. *Id.,* 702 N.E.2d at 294.

519. *Id.*

520. *Id.*

521. *Id.*

522. *Id.,* 702 N.E.2d at 295.

523. *Id.,* 702 N.E.2d at 296. *But see* People v. Norris, 303 Ill. App. 3d 163, 707 N.E.2d 628 (1st Dist. 1999) (failure by state to disclose all knowledge of victim who was unable to identify anyone as perpetrator did not prejudice defendant).

524. S. Ct. Rule 413(a), 413(c), and 413(d). In *People v. Feldmeier,* 286 Ill. App. 3d 602, 676 N.E.2d 723 (2d Dist. 1997), the court held that the state's attorney abused its subpoena power in obtaining defendant's financial and bank records by issuing a grand jury subpoena returnable to the state's attorney's office. *Id.,* 676 N.E.2d at 724. By not making the records returnable to the court, the prosecutor could obtain constitutionally protected private matters. *Id.*

525. S. Ct. Rule 411.

526. People v. Ramshaw, 75 Ill. App. 3d 123, 394 N.E.2d 21 (5th Dist. 1979).

527. S. Ct. Rule 413.

reciprocal discovery to the defense.[528] The defendant may be ordered to produce handwriting exemplars,[529] fingerprints,[530] and blood samples.[531] The state may place the defendant in a line-up[532] and conduct photographic identification.[533]

The state may also request, and the court may order, an in camera inspection of the notes of the *defense* investigator to determine whether they contain statements of a witness that the defense might use for the purposes of impeachment.[534]

§ 4.34   Sanctions Against the Defense for Discovery Violations

The trial judge may order the defense to provide discovery of previously undisclosed materials, grant the state a continuance, grant other just remedies,

---

528. Wardius v. Oregon, 412 U.S. 470 (1973); Williams v. Florida, 399 U.S. 78 (1970); S. Ct. Rule 413(d)(iii).

529. Gilbert v. California, 388 U.S. 263 (1967); S. Ct. Rule 413(a)(viii).

530. Schmerber v. California, 384 U.S 757 (1966); S. Ct. Rule 413(a)(iii). *But see* People v. Bailey, 164 Ill. App. 3d 555, 517 N.E.2d 570, 575 (1st Dist. 1987) (this rule does not contemplate police entering a jail cell while the defendant is awaiting trial to take finger and palm prints without prior judicial approval or constitutional safeguards). *But see* People v. Sims, 166 Ill. App. 3d 289, 519 N.E.2d 921, 931 (1st Dist. 1987) (even though the defendant was convicted and prints were taken without presence of counsel, the rule was not violated), *cert. denied*, 488 U.S. 844 (1988).

531. Schmerber v. California, 384 U.S. 757 (1966); S. Ct. Rule 413(a)(vii). In *People v. Nohren,* 283 Ill. App. 3d 753, 670 N.E.2d 1208 (4th Dist. 1996), the court held that the state may use a *subpoena duces tecum* to investigate a crime for which a defendant has not yet been charged. *Id.,* 670 N.E.2d at 1211. In this case, it was proper for the state to issue a subpoena to the hospital where the defendant was taken after he was involved in a one car accident for results of blood alcohol tests. *Id.,* 670 N.E.2d at 1212. The court rejected defendant's contention that the state was on a "fishing expedition" when it sought the results, finding that when the state issued the subpoena it had probable cause to believe the defendant was intoxicated on the night in question. *Id.,* 670 N.E.2d at 1212–13.

532. United States v. Wade, 388 U.S. 218 (1967); S. Ct. Rule 413(a)(i). *But see Bailey,* 164 Ill. App. 3d 555, 517 N.E.2d at 577 (when the defendant is under the jurisdiction of court, police have no unbridled power to subject defendant to a line-up without constitutional restraints).

533. United States v. Ash, 413 U.S. 300 (1973); S. Ct. Rule 413(a)(iv).

534. People v. Boclair, 119 Ill. 2d 368, 519 N.E.2d 437 (1987), *appeal dismissed,* 484 U.S. 950 (1987); S. Ct. Rule 413(e). *See* People v. Mudge, 143 Ill. App. 3d 193, 492 N.E.2d 1050, 1051 (5th Dist. 1986) (the taped statement of a defendant to attorney given at the attorney's direction is protected by attorney-client privilege).

or exclude defense evidence or witnesses.[535] The exclusion option should be rarely used by the trial court, and if it is used, it should be of last resort because such exclusion may violate the defendant's constitutional right to present witnesses and a defense.[536] Exclusion of defense evidence is very drastic and should be exercised only when the defendant's discovery violation is flagrant or demonstrates a willful disregard of court orders.[537]

As an example of a defendant's discovery violation that is flagrant or demonstrates a willful disregard of court orders, defense counsel should be aware of *Taylor v. Illinois*.[538] In *Taylor,* the trial judge prevented the defense from calling a witness (arguably critical to the defendant) whose name was provided to the prosecution and the court after the prosecution's two principal witnesses had completed their testimony. The defense attorney represented to the court that it was only in the course of the state's two witnesses' testimony that he became aware (from his client) of the existence of this new witness. At a voir dire hearing conducted the next morning, at which this "new" witness was produced, the witness testified that he had talked to defense counsel a week before the trial began. In barring the witness from testifying, the trial judge found that "this [was] a blatant [sic] violation of the discovery rules."[539]

---

535. S. Ct. Rule 415(g)(i). *See, e.g.,* People v. Trice, 217 Ill. App. 3d 967, 577 N.E.2d 1195, 1202 (1st Dist. 1991) (proper to exclude a letter from a witness to the defendant because the defense did not disclose it to the state during discovery); People v. McCarthy, 213 Ill. App. 3d 873, 572 N.E.2d 1219, 1226 (4th Dist. 1991) (it was not abuse to exclude a letter not provided to the state in discovery where the contents were irrelevant to issues of the defendant's guilt).

536. U.S. CONST. amend. VI. *See* People v. Stack, 261 Ill. App. 3d 191, 633 N.E.2d 42, 47 (4th Dist. 1994) (trial court has *discretion* to bar the defendant's defense but is not *required* to, where the defendant violates discovery; trial court committed reversible error by not exercising discretion); People v. Shriner, 198 Ill. App. 3d 748, 555 N.E.2d 1257, 1262 (2d Dist. 1990) (abuse to exclude alibi witness, but harmless because of overwhelming evidence of guilt).

537. People v. Ramshaw, 75 Ill. App. 3d 123, 394 N.E.2d 21 (5th Dist. 1979); People v. Daniels, 75 Ill. App. 3d 35, 393 N.E.2d 667 (1st Dist. 1979); People v. Williams, 55 Ill. App. 3d 752, 370 N.E.2d 1261 (1st Dist. 1977); People v. Rayford, 43 Ill. App. 3d 283, 356 N.E.2d 1274 (5th Dist. 1976). *See, e.g.,* People v. Morgan, 142 Ill. 2d 410, 568 N.E.2d 755, 768 (1991) (defendant has a continuing duty to promptly notify the state of a new alibi if discovered during trial; where the defendant failed to do so, exclusion of testimony is not abuse), *rev'd on other grounds,* 504 U.S. 719 (1992). *But see* People v. Brooks, 277 Ill. App. 3d 392, 660 N.E.2d 270, 275 (1st Dist. 1996) (convictions reversed and remanded due to trial court's refusal to allow presentation of alibi defense "offending our system's fundamental tenets of due process").

538. 484 U.S. 400 (1988).

539. *Id.* at 405.

In the Illinois Appellate Court below, which affirmed the conviction,[540] and before the United States Supreme Court, the state argued that "the Compulsory Process Clause of the Sixth Amendment is merely a guarantee that the accused shall have the power to subpoena witnesses, and simply does not apply to rulings on the admissibility of evidence."[541] The defense, on the other hand, argued that the Sixth Amendment "creates an absolute bar to the preclusion of testimony" of any witness, including a surprise witness.[542] The United States Supreme Court rejected both contentions.

"The right of the defendant to present evidence 'stands on no lesser footing that the other Sixth Amendment rights that we have previously held applicable to the states.' "[543] Thus the state's argument that the Sixth Amendment right "may never be offended by the imposition of a discovery sanction" is not an acceptable proposition.[544] Neither, however, would the Court accept the defendant's argument that preclusion is never permissible in light of the valid purposes of the discovery rules, which ensure fairness and avoid surprise in the adversarial setting. The Sixth Amendment, said the Court, cannot be used to defeat the "fair and efficient administration of justice," on which discovery rules are predicated.[545]

Finally, the Court also rejected the argument that although it was the lawyer who committed the discovery violations, the client should not suffer as a consequence of the lawyer's acts. "Although there are basic rights that the attorney cannot waive without the fully informed and publicly acknowledged consent of the client . . . the lawyer has—and must have—full authority to manage the conduct of the trial."[546] The Court observed "Whenever a lawyer makes use of the sword provided by the Compulsory Process Clause, there is some risk that he may wound his own client."[547] However, in *People v. Foster*,[548] the appellate court held that the trial court abused its discretion in

---

540. People v. Taylor, 141 Ill. App. 3d 839, 491 N.E.2d 3 (1st Dist. 1986), *aff'd*, 484 U.S. 400 (1988). *See* Michigan v. Lucas, 500 U.S. 145 (1991). *But see* People v. Flores, 168 Ill. App. 3d 284, 522 N.E.2d 708, 714 (1st Dist. 1988) (abuse of discretion to preclude defense expert from testifying, since defense discovery violations were not "deliberate, contumacious or demonstrated unwarranted disregard for the trial court's authority so as to merit exclusion of a material witness").

541. *Taylor,* 484 U.S. at 406.

542. *Id.* at 409.

543. *Id.* (quoting Washington v. Texas, 388 U.S. 14, 19 (1967)).

544. *Taylor,* 484 U.S. at 409.

545. *Id.* at 414.

546. *Id.* at 417–18.

547. *Id.* at 418.

548. 271 Ill. App. 3d 562, 648 N.E.2d 337 (4th Dist. 1995).

denying defendant his right to present evidence of self-defense as a sanction for violating discovery.[549] The court found that a trial judge should first consider sanctioning defense counsel personally rather than denying the defendant a right to present a defense, particularly when it is his or her only defense.[550] In *People v. Brooks*,[551] the appellate court held that the trial court erred in barring defendant's alibi testimony as a discovery violation sanction, and the prejudice to defendant was obvious because his attorney had promised an alibi defense in opening statement.[552] The trial court barred the testimony due to a minor discrepancy between the address listed in defendant's supplemental discovery and that given by defendant's alibi witness.[553] The appellate court, in reversing, found that the error in the answer was not intentional and the state was not prejudiced, particularly since the address given by the witness was the same address listed in the discovery as one belonging to another alibi witness.[554] In conclusion, the court stated that the case did not involve willful violation of discovery and was "not a case where the state was lulled into a false sense of security."[555]

§ 4.35   Motion to Suppress Identification

Although successful cases are few and far between,[556] the motion to suppress pretrial identification evidence is an essential weapon in the arsenal of the criminal defense attorney.[557] It has developed into an important method of offsetting the inherent inequities of the identification process,[558] as well as a method of assuring that police officers do not engage in unnecessarily

---

549. *Id.*, 648 N.E.2d at 342.

550. *Id.*, 648 N.E.2d at 341.

551. 277 Ill. App. 3d 392, 660 N.E.2d 270 (1st Dist. 1996).

552. *Id.*, 660 N.E.2d at 274–75.

553. *Id.*, 660 N.E.2d at 273 (one block).

554. *Id.*, 660 N.E.2d at 274.

555. *Id.*

556. People v. Taylor, 163 Ill. App. 3d 346, 516 N.E.2d 649 (1st Dist. 1987).

557. P. WALL, *Eyewitness Identification in Criminal Cases* 27–29 (1966).

558. As the court stated in *Crume v. Beto*, 383 F.2d 36, 40 (5th Cir. 1967), *cert. denied*, 395 U.S. 964 (1969):

> Once a faint glimmer of recognition strikes a witness, his tendency may be to do everything in his power to reinforce that recognition and come to a positive identification. To compensate a fair practice might be to require the police to take every reasonable precaution to insure that the witness is not overly influenced by his original impression, and that he arrives at an objective and accurate identification.

suggestiveidentificationprocedures.[559] In addition, the hearing on the motion to suppress often provides fertile grounds by which counsel can "test the waters" of the pending case, evaluate the witnesses' ability to testify, obtain certain discovery, determine the strengths of the opposition, and observe the judge's overall impression of the case.

This section deals only with identification evidence that is the alleged product of unnecessarily suggestive police procedures. It does not treat the issue of identification evidence that the defense seeks to suppress as the product of an illegal arrest.[560] The pretrial identification of a defendant by a witness may occur by virtue of a lineup,[561] show-up,[562] one-on-one unplanned confrontation, or photographic array. The type of identification process, as well as the timing, are both considerations that will significantly bear on the court's ultimate determination of the fairness of the procedures employed and the admissibility of the identification evidence.

The United States Supreme Court has recognized that lineups must meet basic due process standards of fundamental fairness.[563] If they do not, evidence of the identification will not be admitted.[564] Thus, lineups in which everyone except the suspect is known to the identifying witness;[565] where the suspect is required to wear distinctive clothing that the culprit allegedly wore;[566] or where

---

559.   The fact that the police themselves have, in a given case, little or no doubt that the man put up for identification has committed the offense, and that their chief pre-occupation is with the problem of getting sufficient proof, . . . involves a danger that this persuasion may communicate itself, even in a doubtful case, to the witness in some way . . . .

Williams & Hammelmann, *Identification Parades I* Crim. L. Rev. 479, 483 (1963).

560.   Brown v. Illinois, 422 U.S. 590 (1975).

561.   A lineup is a multiple person confrontation.

562.   A show-up is a one-on-one police-planned confrontation.

563.   Stovall v. Denno, 388 U.S. 293 (1967); Gilbert v. California, 388 U.S. 263 (1967); United States v. Wade, 388 U.S. 218 (1967). *See also* Johnson v. Hanks, 1996 U.S. App. Lexis 17761 (7th Cir. 1996) (photographs of defendant taken at the scene of the crime after a witness identified him were admissible because probative value exceeded unfair prejudice) (unpublished).

564.   People v. Blumenshine, 42 Ill. 2d 508, 250 N.E.2d 152 (1969).

565.   People v. Boney, 28 Ill. 2d 505, 192 N.E.2d 920 (1963).

566.   People v. Crenshaw, 15 Ill. 2d 458, 155 N.E.2d 599, *cert. denied*, 359 U.S. 997 (1959); People v. Franklin, 22 Ill. App. 3d 775, 317 N.E.2d 611 (1st Dist. 1974). *See also* People v. Simpson, 172 Ill. 2d 117, 665 N.E.2d 1228, 1240 (lineup not unnecessarily suggestive; record did not demonstrate participants were "grossly dissimilar" or that defendant's hairstyle so distinctive), *cert. denied,* 519 U.S. 982 (1996).

other participants in the lineup are grossly dissimilar in appearance to the suspect[567] have all been held unnecessarily suggestive.

The courts initially saw show-ups, in which the police show a suspect standing alone, as unnecessarily suggestive and a denial of the defendant's right to due process, especially where the showing was intentional and not inadvertent.[568] However, there has been a gradual erosion of this rule. For example, the following confrontations have been approved by the courts: where the viewing in a hospital was "imperative" because it was uncertain that the wounded victim would survive;[569] where the victim had an excellent opportunity to observe the defendant at the time of the crimes;[570] and where the identifying witness knew the defendant before the crime.[571] In all of the one-on-one confrontations, the courts have looked both to the perceived need of an immediate showing of the defendant and to the intent of the police.[572]

The Illinois Supreme Court has expressed some disfavor toward using photographs for pretrial identification when the defendant is already in custody and available for a lineup.[573] However, one problem for defense counsel is that even when the accused is in custody, the defendant still must demonstrate that use of the photograph was unnecessarily suggestive and led to a substantial likelihood of misidentification.[574]

Photographic arrays, as opposed to the showing of one photograph, are seldom found to be prejudicial. In those cases where photographic arrays are challenged, courts usually find the procedure to be nonsuggestive. Court-sanctioned examples include situations where the defendant's photograph was the only one in the array that was in color;[575] where the defendant's photograph was the only one without any writing on it and without two views of its

---

567. People v. Adell, 75 Ill. App. 2d 385, 221 N.E.2d 72 (1st Dist. 1966), *cert. denied,* 389 U.S. 860 (1967).

568. Neil v. Beggers, 409 U.S. 188 (1972); People v. Gardner, 35 Ill. 2d 564, 221 N.E.2d 232 (1966).

569. Stovall v. Denno, 388 U.S. 293 (1967).

570. People v. Speck, 41 Ill. 2d 177, 242 N.E.2d 208 (1968), *rev'd on other grounds,* 403 U.S. 946 (1971).

571. People v. Robinson, 73 Ill. 2d 192, 383 N.E.2d 164, 168 (1978).

572. A defendant paraded in handcuffs before the witness is viewed differently from a defendant who is being processed as the witness enters the station.

573. People v. Williams, 60 Ill. 2d 1, 322 N.E.2d 819 (1975), *overruled on other grounds* by People v. King, 66 Ill. 2d 551, 363 N.E.2d 838, 841, *cert. denied,* 434 U.S. 894 (1977); People v. Holiday, 47 Ill. 2d 300, 265 N.E.2d 634 (1970).

574. People v. Duarte, 79 Ill. App. 3d 110, 398 N.E.2d 332 (1st Dist. 1979); People v. Mikel, 73 Ill. App. 3d 21, 391 N.E.2d 550 (4th Dist. 1979).

575. People v. Hudson, 7 Ill. App. 3d 333, 287 N.E.2d 297 (3d Dist. 1972).

subject;[576] where the defendant's picture was larger than the rest;[577] or where the defendant was the only person depicted without a shirt.[578]

The defendant, regardless of the type of pretrial identification, has the right to a pretrial hearing to determine whether a witness's identification was based solely on his or her independent observation of the crime and the offender or whether it was influenced by unnecessarily suggestive police procedures or other extraneous factors that may have unfairly affected the judgment and conclusion of the witness.[579]

At the hearing, the initial burden is on the defendant to establish that within the totality of the circumstances, the pretrial identification was so unnecessarily suggestive that it gave rise to a substantial likelihood of irreparable mistaken identification.[580] If the defendant meets this burden, the out-of-court pretrial identification will be held inadmissible.[581]

Even if the pretrial identification is found to be improper, however, an in-court identification by the witness may still be allowed, provided the state establishes by clear and convincing evidence that his identification is based on an observation independent of and before the tainted out-of-court identification.[582] Factors that go into the court's determination of suggestiveness and independent basis include the opportunity of the witness to view the criminal act, the witness's degree of attention, the accuracy of prior descriptions of the offender, the level of certainty demonstrated by the witness at the confrontation, and the time between the crime and the confrontation.[583]

---

576. People v. Witted, 79 Ill. App. 3d 156, 398 N.E.2d 68 (1st Dist. 1979).

577. People v. Hart, 10 Ill. App. 3d 857, 295 N.E.2d 63 (3d Dist. 1973).

578. People v. Johnson, 43 Ill. App. 3d 649, 357 N.E.2d 151 (1st Dist. 1976).

579. People v. Robinson, 46 Ill. 2d 229, 263 N.E.2d 57 (1970).

580. Stovall v. Denno, 388 U.S. 293, 301–02 (1967); People v. Jackson, 24 Ill. App. 3d 700, 321 N.E.2d 420, 423 (1st Dist. 1974). *See* Taylor v. Illinois, 484 U.S. 400 (1988).

581. *Jackson,* 24 Ill. App. 3d 700, 321 N.E.2d at 421.

582. Stovall v. Denno, 388 U.S. 293 (1967); Gilbert v. California, 388 U.S. 263 (1967); United States v. Wade, 388 U.S. 218 (1967).

583. Manson v. Brathwaite, 432 U.S. 98, 114 (1977). *See also* People v. Tedder, 83 Ill. App. 3d 874, 404 N.E.2d 437 (1st Dist. 1980). *See* People v. Enis, 163 Ill. 2d 367, 645 N.E.2d 856, 870 (1994) (although a single photograph showup to two identification witnesses was suggestive and improper, the state met the burden of showing that the identifications were sufficiently independent of viewing the photograph to deny suppression; witnesses had sufficient opportunity to view the defendant, viewed him in daylight, looked directly at his face, gave a description to police, were certain of their initial identification of him, testified that their identification was based on recollection and not on having seen a photograph of

Aside from, or perhaps in addition to, the alleged suggestiveness of pretrial identification procedures, another area of concern to counsel representing a defendant who has been identified in a pretrial procedure is that of the right to counsel. A pretrial lineup is a critical stage of the criminal prosecution[584] and as such may require the presence of counsel. If the lineup or any intentional identification confrontation occurs after the initiation of "adversarial judicial proceedings," the defendant is constitutionally entitled to counsel.[585] In Illinois, prosecutions are commenced by the filing of a complaint, indictment, or information.[586] This filing process is the commencement of adversarial judicial proceedings that triggers the defendant's right to counsel at any lineup or identification process.[587] Thus, absent a valid waiver of counsel by the defendant,[588] a pretrial, postcommencement-of-adversarial-judicial-proceedings-confrontation is a proper subject of a motion to suppress, even in the absence of suggestiveness.[589] In *People v. Garrett*,[590] the court held that defendant was not denied his right to counsel at a lineup. Approximately one month after his arrest and initial appearance in court, he was requested to appear in a lineup. He was then identified. Defendant filed a motion to suppress, contending that he was denied his right to counsel at the lineup. A "lineup rights sheet" was prepared. Defendant signed the sheet, stating that he did not wish the representation of the public defender's office because he was represented by a private attorney. The police testified that he refused to disclose who this attorney was, although he did advise them he had private counsel. Defendant testified that he requested counsel but the police ignored his request. The public defender

---

him, and that they were under no compulsion to identify defendant), *cert. denied*, 516 U.S. 827 (1995).

584. Moore v. Illinois, 434 U.S. 220, 229–32 (1977); *Gilbert*, 388 U.S. at 272; *Wade*, 388 U.S. at 227–37; People v. Curtis, 132 Ill. App. 3d 241, 476 N.E.2d 1162 (1st Dist. 1985), *rev'd on other grounds*, 113 Ill. 2d 136, 497 N.E.2d 1004, 1012 (1986), *cert. denied*, 481 U.S. 1014 (1987).

585. *Moore*, 434 U.S. at 226; *Curtis*, 132 Ill. App. 3d 241, 476 N.E.2d at 1167; People v. Green, 282 Ill App. 3d 510, 668 N.E.2d 158 (1st Dist. 1996).

586. 725 ILCS 5/111-2.

587. *Curtis*, 132 Ill. App. 3d 241, 476 N.E.2d at 1168.

588. "A waiver is an intentional abandonment of a known right." Johnson v. Zerbst, 304 U.S. 458, 464 (1938); People v. Swift, 91 Ill. App. 3d 361, 414 N.E.2d 895, 898 (3d Dist. 1980).

589. "[O]nly a *per se* exclusionary rule as to such testimony and evidence can be an efficacious sanction to assure that law enforcement authorities will respect an accused's constitutional right to assistance of counsel at all critical stages. . . . Thus, . . . the State [is] not entitled to show . . . an independent source [of the in-court identification]." *Curtis*, 132 Ill. App. 3d 241, 476 N.E.2d at 1171.

590. 179 Ill. 2d 239, 688 N.E.2d 614 (1997).

testified that the defendant gave him the name of his counsel and that defendant was not given an opportunity to call counsel while he was present. He further stated that he never heard defendant make such a request either. The public defender left because defendant did not desire his services. When he returned to his office, he contacted defendant's counsel. The trial court denied defendant's motion to suppress. On appeal, the defendant contended that the lineup was a critical stage and his Sixth Amendment right to counsel had attached. The court disagreed, finding that the adversarial process had not begun at the time of the lineup. There were no formal charges against defendant or significant prosecutorial involvement at that time.[591] Specifically, the complaint against defendant was filed by the police and his arrest warrant was issued without the assistance of the state's attorney. Moreover, the filing of a complaint does not represent a formal commitment by the state to prosecute.[592] The only involvement by the assistant state's attorney was attendance at two hearings; one being a bond hearing and the second a continuance of the preliminary hearing. The court did not find the fact that defendant was in jail for twenty-two days after this hearing of import. Finally, it noted that the state's attorney was not present at the lineup in any capacity. Therefore, the adversarial process had not yet begun, and defendant's Sixth Amendment right to counsel had not yet attached.[593]

In spite of all the apparent difficulties in successfully presenting a motion to suppress identification based on unnecessarily suggestive procedures, and regardless of whether adversarial proceedings have been commenced, whenever the defendant is the subject of a pretrial identification, especially when the defendant was shown alone, either in person or through a photograph to the victim, counsel should consider filing a motion to suppress. If the identification procedures are deemed by the court to have been unnecessarily suggestive, evidence of the identification will not be admitted,[594] unless the state proves that the in-court identification is based on observation independent of the out-of-court identification procedure.[595] If the defendant lacked counsel and adversarial judicial proceedings had already commenced, even if the procedures were not suggestive and there was an independent basis for the identification, identification testimony may not be allowed at trial.[596] Absent identification evidence at trial, dismissal of the charges may be the only recourse.

---

591. *Id.*, 688 N.E.2d at 619.

592. *Id.*

593. *Id.*

594. Stovall v. Denno, 388 U.S. 293, 301–02 (1967); People v. Jackson, 24 Ill. App. 3d 700, 321 N.E.2d 420, 423 (1st Dist. 1974).

595. People v. Johnson, 104 Ill. App. 3d 572, 432 N.E.2d 1232 (1st Dist. 1982).

596. *Curtis,* 132 Ill. App. 3d 241, 476 N.E.2d at 1171.

Finally, defense counsel must consider what use, if any, the state can make of defendants' testimony at a hearing on a motion to suppress identification of allegations that defendants had made in the written motion filed with the court. While the prosecution may not use defendants' pretrial testimony given at the hearing on a motion to suppress identification as substantive evidence of defendants' guilt in the state's case-in-chief,[597] defendants' testimony or documents to which they voluntarily attested may be used for purposes of impeachment.[598] Although as a practical matter, defendants' testimony at a motion to suppress identification would rarely contain statements that would impeach them should they choose to testify at trial, defense counsel should not forget the potential use.

§ 4.36 Motions to Bar Use of Evidence of Prior Convictions

Few things can more seriously undermine any witness's testimony, especially that of the defendant, than introduction of proof that the witness was previously convicted of another crime. Yet on the rationale that such prior crimes evidence bears heavily on the issue of credibility, "provables" are frequently introduced against witnesses, usually the defendant, after they testify[599] and sometimes, though for reasons other than credibility, even in the state's case-in-chief.[600] This section discusses three situations most often encountered where prior crime evidence becomes an issue: (1) where the state seeks to introduce evidence of a prior conviction of the defendant after he or she testifies to impeach his or her credibility; (2) where either the state or the defense seeks to introduce impeachment evidence of a prior conviction of a witness other than the defendant; and (3) where the state seeks to introduce substantive evidence of a prior conviction of the defendant, whether or not he testifies, to prove motive, intent, identity, absence of mistake, or some other issue other than credibility.

In all three circumstances the appropriate vehicle by which the defense seeks to preclude prior crimes evidence is a motion to bar use of evidence of prior convictions. In each of the three situations, however, both the law, and more especially, practical considerations differ.

---

597. United States v. Salvucci, 448 U.S. 83 (1980); People v. Dowery, 174 Ill. App. 3d 239, 528 N.E.2d 214 (1st Dist. 1988).

598. People v. Sturgis, 58 Ill. 2d 211, 317 N.E.2d 545 (1974), *cert. denied,* 420 U.S. 936 (1975). *See also* People v. Mulero, 176 Ill. 2d 444, 680 N.E.2d 1329 (1997).

599. People v. Montgomery, 47 Ill. 2d 510, 268 N.E.2d 695, 698–700 (1971); People v. Ray, 54 Ill. 2d 377, 297 N.E.2d 168, 170–71 (1973) (discretionary power of judge applies prospectively); People v. Shelton, 264 Ill. App. 3d 763, 636 N.E.2d 675 (1st Dist. 1993).

600. People v. Scott, 100 Ill. App. 2d 473, 241 N.E.2d 579, 582–83 (1st Dist. 1968).

§ 4.37 — To Impeach the Defendant's Credibility

People v. Montgomery[601] establishes the basic circumstances under which the state may impeach a defendant with a prior conviction after he or she has testified. In *Montgomery*, the Illinois Supreme Court adopted proposed Federal Rule of Evidence 609, specifically, a defendant may be impeached by evidence that he or she was previously convicted of a crime if that conviction was for a felony[602] or involved dishonesty or false statement,[603] regardless of the punishment, unless in either case, the judge determines that the probative value of the evidence of the crime is substantially outweighed by the danger of unfair prejudice.[604] In both cases, a conviction (or release from confinement) that occurred more than ten years before the time admission is sought is inadmissible.[605]

Because *Montgomery* vests the trial judge with absolute discretion in balancing the prejudicial effect against the probative value of prior crimes evi-

---

601. *Montgomery*, 47 Ill. 2d 510, 268 N.E.2d at 698–700.

602. A felony is "an offense for which a sentence of death or to a term of imprisonment in a penitentiary for one year or more is provided." 720 ILCS 5/2-7.

603. Any offense "which has as its basis lying, cheating, deceiving or stealing bears a reasonable relation to testimonial deceit" and is considered a crime of dishonesty or false statement. People v. Spates, 77 Ill. 2d 193, 395 N.E.2d 563, 569 (1979); People v. Woodard, 276 Ill. App. 3d 242, 658 N.E.2d 55 (5th Dist. 1995), *aff'd,* 175 Ill. 2d 435, 677 N.E.2d 935 (1997); People v. Whitelow, 215 Ill. App. 3d 1, 574 N.E.2d 253 (5th Dist. 1991). *Cf.* People v. Strother, 53 Ill. 2d 95, 290 N.E.2d 201, 204 (1972) (because "habitual users of narcotics become notorious liars," argument can be made that multiple prior convictions of narcotics offenses, even if misdemeanors that indicate habitual use, may be used to impeach witnesses under the Montgomery balancing test; however, such use against defendant is probably not ever warranted because of prejudicial effect). *See also* People v. Adams, 109 Ill. 2d 102, 485 N.E.2d 339 (1985), *cert. denied,* 475 U.S. 1088 (1986); People v. Mercado, 244 Ill. App. 3d 1040, 614 N.E.2d 284 (1st Dist. 1993); People v. Smith, 70 Ill. App. 3d 250, 387 N.E.2d 901 (1st Dist. 1979).

604. *Montgomery*, 47 Ill. 2d 510, 268 N.E.2d at 699–700, adopted this balancing test, which finds its origins in the proposed (not as finally adopted) rule 609 of the Federal Rules of Evidence (Committee on Rule of Practice Procedure of the Judicial Conference United States) that was predicated on *Luck v. United States,* 348 F.2d 763 (D.C. Cir. 1965), and *Gordon v. United States,* 383 F.2d 936 (D.C. Cir. 1967). Rule 609 as enacted presumes a prejudicial effect of prior convictions that must be overcome by a showing of greater probative value. *Montgomery* presumes a probative value of prior conviction evidence that is not overcome absent a showing that the probative value is substantially outweighed by the prejudice.

605. *Montgomery*, 47 Ill. 2d 510, 268 N.E.2d at 697.

dence,[606] in all cases where a defendant faces trial having previously been convicted of a crime, defense counsel is well advised to seriously consider filing a motion to bar the use of prior crimes evidence for impeachment. Obviously, if the accused suffered a conviction and release from confinement more than ten years before the present trial, the judge has no discretion to allow the evidence. The absolute ten-year rule bars the evidence.[607] If the conviction was for neither a felony nor a nonfelonious crime involving dishonesty or false statement (for example, many misdemeanors, ordinance violations, and traffic offenses), *Montgomery* also requires preclusion.[608] "[I]f (1) the conviction has been the subject of a pardon, annulment, certificate of rehabilitation, or other equivalent procedure, and (2) the procedure under which the same was granted or issued required a substantial showing of rehabilitation or was based on innocence" (most of these terms refer to proceedings available in states other than Illinois), the conviction should be barred,[609] as well as convictions that were reversed on appeal.[610] If the conviction was a juvenile adjudication, ordinarily it will be inadmissible against the defendant,[611] although it may be used against witnesses other than the defendant.[612]

It is only for those prior convictions within ten years that are felonies or crimes of dishonesty or false statements that *Montgomery* requires the trial judge to exercise discretion and balance the prejudicial effect on the defendant against the probative value to the state. With respect to such prior offenses,

---

606. "The trial court is not *required* to allow impeachment by prior conviction . . . [but rather is left] . . . room for the operation of a sound judicial discretion to play upon the circumstances as they unfold in a particular case." Montgomery, 47 Ill. 2d 510, 268 N.E.2d at 699. *See* People v. McGee, 286 Ill. App. 3d 786, 676 N.E.2d 1341, 1346-47 (1st Dist. 1997) (trial court erred in failing to weigh probative value against unfair prejudice of defendant's two prior drug convictions). *See also* People v. Georgakapoulous, 303 Ill. App. 3d 1001, 708 N.E.2d 1196 (1st Dist. 1999).

607. 268 N.E.2d at 699. *See also People v. Yost,* 78 Ill. 2d 292, 297, 399 N.E.2d 1283, 1284–85 (1980), where the supreme court laid to rest the argument (predicated on *People v. Ray,* 54 Ill. 2d 377, 297 N.E.2d 168 (1973)) that release on parole or probation was also within the ten-year rule provisions. "The 10 year time limit for impeachment stated in *Montgomery* [date of conviction or release from confinement] is the standard to be applied." *Yost,* 78 Ill. 2d 292, 399 N.E.2d at 1285. *See also* People v. McLaurin, 184 Ill. 2d 58, 703 N.E.2d 11 (1998), *cert. denied,* 119 S. Ct. 1506 (1999).

608. *Montgomery,* 47 Ill. 2d 510, 268 N.E.2d at 698.

609. *Id.*

610. People v. Shook, 35 Ill. 2d 597, 221 N.E.2d 290, 292 (1966).

611. *Montgomery,* 47 Ill. 2d 510, 268 N.E.2d at 699.

612. *Id.*

however, that discretion is broad.[613] The *Montgomery* court apparently recognized that it may become a practical impossibility for a defendant to testify in front of a jury if the state could automatically impeach his or her testimony with evidence of a prior conviction, because once the jury learns that the defendant is a convicted felon (or dishonest misdemeanant) it is likely that it would disbelieve anything that he or she said.[614]

The court revisited the admissibility of prior convictions in *People v. Williams*.[615] After a review of the history of *Montgomery*, both before and after its inception, the court observed that there has been "a regression toward allowing the State to introduce evidence of virtually all types of felony convictions for the purported reason of impeaching a testifying defendant."[616] However, the rule has long been that if evidence of other crimes is introduced only to show or suggest a propensity to commit crimes, this is improper and such other crimes' evidence is inadmissible.[617] In *Williams*, the court held that "*Montgomery* . . . does not . . . allow for the admission of evidence of any and all prior crimes. The focus of *Montgomery* was on crimes which bear upon the defendant's truthfulness as a witness."[618]

---

613. Rule 609 of the Federal Rules of Evidence, as adopted, limits the trial judge admissibility discretion to crimes that are not those of dishonesty or false statements. Crimes of dishonesty or false statements are always automatically admissible under the federal rule. In Illinois, however, the trial court may bar the use of any conviction, regardless of its nature or characterization. "It is still the province of the trial court to weigh the probative value of a conviction . . . against the potential for unfair prejudice . . . ." People v. Spates, 77 Ill. 2d 193, 395 N.E.2d 563, 569 (1979); *Montgomery,* 47 Ill. 2d 510, 268 N.E.2d at 699; People v. Smith, 73 Ill. App. 3d 577, 392 N.E.2d 347, 349 (5th Dist. 1979).

614. *Smith,* 73 Ill. App. 3d 577, 392 N.E.2d at 349; *Montgomery,* 47 Ill. 2d 510, 268 N.E.2d at 697 ("On the other hand, the prejudicial effect of this [prior conviction] evidence is unmistakable . . . . 'The defendant is a dead duck once he is on trial before a jury and you present a record that he was convicted . . . . If it's any way close, the jury is going to hang him on that record, not on the evidence.' ").

615. 161 Ill. 2d 1, 641 N.E.2d 296 (1994).

616. *Id.,* 641 N.E.2d at 311–12.

617. *Id.,* 641 N.E.2d at 312.

618. *Id. See also* People v. McGee, 286 Ill. App. 3d 786, 676 N.E.2d 1341, 1346 (1st Dist. 1997) (admission of four felony convictions was a reversible error since the trial judge failed to conduct a meaningful balancing test); People v. Jordan, 282 Ill. App. 3d 301, 668 N.E.2d 90, 93 (1st Dist. 1996) (reminding trial judges that they have "discretion to refuse such evidence for impeachment purposes if . . . [they] believe [ ] that the prejudicial effect of the impeachment outweighs the probative value of the prior conviction as to the issue of credibility"); People v. Adams, 281 Ill. App. 3d 339, 666 N.E.2d 769, 773 (1st Dist. 1996) (prior convictions for aggravated battery and possession were not admissible in defen-

The use of juvenile adjudications to impeach witnesses is another area of controversy. Are they to be treated the same as "provable" convictions subject to the *Montgomery* balancing test? The Fourth District recognized that the Juvenile Court Act "supplanted [the older provisions barring use of juvenile adjudications for impeachment] and prior adjudications are now freely admissible for purposes of impeachment without the balancing test required in Rule 609(d)."[619]

Note that in all cases, the trial judge must conduct the *Montgomery* balancing test.[620] However, *Montgomery* precludes use of juvenile adjudication against a defendant.[621]

What, then, are the factors that a motion to bar use of evidence of a defendant's prior conviction must address in hopes of persuading the trial judge to exercise his or her discretion on the defendant's behalf? If the prior crime the defendant was convicted of is so factually similar to the one he or she is presently charged with, a strong argument can be made for barring that prior conviction because it bears less on his or her credibility than on a general propensity to commit such crimes (for example, "if he did it then, he must be guilty now"), which is a clearly improper purpose.[622] Also, if the prior crime occurred just barely within the ten-year period,[623] or it occurred more than ten years ago but the defendant was discharged from confinement within the ten-year period;[624] the defendant was a youthful offender at the time of the prior conviction and has since led a crime-free life; or the prior incident occurred under unusual circumstances, such as the breakup of a marriage or death of a

---

dant's trial for aggravated battery and armed violence because they were not relevant to his testimonial credibility). *See* People v. Williams, 173 Ill. 2d 48, 670 N.E.2d 638, 655 (1996) (reiterating that three-prong test of *Montgomery* is still law in Illinois), *cert. denied,* 520 U.S. 1122 (1997). *Cf., e.g.,* People v. Robinson, 299 Ill. App. 3d 426, 701 N.E.2d 231, 243 (1st Dist. 1998); People v. Williams, 289 Ill. App. 3d 24, 681 N.E.2d 115, 119 (1st Dist. 1997).

619. People v. McClendon, 146 Ill. App. 3d 1004, 497 N.E.2d 849, 853 (4th Dist. 1986).

620. People v. Williams, 161 Ill. 2d 1, 641 N.E.2d 296, 309 (1994); People v. Jennings, 279 Ill. App. 3d 406, 664 N.E.2d 699, 703 (4th Dist. 1996); People v. Maxwell, 272 Ill. App. 3d 57, 650 N.E.2d 298, 301 (4th Dist. 1995).

621. People v. Sneed, 274 Ill. App. 3d 287, 653 N.E.2d 1349, 1355 (1st Dist. 1995); People v. Kerns, 229 Ill. App. 3d 938, 595 N.E.2d 207, 208 (4th Dist. 1992).

622. *Montgomery,* 47 Ill. 2d 510, 268 N.E.2d at 697; People v. Clark, 3 Ill. App. 3d 196, 278 N.E.2d 511, 515 (1st Dist. 1971).

623. *Montgomery,* 47 Ill. 2d 510, 268 N.E.2d at 698.

624. The court may not presume release within the ten-year period just because a defendant was convicted barely beyond the ten years. Proof is required. People v. Yost, 78 Ill. 2d 292, 399 N.E.2d 1283, 1285 (1980).

loved one, preclusion of the use of the prior conviction should be urged.[625] If it is only through the testimony of the defendant that a defense can be presented, a persuasive argument can be made to bar the prior crimes evidence.[626] It must be remembered, however, that because all of these arguments are directed to the judge's discretion, it is only if the judge abuses[627] or refuses to exercise that discretion[628] in balancing the prejudicial effect to the defendant against the probative value to the state that reversible error is committed. Moreover, although the critical need for an early ruling on admissibility is obvious,[629] the trial judge may reserve his or her ruling until after the state presents its case[630] or even until after the defendant has testified,[631] a fate almost as detrimental as an adverse ruling on the admissibility question itself.

---

625. "In exercising discretion . . . a number of factors might be relevant, such as the nature of the prior crimes, . . . length of the criminal record, the age and circumstances of the defendant, and, above all, the extent to which it is more important for the search for truth in a particular case for the jury to hear the defendant's story than to know of a prior conviction." *Montgomery,* 47 Ill. 2d 510, 268 N.E.2d at 699.

626. Counsel must attempt to convince the court that the only way the defendant can present any defense is if he or she testifies. If the defendant testifies, however, and the state is permitted to impeach his or her testimony with evidence of a prior conviction, it is likely that the jury will reject his or her defense. "It is [under these circumstances] more important to the search for truth . . . for the jury to hear the defendant's story than to know of a prior conviction." *Montgomery,* 47 Ill. 2d 510, 268 N.E.2d at 699. Of course, the state's response is that because the defense case will in large part rest on the defendant's testimony, it becomes even more important for the jury to know that the defendant is a convicted felon (or "dishonest" misdemeanant) in judging his or her credibility. *Cf.* People v. Pruitt, 165 Ill. App. 3d 947, 520 N.E.2d 867, 870 (1st Dist. 1988); People v. Medreno, 99 Ill. App. 3d 449, 425 N.E.2d 588, 591–92 (3d Dist. 1981); People v. Ramey, 70 Ill. App. 3d 327, 388 N.E.2d 196, 199 (1st Dist. 1979). *But see* People v. Redd, 135 Ill. 2d 252, 553 N.E.2d 316 (1990); People v. Robinson, 299 Ill. App. 3d 426, 701 N.E.2d 231 (1st Dist. 1998).

627. People v. Wright, 51 Ill. App. 3d 461, 366 N.E.2d 1058, 1062 (4th Dist. 1977) (aggravated battery conviction "has no bearing whatsoever on honesty and veracity").

628. *Yost,* 78 Ill. 2d 510, 399 N.E.2d at 1283.

629. The theory of the defense, what witnesses may be called, opening statements, and cross-examination of the state's witnesses may all hinge on whether the defendant will testify, which in turn may hinge on whether a prior conviction will be admissible. The defendant's testimony on direct examination also may be affected by whether he or she can be impeached by a prior conviction.

630. People v. Barksdale, 24 Ill. App. 3d 489, 321 N.E.2d 489, 494–95 (1st Dist. 1974).

631. *Id.*

Finally, even if the court opts for allowing the state to impeach a testifying defendant with a prior conviction, the question still remains as to what the factfinder may hear about the prior conviction. While the *fact* of the prior conviction may be relevant in assessing credibility, what about the name of the crime? the date of conviction? the circumstances of the crime that led to conviction? the sentence? whether the defendant pled guilty or was found guilty after trial?

The defense bar, as well a some trial judges, have suggested that since the only legitimate purpose for which a "provable" is introduced is to affect credibility, the conviction should be "sanitized," allowing only the *fact* of a felony conviction and nothing else. With proper instructions this approach would appear to most closely meet the true purposes for which "provable convictions" should be considered.[632]

The United States Supreme Court addressed this issue in a related context. Johnny Lynn Old Chief was charged under a federal indictment with inter alia possession of a firearm by a convicted felon. Prior to trial, Old Chief offered to stipulate to the fact of the prior conviction, an element of the charged offense which the government had to prove. Old Chief argued that the name and nature of the prior conviction, "assault causing serious bodily injury," was inadmissible under Federal Rule of Evidence 403 since its "probative value [was] substantially outweighed by the danger of unfair prejudice."[633] The government rejected Old Chief's offer to stipulate and introduced the entire judgment of conviction, including the name and nature of the offenses.[634]

The Supreme Court first recognized that while the fact of the prior conviction was relevant and admissible, and that in most situations the "prosecution is entitled to prove its case free from any defendant's option to stipulate the evidence away," that authority "has no application when the

---

632. See Justice Steigmann's special concurrence in *People v. Kunze*, 193 Ill. App. 3d 708, 550 N.E.2d 284, 297–303 (4th Dist. 1990), that discusses the "mere fact" rule and prior convictions. People v. Atkinson, 288 Ill. App. 3d 102, 679 N.E.2d 1266 (4th Dist. 1997) (accepting "mere fact rule"); People v. Scott, 278 Ill. App. 3d 468, 663 N.E.2d 97, 102 (4th Dist. 1996) (recognizing that "mere fact rule" "is the best way to impeach a defendant" but not a required method of impeachment). *But see* People v. Thomas, 220 Ill. App. 3d 110, 580 N.E.2d 1353, 1359 (2d Dist. 1991) (rejecting "mere fact rule").

633. Johnny Lynn Old Chief v. United States, 519 U.S. 172, 180 (1997). Rule 403 provides for the exclusion of relevant evidence on the grounds of prejudice, confusion, or waste of time and states: "Although relevant, evidence may be excluded if its probative value is substantially outweighed by the danger of unfair prejudice, confusion of the issues, or misleading the jury, or by considerations of undue delay, waste of time, or needless presentation of cumulative evidence."

634. *Id.* at 175–76.

point at issue is a defendant's legal status."[635] Observing that the issue before it "is the scope of the trial judge's discretion under Rule 403," the Court held that the trial judge abused his discretion by allowing the entire record. The Court found that the name and the nature of the offense risked unfair prejudice which substantially outweighed any probative value in light of the defendant's offered stipulation.[636]

§ 4.38 — To Impeach Witnesses Other than the Defendant[637]

The rules set forth in *People v. Montgomery* for impeachment of a witness by prior convictions apply to all witnesses called to testify, not just the defendant, and regardless of whether the witness is called by the defense or the state.[638] However, although in each case the court must balance the prejudicial effect on the witness in admitting the prior conviction against its probative value, "there is less possibility of unfair prejudice when a prior conviction is used to impeach a witness . . . [other than the defendant because it is only the] defendant . . . [who] may be convicted . . . ."[639] If the trial court sustains a state motion in limine to bar use by the defense of a prior conviction[640] against a state witness without conducting the *Montgomery* balancing test, an abuse of discretion may be found and reversal may be required.[641]

§ 4.39 — Prior Convictions and Other Bad Acts as Substantive Evidence

The most frequently encountered use of evidence of prior convictions is for impeachment purposes after a witness, including the defendant, has testified. Equally, if not more devastating, however, is the introduction by the prosecution in its case-in-chief, as substantive evidence of guilt of the accused, of prior

---

635. *Id.* at 189–90.

636. *Id.* at 191–92.

637. People v. Rollins, 108 Ill. App. 3d 480, 438 N.E.2d 1322, 1329 (1st Dist. 1982). "Illinois law . . . permits trial courts to exercise discretion in deciding whether to preclude impeachment of *prosecution* witnesses with evidence of prior convictions." *Id.,* 438 N.E.2d at 1330. *See also* People v. Warmack, 73 Ill. App. 3d 783, 392 N.E.2d 334, 339 (1st Dist. 1979), *rev'd,* 83 Ill. 2d 112, 413 N.E.2d 1254 (1980) (impeachment of state's witness must comply with proposed rule 609); People v. Thomas, 58 Ill. App. 3d 402, 405, 374 N.E.2d 743, 746 (1st Dist. 1978).

638. *Thomas,* 58 Ill. App. 3d 402, 374 N.E.2d at 746.

639. *Id.* (qualifying felony or crime of dishonesty within 10 years).

640. People v. Groves, 71 Ill. App. 3d 570, 389 N.E.2d 1279, 1283 (1st Dist. 1979).

641. People v. Nuccio, 43 Ill. 2d 375, 253 N.E.2d 353 (1969).

"bad acts" or other offenses allegedly committed by the accused, even if the defendant was not convicted of the offenses and even if they occurred after the offense for which the accused now stands trial.

For purposes of this section, "other crimes" evidence refers to incidents with which the defendant may or may not have been charged, for which the defendant may or may not have been prosecuted, of which the defendant may or may not have been convicted, and which may have occurred before or after the commission of the presently pending charge.

Generally, evidence of other crimes is inadmissible as substantive evidence,[642] "not because it has no appreciable probative value, but because it has too much."[643] Evidence of other crimes tends to imply that the defendant has a propensity to commit crimes. "The law distrusts [or at least recognizes the danger of] the inference that because a man has committed other crimes he is more likely to have committed the current crime."[644] Thus, where the prosecution attempts to introduce evidence of other crimes solely to show the defendant's propensity to commit crimes, it is inadmissible.[645]

However, evidence of a defendant's other crimes may be admissible as substantive evidence if it is relevant for any purpose other than to show the defendant's propensity to commit crime.[646] Such evidence may be admitted to show modus operandi, a fact in issue, motive, intent, identity, absence of mistake or accident, knowledge, or common scheme or design.[647] Because evidence of other offenses, even when properly admitted, is so prejudicial to the defendant, it is almost always in the defendant's best interests to exclude

---

642. People v. Manning, 182 Ill. 2d 193, 695 N.E.2d 423 (1998); People v. Lehman, 5 Ill. 2d 337, 125 N.E.2d 506, 509 (1955).

643. *Id.*

644. *Id.*

645. People v. Thingvold, 145 Ill. 2d 441, 584 N.E.2d 89, 93–94 (1991) (trial court erred in admitting testimony to show motive and intent where it merely demonstrated defendant's propensity to commit crime); People v. Wydra, 265 Ill. App. 3d 597, 637 N.E.2d 741, 754 (1st Dist. 1994) (evidence of defendant's alleged battery of ex-girlfriend's new boyfriend was irrelevant). *See* People v. Johnson, 239 Ill. App. 3d 1064, 608 N.E.2d 36 (1st Dist. 1992).

646. People v. Lehman, 5 Ill. 2d 337, 125 N.E.2d 506, 509 (1955). The named list is not all-inclusive. As long as the evidence is being used for some purpose other than to show propensity, the evidence may be admissible. People v. Manning, 182 Ill. 2d 193, 695 N.E.2d 423 (1998); People v. Biggers, 273 Ill. App. 3d 116, 652 N.E.2d 474 (4th Dist. 1995).

647. Note that although the courts often treat modus operandi, common cause or design, and intent as separate and distinctive theories of admission of other offense evidence, the line between the theories is often broken if not completely indistinguishable.

the evidence. The vehicle by which such evidence may be excluded is a motion in limine to preclude the state from introducing other crimes evidence. At a hearing, the court must closely scrutinize the offered evidence to determine the purpose for which it is offered and the context in which it is offered. If the prosecution cannot establish that the evidence is relevant and admissible for a purpose other than to show the defendant's propensity to commit crime, it should be kept out.[648]

In ruling on the motion, the court must consider a number of factors beyond the purpose for which the evidence is purportedly offered. That is, the state must establish that the other crime actually took place and that the defendant was involved in its commission.[649] How involved the defendant was in the other offense will be determined on a case-by-case basis. The state will not be required to prove beyond a reasonable doubt that the defendant was involved in the other offense,[650] but mere suspicion[651] or the defendant's mere presence at the scene of the other offense is usually not enough to allow its admission.[652] Note, however, that a prior offense may be admissible for a legitimate non-propensity purpose even if the defendant, now on trial, was acquitted of the prior offense.[653]

Finally, before admitting other crimes evidence the judge must balance the probative value of the evidence against its prejudicial effect,[654] considering both

---

648. People v. Smith, 122 Ill. App. 3d 609, 461 N.E.2d 534 (3d Dist. 1984); People v. Miller, 55 Ill. App. 3d 421, 370 N.E.2d 1155 (1st Dist. 1977).

649. *Miller,* 55 Ill. App. 3d 421, 370 N.E.2d at 1159. *But see* People v. Vozel, 346 Ill. 209, 178 N.E. 473 (1931); People v. Wolf, 334 Ill. 218, 165 N.E. 619 (1929) (where other arsons occurred at or about same time as crime charged and in same area, evidence of other arsons was admissible to show that arsons were purposefully set by defendant as part of common scheme or design).

650. People v. Miller, 55 Ill. App. 3d 421, 370 N.E.2d 1155 (1st Dist. 1977).

651. *Id.,* 370 N.E.2d at 1159.

652. People v. Rodriguez, 107 Ill. App. 3d 43, 437 N.E.2d 441, 445 (2d Dist. 1982).

653. Dowling v. United States, 493 U.S. 342, 361–62 (1990). In *Dowling,* the identity of the defendant, accused bank robber, was at issue. The Supreme Court held that the defendant's prior charges of which he had been acquitted were admissible, since identification of Dowling as the prior offender, though not enough to convict him of the prior offenses, was relevant to the description and identification of Dowling as the bank robber in the present trial. *Id.* Note that the Court also rejected the defense's double jeopardy bar contention. *Id.* at 348–49. *See also* People v. Scott, 148 Ill. 2d 479, 594 N.E.2d 217 (1992), *cert. denied,* 507 U.S. 989 (1993).

654. People v. Lindgren, 79 Ill. 2d 129, 402 N.E.2d 238 (1980); *Rodriguez,* 107 Ill. App. 3d 43, 437 N.E.2d at 445; People v. Triplett, 99 Ill. App. 3d 1077, 425 N.E.2d 1236 (1st Dist. 1981).

the relevance and necessity of the offered evidence to the state's case.[655] Thus, where the state argued that evidence of another gas station robbery was relevant and necessary in a gas station armed robbery prosecution to show that the defendant knew the gas station's procedures, the appellate court reversed because the defendant had also worked at other gas stations.[656] The state failed to show the necessity for introduction of other crimes evidence, and the prejudicial effect on the defendant outweighed any probative value.[657]

With these principles in mind, the following areas should be considered.

§ 4.40 — — Modus Operandi

Evidence of other offenses committed by the defendant may be introduced on the theory of proving modus operandi, which refers to a "pattern of criminal behavior so distinctive that separate crimes are recognizable as the handiwork of the same wrongdoer."[658] That is, the other crimes are the defendant's "signature" through which he or she may now be identified.

Before the courts will allow such evidence to be admitted, however, the prosecution must make a strong and persuasive showing of similarity between the offense presently charged and that previously committed.[659] Furthermore, it is not merely the similarity of the offenses that governs but rather the similarity of the underlying facts in both cases.[660] Thus, in *People v. Barbour*,[661]

---

655. *Triplett,* 99 Ill. App. 3d 1077, 425 N.E.2d at 1240.

656. *Id. See also* People v. Barbour, 106 Ill. App. 3d 993, 436 N.E.2d 667, 672 (1st Dist. 1982) (evidence of prior rapes excluded to show modus operandi because there was no issue about identity; defense was consent); People v. Johnson, 81 Ill. App. 3d 359, 401 N.E.2d 288 (2d Dist. 1980) (not necessary to introduce evidence of prior burglary to show identity or knowledge).

657. People v. Alford, 111 Ill. App. 3d 741, 444 N.E.2d 576, 578 (1st Dist 1982). *But see* People v. Bragg, 277 Ill. App. 3d 468, 659 N.E.2d 1378 (1st Dist.1995); People v. Hayes, 168 Ill. App. 3d 816, 522 N.E.2d 1279 (1st Dist. 1988).

658. *Barbour,* 106 Ill. App. 3d 993, 436 N.E.2d at 672.

659. People v. Friedman, 79 Ill. 2d 341, 403 N.E.2d 229 (1980).

660. People v. Barbour, 106 Ill. App. 3d 993, 436 N.E.2d 667 (1st Dist. 1982). *See also* People v. Johnson, 107 Ill. App. 3d 156, 437 N.E.2d 436, 438 (3d Dist. 1982) (court reiterated that while the "other crimes do not have to be identical in every minute detail[ ] [t]he similarity [must] only be striking or distinctive"). *See* People v. Howard, 303 Ill. App. 3d 726, 708 N.E.2d 1212, 1216 (1st Dist. 1999) (defendant's conviction reversed because prior offense did not have enough distinctive similarity when compared to present one, state did not need evidence of prior offense because its case was strong, and prejudicial effect was thus enhanced since jury would probably use prior offense as propensity evidence).

661. *Barbour,* 106 Ill. App. 3d 993, 436 N.E.2d at 672–73.

reversal was required where two previous rape victims were permitted to testify in the defendant's rape prosecution under the guise of modus operandi. Because the two previous victims had been raped in their apartments and the present incident allegedly occurred in the defendant's car, the incidents did not bear enough similarity to be the signature of the defendant.[662] Moreover, though the state argued 19 similarities between the past and present occurrences, many were either "irrelevant coincidences" or "merely descriptive of the crime of rape."[663] Although the state is not required to show that the similarities are so unique that they exclude all other persons, it must demonstrate some "distinctive features that are not common to most offenses of that type."[664] Thus, in an armed robbery prosecution, it is improper to introduce other crimes evidence merely because all offenses have in common the use of a gun, the occurrence is at night near the victims' cars, and the statement by the offender in each instance is "If you move, I'll shoot."[665]

---

662. *Id.* For example, force was used in all three attacks.

663. *Id. See also* People v. Tate, 87 Ill. 2d 134, 429 N.E.2d 470, 475 (1981). In addition, the *Barbour* court emphasized that modus operandi goes to show identity. But since identity was not an issue, the evidence of other crimes was not relevant. *Barbour,* 106 Ill. App. 3d 993, 436 N.E.2d at 672–73. Furthermore, consent and force are issues for the trier of fact, and evidence of other crimes may not be admitted to enhance the credibility of witnesses. *Id. See, e.g.,* People v. Willer, 281 Ill. App. 3d 939, 667 N.E.2d 708, 719 (2d Dist. 1996) (many similarities argued by state were common to the offense of aggravated criminal sexual abuse and others were merely descriptive of the crime itself); People v. Howard, 303 Ill. App. 3d 726, 708 N.E.2d 1212, 1216 (1st Dist. 1999) (purported similarities were not distinct enough).

664. *Barbour,* 106 Ill. App. 3d 993, 436 N.E.2d at 672. The state also unsuccessfully argued admissibility under common scheme or design, reason for arrest, design, knowledge, and presence. *But cf.* People v. Johnson, 107 Ill. App. 3d 156, 437 N.E.2d 436 (3d Dist. 1982) (evidence of prior rape and prior attempt was sufficiently similar to crime charged to be properly admitted). *See also* People v. McDonald, 62 Ill. 2d 448, 343 N.E.2d 489 (1975); People v. Copeland, 66 Ill. App. 3d 556, 384 N.E.2d 391 (1st Dist. 1978); People v. Sievers, 56 Ill. App. 3d 880, 372 N.E.2d 705 (4th Dist. 1978). In *Copeland,* the defendant was accused of robbing a gas station. Evidence that the defendant robbed another gas station less than a mile away two hours earlier using the same method (asking for change for a five dollar bill for cigarettes) was admissible because the defendant used a revolver that was stolen from the prior robbery. *Copeland,* 66 Ill. App. 3d 556, 384 N.E.2d at 394. *See* People v. Howard, 303 Ill. App. 3d 726, 708 N.E.2d 1212, 1216 (1st Dist. 1999), and *supra* note 660.

665. People v. Connors, 82 Ill. App. 3d 312, 402 N.E.2d 773, 778 (1st Dist. 1980).

§ 4.41 — — Common Scheme or Design

A second often-encountered attempt by the prosecution to introduce other crimes evidence involves common scheme or design, which "refers to a larger criminal scheme of which the crime charged is only a portion."[666] For example, where the defendant was on trial for armed robbery, evidence of three armed robberies occurring within 45 minutes just before the offense charged was admissible to show common scheme or design.[667] But where the defendants were charged with residential burglary, the court excluded evidence of their involvement in a robbery the day after, stating that the evidence after the burglary was not part of a common plan such as to justify its admission.[668]

§ 4.42 — — Consciousness of Guilt

The prosecution may also attempt to introduce other crimes evidence to show the defendant's consciousness of guilt of the crime charged. The classic example is evidence of the defendant's escape, which is evidence of another crime, from police custody while being questioned about the charge for which he or she was arrested. The rationale is that only a guilty individual would try to escape from the police, and the evidence of the escape is relevant to prove the defendant's consciousness of guilt of the offense for which he or she was initially apprehended. Relevance, however, is the key. Thus, evidence that the defendant attempted to kill an eyewitness to the shooting with which the defendant was charged is relevant and admissible,[669] while evidence of an unrelated arson committed within hours, at a different location, of the murder

---

666. People v. Alford, 111 Ill. App. 3d 741, 444 N.E.2d 576, 578 (1st Dist. 1982).

667. People v. Armstrong, 41 Ill. 2d 390, 243 N.E.2d 825 (1968), *cert. denied,* 394 U.S. 992 (1969).

668. People v. Romero, 66 Ill. 2d 325, 362 N.E.2d 288 (1977). *See e.g.,* People v. Overton, 281 Ill. App. 3d 209, 666 N.E.2d 753, 758 (1st Dist. 1996) (evidence of radio dispatch of earlier robbery with which defendant had been charged and acquitted required reversal since it was too tenuous to establish modus operandi); People v. Williams, 285 Ill. App. 3d 394, 673 N.E.2d 1169, 1173–74 (4th Dist. 1996) (facts of three crimes did not support the application of modus operandi because the modus operandi was different in each; but evidence properly demonstrated that all three crimes were connected since the same gun was used in each).

669. People v. Cruz, 162 Ill. 2d 314, 643 N.E.2d 636 (1994); People v. Baptist, 76 Ill. 2d 19, 389 N.E.2d 1200, 1204 (1979). *See also* People v. Lucas, 151 Ill. 2d 461, 603 N.E.2d 460, 471 (1992) (evidence of other crimes may be admissible as to consciousness of guilt if other crime is related to offense for which defendant is on trial), *cert. denied,* 508 U.S. 916 (1993).

with which the defendant was charged was not relevant to the defendant's "guilty conscience" and thus not admissible.[670]

§ 4.43 — — Motive, Intent, and Absence of Mistake

If the other crime was committed by the defendant and is relevant to prove his or her motive or intent, or it demonstrates lack of mistake in response to or in anticipation of a claim of mistake, evidence of other crimes will be admissible. Thus, the prosecution was permitted to introduce outstanding arrest warrants as relevant to a defendant's motive in subsequently killing a police officer.[671] Whether the defendant had knowledge of the warrants (lack of knowledge would seem to initiate the motive-relevance theory) at the time of the killing is apparently left to explanation by the defendant, argument, or both.

The prosecution may also introduce other crimes evidence to demonstrate that the defendant intended to act in the manner presently charged as an offense,[672] acted knowingly and intentionally, or not by mistake.[673] In addition, evidence of other crimes may be introduced to place a defendant in the general proximity of the crime charged,[674] assuming that the defendant does not admit that he or she was in the area.[675] Note, however, that even if other crimes evidence is ruled inadmissible to show proximity, it may still be admitted to

---

670. People v. Lindgren, 79 Ill. 2d 129, 402 N.E.2d 238, 242 (1980) (citing People v. Spaulding, 309 Ill. 292, 141 N.E. 196, 202 (1923)). *See also* People v. Bean, 137 Ill. 2d 65, 560 N.E.2d 258 (1990), *cert. denied,* 499 U.S. 932 (1991).

671. People v. Witherspoon, 27 Ill. 2d 483, 190 N.E.2d 281, 284 (1963). *But see* People v. Wilson, 116 Ill. 2d 29, 506 N.E.2d 571, 581 (1987) (court observed that "[u]nless the defendant knew about the warrant . . ., the existence of the warrant does not establish anything about the defendant's state of mind."); People v. Ranstrom, 304 Ill. App. 3d 664, 710 N.E.2d 61, 69 (1st Dist. 1999) (evidence of defendant's stalking of one victim was admissible as evidence of motive for attack on victim's boyfriend).

672. People v. Tiller, 94 Ill. 2d 303, 447 N.E.2d 174 (1982), *cert. denied,* 461 U.S. 944 (1983). *But see* People v. Friedman, 79 Ill. 2d 341, 403 N.E.2d 229 (1980) (state unable to show probative value of other crime as to intent).

673. People v. Tuczynski, 62 Ill. App. 3d 644, 378 N.E.2d 1200, 1206 (1st Dist. 1978).

674. People v. Wilson, 46 Ill. 2d 376, 263 N.E.2d 856, 859 (1970).

675. If the defendant admits that he or she was in the area of the crime charged, proximity evidence is unnecessary and therefore inadmissible. People v. Lindgren, 79 Ill. 2d 129, 402 N.E.2d 238, 243 (1980); People v. Copeland, 66 Ill. App. 3d 556, 384 N.E.2d 391, 394 (1st Dist. 1978).

show the defendant's knowledge,[676] common scheme or design,[677] or modus operandi.

A final issue in connection with the use of "bad acts" for impeachment involves a defendant's use of a state witness's "bad act" in order to impeach the state witness. While *People v. Goose* (what's good for the goose is good for the gander) ought to govern, the law with respect to this issue is sketchy at best. Depending upon a police officer's number and type of prior disciplinary suspensions, defense counsel is entitled to cross-examine the officer regarding prior disciplinary suspensions; these may be relevant to a possible motive to testify falsely in the case of trial, since the officer does not want to be suspended again.[678] Whether or how far this point can be expanded is subject to the defense's creativity.

§ 4.44 Fitness to Stand Trial

The Supreme Court of the United States has long held that the trial and conviction of a person accused of a crime who is unfit to stand trial because of a physical or mental incapacity violates due process.[679] Consequently, the state has an obligation to establish procedures adequate to protect the unfit defendant until the time, if ever, he or she becomes fit.[680] Section 104 of chapter 725[681] is Illinois'

---

676. *Wilson,* 46 Ill. 2d 376, 263 N.E.2d at 859.

677. *Copeland,* 66 Ill. App. 3d 556, 384 N.E.2d at 394; People v. Armstrong, 41 Ill. 2d 390, 243 N.E.2d 825, 829 (1968), *cert. denied,* 394 U.S. 992 (1969); People v. Tranowski, 20 Ill. 2d 11, 169 N.E.2d 347, *cert. denied,* 364 U.S. 923 (1960).

678. People v. Phillips, 95 Ill. App. 3d 1013, 420 N.E.2d 837 (1st Dist. 1981). *See also* People v. Robinson, 163 Ill. App. 3d 754, 516 N.E.2d 1292, 1312 (1st Dist. 1987) (cross-examination of state witness to show motive, intent, or bias is allowed).

679. U.S. CONST. amend. XIV; Pate v. Robinson, 383 U.S. 375, 378 (1966); People v. Nitz, 173 Ill. 2d 151, 670 N.E.2d 672, 674 (1996), *cert. denied,* 520 U.S. 1139 (1997); People v. Birdsall, 172 Ill. 2d 464, 670 N.E.2d 700, 706 (1996); People v. Murphy, 72 Ill. 2d 421, 381 N.E.2d 677, 682 (1978); People v. Burson, 11 Ill. 2d 360, 143 N.E.2d 239, 244 (1957). *See also* Cooper v. Oklahoma, 517 U.S. 348, 369 (1996) (Oklahoma law that presumed a defendant was competent to stand trial unless he proved incompetency by clear and convincing evidence violated the Due Process Clause where defendant had already demonstrated by a preponderance of the evidence that he was more likely than not incompetent).

680. Drope v. Missouri, 420 U.S. 162, 172 (1975); *Murphy,* 72 Ill. 2d 421, 381 N.E.2d at 682. If the state fails to protect the defendant against being tried while unfit, the defendant's conviction will be reversed. People v. Turner, 88 Ill. App. 3d 793, 410 N.E.2d 1151, 1154 (1st Dist. 1980). *See also* People v. Newell, 196 Ill. App. 3d 373, 553 N.E.2d 722 (3d Dist. 1990).

681. 725 ILCS 5/104.

response to the Supreme Court's mandate to protect the unfit defendant. Because, however, even cursory consideration of all of the provisions dealing with unfit defendants in criminal cases would require a multi-volume treatise, only those aspects most frequently encountered are discussed here.

Counsel should take note that the "Fitness to Stand Trial or Be Sentenced" provisions have been amended in a number of respects, and that several significant decisions have been handed down, as discussed below. Because this area of the law is particularly fluid, check closely to make sure that you are preparing your case under the latest statutory amendments and case law.

§ 4.45   — Raising the Issue

Illinois statutorily presumes that a defendant charged with a criminal offense is fit to stand trial.[682] What constitutes unfitness is also statutorily defined: a defendant is considered unfit if, because of some physical or mental condition, he or she is unable to understand the nature and purpose of the proceedings against him or her or is unable to assist in his or her defense.[683] This requires the court to consider whether the defendant has "sufficient present ability to consult with counsel with a reasonable degree of rational understanding and whether the defendant has both a rational and factual understanding of the proceedings."[684] Note that "a defendant who is receiving psychotropic drugs shall not be presumed to be unfit to stand trial solely by virtue of the receipt of those drugs or medications."[685]

---

682. 725 ILCS 5/104-10. This article applies to felonies, misdemeanors, and proceedings under the Illinois Vehicle Code. People v. Brown, 131 Ill. App. 3d 859, 476 N.E.2d 469, 473 (2d Dist. 1985). In addition, it applies to juvenile proceedings. People v. T.D.W., 109 Ill. App. 3d 852, 441 N.E.2d 155, 157 (4th Dist. 1982). However, this section is not applicable to post-conviction proceedings. People v. Owens, 139 Ill. 2d 351, 564 N.E.2d 1184, 1191 (1990), *cert. denied,* 469 U.S. 963 (1984).

The defendant has the burden of raising a real, substantial, and legitimate doubt as to his or her mental capacity which is determined by an objective test. People v. Eddmonds, 143 Ill. 2d 501, 578 N.E.2d 952, 959 (1991), *cert. denied,* 503 U.S. 942 (1992). The preponderance of the evidence standard governs. People v. Ralon, 211 Ill. App. 3d 927, 570 N.E.2d 742, 751 (1st Dist. 1991).

683. 725 ILCS 5/104-10; People v. Thomas, 246 Ill. App. 3d 708, 616 N.E.2d 695 (2d Dist. 1993). The test for competency to plead guilty is the same as that for competency to stand trial. People v. Heral, 62 Ill. 2d 329, 342 N.E.2d 34 (1976).

684. People v. Turner, 111 Ill. App. 3d 358, 443 N.E.2d 1167, 1171 (2d Dist. 1982).

685. 725 ILCS 5/104-21. See discussion at end of section on this provision.

The defense, state, or trial judge may raise the issue of fitness at any time the criminal case is pending.[686] However, the mere raising of the fitness issue does not require the court to hold a hearing to determine fitness.[687] Rather, the court is required to conduct a fitness hearing only when the facts before it raise a bona fide doubt about the defendant's fitness to stand trial, plead, or be sentenced.[688] Although it is within the court's discretion to determine whether a bona fide doubt exists[689] and whether to appoint an expert to examine the defendant,[690] it is an abuse of discretion if the court fails to order a fitness hearing once a bona fide doubt is a matter of record.[691]

---

686. The issue may be raised before, during, or after trial. 725 ILCS 5/104-11(a); People v. Ralon, 211 Ill. App. 3d 927, 570 N.E.2d 742 (1st Dist. 1991).

687. People v. Foster, 76 Ill. 2d 365, 392 N.E.2d 6, 12 (1979).

688. 725 ILCS 5/104-11(a); People v. Nitz, 173 Ill. 2d 151, 670 N.E.2d 672, 674 (1996), *cert. denied*, 117 S. Ct. 1289 (1997); People v. Murphy, 72 Ill. 2d 421, 381 N.E.2d 677, 682 (1978); People v. McLain, 37 Ill. 2d 173, 226 N.E.2d 21, 24 (1967); People v. Thomas, 246 Ill. App. 3d 708, 616 N.E.2d 695 (2d Dist. 1993). The court may consider facts presented before it, either from observation of the defendant or by suggestion of counsel. People v. Stribling, 104 Ill. App. 3d 969, 433 N.E.2d 967, 968 (1st Dist. 1982). *See also* People v. Johnson, 183 Ill. 2d 176, 700 N.E.2d 996 (1998), *cert. denied*, 119 S. Ct. 1150 (1999).

689. 725 ILCS 5/104-11(b); People v. Johnson, 183 Ill. 2d 176, 700 N.E.2d 996 (1998), *cert. denied*, 119 S. Ct. 1150 (1999); People v. Fowler, 222 Ill. App. 3d 157, 583 N.E.2d 686 (2d Dist. 1991); People v. Hall, 186 Ill. App. 3d 123, 541 N.E.2d 1369 (1st Dist. 1989).

690. 725 ILCS 5/104-11(b). The fact that the defense attorney requests in good faith a psychiatric examination to determine bona fide doubt (or fitness) does not, in itself, require the court to exercise its discretion. People v. Banks, 94 Ill. App. 3d 122, 418 N.E.2d 510, 515 (3d Dist. 1981). To do so would divest the trial court of its discretion. *Id. See, e.g.*, People v. Allen, 218 Ill. App. 3d 930, 578 N.E.2d 1193, 1195 (1st Dist. 1991) (although judge ordered examination for defendant, defendant refused to participate and counsel never requested fitness hearing prior to trial; fact that counsel asked for examination did not, in itself, bring issue of defendant's fitness into question so that judge should have ordered hearing sua sponte), *rev'd on other grounds*, 153 Ill. 2d 145, 606 N.E.2d 1149 (1992). However, the judge may appoint an expert to make an initial determination of whether a bona fide doubt exists. People v. Thomas, 246 Ill. App. 3d 708, 616 N.E.2d 695, 698 (2d Dist. 1993). However, defense counsel requesting a psychiatric examination alone does not trigger the court's duty to exercise discretion in this matter. People v. Haynes, 174 Ill. 2d 204, 673 N.E.2d 318, 341 (1996) (trial court did not err in refusing to reevaluate defendant's fitness prior to sentencing him where defendant was found fit to stand trial after lengthy pretrial hearing), *cert. denied*, 520 U.S. 1231 (1997).

691. People v. Queen, 108 Ill. App. 3d 1088, 440 N.E.2d 126, 131 (5th Dist. 1982). *See* People v. Rice, 257 Ill. App. 3d 220, 628 N.E.2d 837, 840 (1st Dist. 1993)

How, then, is the existence of a bona fide doubt of the defendant's fitness to stand trial established? Whether a bona fide doubt exists depends on the facts and circumstances of each case.[692] The court may consider testimony of expert and lay witnesses on the issue,[693] and it should also consider facts of which it is made aware during the pendency of the litigation.[694] Such evidence may include the defendant's prior psychiatric history,[695] irrational behavior,[696] and demeanor in court.[697] Because each case is decided on its own

---

(limited mental impairment does not in and of itself raise bona fide doubt of fitness).

692. *Nitz*, 173 Ill. 2d 151, 670 N.E.2d at 674; People v. Birdsall, 172 Ill. 2d 464, 670 N.E.2d 700, 706–07 (1996); *Murphy,* 72 Ill. 2d 421, 381 N.E.2d at 684.

693. People v. Robinson, 102 Ill. App. 3d 884, 429 N.E.2d 1356, 1362 (1st Dist. 1981). *See* People v. Fosdick, 166 Ill. App. 3d 491, 519 N.E.2d 1102, 1109 (1st Dist. 1988) (if expert testimony conflicts, court may accept one opinion over other).

694. People v. McLain, 37 Ill. 2d 173, 226 N.E.2d 21, 24 (1967).

695. *Id.* The fact that the defendant has previously been adjudicated unfit to stand trial is a factor to consider when deciding the issue of bona fide doubt. People v. Stribling, 104 Ill. App. 3d 969, 433 N.E.2d 967, 969 (1st Dist. 1982). However, in determining the defendant's fitness, psychiatric reports and opinions are not necessarily conclusive, even in making the initial determination about bona fide doubt. People v. Turner, 111 Ill. App. 3d 358, 443 N.E.2d 1167, 1173 (2d Dist. 1982). *See, e.g.*, People v. Fowler, 222 Ill. App. 3d 157, 583 N.E.2d 686, 692 (2d Dist. 1991) (fact that the defendant suffered a mental disturbance or required psychiatric treatment did not necessarily raise bona fide doubt); People v. Allen, 218 Ill. App. 3d 930, 578 N.E.2d 1193, 1195 (1st Dist. 1991) (even if defendant is known to suffer from mental disturbance, bona fide doubt not created since fitness speaks to person's ability to function in context of trial, not to competence in other areas), *rev'd on other grounds*, 153 Ill. 2d 145, 606 N.E.2d 1149 (1992).

696. Pate v. Robinson, 383 U.S. 375, 378 (1966); *Murphy,* 72 Ill. 2d 421, 381 N.E.2d at 684. *See, e.g.*, People v. Smith, 253 Ill. App. 3d 948, 625 N.E.2d 897, 901 (4th Dist. 1993) (evidence of extreme disruptive behavior and sociopath personality does not compel conclusion that bona fide doubts exists).

697. Drope v. Missouri, 420 U.S. 162, 179 (1975); *Murphy,* 72 Ill. 2d 421, 381 N.E.2d at 684; People v. Queen, 108 Ill. App. 3d 1095, 440 N.E.2d 126 (5th Dist. 1982). The *Queen* court further stated that the trial court may consider evidence of the defendant's behavior as outlined in police reports, as well as the defendant's demeanor in court. *Id.,* 440 N.E.2d at 131. *See also* People v. Strickland, 154 Ill. 2d 489, 609 N.E.2d 1366, 1376 (1992) (judge may use own observations of the defendant's ability to comprehend proceedings and assist counsel in making fitness decision), *cert. denied,* 510 U.S. 858 (1993); People v. Anderson, 266 Ill. App. 3d 947, 641 N.E.2d 591 (1st Dist. 1994) (defendant's discussions with court and testimony that was responsive to questions posed gave court ability to judge such that no bona fide doubt as to fitness existed), *cert. denied,* 516 U.S. 834

facts, however, there is no one condition, factor, or symptom that automatically must result in a finding of bona fide doubt.[698]

For example, in *People v. McLain*,[699] the court held that the combination of previous judicially ordered commitments for mental illness, attempted suicides, efforts to escape from a psychiatric institution, testimony of expert witnesses indicating the defendant's instability, and the fact that the defendant was brought immediately from psychiatric confinement to arraignment did raise a bona fide doubt. Furthermore, the opinion of one doctor stating that the defendant was fit did not counterbalance the other facts to negate a finding of bona fide doubt.[700] In *People v. Thomas*,[701] the court also held a bona fide doubt existed. In this case, the defendant, who believed his lawyer was God, would not cooperate with his appointed attorney and was of below average

---

(1995); People v. Rogers, 263 Ill. App. 3d 120, 635 N.E.2d 889, 896 (1st Dist. 1994) (trial judge did not abuse discretion in finding no bona fide doubt where judge observed defendant over the past year and could not discern anything from appearance or statements that would indicate the presence of mental disease; more importantly, the defendant testified at trial during which time the judge observed or heard nothing which would suggest incompetence).

698. *Strickland*, 154 Ill. 2d 489, 609 N.E.2d at 1375 (where the only evidence the defendant presented to show he was unfit was that he received Mellaril before and during trial and alleged difficulty in identifying scenes in exhibits, the trial judge properly found him fit, particularly where evidence showed Mellaril dosage would have enhanced rather than compromised defendant's fitness); People v. Rice, 257 Ill. App. 3d 220, 628 N.E.2d 837, 840 (1st Dist. 1993) (limited mental capacity insufficient in itself to raise bona fide doubt). *See also* People v Coleman; 168 Ill. 2d 509, 660 N.E.2d 919, 928 (1995) (person may be fit to stand trial even though his mind is "otherwise unsound"), *cert. denied*, 519 U.S. 827 (1996); People v. Walker, 292 Ill. App. 3d 500, 685 N.E.2d 997 (1st Dist. 1997); People v. Torry, 212 Ill. App. 3d 759, 571 N.E.2d 827, 831 (1st Dist. 1991) (fitness was established by preponderance of evidence where psychiatrist testified the defendant was aware of the nature and consequences of the proceedings, defendant did not suffer from any organic disorder, and based on an interview with the defendant, the psychiatrist testified that the defendant was untruthful about his ability to remember); People v. Bleitner, 189 Ill. App. 3d 971, 546 N.E.2d 241, 244 (4th Dist. 1989) (where the defendant knew who his attorneys were and expressed an opinion about one attorney being better than other, understood the charge against him, understood the roles of judge, jury, and prosecutor, the plea-bargaining system and the nature of a motion to suppress, that his lawyer's role was to help him, and that penalties against him were possible, the judge did not err in finding defendant fit).

699. *McLain*, 37 Ill. 2d 173, 226 N.E.2d at 24.

700. *Id.*

701. 43 Ill. 2d 328, 253 N.E.2d 431, 434 (1969).

intelligence.[702] The court said that when the defendant is unwilling to cooperate with counsel because of lack of mental capacity, counsel is denied access to the defendant's knowledge of facts surrounding the charges against him or her and to information that may aid in his or her defense.[703]

Similarly, in *People v. Burson,*[704] the court held that a bona fide doubt existed where the defendant refused to cooperate with counsel.[705] The fact that the defendant had a persecution complex, suffered delusions of grandeur in connection with his identification with God, and was unruly in court were all factors leading to a finding of bona fide doubt.[706]

Finally, in *People v. Eddmonds,*[707] the defendant sought postconviction relief on a claim of ineffective assistance of counsel.[708] Defendant's claim was premised on his counsel's failure to request a fitness hearing before trial.[709] The court found that the defendant had the burden of proof, at the time of the request, to raise a bona fide doubt as to his mental capacity to participate in his defense and cooperate with counsel.[710] The trial court must access several essential factors in determining whether defendant has raised a bona fide doubt of fitness to stand trial which include: defendant's irrational behavior; his or her demeanor at trial; any prior medical opinions on his or her competence to stand trial; and defense counsel's opinion concerning fitness.[711] The court observed that *some* doubt is not necessarily a bona fide doubt.[712]

---

702. *Id.,* 253 N.E.2d at 432.

703. *Id.,* 253 N.E.2d at 433. However, in *People v. Beacham,* 87 Ill. App. 3d 457, 410 N.E.2d 87, 97 (1st Dist. 1980), the court held there was no bona fide doubt even where the defendant refused to leave his jail cell, would not communicate with his attorney, and refused to answer the court's questions. *See also* People v. Joseph, 176 Ill. App. 3d 636, 531 N.E.2d 432, 434 (2d Dist. 1988) (defendant's repeated refusals to cooperate did not require a finding that he was unable to); People v. Moore, 159 Ill. App. 3d 850, 513 N.E.2d 24, 27 (1st Dist. 1987) (unwillingness to cooperate does not equate to inability to do so).

704. 11 Ill. 2d 360, 143 N.E.2d 239 (1957).

705. *Id.,* 143 N.E.2d at 245. The defendant also called his attorneys as witnesses to illustrate a conspiracy against him and delivered his own closing arguments.

706. *Id. See* People v. Allen, 71 Ill. App. 2d 283, 218 N.E.2d 837 (1st Dist. 1966) (defendant was entitled to fitness hearing where he had interrupted trial with ravings 119 times).

707. 143 Ill. 2d 501, 578 N.E.2d 952 (1991), *cert. denied,* 503 U.S. 942 (1992).

708. *Eddmonds,* 143 Ill. 2d 501, 578 N.E.2d at 956.

709. *Id.*

710. *Id.*

711. *Id.,* 578 N.E.2d at 959.

712. *Id.,* 578 N.E.2d at 962.

In *People v. Sandham*,[713] the Illinois Supreme Court, under a plain error analysis (the fitness issue was not raised at trial or in posttrial motions), reversed defendant's conviction who at trial did not have a fitness hearing.[714] The court considered among other factors as raising a bona fide doubt, the following:

1. although his public defender had requested a psychiatric evaluation for fitness and although an evaluation was ordered, prior to any examination, the public defender was replaced by private counsel who did not pursue the issue;

2. a continuance was granted on the new attorney's motion based on the commitment of the defendant to a psychiatric hospital;

3. before and during his commitment, the defendant sent rambling letters to the judge;

4. the defendant also made several threatening phone calls to the judge;

5. at his sentencing hearing, the defendant's parents related his bizarre behavior;

6. the defendant's father indicated his son had been considered schizophrenic, and while incarcerated was on lithium, prolixin and ativan.[715]

Finally, at the sentencing hearing the judge was made aware that the defendant was still on medication, and the defendant suggested that the judge "cut my brain out." The judge, after observing this, stated that the defendant apparently "[did not] even seem to understand what's going on . . .," yet sentenced him.[716]

The court, in reversing the conviction, sidestepped the psychotropic medication issue under *People v. Kinkead*[717] and section 104-21(a).[718] Rather, the court held that the trial court's failure, sua sponte, to conduct a fitness hearing, in light of the above incidents, mandated reversal. "[A] trial court's discre-

---

713. 174 Ill. 2d 379, 673 N.E.2d 1032 (1996).

714. *Id.*, 673 N.E.2d at 1036.

715. *Id.*

716. *Id.*

717. 168 Ill. 2d 394, 660 N.E.2d 852 (1995), *superseded by statute as stated in* People v. Nitz, 173 Ill. 2d 151, 670 N.E.2d 672, 675 (1996), *cert. denied*, 520 U.S. 1139 (1997). See discussion at end of section.

718. 725 ILCS 5/104-21(a). See discussion at end of section.

tion . . . is not unbridled."[719] The court concluded that the "events and testimony combined to raise a bona fide doubt as to defendant's fitness."[720]

Yet, because of the case-by-case treatment, even in the presence of irrational behavior, unruly demeanor in court, or prior psychiatric hospitalizations, the court may conclude that a bona fide doubt does not exist.[721] The ordering of psychological examinations by the court also does not in itself raise a bona fide doubt,[722] nor does defense counsel's assertion that a defendant may be unfit[723] or the suggestion that the defendant has a limited mental capacity.[724] Because the issue of a defendant's fitness to stand trial relates only to the defendant's ability to function at trial,[725] a defendant may be fit and no bona fide doubt may exist even though his or her mind is otherwise unsound.[726]

Because the existence of a bona fide doubt of the defendant's fitness to stand trial is the essential prerequisite for the court to conduct a fitness hearing, the establishment of a bona fide doubt based on the particular facts and the creative and aggressive presentation of those facts to the court may be outcome

---

719. *Sandham*, 174 Ill. 2d 379, 673 N.E.2d at 1036–37.

720. *Id.*, 673 N.E.2d at 1036.

721. Even where a defendant had at one time been committed to a state hospital for psychiatric treatment, the court held that no bona fide doubt existed. People v. Richeson, 24 Ill. 2d 182, 181 N.E.2d 170, 171 (1962). Although commitment to an institution may indicate the defendant needs some psychiatric care, it does not automatically follow that he or she is unfit. *Id.*

722. People v. Wilson, 124 Ill. App. 3d 831, 464 N.E.2d 1158 (1st Dist. 1984); People v. Leiker, 115 Ill. App. 3d 752, 450 N.E.2d 37, 40–41 (3d Dist. 1983).

723. People v. Eddmonds, 143 Ill. 2d 501, 578 N.E.2d 952 (1991), *cert. denied*, 503 U.S. 942 (1992). *See also* People v. Hall, 186 Ill. App. 3d 123, 541 N.E.2d 1369, 1375 (1st Dist. 1989) (where counsel's request for a fitness examination was not based on knowledge that the defendant was not taking medication, even though counsel informed the court that the defendant failed to take medication on the day of the hearing, and counsel stated that the defendant "could be fit" for that day's and all prior proceedings, there was no abuse in denying a request for a fitness examination because counsel's concern was speculative).

724. People v. Murphy, 72 Ill. 2d 421, 381 N.E.2d 677, 683 (1978); People v. Rice, 257 Ill. App. 3d 220, 628 N.E.2d 837 (1st Dist. 1993).

725. People v. Lang, 76 Ill. 2d 311, 391 N.E.2d 350, 356–57, *cert. denied*, 444 U.S. 954 (1979).

726. *Murphy,* 72 Ill. 2d 421, 381 N.E.2d at 683. *See* People v. Lopez, 216 Ill. App. 3d 83, 576 N.E.2d 246, 248 (1st Dist. 1991) (fitness implicates the defendant's ability to be fit for trial and does not refer to sanity or competence in other areas; therefore, a prior suicide attempt, use of psychotropic medication, recent refusal to take medication, and a report recommending ongoing psychiatric services do not raise bona fide doubt).

determinative. Therefore, it is imperative that counsel, in any case where the defendant's fitness to stand trial may be an issue, gather the facts as early and completely as possible. One especially important tool by which the facts may be gathered, honed, and eventually presented to the court is the fitness examination.[727]

One might question whether a defendant for whom there exists a bona fide doubt of fitness is "fit" to waive a jury for a fitness hearing. That issue was put to rest in *People v. Brown*.[728] The *Brown* decision apparently rests on the principle of *ipse dixit* (*i.e.,* because we say so!), as the court recently observed in reaffirming *Brown*. While the defendant's argument "has some surface appeal . . ., we do not think it makes a tendered jury waiver a nullity."[729]

In *People v. Haynes*,[730] the court had before it a defendant charged with killing a Wilmette, Illinois, plastic surgeon targeted by the defendant because "he decided to kill a plastic surgeon and [the doctor] had the largest advertisement in the Yellow Pages."[731] He had killed another person in San Francisco and tried to kill the president of a contact lens manufacturer.[732] At the fitness hearing expert testimony was presented on both sides, with the court eventually finding the defendant fit.[733] The defendant, who went on to represent himself and waived his right to a jury for both trial and sentencing, was sentenced to death.[734]

Until December 31, 1996, when a defendant was taking psychotropic medication, a fitness hearing was required.[735] However, in response to a series of cases,[736] section 104-21(a) was amended to read: "A defendant who is receiving psycho-tropic drugs shall not be presumed to be unfit to stand trial solely by virtue of the receipt of those drugs or medications."[737] There will be

---

727. 725 ILCS 5/104-11(b).

728. 43 Ill. 2d 79, 250 N.E.2d 647, 649 (1969).

729. *Id.,* 250 N.E.2d at 649.

730. 174 Ill. 2d 204, 673 N.E.2d 318 (1996), *cert. denied,* 520 U.S. 1231 (1997).

731. *Id.,* 673 N.E.2d at 323.

732. *Id.,* 673 N.E.2d at 323–24.

733. *Id.,* 673 N.E.2d at 330.

734. *Id.,* 673 N.E.2d at 322.

735. 725 ILCS 5/104-21(a).

736. People v. Brandon, 162 Ill. 2d 450, 643 N.E.2d 712 (1994); People v. Gevas, 166 Ill. 2d 461, 655 N.E.2d 894 (1995), *superseded by statute as stated in* People v. Nitz, 173 Ill. 2d 151, 670 N.E.2d 672, 675 (1996), *cert. denied,* 520 U.S. 1139 (1997); People v. Birdsall, 172 Ill. 2d 464, 670 N.E.2d 700, 706–07 (1996).

737. 725 ILCS 5/104-21(a). Several courts have held that this provision does not apply retroactively because it is a substantive change in the law. People v. Smith, 296 Ill. App. 3d 435, 694 N.E.2d 681, 683 (4th Dist. 1998); People v. Jamerson, 292 Ill. App. 3d 944, 687 N.E.2d 329, 332 (3d Dist. 1997); People v. Jones, 291 Ill.

some circumstances where the use of psychotropic medication could affect the defendant's mental function in such a way that relief may be warranted.[738]

In 1998, the Illinois Supreme Court reversed and remanded the lower court's findings of a defendant's fitness in *People v. Kinkead* (*Kinkead II*).[739] The court held that the 1996 amendment of section 104-21(a), which provides that a lack of fitness shall not be presumed solely because of the defendant's use of psychotropic drugs, cannot be applied retroactively[740] based upon the holdings of *Cortes*,[741] *Birdsall*,[742] and *Nitz*.[743] The court went on to determine that there was a "*bona fide* doubt as to [Kinkead's] competency at the time he pleaded guilty" and was sentenced.[744] The court held that a fitness hearing should have been held in the original proceedings, and since the original proceedings were over five years earlier, a retrospective fitness hearing would be inappropriate, thus reversing the conviction and remanding the case.[745]

In *People v. Akers*,[746] the state charged the defendant with criminal sexual assault and sexual relations within families. Later, the state successfully petitioned the court to have the defendant declared a sexually dangerous person (SDP) under the Sexually Dangerous Persons Act.[747] The defendant appealed the SDP declaration, claiming he had a right to a fitness hearing during the

---

App. 3d 231, 684 N.E.2d 772, 776 (5th Dist. 1996). *But see* People v. Gibson, 292 Ill. App. 3d 842, 687 N.E.2d 1076, 1080 (5th Dist. 1997) (amendment applied retroactively because case pending on direct appeal at time amendment became effective; however, 15-year-old who was taking sinequan, a psychotropic drug, at time he entered *Alford* plea entitled to hearing on fitness to enter plea).

738. People v. Burgess, 176 Ill. 2d 289, 680 N.E.2d 357, 363 (1997). *See also* People v. Jamerson, 292 Ill. App. 3d 944, 687 N.E.2d 329, 332 (3d Dist. 1997) (declining to apply amended statute retroactively, court further declined to apply automatic reversal rule but instead ordered limited remand for fitness hearing).

739. 182 Ill. 2d 316, 695 N.E.2d 1255 (1998).

740. *Id.*, 695 N.E.2d at 1263.

741. People v. Cortes, 181 Ill. 2d 249, 692 N.E.2d 1129, *cert. denied*, 119 S. Ct. 1901 (1998).

742. People v. Birdsall, 172 Ill. 2d 464, 670 N.E.2d 700 (1996).

743. People v. Nitz, 173 Ill. 2d 151, 670 N.E.2d 672 (1996), *cert. denied*, 520 U.S. 1139 (1997).

744. *Kinkead II*, 102 Ill. 2d 316, 695 N.E.2d at 1267.

745. *Id.*, 695 N.E.2d at 1270. *But see* People v. Hill, 297 Ill. App. 3d 500, 697 N.E.2d 316 (1st Dist. 1998) (holding that retrospective fitness hearing is appropriate for defendant taking psychotropic medication).

746. 301 Ill. App. 3d 745, 704 N.E.2d 452 (4th Dist. 1998).

747. 725 ILCS § 205/0.01 *et seq.*

SDP proceeding because of a bona fide doubt as to his fitness.[748] The court reasoned that the right to a fitness hearing, if appropriate, only attaches with the prosecution of the defendant.[749] Since SDP proceedings are civil in nature, the defendant was not entitled to a fitness hearing pertaining to the SDP declaration.[750]

§ 4.46 — Court-Ordered Examination

The court is vested with discretion to order an examination of a defendant to determine whether he or she is fit to stand trial or whether a bona fide doubt of fitness exists.[751] When the issue of fitness concerns the defendant's mental condition, the court must appoint one or more psychiatrists, clinical psychologists, or licensed physicians to examine the defendant.[752] When the defendant's fitness concerns a physical condition, the court must appoint one or more physicians and any other experts necessary to examine the defendant.[753] The examination will be performed at the time and place designated by the examiner,[754] though if the defendant is in custody, the examination will take place at a location chosen by the court.[755] Because the circumstances and conditions under which an examination takes place may affect the defendant's ability to concentrate or communicate,[756] counsel should vigorously attempt to persuade the court to allow an in-custody defendant to be transported to the examiner's office rather than having the examination occur under the stilted and emotionally and physically confining aura of a

---

748. *Akers*, 301 Ill. App. 3d 745, 704 N.E.2d at 453.

749. *Id.,* 704 N.E.2d at 455; People v. Nitz, 173 Ill. 2d 151, 670 N.E.2d 672, 673–74 (1996).

750. *Akers*, 704 N.E.2d at 455; People v. Allen, 107 Ill. 2d 91, 481 N.E.2d 690, 696 (1985), *aff'd,* 478 U.S. 364 (1986).

751. 725 ILCS 5/104-11(b).

752. 725 ILCS 5/104-13(a) ("The experts will be chosen by the court. However, no physician, clinical psychologist or psychiatrist employed by the Department of Human Services shall be ordered to perform, in his official capacity, an examination under this Section.").

753. 725 ILCS 5/104-13(b).

754. 725 ILCS 5/104-13(c) ("No examinations under this Section shall be ordered to take place at facilities operated by the Department of Human Services.").

755. *Id.* The court may order the defendant to be admitted to an appropriate facility for examination, other than a screening examination, as provided in section 5/104-13(c). However, the defendant may not be admitted for longer than seven days unless the court grants an additional seven days to complete the examination on a showing of a good cause.

756. L. KOLB, MODERN CLINICAL PSYCHIATRY, 148 (8th ed. 1973).

jail. In any event, the ordering of an examination of an out-of-custody defendant will not operate as a revocation of his or her release on bail or recognizance,[757] nor will it affect the incarcerated defendant's application for bail or recognizance.[758]

Defense counsel should be aware that on request, if the defendant is indigent, the court may appoint an expert selected by the defendant, in addition to those examiners already appointed by the court,[759] whose reasonable fee for services, after the filing of a verified statement of services rendered, will be paid by the county treasurer.[760] This provision thus allows for payment of expert expenses separate from expert witness fees provided for generally.[761]

Of considerable concern to the defendant as well as to counsel is the use that can be made of statements made and information provided the examiner during the examination. Statements made by the defendant and information gathered during any examination are not generally admissible against him or her in subsequent proceedings.[762] They are, however, admissible if the defendant, at trial, raises the defenses of insanity, intoxication, or drugged condition, though their admissibility is limited to those issues.[763] Accordingly, the court must advise the defendant that his or her statements may be used against him or her

---

757. 725 ILCS 5/104-13(d).

758. *Id.*

759. 725 ILCS 5/104-13(e).

760. 725 ILCS 5/104-11(b), 5/104-13(3). An indigent defendant may be en titled to funds for an expert examination where expert testimony is crucial to a proper defense. People v. Clay, 19 Ill. App. 3d 296, 311 N.E.2d 384 (2d Dist. 1974). *See* People v. Kinion, 97 Ill. 2d 322, 454 N.E.2d 625, 630–31 (1983). Where an indigent defendant seeks to have the state pay witness fees in excess of the statutory amount (section 5/113-3), the defendant should petition for the greater sum before presenting it. *See also* People v. Bracy, 38 Ill. 2d 358, 231 N.E.2d 455, 456 (1967) (defendant's constitutional rights were not violated by refusal to furnish him with funds for psychiatric examination). *See* discussion in § 4.09 regarding payment of expert witness fees.

761. 725 ILCS 5/113-3.

762. 725 ILCS 5/104-14(a).

763. Statements will be admissible if the defendant raises the defense of insanity or drugged or intoxicated condition. However, the statements will only be admissible as to these issues. *Id. See* People v. Childers, 94 Ill. App. 3d 104, 418 N.E.2d 959 (3d Dist. 1981), *cert. denied,* 455 U.S. 947 (1982); 725 ILCS 5/104-14(a), (b). *But see* People v. Brock, 262 Ill. App. 3d 485, 633 N.E.2d 735, 742 (1st Dist. 1992) (state allowed to utilize information and statements obtained during examination to impeach defendant and rebut theory that his diminished intellectual capacity prevented him from comprehending the full import of his *Miranda* rights).

and of the extent to which they may be used.[764] Further, the court must advise the defendant that he or she has the right to refuse to cooperate with the examining expert.[765] Note, however, two significant consequences that follow if a defendant refuses to cooperate with the examiner in a court-ordered fitness examination: (1) the refusal may be admissible to determine his or her physical or mental condition;[766] and (2) although refusal to cooperate does not preclude the defendant from later raising the defense of insanity or drugged or intoxicated condition, he or she will be precluded from "offering expert evidence or testimony tending to support such defenses if the expert evidence or testimony is based upon the expert's examination of the defendant."[767]

§ 4.47 — Report

Following a court-ordered examination, the examiner must submit a written report to the court, state, and defendant.[768] The report must satisfy a number of statutory requirements.[769] The examiner must include a diagnosis[770] and a description of the defendant's mental or physical disability, if any;[771] facts on which the diagnosis was based;[772] an explanation of how the diagnosis was reached;[773] a description of the severity of the defendant's disability; and an

---

764. 725 ILCS 5/104-14(c). *But see* People v. Scott, 148 Ill. 2d 479, 594 N.E.2d 217, 237 (1992) (where defendant was allowed to present expert testimony to support his insanity defense, the judge's failure to admonish him with respect to fitness interviews is harmless error), *cert. denied,* 507 U.S. 989 (1993).

765. 725 ILCS 5/104-14(c).

766. People v. Kaufman, 67 Ill. App. 3d 36, 384 N.E.2d 468 (3d Dist. 1978).

767. 725 ILCS 5/104-14(a).

768. 725 ILCS 5/104-15(a). The report should be submitted within 30 days of the date of the order for examination.

769. People v. Harris, 113 Ill. App. 3d 663, 447 N.E.2d 941, 945 (1st Dist. 1983).

770. 725 ILCS 5/104-15(a)(1).

771. 725 ILCS 5/104-15(a)(2).

772. 725 ILCS 5/104-15(a)(1).

773. *Id. See also Harris,* 113 Ill. App. 3d 663, 447 N.E.2d at 945 (report tendered failed to comply with statutory requirements because it did not render explanation about how diagnosis was reached and was conclusory, thus precluding court from independently evaluating report). *But see* People v. Bennett, 159 Ill. App. 3d 172, 511 N.E.2d 1340, 1348 (1st Dist. 1987) (two psychiatric reports, relied on by judge, were statutorily insufficient because they failed to explain how diagnoses were obtained and failed to delineate facts upon which conclusions were based; however, deficiencies were harmless, technical error because the question of the defendant's fitness was raised prior to trial and court observed, talked to defendant, and had ample opportunity to make independent determination that the

opinion on whether and to what extent the disability impairs the defendant's fitness to stand trial.[774]

In addition, if the report indicates that in the examiner's opinion the defendant is not fit, it must also include an opinion on the likelihood that the defendant will attain fitness within one year if he or she is provided with treatment.[775] If the person preparing the report cannot provide such an opinion, the report must explain why.[776] Finally, the report must also include any information that the examiner believes might be harmful to the patient-defendant if made known to him or her.[777]

The importance of the report to defense counsel cannot be overestimated. Not only is it a valuable source of discovery relative to the issue of fitness, it may be equally valuable to establishing a defense at trial. It is thus incumbent on defense counsel, when an examination is requested, and it is known that a report will be prepared, to amass background information on the defendant (including prior hospitalization, outpatient treatment, and incidents at school, work, and home) and to provide that information to the examiner. Providing the information may in fact tip the scales in favor of the desired result on the fitness issue, and it may also legitimize and lend credence to a psychiatric defense, if one is utilized at trial,[778] because much of the information the examiner relies on in forming his or her opinion may be considered by the fact finder at trial.[779]

---

defendant understood the nature and purpose of proceedings). *See* People v. Williams, 274 Ill. App. 3d 793, 655 N.E.2d 470, 477 (4th Dist. 1995) (although report did not state specific medical diagnoses, it was in compliance in all other aspects of statutory requirements and "did not prejudice the defendant").

774. 725 ILCS 5/104-15(a)(2).

775. 725 ILCS 5/104-15(b).

776. *Id.* The report may contain a description of the treatment needed and the least physically restrictive form of treatment appropriate.

777. 725 ILCS 5/104-15(c).

778. As significant as the report might be, counsel is always faced with the possibility that the report may be returned with a conclusion adverse to his or her client's best interests. It should again be noted that the report is not necessarily dispositive of the issue of bona fide doubt of fitness. The defendant's abnormal behavior (*People v. Thomas*, 43 Ill. 2d 328, 253 N.E.2d 431, 433 (1969)), information from counsel [*See* footnote 688 this chapter.], the defendant's psychiatric history [*See* footnote 695.], and hearsay reports [*See* footnote 697.] may all raise bona fide doubts of fitness even in the face of an expert's report to the contrary. *Id.,* 253 N.E.2d at 433.

779. *Wilson v. Clark*, 84 Ill. 2d 186, 417 N.E.2d 1322, *cert. denied,* 454 U.S. 836 (1981), adopts Federal Rules of Evidence 703 and 705. Rule 703 provides:

The facts or data in the particular case upon which an expert bases an opinion or inference may be those perceived by or made known to him

§ 4.48 — Hearing

Within forty-five days of receiving the final written report on the defendant's fitness examination, and assuming the existence of a bona fide doubt[780] in the report or elsewhere, the court must conduct a hearing to decide the issue of fitness.[781] The defendant always has the right to be present at the hearing[782] and in fact is only rarely allowed to waive his or her presence.[783] The rules of evidence applicable to a trial apply,[784] and the trier of fact, subject to those rules, may consider any evidence in reaching a decision on fitness, though some statutory guidance is provided.[785] The state has the burden of proving by a preponderance of the evidence that the

---

at or before the hearing. If of a type reasonably relied upon by experts in the particular field in forming opinions or inferences upon the subject, the facts or data need not be admissible in evidence.

Rule 705 provides, inter alia: "The expert may testify in terms of opinion or inference and give his reason therefor . . . ."

780. People v. Rangel, 104 Ill. App. 3d 695, 432 N.E.2d 1141, 1143 (1st Dist. 1982); People v. Beacham, 87 Ill. App. 3d 457, 410 N.E.2d 87, 96–97 (1st Dist. 1980).

781. 725 ILCS 5/104-11(a). *See* People v. Joseph, 176 Ill. App. 3d 636, 531 N.E.2d 432, 434 (2d Dist. 1988) (where psychologist's consistent opinion was that defendant was fit for trial, including the day before trial, the court's failure to order a second fitness hearing during the only day of trial was not error because the defendant was found fit within the last 24 hours); People v. Thompson, 158 Ill. App. 3d 860, 511 N.E.2d 993, 996 (3d Dist. 1987) (prior adjudication of unfitness raises the presumption that the defendant remains unfit and the presumption continues until a valid subsequent hearing adjudicates him fit; finding of fitness may not be based on a stipulation to psychiatric conclusions); People v. Durham, 142 Ill. App. 3d 473, 491 N.E.2d 832, 840 (4th Dist. 1986) (delay in holding a fitness hearing does not require discharge; there is no sanction in the section for tardiness violation).

782. 725 ILCS 5/104-16(c).

783. Section 5/104-16(c) provides, inter alia, that to waive his or her presence the defendant must file a certificate stating that he or she is physically unable to be present. The certificate must be signed by a licensed physician who examined the defendant within seven days of the filing of the certificate.

784. 725 ILCS 5/104-16(b).

785. 725 ILCS 5/104-16(b).

(b) Subject to the rules of evidence, matters admissible on the issue of the defendant's fitness include, but are not limited to, the following:

(1) The defendant's knowledge and understanding of the charge, the proceedings, the consequences of a plea, judgment or sentence, and the functions of the participants in the trial process;

defendant is fit,[786] though the court may call its own witnesses and conduct its own inquiry.[787]

Who decides the issue of a defendant's fitness to stand trial—bench or jury—raises a number of interesting issues. A defendant does not have a constitutional right to a trial by jury at a fitness hearing,[788] but the Illinois Legislature has granted him or her the right to have a jury determine fitness,[789] although, of course, that right may be waived.[790]

A dilemma faced by defense counsel is that the defendant's waiver of a jury determination of fitness must be voluntarily and knowingly made by the defendant.[791] Thus, counsel must establish that even though a bona fide doubt of fitness exists, the defendant is still fit enough to make a voluntary and knowing jury waiver. That dilemma is resolved in part by the statutory presumption of fitness[792] that continues until a determination of unfitness is made. The dilemma is further resolved by the fact that it is not only the defendant who has the right to a jury determination of fitness; the state or even the court on its

---

> (2) The defendant's ability to observe, recollect and relate oc curences, especially those concerning the incidents alleged, and to communicate with counsel;
>
> (3) The defendant's social behavior and abilities; orientation as to time and place; recognition of persons, places and things; and performances of motor processes.

725 ILCS 5/104-16(b)(1), (2), (3).

786. 725 ILCS 5/104-16(c). The state also has the burden of production. People v. Hubert, 51 Ill. App. 3d 394, 366 N.E.2d 909 (1st Dist. 1977). *See, e.g.*, People v. Mahaffey, 166 Ill. 2d 1, 651 N.E.2d 1055, 1063–64 (trial court did not err in finding the defendant fit to stand trial even though he claimed he was under a religious delusion that he could not be found guilty or sentenced to death, where the judge heard expert testimony from both sides and observed the defendant), *cert. denied*, 516 U.S. 977 (1995).

787. 725 ILCS 5/104-11(c).

788. People v. Welsh, 30 Ill. App. 3d 887, 333 N.E.2d 572, 573 (2d Dist. 1975); People v. Shanklin, 26 Ill. App. 3d 167, 324 N.E.2d 711, 713 (5th Dist. 1975); People v. White, 131 Ill. App. 2d 652, 264 N.E.2d 228, 232 (3d Dist. 1970).

789. 725 ILCS 5/104-12. Either the state or the defense may demand a jury, or the court may impanel a jury on its own motion.

790. People v. Brown, 43 Ill. 2d 79, 250 N.E.2d 647, 649 (1969).

791. People v. Shadowens, 44 Ill. 2d 70, 254 N.E.2d 484, 485 (1969). *See* People v. Strickland, 154 Ill. 2d 489, 609 N.E.2d 1366, 1379 (1992) (where the defendant failed to show a connection between alleged fears for personal safety in jail and a decision to waive juries, inquiries by judge showed waivers knowing, intelligent, and voluntary), *cert. denied*, 510 U.S. 858 (1993).

792. 725 ILCS 5/104-10.

own motion may order a jury determination.[793] Thus, if defense counsel, the state, or the court doubts the ability of the defendant to make a valid waiver, all participants might be well advised to opt for having the fitness determination made by a jury. By so doing the rights of the defendant are scrupulously honored, the court is insulated from reversal on appeal, and defense counsel is protected against a later claim of incompetency on appeal or through collateral attack. Note that while Illinois apparently has no problem with the procedure, the United States Supreme Court long ago observed that "it is contradictory to argue that a defendant may be incompetent, and yet knowingly or intelligently 'waive' his right to have the court determine his capacity to stand trial."[794]

At the hearing, although the rules of evidence apply, the judge or jury may also base the decision, in part, on the defendant's demeanor and irrational behavior.[795] These two factors, it would seem, though not sanctioned by the rules of evidence, are certainly within the scope of logic, common sense, and human experience. Note, however, that although all of the factors articulated in the statute,[796] as well as those outside the statute, are relevant, none is necessarily dispositive of the issue of fitness.[797] The trier may consider testimony of lay witnesses as well as that of experts.[798] Because conclusions of

---

793. 725 ILCS 5/104-12.

794. Pate v. Robinson, 383 U.S. 375, 384 (1966); see further discussion of the issue of jury waiver by a questionably fit defendant at § 4.45.

795. *See* footnotes 696–697 in this chapter.

796. 725 ILCS 5/104-16(b).

797. The mere fact that a defendant has a history of mental disorder is not conclusive that he or she lacks capacity to stand trial. People v. Cole, 61 Ill. App. 3d 1007, 378 N.E.2d 381, 383 (5th Dist. 1978). Depravity of character, abandoned habits, or commission of an atrocious crime are not in themselves evidence of insanity. People v. Robinson, 22 Ill. 2d 162, 174 N.E.2d 820, 823 (1961), *cert. denied,* 368 U.S. 995 (1962). The defendant's demeanor at trial is not dispositive of the issues of his or her fitness to stand trial. People v. Count, 42 Ill. App. 3d 715, 356 N.E.2d 435, 437 (3d Dist. 1976). *See also* People v. Haynes, 174 Ill. 2d 204, 673 N.E.2d 318 (1996) (see discussion of *Haynes* in text of § 4.45 and notes 728–734.)

798. In *People v. Robinson*, 102 Ill. App. 3d 884, 429 N.E.2d 1356, 1362 (1st Dist. 1981), the court stated that a lay witness who has an opportunity to observe the defendant may give an opinion about the defendant's mental condition as long as the testimony includes sufficient facts and circumstances forming the basis for the opinion. *See also* People v. Aspelmeier, 250 Ill. App. 3d 803, 621 N.E.2d 228, 250 (3d Dist. 1993) (lay testimony supported trial court's finding that defendant was sane); People v. Glenn, 233 Ill. App. 3d 666, 599 N.E.2d 1220, 1228 (1st Dist. 1992) (lay testimony was properly accepted over expert testimony); People v. Clark, 102 Ill. App. 3d 414, 429 N.E.2d 1255, 1257–60 (1st Dist. 1981) (lay witnesses' opinion may overcome expert's opinion regarding sanity); People v. Gindorf, 159 Ill. App. 3d 647, 512 N.E.2d 770, 776 (2d Dist. 1987); People v.

experts are only as valid as the bases or reasons for them,[799] neither the trial judge nor a jury is obliged as a matter of law to accept the opinions of expert witnesses.[800] Where there is uncontradicted expert testimony, however, that a defendant is not fit to stand trial, the factfinder is not free to reject the testimony in the absence of other evidence indicating the defendant is fit,[801] nor may it reject the expert testimony solely on its own opinion from "brief conversations and common sense interpretation" of opinions that the defendant is fit.[802]

Assuming a finding of unfitness is made,[803] the trier of fact must also determine whether there is a substantial probability that the defendant will attain fitness within one year if provided with treatment.[804] If a substantial probability is found, or if the trier cannot determine whether the probability exists, "the court shall order the defendant to undergo treatment for the purpose of rendering him fit."[805]

§ 4.49 — Posthearing Issues: Treatment and Restoration of the Unfit Defendant

Once a defendant is found unfit to stand trial but is expected to be fit within one year, the court must order treatment in conjunction with the Illinois Department of Human Services, subject to a series of complex provisions that are determinative of inpatient or outpatient status, where the defendant will be

---

Chambers, 36 Ill. App. 3d 838, 345 N.E.2d 119, 123–24 (1st Dist. 1976). *See also* People v. Whitten, 269 Ill. App 3d 1037, 647 N.E.2d 1062 (5th Dist. 1995) (expert's opinion is matter of weight).

799. People v. Walker, 77 Ill. App. 3d 227, 395 N.E.2d 1087 (1st Dist. 1979).

800. People v. Thomas, 43 Ill. 2d 328, 253 N.E.2d 431, 433 (1969) (expert's report indicating that defendant was fit could not be viewed as conclusive in presence of defendant's abnormal behavior). *See also* People v. Bleitner, 189 Ill. App. 3d 971, 546 N.E.2d 241, 245 (4th Dist. 1989) (mere fact that a psychiatrist expressed an opinion that the defendant was unfit not mandate a similar finding by the judge; ultimate issue for the judge to decide); People v. Baldwin, 185 Ill. App. 3d 1079, 541 N.E.2d 1315, 1321 (1st Dist. 1989) (where uncontroverted expert testimony presented showed the defendant unfit, the judge could not reject an expert's conclusions without other testimony or evidence that the defendant was fit). *See* People v. McMillen, 281 Ill. App. 3d 247, 666 N.E.2d 812 (1st Dist. 1996); People v. Gilyard, 237 Ill. App. 3d 8, 602 N.E.2d 1335 (2d Dist. 1992).

801. People v. Baldwin, 185 Ill. App. 3d 1079, 541 N.E.2d 1315 (1st Dist. 1989).

802. People v. Williams, 87 Ill. App. 3d 860, 409 N.E.2d 439, 442 (3d Dist. 1980).

803. Note that an order finding the defendant unfit is a final order for purposes of appeal. 725 ILCS 5/104-16(e).

804. 725 ILCS 5/104-16(d).

805. *Id.*

housed, and reporting requirements.[806] Those provisions are beyond the scope of this chapter.

There are two other significant areas of pretrial fitness issues, however, with which counsel must also be familiar. The first area concerns the "restoration" of the previously unfit defendant to fitness and trial. The second area involves the defendant who was found unfit and unlikely to attain fitness within one year.

Both the statutory provisions and the supporting law are relatively straight-forward concerning the restoring to fitness of a defendant previously adjudged unfit. Within 90 days of the initial entry or a continuation of a previously entered order of treatment,[807] or at any other time when notified by the defendant's treatment supervisor that the defendant is now fit, the court must order a new hearing to determine that issue.[808] The defendant is entitled to be represented by counsel,[809] and the procedural requirements of the hearing are as stringent as those of the original fitness hearing.[810] The defendant is not, however, entitled to have the restoration of fitness decision made by a jury.[811]

At the restoration hearing, the burden of proving the defendant's fitness by a preponderance of the evidence is still on the state, as it was at the initial fitness hearing.[812]

---

806. 725 ILCS 5/104-16 through 5/104-23.

807. The order of treatment was entered upon the initial finding of unfitness and that the defendant would be fit within one year, or the finding of unfitness and the inability to decide if the defendant would be fit within one year. 725 ILCS 5/104-16(d).

808. 725 ILCS 5/104-20. *See* People v. Ralon, 211 Ill. App. 3d 927, 570 N.E.2d 742, 751 (1st Dist. 1991) (after treatment where the defendant was reported to be fit, the judge's inquiry at the restoration hearing is to determine fitness or unfitness based on evidence which includes professional evaluation by medical experts).

809. People v. Lewis, 115 Ill. App. 3d 389, 450 N.E.2d 886 (1st Dist. 1983), *rev'd*, 103 Ill. 2d 111, 468 N.E.2d 1222 (1984), *cert. denied*, 470 U.S. 1006 (1985).

810. *Lewis*, 115 Ill. App. 3d 389, 450 N.E.2d at 891–92. *See* People v. Thompson, 158 Ill. App. 3d 860, 511 N.E.2d 993, 996 (3d Dist. 1987) (where a fitness hearing failed to meet minimal due process necessary to find the defendant fit, the judge's finding at the post-conviction hearing that the defendant was restored was against the manifest weight of the evidence).

811. 725 ILCS 5/104-12, 5/104-20, 5/104-27.

812. 725 ILCS 5/104-11(c); People v. Phillips, 110 Ill. App. 3d 1092, 443 N.E.2d 655, 661 (1st Dist. 1982). *See* People v. Brown, 252 Ill. App. 3d 377, 625 N.E.2d 100, 104 (1st Dist. 1993) (even though the judge's comments at the restoration hearing indicated that the judge believed the defendant had the burden of proving fitness, was not reversible error because the defendant was found fit in two prior restoration hearings, one expert testified that the defendant was fit for trial while on medication, no other expert presented, and the defendant's testimony was coherent although he expressed dissatisfaction with his attorney); People v.

The manner by which evidence of fitness is admitted at the restoration hearing has generated some controversy. In large metropolitan areas of the state where the volume of cases is great and the number of experts available at any given time is limited, the question arises whether stipulated testimony is allowable in lieu of live witness testimony. Defense counsel, as in the jury waiver situation,[813] must act for a defendant who is still under a finding of unfitness and thus is presumptively unable to assist or cooperate with his or her counsel[814] (he or she may be psychiatrically but not yet legally fit) and decide whether the entire hearing will be predicated on stipulated testimony.

For a short time, *People v. Greene*[815] provided an answer to the apparent dilemma. In *Greene,* following reexamination of a previously adjudicated unfit defendant and on a motion for a fitness hearing, the assistant state's attorney read into the record a letter of one psychiatrist. Counsel for the state and defense counsel stipulated to the qualifications of both examining psychiatrists and "to their findings that the defendant is fit to stand trial"[816] following which the trial court found the defendant fit to stand trial. In reversing the defendant's conviction, the appellate court held that "[a] judicial determination of defendant's fitness cannot be based upon mere stipulation to the existence of psychiatric conclusions."[817] Without an "affirmative showing" in the record below that the defendant was "fit to stand trial, there was in effect no fitness hearing at all."[818] Thus, either live witness testimony or at least something more by way of stipulation than was done in *Greene* must occur before a previously adjudicated unfit defendant can be judicially restored to fitness. What that "something more" is was given a questionable definition in *People v. Lewis.*[819]

In *Lewis,* the supreme court reviewed several consolidated First District Appellate Court decisions of defendants who, as in *Greene,* had been restored to fitness status solely on the basis of stipulated testimony. The appellate court,

---

Ralon, 211 Ill. App. 3d 927, 570 N.E.2d 742, 749 (1st Dist. 1991) (preponderance of the evidence standard applies at both).

813. *See* the discussion in footnotes 791–793 in this chapter.

814. People v. Greene, 102 Ill. App. 3d 639, 430 N.E.2d 219, 221–22 (1st Dist. 1981).

815. 102 Ill. App. 3d 639, 430 N.E.2d 219 (1st Dist. 1981).

816. *Id.,* 430 N.E.2d at 220.

817. *Id.,* 430 N.E.2d at 222.

818. *Id.*

819. 103 Ill. 2d 111, 468 N.E.2d 1222 (1984), *cert. denied,* 470 U.S. 1006 (1985). *See also* People v. Williams, 274 Ill. App. 3d 793, 655 N.E.2d 470, 477 (4th Dist. 1995) (even though parties stipulated to fact that the psychologist made certain findings and conclusions that the court could consider, the trial court's finding of fitness was not based on mere stipulation; the trial court relied not only on report but also on observance of the defendant on several occasions).

in each case, had reversed the conviction on the rationale and authority of *Greene*. That is, in each case, "[t]he appellate court reasoned that since there was 'no affirmative showing . . . that the trial court exercised discretion in finding [the defendant] fit to stand trial, there was in effect no fitness hearing at all.' "[820]

The supreme court, in what appears to be more an affirmation of the sometimes practical problem of arranging for live witness testimony than a well-reasoned analysis of the rights of an unfit defendant, reversed each appellate court determination of unfitness. The supreme court distinguished the Lewis determinations from *Greene*, finding that in *Greene*

> defense counsel stipulated to the "findings of the two psychiatrists as contained in the reports and * * * to the fact that the defendant is fit for trial" [citation omitted]. Here, however, it was stipulated that, if called to testify, qualified psychiatrists who had examined defendants would testify that in their opinions the defendant was mentally fit to stand trial.[821]

It is perhaps a difference without a distinction, but apparently a previously adjudged unfit defendant may be restored to fitness on stipulated testimony alone, assuming that counsel is cautious about the wording used in the stipulation.[822]

In any event, whether the hearing proceeds by way of stipulation,[823] live witness testimony, or both, the court must (1) find that the defendant is fit to stand trial and accordingly set the matter on the trial call;[824] or (2) find

---

820. *Id.*, 468 N.E.2d at 1224.

821. *Id.*

822. Justice Simon in his dissent argued that the "court relies on a semantic technicality to emasculate the long standing Illinois principle that defendants who have once been adjudicated incompetent require the special protection of the courts and cannot stipulate that protection away by their own actions or the actions of their attorneys." To allow a defendant who is still legally presumptively unable to cooperate with the counsel or understand the nature of the proceedings through his or her counsel, to stipulate to unsworn expert testimony would "make a sham" out of the fitness hearing. *Id.*, 468 N.E.2d at 1227. *But see* People v. Robinson, 221 Ill. App. 3d 1045, 582 N.E.2d 1299, 1303 (1st Dist. 1991) (the trial court properly found defendant restored based not only on the stipulation of the defense counsel but also on the fact that he reviewed the doctors' reports, observed defendant's demeanor, and confirmed the fact that she was taking medication).

823. 725 ILCS 5/104-20(a).

824. 725 ILCS 5/104-20(a)(1), 5/104-20(b). *See* People v. Lang, 113 Ill. 2d 407, 498 N.E.2d 1105, 1122–23 (1986) (defendant adjudicated unfit to stand trial more than five years earlier had substantial interest in clearing his name and record of

that the defendant is still unfit and decide whether the defendant is making progress toward attaining fitness.[825] If the court concludes that the defendant is making progress toward attaining fitness, the original or a modified treatment plan[826] continues.[827] If, however, the court finds that the defendant is "not making progress . . . such that there is not a substantial probability that he will attain fitness within one year from the . . . original finding of unfitness,"[828] the defendant is then placed in the same position as the unfit defendant for whom it was initially decided that fitness within one year was not a probability and for whom no "special provisions or assistance" can ever make him or her fit.[829]

It is with respect to this final area—that of the unfit defendant who may never become fit, or at least not within one year—that the court and counsel may have a profound impact on the defendant's future. Unfortunately, because of the newness of the applicable statutory provisions,[830] there are few Illinois cases to which counsel may look for guidance.

§ 4.50 — The Discharge Hearing

Where the defendant is found unfit to stand trial and there is no substantial probability of his or her restoration to fitness within one year, the defendant may move for a discharge hearing under section 104-25.[831] The court must

---

an alleged murder for which he was indicted more than 15 years earlier and was entitled to a hearing regarding his fitness to stand trial).

825. 725 ILCS 5/104-20(a)(1), 5/104-20(c).

826. 725 ILCS 5/104-17.

827. 725 ILCS 5/104-20(c).

828. 725 ILCS 5/104-20(d).

829. 725 ILCS 5/104-23. *See* People v. Burton, 166 Ill. App. 3d 143, 519 N.E.2d 947, 949 (3d Dist. 1988) (where a one year period from the date of the original unfitness finding elapsed, the state was required to request the court to conduct a discharge hearing).

830. 725 ILCS 5/104-25.

831. 725 ILCS 5/104-23(a). The discharge hearing may be requested by the defendant at any time, or by the state where the defendant has remained unfit for a year after the original unfitness finding or where there is no substantial probability that the defendant will attain fitness within one year. People v. Rink, 97 Ill. 2d 533, 455 N.E.2d 64, 66 (1983). *See* People v. Lavold, 262 Ill. App. 3d 984, 635 N.E.2d 919, 924–25, 929 (1st Dist. 1994) (where a trial judge exceeded maximum treatment term, without hearing, by a little over two years, the delay did not deprive the court of jurisdiction because the section does not authorize automatic release of an unfit defendant as soon as treatment period expires).

conduct the hearing within 120 days of the filing of the motion, unless the defendant causes a delay.[832]

The purpose of the discharge hearing is to determine the sufficiency of evidence against the defendant.[833] It is an "innocent only" hearing—that is, a proceeding to determine whether the evidence is insufficient to prove the defendant guilty or to determine if he or she had a meritorious defense that entitles him or her to an acquittal. It is not a hearing to determine his or her guilt,[834] although evidence relevant to the defendant's guilt is of course admissible.[835] If the evidence introduced fails to prove the defendant's guilt beyond a reasonable doubt (because of insufficient evidence or meritorious defense), the defendant must be acquitted.[836] If the acquitted defendant is still in need of psychiatric care, however, the court may commit him or her to the Illinois Department of Mental Health and Developmental Disabilities, under either the Mental Health and Disabilities Code[837] or the Unified Code of Corrections,[838]

---

832. 725 ILCS 5/104-23(a). *See* People v. Cain, 171 Ill. App. 3d 468, 525 N.E.2d 1194, 1198–99 (4th Dist. 1988) (court did not err in denying discharge for denial of right to speedy trial where the defendant's refusal to cooperate with examination during the fitness proceeding was delaying conduct and basis for tolling 120-day period).

833. 725 ILCS 5/104-25.

834. *Rink,* 97 Ill. 2d 533, 455 N.E.2d at 68. *See* People v. Lang, 225 Ill. App. 3d 229, 587 N.E.2d 490, 493 (1st Dist. 1992) (state is required to prove a defendant's guilt beyond a reasonable doubt but the judge's determination that the state met the burden does not constitute technical determination of guilt); People v. Lang, 189 Ill. App. 3d 384, 545 N.E.2d 327, 328 (1st Dist. 1989) (a discharge hearing is like a criminal trial because the defendant may be acquitted outright or on grounds of insanity and is unlike a criminal trial since the defendant cannot be convicted).

835. 725 ILCS 5/104-25; *Rink,* 97 Ill. 2d 533, 455 N.E.2d at 68. The court may admit hearsay or affidavit evidence on secondary matters such as testimony to establish chain of possession of physical evidence, laboratory reports, authentication of transcripts, records, and public documents.

836. 725 ILCS 5/104-25(b). *See* People v. Lang, 113 Ill. 2d 407, 498 N.E.2d 1105, 1122 (1986) (failure of the state to prove the defendant guilty beyond a reasonable doubt results in acquittal; if the state sustains its burden, the defendant is remanded for further treatment).

837. 405 ILCS 5/1-100.

838. 730 ILCS 5/5-2-4.

depending on the particular basis of the finding of not guilty.[839] The length of commitment, appeal rights, and so forth are fully set out in the code.[840]

The biggest problem in proceeding under the discharge hearing provisions[841] is identical to that encountered by counsel in the initial fitness hearing—bench or jury determination[842]—and in the stipulated testimony versus live witness dilemma faced at the restoration hearing.[843] Counsel must go to trial, or at least a "hearing," in a situation where his or her client is unfit to stand trial because "he is unable to understand the nature and purpose of the proceedings against him or to assist in his defense."[844] How, then, can counsel provide effective assistance as he or she is required to do and as the client is entitled to have?[845]

The dilemma is enhanced by the fact that it is the defendant who may set into operation the discharge hearing machinery by demanding a hearing.[846]

---

839. *But see* People v. Bocik, 211 Ill. App. 3d 801, 570 N.E.2d 671, 675 (1st Dist. 1991) (where there is no evidence the defendant would ever be fit for trial, the judge could not proceed with a criminal trial; because the judge's order did not find the defendant subject to involuntary commitment, he was required to release the defendant).

840. 725 ILCS 5/104-25(d), (e), (f), (g). *See, e.g.*, People v. Rasgaitis, 222 Ill. App. 3d 855, 584 N.E.2d 451, 454–55 (1st Dist. 1991) (although there was sufficient evidence to support a determination that the defendant was subject to involuntary admission and a threat to public safety, the trial judge erred in ordering a period of treatment, up to 40 years, commencing on date of court's hearing; under paragraph (g)(4) defendant's treatment period cannot be extended beyond the maximum sentence he would have received had he been convicted of murder, *e.g.*, 40 years which began to run from date of original finding of defendant's unfitness to stand trial more than 10 years prior); People v. Young, 220 Ill. App. 3d 98, 581 N.E.2d 371, 377 (2d Dist. 1991) (even where term of treatment expires before completion of appellate review, appeal from order of commitment at discharge hearing is ordinarily not considered moot); Yiadom v. Kiley, 204 Ill. App. 3d 418, 562 N.E.2d 310, 313 (1st Dist. 1990) (since orders of commitment normally expire before appellate review, thereby invoking mootness doctrine, and since dismissal for mootness would eliminate appellate review, doctrine must be held inapplicable); People v. McBrien, 144 Ill. App. 3d 489, 494 N.E.2d 732, 735 (4th Dist. 1986) (any order denying acquittal is directly appealable).

841. 725 ILCS 5/104-25.

842. *See* the discussion at footnotes 791–793 in this chapter.

843. *See* the discussion at footnotes 814–822 in this chapter.

844. 725 ILCS 5/104-10.

845. U.S. Const. amend. VI.

846. 725 ILCS 5/104-23. *See* People v. Christy, 206 Ill. App. 3d 361, 564 N.E.2d 238, 242 (4th Dist. 1990) (once defendant is released after the hearing conducted pursuant to paragraph (b)(3), the judge and not the state must determine whether to hold a discharge hearing or dismiss charges with prejudice; where a discharge

Although it is true that a defendant who proceeds under the discharge hearing provisions cannot be found guilty, the rules of evidence are significantly relaxed[847] and "transcripts of testimony taken at a discharge hearing may be admitted in evidence at a subsequent trial of the case [if the defendant is not acquitted.]"[848] Moreover, the length of potential civil commitment may be based on the discharge hearing findings.[849]

Counsel, then, might be well advised before demanding a discharge hearing to seriously consider whether the client, who cannot cooperate or understand the nature of the proceedings, can provide enough information to warrant a hearing demand. If, through the client and counsel's own investigative efforts, it is concluded that the defendant has a meritorious defense or the evidence is insufficient to convict, the risks of proceeding with the hearing are obviously minimized, and the benefits of removing the innocent and unfit defendant from criminal to civil proceedings are worth the risk. If, however, the client's understanding and cooperation are fundamental to the development of a defense, the "commit or release" rationale of the statute[850] must be heavily weighed against the client's right to effective assistance of counsel which, at least arguably, cannot be provided by a lawyer who is without his or her client's full understanding and cooperation.

---

hearing is held, the judge has no other option than to proceed under paragraph (b)(2) and dismiss with prejudice; the section does not provide for a reevaluation hearing). *But see* People v. Rasgaitis, 222 Ill. App. 3d 855, 584 N.E.2d 451, 455 (1st Dist. 1991) (where a defendant charged with murder and involuntarily committed, periodic hearings to reevaluate continued need for involuntary admission and continued unfitness to stand trial must be held).

847. "The court may admit hearsay or affidavit evidence on secondary mat ters . . . ." 725 ILCS 5/104-25(a). *See* People v. Fosdick, 166 Ill. App. 3d 491, 519 N.E.2d 1102, 1109 (1st Dist. 1988) (state need not produce an expert witness as to defendant's sanity at time of offense, but may rely on facts in evidence and inferences drawn therefrom; factfinder may reject expert testimony that the defendant was insane at the time and conclude that the defendant is sane based solely on lay testimony).

848. "(e) Transcripts of testimony taken at a discharge hearing may be admitted in evidence at a subsequent trial of the case, subject to the rules of evidence, if the witness who gave such testimony is legally unavailable at the time of the subsequent trial." 725 ILCS 5/104-25(e).

849. 725 ILCS 5/104-25(d), (g).

850. *See* Jackson v. Indiana, 406 U.S. 715 (1972).

§ 4.51   Motion to Dismiss the Charge

An indictment, information, or complaint may be dismissed on any of the 11 enumerated grounds of dismissal in chapter 725[851] as well as where the defendant's rights to due process have been violated. This section discusses each of the specific 11 grounds of dismissal and those types of due process violations that have been held to vest the trial court with the inherent authority to dismiss the charge. Under most circumstances the motion must be "filed within a reasonable time after the defendant has been arraigned."[852] The statute

---

851. The eleven grounds are, in summary:

(1) The defendant's statutory speedy trial rights were violated;

(2) The offense is beyond the statute of limitations or the defendant's double jeopardy rights were violated;

(3) The defendant was granted immunity from prosecution;

(4) The grand jury that returned the indictment was improperly selected resulting in substantial injustice to the defendant;

(5) The grand jury that returned the indictment (1) acted contrary to statute (2) to the defendant's prejudice;

(6) The court lacks jurisdiction;

(7) Venue is improper;

(8) The charge does not state an offense;

(9) The indictment is based solely on the testimony of an incompetent witness;

(10) The defendant (1) is misnamed (2) to his or her prejudice;

(11) The indictment was not returned or a preliminary hearing was not held in a timely fashion as set forth in section 109-3.1.

725 ILCS 5/114-1. The grounds for dismissal under this section are not exclusive. People v. Heinzmann, 232 Ill. App. 3d 557, 597 N.E.2d 942, 944 (5th Dist. 1992). *But see* People v. Sullivan, 201 Ill. App. 3d 1011, 559 N.E.2d 508, 509 (3d Dist. 1990) (judge may dismiss charge prior to trial only when presented with grounds specifically set forth in the section or where clear denial of due process exists resulting in prejudice to the defendant; judge has no authority to dismiss simply because victim no longer wished to pursue the matter and judge believed allowing the case to proceed to be waste of resources).

852. 725 ILCS 5/114-1(b). The exceptions to the requirement of timely filing are where (1) the court lacks jurisdiction, or (2) the charging instrument fails to state an offense. *See* People v. Marty, 241 Ill. App. 3d 266, 608 N.E.2d 1326, 1328 (4th Dist. 1993) (where dismissal was made after the jury was sworn, opening statements made and the state had called their first witness, dismissal did not fall within this pretrial dismissal section); People v. Covelli, 184 Ill. App. 3d 114, 540 N.E.2d 569, 572 (2d Dist. 1989) (motion to dismiss brought more than one year after arraignment is not untimely, where judge ordered pretrial motions need not be filed until discovery is complete); People v. Moats, 165 Ill. App. 3d 413, 519 N.E.2d 52, 54 (3d Dist. 1988)

is clear about the procedures the trial court must employ in ruling on a motion to dismiss:

> (c) If the motion presents only an issue of law the court shall determine it without the necessity of further pleadings. If the motion alleges facts not of record in the case the State shall file an answer admitting or denying each of the factual allegations of the motion.
>
> (d) When an issue of fact is presented by a motion to dismiss and the answer of the State the court shall conduct a hearing and determine the issues.
>
> (d-5) When a defendant seeks dismissal of the charge upon the ground set forth in subsection (a)(7) of this Section, the defendant shall make a prima facie showing that the county is an improper place of trial. Upon such showing, the State shall have the burden of proving, by a preponderance of the evidence, that the county is the proper place of trial.[853]

The consequences of a favorable ruling on a motion to dismiss are also articulated:

> (e) Dismissal of the charge upon the grounds [of improper grand jury selection,[854] or conduct,[855] lack of jurisdiction in the court,[856] improper venue,[857] failure of the charge to state an offense,[858] the charge was based solely on the testimony of an incompetent witness,[859] the defendant is misnamed,[860] or the defendant was not timely indicted or did not have a timely preliminary hearing[861]] shall not prevent the return of a new indictment or the filing of a new charge . . . . [862]

(judge erred in denying defendant's speedy trial motion to dismiss as untimely even though it violated local rules, where judge could not properly determine when defendant should reasonably have known of possible violation).

853. 725 ILCS 5/114-1(c), (d), (d-5).

854. 725 ILCS 5/114-1(a)(4).

855. 725 ILCS 5/114-1(a)(5).

856. 725 ILCS 5/114-1(a)(6).

857. 725 ILCS 5/114-1(a)(7).

858. 725 ILCS 5/114-1(a)(8).

859. 725 ILCS 5/114-1(a)(9).

860. 725 ILCS 5/114-1(a)(10).

861. 725 ILCS 5/114-1(a)(11).

862. 725 ILCS 5/114-1(e).

Of more than passing interest is the court's power over the defendant even upon dismissal of the charge for the above reasons: "[T]he court may order that the defendant be held in custody or if he had been previously released on bail that his bail be continued for a specified time pending the return of a new indictment or the filing of a new charge."[863] Finally, if the grounds of a motion to dismiss are improper venue or lack of jurisdiction, the trial court may "instead of dismissal, order the cause transferred to a court of competent jurisdiction or to a proper place of trial."[864] It is only with respect to motions sustained on speedy trial violations[865] immunity grants,[866] the statute of limitations, double jeopardy violations,[867] or due process violations that a defendant may not be reindicted or otherwise recharged. The state has a right to appeal any case where the court's judgment has the substantial effect of dismissing the case.[868]

§ 4.52   — Speedy Trial Violations

If a defendant has not been brought to trial within the statutory scheme of chapter 725, section 5/103-5,[869] the court may dismiss the charge against him or her[870] and new charges predicated on the same offense may not

---

863. 725 ILCS 5/114-1(e).

864. 725 ILCS 5/114-1(f).

865. 725 ILCS 5/103-5, 5/114-1(a)(1).

866. 725 ILCS 5/114-1(a)(3).

867. 720 ILCS 5/3-3 through 5/3-8; 725 ILCS 5/114-1(a)(12).

868. People v. Carpenter, 221 Ill. App. 3d 58, 581 N.E.2d 683, 688 (5th Dist. 1991), *cert. denied,* 506 U.S. 825 (1992).

869. 725 ILCS 5/114-1(e), (f).

870. 725 ILCS 5/114-1(a)(1). *See* People v. Woolsey, 139 Ill. 2d 157, 564 N.E.2d 764, 769–70 (1990) (judge should dispose of defendant's speedy trial motion before allowing the state to *nolle pros* where a potentially dispositive defense motion was filed before the state's motion); People v. Schmidt, 233 Ill. App. 3d 512, 599 N.E.2d 201, 204 (3d Dist. 1992) (dismissal mandatory, not discretionary, when speedy trial period is violated unless the delay is charged to defendant); People v. Young, 220 Ill. App. 3d 488, 581 N.E.2d 241, 244 (1st Dist. 1991) (to prevail on a motion to dismiss based on allegations of delay between crime and charge, defendant must show actual and substantial prejudice). *See also In re A.F.,* 282 Ill. App. 3d 930, 668 N.E.2d 1168, 1170 (1st Dist. 1996) (state's nolle prosequi of charge tolled speedy trial period until refiled where there was no evidence state used the time to gain tactical advantage). *But see* People v. Ladd, 294 Ill. App. 3d 928, 691 N.E.2d 896, 903 (5th Dist. 1998) (trial court abused its discretion in dismissing prematurely filed motion for discharge on basis of speedy trial where speedy trial period expired while motion pending).

be brought.[871] See the discussion of speedy trial issues in section 4.81 of this text.

§ 4.53 — Statute of Limitation Problems

A motion to dismiss the charge will also lie where the applicable statute of limitations has run.[872] Generally, "a prosecution for first degree murder, second degree murder, involuntary manslaughter, reckless homicide, concealment of homicidal death, treason, arson, aggravated arson, or forgery may be commenced at any time."[873] All other felonies have a three-year limitation period, unless otherwise specified or extended.[874] Misdemeanors may be tried within eighteen months of the date of the offense.[875] Under some

---

871. 725 ILCS 5/114-1(e). *See* People v. Quigley, 183 Ill. 2d 1, 697 N.E.2d 735 (1998) (dismissal of misdemeanor DUI on speedy trial grounds required dismissal of felony DUI brought for same offense); People v. Rhoads, 110 Ill. App. 3d 1107, 443 N.E.2d 673, 679 (1st Dist. 1982) (state cannot drop charges and thereafter file new charge based on same offense when defendant entitled to dismissal based on speedy trial violations). *But see* People v. Crowe, 195 Ill. App. 3d 212, 552 N.E.2d 5, 10 (4th Dist. 1990) (double jeopardy not applicable where case dismissed for speedy trial violation because question of defendant's guilt or innocence never submitted to jury).

872. 725 ILCS 5/114-1(a)(2). *See* People v. Gwinn, 255 Ill. App. 3d 628, 627 N.E.2d 699, 701 (2d Dist. 1994) (charging instrument must allege defendant committed offense at some time prior to return of indictment or information and within period fixed by statute of limitations).

873. 720 ILCS 5/3-5(a).

874. 725 ILCS 5/3-5(b). *See* People v. Berg, 277 Ill. App. 3d 549, 660 N.E.2d 1003, 1004–05 (2d Dist. 1996) (aggravated arson charge had to be dismissed because not brought within three years of incident; legislature did not include aggravated arson in section 3-5(a) and court was not willing to find aggravated arson same as arson; section now amended to include aggravated arson but no retroactive application). *See, e.g.*, People v. Calderon, 261 Ill. App. 3d 558, 633 N.E.2d 890, 892 (1st Dist. 1994) (sexual assault charges could be brought by victim, age 20, against father accused of sexual intercourse with daughter despite specific statute of limitations applying to sexual conduct between underage victim and defendant who was family member called for prosecution within one year of victim attaining age of 18; that statute extends time in cases where general three year statute would not apply and action in present case could be brought under general statute), *vacated*, 157 Ill. 2d 508, 640 N.E.2d 946 (1994) (conviction reversed).

875. 725 ILCS 5/3-5(b).

circumstances and for certain offenses, the above limitation periods may be extended.[876]

---

876.   Sec. 3-6. Extended limitations. The period within which a prosecution must be commenced under the provisions of Section 3-5 [720 ILCS 5/3-5] or other applicable statute is extended under the following conditions:

(a) A prosecution for theft involving a breach of a fiduciary obligation to the aggrieved person may be commenced as follows:

(1) If the aggrieved person is a minor or a person under legal disability, then during the minority or legal disability or within one year after the termination thereof.

(2) In any other instance, within one year after the discovery of the offense by an aggrieved person, or by a person who has legal capacity to represent an aggrieved person or has a legal duty to report the offense, and is not himself or herself a party to the offense; or in the absence of such discovery, within one year after the proper prosecuting officer becomes aware of the offense. However, in no such case is the period of limitation so extended more than 3 years beyond the expiration of the period otherwise applicable.

(b) A prosecution for any offense based upon misconduct in office by a public officer or employee may be commenced within one year after discovery of the offense by a person having a legal duty to report such offense, or in the absence of such discovery, within one year after the proper prosecuting officer becomes aware of the offense. However, in no such cases is the period of limitation so extended more than 3 years beyond the expiration of the period otherwise applicable.

(c) A prosecution for any offense involving sexual conduct or sexual penetration, as defined in Section 12-12 of this Code [720 ILCS 5/12-12], where the victim and defendant are family members, as defined in Section 12-12 of this Code [725 ILCS 5/12-12], may be commenced within one year of the victim attaining the age of 18 years.

(d) A prosecution for child pornography, indecent solicitation of a child, soliciting for a juvenile prostitute, juvenile pimping or exploitation of a child may be commenced within one year of the victim attaining the age of 18 years. However, in no such case shall the time period for prosecution expire sooner than 3 years after the commission of the offense. When the victim is under 18 years of age, a prosecution for criminal sexual assault, aggravated criminal sexual assault, criminal sexual abuse or aggravated criminal sexual abuse may be commenced within one year of the victim attaining the age of 18 years. However, in no such case shall the time period for prosecution expire sooner than 3 years after the commission of the offense.

(e) A prosecution for any offense involving sexual conduct or sexual penetration, as defined in Section 12-12 of this Code [725 ILCS 5/12-12], where the defendant was within a professional or fiduciary relationship or a purported professional or fiduciary relationship with the victim at the time of the commission of the offense may be commenced within one year after the discovery of the offense by the victim.

Under all circumstances the time clock does not run if the defendant is not living in the state,[877] if "[t]he defendant is a public officer and the offense charged is theft of public funds while in public office,"[878] or if the case is pending, "even if the [charge is dismissed by the court] . . . or the proceedings thereon are set aside, or are reversed on appeal."[879]

The fact that the charge is commenced within the statutory period is a material element of any indictment or information and must always be pleaded and proved.[880] If there are factors that operate to toll the running of the statute, those factors must also be alleged within the charging instrument and proven by the prosecution.[881] Any indictment that shows on its face that the offense charged is beyond the limitation period is subject to dismissal on motion.[882]

(f) A prosecution for any offense set forth in Section 44 of the "Environmental Protection Act", approved June 29, 1970, as amended [415 ILCS 5/44], may be commenced within 5 years after the discovery of such an offense by a person or agency having the legal duty to report the offense or in the absence of such discovery, within 5 years after the proper prosecuting officer becomes aware of the offense.

(g) A prosecution for attempt to commit first degree murder may be commenced within 7 years after commission of the offense.

(h) A prosecution for criminal sexual assault or aggravated criminal sexual assault may be commenced within 5 years of the commission of the offense if the victim reported the offense to law enforcement authorities within 6 months after the commission of the offense.

Nothing in subdivision (h) shall be construed to shorten a period within which a prosecution must be commenced under any other provision of this Section.

720 ILCS 5/3-6. "When an offense is based on a series of acts performed at different times, the period of limitations prescribed by this Article starts at the time when the last such act is committed." 720 ILCS 5/3-8.

877. 720 ILCS 5/3-7(a).

878. 720 ILCS 5/3-7(b).

879. 720 ILCS 5/3-7(c).

880. People v. Munoz, 23 Ill. App. 3d 306, 319 N.E.2d 98 (2d Dist. 1974).

881. People v. Strait, 72 Ill. 2d 503, 381 N.E.2d 692 (1978).

882. People v. Hawkins, 34 Ill. App. 3d 566, 340 N.E.2d 223 (1st Dist. 1975). *But see* People v. Gwinn, 255 Ill. App. 3d 628, 627 N.E.2d 699, 701 (2d Dist. 1994) (if charging instrument shows on face that defendant committed offense after limitations period has run, charge must allege facts which would extend limitations period or toll running of limitations period). *See* People v. Cray, 209 Ill. App. 3d 60, 567 N.E.2d 598, 620 (4th Dist. 1991) (dismissal based on expiration of statute of limitations subject only to state's appeal; reindictment not possible absent reversal on appeal).

§ 4.54 — Double Jeopardy Violations

The state is also precluded from bringing to trial a defendant who was previously brought to trial for the same offense with which he or she is presently charged.[883] This additional protection is the statutory embodiment[884] of the

---

883. 720 ILCS 5/3-3, 5/3-4.

884.   Sec. 3-3. Multiple prosecutions for same act. (a) When the same conduct of a defendant may establish the commission of more than one offense, the defendant may be prosecuted for each such offense.

           (b) If the several offenses are known to the proper prosecuting officer at the time of commencing the prosecution and are within the jurisdiction of a single court, they must be prosecuted in a single pro secution, except as provided in Subsection (c), if they are based on the same act.

           (c) When 2 or more offenses are charged as required by Subsection (b), the court in the interest of justice may order that one or more of such charges shall be tried separately.

       720 ILCS 5/3-3.

           Sec. 3-4. Effect of former prosecution. (a) A prosecution is barred if the defendant was formerly prosecuted for the same offense, based upon the same facts, if such former prosecution:

           (1) Resulted in either a conviction or an acquittal or in a determination that the evidence was insufficient to warrant a conviction; or

           (2) Was terminated by a final order or judgment, even if entered before trial, which required a determination inconsistent with any fact or legal proposition necessary to a conviction in the subsequent prosecution; or

           (3) Was terminated improperly after the jury was impaneled and sworn or, in a trial before a court without a jury, after the first witness was sworn but before findings were rendered by the trier of fact, or after plea of guilty was accepted by the court.

           A conviction of an included offense is an acquittal of the offense charged.

           (b) A prosecution is barred if the defendant was formerly prosecuted for a different offense, or for the same offense based upon different facts, if such former prosecution:

           (1) Resulted in either a conviction or an acquittal, and the subsequent prosecution is for an offense of which the defendant could have been convicted on the former prosecution; or was for an offense with which the defendant should have been charged on the former prosecution, as provided in Section 3-3 of this Code [720 ILCS 5/3-3] (unless the court ordered a separate trial of such charge); or was for an offense which involves the same conduct, unless each prosecution requires proof of a fact not required on the other prosecution, or the offense was not consummated when the former trial began; or

           (2) Was terminated by a final order or judgment, even if entered before trial, which required a determination inconsistent with any fact necessary to a conviction in the subsequent prosecution; or

double jeopardy clauses of both the United States Constitution[885] and the Constitution of the State of Illinois.[886] To understand how the statute, which entitles a defendant to dismissal of charges, operates, at least a cursory discussion of what the statute and the clauses were intended to do is required.

The primary purpose of the statutory provisions is to preserve the integrity of final judgments[887] while as the same time protecting the defendant's interest in avoiding multiple prosecutions for the same offense.[888] The double jeopardy clauses and their statutory counterparts also ensure that a defendant will not be punished repeatedly for the same offense.[889]

---

(3) Was terminated improperly under the circumstances stated in Subsection (a), and the subsequent prosecution is for an offense of which the defendant could have been convicted if the former prosecution had not been terminated properly.

(c) A prosecution is barred if the defendant was formerly prosecuted in a District Court of the United States or in a sister State for an offense which is within the concurrent jurisdiction of this State, if such former prosecution:

(1) Resulted in either a conviction or an acquittal, and the subsequent prosecution is for the same conduct, unless each prosecution requires proof of a fact not required in the other prosecution, or the offense was not consummated when the former trial began; or

(2) Was terminated by a final order or judgment, even if entered before trial, which required a determination inconsistent with any fact necessary to a conviction in the prosecution in this State.

(d) However, a prosecution is not barred within the meaning of this Section 3-4 [720 ILCS 5/3-4] if the former prosecution:

(1) Was before a court which lacked jurisdiction over the defendant or the offense; or

(2) Was procured by the defendant without the knowledge of the proper prosecuting officer, and with the purpose of avoiding the sentence which otherwise might be imposed; or if subsequent proceedings resulted in the invalidation, setting aside, reversal, or vacating of the conviction, unless the defendant was thereby adjudged not guilty.

720 ILCS 5/3-4.

885. "[N]or shall any person be subject for the same offense to be twice put in jeopardy of life or limb . . . ." U.S. CONST. amend. V.

886. "No person shall be . . . twice put in jeopardy for the same offense." ILL. CONST. art. I, § 10.

887. Crist v. Bretz, 437 U.S. 28, 33 (1978); People v. Woollums, 63 Ill. App. 3d 602, 379 N.E.2d 1385 (4th Dist. 1978).

888. United States v. Scott, 437 U.S. 82, 92 (1978); Illinois v. Somerville, 410 U.S. 458 (1973).

889. Ohio v. Johnson, 467 U.S. 493 (1984); People v. Franklin, 167 Ill. 2d 1, 656 N.E.2d 750, 756 (1995) (defendant cannot be granted new trial on collateral

It is clear that once a defendant has been acquitted of the charges against him or her, retrial for the same offense is barred,[890] though it is not always clear what constitutes an acquittal. In addition to the case of the previously acquitted defendant, other double jeopardy areas warranting consideration are: the defendant whose conduct constitutes multiple offenses arising from the same act or acts; the defendant whose case was reversed on appeal; the defendant whose case was dismissed; and the defendant whose case went to trial earlier but resulted in a mistrial.

§ 4.55 — — The Previously Acquitted Defendant

A defendant who has been tried and acquitted (or, for that matter, convicted) cannot be retried on the same charge for which he or she was acquitted.[891] This is the essence of the double jeopardy clause and applicable statutes.[892] Assuming a prior acquittal on the now-charged offense is established, a motion to dismiss the new charge will lie.[893] The problem sometimes arises, however, as to what an acquittal is.

An acquittal, by definition, occurs when the trier of fact renders a finding of not guilty.[894] An acquittal also occurs when a defendant is tried for an offense

---

estoppel grounds on basis that co-defendant was granted a new trial; defendant was not a party to co-defendant's trial nor to co-defendant's appeal), *cert. denied,* 517 U.S. 1122 (1996).

890. *Arizona v. Washington,* 434 U.S. 497 (1978), articulated that the public interest in the finality of criminal judgment is so strong that an acquitted defendant may not be retried even though the "acquittal was based upon egregiously erroneous foundation." *See* Fong Foo v. United States, 369 U.S. 141, 143 (1962).

891. 720 ILCS 5/3-4(a)(1); U.S. CONST. amend. V; ILL. CONST. art. I, § 6; Arizona v. Washington, 434 U.S. 497 (1978); *Fong Foo,* 369 U.S. at 143. *But see* discussion of *People v. Aleman,* 281 Ill. App. 3d 991, 667 N.E.2d 615 (1st Dist. 1996), *cert. denied,* 519 U.S. 1128 (1997), which follows in text and in notes 897–899.

892. 720 ILCS 5/3-3, 3-4.

893. 725 ILCS 5/114-1(a)(2).

894. 720 ILCS 5/2-1. *But see* People v. Schram, 283 Ill. App. 3d 1056, 672 N.E.2d 1237, 1241–42 (1st Dist. 1996) (dismissal of charges under Illinois Motor Fuel Tax Act did not equate to an acquittal and thus did not bar subsequent prosecution for forgery where prior charges were dismissed due to technical insufficiency of indictment); People v. Williams, 279 Ill. App. 3d 22, 664 N.E.2d 164 (1st Dist. 1996) (where defendant's conviction later vacated for constitutional reasons generally not considered functional equivalent of acquittal for double jeopardy purposes absent evidence of insufficient evidence to convict); People v. Smith, 275 Ill. App. 3d 207, 655 N.E.2d 1129, 1135 (1st Dist. 1995) (trial judge did not direct a finding of acquittal and double jeopardy principles were not violated

and is convicted only of a lesser included offense.[895] Under either of these two circumstances, retrial of the defendant for the same offense, or a lesser or greater offense arising out of the same transaction, is barred.[896]

One of the most fascinating and creative analyses of the double jeopardy clauses of the United States and Illinois Constitutions involves Harry Aleman, a defendant, who in 1977 was acquitted in a bench trial in the Circuit Court of Cook County.[897] In spite of his acquittal and the passage of time, the state reindicted Aleman, claiming that his acquittal was occasioned by a corrupt judge who accepted a bribe in exchange for the not guilty finding. The state maintained that since the judge agreed not to convict in exchange for the payoff, the defendant had never been in "jeopardy" of being convicted in the first place, and therefore the reindictment did not violate his double jeopardy protections.

The trial judge, in denying Aleman's motion to dismiss, detailed an exhaustive analysis of double jeopardy cases which included an historical perspective for the inclusion of the double jeopardy clause in the Fifth Amendment. Following an evidentiary hearing in which the corrupt lawyer who had bribed the judge some fifteen years earlier testified, the trial judge denied

---

where court allowed defendant to argue motion for directed verdict before state finished its case, later admitted additional evidence, and then denied defendant's motion).

895. Brown v. Ohio, 432 U.S. 161 (1977); In re Vitale, 71 Ill. 2d 229, 375 N.E.2d 87 (1978) (law unclear as to whether careless failure to reduce speed to avoid accident is a lesser included offense of involuntary manslaughter), *vacated,* 447 U.S. 410 (1980). *See also* People v. Fisher, 259 Ill. App. 3d 445, 632 N.E.2d 689, 695 (5th Dist. 1994) (where jury found defendant guilty of aggravated battery, a lesser included offense of armed violence, jury impliedly acquitted defendant of armed violence and double jeopardy principles barred retrial on armed violence); People v. Brown, 218 Ill. App. 3d 890, 578 N.E.2d 1168, 1173 (1st Dist. 1991) (conviction for second-degree murder implied acquittal of first degree murder; if defendant's appeal of second degree murder conviction is overturned and remanded for new trial, double jeopardy bars retrial of first degree murder).

896. 720 ILCS 5/3-3, 3-4(a), (b); People v. Woods, 23 Ill. App. 3d 480, 319 N.E.2d 263 (4th Dist. 1974). *See* People v. Carrillo, 164 Ill. 2d 144, 646 N.E.2d 582, 586 (defendant could not be subsequently charged with felony murder predicated upon armed robbery or murder based upon intent to kill or harm where previously acquitted on attempted murder, aggravated battery, and armed robbery charges), *cert. denied,* 515 U.S. 1146 (1995). *But cf.* People v. Jones, 301 Ill. App. 3d 608, 703 N.E.2d 994 (5th Dist. 1998) (rejecting defendant's contentions that prison disciplinary committee finding defendant not guilty of attack on another person precluded criminal charges for same behavior).

897. People v. Aleman, 281 Ill. App. 3d 991, 667 N.E.2d 615 (1st Dist. 1996), *cert. denied,* 519 U.S. 1128 (1997).

the motion to dismiss. The Illinois Appellate Court affirmed, stating that "[b]y bribing the [original trial] judge, Aleman prevented a fair 'resolution' of the first proceeding."[898] "It is ludicrous," observed the court, "to suggest that Aleman has a vested right to a prejudiced fact finder."[899]

§ 4.56   — — Multiple Offenses Arising from One Transaction

When a defendant is charged with a number of offenses that allegedly arose from the same criminal act or transaction, separate prosecutions for the separate offenses are not barred, provided that the acts alleged are legally separate and distinct.[900] This is true regardless of how closely related the offenses are in point of fact.[901] In determining whether the offenses are legally separate and distinct, the test is whether each offense requires proof of a fact or facts that the other does not.[902]

The United States Supreme Court in *United States v. Dixon*,[903] held that although double jeopardy may bar a subsequent prosecution for separate

---

898. *Id.*, 667 N.E.2d at 626.

899. *Id.*

900. In re Vitale, 71 Ill. 2d 229, 375 N.E.2d 87 (1978). *See* People v. Brookhouse, 289 Ill. App. 3d 1079, 682 N.E.2d 1200, 1202–03 (3d Dist. 1997) (double jeopardy not a bar where defendant found to be in simultaneous constructive possession of two quantities of the same controlled substance in two different locations because they are two offenses; defendant found in possession of controlled substance in home and at same time a controlled substance found in his locker at the bowling alley).

901. *Vitale,* 71 Ill. 2d 229, 375 N.E.2d at 90.

902. Blockburger v. United States, 284 U.S. 299 (1932), *overruled on other grounds by* Whalen v. United States, 445 U.S. 684, 693–94 (1980); People v. Woollums, 63 Ill. App. 3d 602, 379 N.E.2d 1385 (4th Dist. 1978). *See* People v. Pudlo, 272 Ill. App. 3d 1002, 651 N.E.2d 676, 678 (1st Dist. 1995) (defendant could be prosecuted under Litter Control Act even though convicted of violating numerous municipal ordinances for the same activities; municipal sections contained elements not required under the Litter Control Act and vice versa, therefore not same offenses; dissent found that some of offenses were same and also found penalty provisions under one of municipal ordinances punitive in nature), *cert. denied,* 517 U.S. 1137 (1996). *But see* People v. Beck, 295 Ill. App. 3d 1050, 693 N.E.2d 897, 907 (2d Dist. 1998) (double jeopardy attaches when defendant is tried for DUI and reckless homicide because DUI is a lesser included offense of reckless homicide); People v. Eggerman, 292 Ill. App. 3d 644, 685 N.E.2d 948, 951 (1st Dist. 1997) (prosecution of defendant for hijacking and robbery in one county barred where defendant had pleaded guilty to possession of stolen vehicle charge in another county based on same conduct).

903. 509 U.S. 688 (1993).

offenses when the government loses an earlier prosecution involving the same facts, double jeopardy does not require the government to bring all of its prosecutions at the same time. The government is free to bring prosecutions separately and acquire convictions in both.[904] *Dixon* overruled the Supreme Court's earlier case of *Grady v. Corbin*,[905] in which the Court established the "same-conduct" test. In addition to satisfying the *Blockburger* "same elements" rule, the *Grady* Court required the government to satisfy the "same-conduct" rule before it could bring a subsequent prosecution. Thus, in *Grady*, the Supreme Court held that "the Double Jeopardy Clause bars a subsequent prosecution if, to establish an essential element of an offense charged in that prosecution, the government will prove *conduct* that constitutes an offense for which the defendant has already been prosecuted."[906] The Court in *Dixon* held that the "same elements" test was the exclusive basis for determining whether a subsequent prosecution may be brought.[907] In overruling *Grady*, the Supreme Court reasoned that the same "conduct" test contradicted an unbroken line of decisions, contained less than accurate historical analysis, and has produced confusion. Moreover, unlike the *Blockburger* test, the *Grady* test "lacks constitutional roots."[908] Finally, *Grady* is totally inharmonious with Supreme Court precedent and contravenes the plain common law understanding of double jeopardy.[909]

However, under Illinois law, "[i]f the several offenses are known to the proper prosecuting officer at the time of commencing the prosecution and are within the jurisdiction of a single court, they must be prosecuted in a single prosecution, except as provided in Subsection (c), if they are based on the same act."[910] Subsection (c) provides that the court may order that separate offenses be tried separately if "the interest of justice" requires.[911]

---

904. *Id.* at 705.

905. 495 U.S. 508 (1990).

906. *Id.* at 510 (emphasis added).

907. *Dixon,* 509 U.S. at 696–97.

908. *Id.* at 704.

909. *Id.*

910. 720 ILCS 5/3-3(b). People v. Zegart, 83 Ill. 2d 440, 415 N.E.2d 341, 342 (1980) (compulsory joinder provision (5/3-3) not applicable to offenses charged by way of uniform citation and complaint forms provided for traffic offenses, certain misdemeanors, and petty offenses), *overruled by* People v. Jackson, 118 Ill. 2d 179, 514 N.E.2d 983, 988 (1987).

911. 720 ILCS 5/3-3(c).

In *People v. Carrillo*,[912] the Illinois Appellate Court held that under *Diaz v. United States*,[913] the double jeopardy clause did not prohibit the state from bringing murder and intentional murder charges against two individuals who had previously been prosecuted for attempted murder, home invasion, armed robbery, burglary, aggravated battery, and armed violence because the defendants could not have been prosecuted for the latter charges until the victim died.[914] According to this court, the *Diaz* exception applies in Illinois without confines of a time limit.[915] The court found that defendant Carrillo could be subsequently charged with felony murder based upon armed robbery, burglary and home invasion; murder based upon intent to kill or cause great bodily harm; and murder based upon knowledge that his actions created a strong probability of death or great bodily harm.[916] In the prior prosecution, Carrillo had pleaded guilty to all charges. The appellate court held that because Carrillo merely pleaded guilty, no issues were litigated and collateral estoppel did not bar the subsequent prosecution. On the other hand, in prior proceedings, the trial court found defendant Stacey guilty of home invasion and burglary but acquitted her on attempted murder, aggravated battery, and armed robbery. Because of the acquittals, any subsequent prosecution for murder based on intent to kill as well as felony murder predicated on armed robbery were foreclosed. The prior court had determined that there was a reasonable doubt that Stacey had the requisite intent to kill or commit armed robbery against the victim thus negating the charging of felony murder based upon armed robbery or murder based upon intent to kill or harm. However, the court did find that Stacey could be charged with felony murder under a theory of home invasion and burglary, and of murder based upon knowledge that her actions would create a strong possibility of death or harm.[917]

In *People v. Krstic*,[918] the court held that where the state is not a party to a first proceeding, either civil or criminal, it is not collaterally estopped from pursuing a subsequent criminal prosecution.[919] Accordingly, in this case, where the domestic relations judge found, in evaluating the wife's petition for a protective order, that defendant had committed "no abuse," the state was not

---

912. 164 Ill. 2d 144, 646 N.E.2d 582 (1995).

913. 223 U.S. 442, 448–49 (1912) (double jeopardy exception exists where the state is unable to proceed on the more serious charge at the beginning because additional facts necessary to sustain the charge have not yet occurred).

914. *Carrillo*, 164 Ill. 2d 144, 646 N.E.2d at 585.

915. *Id.*

916. *Id.*, 646 N.E.2d at 586.

917. *Id.*

918. 292 Ill. App. 3d 720, 686 N.E.2d 692 (1st Dist. 1997).

919. *Id.*, 686 N.E.2d at 693.

barred from prosecuting defendant for domestic battery and violation of a prior protective order based on the same events. The court concluded that the state cannot be collaterally estopped unless it is a party to a prior action.[920]

§ 4.57 — — The Defendant Whose Case Was Previously Dismissed

A dismissal of the charges against a defendant usually does not bar reinstituting those charges, although the reasons the charges were dismissed and by whom—the court or the state—are both important aspects of a double jeopardy claim that may warrant dismissal of the new charge.

To bar a subsequent prosecution following a dismissal of charges, the dismissal must have had the substantive effect of an acquittal[921]—that is, some or all of the elements of the crime charged must have been resolved in the defendant's favor.[922] Where the state's motion to nolle prosequi is sustained, the state may reinstate the charges at a later date without running afoul of the double jeopardy or statutory provisions,[923] because the substantive effect is not of an acquittal. Because jeopardy had not attached to the original charge, the defendant who is recharged has not been twice put in jeopardy.[924] Note,

---

920. *Id.*, 686 N.E.2d at 694.

921. People v. Shields, 76 Ill. 2d 543, 394 N.E.2d 1161 (1979), *cert. denied*, 445 U.S. 917 (1980). *See also* Village of Round Lake v. Sams, 96 Ill. App. 3d 683, 421 N.E.2d 1008, 1011 (2d Dist. 1981) ("While the State would be barred from proceeding on the charges which were dismissed this bar would exist by virtue of the terms of the plea agreement and not because of the double jeopardy provisions . . . ."). 720 ILCS 5/3-4(a)(1).

922. United States v. Martin Linen Supply Co., 430 U.S. 564 (1977); People v. Williams, 279 Ill. App. 3d 22, 664 N.E.2d 164 (1st Dist. 1996). *But see* People v. Creek, 94 Ill. 2d 526, 447 N.E.2d 330 (1983); 720 ILCS 5/3-4(a)(2).

923. People v. Mooar, 92 Ill. App. 3d 852, 416 N.E.2d 81 (2d Dist. 1981). *See also* People v. Newell, 83 Ill. App. 3d 133, 403 N.E.2d 775 (3d Dist. 1980). *But see* People v. Blake, 287 Ill. App. 3d 487, 678 N.E.2d 761, 764 (1st Dist. 1997) (*nolle prose* of counts, after jeopardy attached bars reinstatement of those counts under double jeopardy provisions).

924.   [W]here the declaration of a mistrial [for a "jurisdictionally" defective indictment] implements a reasonable state policy and aborts a proceeding that at best would have produced a verdict that could have been upset at will by one of the parties, the defendant's interest in proceeding to verdict is outweighed by the competing and equally legitimate demand for public justice.

Illinois v. Somerville, 410 U.S. 458, 471 (1973); People v. Barfield, 288 Ill. App. 3d 578, 680 N.E.2d 805 (5th Dist. 1997); People v. Aleman, 281 Ill. App. 3d 991, 667 N.E.2d 615 (1st Dist. 1996), *cert. denied*, 519 U.S. 1128 (1997).

however, apart from double jeopardy protection, if charges were previously dismissed because of a speedy trial violation, new charges arising out of the same offense are barred.[925]

§ 4.58 — — The Defendant Whose Case Was Reversed on Appeal

Whether the defendant whose case was reversed on appeal has a sustainable double jeopardy claim depends on the basis of the reversal. If the conviction was reversed because the prosecution failed to prove the defendant guilty beyond a reasonable doubt, a new trial is prohibited.[926] This is to be distinguished from a reversal predicated on the guilty verdict being against the weight of the evidence, which does not bar retrial.[927] The articulated distinction between weight of evidence and sufficiency of evidence is that when no rational factfinder could have found the defendant guilty beyond a reasonable doubt, there is insufficient evidence to convict and retrial is barred.[928] When a rational factfinder might have found the defendant guilty but the trier of fact determined "that a greater amount of credible evidence supports one side of an issue or cause than the other," reversal may be warranted but retrial is permitted. Essentially, the appellate court puts itself in the position of a thirteenth juror with the power to prevent a conviction by reversal but not to bar retrial.[929] In *People v. Woolsey*,[930] the court held that defendant's double jeopardy rights were not violated where the defendant was resentenced to correct an illegal sentence. In this case the trial judge had imposed supervision for domestic violence which it had no authority to do. Therefore, the original sentence was void.[931]

In *People v. Ousley*,[932] the defendant was found guilty of two counts of aggravated criminal sexual assault and various other counts, but not guilty on

---

925. 720 ILCS 5/3-4(a)(2); 725 ILCS 5/114-1(e).

926. 720 ILCS 5/3-4; Justices of Boston Mun. Court v. Lydon, 466 U.S. 294 (1984). Note also that an order for new trial that is predicated on the state's failure to prove the defendant guilty beyond a reasonable doubt is tantamount to a finding of not guilty, which bars reprosecution. People v. Woodall, 61 Ill. 2d 60, 329 N.E.2d 203 (1975).

927. Tibbs v. Florida, 457 U.S. 31 (1982).

928. *Id.* at 37–38.

929. *Id.*

930. 278 Ill. App. 3d 708, 663 N.E.2d 763 (2d Dist. 1996). *See also* City of Chicago v. Roman, 184 Ill. 2d 504, 705 N.E.2d 81 (1998).

931. *Id.*, 663 N.E.2d at 764.

932. 297 Ill. App. 3d 758, 697 N.E.2d 926, 927 (3d Dist. 1998).

a charge of criminal sexual assault, all of which arose out of a single incident. On appeal, the defendant argued that the two aggravated criminal sexual assault convictions were legally inconsistent with the not guilty verdict for the predicate offense.[933] The court agreed and reversed the aggravated criminal sexual assault convictions and held that the doctrine of collateral estoppel and double jeopardy precluded retrying the defendant on these two charges.[934]

§ 4.59 — — Mistrial and Retrial

Whether a mistrial will bar retrial for the same offense depends in large part on the reason the mistrial was granted. Ordinarily, if there was a "manifest necessity" to grant a mistrial to "further the ends of justice," retrial will be permitted.[935] Whether manifest necessity requires a mistrial is decided on a case-by-case basis. If something occurs during the trial that makes it no longer possible to fairly conduct the trial or to reach a just verdict, manifest necessity will be found.[936] The classic example of manifest necessity that requires a mistrial but does not bar retrial is that of the deadlocked jury.[937] Although the prospect of another trial is not particularly pleasing, it can be seen that because neither side nor the judge did anything to provoke or evoke the manifest necessity, retrial should not be barred.

Whether the state's attorney or the court did something to cause the necessity of granting a mistrial that will bar retrial is somewhat more problematic.

---

933. *Id.,* 697 N.E.2d at 929.

934. *Id.,* 697 N.E.2d at 930.

935. United States v. Jorn, 400 U.S. 470 (1971). *See* Oregon v. Kennedy, 456 U.S. 667, 679 (1982) ("the circumstances under which such a defendant may invoke the bar of double jeopardy in a second effort to try him are limited to those cases in which the conduct giving rise to the successful motion for a mistrial was intended to provoke the defendant into moving for a mistrial"); People v. Ryan, 259 Ill. App. 3d 611, 631 N.E.2d 348, 352 (2d Dist. 1994) (motion by the defendant for mistrial deemed to be a deliberate decision to abandon the right to have guilt or innocence determined before first trier of fact, such a motion is generally deemed to remove the double jeopardy bar and the state may reprosecute even when there is error prompting motion attributable to state), *cert. denied,* 541 U.S. 1064 (1995); People v. Turner, 105 Ill. App. 3d 393, 434 N.E.2d 428 (1st Dist. 1982); People v. Partee, 52 Ill. App. 3d 178, 367 N.E.2d 188 (1st Dist. 1977), *cert. denied,* 436 U.S. 928 (1978).

936. People v. Yarbrough, 179 Ill. App. 3d 198, 534 N.E.2d 695 (5th Dist. 1989); People v. Turner, 105 Ill. App. 3d 393, 434 N.E.2d 428 (1st Dist. 1982); People v. Pendleton, 75 Ill. App. 3d 580, 394 N.E.2d 496 (1st Dist. 1979).

937. United States v. Sanford, 429 U.S. 14 (1976).

Usually improper closing arguments and remarks by the prosecutor,[938] improper questioning,[939] trial errors committed by either party, and rulings by the court that result in mistrial will not preclude subsequent prosecution. Where, however, the mistrial motion by the defendant becomes manifestly necessary because of prosecutorial or judicial overreaching,[940] retrial will be forbidden.[941]

§ 4.60 — — Multiple Jurisdiction Problems

Another double jeopardy problem counsel must consider is that of the Illinois defendant who, in the federal courts, is or was charged with or was convicted or acquitted of an offense stemming from the same act that forms the basis of his or her present Illinois charge. The double jeopardy clause of the Fifth Amendment does not preclude the federal government from bringing to trial on federal charges a defendant who was, relative to the same incident, previously convicted or acquitted in state court on the rationale that separate jurisdictions—the United States government and the State of Illinois—may charge separately for violation of their respective statutes. However, Illinois, by statute, has barred state prosecution if the defendant was formerly prosecuted in a District Court of the United States or in a sister State for an offense which is within the concurrent jurisdiction of this State if such former prosecution:

> (1) Resulted in either a conviction or an acquittal, and the subsequent prosecution is for the same conduct, unless each prosecution requires proof of a fact not required in the other prosecution, or the offense was not consummated when the former trial began; or

> (2) Was terminated by a final order or judgment, even if entered before trial, which required a determination inconsistent with any fact necessary to a conviction in the prosecution in this State.[942]

---

938. People v. Estrada, 91 Ill. App. 3d 228, 414 N.E.2d 512 (3d Dist. 1980).

939. People v. Gomez, 84 Ill. App. 3d 785, 406 N.E.2d 886 (3d Dist. 1980).

940. *Overreaching* is misconduct designed to produce a mistrial to secure a more favorable opportunity to convict the defendant in a later trial (*United States v. Dinitz*, 424 U.S. 600 (1976)), or motivated by bad faith, or undertaken to harrass the defendant (*Id.* at 611). *See also* United States v. Tateo, 377 U.S. 463 (1964); People v. Hill, 34 Ill. App. 3d 193, 339 N.E.2d 405 (5th Dist. 1975).

941. People v. Pendleton, 75 Ill. App. 3d 580, 394 N.E.2d 496 (1st Dist. 1979).

942. 720 ILCS 5/3-4(c).

If a defendant faces Illinois charges and falls within the statutory preclusion, a motion to dismiss will lie.[943]

§ 4.61 — — Forfeiture

Another double jeopardy issue which has emerged focuses on circumstances under which an individual may be subjected to a civil penalty, such as forfeiture or tax liability, and be prosecuted as well for the criminal offense which led to the civil sanction.

In *United States v. Halper*,[944] the Supreme Court set forth a test for establishing when a civil penalty is punishment for double jeopardy purposes, and therefore bars subsequent prosecution for criminal charges or imposition of civil sanctions. The label *civil* or *criminal* is not controlling.[945] Instead, trial courts must look to the actual purposes served by the penalty to determine whether it constitutes punishment.[946] If the purpose of the sanction is not solely remedial, but instead also serves retribution or deterrence, it is punishment for double jeopardy purposes.[947] "Where a defendant previously has sustained a criminal penalty and the civil penalty sought in the subsequent proceeding bears no rational relation to the goal of compensating the Government for its loss, but rather appears to qualify as 'punishment' in the plain meaning of the word, then the defendant is entitled to an accounting of the Government's damages and costs to determine if the penalty sought in fact constitutes a second punishment."[948] In *Austin v. United States*,[949] the Court affirmed the *Halper* test and held that the federal forfeiture statute constituted punishment even though it may have served some remedial purpose.[950] In *Department of Revenue*

---

943. 725 ILCS 5/114-1(a)(2).

944. 490 U.S. 438 (1989).

945. *Id.* at 448.

946. *Id.*

947. *Id.*

948. *Id.* at 449.

949. 509 U.S. 602 (1993).

950. *Id.* at 608. *See, e.g.*, United States v. $405,089.23 United States Currency, 33 F.3d 1210 (9th Cir. 1994) (finding criminal prosecution brought separately from civil forfeiture barred under double jeopardy where civil sanction is punishment). *But see* Bennis v. Michigan, 516 U.S. 442, 446 (1996) (petitioner was not denied due process and Michigan did not violate the Takings Clause of the Fifth Amendment despite petitioner's assertion that she was an innocent owner and that she did not know her husband would use a car they jointly owned to have sex with a prostitute, where her car was forfeited to the state as a result of her husband's deeds); Smith v. United States, 76 F.3d 879, 882 (7th Cir. 1996) (drug trafficking prosecution following forfeiture of automobile and cash from drug

v. Kurth Ranch,[951] the Court held that a tax on possession of illegal drugs imposed after imposition of criminal penalties may count as separate jeopardy. The Court noted that *Halper's* test did not work in tax statute cases, since the purpose of tax statutes is to raise revenue rather than to punish. In addition, a tax may be high and intend some deterrent effect and still not be considered punitive.[952] In finding the tax in *Kurth* the functional equivalent of a criminal prosecution, the Court looked to the unique characteristics of the tax: it was conditioned on the commission of crime; it was assessed only after the taxpayer had been arrested, paid all fines and forfeitures; the tax was levied on goods the taxpayer no longer owned or possessed; and the tax had no legitimate revenue raising purpose which could not have been accomplished by increasing fines against defendants.[953]

Finally, the court in *Hudson v. United States* held that the double jeopardy clause "protects only against the imposition of multiple criminal punishments for the same offense, . . . when such occurs in successive proceedings."[954] Here, bank officers who had previously been subject to monetary penalties and occupational disbarment were indicted.[955] The court concluded that Congress "intended [the] sanctions to be civil in nature" and not in violation of the double jeopardy clause.[956] The court, though not overruling *Halper*,[957] considered *Halper* abrogated.[958] Similarly, a petition for wardship based on the same

---

proceeds not barred by double jeopardy where forfeiture remedial and not punishment; defendant had no claim to drug proceeds and proceeds were directly proportional to loss to government and society). *But see* Degen v. United States, 517 U.S. 820, 825 (1996) (trial court erred by disentitling the defendant, a fugitive from criminal prosecution, from participating in a related civil forfeiture proceeding against him, where there was no risk of delay or danger that the court would waste its time rendering an unenforceable judgment, since the court's jurisdiction over the defendant's property was secure in spite of his absence; the court further noted that although there was a risk that the civil case might compromise the government's criminal case, because of the more liberal discovery allowed in civil cases, the criminal case could be protected by the trial court's discretionary power to limit discovery through protective orders, the form of proof allowed at trial, or sanctions in the event of noncompliance with legitimate court orders).

951. 511 U.S. 767 (1994).

952. *Id.* at 779–81.

953. *Id.* at 781–83.

954. 522 U.S. 93, 99 (1997).

955. *Id.* at 97.

956. *Id.* at 103.

957. United States v. Halper, 490 U.S. 438 (1989).

958. *Hudson*, 522 U.S. at 101–02.

conduct for which the minor had been expelled from school was not barred by double jeopardy.[959] Also, an inmate previously found not guilty of a battery by a prison disciplinary committee could be prosecuted criminally for the same behavior.[960]

In *United States v. Ursery*,[961] the Supreme Court held that "civil forfeitures [under sections 881 and 981] (and civil forfeitures generally) . . . do not constitute 'punishment' for purposes of the Double Jeopardy Clause."[962] The Supreme Court distinguished *Halper*, *Austin*, and *Kurth Ranch*. *Halper*, observed the Court, dealt with *in personam* civil penalties applying a case specific inquiry to determine whether the civil penalty is so disproportionate to constitute punishment that would violate double jeopardy.[963] The decision was limited to civil penalties and did not address civil forfeitures which are distinct; the case by case approach applies only to the former.[964] *Austin* dealt with an excessive fine analysis under the Eighth Amendment in which the Court's only conclusion was that forfeitures were subject to the Eighth Amendment's Excessive Fines Clause.[965] Finally, *Kurth Ranch* dealt with a punitive tax imposed on marijuana. The Court concluded that none of these cases involved the issue now before it, *e.g.*, *in rem* civil forfeitures.

The Court, in its analysis, rejected a case specific analysis and stated that none of these cases overruled the test set forth in *United States v. One Assortment of 89 Firearms*.[966] That test explores what the congressional intent in enacting the provision was and whether the scheme was punitive in purpose or effect as to negate congressional purpose to establish a civil remedial remedy."[967] Applying this test to the case before it, the Court concluded that *in rem* civil forfeitures were not punishment. First, the Court found that Congress clearly intended forfeitures to be civil in nature based on the procedural nature of such proceedings. The notice requirements, for example, are comparable to civil actions, and the burden of proof is that of a civil action.[968] As to the second prong, although forfeitures may have punitive aspects, they serve two important

---

959. *In re* K.B., 301 Ill. App. 3d 926, 704 N.E.2d 791 (1st Dist. 1998); *In re* S.J., 291 Ill. App. 3d 703, 684 N.E.2d 1009 (5th Dist. 1997).

960. People v. Jones, 301 Ill. App. 3d 608, 703 N.E.2d 994 (5th Dist. 1998).

961. 518 U.S. 267 (1996).

962. *Id.* at 270–71.

963. *Id.* at 279–80.

964. *Id.* at 282–83.

965. *Id.* at 281, 286–87.

966. 465 U.S. 358 (1984).

967. *Ursery*, 518 U.S. at 277–78, citing *89 Firearms*, 465 U.S. at 365, citing United States v. Ward, 448 U.S. 242, 248–49 (1980).

968. *Ursery*, 518 U.S. at 288–89.

nonpunitive functions. First, they "encourage[] property owners to take care in managing their property and ensure[] that they will not permit that property to be used for illegal purposes."[969] Second, the forfeiture provisions applied to "'proceeds' of illegal drug activity, [which] serves the additional nonpunitive goal of ensuring that persons do not profit from their illegal acts."[970] Additional factors which led the Court to conclude that forfeiture proceedings were not punishment were: the fact that *in rem* proceedings have historically not been regarded as punishment; that there is no requirement that the government prove scienter on the part of the respondent; that although they may serve the purpose of deterrence, deterrence can be civil or criminal; and finally, the fact that forfeiture proceedings are tied to criminal activity were all insufficient to render them punishment.[971]

In *Hudson v. United States*,[972] the Court disavowed the analysis employed in *Halper* and reaffirmed its previous rule of *United States v. Ward*.[973] It then held that the defendants' subsequent criminal convictions were not barred where they had previously been fined and disbarred because the first proceeding was administrative and civil, not criminal.[974] Here, the Office of Comptroller of the Currency imposed a monetary penalty on defendants as well as an occupational disbarment. The defendants were bank officials who caused the making of unlawful loans that were to their benefit. They were later criminally charged based on the same conduct.

According to the Court, the double jeopardy clause prohibits only imposition of "multiple *criminal* punishments for the same offense."[975] It referenced the factors listed in *Kennedy v. Mendoza-Martinez*[976] to evaluate whether a civil penalty constitutes a criminal punishment.[977] The Court did note that *Halper*

---

969   *Id.* at 290.

970. *Id.* at 291.

971. *Id.* at 291–92.

972. 118 S. Ct. 488 (1997).

973. 448 U.S. 242 (1980).

974. *Hudson*, 118 S. Ct. at 492.

975. *Id.* at 493 (emphasis in original).

976. 372 U.S. 144 (1963). These factors were: (1) "whether the sanction involves an affirmative disability or restraint"; (2) "whether it has historically been regarded as a punishment"; (3) "whether it comes into play only on a finding of scienter"; (4) "whether its operation will promote the traditional aims of punishment— retribution and deterrence"; (5) "whether the behavior to which it applies is already a crime"; (6) "whether an alternative purpose to which it may rationally be connected is assignable for it"; and (7) "whether it appears excessive in relation to the alternative purpose assigned." *Id.* at 168–69.

977. *Hudson*, 118 S. Ct. at 493–94.

was the first time it applied the double jeopardy clause to a sanction without first determining whether it was criminal in nature.[978] It concluded that the approach there deviated from traditional double jeopardy analysis in two respects. First, *Halper* bypassed the threshold question of whether a successive punishment was *criminal* punishment. Instead, *Halper* focused on whether the penalty was "grossly disproportionate" to the harm to constitute a punishment. Thus, it considered only one of the *Kennedy* factors.[979] Further, the *Halper* Court assessed the character of the sanction imposed rather than assessing the statutory provision that authorized the penalty to determine whether the provision provided for a criminal sanction.[980] The Court concluded that this departure was "ill considered" and has proven unworkable. In lieu of this analysis, the Court applied the traditional principles of double jeopardy and concluded that in the instant case double jeopardy was not violated. The Office of Comptroller of the Currency's penalties were clearly meant to be civil in nature. Further, there was no evidence that the penalties were "so punitive in form and effect as to render them criminal."[981] Neither had been historically viewed as punishment.[982] Neither involved an "affirmative disability or restraint."[983] Neither came into play only upon a finding of "scienter." Further, even though the conduct upon which the penalties were based could also result in criminal prosecution, this was insufficient to render them punitive. Finally, even though the civil penalties may have a deterrent effect, this too was insufficient to render them punitive.[984]

Illinois courts have also addressed the issue. In *People v. Towns*,[985] the appellate court held that forfeiture under the Illinois Controlled Substance Act constituted punishment within the meaning of the double jeopardy clause.[986]

In *People v. Smith*,[987] the Illinois Appellate Court held that a nonjudicial forfeiture of defendant's property which was later declared void *ab initio* for lack of proper notice was not punishment for purposes of double jeopardy.[988]

---

978. *Id.* at 494.

979. *Id.*

980. *Id.*

981. *Id.* at 495.

982. *Id.*

983. *Id.* at 496.

984. *Id.*

985. 269 Ill. App. 3d 907, 646 N.E.2d 1366 (2d Dist. 1995). This decision was reversed *sub. nom* by *People v. P.S.*, 169 Ill. 2d 260, 661 N.E.2d 329 (1996).

986. *Towns*, 269 Ill. App. 3d 907, 646 N.E.2d at 1371.

987. 275 Ill. App. 3d 844, 656 N.E.2d 797 (2d Dist. 1995).

988. *Id.*, 656 N.E.2d at 799.

According to the court, the effect of finding the forfeiture void rendered the forfeiture proceeding null and ineffective as to defendant.[989] Where the state's attorney failed to give proper notice to the defendant, as required by statute, this rendered the forfeiture proceeding void for lack of jurisdiction,[990] and had no legal force or binding effect.[991] Because the procedure was void, "neither defendant nor his purported ownership interest in the property was effectively at risk or in jeopardy, and there was no 'punishment' for double jeopardy purposes."[992] Although there was a due process violation, it was not punishment for double jeopardy purposes.[993]

In *People v. Dvorak*,[994] in a case of first impression, the court held that summary suspension of one's driver's license under the implied-consent statute for driving under the influence was not punishment within the meaning of double jeopardy.[995] In arriving at its decision, the court reviewed the Supreme Court cases and stated it did not believe they stood for the proposition that any sanction will be automatically classified as punishment unless it solely serves a remedial purpose.[996] Instead, the test is "a particularized assessment of the characteristics of the sanction (penalty or exaction) as a whole; the purposes that it may fairly be said to serve; and whether the sanction may be 'fairly characterized' as remedial or as punishment, taking into consideration its deterrent or retributive purposes, and, if helpful to the inquiry, its historical or traditional treatment."[997] In this case, the court explained that a driver's license was a privilege and suspension of the right to drive did not amount to suspension of a fundamental right.[998] In addition, the statute governing drunk driving sought to protect the safety of the public, not punish the driver. Therefore, suspension serves a remedial purpose.[999] The court further concluded that recision of a summary suspension is not tantamount to an acquittal for double jeopardy purposes.[1000]

---

989.   *Id.*, 656 N.E.2d at 800.

990.   *Id.*, 656 N.E.2d at 801.

991.   *Id.*, 656 N.E.2d at 802.

992.   *Id.*

993.   *Id.*, 656 N.E.2d at 803.

994.   276 Ill. App. 3d 544, 658 N.E.2d 869 (2d Dist. 1995).

995.   *Id.*, 658 N.E.2d at 875.

996.   *Id.*, 658 N.E.2d at 874.

997.   *Id.*, 658 N.E.2d at 875.

998.   *Id.*

999.   *Id.*

1000.   *Id.*, 658 N.E.2d at 876. *See also* People v. Eck, 279 Ill. App. 3d 541, 664 N.E.2d 1147, 1149 (5th Dist. 1996) (statutory summary suspension of defendant's

In *People v. P.S.*,[1001] the Illinois Supreme Court addressed the issue of forfeiture and criminal prosecutions. The issue before the court was whether double jeopardy prohibits a criminal prosecution following a civil forfeiture based on the same conduct.[1002] The court answered the question in both the affirmative and the negative. Three cases were consolidated: defendant Turner, defendant P.S. (a minor), and defendant Kimery. Defendants Turner and P.S. were charged with possession of and intent to deliver and Turner with failing to have a tax stamp. Prior to Turner's criminal trial, a sum of cash was forfeited in a civil proceeding. Prior to P.S.'s criminal trial, cash and an automobile were forfeited. Defendant Kimery was charged with possession of and his vehicle was forfeited based on its use in a drug transaction. In determining whether any of the subsequent criminal prosecutions of these defendants were barred, the court set forth the test as: "(1) whether the civil forfeitures in the instant cases constitute 'punishment' for double jeopardy purposes; (2) whether the civil forfeitures and criminal prosecutions constitute punishment for the same offenses; and (3) whether the civil forfeitures and criminal prosecutions are separate proceedings."[1003]

The test which the court used to determine whether a civil sanction and a criminal prosecution are separate offenses is the *Blockburger* same-elements test. If each offense contains an element not present in the other offense, they are not the same offenses. Therefore, double jeopardy would not bar both prosecutions.[1004] The court held that defendant Turner and defendant P.S. were charged with separate offenses. The elements necessary to establish the criminal charges were clearly distinguishable from those necessary to establish grounds for forfeiture. None of the elements necessary for forfeiture was included in the elements necessary to establish the three criminal charges.[1005] As to defendant Kimery, the court held that the civil forfeiture and criminal proceedings were prosecutions for the same offense. In his case, the elements necessary to prove forfeiture required proof of the criminal conduct, *viz.*, the criminal offense was "subsumed" by the forfeiture statute and the elements

---

driver's license in DUI case did not constitute punishment for double jeopardy purposes because it was not a forfeiture of a fundamental property right, but rather a temporary suspension of a privilege).

1001.   169 Ill. 2d 260, 661 N.E.2d 329 (1996), *vacated and remanded*, 518 U.S. 1031 (1996) (for reconsideration in light of *United States v. Ursery*), *on remand*, 175 Ill. 2d 79, 676 N.E.2d 656 (1997). See discussion below.

1002.   *P.S.*, 169 Ill. 2d 260, 661 N.E.2d at 331.

1003.   *Id.*, 661 N.E.2d at 335–36.

1004.   *Id.*, 661 N.E.2d at 336.

1005.   *Id.*, 661 N.E.2d at 337.

were the same. Therefore, any subsequent prosecution of Kimery was barred.[1006]

The court then went on to address the elements for determining whether a civil sanction is punishment. It reviewed the Supreme Court decisions and stated that if the forfeiture served, in part, to punish the defendant, it would be considered punishment for double jeopardy purposes.[1007] The court held that forfeiture under section 2 of the Illinois Forfeiture Act constituted punishment. First, the Illinois statute was patterned after the federal statute which had been found to constitute punishment. Second, the objective of the statute is to deter criminal behavior. Third, the statute is not triggered until there is a criminal violation. Finally, in both the federal and state statutes, there is an exception for innocent-owners. Therefore, based on interpretation of the federal statute and our statute's similarity to it, the court held that forfeiture of Kimery's car was punishment.[1008]

Finally, the court addressed the issue of whether the civil forfeiture against Kimery and the criminal proceedings were separate proceedings. The court first noted that it was clear that the government may seek both a civil remedy and criminal prosecution in the same proceeding as long as the punishment does not exceed that authorized by law.[1009] In this case, however, the two proceed-

---

1006.   *Id.*, 661 N.E.2d at 338.

1007.   *Id.*, 661 N.E.2d at 340.

1008.   *Id. But see* People v. Ratliff, 282 Ill. App. 3d 707, 669 N.E.2d 122, 126 (2d Dist. 1996) (defendant, who was charged with unlawful possession of a gun by a felon and with possession of a firearm without an identification card after a gun was found in his car, was not subjected to double jeopardy where local ordinance imposed a $500 fine upon defendant and required him to pay towing and storage fees for using a motor vehicle to commit the predicate offense of aggravated assault because those sanctions did not constitute punishment for double jeopardy purposes under either the Federal or Illinois Constitutions since the fine and fee were neither so extreme nor so divorced from nonpunitive purpose of compensating the city for damages done by the defendant); People v. $5,970 United States Currency, 279 Ill. App. 3d 583, 664 N.E.2d 1115, 1120–22 (2d Dist. 1996) (defendant's forfeiture of $5,970 was proper where the arresting officer found the money in a box on the passenger floorboards of the defendant's car next to a baggie containing cocaine residue, and where the evidence demonstrated a sufficient nexus between the currency and the drugs; court also rejected defendant's claim that the forfeiture violated the Eighth Amendment's Excessive Fines Clause, because it involved money and not real property and because a possession of cocaine charge was a serious offense that allowed the trial court to impose a fine of up to $15,000.00 for possession of even a small quantity).

1009.   *P.S.*, 169 Ill. 2d 260, 661 N.E.2d at 342.

ings were completely separate.[1010] The proceedings were brought and tried separately; they were initiated and docketed separately; they were tried before different judges and by different attorneys; and there was no indication of communication between the prosecuting authorities.[1011] Thus, the two proceedings were not part of a single, coordinated procedure.[1012] Based on this, the court found that the prosecution of defendant Kimery following the civil forfeiture of his vehicle was barred by the double jeopardy clause. In contrast, the subsequent criminal prosecutions of the defendants Turner and P.S. were not barred.

However, the Illinois Supreme Court revisited Kimery's proceedings after the United States Supreme Court advised it to review its prior decision in light of *Ursery*.[1013] In *P.S. II*, the Illinois Supreme Court held that forfeitures under section 505(a)(3) of the Controlled Substance Act do not constitute punishment and therefore, Kimery could be subsequently prosecuted for the related drug offense.[1014] The supreme court adopted in full the rationale and reasoning set forth in *Ursery*, finding that Illinois statutory provisions and the Illinois Constitution were interpreted in a manner consistent with that of the United States Constitution.[1015] Accordingly, the court reversed it prior decision and remanded to the circuit court for further proceedings.

In *Wilson v. Department of Revenue*,[1016] the court held that Illinois Cannabis and Controlled Substances Tax Act was unconstitutional as it is the functional equivalent of a subsequent criminal prosecution which places defendants in jeopardy a second time for the same offense.[1017] In rendering its decision, the court looked to *Kurth* and found that the elements of the tax statute in Illinois was virtually identical to those in *Kurth*. First, criminal conduct is a prerequisite to tax liability under the act because the only persons who are liable for the tax are "dealers." To qualify as a "dealer," an individual must have been tried and convicted of the underlying offense.[1018] Moreover, its punitive nature is under-

---

1010. *Id.*, 661 N.E.2d at 343.

1011. *Id.*

1012. *Id.*, 661 N.E.2d at 344.

1013. 175 Ill. 2d 79, 676 N.E.2d 656 (1997).

1014. *Id.*, 676 N.E.2d at 659.

1015. *Id.*, 676 N.E.2d at 659–61. *See also* People v. Felix, 282 Ill. App. 3d 621, 668 N.E.2d 644, 645–46 (4th Dist. 1996) (defendant's *in rem* asset forfeiture did not implicate double jeopardy under the Federal or Illinois Constitutions, pursuant to *Ursery*, because it was not punishment for double jeopardy purposes, where defendant forfeited $1,800 in cash and 1.6 grams of cocaine after drug arrest).

1016. 169 Ill. 2d 306, 662 N.E.2d 415 (1996).

1017. *Id.*, 662 N.E.2d at 421.

1018. *Id.*, 662 N.E.2d at 420.

scored by the fact that individuals cannot avoid the penalty and interest provisions because the state can only collect the tax following a criminal conviction, despite the fact the tax accrued at the time the individual came into possession of the drugs long before criminal prosecution. In addition, as in *Kurth*, when the state seeks to impose the tax, the individual no longer possesses the contraband which is being taxed.[1019] The final similar characteristic is that the same sovereign is attempting to impose tax liability on an activity which it has already forbidden under the criminal law.[1020] The court also noted that "there is no point in entertaining the pretense that the tax scheme at issue here is actually supposed to be some kind of money-maker for the State," where its entire purpose is to put the drug trade out of business.[1021]

However, in *People v. Medina*,[1022] the court determined that defendant's criminal conviction for possession of cocaine with intent to deliver was not barred by double jeopardy principles where the Department of Revenue had previously issued a jeopardy tax assessment against the defendant and a lien on his property, pursuant to the Cannabis and Controlled Substance Tax Act, where jeopardy did not attach on the tax penalty until after jeopardy had attached on the criminal matter.[1023] Consequently, the defendant was not entitled to postconviction relief. First, the court concluded that jeopardy attached to defendant's criminal matter on January 13, 1992, when the state's first witness was sworn. It further concluded that jeopardy attached to the tax proceeding, at the earliest, at the beginning of the protest hearing when the tax claim was adjudicated, rejecting defendant's contention that jeopardy attached at the time of notice in March of 1991.[1024] In *Kurth Ranch* and its progeny, it was "the proceeding to impose or enforce the tax [that] was the equivalent of a second impermissible criminal proceeding placing the defendants 'at risk' for a prohibited (second) punishment for the same criminal conduct."[1025] Jeopardy did not attach to the notice of tax assessment.[1026] The court found that this type of tax proceeding equated to a criminal prosecution. It then reasoned that notice of assessment or lien was equivalent to being charged with a crime and that jeopardy did not attach at this time. Instead, the tax assessment was not adjudicated until January 17, 1992, four days after defendant's criminal trial began. In conclusion, the court held that where a defendant protests a tax (unlike

---

1019. *Id.*

1020. *Id.*

1021. *Id.*, 662 N.E.2d at 420–21.

1022. 287 Ill. App. 690, 679 N.E.2d 487 (2d Dist. 1997).

1023. *Id.*, 679 N.E.2d at 491.

1024. *Id.*

1025. *Id.*, 679 N.E.2d at 492.

1026. *Id.*, 679 N.E.2d at 493.

an *in rem* forfeiture), jeopardy does not attach until the tax hearing begins and the trier begins to hear evidence.[1027] In *Medina*, there was no constitutional violation even if the tax was unconstitutionally applied because the tax proceeding was outside the reach of the postconviction hearing act. Accordingly, defendant's remedy lay elsewhere.[1028] The court declined to determine when jeopardy would attach if defendant fails to protest the tax and declined to determine whether *Kurth Ranch* should apply retroactively.[1029]

§ 4.62 — Immunity from Prosecution

A defendant who was granted immunity from prosecution may not be prosecuted for the offense for which he or she was granted immunity and is entitled to a favorable ruling on a motion to dismiss the charge.[1030] The procedures for securing immunity, as well as the nature of immunity, are beyond the scope of this chapter.

In *People v. Weilmuenster*,[1031] the defendant was granted immunity from prosecution in Cook County on calculated criminal cannabis conspiracy and cannabis trafficking charges. The indictment was transferred to Kane County where the trial court dismissed it upon defendant's motion. The state appealed, contending that defendant was only granted use immunity, not transactional immunity, and, thus, could be prosecuted in Kane County. The court disagreed. It noted that there was a factual issue that was resolved by the Kane County court in defendant's favor. Defendant testified that he was not familiar with the different types of immunity. He was not offered assistance of counsel and believed that he did not require counsel based on the state's representations.[1032] The assistant attorney general who spoke with defendant could not remember whether she explained the different types of immunity and testified that it was her intent that defendant not serve more time in jail.[1033] The order of immunity, present in the record, was not the original and had been signed ex parte one year after the agreement had been reached. Finally, a state police officer involved in the investigation stated that it was his impression that defendant would not be further prosecuted if he cooperated. The court concluded that the Kane County court did not err in resolving the ambiguity of the agreement between the parties in defendant's favor.

1027. *Id.*

1028. *Id.*, 679 N.E.2d at 494.

1029. *Id.*

1030. 725 ILCS 5/114-1(a)(3).

1031. 283 Ill. App. 3d 613, 670 N.E.2d 802 (2d Dist. 1996).

1032. *Id.*, 670 N.E.2d at 809.

1033. *Id.*

We hold that fundamental fairness requires that a defendant—particularly one unrepresented by counsel—who is called upon to surrender his privilege against self-incrimination in return for a grant of immunity, must be fully and fairly informed by the State of the scope of the protection being afforded; an oblique or perfunctory reference to the type of immunity offered is insufficient.[1034]

§ 4.63   — Improperly Selected Grand Jury

The fourth statutorily articulated ground on which the trial court is authorized to dismiss the charging instrument is where the indictment was returned by an improperly selected grand jury and where the improper selection "result[ed] in substantial injustice to the defendant."[1035] Courts have interpreted the statutory provisions governing grand juror selection[1036] as directory rather than mandatory.[1037] Unless there is proof of substantial prejudice to the defendant because of the selection process, and as long as there was "compliance or substantial compliance with the law," a motion to dismiss based on improper grand jury selection will not be sustained.[1038]

However, no indictment may withstand a motion to dismiss where it is alleged and subsequently proven that prospective grand jurors were excluded because of race.[1039] In fact, even a defendant eventually convicted by a properly selected petit jury may be entitled to a reversal of conviction if the grand jury that initially returned the charge against him or her was selected in a racially discriminatory manner.[1040]

§ 4.64   — Improper Grand Jury Conduct

An area of more frequent, though not necessarily more fertile, attack on a charging instrument via a motion to dismiss is that of conduct before a properly selected grand jury, usually by the prosecutor or a witness, or by

---

1034. *Id.*, 670 N.E.2d at 810.

1035. 725 ILCS 5/114-1(a)(4).

1036. 705 ILCS 310/1-1 through 310/1-12.

1037. People v. Petruso, 35 Ill. 2d 578, 221 N.E.2d 276 (1966).

1038. *Id.,* 221 N.E.2d at 279.

1039. Whitus v. Georgia, 385 U.S. 545 (1967).

1040. Campbell v. Louisiana, 523 U.S. 392 (1998); Rose v. Mitchell, 443 U.S. 545 (1979).

the grand jury itself contrary to chapter 725, section 5/112.[1041] Because the grand jury does not adjudicate guilt or innocence, traditionally Illinois courts have allowed the grand jury wide latitude in deciding what evidence to hear[1042] and from whom,[1043] regardless of its source, including illegal seizure.[1044] As long as there is some evidence as to some elements presented, regardless of how scanty that evidence is, reviewing courts will usually affirm the trial judge's decision to deny a motion to dismiss.[1045] A violation of grand jury secrecy, although improper, does not justify dismissal of the indictment if the violation does not affect the grand jury's deliberations.[1046]

Although defendants have been offered few and limited procedural safe-guards related to grand jury proceedings,[1047] counsel should not be dissuaded from moving to dismiss an indictment because of improper conduct before or by the grand jury. As limited as such rights are, neither the prosecutor nor the grand jury is permitted to proceed against a defendant with a total disregard of his or her due process rights.[1048] Grand jury investigations into the personal affairs of citizens where no criminal activity is involved or where the court lacks subject matter jurisdiction will not be condoned.[1049] Illinois courts have a

---

1041. Chapter 725, section 5/112 provides, inter alia, for the number of grand jurors and their duties, the duties of the state's attorney, and the duties and rights of targets of grand jury investigations and their counsel.

1042. Hearsay is a permissible method of securing an indictment. Costello v. United States, 350 U.S. 359 (1956); People v. Creque, 72 Ill. 2d 515, 382 N.E.2d 793 (1978), cert. denied, 441 U.S. 912 (1979).

1043. The testimony of an incompetent witness may in part be a basis of an indictment. People v. Jones, 19 Ill. 2d 37, 166 N.E.2d 1, 3 (1960); People v. Edwards, 243 Ill. App. 3d 280, 611 N.E.2d 1196 (1st Dist. 1993), cert. denied, 511 U.S. 1071 (1994). See, however, 725 ILCS 5/114-1(a), which provides that a motion to dismiss does lie if "the indictment is based solely on the testimony of an incompetent witness."

1044. United States v. Calandra, 414 U.S. 338 (1974). See Arizona v. Evans, 514 U.S. 1, 10 (1995) (reaffirmation of Calandra doctrine); People v. J.H., 136 Ill. 2d 1, 554 N.E.2d 961, 965 (misconduct by prosecutor is not enough to warrant dismissal of indictment), cert. denied, 498 U.S. 942 (1990).

1045. J.H., 136 Ill. 2d 1, 554 N.E.2d at 965; People v. Rodgers, 92 Ill. 2d 283, 442 N.E.2d 240 (1982); People v. Chatman, 297 Ill. App. 3d 57, 696 N.E.2d 1159 (2d Dist. 1998).

1046. People v. DiVincenzo, 183 Ill. 2d 239, 700 N.E.2d 981, 991 (1998).

1047. Rodgers, 92, Ill. 2d 283, 442 N.E.2d at 243–44.

1048. People v. Sears, 49 Ill. 2d 14, 273 N.E.2d 380, 392 (1971). But see People v. Fassler, 153 Ill. 2d 49, 605 N.E.2d 576 (1992) (failure to follow required procedures does not warrant dismissal of indictment per se).

1049. Id.

supervisory power and duty to see that the grand jury process is not abused.[1050] Thus, where the defense alleges prosecutorial or grand jury misconduct in clear factual terms, an indictment predicated on such conduct may be challenged.[1051]

Moreover, when a motion to dismiss alleges improper conduct by or before the grand jury, the trial court may, pursuant to its inherent authority, review transcripts of the grand jury proceedings to determine whether improprieties occurred or whether *any* evidence was presented that tended to connect the defendant with the offense charged.[1052] Although the prosecutor may introduce evidence that is entirely hearsay, if it is likely to mislead the grand jurors, the prosecutor has an obligation to advise the grand jury that the evidence presented is hearsay.[1053]

In addition, the trial court may examine the grand jury transcript to determine if the prosecutor complied with his or her statutory obligation to advise the grand jurors that they have "the right to subpoena and question any person against whom the State's Attorney is seeking a Bill of Indictment, or any other person, and to obtain and examine any documents or transcripts relevant to the matter being prosecuted by the State's Attorney."[1054] The prosecutor must also advise the grand jurors if there was a previous preliminary hearing at which a finding of no probable cause was entered, as well as of the jurors' right to

> subpoena and question any witness who testified at the preliminary hear-
> ing, or who is believed to have knowledge of such offense, and of [their]
> right to obtain and examine the testimony heard at the preliminary hearing,
> either through the production of a transcript of the proceedings, or through
> the verbatim testimony of the court reporter who attended the preliminary
> hearing.[1055]

Finally, the trial court may examine transcripts of the grand jury proceedings to determine if the prosecutor misadvised the grand jury about their power to act in a particular manner, such as by telling the jurors in a case where the state

---

1050. *Id.*

1051. People v. Linzy, 62 Ill. App. 3d 97, 379 N.E.2d 58, 60, *rev'd on other grounds,*
        78 Ill. 2d 106, 398 N.E.2d 1 (1979). *See also* People v. DiVincenzo, 183 Ill. 2d
        239, 700 N.E.2d 981 (1998).

1052. *Linzy,* 62 Ill. App. 3d 97, 379 N.E. 2d at 60.

1053. People v. Creque, 72 Ill. 2d 515, 382 N.E.2d 793, 796 (1978), *cert. denied,* 441
        U.S. 912 (1979).

1054. 725 ILCS 5/112-4(b).

1055. *Id. See* People v. Valenzuela, 180 Ill. App. 3d 671, 536 N.E.2d 160, 164 (2d
        Dist. 1989) (although an indictment may be dismissed where the grand jury was
        not properly advised, the state is not barred from returning a new indictment).

seeks an indictment for murder that the grand jury cannot return an indictment for manslaughter.[1056] Any prosecutorial misconduct that results in actual substantial prejudice to the defendant[1057] or is predicated on racial, religious, or sexual discrimination[1058] entitles the defendant to a favorable ruling on a motion to dismiss.

Regardless of the nature of the alleged misconduct, the defendant moving to dismiss an indictment predicated on prosecutorial misconduct has a heavy burden of presenting proof supportive of the allegations, in part because every prosecution is presumed to be in good faith.[1059] Moreover, any doubts caused by an incomplete record will be resolved against the defendant,[1060] and the trial court will be presumed to have acted properly in denying the motion to dismiss.[1061] All such determinations will be made, however, on a case-by-case basis.[1062]

§ 4.65 — Lack of Jurisdiction

The sixth enumerated ground on which a charging instrument may be dismissed is where the court before whom the matter is pending lacks jurisdiction to hear the matter.[1063] A trial court lacks jurisdiction to try an offense if the county in which the defendant is being tried is an improper place for the trial,[1064] if double jeopardy or a previous dismissal bars retrial,[1065] or if the indictment contains

---

1056.   *Linzy,* 62 Ill. App. 3d 97, 379 N.E.2d at 60.

1057.   People v. Mack, 107 Ill. App. 3d 164, 437 N.E.2d 396 (4th Dist. 1982).

1058.   People v. Lewis, 73 Ill. App. 3d 361, 386 N.E.2d 910 (3d Dist. 1979). *See* People v. Brandstetter, 103 Ill. App. 3d 259, 430 N.E.2d 731 (4th Dist.), *cert. denied,* 459 U.S. 988 (1982).

1059.   *See also* People v. Golz, 53 Ill. App. 3d 654, 368 N.E.2d 1069 (2d Dist. 1977), *cert. denied,* 437 U.S. 905 (1978).

1060.   People v. Easter, 102 Ill. App. 3d 974, 430 N.E.2d 612 (1st Dist. 1981).

1061.   *Id.,* 430 N.E.2d at 616.

1062.   People v. Stanley, 95 Ill. App. 3d 910, 420 N.E.2d 727 (1st Dist. 1981).

1063.   725 ILCS 5/114-1(a)(6). Jurisdiction must be proven beyond a reasonable doubt. People v. Moreland, 292 Ill. App. 3d 616, 686 N.E.2d 597 (1st Dist. 1997); People v. Blanck, 263 Ill. App. 3d 224, 635 N.E.2d 1356, 1360 (2d Dist. 1994).

1064.   725 ILCS 5/114-1(a)(7). A defendant has a constitutional right to be tried within the county in which the offense is alleged to have been committed. ILL. CONST. art. I, § 8. *But see* 725 ILCS 5/114-1(f). The further provision of section 5/114-1(f) is that in lieu of dismissal on account of an improper place for trial, the court may transfer the cause to proper venue.

1065.   725 ILCS 5/114-1(e).

uncertain allegations about the offense charged or any of its essential elements is missing.[1066] A trial court lacks jurisdiction to try a juvenile defendant unless the state and the juvenile court complied with statutory and constitutional prerequisites allowing a criminal prosecution.[1067] Where no judicial determination to transfer was made or where the juvenile court judge had objected to the transfer, the trial court must dismiss the indictment on the defendant's motion.[1068]

The issue of lack of jurisdiction over the defendant may be raised at any time. Thus, even if a motion to dismiss based on lack of jurisdiction is not presented in the pretrial stage, the issue is not considered waived.[1069] However, a dismissal predicated on lack of jurisdiction does not bar reindictment or the filing of a new information.[1070] As an alternative to dismissal, the court may "order the cause transferred to a court of competent jurisdiction."[1071]

§ 4.66 — Improper Venue

If the county in which the prosecution is commenced is improper,[1072] the trial court may dismiss the indictment or information predicated on that

---

1066. People v. Billingsley, 67 Ill. App. 2d 292, 213 N.E.2d 765 (2d Dist. 1966). *Cf.* People v. Davis, 281 Ill. App. 3d 984, 668 N.E.2d 119, 123 (1st Dist. 1996) (three counts of official misconduct in indictment failed to comply with section 111-3(a) because they failed to allege conduct that described the nature and elements of the offense).

1067. People v. Boclaire, 33 Ill. App. 3d 534, 337 N.E.2d 728 (1st Dist. 1975).

1068. *Id.,* 337 N.E.2d at 733.

1069. The defense attorney may attack the pleadings at the pretrial stage. However, if the defense elects to do so, he or she must remember that the state, after dismisssal of the charge, may recharge the defendant. The defense attorney must, therefore, make a tactical decision about whether to attack the charge or go to trial on defective pleadings, and in the event of an adverse decision, raise the matter in a posttrial motion in arrest of judgment. People v. Gresham, 104 Ill. App. 3d 81, 432 N.E.2d 654 (4th Dist. 1982).

1070. 725 ILCS 5/114-1(e).

1071. 725 ILCS 5/114-1(f).

1072.   Sec. 1-6. Place of trial. (a) Generally. Criminal actions shall be tried in the county where the offense was committed, except as otherwise provided by law. The State is not required to prove during trial that the alleged offense occurred in any particular county in this State. When a defendant contests the place of trial under this Section, all proceedings regarding this issue shall be conducted under Section 114-1 of the Code of Criminal Procedure of 1963. All objections of improper place of trial are waived by a defendant unless made before trial.

          (b) Assailant and Victim in Different Counties. If a person committing an offense upon the person of another is located in one county and his victim is located in another county at the time of the commission of the offense, trial may be had in either of said counties.

(c) Death and Cause of Death in Different Places or Undeter mined. If cause of death is inflicted in one county and death ensues in another county, the offender may be tried in either county. If neither the county in which the cause of death was inflicted nor the county in which death ensued are known before trial, the offender may be tried in the county where the body was found.

(d) Offense Commenced Outside the State. If the commission of an offense commenced outside the State is consummated within this State, the offender shall be tried in the county where the offense was consummated.

(e) Offenses Committed in Bordering Navigable Waters. If an of fense is committed on any of the navigable waters bordering on this State, the offender may be tried in any county adjacent to such navigable water.

(f) Offenses Committed While in Transit. If an offense is commit ted upon any railroad car, vehicle, watercraft or aircraft passing within this State, and it cannot readily be determined in which county the offense was committed, the offender may be tried in any county through which such railroad car, vehicle, watercraft or aircraft has passed.

(g) Theft. A person who commits theft of property may be tried in any county in which he exerted control over such property.

(h) Bigamy. A person who commits the offense of bigamy may be tried in any county where the bigamous marriage or bigamous cohabitation has occurred.

(i) Kidnapping. A person who commits the offense of kidnapping may be tried in any county in which his victim has traveled or has been confined during the course of the offense.

(j) Pandering. A person who commits the offense of pandering may be tried in any county in which the prostitution was practiced or in any county in which any act in furtherance of the offense shall have been committed.

(k) Treason. A person who commits the offense of treason may be tried in any county.

(l) Criminal Defamation. If criminal defamation is spoken, printed or written in one county and is received or circulated in another or other counties, the offender shall be tried in the county where the defamation is spoken, printed or written. If the defamation is spoken, printed or written outside this state, or the offender resides outside this state, the offender may be tried in any county in this state in which the defamation was circulated or received.

(m) Inchoate Offenses. A person who commits an inchoate offense may be tried in any county in which any act which is an element of the offense, including the agreement in conspiracy, is committed.

(n) Accountability for Conduct of Another. Where a person in one county solicits, aids, abets, agrees, or attempts to aid another in the planning or commission of an offense in another county, he may be tried for the offense in either county.

(o) Child Abduction. A person who commits the offense of child abduction may be tried in any county in which his victim has traveled, been detained, concealed or removed to during the course of the offense. Notwithstanding the foregoing, unless for good cause shown, the preferred place of trial shall be the county of the residence of the lawful custodian.

(p) A person who commits the offense of narcotics racketeering may be tried in any county where cannabis or a controlled substance which is the basis for the charge of narcotics racketeering was used; acquired; transferred or distributed to, from or through; or any county where any act was performed to further the use; acquisition, transfer or distribution of said cannabis or controlled substance; any money, property, property interest, or any other asset generated by narcotics activities was acquired, used, sold, transferred or distributed to, from or through; or, any enterprise interest obtained as a result of narcotics racketeering was acquired, used, transferred or distributed to, from or through, or where any activity was conducted by the enterprise or any conduct to further the interest of such an enterprise.

(q) A person who commits the offense of money laundering may be tried in any county where any part of a financial transaction in criminally derived property took place or in any county where any money or monetary instrument which is the basis for the offense was acquired, used, sold, transferred or distributed to, from or through.

(r) A person who commits the offense of cannabis trafficking or controlled substance trafficking may be tried in any county.

720 ILCS 5/1-6.

While venue was a material allegation which the state had to prove beyond a reasonable doubt as with any other element of an offense (*People v. Adams*, 161 Ill. 2d 333, 641 N.E.2d 514, 518 (1994)), section 1-6 was amended, effective August 11, 1995, to delete such a requirement. This amendment, however, does not apply retroactively. People v. Digirolama, 179 Ill. 2d 24, 688 N.E.2d 116, 128–29 (1997).

See, e.g., People v. Carroll, 260 Ill. App. 3d 319, 631 N.E.2d 1155, 1162 (1st Dist. 1992) (although sexual assault of the victim occurred in a county other than the one in which the defendants were tried, venue is proper in any county in which a defendant began to aid and abet others in committing the assault; thus the county from which the victim was abducted at gunpoint was proper); People v. Barraza, 253 Ill. App. 3d 850, 626 N.E.2d 275, 279 (4th Dist. 1993) (prosecution for cannabis trafficking in the county through which the defendant traveled with cannabis held proper, even though the venue is generally only proper in the county where the defendant caused drugs to be brought into the state, because the court could not ascertain which county defendant entered when he first brought drugs into the state). *But see* People v. Allen, 288 Ill. App.

fact.[1073] However, a dismissal for improper venue does not bar subsequent prosecution,[1074] and as an alternative to dismissal, the court may order the cause transferred to a proper county for trial.[1075]

§ 4.67 — Charge Does Not State an Offense

The failure of the charging instrument to state the nature and essential elements of the offense is grounds for dismissal.[1076] The nature and elements

---

3d 502, 680 N.E.2d 795, 800–801 (4th Dist. 1997) ("[t]he State's complete failure to prove venue is fatal to a judgment of conviction, and the issue may be considered for the first time on appeal," noting that section 1-6(a) has since been amended such that state no longer needs to prove offense occurred where prosecution is instituted).

1073. 725 ILCS 5/114-1(a)(7). In *People v. Digirolamo*, 179 Ill. 2d 24, 688 N.E.2d 116 (1997), the court reversed the defendant's conviction for obstructing justice, pursuant to section 1-6(a) that provides that criminal actions shall be tried in the county where the offense was committed. The court found that the prosecution failed to prove beyond a reasonable doubt that the defendant committed the act of obstructing justice in the same county in which he was prosecuted. *Id.*, 688 N.E.2d at 129. The court also noted that the statute had been amended subsequent to the defendant's trial to eliminate the requirement that the state prove venue in any particular county, but stated that because the amendment affected substantive rights, it could not be applied retroactively to the defendant. *Id.*, 688 N.E.2d at 128.

1074. 725 ILCS 5/114-1(e).

1075. 725 ILCS 5/114-1(e).

1076. 725 ILCS 5/114-1(f). *See* People v. Harris, 205 Ill. App. 3d 873, 563 N.E.2d 874, 876 (1st Dist. 1990) (contention that the complaint failed to apprise the defendant of the precise offense with sufficient specificity was upheld because the defendant failed to move to dismiss the complaint, but instead raised question in a motion for acquittal at the end of the state's case); People v. Gerdes, 173 Ill. App. 3d 1024, 527 N.E.2d 1310, 1313 (5th Dist. 1988) (defendant's statements made in an affidavit relied upon in the charging document fell within "exculpatory denial" doctrine and, therefore, could not serve as predicate for a charge of obstructing justice; thus, the information failed to state the cause of action, was constitutionally void, and would not be allowed to stand); People v. Gresham, 104 Ill. App. 3d 81, 432 N.E.2d 654, 657 (4th Dist. 1982) (indictment which failed to charge the offense is subject to dismissal at any time). *But see* People v. DiLorenzo, 169 Ill. 2d 318, 662 N.E.2d 412, 415 (1996) (indictment charging aggravated criminal sexual assault was sufficient even though it failed to include "for the purpose of gratification," failed to define "sexual conduct," and failed to specifically describe the conduct defendant engaged in).

of the crime must be alleged with sufficient particularity to give the defendant notice of why he or she is being tried.[1077] An indictment or information that fails to adequately state an offense will not support a judgment, and a prosecution on such an instrument may deny a defendant due process.[1078] Generally it is adequate for a complaint, indictment, or information to allege an offense in the language of the statute, but the statutory language must particularize the offense so that it sufficiently informs the defendant of the precise crime with which he or she is charged.[1079] When a charge does not describe the acts that constitute the crime or where by its generality it may embrace conduct which the statute does not intend to punish, a charge stated solely in the language of the statute is not sufficient.[1080] The dismissal of a charging instrument based on its failure to state an offense does not bar recharging of the defendant at a later date.[1081]

§ 4.68 — Incompetent Witness Testimony

Although an indictment or information predicated entirely on incompetent testimony before the grand jury may be dismissed,[1082] the key to dismissal is proof that all of the testimony presented was in fact incompetent.[1083] The only time Illinois courts find testimony to be incompetent is where the witness who

---

1077. People v. Leach, 3 Ill. App. 3d 389, 279 N.E.2d 450 (1st Dist. 1972). *See* People v. Brouder, 168 Ill. App. 3d 938, 523 N.E.2d 100 (1st Dist. 1988).

1078. People v. Heard, 47 Ill. 2d 501, 266 N.E.2d 340 (1970); People v. Billingsley, 67 Ill. App. 2d 292, 213 N.E.2d 765 (2d Dist. 1966). *See also* People v. Brown, 157 Ill. App. 3d 61, 510 N.E.2d 71, 73 (1st Dist. 1987) (failure to state nature and elements of the offense charged in the complaint constitutes due process deprivation).

1079. People v. Sims, 393 Ill. 238, 66 N.E.2d 86 (1946); People v. Leach, 3 Ill. App. 3d 389, 279 N.E.2d 450 (1st Dist. 1972). *See also* People v. Morissette, 225 Ill. App. 3d 1044, 589 N.E.2d 144, 146 (4th Dist. 1992) (trial judge must only look to the charging instrument when addressing a claim of insufficiency and cannot look at the entire record); People v. Williams, 223 Ill. App. 3d 692, 585 N.E.2d 1188, 1197 (3d Dist. 1992) (standard to determine whether the charge is sufficient is whether it complies with 725 ILCS 5/111-1; if it meets this criteria, it should not be dismissed).

1080. People v. Peters, 10 Ill. 2d 577, 141 N.E.2d 9 (1957); People v. Leach, 3 Ill. App. 3d 389, 279 N.E.2d 450 (1st Dist. 1972).

1081. 725 ILCS 5/114-1(e).

1082. 725 ILCS 5/114-1(a)(9).

1083. People v. Melson, 49 Ill. App. 3d 50, 363 N.E.2d 888 (5th Dist. 1977).

presents it is disqualified by law. "[O]therwise if a witness was competent, his testimony was competent."[1084]

§ 4.69 — Misnamed Defendant

A charge may be dismissed if the defendant is misnamed and the misnomer results in substantial prejudice to the defendant.[1085]

§ 4.70 — Timeliness Violations

The final enumerated ground for dismissing a charging instrument involves an incarcerated defendant who did not receive a preliminary hearing or was indicted within 30 days of his or her arrest.[1086] If the defendant is not in custody, the time period is 60 days.[1087] Failure to timely charge the defendant or grant a preliminary hearing as required by chapter 725, section 5/109-3.1, which results in a dismissal, does not bar recharging at a later date.[1088]

1084. *Id.,* 363 N.E.2d at 891.

1085. 725 ILCS 5/114-1(a)(10).

1086. 725 ILCS 5/109-3.1(b), 114-1(a).

1087. 725 ILCS 5/109-3.1(b). *See* People v. Clarke, 231 Ill. App. 3d 504, 596 N.E.2d 872, 874 (5th Dist. 1992) (judge did not abuse discretion in denying the defendant's motion to dismiss on failure to hold a prompt preliminary hearing within the time frame outlined in the section); People v. Roby, 200 Ill. App. 3d 1063, 558 N.E.2d 729, 731 (5th Dist. 1990) (section sets a time limit of 30 or 60 days on constitutional right to a "prompt" preliminary hearing). *But see* People v. Ladd, 294 Ill. App. 3d 928, 691 N.E.2d 896 (5th Dist. 1998) (delay does not entitle defendant to release), *aff'd,* 185 Ill. 2d 602, 708 N.E.2d 359 (1999).

1088. 725 ILCS 5/114-1(e). *See, e.g.,* People v. Roby, 200 Ill. App. 3d 1063, 558 N.E.2d 729, 732 (5th Dist. 1990) (state may file a new information charging the defendant with the same offense as the information dismissed for failure to provide prompt preliminary hearing; no violation of Art. I, sections 7 or 12 of Illinois Constitution); People v. Bartee, 177 Ill. App. 3d 937, 532 N.E.2d 997, 999 (2d Dist. 1988) (state may return a new indictment where the previous charge dismissed on the state's delay in scheduling a preliminary hearing; defendant's contention that reindictment is barred where dismissal of the original charge came more than 60 days after defendant's arrest was rejected because such interpretation would render the state's right to bring a new charge meaningless).

§ 4.71 — Due Process

Although generally the trial court is authorized to dismiss a charging instrument only on those specifically enumerated grounds in chapter 725,[1089] courts do have the inherent authority to dismiss charges where there has been a clear denial of the due process protections to which the defendant is entitled.[1090] This is so because courts have an absolute obligation to ensure defendants a fair trial.[1091] Thus, where there was a substantial delay between charging the defendant and knowledge in the prosecutor's office of the alleged offense by the defendant,[1092] or where the prosecutor's conduct made it impossible for the defendant to receive a fair trial,[1093] it was appropriate for the court to dismiss the charging instrument even though the conduct complained of did not fall within any of the statutorily listed grounds for dismissal.[1094] As in so many other instances, creative lawyering in articulating the alleged conduct that may have violated the defendant's due process rights may be outcome determinative.

§ 4.72 Motion for Change of Place of Trial

Generally, "[c]riminal actions shall be tried in the county where the offense was committed."[1095] However, when it appears that the defendant cannot receive a fair trial in the county where venue is proper, usually because of

---

1089.   725 ILCS 5/114-1(a)(1) through 5/114-1(a)(11); People v. Lawson, 67 Ill. 2d 449, 367 N.E.2d 1244 (1977).

1090.   *Lawson,* 67 Ill. 2d 449, 367 N.E.2d at 1246 ("Due process is a fundamental premise of our system of justice and is constitutionally guaranteed by the fourteenth amendment. It does not need enabling legislation"); People v. Hunter, 298 Ill. App. 3d 126, 698 N.E.2d 230 (2d Dist. 1998) (where previous indictment is dismissed for due process violation, state may not reindict).

1091.   People v. Yaeger, 84 Ill. App. 3d 415, 406 N.E.2d 555 (3d Dist. 1980); People v. Nichols, 60 Ill. App. 3d 919, 377 N.E.2d 815 (3d Dist. 1978). *See* People v. Singleton, 278 Ill. App. 3d 296, 662 N.E.2d 580 (1st Dist. 1996) (50-month delay between indictment and arrest warranted dismissal because defendant's federal constitutional speedy trial rights were violated); In the Interest of A.J., 135 Ill. App. 3d 494, 481 N.E.2d 1060 (1st Dist. 1985) (nearly 700-day delay from arraignment to hearing warranted discharge of minor).

1092.   *Nichols,* 60 Ill. App. 3d 919, 377 N.E.2d at 818–19.

1093.   People v. Silverstein, 19 Ill. App. 3d 826, 313 N.E. 2d 309 (1st Dist. 1974) (prosecutor advised state's key witness not to discuss his testimony with defense counsel), *rev'd on other grounds,* 60 Ill. 2d 464, 328 N.E.2d 316 (1975).

1094.   *Silverstein,* 19 Ill. App. 3d 826, 313 N.E.2d at 314.

1095.   720 ILCS 5/1-6(a).

extensive pretrial publicity, the appropriate vehicle to remove the case to a different county is a motion for change of place of trial, commonly referred to as a change of venue.[1096] This should not be confused with a motion for substitution of judges[1097] by which the case is transferred from one judge to another but remains in the same county.[1098]

The courts have developed a two-pronged test by which a motion for change of place of trial should be decided: (1) Does prejudice against the defendant actually exist? and (2) Is it reasonably likely that such prejudice will make it impossible for the defendant to be fairly tried?[1099]

As with most other motions, the decision to grant or deny a motion for change of place of trial is addressed to the sound discretion of the trial judge,[1100] although as a practical matter the motion is rarely granted. In denying the motion, the court may look to a number of less drastic means to dissipate the purported prejudice. These include a lengthy delay of the proceedings to lessen public interest[1101] and specialized voir dire designed, at least in principle, to discover and avoid prejudiced jurors.[1102] In fact, failure of defense counsel to exhaust available peremptory challenges,[1103] and retrospective evaluation of

---

1096. 725 ILCS 5/114-6(a).

1097. 725 ILCS 5/114-5.

1098. *See* the discussion in §§ 4.73–4.77.

1099. People v. Knippenberg, 70 Ill. App. 3d 496, 388 N.E.2d 806 (5th Dist. 1979). *Cf.* Morgan v. Dickstein, 292 Ill. App. 3d 822, 686 N.E.2d 56 (5th Dist. 1997) (even strong showing of prejudice in community is not sufficient, standing alone, to warrant change of place of trial without showing that 12 fair and impartial jurors cannot be found).

1100. Morgan v. Dickstein, 292 Ill. App. 3d 822, 686 N.E.2d 56 (5th Dist. 1997); People v. Farris, 82 Ill. App. 3d 147, 402 N.E.2d 629 (4th Dist. 1980).

1101. People v. Speck, 41 Ill. 2d 177, 242 N.E.2d 208 (1968), *rev'd on other grounds,* 403 U.S. 946 (1971); People v. Knippenberg, 70 Ill. App. 3d 496, 388 N.E.2d 806 (5th Dist. 1979).

1102. People v. Speck, 41 Ill. 2d 177, 242 N.E.2d 208 (1968), *rev'd on other grounds,* 403 U.S. 946 (1971) (where large number of venire persons excused for cause, this demonstrates that trial court exercised care in assuring that defendant was tried by fair and impartial jury). *See also* People v. Fort, 248 Ill. App. 3d 301, 618 N.E.2d 445 (1st Dist. 1993), *cert. denied,* 510 U.S. 1134 (1994). People v. Grover, 93 Ill. App. 3d 877, 417 N.E.2d 1093 (4th Dist. 1981); People v. Carmack, 50 Ill. App. 3d 983, 366 N.E.2d 103 (3d Dist. 1977); People v. Campbell, 28 Ill. App. 3d 480, 328 N.E.2d 608 (5th Dist. 1975).

1103. People v. Townes, 130 Ill. App. 3d 844, 474 N.E.2d 1334 (4th Dist. 1985); People v. Knippenberg, 70 Ill. App. 3d 496, 388 N.E.2d 806 (5th Dist. 1979); People v. Aprile, 15 Ill. App. 3d 461, 304 N.E.2d 642 (4th Dist. 1973); Fleeman v. Fischer, 244 Ill. App 3d 753, 613 N.E.2d 836 (5th Dist. 1993) (failure to exhaust peremptory challenges waives complaint about "unfair" jury).

the trial that reveals "fairness and impartiality" in spite of community preju-dice[1104] would vitiate any defense hopes of appellate relief.

The motion for change of place of trial must be in writing and supported by affidavits stating facts that disclose the alleged prejudice against the defen-dant.[1105] In opposition the state may file responsive affidavits.[1106] The court must conduct a hearing on the merits of the motion,[1107] and if the court determines that there is prejudice that will prevent the defendant from receiving a fair and impartial trial, the case must be transferred to a county where a fair trial can be conducted.[1108]

In addition to the legal hurdles that defense counsel must overcome to convince the court of the propriety of changing the place of trial (for example, establishing the record of a prejudicial atmosphere that makes a fair trial impossible), a number of practical issues are also worthy of consideration. Although the county that is responsible for prosecuting the case (the transfer-ring county) must pay for the costs of the prosecution,[1109] the problems facing the defense may be substantially greater than financial considerations. The defendant and his or her attorney will be facing trial among unfamiliar court personnel, will be far removed from family and friends, and will be away from counsel's office and staff. These obvious difficulties and potential hardship on witnesses and on counsel's practice should be carefully considered. Finally, the motion for change of place of trial is viewed as a delay attributable to the defendant that tolls the running of the speedy trial clock.[1110]

In an apparent attempt to obviate the problems faced by both the prosecution and the defense and to minimize the expense to taxpayers, courts have developed some rather creative alternatives. One approach has been to grant the motion in part by providing for the selection of the jury in another county but conducting the actual trial in the county where change was sought.[1111] This arguably affords the defendant a nonprejudicial jury with minimal inconvenience and lower costs. Other possible alternatives are jury

---

1104. People v. Knippenberg, 70 Ill. App. 3d 496, 388 N.E.2d 806 (5th Dist. 1979).

1105. 725 ILCS 5/114-6(b). *See* People v. Coddington, 123 Ill. App. 2d 351, 259 N.E.2d 382, 390 (5th Dist. 1970) (absence of a defense affidavit showing prejudice in conjunction with the state's affidavits countering allegations were sufficient to uphold denial of motion).

1106. 725 ILCS 5/114-6(b).

1107. *Id.*

1108. 725 ILCS 5/114-6(c).

1109. 725 ILCS 5/114-6(h).

1110. People v. Ortiz, 70 Ill. App. 3d 684, 388 N.E.2d 891 (5th Dist. 1979).

1111. People v. Gacy, 103 Ill. 2d 1, 468 N.E.2d 1171 (1984), *cert. denied,* 470 U.S. 1037 (1985).

sequestration,[1112] individual voir dire of prospective jurors out of the presence of the rest of the venire,[1113] additional peremptory challenges beyond the statutory amount,[1114] allowing the attorneys to personally conduct the voir dire,[1115] and publicity surveys.[1116] Finally, although counsel should recognize that none of the above alternatives to a motion for change of place of trial is constitutionally mandated[1117] and that courts are prone to deny many of the suggested requests, failure to raise the issue will result in waiver.[1118] In an appropriate case and with an issue-preserved record, a denial of any of the above defense requests may bear on the appellate relief sought.

§ 4.73   Substitution of Judges

The vehicle by which a case may be transferred from one judge to another based on the alleged inability of the first judge to be fair, and absent a voluntary recusal by the judge himself or herself, is the motion or petition for substitution of judges.[1119] Under some circumstances discussed below,

---

1112. *But see* United States v. Haldeman, 559 F.2d 31, 85 (D.C. Cir. 1976) (court hypothesized that sequestered jury might take out their anger at being "locked up" on defendant, who is perceived as cause of jury's situation), *cert. denied*, 431 U.S. 933 (1977).

1113. People v. Gacy, 103 Ill. 2d 1, 468 N.E.2d 1171 (1984), *cert. denied*, 470 U.S. 1037 (1985).

1114. *But see Id.*, 468 N.E.2d at 1185.

1115. Supreme Court Rule 234 now entitles the attorneys to personally conduct voir dire examination. "The Court . . . shall permit the parties to supplement the examination by such direct inquiry as the court deems proper for a reasonable time . . . ." Although trial judges are following the amended rule, many apparently are not pleased with the change and have imposed drastic limitations on the attorney-conducted voir dire as to time and content.

1116. *See* NATIONAL JURY PROJECT, Jurywork: Systematic Techniques 21–49 (1979).

1117. *Gacy,* 103 Ill. 2d 1, 468 N.E.2d at 1188.

1118. *Id.*

1119.   § 114-5. Substitution of Judge. (a) Within 10 days after a cause involving only one defendant has been placed on the trial call of a judge the defendant may move the court in writing for a substitution of that judge on the ground that such judge is so prejudiced against him that he cannot receive a fair trial. Upon the filing of such a motion the court shall proceed no further in the cause but shall transfer it to another judge not named in the motion. The defendant may name only one judge as prejudiced, pursuant to this subsection; provided, however, that in a case in which the offense charged is a Class X felony or may be punished by death or life imprisonment, the defendant may name two judges as prejudiced.

(b) Within 24 hours after a motion is made for substitution of judge in a cause with multiple defendants each defendant shall have the right to move in accordance with subsection (a) of this Section for a substitution of one judge. The total number of judges named as prejudiced by all defendants shall not exceed the total number of defendants. The first motion for substitution of judge in a cause with multiple defen dants shall be made within 10 days after the cause has been placed on the trial call of a judge.

(c) Within 10 days after a cause has been placed on the trial call of a judge the State may move the court in writing for a substitution of that judge on the ground that such judge is prejudiced against the State. Upon the filing of such a motion the court shall proceed no further in the cause but shall transfer it to another judge not named in the motion. The State may name only one judge as prejudiced, pursuant to this subsection.

(d) In addition to the provisions of subsections (a), (b) and (c) of this Section the State or any defendant may move at any time for substitution of judge for cause, supported by affidavit. Upon the filing of such motion a hearing shall be conducted as soon as possible after its filing by a judge not named in the motion; provided, however, that the judge named in the motion need not testify, but may submit an affidavit if the judge wishes. If the motion is allowed, the case shall be assigned to a judge not named in the motion. If the motion is denied the case shall be assigned back to the judge named in the motion.

725 ILCS 5/114-5.

The standard of review in determining prejudice or absence of prejudice is by a preponderance of the evidence. People v. Smeathers, 297 Ill. App. 3d 711, 698 N.E.2d 181 (2d Dist. 1998); People v. Mercado, 244 Ill. App. 3d 1040, 614 N.E.2d 284, 287 (1st Dist. 1993). This section is not applicable to postconviction proceedings (*People v. Meeks*, 249 Ill. App. 3d 152, 618 N.E.2d 1000, 1005 (1st Dist. 1993)), at retrial, or in defendant's criminal contempt proceeding. *In re Peasley*, 189 Ill. App. 3d 865, 545 N.E.2d 792, 795 (4th Dist. 1989). *See also* People v. Ryan, 264 Ill. App. 3d 1, 636 N.E.2d 1126, 1128 (2d Dist. 1994) (reviewing court's remand does not operate to initiate separate and distinct prosecution which would begin defendant's right to substitution anew without regard to his exercise of right on remand; remand is continuation for purpose of this section). *But see* People v. Thompkins, 181 Ill. 2d 1, 690 N.E.2d 984, 994 (1998) (while statutory provisions for substitution of judges do not apply to postconviction proceedings, there are circumstances where postconviction judge should recuse himself or herself because of bias or prejudice, such as where judge may be material witness, has knowledge outside record "concerning the truth or falsity of allegations made," or where judge has "direct, personal and substantial pecuniary interest in a criminal case"); People v. Brim, 241 Ill. App. 3d 245, 608 N.E.2d 958 (4th Dist. 1993) (postconviction judge should have granted defendant's motion for substitution of judge, since allegation of prejudice was against judge himself).

the motion must be granted and the matter is automatically reassigned,[1120] while under other situations the granting of the motion is discretionary.[1121] A third scenario involves a situation where a mandatory motion is filed but the judge to whom the motion is addressed has already ruled on other substantive matters in the case. In this situation the mandatory substitution of judges provision no longer applies.[1122] Under no circumstances should the motion for substitution of judges be confused with either a motion for change of place of trial[1123] or a motion for change of venue[1124] which are addressed elsewhere in this chapter.[1125]

§ 4.74 — Ten-Day Rule

The so-called ten-day rule gives a defendant charged alone in the case an absolute and automatic right[1126] to change judges if the motion is filed within ten days of the time that the case was placed on the trial call of the judge named in the motion.[1127] The motion must be in writing.[1128] Although the motion

---

1120. 725 ILCS 5/114-5(a).

1121. 725 ILCS 5/114-5(c).

1122. People v. Cazaux, 119 Ill. App. 2d 11, 254 N.E.2d 797 (1st Dist. 1969).

1123. 725 ILCS 5/114-6.

1124. *Id.*

1125. 725 ILCS 5/114-5(a).

1126. The defendant's right under this statute is absolute. People v. Pace, 225 Ill. App. 3d 415, 587 N.E.2d 1257, 1264 (2d Dist. 1992).

1127. 725 ILCS 5/114-5(a). *But see* People v. Lackland, 248 Ill. App. 3d 426, 618 N.E.2d 508, 512 (1st Dist. 1993) (judge erred in denying a defendant's motion for automatic substitution on grounds that the motion was untimely; although case on call on December 22, 1988, the judge did not make a ruling on the defendant's fitness until June 28, 1989; prior to June 28th, the defendant was not fit to exercise right to automatic substitution).

1128. 725 ILCS 5/114-5(a). *See* People v. Langford, 246 Ill. App. 3d 460, 616 N.E.2d 628, 633 (5th Dist. 1993) (where facts show that the defendant made a mistake in filing a motion for substitution, then requested to correct the mistake, the rule favors amendment; denying a motion for failure to comply with strict construction of the statute without a chance to amend defeats rather than promotes the purpose of the law). *But see* People v. Burns, 188 Ill. App. 3d 716, 544 N.E.2d 466, 468 (4th Dist. 1989) (where defendant filed motion for substitution within 10 day period but filed amended petition containing required allegation of prejudice after 10 day period, defendant failed to meet minimal requirement for automatic substitution).

In addition, the motion must comply with the statutory requirements and defendant must clearly and unequivocally request a substitution of judge and

allows a defendant to have his or her case removed from the trial call of an allegedly prejudiced judge, it does not on its face allow the defendant to select a judge into whose courtroom he or she wishes to have the case transferred. As a practical matter, however, depending on the number of available judges in any county, some "forum shopping" is inevitable.

The statute provides that "[up]on the filing of . . . [the motion] the court shall proceed no further in the cause but shall transfer it to another court or judge not named in the motion."[1129] If the judge has not ruled on any substantive issues in the case[1130] or held a pretrial conference,[1131] and the motion was timely filed, any proceedings held before that judge after the filing of the motion are void.[1132] Although the language of the statute seems clear, some courts have held that it is the good faith knowledge of the defendant as to when the matter was first

---

must do so without contingency, e.g., no alternative pleading is permitted by the statute. People v. Morrison, 260 Ill. App. 3d 775, 633 N.E.2d 48, 59 (4th Dist.) (denial of the defendant's motion for substitution was proper where the defendant did not clearly request substitution of the judge and the motion did not contain any allegation that the judge was prejudiced against the defendant), *vacated and remanded*, 157 Ill. 2d 514, 640 N.E.2d 630 (1994) (trial court was ordered to grant defendant's motion for recusal or other relief and transfer case to another judge); People v. Smeathers, 297 Ill. App. 3d 711, 698 N.E.2d 181 (2d Dist. 1998).

1129. People v. Massarella, 80 Ill. App. 3d 552, 400 N.E.2d 436, 445 (1st Dist. 1979), *cert. denied*, 449 U.S. 1077 (1981). *See* People v. Williams, 217 Ill. App. 3d 791, 577 N.E.2d 944, 946 (5th Dist. 1991) (once a proper motion is filed, the judge losses all power and authority over the case except to effectuate substitution); People v. Banks, 213 Ill. App. 3d 205, 571 N.E.2d 935, 940 (4th Dist. 1991) (order entered by the judge who earlier had been substituted is void, because once a motion is brought, the judge losses all authority and power over defendant's case except to make all necessary orders to effectuate change).

1130. People v. Cazaux, 119 Ill. App. 2d 11, 254 N.E.2d 797, 800 (1st Dist. 1969). *See* People v. Flanagan, 201 Ill. App. 3d 1071, 559 N.E.2d 1105, 1111 (4th Dist. 1990) (motion for substitution of judge must be timely made and also prior to judicial action on merits; a litigant is precluded from testing judicial attitude on issues and then later asserting prejudice when judge fails to support that party).

1131. S. Ct. Rule 402; *Cazaux*, 119 Ill. App. 2d 11, 254 N.E.2d at 800.

1132. People v. Samples, 107 Ill. App. 3d 523, 437 N.E.2d 1232 (5th Dist. 1982), *disagreed with by* People v. Williams, 217 Ill. App. 3d 791, 577 N.E.2d 944 (5th Dist. 1991). In *Williams,* the court found that in *People v. Walker*, 119 Ill. 2d 465, 519 N.E.2d 890 (1988), the Illinois Supreme Court addressed the constitutionality of section 114-5(a) [current section 5/114-5(a)] and concluded that the automatic substitution of judge provision makes it clear that its protections may be invoked only after assignment to the judge and then only within ten days after the case has been placed on the trial calendar of the assigned judge.

placed on the named judge's trial call that governs the commencement of the ten-day period, rather than when the matter was actually placed on that judge's trial call.[1133]

§ 4.75 — Number of Judges Allowed

The statute allows a single defendant to name one judge, unless the "offense charged is a Class X felony or may be punished by death or life imprisonment," in which case he or she may name two judges as prejudiced.[1134] For a single defendant who contemplates filing a motion for substitution of judges under the ten-day rule provisions,[1135] the statute's operation is simple. Only three questions need to be addressed, the answers to which either assure or defeat the defendant's absolute right under the rule:

1.   Did the defendant in good faith know when the case was placed on the judge's call or has the matter actually been assigned to the named judge's trial call for ten days or less?[1136]

2.   Even if the matter is on the named judge's trial call for ten days or less, has anything substantively occurred that acts as a waiver of the defendant's otherwise absolute right to a substitution of judges?[1137]

3.   Is the defendant charged with an offense that allows him or her to name one or two judges?[1138]

1133.   People v. Thomas, 58 Ill. App. 3d 460, 374 N.E.2d 795 (1st Dist. 1978). *See* People v. Pace, 225 Ill. App. 3d 415, 587 N.E.2d 1257 (2d Dist. 1992) (defendant is not charged with notice of assignment for 10-day rule purposes where no paperwork indicating assignment exists).

1134.   725 ILCS 5/114-5(a), (b).

1135.   725 ILCS 5/114-5(a).

1136.   725 ILCS 5/114-5(a). *See* People v. Williams, 217 Ill. App. 3d 791, 577 N.E.2d 944, 948 (5th Dist. 1991) (presence of the defendant's case on a judge's docket call is insufficient itself to charge the defendant with knowledge that the judge is assigned to the case).

1137.   People v. Taylor, 101 Ill. 2d 508, 463 N.E.2d 705 (defendant cannot complain about denial of motion made after judge rules on number of substantive issues including motion to quash arrest, motion to suppress statements, made to state's attorney, and motion seeking to bar use of evidence of other crimes), *cert. denied,* 469 U.S. 866 (1984). *See also* People v. Pace, 225 Ill. App. 3d 415, 587 N.E.2d 1257 (2d Dist. 1992).

1138.   Class X offense or one punishable by death or life imprisonment. 725 ILCS 5/114-5(a).

An example of the principle that bad advice is bad advice even if it comes from a judge is *People v. Posey*.[1139] In *Posey,* when the defendant who was charged with a Class X offense was arraigned, he moved to substitute the judge assigned to preside at his trial.[1140] Posey also inquired of the arraignment judge whether he should at the same time name the second judge he wished to substitute.[1141] The judge responded that Posey could wait until his case was reassigned.[1142] Later, long after ten days had run, Posey appeared before the new judge to whom his case had been reassigned and made an oral motion to substitute that judge.[1143] Within ten days of this appearance Posey followed up his oral motion with a written one.[1144] The motion was denied.[1145] On appeal, the appellate court found that under section 114-5(a) (current 725 ILCS 5/114-5(a)), a defendant charged with a Class X felony or an offense punishable by death or life imprisonment, may move to substitute two judges, however the defendant is entitled to only one motion naming both at that time.[1146] The court recognized that the arraignment judge had misinformed Posey about the proper procedures for substituting judges and granted him a new trial.[1147] Bad advice by a judge can not inure to the defendant's detriment.[1148]

In the prosecution of multiple defendants, however, the issue becomes somewhat more complex and the consequences somewhat less clearly ascertainable, because each defendant can name only one judge in his or her motion, even if the offense is a Class X or a felony punishable by life imprisonment or death.[1149] Moreover, the total number of judges named by all defendants cannot exceed the total number of defendants.[1150] For example, three defendants

---

1139.   206 Ill. App. 3d 1017, 564 N.E.2d 1323 (1st Dist. 1990).

1140.   *Id., * 564 N.E.2d at 1324.

1141.   *Id.*

1142.   *Id.*

1143.   *Id.*

1144.   *Id.*

1145.   *Id.*

1146.   *Id.*

1147.   *Id.*

1148.   *Id.* In the experience of this writer, some judges still misinform defendants in multi-defendant cases that after the first defendant has filed his or her motion for substitution of judges, the other defendants have 10 days to file theirs. As discussed in the text above, that is not an accurate statement of the law.

1149.   725 ILCS 5/114-5(b). This section does not violate defendant's due process rights (*People v. Williams*, 124 Ill. 2d 300, 529 N.E.2d 558, 561 (1988)) nor does it violate separation of powers. People *ex rel.* Baricevic v. Wharton, 136 Ill. 2d 423, 556 N.E.2d 253, 257 (1990).

1150.   725 ILCS 5/114-5(b).

charged with a Class X offense or an offense punishable by life imprisonment or death can together name only a total of three judges. Also, within 24 hours of the time that one defendant files his or her motion, all other defendants must make their motions or the right is lost.[1151]

If all of the multiple-charged defendants can agree on the judges they want to name in their respective motions, the statute may in fact work to their advantage over the individually charged defendant as far as ending up in front of a desirable judge. A few examples demonstrate the principles involved.

1. Defendant 1 is singularly charged with a Class X offense. He timely files a motion for substitution of judges in which he names Judge A, on whose trial call his case was originally placed, and Judge B as prejudiced. Having timely filed his motion, Defendant 1's case must be reassigned, and his case ends up on the trial call of Judge C.

2. Defendants 1 and 2 are jointly charged with a Class X offense. Their case is initially assigned to Judge A. Defendant 1 timely files her motion for substitution of judges, naming Judge A as prejudiced, and the matter is reassigned to Judge B. Because the defendants were jointly charged[1152] and to avoid severing the defendants from one another, Defendant 2 is also administratively reassigned to Judge B. Defendant 2, within 24 hours, files his motion for substitution of judges, naming Judge B.[1153] Defendant's 2's case is reassigned to Judge C, and again to avoid severance of defendants, Defendant 1's case is also reassigned to Judge C.

3. Defendants 1, 2, and 3 are jointly charged with a Class X offense. Defendant 1 files a motion for substitution of judges, naming Judge A, to whom the case was initially assigned. He and Defendants 2 and 3, for the administrative reasons discussed above, are all reassigned to Judge B. Defendant 2, within 24 hours, names Judge B as prejudiced, and she and Defendants 1 and 3, for the reasons discussed above, are all reassigned to Judge C. Defendant 3 now files timely his motion for substitution of judges, naming Judge C as prejudiced, and all three defendants, again for the reasons discussed above are all reassigned to Judge D.

The advantage under these circumstances becomes apparent. Had each defendant been charged alone, he or she could have named only two judges as prejudiced.[1154] But because they were jointly charged, each defendant as a practical matter is able to avoid three rather than two prejudiced judges.

1151. *Id.*

1152. 725 ILCS 5/114-5(b).

1153. *Id.*

1154. *Id.*

Whatever advantage the statute apparently gives to jointly charged defendants when their number is three or greater, the statute presupposes that all of the defendants either desire to name the same judges as prejudiced, and therefore have no objection to being administratively transferred when a co-defendant has actually made the motion, or that all defendants want to stay in front of the same judge and all of the co-defendants decline the right to make a motion. It is not difficult to imagine circumstances, however, in which it is not in the joint interests of the multiple charged defendants to either remain in the courtroom the case was originally assigned to or to be transferred to another courtroom. A few more examples demonstrate the problems involved:

4.   Two defendants are charged with a Class X offense and are initially assigned to the trial call of Judge A. Defendant 1 is satisfied with the fairness of Judge A and wants to have her case tried by that judge. Defendant 2, however, was convicted on a previous occasion by Judge A and thus files a motion for substitution of judges within the ten-day period, naming as prejudiced Judge A. Having timely filed her motion, the matter must be reassigned to a different judge, and for administrative reasons previously discussed, Defendant 1's case is reassigned as well. Both defendants have been reassigned to Judge B. Defendant 1, fearing that Judge B is prejudiced, files her motion for substitution of judges within the required 24-hour period, and both defendants are then reassigned to Judge C. Defendant 1, however, was previously convicted of another offense by Judge C and therefore fears that Judge C will be prejudiced against her. The defendants were jointly charged and by the specification of the statute, the total number of judges named cannot exceed the total number of defendants. Therefore, Defendant 1, absent any "cause," as discussed below, cannot name Judge C as prejudiced and accordingly, must remain in that courtroom. In this example Defendant 1's interests are affected in two ways. Were she not jointly charged, she would have been able to remain in the courtroom of Judge A rather than being transferred to another courtroom. Also, because of the statute's application to multiple defendants, Defendant 1 is only able to name one judge as prejudiced rather than the two she would have been able to name had she been individually charged with a Class X offense.

5.   Two defendants, jointly charged with a Class X offense, are initially assigned to the courtroom of Judge A, whose reputation is for holding the state stringently to its burden of proof. Defendant 1 has negotiated an agreement with the prosecutor related to a reduction of charges in exchange for testimony against Defendant 2. Until the testimony occurs, however, Defendant 1 continues to be a defendant of record who is entitled to all the rights of a defendant for whom an agreement has not been negotiated. At the urging of the assistant

state's attorney, Defendant 1 files a petition for substitution of judges naming Judge A as prejudiced. The state's attorney would prefer a transfer of the defendants to any other courtroom in the county rather than remaining before Judge A. The case is then reassigned to Judge B, and for administrative reasons Defendant 2's case is assigned to Judge B's courtroom as well. Defendant 2, aware of Judge B's reputation as a "prosecution-oriented" judge, files his motion for substitution of judges, naming Judge B as prejudiced, and both Defendants 1 and 2 are then reassigned to the trial call of Judge C, another "prosecution-oriented" judge. Because they are jointly charged defendants and the total number of judges named in a petition for substitution of judges cannot exceed the total number of defendants, the case must now remain before Judge C. Again, as in the previous example, had Defendant 2 been charged alone, he would have had the benefit of naming two judges rather than one under the statute.

This writer has been unable to find any decision in which a multiple charged defendant successfully attacked his or her conviction on the ability to name only one judge as prejudiced instead of naming two that he or she might have been able to name had he or she been singly charged with a Class X offense or any other felony punishable by death or life imprisonment.

§ 4.76 — Substitution of Judges for Cause

In addition to the previously discussed provisions, a defendant may seek substitution of a judge at any time for cause supported by affidavit.[1155] The cause alleged under this section of the statute[1156] is entirely different from the prejudice feared and alleged under the ten-day rule.[1157]

Although a motion for substitution of judges based on cause may be filed at any time the case is pending,[1158] the alleged bias must be shown to have stemmed from an extrajudicial source and resulted "in an opinion on the merits on some basis other than what the judge learned from his participation in the case."[1159] It is easier to ascertain what is not cause for substitution under this

---

1155.   725 ILCS 5/114-5(c).

1156.   725 ILCS 5/114-5(c).

1157.   725 ILCS 5/114-5(a); People v. Covington, 92 Ill. App. 3d 598, 416 N.E.2d 61 (5th Dist. 1981).

1158.   725 IlCS 5/114-5(d). Both the defendant and the state have a right to challenge a judge for cause. People v. Walker, 119 Ill. 2d 465, 519 N.E.2d 890, 895 (1988).

1159.   People v. Massarella, 80 Ill. App. 3d 552, 400 N.E.2d 436, 447 (1st Dist. 1979), cert. denied, 449 U.S. 1077 (1981). See People v. Walsh, 273 Ill. App. 3d 453, 652 N.E.2d 1102 (1st Dist. 1995); People v. Damnitz, 269 Ill. App. 3d 51, 645

section of the statute than to define what is. Cause for substitution is not established merely because the judge had accepted guilty pleas of co-defendants[1160] or "even because he presided at a prior trial of the same defendant in the same cause." [1161] However, if the motion is in writing,[1162] is accompanied by an affidavit,[1163] and contains an allegation of the judge's bias that is supported by facts,[1164] the defendant is entitled to an evidentiary hearing on the merits of the motion before a judge other than the one he or she alleges cannot give him or her a fair trial.[1165] Although denial of the hearing itself

---

N.E.2d 465 (1st Dist. 1995). *See also* People v. Blanck, 263 Ill. App. 3d 224, 635 N.E.2d 1356, 1363 (2d Dist. 1994) (isolated comment by a judge during a momentary lapse of judicial composure does not automatically disqualify judge; concern is whether a pervasive attitude of animosity, hostility, ill will, or distrust exists, which might affect the performance of judicial duties in the particular case).

1160.   *Massarella*, 80 Ill. App. 3d 552, 400 N.E.2d at 447 (citing People v. Smith, 29 Ill. App. 3d 519, 331 N.E.2d 99 (1st Dist. 1975), *cert. denied,* 424 U.S. 925 (1976)).

1161.   *Massarella*, 80 Ill. App. 3d 552, 400 N.E.2d at 447 (citing United States v. Dichiarinte, 445 F.2d 126 (7th Cir. 1971)).

1162.   725 ILCS 5/114-5(d). *See* People v. Johnson, 256 Ill. App. 3d 728, 632 N.E.2d 37, 38–39 (1st Dist. 1993) (this section fails to give a trial judge discretionary authority to find the defendant has moved for substitution of judge for cause when the defendant never made such a motion; trial judge's characterization of defendant's complaint to Judicial Inquiry Board as request for substitution was improper, particularly in light of defendant's statement to the contrary).

1163.   725 ILCS 5/114-5(d). *See* People v. Amos, 204 Ill. App. 3d 75, 561 N.E.2d 1107, 1116 (1st Dist. 1990) (motion for substitution is properly denied where oral, not supported by affidavit or evidence in record, and there is only a claim by the defendant that he believed the judge to be hostile); People v. Marshall, 165 Ill. App. 3d 968, 521 N.E.2d 538, 542 (1st Dist. 1988) (where the judge stated that the defendant's motion for substitution of judge contained only a cursory allegation of prejudice, was not specific, was not supported by affidavit, and while defendant had appeared before him in an earlier trial he had no recollection of the outcome, prejudice is not shown).

1164.   725 ILCS 5/114-5(d).

1165.   725 ILCS 5/114-5(d). *See* People v. Brim, 241 Ill. App. 3d 245, 608 N.E.2d 958, 961 (4th Dist. 1993) (judge abused discretion by ruling on a motion for substitution when the motion sufficiently indicated that the judge could be prejudiced). *But see* People v. Jimenez, 191 Ill. App. 3d 13, 547 N.E.2d 616, 625 (1st Dist. 1989) (where defendant did not object to judge's ruling on the motion, he waived the issue on appeal).

In *People v. Bell*, 276 Ill. App. 3d 939, 658 N.E.2d 1372 (2d Dist. 1995), the court held that once a motion for substitution of judge for cause is brought, the

constitutes reversible error,[1166] the granting or denial of the motion of substitution of judges for cause is discretionary, and the only requirement is that the defendant have an opportunity to present evidence.[1167] Unlike an improperly denied motion for substitution of judges filed under the ten-day provision,[1168] which makes all subsequent proceedings void,[1169] an improperly denied motion for substitution of judges for cause, although it potentially provides a defendant with one more issue for appeal, does not render subsequent proceedings void.[1170] At the hearing the burden of proof is on the defendant to prove that he or she has cause for substitution of the judge,[1171] and the judge who is named in the motion may present evidence in opposition at the hearing either by testimony or affidavit.[1172] "If the motion is allowed, the case shall be assigned to a judge not named in the motion. If the motion is denied, the case shall be assigned back to the judge named in the motion."[1173] Proving that there is cause to have a case removed from the trial call of a judge is difficult, to say the least, because it is the court itself that is held to be in the best position to determine whether it may be prejudiced against the defendant.[1174] Counsel should not be dissuaded, however, from filing a motion in an appropriate case because the record may demonstrate

---

allegedly biased judge loses all power and authority over the case and has no power to hear the motion, just as with the 10-day automatic substitution rule. *Id.*, 658 N.E.2d at 1378.

1166. People v. Wolfe, 124 Ill. App. 2d 349, 260 N.E.2d 424 (1st Dist. 1970).

1167. People v. Evans, 75 Ill. App. 3d 949, 394 N.E.2d 710, 715 (4th Dist. 1979).

1168. 725 ILCS 5/114-5(a).

1169. People v. Pace, 225 Ill. App. 3d 415, 587 N.E.2d 1257 (2d Dist. 1992). People v. Samples, 107 Ill. App. 3d 523, 437 N.E.2d 1232, 1235–36 (5th Dist. 1982).

1170. People v. Robinson, 18 Ill. App. 3d 804, 310 N.E.2d 652 (1st Dist. 1974).

1171. People v. Covington, 92 Ill. App. 3d 598, 416 N.E.2d 61, 64 (5th Dist. 1981). *See* People v. Damnitz, 269 Ill. App. 3d 51, 645 N.E.2d 465, 469–70 (1st Dist. 1994) (substitution for cause and hearing by a different judge is not required based on evidentiary rulings of the trial judge or on the judge's statement to the jury after the verdict that he would have convicted the defendant of a different felony of which the jury found the defendant not guilty).

1172. 725 ILCS 5/114-5(a); *In re* Santa Cruz, 179 Ill. App. 3d 611, 534 N.E.2d 636, 644 (2d Dist. 1989) (although the judge had personal knowledge of the proceedings from the outcome, where he stated he would keep an open mind and would listen to any appropriate arguments, the defendant failed to meet the burden of establishing cause to substitute a new judge, particularly in light of the judge's assurances of impartiality and where the judge is in the best position to determine whether prejudice exits).

1173. 725 ILCS 5/114-5(c).

1174. In the Interest of C.S., 215 Ill. App. 3d 600, 575 N.E.2d 1 (3d Dist. 1991); People v. Massarella, 80 Ill. App. 3d 552, 400 N.E.2d 436, 445–46 (1st Dist. 1979),

the inability of the judge to be fair although he or she denied that inability at the evidentiary hearing.

§ 4.77 — State's Right

As of July 1, 1987, the state was granted the right to move to substitute a judge.[1175]

§ 4.78 Continuances

Section 5/114-4(b) provides specific grounds on which an accused can request a continuance, although the court may grant continuances on other grounds if "the interests of justice so require."[1176] The granting of a continuance is within the "discretion of the trial court and shall be considered in the light of the diligence" shown by the movant.[1177] Any motion for a continuance made

---

    cert. denied, 449 U.S. 1077 (1981); People v. Nickols, 41 Ill. App. 3d 974, 354 N.E.2d 474 (3d Dist. 1976).

1175. 725 ILCS 5/114-5(c):

> (c) Within 10 days after a cause has been placed on the trial call of a judge the State may move the court in writing for a substitution of that judge on the ground that such judge is prejudiced against the State. Upon the filing of such a motion the court shall proceed no further in the cause but shall transfer it to another judge not named in the motion. The state may name only one judge as prejudiced, pursuant to this subsection.

> (d) In addition to the provisions of subsections (a), (b) and (c) of this Section the State or any defendant may move at any time for substitution of judge for cause, supported by affidavit. Upon the filing of such motion a hearing shall be conducted as soon as possible after its filing by a judge not named in the motion; provided, however, that the judge named in the motion need not testify, but may submit an affidavait if the judge wishes. If the motion is allowed, the case shall be assigned to a judge not named in the motion. If the motion is denied the case shall be assigned back to the judge named in the motion.

> *See* People v. Marshall, 256 Ill. App. 3d 310, 629 N.E.2d 64, 68 (1st Dist. 1993) (state has the right to a change of venue if the motion is timely and in proper form); People v. Ross, 244 Ill. App. 3d 868, 614 N.E.2d 182, 189 (1st Dist. 1993) (when opposing the substitution of the judge, the defendant must at least allege facts which, if true, would require the judge to conduct a hearing; when the motion for substitution is presented by the state, the judge need not, sua sponte, announce the absence or presence of prima facie case of abuse).

>   The state's right to appeal under this section is constitutional. People *ex rel.* Baricevic v. Wharton, 136 Ill. 2d 423, 556 N.E.2d 253, 257–58 (1990).

1176. 725 ILCS 5/114-4(d).

1177. 725 ILCS 5/114-4(e). *See* People v. Sullivan, 234 Ill. App. 3d 328, 600 N.E.2d 457, 460 (2d Dist. 1992) (discretion of court standard).

more than 30 days after arraignment must be in writing and supported by affidavit.[1178]

Legitimate requests for a pretrial continuance generally arise out of two broadly overlapping situations: (1) the need for more time so that the accused can obtain the services and representation of counsel of his or her choice,[1179] and (2) the need for more time so that counsel can adequately prepare the case for trial.[1180]

The framework within which a trial court should consider the request for a continuance has been succinctly stated by the Illinois Supreme Court:

> The granting of a continuance to permit preparation for a case, or for the substitution of counsel, necessarily depends upon the particular facts and circumstances surrounding the request, and is a matter resting within the sound judicial discretion of the trial court. (People v. Surgeon, 15 Ill. 2d 236; People v. Clark, 9 Ill. 2d 46.) Before a judgment of conviction will be reversed because of the denial of such a motion, it must appear that the refusal of additional time in some manner embarrassed the accused in preparing his defense and prejudiced his rights.[1181]

The discretion of the trial judge will be considered to have been abused only on a clear showing of embarrassment to the accused in preparing his or her defense whereby his or her rights were prejudiced.[1182] The judge must at least make some inquiry as to whether the continuance sought is for delay.[1183]

1178.   725 ILCS 5/114-4(a).

1179.   People v. Green, 42 Ill. 2d 555, 248 N.E.2d 116, 117 (1969). *See* People v. Hardin, 299 Ill. App. 3d 33, 700 N.E.2d 1057 (1st Dist. 1998).

1180.   People v. Jefferson, 35 Ill. App. 3d 424, 342 N.E.2d 185, 187 (1st Dist. 1976).

1181.   People v. Solomon, 24 Ill. 2d 586, 182 N.E.2d 736, 738, *cert. denied,* 371 U.S. 853 (1962); People v. Sullivan, 234 Ill. App. 3d 328, 600 N.E.2d 457 (2d Dist. 1992).

1182.   People v. McDonald, 227 Ill. App. 3d 92, 590 N.E.2d 1003 (2d Dist. 1992); People v. Cates, 111 Ill. App. 3d 681, 444 N.E.2d 543, 547 (1st Dist. 1982). *See* People v. Kagan, 283 Ill. App. 3d 212, 669 N.E.2d 1239, 1242 (2d Dist. 1996) (defendant's cardiovascular problems did not warrant continuance of his trial for solicitation of murder for hire and attempted first-degree murder where the trial judge observed defendant in court and had found that he was not prevented from presenting an adequate defense or cooperating with counsel, especially since defendant refused the state's offer of a furlough to seek medical treatment).

1183.   People v. Basler, 304 Ill. App. 3d 230, 710 N.E.2d 431 (5th Dist. 1999).

§ 4.79 — To Secure Counsel of Choice

The accused in a criminal case, within bounds, has the constitutional right to be represented by retained counsel of his or her choice.[1184] It is reversible error for a court to deny a continuance requested by the accused to effectuate that right or to use coercive tactics to inhibit the assertion of the right.[1185] For example, when the accused showed the court the business card of an attorney she had contacted but who was unable to be present on that day, the denial of her request for a continuance was reversible error because there was uncontradicted evidence of her exercising diligence in attempting to procure an attorney.[1186] Reversible error also occurred when the trial judge forced a defendant to go to trial with an inexperienced associate of the attorney of record, notwithstanding the defendant's request for a continuance so that the attorney could be present.[1187]

The request for a continuance in order to secure counsel of one's choice will not, however, be allowed to abuse the criminal justice system. The right to be represented by the counsel of one's own choosing "may not be employed as a weapon to indefinitely thwart the administration of justice, or to otherwise embarrass the effective prosecution of crime."[1188] Although

---

1184. People v. Canaday, 49 Ill. 2d 416, 275 N.E.2d 356 (1971). *Accord* People v. Williams, 92 Ill. 2d 109, 440 N.E.2d 843, 847 (1982); People v. Basler, 304 Ill. App. 3d 230, 710 N.E.2d 431 (5th Dist. 1999); People v. Spurlark, 67 Ill. App. 3d 186, 384 N.E.2d 767, 774 (1st Dist. 1978).

1185. People v. Green, 42 Ill. 2d 555, 248 N.E.2d 116, 117 (1969). *Accord* People v. Payne, 46 Ill. 2d 586, 264 N.E.2d 167, 169 (1970). *See* People v. Jackson, 216 Ill. App. 3d 1, 574 N.E.2d 719, 723 (1st Dist. 1991) (where defendant fails to articulate reason for request for new counsel, there is no abuse of discretion in denial of request for continuance).

1186. People v. Lyons, 26 Ill. App. 3d 358, 325 N.E.2d 89, 90–91 (3d Dist. 1975).

1187. People v. Myles, 49 Ill. App. 3d 325, 364 N.E.2d 323, 327 (1st Dist. 1977). *See also* People v. Jackson, 216 Ill. App. 3d 1, 574 N.E.2d 719, 723 (1st Dist. 1991) (where private counsel retained or appearance filed, abuse of discretion to deny continuance and to proceed to trial without presence of counsel or verifying claim of employment of counsel). *Cf.* People v. Childress, 276 Ill. App. 3d 402, 657 N.E.2d 1180 (1st Dist.1995) (where court failed to ascertain length of continuance desired, even though court found that request was for retained counsel and not to delay, court abused discretion in denying continuance).

1188. People v. Friedman, 79 Ill. 2d 341, 403 N.E.2d 229, 233 (1980) (request to substitute retained counsel for public defender on day set for trial was not timely made and therefore was properly denied); People v. Wanke, 303 Ill. App. 3d 772, 708 N.E.2d 833, 841 (2d Dist. 1999) (indigent defendant has "no right to choose his appointed counsel or insist on representation by a particular public defender").

each case is assessed on its own facts and circumstances, a common theme appears in those cases where a request for a continuance was deemed to have been properly denied: the continuance request was not timely made. A continuance sought on the day before trial to secure new counsel was properly denied because the attorney of record had represented the accused for five months and the accused had not expressed dissatisfaction with that representation.[1189] An attempt to substitute private counsel for the public defender on the day of the trial was properly denied because the request was made only for the purpose of delay.[1190] A request for new counsel when present counsel was experienced and had ably represented the accused was looked on with disfavor by the courts,[1191] and the request for a continuance to substitute new counsel on the day a retrial was to begin, allegedly because of a "communications breakdown" between the accused and his attorney, was held not to have been made in good faith.[1192] Thus, if the accused wants to substitute attorneys, the request for a continuance

---

1189.   People v. Johnson, 66 Ill. App. 3d 84, 383 N.E.2d 648, 653 (5th Dist. 1978).

1190.   People v. Gatheright, 9 Ill. App. 3d 1058, 293 N.E.2d 734, 737 (1st Dist. 1973), *cert. denied,* 414 U.S. 1132 (1974); People v. Jackson, 216 Ill. App. 3d 1, 574 N.E.2d 719 (1st Dist. 1991) (trial day request for continuance to retain private counsel properly denied). *See* People v. Childress, 276 Ill. App. 3d 402, 675 N.E.2d 1180 (1st Dist. 1995); United States *ex rel.* Lopez v. Nelson, No. 97 C 0357, 1997 WL 269624 (N.D. Ill. May 14, 1997). *But see* People v. Hardin, 299 Ill. App. 3d 33, 700 N.E.2d 1057 (1st Dist. 1998) (trial court abused discretion in denying continuance on day of trial to newly retained counsel who was unaware case was set for trial).

1191.   People v. Mims, 111 Ill. App. 3d 814, 444 N.E.2d 684, 686 (1st Dist. 1982). *Accord* People v. Langdon, 73 Ill. App. 3d 881, 392 N.E.2d 142, 147 (1st Dist. 1979). *See* People v. Robinson, 254 Ill. App. 3d 906, 626 N.E.2d 1242, 1247 (1st Dist. 1993) (granting of continuance to substitute counsel rests within discretion of judge and must be considered in light of diligence shown on part of defendant); People v. Johnson, 220 Ill. App. 3d 550, 581 N.E.2d 118, 125–26 (1st Dist. 1991) (where defendant's counsel requested continuance based on defendant's disagreement with counsel about trial strategy and personality conflict and not because counsel unprepared, and where defendant's conviction not due to lack of preparation, competency, or advocacy by counsel but on strength of evidence against him, trial judge not abuse discretion in denying defendant's motion for continuance based on dissatisfaction with counsel); People v. Jackson, 216 Ill. App. 3d 1, 574 N.E.2d 719, 723 (1st Dist. 1991) (where defendant failed to articulate acceptable reason for desiring new counsel and already represented by experienced, court-appointed criminal attorney, no abuse to deny defendant's request on day of trial for continuance).

1192.   People v. Isenberg, 60 Ill. App. 3d 325, 376 N.E.2d 778, 780 (4th Dist. 1978).

must be timely made. The accused will not be permitted to engage in "dilatory tactics."[1193]

If the trial court does allow substitution of attorneys but denies a continuance to the new lawyer on the day before trial, the reviewing court will determine whether the accused was prejudiced at trial by the performance of the new attorney who conducted the defense.[1194] For example, where a privately re-tained attorney had represented the defendant for two and one-half months before trial, the trial court properly denied a continuance on the day set for trial so that a newly engaged, more experienced co-counsel could familiarize himself with the case but who declined to enter the case when the continuance was denied.[1195] Although the defendant who retains counsel has both the choice and control over the representation he or she receives, he or she will not be allowed to use that choice to abuse the criminal prosecution process. "It is clear that the right to a reasonable time in which to prepare for trial cannot be construed to permit a defendant to postpone his trial date indefinitely by changing counsel on the day of the trial."[1196]

§ 4.80   — For Preparation of Case

Of more concern to the attorney as well as to the defendant is the principle that the accused must be given a reasonable time in which to prepare his or her case. "All persons charged with crime are entitled to a reasonable time to prepare a defense."[1197] The accused must have a "fair opportunity to de-fend,"[1198] and the trial judge must exercise his or her discretion on the basis of

---

1193. People v. Cross, 77 Ill. 2d 396, 396 N.E.2d 812, 820 (1979), *cert. denied,* 445 U.S. 929 (1980). *See, e.g.,* People v. Sullivan, 234 Ill. App. 3d 328, 600 N.E.2d 457, 460 (2d Dist. 1992) (granting of continuance to permit preparation or for substitution of counsel depends on circumstances surrounding request and within sound discretion of trial judge).

1194. People v. Hayes, 52 Ill. 2d 170, 287 N.E.2d 465, 467 (1972); People v. Flores, 269 Ill. App. 3d 196, 645 N.E.2d 1050 (1st Dist. 1995). *Accord* People v. Pruden, 110 Ill. App. 3d 250, 442 N.E.2d 284, 290 (4th Dist. 1982) ("His new counsel showed himself thoroughly familiar with the case, ably cross-examined the State's witnesses and presented his own case in chief").

1195. People v. Gore, 6 Ill. App. 3d 51, 284 N.E.2d 333, 335 (1st Dist. 1972), *cert. denied,* 411 U.S. 907 (1973).

1196. People v. Crawford, 23 Ill. 2d 605, 179 N.E.2d 667, 669 (1962); People v. Childress, 276 Ill. App. 3d 402, 657 N.E.2d 1180 (1st Dist. 1995); People v. Phelps, 197 Ill. App. 3d 954, 557 N.E.2d 235 (1st Dist. 1990).

1197. People v. Trimble, 345 Ill. 82, 177 N.E. 696, 697 (1931).

1198. People v. Shrum, 12 Ill. 2d 261, 146 N.E.2d 12, 13 (1957). For an excellent analysis, albeit in dictum, of the right to a continuance, see Justice Wolfson's

the facts and circumstances of each case.[1199] "There is no mechanical test, statutory or other, for determining the point at which the denial of a continuance in order to accelerate the judicial proceedings violates the substantive right of the accused to properly defend."[1200]

Although the test may not be mechanical, the seriousness of the charge and the complexity of the case are crucial factors in determining whether a continuance should be granted for preparation purposes. A capital case requires special attention. "Ten or eleven days to investigate 48 State witnesses and to prepare for cross-examination thereof and to prepare the defense in chief in a capital case can hardly be deemed reasonable and the trial court should have continued the case to a later date."[1201] When the case is less complex or less serious, lack of time to prepare is less likely to serve as a ground for a continuance.[1202] Each case, however, will be determined on its own merits.

Forcing a public defender to conduct a burglary trial the day she was appointed, one day after the arraignment, notwithstanding her diligent request for a continuance in order to prepare, was an abuse of discretion to the prejudice of the defendant.[1203] Where no motion for continuance or postponement was made, there was no abuse of discretion in a battery case when a public defender conducted trial four hours after appointment. "If he needed time to prepare, he should have moved the trial court for a continuance or postponement for a reasonable period to enable him to make his preparation."[1204] The trial court must be given reason to believe that additional time is needed for preparation.[1205] One such reason is the lack of "full and complete discovery."[1206]

---

opinion in *People v. Gardner*, 282 Ill. App. 3d 209, 668 N.E.2d 125, 129 (1st Dist. 1996).

1199. People v. Clark, 9 Ill. 2d 46, 137 N.E.2d 54, 55–56 (1956), *cert. denied*, 352 U.S. 1002 (1957). *See also* People v. Brown, 172 Ill. 2d 1, 665 N.E.2d 1290, 1307 (defendant not prejudiced by trial judge's denial of continuance to obtain evidence to impeach witness where impeaching fact contained in police report), *cert. denied*, 519 U.S. 970 (1996).

1200. People v. Lott, 66 Ill. 2d 290, 362 N.E.2d 312, 315 (1977). *See also* Ungar v. Sarafite, 376 U.S. 575 (1964).

1201. People v. Crump, 5 Ill. 2d 251, 125 N.E.2d 615, 622 (1955).

1202. People v. Sullivan, 52 Ill. App. 3d 666, 367 N.E.2d 1042, 1045 (4th Dist. 1977). *See, e.g.*, People v. Westpfahl, 295 Ill. App. 3d 327, 692 N.E.2d 831, 837 (3d Dist. 1998) (where discovery had been completed, defense request for continuance to secure additional records that had not been earlier subpoenaed or requested was properly denied).

1203. People v. Jefferson, 35 Ill. App. 3d 424, 342 N.E.2d 185, 187 (1st Dist. 1976).

1204. People v. Villareal, 114 Ill. App. 3d 389, 449 N.E.2d 198, 200 (2d Dist. 1983).

1205. People v. Smith, 23 Ill. 2d 512, 179 N.E.2d 20, 21–22 (1961).

1206. *Jefferson*, 35 Ill. App. 3d 424, 342 N.E.2d at 187.

The need to procure additional witnesses is a frequent reason given for seeking a continuance in order to prepare the defense.[1207] Where the accused's sanity was in issue, the court improperly denied counsel's request for a continuance to subpoena psychiatrists and psychologists.[1208] The testimony of the witness being sought must be material to the case,[1209] and the defendant must show diligent efforts to locate the witness.[1210] Moreover, the state must be given an opportunity to stipulate to the testimony of an absent defense witness. If the state is not asked to stipulate by the defense, the motion for a continuance may be denied.[1211] In all instances the accused must show that the denial of a continuance requested for the purpose of securing a witness will prejudice his or her defense.[1212]

1207.   725 ILCS 5/114-4(b)(3).

1208.   People v. Wilson, 120 Ill. App. 3d 950, 458 N.E.2d 1081, 1088 (1st Dist. 1983).

1209.   People v. Arndt, 50 Ill. 2d 390, 280 N.E.2d 230, 233 (1972) (witness testifying to accused's intoxication in case of involuntary manslaughter was not material because intoxication is not defense to involuntary manslaughter). *See* People v. Williams, 96 Ill. App. 3d 958, 422 N.E.2d 199 (1st Dist. 1981).

1210.   People v. Hanson, 120 Ill. App. 3d 84, 457 N.E.2d 1048, 1051 (5th Dist. 1983). *Accord* People v. Rivera, 64 Ill. App. 3d 49, 380 N.E.2d 1018 (1st Dist. 1978). *See* People v. Clamuextle, 255 Ill. App. 3d 504, 626 N.E.2d 741, 745 (2d Dist. 1994) (motion for continuance sought to secure presence of witness should be granted where defendant diligent in attempting to secure witness for trial, proposed testimony material and might affect jury verdict, and failure to grant would prejudice defendant). *But see* People v. Rodgers, 288 Ill. App. 3d 167, 680 N.E.2d 437, 440–41 (5th Dist. 1997) (defendant failed to demonstrate diligence in obtaining a witness where no attempt was made to contact the witness after the first day of trial and before the second day of trial).

1211.   People v. Robinson, 27 Ill. 2d 289, 189 N.E.2d 243, 246 (1963). *Accord* People v. Prochut, 27 Ill. 2d 298, 189 N.E.2d 290, 292 (1963); People v. Petrovic, 102 Ill. App. 3d 282, 430 N.E.2d 6, 11 (1st Dist. 1981); People v. Kane, 31 Ill. App. 3d 500, 333 N.E.2d 247 (1st Dist. 1975).

1212.   People v. Arndt, 50 Ill. 2d 390, 280 N.E.2d 230 (1972); People v. Villareal, 114 Ill. App. 3d 389, 449 N.E.2d 198 (2d Dist. 1983). *See* People v. Ward, 154 Ill. 2d 272, 609 N.E.2d 252, 266 (1992) (factors considered in reviewing denial of request for continuance include defendant's diligence, witness' testimony materiality, whether it affected the jury verdict, and whether defendant was prejudiced), *cert. denied,* 510 U.S. 873 (1993); People v. Easley, 288 Ill. App. 3d 487, 680 N.E.2d 776, 781 (3d Dist. 1997) (no abuse of discretion where court denied continuance request of defendant's to relitigate issues previously decided), *cert. denied,* 119 S. Ct. 1144 (1999); People v. Flores, 269 Ill. App. 3d 196, 645 N.E.2d 1050, 1054 (1st Dist. 1995) (no abuse of discretion in denying defendant's motion for continuance when defendant's counsel failed to exercise diligence in investigation or obtaining records); People v. Dotson, 263 Ill. App.

If counsel is on trial in another case, the defendant is statutorily entitled to a continuance,[1213] and appointed counsel, busy with other trial commitments, must be given a reasonable time to prepare,[1214] especially for a complex murder case.[1215] Note, however, that where a continuance is occasioned by defense counsel who is engaged elsewhere, the delay is properly charged to the defendant for purposes of tolling the speedy trial act.[1216] The review of the denial of a continuance sought for purposes of preparation will be examined in terms of the whole trial record to see if the denial prejudiced the defense.[1217]

A continuance may be sought because of the illness or death of the attorney of record.[1218] If the continuance is denied, the absence of the accused's attorney will be reviewed in the total context of the case. Where the case had been continued 21 times and on the day of trial counsel was incapacitated by oral surgery, the court did not abuse its discretion by denying a continuance because an associate of the absent attorney was qualified to try the case.[1219] Moreover, the death of counsel's mother on the first day of trial was not sufficient cause for a continuance when co-counsel was available.[1220] Nor was the death of the accused's daughter grounds for a continuance when the death was not unexpected and the accused did not show that he was mentally or physically incapacitated by the tragic event.[1221] Obviously, the key factors for granting or denying continuances in instances of illness or death are the time of the occurrence and the availability of substitute counsel.[1222] Courts will normally grant continuances for such events as a matter of course. The issue arises on

---

3d 571, 635 N.E.2d 559, 564 (1st Dist. 1994) (no error in denying one day continuance during trial to allow defendant to subpoena witnesses where defendant's theory of innocence was that he was "set up").

1213.   725 ILCS 5/114-4(b)(1).

1214.   People v. Kenzik, 9 Ill. 2d 204, 137 N.E.2d 270, 274 (1956).

1215.   People v. Crump, 5 Ill. 2d 251, 125 N.E.2d 615, 621 (1955).

1216.   People v. Logan, 117 Ill. App. 3d 753, 453 N.E.2d 1317, 1319 (1st Dist. 1983), *cert. denied,* 480 U.S. 907 (1987).

1217.   People v. Weaver, 8 Ill. App. 3d 299, 290 N.E.2d 691, 695 (1st Dist. 1972).

1218.   725 ILCS 5/114-4(b)(1).

1219.   People v. Cates, 111 Ill. App. 3d 681, 444 N.E.2d 543, 547–48 (1st Dist. 1982). *Accord* People v. Sedlacko, 65 Ill. App. 3d 659, 382 N.E.2d 363, 370–71 (1st Dist. 1978).

1220.   People v. Nobles, 83 Ill. App. 3d 711, 404 N.E.2d 330 (4th Dist. 1980). *See also* People v. Hardin, 299 Ill. App. 3d 33, 700 N.E.2d 1057 (1st Dist. 1998).

1221.   People v. Rodriguez, 121 Ill. App. 3d 50, 459 N.E.2d 254, 258 (1st Dist. 1983).

1222.   People v. Parks, 168 Ill. App. 3d 978, 523 N.E.2d 130 (1st Dist. 1988) (emergency appendectomy of public defender did not require continuance, since second public defender could take over).

appeal only when the event occurs near or at the time of trial, thereby requiring the trial court to balance the need of the defense for a continuance with the state's interest in the effective and efficient administration of justice. Absent clear abuse, the trial court's determination need not be overturned.

Finally, the defendant may seek a continuance to avoid "prejudice against . . . [him] on the part of the community" caused by "pretrial publicity concerning the case,"[1223] or because of substantive amendments to the charge or bill of particulars that take him or her by surprise and that prevent him or her from fairly defending himself or herself without a continuance.[1224] The later situation arises so rarely that further discussion is unwarranted.

§ 4.81 Speedy Trial

Every defendant in a criminal case has a federal[1225] and state[1226] right to a speedy trial. To implement this right, Illinois has adopted a speedy trial statute,[1227] although the Illinois statutory time period is not necessarily

---

1223.   (b) A written motion for continuance made by the defendant more than 30 days after arraignment may be granted when: . . .

             (5) Pretrial publicity concerning the case has caused a prejudice against defendant on the part of the community. . . .

        725 ILCS 5/114-4(b)(5).

1224.   (b) A written motion for continuance made by the defendant more than 30 days after arraignment may be granted when: . . .

             (6) The amendment of a charge or a bill of particulars has taken the defendant by surprise and he cannot fairly defend against such an amendment without a continuance.

        725 ILCS 5/114-5(b)(6).

1225.   "In all criminal prosecutions, the accused shall enjoy the right to a speedy . . . trial." U.S. CONST. amend. VI. See People v. Moore, 263 Ill. App. 3d 1, 635 N.E.2d 507, 513 (1st Dist. 1994) (United States Supreme Court has identified factors in determining constitutional speedy trial claim: length of delay; reason for delay; defendant's assertion of right; prejudice to defendant; and who is to blame for delay). But see Reed v. Farley, 512 U.S. 339 (1994) (defendant's Sixth Amendment right to speedy trial not violated when tried 54 days after 120 day period of Interstate Agreement on Detainers expired where defendant failed to show prejudice).

1226.   "In criminal prosecutions, the accused shall have the right to a speedy . . . trial." ILL. CONST. art. I, § 8.

1227.   Sec. 103-5. Speedy trial. (a) Every person in custody in this State for an alleged offense shall be tried by the court having jurisdiction within 120 days from the date he was taken into custody unless delay is occasioned by the defendant, by an examination for fitness ordered pursuant to Section 104-13 of this Act [725 ILCS 5/104-13], by a fitness hearing, by an adjudication of unfitness to stand trial, by a continuance allowed pursuant to Section 114-4 of this Act [725 ILCS 5/114-4] after a court's determination of the defendant's physical incapacity for trial, or by an interlocutory appeal. [Note that effective January 1, 1999, the statute was amended to include:] Delay shall be considered to be agreed to by the defendant unless he or she objects to the delay by making a written demand for trial or an oral demand for trial on the record.

(b) Every person on bail or recognizance shall be tried by the court having jurisdiction within 160 days from the date defendant demands trial unless delay is occasioned by the defendant, by an examination for fitness ordered pursuant to Section 104-13 of this Act [725 ILCS 5/104-13], by a fitness hearing, by an adjudication of unfitness to stand trial, by a continuance allowed pursuant to Section 114-4 of this Act [725 ILCS 5/114-4] after a court's determination of the defendant's physical incapacity for trial, or by an interlocutory appeal.

For purposes of computing the 160 day period under this subsection, every person who was in custody for an alleged offense and demanded trial and is subsequently released on bail or recognizance and demands trial, shall be given credit for time spent in custody following the making of the demand while in custody. Any demand for trial made under this provision shall be in writing; and in the case of a defendant not in custody, the demand for trial shall include the date of any prior demand made under this provision while the defendant was in custody.

(c) If the court determines that the State has exercised without success due diligence to obtain evidence material to the case and that there are reasonable grounds to believe that such evidence may be obtained at a later day the court may continue the cause on application of the State for not more than an additional 60 days. If the court determines that the State has exercised without success due diligence

to obtain results of DNA testing that is material to the case and that there are reasonable grounds to believe that such results may be obtained at a later day, the court may continue the cause on application of the State for not more than an additional 120 days.

(d) Every person not tried in accordance with subsections (a), (b) and (c) of this Section shall be discharged from custody or released from the obligations of his bail or recognizance.

(e) If a person is simultaneously in custody upon more than one charge pending against him in the same county, or simultaneously demands trial upon more than one charge pending against him in the same county, he shall be tried, or adjudged guilty after waiver of trial, upon at least one such charge before expiration relative to any of such pending charges of the period prescribed by subparagraphs (a) and (b) of this Section. Such person shall be tried upon all of the remaining charges thus pending within 160 days from the date on which judgment relative to the first charge thus prosecuted is rendered pursuant to the Unified Code of Corrections [730 ILCS 5/1-1-1 et seq.] or, if such trial upon such first charge is terminated without judgment and there is no subsequent trial of, or adjudication of guilt commensurate with that under federal constitutional provisions.[1228] The importance of the Illinois statute is that if an accused is not brought to trial within the period of time specified by the statute, the trial court will discharge an incarcerated defendant from custody and release a bonded defendant from the obligation of bond,[1229] and dismiss the charges against the accused.[1230]

---

after waiver of trial of, such first charge within a reasonable time, the person shall be tried upon all of the remaining charges thus pending within 160 days from the date on which such trial is terminated; if either such period of 160 days expires without the commencement of trial of, or adjudication of guilt after waiver of trial of, any of such remaining charges thus pending, such charge or charges shall be dismissed and barred for want of prosecution unless delay is occasioned by the defendant, by an examination for fitness ordered pursuant to Section 104-13 of this Act [725 ILCS 5/104-13], by a fitness hearing, by an adjudication of unfitness for trial, by a continuance allowed pursuant to Section 114-4 of this Act [725 ILCS 5/114-4] after a court's determination of the defendant's physical incapacity for trial, or by an interlocutory appeal; provided, however, that if the court determines that the State has exercised without success due diligence to obtain evidence material to the case and that there are reasonable grounds to believe that such evidence may be obtained at a later day the court may continue the cause on application of the State for not more than an additional 60 days.

(f) Delay occasioned by the defendant shall temporarily suspend for the time of the delay the period within which a person shall be tried as pre scribed by subparagraphs (a), (b) or (e) of this Section and on the day of expiration of the delay the said period shall continue at the point at which it was suspended. Where such delay oc curs within 21 days of the end of the period within which a person shall be tried as prescribed by subparagraphs (a), (b), or (e) of this Section, the court may continue the cause on application of the State for not more than an additional 21 days beyond the period prescribed by subparagraphs (a), (b), or (e). This subsection (f) shall become effective on, and apply to persons charged with alleged offenses committed on or after March 1, 1977.

725 ILCS 5/103-5.

1228. People v. Nowak, 45 Ill. 2d 158, 258 N.E.2d 313 (1970) (statutory rights are not to be seen as co-extensive within constitutional scheme). *See* People v. Fly, 249 Ill. App. 3d 730, 619 N.E.2d 821, 823 (4th Dist. 1993) (existence of specific time limits under this section which are not found in United States or Illinois Constitution creates a possibility of violating the statutory guaranty to speedy trial without violating constitutional guarantees).

1229. 725 ILCS 5/103-5(d).

1230. 725 ILCS 5/114-(a)(1); People v. Reimolds, 92 Ill. 2d 101, 440 N.E.2d 872 (1982). *See* People v. Schmidt, 233 Ill. App. 3d 512, 599 N.E.2d 201, 204 (3d Dist. 1992) (dismissal mandatory, not discretionary, when speedy trial period expired and delay not attributable to defendant); People v. Hinkle, 234 Ill. App. 3d 663, 600 N.E.2d 535, 538 (5th Dist. 1992) (where it appeared unlawful use

Although the statute on its face requires that every person in custody in Illinois be tried within 120 days from the date he or she was taken into custody[1231] and that every person on bail or recognizance must be tried within 160 days from the date he or she demands trial,[1232] exceptions exist because of a delay occasioned by the defendant; an examination for fitness; a fitness hearing; an adjudication of unfitness for trial; a court's determination of the defendant's physical incapacity for trial; or an interlocutory appeal.[1233] In

---

of weapon charge based on sexual assault, offenses were subject to compulsory joinder and defendant denied speedy trial right where state had knowledge of facts underlying both charges at time original charge filed but did not file aggravated sex charge until five months later; dismissal of criminal sexual assault charge proper). Note that *Hinkle* was abrogated by *People v. Reedy,* 186 Ill. 2d 1, 708 N.E.2d 1114 (1999). *But see* People v. Gooden, 296 Ill. App. 3d 205, 694 N.E.2d 215 (5th Dist. 1998) (where court chose to disregard its earlier reasoning in *Hinkle,* holding that continuance requested by defendant on original charge is delay as to later charge filed based on same original conduct; here several assault charges were added in amended information, the original information only alleging one invasion), *appeal granted,* 183 Ill. 2d 579, 712 N.E.2d 820 (1999). *Cf.* People v. Quigley 183 Ill. 2d 1, 697 N.E.2d 735 (1998); People v. Dortch, 303 Ill. App. 3d 839, 709 N.E.2d 280 (3d Dist. 1999).

1231.   725 ILCS 5/103-5a. *See* People v. Hamblin, 217 Ill. App. 3d 460, 577 N.E.2d 544, 546 (4th Dist. 1991) (120 day requirement does not dictate continuous period of incarceration; different periods of custody must be combined to determine whether exceeds 120 days). *But see* People v. Torres, 289 Ill. App. 3d 513, 682 N.E.2d 261, 263 (1st Dist. 1997) (defendant who is out on bond from an agreement on detainers is not incarcerated for purposes of speedy trial time); People v. Arsberry, 242 Ill. App. 3d 1034, 611 N.E.2d 1285, 1289 (1st Dist. 1993) (120 day period not run while defendant in custody of federal government).

1232.   725 ILCS 5/103-5(b). *See* People v. Staten, 159 Ill. 2d 419, 639 N.E.2d 550, 553 (where defendant's demand for jury trial cited paragraph (b) rather than intrastate detainer statute, defendant failed to satisfy applicable speedy trial statute and 160 day period never began to run), *cert. denied,* 513 U.S. 1063 (1994); People v. Moore, 263 Ill. App. 3d 1, 635 N.E.2d 507, 510 (1st Dist. 1994) (person committed to Department of Corrections with charge pending against him in any county in state is subject to 160 speedy trial period in paragraph (b); in this situation, § 3-8-10 of the Unified Code of Corrections governs and speedy trial term does not begin to run until defendant files a speedy trial demand).

1233.   725 ILCS 5/103-5(b). *See, e.g.,* People v. East-West University, Inc., 265 Ill. App. 3d 557, 637 N.E.2d 594, 598 (1st Dist. 1994) (trial judge's order joining theft and conspiracy charges interlocutory and nonappealable; pendency of appeal not toll running of speedy trial period). *But see* People v. Sojack, 273 Ill.

addition, if the court determines that the state has, without success, exercised "due diligence" in obtaining material evidence and that there are reasonable grounds to believe that the evidence may be obtained at a later date, the court may continue the case for an additional sixty days beyond the 120- or 160-day applicable period.[1234] The problem of a defendant who has more than one charge[1235] pending against him or her in the same county is also anticipated in the statute: trial on any one of the charges must commence before the expiration of the statutory period for any of the charges, and all remaining charges must then be tried within 160 days after judgment is rendered in the first trial.[1236]

App. 3d 579, 652 N.E.2d 1061 (1st Dist. 1995) (delay properly charged to defendant because "his lawyer was engaged elsewhere"); People v. Alerte, 239 Ill. App. 3d 1050, 608 N.E.2d 1, 4 (1st Dist. 1992) (time during which state's appeal pending in federal court not counted since state not obligated to commence retrial in state court until relevant matters pending in federal court disposed of).

1234. 725 ILCS 5/103-5(c).

1235. 725 ILCS 5/102-8 (" 'Charge' means a written statement presented to a court accusing a person of the commission of an offense and includes complaint, information, and indictment").

1236. 725 ILCS 5/103-5(e). *See* People v. Goins, 119 Ill. 2d 259, 518 N.E.2d 1014, 1015 (1988) (because defendant incarcerated in one county for same offense for which charged and convicted in another county, 120 day period commenced on date of incarceration in first county); People v. Cavitt, 246 Ill. App. 3d 514, 616 N.E.2d 666, 670 (5th Dist. 1993) (as demand for speedy trial by defendant in custody assumed by statute and is automatic, there were simultaneous demands for speedy trial on murder and drug charges, state had additional 160 days from date judgment rendered on drug charge in which to try defendant on murder charge even though defendant never made formal demand for speedy trial on drug charge); People v. Crowe, 195 Ill. App. 3d 212, 552 N.E.2d 5, 7 (4th Dist. 1990) (if newly charged offenses known to state at time of original prosecution and arise from same facts, new offense subject to speedy trial limits that apply to original charge regardless when new charges filed). *Cf.* People v. Quigley, 183 Ill. 2d 1, 697 N.E.2d 735 (1998). *See* People v. Clark, 188 Ill. App. 3d 130, 544 N.E.2d 32, 33 (5th Dist. 1989) (where defendant present in county for approximately 3½ months as prisoner of United States but not county, 120 day limit not begin to run until state had custody some four years later). *But see* People v. Gooden, 296 Ill. App. 3d 205, 694 N.E.2d 215, 219 (5th Dist. 1998) (where state added aggravated criminal sexual charge to charge of home invasion where both charges arose out of same facts and home invasion in process of trial and state requested a continuance of original charge, continuance attributed to assault charge for purposes of speedy trial act, even though state had knowledge of added charges at time of original charge, because no evidence state waited to amend to violate speedy trial act or to hinder defendant's defense).

The consequences of a delay occasioned by the defendant in calculating the time left in which he or she must be tried is also clearly stated: the running of the statutory period is temporarily suspended until the time of delay is over. At that point, the statutory period again continues to run without loss of the time during the suspended period.[1237] If delay occurs within twenty-one days of the end of the "term" period, the court may continue the case on application of the state for a period not to exceed twenty-one days.[1238]

Three frequently encountered problem areas are (1) figuring the time at which the term begins to run; (2) determining what is delay occasioned by the defendant; and (3) determining under what circumstances the term may legitimately be extended beyond the 120- or 160-day statutory period.

§ 4.82 — The Term Begins

Computation of the statutory period begins immediately when the defendant is taken into custody.[1239] However, when a defendant is on bail or

---

1237. 725 ILCS 5/103-5(f). *See* People v. McKinney, 59 Ill. App. 3d 536, 375 N.E.2d 854, 855 (5th Dist. 1978) ("that with respect to offenses committed prior to March 1, 1977 . . . delay occasioned by defendant tolls the running of the statute and a new statutory period commences to run from the date to which the case has been delayed. [citation omitted]. With respect to offenses committed on or after March 1, 1977, delay occasioned by the defendant only temporarily suspends for the time of the delay the period in which defendant is to be tried."). *But see* People v. Andrade, 279 Ill. App. 3d 292, 664 N.E.2d 256 (1st Dist. 1996) (motion to discharge on speedy trial grounds that required one-day extension for state response was chargeable to defendant).

1238. 725 ILCS 5/103-5(f); People v. McKinney, 59 Ill. App. 3d 536, 375 N.E.2d 854 (5th Dist. 1978).

1239. People v. Mrozek, 52 Ill. App. 3d 500, 367 N.E.2d 783, 786 (3d Dist. 1977) (accused who is in custody has no duty to demand trial in order to later assert his rights under speedy trial). The 120-day period only begins to run when an accused is in the custody of the State of Illinois. *See also* People v. Hayes, 23 Ill. 2d 527, 179 N.E.2d 660, 662 (1962). The statutory period begins to run only when the accused is confined in connection with the subsequently prosecuted charges. People v. Jones, 33 Ill. 2d 357, 211 N.E.2d 261, 263 (1965), *cert. denied,* 385 U.S. 854 (1966); People v. Adams, 106 Ill. App. 3d 467, 435 N.E.2d 1203 (1st Dist. 1982). *See* People v. Bryant, 223 Ill. App. 3d 971, 585 N.E.2d 1233, 1235 (4th Dist. 1992) (limitation period not tolled by delay occasioned by defendant before incarceration when he failed to appear for trial, since 120 day limitation period extended from date defendant taken into custody; failure of defendant to appear for trial occurred before statutory period began to run).

recognizance, the statute does not begin to run until an actual demand for trial is made.[1240]

Counsel must be cautioned that although a demand for trial for persons in custody need not be in writing, and no specific words are required,[1241] there must be some affirmative conduct by the defendant, especially the out-on-bail defendant, informing the court of his or her demand.[1242] Persons on bond must make a written demand,[1243] as must persons incarcerated in the Illinois Department of Corrections.[1244] The demand must be "clear, unequivocal and apparent

---

1240.   725 ILCS 5/103-5(b). *See, e.g.*, People v. Lock, 266 Ill. App. 3d 185, 640 N.E.2d 334, 338 (2d Dist. 1994) (where defendants out on bond and did not make speedy trial request before filing motion to dismiss, no violation of right to speedy trial). *But see* People v. Garrett, 136 Ill. 2d 318, 555 N.E.2d 353, 359 (1990) (demand under paragraph (b) by accused was premature and had no effect); People v. Baker, 273 Ill. App. 3d 327, 652 N.E.2d 858, 860 (5th Dist. 1995) (bonded defendant's first demand for speedy trial null and void because made before he was arrested); People v. Prince, 242 Ill. App. 3d 1003, 611 N.E.2d 105, 110 (3d Dist. 1993) (where defendant justifiably under impression charges no longer pending against him, failure to demand trial not waiver of right to speedy trial); People v. Daniels, 190 Ill. App. 3d 224, 546 N.E.2d 645, 646 (1st Dist. 1989) (demand meaningless if made at time when no charges pending against defendant); People v. Stevens, 185 Ill. App. 3d 261, 541 N.E.2d 239, 241 (2d Dist. 1989) (same). *See generally* People v. Meyer, 294 Ill. App. 3d 954, 691 N.E.2d 1191 (5th Dist. 1998) (demand for trial for defendant not in custody must be made to start the time clock running)

1241.   Though local circuit court rules may provide otherwise. For example, Rule 14.2 of the Rules of the Circuit Court of Cook County provides: "Any demand for trial . . . shall be in written form. No demand for trial shall be accepted . . . unless filed in accordance with this rule." Although in most instances, counsel should file a written demand to ensure the running of the speedy trial "time clock," failure to file the demand in writing probably has no effect on the time computation because the statute (chapter 725, section 5/103-5) contains no "in writing" requirement. Any local rule would almost certainly be preempted by the statutory and constitutional speedy trial provisions. *See* People v. Meyer, 294 Ill. App. 3d 954, 691 N.E.2d 1191 (5th Dist. 1998) (local rule requiring speedy trial demand to be in writing is within inherent power of the circuit court). Note, however, that the defendant's purported trial demand did not comply with the statute.

1242.   People v. Schoo, 55 Ill. App. 3d 163, 371 N.E.2d 86 (2d Dist. 1977); People v. Placek, 25 Ill. App. 3d 945, 323 N.E.2d 410 (2d Dist. 1975). *See* People v. Ground, 257 Ill. App. 3d 956, 629 N.E.2d 783, 785 (4th Dist. 1994) (to trigger this section, there must be affirmative statement in record showing defendant requests speedy trial).

1243.   725 ILCS 5/103-5(b).

1244.   Unified Code of Corrections, 730 ILCS 5/3-8-10.

from the record of the case."[1245] Clarity could be assured by the filing of a demand in writing. An in-custody defendant need not make a demand for trial to start the running of the term.[1246] However, when he or she subsequently posts bail, a prior demand for trial made while he or she was in custody does not trigger the running of the 160-day period that is applicable to him or her now that he or she is on bail.[1247] Rather, the defendant must renew the demand for trial to be eligible for the 160-day speedy trial provision.[1248] In *People v. McDonald*,[1249] the court held that under the Interstate Agreement on Detainers Act, defendants in custody of Illinois prisons or other jurisdictions must meet the requirements of that act, *viz.*, send written notice and request a final disposition of his or her case before the 180-day term begins to run.[1250]

1245.   In order to commence the running of the 160-day period, the defen dant must make a demand for trial which is clear, unequivocal and apparent from the record of the case . . . . [Therefore], a request for a jury trial does not meet these requirements of § 103-5(b).

People v. Althide, 71 Ill. App. 3d 963, 389 N.E.2d 240, 242 (3d Dist. 1979). *See also Baker,* 273 Ill. App. 3d 327, 652 N.E.2d at 861 (defendant's second demand for speedy trial which failed to make reference to the statute was insufficient to constitute a clear and unequivocal demand); People v. Erickson, 266 Ill. App. 3d 273, 639 N.E.2d 979, 982 (2d Dist. 1994) (because defendant's purported speedy trial request was not in document with proper heading, did not state she demanded "a speedy trial," and did not cite to statutory section, defendant failed to make effective speedy trial demand within meaning of paragraph (b)); People v. Milsap, 261 Ill. App. 3d 827, 635 N.E.2d 1043, 1046 (4th Dist. 1994) (although no evidence defendant intentionally tried to mislead state, request not clear enough to put it on notice that defendant requesting speedy trial); People v. Ground, 257 Ill. App. 3d 956, 629 N.E.2d 783, 785 (4th Dist. 1994) (defendant's demand under paragraph (b) must be set forth in title or heading of pleading containing the demand; title or heading must say that defendant "demands a speedy trial"); People v. Mills, 234 Ill. App. 3d 368, 599 N.E.2d 1362, 1367 (5th Dist. 1992) (defendant must, through some affirmative conduct, demand speedy trial either in writing or in unambiguous language designed to communicate demand to trial court by formal motion preserved in record), *vacated on other grounds,* 149 Ill. 2d 657, 610 N.E.2d 83 (1993) (for reconsideration in light of *People v. Schaefer,* 154 Ill. 2d 250, 609 N.E.2d 329 (1993)).

1246.   People v. Cornwell, 9 Ill. App. 3d 799, 293 N.E.2d 139 (5th Dist. 1973).

1247.   People v. Toney, 58 Ill. App. 3d 364, 374 N.E.2d 695 (1st Dist. 1978).

1248.   *Id.,* 374 N.E.2d at 697.

1249.   168 Ill. 2d 420, 660 N.E.2d 832 (1995), *cert. denied,* 518 U.S. 1024 (1996); People v. Moore, 263 Ill. App. 3d 1, 635 N.E.2d 507 (1st Dist. 1994).

1250.   *Id.,* 660 N.E.2d at 839.

§ 4.83 — Delay Occasioned by the Defendant

The second problem area of concluding what delays are occasioned by the defendant is somewhat more complex, though just as critical. Depending on the districts, cases seem to be all over the spectrum. If the court determines that it is the defendant who has caused a delay in the proceedings, the statutory period will be suspended for the length of the delay.[1251] The articulated criterion in attributing delay is whether the defendant's acts in fact caused or contributed to a delay,[1252] although obviously each case must

---

1251. 725 ILCS 5/103-5(f). *See* People v. Bowman, 138 Ill. 2d 131, 561 N.E.2d 633, 641 (1990) (defendant could not contend unfair to force him to choose between speedy trial and effective assistance of counsel; these rights are separate but related and both are designed to assure accused a fair trial, and to prevent undue delay in one instance and undue haste in the other; defendant may have right, even of constitutional dimension, to pursue whichever course he may, but constitution does not forbid requiring him to choose); People v. Williams, 299 Ill. App. 3d 143, 700 N.E.2d 753 (1st Dist. 1998) (defendant's speedy trial rights were not violated in trial six years after defendant was originally arrested and charged with residential burglary because he used fictitious names and dates of birth in twelve unrelated arrests during six-year span).

1252. People v. Fosdick, 36 Ill. 2d 524, 224 N.E.2d 242 (1967). *See* People v. Andrade, 279 Ill. App. 3d 292, 664 N.E.2d 256, 263 (1st Dist. 1996) (continuances granted to the state beyond the 120-day period after defendant filed a motion to discharge on the 120th day did not violate defendant's right to a speedy trial where confusion existed as to which side caused various delays in setting a trial date and where such delays were ultimately attributable to defendant); People v. Smith, 251 Ill. App. 3d 839, 623 N.E.2d 857, 860 (2d Dist. 1993) (if two reasons cause delay and one attributable to state and one attributable to defendant, fact delay partially due to defendant sufficient to toll period); People v. Arsberry, 242 Ill. App. 3d 1034, 611 N.E.2d 1285, 1289 (1st Dist. 1993) (although record failed to reflect express articulation of party responsible for delay, defendant's actions contributed almost habitually to every delay and defendant resoundingly failed to sustain burden of showing violation of right to speedy trial). *But see* People v. Ladd, 185 Ill. 2d 602, 708 N.E.2d 359 (1999) (over three-month delay together with silent record was not delay attributable to defendant); People v. Healy, 293 Ill. App. 3d 684, 688 N.E.2d 786, 792 (1st Dist. 1997) (murder conviction reversed for violation of speedy trial act where defendant did not agree to continuances requested by state; there was no affirmative act by defendant to show that he contributed to the delays) (acquiescence to date suggested by court not affirmative act attributable to defendant); People v. Schmidt, 233 Ill. App. 3d 512, 599 N.E.2d 201, 205 (3d Dist. 1992) (defendant adequately showed elements of violation of right to speedy trial where incarcerated, given no bail, and not tried within 120 days; defendant was not accountable for delay that took case outside term). *See also* People v. Quigley,

be decided on its own facts.[1253]

What acts of the defendant cause delay? A motion for a continuance, either requested or agreed to by the defendant, is usually deemed a delay attributable to him or her.[1254] However, mere acquiescence by the defendant to a date

---

183 Ill. 2d 1,697 N.E.2d 735 (1998) (defendant who was in custody on drug charge when he made demand on murder charge, made simultaneous demand on both; thus state had only 160 days after judgment was entered on drug charge to try him for murder, since term on in-custody defendant renews even without formal demand).

1253. People v. Bombacino, 51 Ill. 2d 17, 280 N.E.2d 697, *cert. denied,* 409 U.S. 912 (1972).

1254. People v. Turner, 128 Ill. 2d 540, 539 N.E.2d 1196, *cert. denied,* 493 U.S. 939 (1989). "Where the defendant specifically requests or agrees to continuance, the statutory 120-day period is tolled . . . [and] [t]he same result occurs if defendant causes a delay in the proceedings, even if he did not expressly seek a continuance." People v. Leonard, 18 Ill. App. 3d 527, 310 N.E.2d 15, 17 (4th Dist. 1974). "If the defendant agrees to continuance during the 120-day statutory period, the period is suspended." People v. Scott, 13 Ill. App. 3d 620, 301 N.E.2d 118, 125 (1st Dist. 1973). *See also* People v. Kliner, 185 Ill. 2d 81, 705 N.E.2d 850, 870 (1998) (repeated failures to call motions and agreement continuances are attributable to defendant), *cert. denied,* 68 U.S.L.W. 3224 (1999); People v. Williams, 272 Ill. App. 3d 868, 651 N.E.2d 532, 540–41 (1st Dist. 1995) (defendant not tried outside term where agreed to continuance; trial judge sought to try case earlier and defense counsel agreed to later date); People v. Colts, 269 Ill. App. 3d 679, 645 N.E.2d 225, 229–30 (1st Dist. 1993) (defendant's right to speedy trial not violated even though trial began 228 days after arrest where defense counsel agreed to continuances totaling 107 days and additional one day delay in conducting trial at end of period caused by defendant's motion to discharge); People v. Moore, 263 Ill. App. 3d 1, 635 N.E.2d 507, 511–12 (1st Dist. 1994) (where defense counsel requested continuance so he could proceed on defendant's motion to vacate guilty plea, delay attributable to defendant since defendant bound by acts of counsel); People v. Burchette, 257 Ill. App. 3d 641, 628 N.E.2d 1014, 1026 (1st Dist. 1993) (same); People v. Medina, 239 Ill. App. 3d 871, 607 N.E.2d 619, 624 (2d Dist. 1993) (defendant not only agreed to a continuance, but failed to provide transcripts with the motion to dismiss which contributed to the delay; therefore the defendant was not denied statutory right to speedy trial); People v. Stuckey, 231 Ill. App. 3d 550, 596 N.E.2d 646, 654 (1st Dist. 1992) (where parties expressly agree to a continuance on record, the affirmative act is attributable to the defendant which suspends 120-day period); People v. Meyer, 294 Ill. App. 3d 954, 691 N.E.2d 1191, 1192 (5th Dist. 1998) (demand for trial must be clear and unequivocal); People v. Brummett, 279 Ill. App. 3d 421, 664 N.E.2d 1074, 1079 (4th Dist. 1996) (motion for substitution of judge is delay attributable to defendant). *But see* People v. Ladd, 185 Ill. 2d 602, 708 N.E.2d 359 (1999) (over three-month delay together with silent record was not delay attributable to defendant); People v. Wynn, 296 Ill. App. 3d 1020,

suggested by the court does not constitute delay attributable to the defendant.[1255] Defense motions that require evidentiary hearings or responses from the prosecutor also are usually considered as occasioning delay for section 103-5 purposes—for example, motions for severance,[1256] motions for substitutions of judges,[1257] motion for change of venue[1258] and motions to suppress evidence.[1259] Although a defendant is entitled to discovery, the filing

---

695 N.E.2d 903, 908 (4th Dist. 1998) (acquiescence to date suggested by court does not constitute delay occasioned by defendants).

1255. People v. Healy, 293 Ill. App. 3d 684, 688 N.E.2d 786 (1st Dist. 1997). *See also* People v. Cichanski, 81 Ill. App. 3d 619, 401 N.E.2d 1315 (2d Dist. 1980).

1256. People v. Bombacino, 51 Ill. 2d 17, 280 N.E.2d 697, *cert. denied,* 409 U.S. 912 (1972).

1257. People v. Grant, 68 Ill. 2d 1, 368 N.E.2d 909 (1977), *superseded by statute as stated in* People v. McClure, 75 Ill. App. 3d 566, 394 N.E.2d 833, 835 (5th Dist. 1979); People v. Murphy, 47 Ill. App. 3d 278, 361 N.E.2d 842 (2d Dist. 1977), *aff'd on other grounds,* 72 Ill. 2d 421, 381 N.E.2d 677, 686 (1978). *See also* People v. Ladd, 185 Ill. 2d 602, 708 N.E.2d 359 (1999) (over three-month delay together with silent record was not delay attributable to defendant); People v. Kliner, 185 Ill. 2d 81, 705 N.E.2d 850 (1998) (motion for substitution of judges is delay caused by defendant), *cert. denied,* 68 U.S.L.W. 3224 (1999); People v. Smith, 268 Ill. App. 3d 1008, 645 N.E.2d 384, 392 (1st Dist. 1994) (although the defendant failed to preserve the issue, the trial judge properly charged continuances to the defendant even though the state tendered a fingerprint report late, where the defendant requested a continuance to include the report in trial preparation; the defendant can be forced to choose between speedy trial and right to effective counsel); People v. Lendabarker, 215 Ill. App. 3d 540, 575 N.E.2d 568, 578 (2d Dist. 1991) (defendant's petition for treatment under Substance Abuse Treatment Program and motion for substitution of judges were both sufficient to toll running of speedy trial statute, as the defendant is charged with the time naturally associated with the processing and disposition of motions he makes), *cert. denied,* 503 U.S. 960 (1992).

1258. People v. Nowak, 45 Ill. 2d 158, 258 N.E.2d 313 (1970) (motions for change of venue); People v. Turley, 235 Ill. App. 3d 917, 601 N.E.2d 305 (5th Dist. 1992).

1259. People v. Spann, 97 Ill. App. 3d 670, 422 N.E.2d 1051 (1st Dist. 1981), *cert. denied,* 455 U.S. 954 (1982). *See also* People v. McDonald, 168 Ill. 2d 420, 660 N.E.2d 832, 840 (1995) (no violation of speedy trial right where defendant filed pro se motion to quash arrest and suppress evidence, which was later withdrawn because continuance granted so defendant could consult with counsel and obtain discovery—delay attributable to defendant; delay to allow state to answer additional motion to quash arrest and suppress evidence and motion to dismiss based on speedy trial grounds delay due to defendant), *cert. denied,* 518 U.S. 1024 (1996). *See* People v. Ladd, 185 Ill. 2d 602, 708 N.E.2d 359 (1999); People v. Kliner, 185 Ill. 2d 81, 705 N.E.2d 850 (1998). *See also* People v. Hinkle, 234

of some discovery motions may delay trial while others will not.[1260] Further-more, a request by the defense for a fitness examination or a hearing is a delay chargeable to the defendant and will suspend the statutory period.[1261] A mere

---

Ill. App. 3d 663, 600 N.E.2d 535, 537 (5th Dist. 1992) (judge did not abuse discretion in refusing to attribute to defendant delay caused by a motion to suppress identification with regard to unlawful use of weapons charge, where a new and additional charge was filed against the defendant and it was clear that the additional charge arose out of same facts and circumstances as the original charge and was known to the state at time of filing of the original charge; time in which trial should begin on the additional charge was subject to same statutory limitations as the original charge). *Cf.* People v. Quigley, 183 Ill. 2d 1, 697 N.E.2d 735, 742 (1998) (relationship of speedy trial provisions and compulsory joinder provisions required discharge of defendant on felony DUI where court had earlier discharged defendant on speedy trial ground on misdemeanor DUI from same incident). *See also* People v. Murphy, 47 Ill. App. 3d 278, 361 N.E.2d 842 (2d Dist. 1977) (motions for suppression of evidence).

1260.   A discovery motion which the State can answer quickly would cause little or no delay; the State should not be permitted to use such a motion as an excuse to toll the statute. . . . On the other hand, a discovery motion that calls for answers which are not quickly available or requests answers replete in detail would cause a legitimate delay; such a motion is properly attributable to a defendant and tolls the running of the statutory period. Whether a motion falls into the former or latter category would depend on the facts of each case.

People v. Scott, 13 Ill. App. 3d 620, 301 N.E.2d 118, 125 (1st. Dist. 1973). *See* People v. Smith, 207 Ill. App. 3d 1072, 566 N.E.2d 797, 800 (5th Dist. 1991) (defendant has the right to discovery and the time necessary to complete it is not delay attributable to defendant); People v. Montenegro, 203 Ill. App. 3d 314, 560 N.E.2d 934, 936–37 (2d Dist. 1990) (not all discovery motions intrinsically dilatory and not every motion extends statutory period; motion which state can answer quickly causes little or no delay, and a motion which requests answers which are not readily available causes delay appropriately charged to defendant; where state must supply lengthy list of witnesses who reside in various locations, numerous exhibits, and large amount of scientific evidence, compliance with discovery properly attributable to defendant; where state can respond almost immediately by supplying police reports, statements of witnesses, and list of potential witnesses request not extraordinary and not occasion delay); People v. Paulsgrove, 178 Ill. App. 3d 1073, 534 N.E.2d 131, 132 (3d Dist. 1989) (where defendant filed discovery motion on August 6th, state provided discovery on August 25th, and sent notice to defendant of arraignment scheduled for September 16th, entire 42 day delay chargeable to defendant).

1261.   People v. Siglar, 49 Ill. 2d 491, 274 N.E.2d 65 (1971); 725 ILCS 5/103-5(a). *See* People v. Moore, 263 Ill. App. 3d 1, 635 N.E.2d 507, 512 (1st Dist. 1994) (counsel's request for additional time so defendant could undergo psychiatric

"arbitrary" suggestion of insanity will not suffice.[1262] Where a jury has been picked but not sworn, and then dismissed, and a new jury is picked from a new venire, the "clock" keeps ticking.[1263]

Will a motion for discharge alleging that the "term" has run be considered a delay attributable to the defendant? While a number of appellate districts have attributed delay under these circumstances to the defendant, the latest Illinois Supreme Court pronouncement refuses to attribute the delay to the defendant.[1264] In all instances, whether and what action of the defendant or the state constitutes good cause for delay rests within the sound discretion of the trial court.[1265]

In *People v. Roberson*,[1266] the court concluded that the defendant was denied his right to a speedy trial and, therefore, reversed his conviction for possession with intent to deliver. Defendant was arrested on April 13, 1995, and pursuant to statute had to be tried by August 11, 1995, unless any delays were attributable to him. The record demonstrated that there were no delays attributed to defendant.

---

examination tolled statutory period); People v. Cabrera, 188 Ill. App. 3d 369, 544 N.E.2d 439, 440 (3d Dist. 1989) (when defendant files pretrial motion he is responsible for the time naturally associated with processing motion and for any delay where his action caused rescheduling of trial). *See also* People v. Seaman, 203 Ill. App. 3d 871, 561 N.E.2d 188, 194 (5th Dist. 1990) (judge did not err in denying the defendant's motion for discharge for violating speedy trial rights where the state raised bona fide doubt as to the defendant's fitness, based on the fact that insanity was raised as a defense and a defense expert made conflicting representation as to defendant's fitness; it was reasonable for the state to seek resolution of fitness issue).

1262. People v. Hundley, 13 Ill. App. 3d 935, 301 N.E.2d 339 (4th Dist. 1973).

1263. People v. Roberson, 289 Ill. App. 3d 344, 681 N.E.2d 1069, 1073–74 (4th Dist. 1997).

1264. People v. Ladd, 185 Ill. 2d 602, 708 N.E.2d 359 (1999). *See also* People v. Tamborski, 415 Ill. 466, 114 N.E.2d 649 (1953).

1265. *See* People v. Howard, 205 Ill. App. 3d 702, 563 N.E.2d 1219, 1224 (5th Dist. 1990) (discretion of trial judge whether the delay is attributable to the defendant); People v. Hagley, 1 Ill. App. 3d 828, 275 N.E.2d 178 (5th Dist. 1971) (state's petition suggesting incompetency that was filed on the 119th day of 120-day statutory period not filed in good faith but made for purposes of delay). *See also McDonald*, 168 Ill. 2d 420, 660 N.E.2d at 841 (good cause shown and delay does not violate speedy trial right where time needed to take defendant's palm print whose hands were disfigured, and it was difficult to obtain fingerprints; key evidence to possibly link defendant to crime).

1266. 289 Ill. App. 3d 344, 681 N.E.2d 1069 (4th Dist. 1997).

A jury was selected on July 15, 1995, but it was not sworn. The case was recessed until July 25 because the state's attorney responsible for the case was hospitalized and the assistant taking over the case was not prepared to proceed on July 20, the next scheduled trial date. At this time, the trial court noted that it would not attribute the delay to either party. The case did not proceed on July 25, and there is no evidence in the record as to the reason. Further, the state did not file a section 103-5(c) motion. On August 14, the state moved for a mistrial. The trial court concluded that because the jury had not been sworn there was no need to declare a mistrial. Instead, it rescheduled trial for August 21. On August 18, defendant filed a motion for discharge under the speedy trial act. This motion was denied. The appellate court reversed. First, it found that the trial court erred in not attributing the original delay to the state. It found that this "skews" the focus of the speedy trial act. The state has no right to a speedy trial within 120 days, only the defendant has that right. The court reasoned that to say the delay was not attributable to the state had the effect of saying it was attributable to defendant.

In order to prove a violation of the speedy trial act two things are required: (1) proof that defendant was not tried within 120 days and (2) proof that defendant did not cause any delay.[1267] Both were proven in the instant case. Moreover, the court rejected the state's argument that the trial commenced on July 17 because a jury was selected on that day. The defendant was not tried by this jury but by another jury picked over a month later. The court agreed with *People v. Perkins*,[1268] wherein the venire was sworn but dismissed before the 120-day period expired. "Where a jury has been selected but not sworn and is later dismissed and a new jury selected from an entirely different venire, a defendant's trial does not commence for purposes of statutory speedy trial rights upon the selection of the first jury."[1269]

Of special significance in calculating when the time clock begins to run is the fact of custody: it is not essential to the starting of the statutory period that criminal charges be pending against the defendant, because the period will begin to run at the time of arrest and before the defendant is formally charged with a crime.[1270] It must be shown that the defendant was in custody for the subsequently prosecuted charges to come within the statute,[1271] although the

---

1267. *Id.*, 681 N.E.2d at 1071.

1268. 90 Ill. App. 3d 975, 414 N.E.2d 110 (1st Dist. 1980).

1269. *Roberson*, 289 Ill. App. 3d 344, 681 N.E.2d at 1072–73.

1270. People v. Nettles, 107 Ill. App. 2d 143, 246 N.E.2d 29 (3d Dist. 1969).

1271. People v. Behning, 130 Ill. App. 2d 536, 263 N.E.2d 607 (2d Dist. 1970). *But see* People v. Martinez, 264 Ill. App. 3d 807, 637 N.E.2d 447, 451 (1st Dist. 1994) (where defendant already in custody for unrelated charge, speedy trial provision begins to run from date of indictment for new offense).

period may begin to run at the time of the defendant's arrest and before the defendant has been formally charged with the crime.[1272]

Finally, when charges are dismissed, the nature of the dismissal usually will determine whether the statutory period has been tolled or whether it continues to run.[1273] The time clock continues to run if the state moves to *nolle prosequi* or strikes the case with leave to reinstate the charges.[1274] Where there is a judicial discharge for want of probable cause, however, the statutory term ends with the proceedings, and new charges result in the commencement of a new term.[1275]

1272. People v. Parsons, 48 Ill. App. 3d 618, 363 N.E.2d 396 (2d Dist. 1977). *But see* People v. King, 8 Ill. App. 3d 2, 288 N.E.2d 672 (1st Dist. 1972) (statutory term had begun to run although no charges were pending against defendant because defendant was in custody and statutory term had begun to run on related charges).

1273. People v. Dace, 171 Ill. App. 3d 271, 524 N.E.2d 1258 (3d Dist. 1988). *Cf.* People v. Miller, 286 Ill. App. 3d 297, 676 N.E.2d 309 (2d Dist. 1997) (where motion to *nolle prose* is not made in bad faith to evade speedy trial provisions, statute is tolled).

1274. People v. Toney, 58 Ill. App. 3d 364, 374 N.E.2d 695 (1st Dist. 1978). *See* People v. Woolsey, 139 Ill. 2d 157, 564 N.E.2d 764, 769 (1990) (trial judge should dispose of defendant's speedy trial motion before allowing state to enter a *nolle pros* indictment); People v. East-West University Inc., 265 Ill. App. 3d 557, 637 N.E.2d 594, 597 (1st Dist. 1994) (state's action in striking theft and conspiracy charges with leave to reinstate did not toll statutory period); People v. Young, 220 Ill. App. 3d 488, 581 N.E.2d 241, 246 (1st Dist. 1991) (*nolle pros* procedure terminates pending charges and requires institution of new proceeding to prosecute for dismissed offense; therefore, when no charge pending against defendant and released from bond, speedy trial provisions do not apply); Mitchell v. Keenan, 858 F. Supp. 105, 107 (N.D. Ill. 1994) (even though stricken off call with leave to reinstate cases may indefinitely toll state statute of limitations; they do not indefinitely toll state speedy trial act; prosecution has 160 days with some exceptions to try defendant who demands trial and any prosecution attempt to reinstate case dismissed SOL after 160 day time period violates act), *aff'd*, 50 F.3d 473 (7th Cir.), *cert. denied*, 516 U.S. 856 (1995); People v. Miller, 286 Ill. App. 3d 297, 676 N.E.2d 309 (2d Dist. 1997) (good faith *nolle prose* tolls statute). *But see* People v. Austin, 195 Ill. App. 3d 17, 551 N.E.2d 1074, 1075 (1st Dist. 1990) (speedy trial term, which began to run on defendant's previous arrest, tolled by *nolle pros* obtained by state; no evidence that *nolle pros* motivated by desire to harass or prejudice defendant or to gain tactical advantage over him); People v. Stevens, 185 Ill. App. 3d 261, 541 N.E.2d 239, 241 (2d Dist. 1989) (defendant not satisfy burden that he was on bail or recognizance after *nolle pros*; therefore the right to speedy trial under paragraph (b) was not violated).

1275. *Toney*, 58 Ill. App. 3d 364, 374 N.E.2d at 698.

§ 4.84 — State's Right to a Continuance

A final area of concern with respect to the operation of the statute is the granting of a continuance to the prosecutor where the state, despite "diligent efforts," is unable to locate material evidence within the period prescribed for bringing a defendant to trial. Under such circumstances, a reasonable extension not to exceed 60 days is permitted if there is good reason to believe that the evidence sought can be obtained in the near future[1276] and if the state shows that it was diligent in seeking that evidence.[1277] Extensions have been approved where a witness could not immediately be located,[1278] where a witness was hospitalized recovering from injuries,[1279] or even where the witness was temporarily absent from the state.[1280] Here, too, the request for time extension is addressed to the sound discretion of the trial court,[1281] whose

---

> A dismissal for lack of probable cause is a judicial determination in favor of the defendant rather than a voluntary act on the part of the State. Where charges are dismissed upon a judicial determination of no probable cause, the State has little opportunity to manipulate the proceedings or to purposefully evade the operation of the statutory term.

1276. People v. Garcia, 251 Ill. App. 3d 473, 621 N.E.2d 1035 (2d Dist. 1993).

1277. People v. Elliott, 68 Ill. App. 3d 873, 386 N.E.2d 579 (1st Dist. 1979). *See* People v. Smith, 268 Ill. App. 3d 1008, 645 N.E.2d 384, 388–39 (1st Dist. 1994) (although the defendant waived issue, the trial judge did not err in granting the state a 60-day continuance, where it was diligent in locating witnesses during the 120-day period, even though it only began searching for witnesses after first scheduled trial date; the state took substantial efforts to locate witness in the initial period and nothing in record indicated the search would have been necessary; finally, defense counsel admitted the case was not ready for trial on originally scheduled date).

1278. People v. Robinson, 44 Ill. App. 3d 447, 358 N.E.2d 43 (1st Dist. 1976); People v. Foster, 297 Ill. App. 3d 600, 697 N.E.2d 357 (1st Dist. 1998) (no abuse of discretion where trial court granted extension to 120-day period to locate witness and defendant did not file motion for discharge prior to trial). *See* People v. Garcia, 251 Ill. App. 3d 473, 621 N.E.2d 1035 (2d Dist. 1993).

1279. People v. Knox, 94 Ill. App. 2d 36, 236 N.E.2d 384 (1st Dist. 1968).

1280. People v. Richards, 81 Ill. 2d 454, 410 N.E.2d 833 (1980); People v. Wollenberg, 37 Ill. 2d 480, 229 N.E.2d 490 (1967). *See* People v. Griffin, 175 Ill. App. 3d 111, 529 N.E.2d 727, 731 (1st Dist. 1988) (judge did not err or abuse discretion in granting the state's request for 20 additional days in which to try defendant based upon unique circumstances related to a difficulty in locating the complaining witness incarcerated in California).

1281. People v. Arndt, 50 Ill. 2d 390, 280 N.E.2d 230 (1972) (witness at sea); People v. Smith, 268 Ill. App. 3d 1008, 645 N.E.2d 384 (1st Dist. 1994) (extension was appropriate where state needed additional time to secure recently discovered

action in granting or denying the request will only be disturbed on review if that discretion was abused.[1282]

Where the state petitions for an extension of the trial term, it must demonstrate due diligence in trying to obtain material evidence.[1283] The test of due diligence is "whether the state commenced its efforts to locate those witnesses in sufficient time to secure their presence before the 120 day [(or 160 day)] term expired . . . rather than diligence in obtaining evidence before the scheduled trial date."[1284] Factual allegations in support of the motion for extension of the term will prima facie satisfy the state's burden to demonstrate due diligence in the absence of a denial by the defendant.[1285] If the defendant denies the truth of the allegations, an evidentiary hearing is required.[1286]

§ 4.85 Joinder and Severance

Either defendants or charges may be the subject of a pretrial motion to consolidate (joinder) or separate (severance). This section discusses both joinder and severance of charges, and of defendants recognizing that the defense will seldom be in the position of moving for joinder and the state seldom in a position of moving for severance.

§ 4.86 — Of Charges

Two or more offenses may be charged in the same charging instrument, in separate counts, if the offenses charged are a part of the same comprehensive

---

fingerprint evidence); People v. Garcia, 251 Ill. App. 3d 473, 621 N.E.2d 1035 (2d Dist. 1993) (state's request for extension 29 days before expiration of term and 5 days before trial properly granted when state alleged that two witnesses would be out of state during scheduled trial period and third witness had sold house and present whereabouts were unknown); People v. Robinson, 41 Ill. App. 3d 433, 354 N.E.2d 551 (1st Dist. 1976) (witness had gone to care for critically ill sister); People v. Stephenson, 12 Ill. App. 3d 201, 298 N.E.2d 218 (1st Dist. 1973) (witness on vacation in South America).

1282. People v. Jones, 76 Ill. App. 2d 186, 221 N.E.2d 771 (1st Dist. 1966).

1283. People v. Elliott, 68 Ill. App. 3d 873, 386 N.E.2d 579 (1st Dist. 1979).

1284. People v. Smith, 268 Ill. App. 3d 1008, 645 N.E.2d 384, 388 (1st Dist. 1994).

1285. People v. Gamble, 41 Ill. App. 3d 394, 353 N.E.2d 136 (1st Dist. 1976). *See also* People v. Hughes, 274 Ill. App. 3d 107, 653 N.E.2d 818, 822 (1st Dist. 1995) (state's request for extension of speedy trial provisions requires no formal or particular language, may be oral or written, and is within trial court's discretion so long as there is showing that witness might be found within extended time).

1286. People v. Moore, 27 Ill. App. 3d 337, 326 N.E.2d 420 (1st Dist. 1975).

transaction.[1287] On motion of either party, the court may order the consolidation of two or more separately filed charges if the offenses charged initially could have been joined in a single charging instrument.[1288]

No precise test exists for determining whether separate offenses are part of the same comprehensive transaction.[1289] Separate offenses may be joined if they are part of the same general transaction or plan or scheme[1290]—for example, charges that the defendant stole an automobile and then two days later took items from inside the car. Because such acts, although separate, are sufficiently related so as to be considered part of the same comprehensive transaction, joinder is appropriate.[1291]

1287.   Sec. 111-4. Joinder of offenses and defendants. (a) Two or more of fenses may be charged in the same indictment, information or complaint in a separate count for each offense if the offenses charged, whether felonies or misdemeanors or both, are based on the same act or on 2 or more acts which are part of the same comprehensive transaction.

725 ILCS 5/111-4(a). *See, e.g.,* People v. Willer, 281 Ill. App. 3d 939, 667 N.E.2d 708 (2d Dist. 1996), *appeal denied*, 168 Ill. 2d 622, 671 N.E.2d 742 (1996) (sexual abuse of two daughters far enough apart and distinct so as not to be part of same "comprehensive transaction" requiring separate trials).

1288.   Sec. 114-7. Joinder of related prosecutions. The court may order 2 or more charges to be tried together if the offenses and the defendants could have been joined in a single charge. The procedure shall be the same as if the prosecution were under a single charge.

725 ILCS 5/114-7.

1289.   People v. Coulter, 230 Ill. App. 3d 209, 594 N.E.2d 1163, 1168 (1st Dist. 1992) (factors to consider: proximity of offenses in time and location; identity of evidence needed to link offenses; whether offenses shared common method; and whether same or similar evidence would establish elements of offenses); *appeal denied*, 146 Ill. 2d 636, 602 N.E.2d 461 (1992); People v. Trail, 197 Ill. App. 3d 742, 555 N.E.2d 68, 71 (4th Dist. 1990) (factors: common method of operation; proximity in time and location of offenses; common type of victim; similarity of offenses; and identity of evidence needed to demonstrate link between offenses). *See also* People v. Gapski, 283 Ill. App. 3d 937, 670 N.E.2d 1116 (2d Dist. 1996).

1290.   People v. Sockwell, 55 Ill. App. 3d 174, 371 N.E.2d 100 (2d Dist. 1977); People v. Gapski, 283 Ill. App. 3d 937, 670 N.E.2d 1116 (2d Dist. 1996); People v. Willer, 281 Ill. App. 3d 939, 667 N.E.2d 708 (2d Dist. 1996).

1291.   People v. Van DeVeire, 47 Ill. App. 3d 289, 361 N.E.2d 1180 (3d Dist. 1977). *See also* People v. Weston, 271 Ill. App. 3d 604, 648 N.E.2d 1068, 1074 (1st Dist. 1995) (no error in joining charges which arose out of same comprehensive transaction: locations three blocks apart, crimes occurred around 10:30 p.m., and motive same—gang rivalry revenge; also charges based on common design, method and evidence: 9 mm gun used, victims shot while outside homes, were not engaging in violent activity, and each victim attempted to escape and

Conversely, joinder is not permitted where charges are not related, the crimes occur several days apart, or there is no common plan or scheme that links the acts.[1292] For example, charges of armed robbery and possession of marijuana occurring days apart were not necessarily part of the same comprehensive transaction.[1293] Moreover, a defendant may not be compelled to go to trial over his or her objection on separate offenses that are not part of the same act or comprehensive transaction, even though charged in one multicount indictment or information.[1294] However, the reviewing courts usually look to see if the defendant was in fact prejudiced by the joined charges.[1295]

At the trial court level, the appropriate motion to separate improperly joined charges is one of severance of offenses.[1296] To preserve the issue for appellate

---

defendant kept shooting); People v. Brock, 262 Ill. App. 3d 485, 633 N.E.2d 735, 744 (1st Dist. 1992) (pattern of continuous conduct in commission of murder and armed robbery where two offenses occurred within minutes of each other and only one block away); People v. Patterson, 245 Ill. App. 3d 586, 615 N.E.2d 11, 13–14 (5th Dist. 1993) (not abuse to deny defendant's motion to sever where charges connected in time and place, evidence necessary to establish element of each charge essentially same, evidence established common method in perpetrating offenses, victims similar although against two different children, trying charges together promoted judicial efficiency, and offenses part of same comprehensive transaction); People v. Wells, 184 Ill. App. 3d 925, 540 N.E.2d 1070, 1073 (1st Dist. 1989) (where two transactions are completed two weeks apart, contingent upon one another and part of an overall plan to furnish an uninterrupted supply of drugs, same comprehensive plan).

1292. People v. Daniels, 35 Ill. App. 3d 791, 342 N.E.2d 809 (1st Dist. 1976). *See* People v. Willer, 281 Ill. App. 3d 939, 667 N.E.2d 708 (2d Dist. 1996) (reversal was required where trial court refused to sever counts that had been based on separate abuses of different victims and not part of "same comprehensive transaction").

1293. People v. Pullum, 57 Ill. 2d 15, 309 N.E.2d 565 (1974). *See also* People v. Karraker, 261 Ill. App. 3d 942, 633 N.E.2d 1250, 1256–57 (3d Dist. 1994) (where charges took place on three separate days, completely unrelated and not part of same comprehensive transaction, paragraph (a) violated, defendant prejudiced, and denied fair trial).

1294. People v. Sockwell, 55 Ill. App. 3d 174, 371 N.E.2d 100 (2d Dist. 1977).

1295. People v. Fornear, 283 Ill. App. 3d 171, 669 N.E.2d 939, 945 (2d Dist. 1996), *aff'd in part, rev'd in part on other grounds*, 176 Ill. 2d 523, 680 N.E.2d 1383 (1997).

1296. Although less often encountered, defense counsel may move for joinder of offenses if the accused faces multiple trials on related but unjoined charges. *See,* *e.g.*, People v. Gacy, 103 Ill. 2d 1, 468 N.E.2d 1171 (1984), *cert. denied,* 470 U.S. 1037 (1985).

review, the motion should be in writing.[1297] Counsel must allege facts demonstrating the separate nature of the joined charges, as well as facts demonstrating how the defendant would be prejudiced by a single joined prosecution. In the absence of demonstrable prejudice, the defendant can be compelled to proceed to trial on unassociated but jointly charged crimes.[1298] When prejudice is demonstrated, however, the trial court may order separate trials or grant other relief as justice requires.[1299] For example, in *People v. Willer*,[1300] the court held that the joinder of two charges of aggravated criminal sexual abuse concerning two victims constituted a reversible error since the evidence of the alleged crimes against one victim would have been inadmissible in a trial concerning the other victim, despite the state's claim that the similarity of the alleged offenses, including the victims' relation to the defendant, the location of the alleged crimes, and the age of victims would have rendered the offenses admissible in separate trials under the modus operandi exception.[1301]

A motion for severance is proper where a co-defendant has made an admission that implicates the defendant or when co-defendants have antagonistic defenses.[1302] A defendant will be prejudiced if the co-defendant's out-of-

---

1297. Although a written motion is not required by the statute (chapter 725, section 5/114-7), it is required by effective advocacy and common sense.

1298. People v. Tomasello, 98 Ill. App. 3d 588, 424 N.E.2d 785 (2d Dist. 1981). *See also* People v. Fornear, 283 Ill. App. 3d 171, 669 N.E.2d 939, 946 (2d Dist.) (trial court did not commit a reversible error by refusing to sever an unrelated unlawful use of weapons charge from an aggravated discharge of a weapon charge where there was uncontradicted evidence that defendant possessed the shotgun involved in both charges and where a separate trial would not have yielded a different result), *aff'd in part, rev'd in part on other grounds*, 176 Ill. 2d 523, 680 N.E.2d 1383 (1997); People v. Trail, 197 Ill. App. 3d 742, 555 N.E.2d 68, 71 (4th Dist. 1990) (where a defendant is charged with two counts of criminal sexual assault which occurred in same household during closely related times and involved similar victims, it is not abuse to try the charges together); People v. Stevens, 188 Ill. App. 3d 865, 544 N.E.2d 1208, 1222 (4th Dist. 1989) (two break-ins are sufficiently similar and close in place and time to warrant joinder). *But see* People v. Collins, 214 Ill. App. 3d 98, 573 N.E.2d 346, 352 (4th Dist. 1991) (defendant has no right to have charges of sexual molestation involving different victims tried at same time where state preferred to try separately).

1299. 725 ILCS 5/114-8.

1300. 281 Ill. App. 3d 939, 667 N.E.2d 708 (2d Dist. 1996).

1301. *Id.*, 667 N.E.2d at 719.

1302. People v. Harris, 123 Ill. 2d 113, 526 N.E.2d 335, *cert. denied*, 488 U.S. 902 (1988); People v. Daugherty, 102 Ill. 2d 533, 468 N.E.2d 969 (1984). *See also* People v. Bramlett, 211 Ill. App. 3d 172, 569 N.E.2d 1139, 1144 (4th Dist. 1991) (actual hostility between two defendants is required to justify severance; for

court statement is admitted but the defendant is unable to cross-examine the co-defendant because he or she does not testify.[1303] A defendant is also prejudiced when his or her defense is antagonistic to that of a co-defendant, and under this circumstance severance is imperative to assure a fair trial for each.[1304] The most common example of antagonistic defenses is where each defendant is "protesting his innocence and condemning the other."[1305]

§ 4.87 — Joinder of Defendants

It is almost axiomatic that persons who are initially charged together should be tried together,[1306] although defendants who could have been charged together but were not may still be jointly tried.[1307] Defendants may be jointly charged or subsequently joined, and therefore tried together, if they are alleged to have participated in the same act or transaction out of which the offense arose,[1308] as, for example, where one defendant shot the victim and the other defendant kicked the victim and told witnesses to keep quiet. Because both defendants participated in the same transaction, they were properly jointly

---

example when one defendant points a finger at the other or where one defendant, protesting his innocence, testifies implicating the other). *See, e.g.,* People v. Spain, 285 Ill. App. 3d 228, 673 N.E.2d 414, 419–21 (1st Dist. 1996) (defendants' first degree murder trial mandated severance where defense was antagonistic because co-defendant implicated defendant and defendant blamed co-defendant). *But see* People v. Rice, 286 Ill. App. 3d 394, 675 N.E.2d 944, 951 (1st Dist. 1996) (defendants' defenses not antagonistic thus severance was not warranted; even though both professed ignorance of the contents of the bag, neither pointed the finger at the other; their defenses were merely contradictory and not hostile).

1303.　*Daugherty,* 102 Ill. 2d 533, 468 N.E.2d at 973.

1304.　*Id.*

1305.　*Id.*

1306.　People v. Earl, 34 Ill. 2d 11, 213 N.E.2d 556 (1966); People v. Bramlett, 211 Ill. App. 3d 172, 569 N.E.2d 1139 (4th Dist. 1991); People v. Sessions, 95 Ill. App. 2d 17, 238 N.E.2d 94 (1st Dist. 1968).

1307.　725 ILCS 5/114-7.

1308.　(b) Two or more defendants may be charged in the same indictment, information or complaint if they are alleged to have participated in the same act or in the same comprehensive transaction out of which the offense or offenses arose. Such defendants may be charged in one or more counts together or separately and all of the defendants need not be charged in each count.

725 ILCS 5/111-4(b).

charged and tried.[1309] Where on three occasions one defendant took coin pouches from a mail truck, put the pouches in a cart, and put the cart on an elevator, and the other two defendants took the cart off the elevator and then hid the pouches, all three defendants were properly joined for trial because each took part in the same transaction out of which the offense arose.[1310]

Two or more defendants may also be charged together or subsequently joined for trial if the offenses were committed in furtherance of a conspiracy.[1311] In the area most frequently encountered, that of accountability,[1312] the accountable defendants may be charged and tried together with the defendant principally responsible.[1313] Finally, when multiple defendants are jointly charged in one charging instrument, each defendant may be charged in one or more counts together or separately.[1314]

Invariably filed by the state, the appropriate motion by which separately charged defendants may be prosecuted in a single trial is the motion for joinder.[1315] Although this motion is usually made by the prosecutor regarding defendants who were inadvertently charged separately, there is no statute or case law that precludes the defense from making the same motion to join defendants who might be prejudiced by separate trials. To preserve the issue, the motion should be in writing and allege with particularity how the separately charged defendants would be prejudiced by separate trials.[1316]

1309. People v. Mumford, 70 Ill. App. 3d 395, 387 N.E.2d 910 (1st Dist. 1979).

1310. United States v. Scott, 413 F.2d 932 (7th Cir. 1969), *cert. denied,* 396 U.S. 1006 (1970).

1311. 725 ILCS 5/111-4(b); United States v. Isaacs, 493 F.2d 1124 (7th Cir.), *cert. denied,* 417 U.S. 976 (1974).

1312. Sec. 5-2. When accountability exists. A person is legally accountable for the conduct of another when:

  (a) Having a mental state described by the statute defining the offense, he causes another to perform the conduct, and the other person in fact or by reason of legal incapacity lacks such a mental state; or

  (b) The statute defining the offense makes him so accountable; or

  (c) Either before or during the commission of an offense, and with intent to promote or facilitate such commission, he solicits, aids, abets, agrees or attempts to aid, such other person in the planning or com mission of the offense . . . .

  725 ILCS 5/5-2(a), (b), (c).

1313. People v. Tanthorey, 404 Ill. 520, 89 N.E.2d 403 (1949).

1314. 725 ILCS 5/111-4(b).

1315. 725 ILCS 5/111-4.

1316. Again, as with a motion for severance of charges, a written motion is not required by statute but rather by common sense and effective advocacy.

§ 4.88 — Severance of Defendants Based on Statements

In a multi-defendant prosecution, the decision of whether the defendants will be tried separately or together will have tremendous impact on the outcome of litigation. The problem of jointly charged defendants who either had made statements implicating each other or whose defenses at trial are antagonistic is familiar to even the most inexperienced defense practitioner. While the problem is enhanced by a number of decisions that have seriously eroded the right of jointly charged defendants to obtain separate trials, at least in Cook County, it is the experience of this writer that the state's attorney's office has opted to err on the side of safety and not oppose a defense motion for severance of defendants based on statements. However, even where severance of defendants based on statements has been granted, defendants may simultaneously still end up being on trial in the same courtroom, at least for portions of the case, albeit in front of separate juries.

To fully appreciate the difficulties encountered in severing defendants, yet to imbue counsel with an understanding that creative lawyering may make a difference in whether a defendant is tried jointly or alone, some historical background is necessary.

The Sixth Amendment to the Constitution of the United States provides that "[i]n all criminal prosecutions, the accused shall enjoy the right . . . to be confronted with the witnesses against him." This right has been held applicable to the states under the Fourteenth Amendment.[1317]

Analytically, if one defendant (D1) had made statements that incriminated himself or herself and a jointly charged co-defendant (D2), the person to whom D1 made the statement is then allowed to testify about the contents of that statement in the joint trial of D1 and D2. If D1 does not testify,[1318] D2 will be unable to confront or cross-examine D1, the out-of-court declarant, who for all practical purposes and certainly in the eyes of the factfinder, is a witness against D2. This is what the Supreme Court of the United States found in *Bruton v. United States*.[1319] The introduction of D1's statement, which incriminated D2, in their joint trial gave substantial, perhaps even critical weight to the government's case in a form not subject to cross-examination because D1 did not take

---

1317.   Pointer v. Texas, 380 U.S. 400 (1965).

1318.   Under the Fifth Amendment to the United States Constitution, D1 cannot be compelled to testify by either the state or D2.

1319.   391 U.S. 123 (1968).

the stand.[1320] Limiting instructions to the jury are not adequate to protect the defendant's rights under the Sixth Amendment.[1321]

For over ten years, the *Bruton* rule made severance decisions relatively simple for all trial participants: if D1's statement, which incriminated D2, was going to be introduced by the state against D1, D2 was entitled to a separate trial. If the state wanted to have the defendants tried together, a number of options were available: try the case without using the statement; excise the statement so as to delete references to D2;[1322] or utilize separate juries for each defendant in a unified trial where D2's jury would be out of the courtroom during admission of D1's statements.[1323] Finally, a somewhat riskier but nonetheless sanctioned procedure is to allow the introduction of D1's statement during the prosecution's case-in-chief against D1 and D2. If D1, in the defense case, testifies, then D2's right to confrontation and cross-examination is preserved. If D1 does not testify, D2 may then be granted a mistrial, thereby effectively severing his or her case from D1. D1's case may then continue to verdict.

The ease of applying the *Bruton* formula was significantly eroded by the United States Supreme Court's plurality decision in *Parker v. Randolph.*[1324] Where D1 and D2 made separate but similar statements to the police about their participation in a crime, such statements were found to be "interlocking." On the rationale that neither defendant would be hurt by a joint trial, at which time their interlocking statements (statements that say substantially the same thing) would be introduced, introduction of the statements was found not to offend the confrontation clause of the Sixth Amendment.[1325]

Two decisions of the United States Supreme Court and one of the Illinois Supreme Court have recognized the tenuousness (at best) of that theory. Recognizing that "a co-defendant's confession inculpating the accused is inherently unreliable," the United States Supreme Court held, in *Lee v. Illinois,*[1326] that absent "sufficient 'indicia of reliability,' flowing from either the

---

1320. *Id.* at 128. *Cf.* People v. Tyner, 30 Ill. 2d 101, 195 N.E.2d 675 (1964); People v. Rodriguez, 289 Ill. App. 3d 223, 680 N.E.2d 757 (2d Dist. 1997).

1321. *Bruton,* 391 U.S. at 129–30; People v. Ruiz, 94 Ill. 2d 245, 447 N.E.2d 148 (1982), *cert. denied,* 462 U.S. 1112 (1983).

1322. People v. Clark, 50 Ill. 2d 292, 278 N.E.2d 782 (1972).

1323. People v. Rainge, 112 Ill. App. 3d 396, 445 N.E.2d 535 (1st Dist. 1983), *cert. denied,* 467 U.S. 1219 (1984).

1324. 442 U.S. 62 (1979).

1325. *Id.* at 74–75.

1326. 476 U.S. 530 (1986), *overruled by* Bourjaily v. United States, 483 U.S. 171 (1987) (out-of-court statements need only fall within well-rooted hearsay exception).

circumstances surrounding the confession or the 'interlocking' character of the confessions," a nontestifying co-defendant's confession cannot be introduced in a joint trial without violating the constitutional right of confrontation.[1327]

What factors go into a determination that the co-defendant's statement bears "sufficient indicia of reliability" such as to justify its admission in a joint trial? One factor the Court looked to was whether the record demonstrated that the co-defendant has a "theoretical motive to distort the facts" to the detriment of the jointly tried defendant in whose trial the confession was introduced.[1328] Without evidence indicating a lack of motive, the Court presumed that "once partners in a crime recognize that 'the jig is up,' they tend to lose any identity of interest and immediately become antagonists, rather than accomplices."[1329] It is that antagonism that provides the confessing co-defendant a motive to inculpate the defendant, a basis for the Court to presume the unreliability of the confession.

In addition to the motive consideration, the Court looked to a second factor in deciding whether the co-defendant's confession bore sufficient indicia of reliability: just how "interlocking" were the confessions? "[W]hen the discrepancies between the statements are not insignificant, the co-defendant's confession may not be admitted."[1330] The gauge of accuracy, the indicia of reliability, is significantly increased "when co-defendants' confessions are identical in all material respects . . . ."[1331] The more interlocking the statements, the more reliable they are assumed to be. It becomes apparent that while *Lee* did not overrule *Parker,* it certainly revitalized the *Bruton* concept. That concept was given even more life in *Cruz v. New York.*[1332]

In *Cruz,* Justice Scalia, writing for the Court, recognized that the *Parker* assessment that interlocking confessions really are not harmful was untenable:

> A codefendant's confession will be relatively harmless if the incriminating story it tells is different from that which the defendant himself is alleged to have told, but enormously damaging if it confirms, in all essential respects, the defendant's alleged confession. It might be otherwise if the defendant were *standing* by his confession, in which case it could be said that the codefendant's confession does no more than support the defendant's very own case. But in the real world of criminal litigation, the defendant is seeking to *avoid* his confession—on the ground that it was

---

1327. *Lee,* 476 U.S. 546.

1328. *Id.* at 544.

1329. *Id.* at 544–45.

1330. *Id.* at 545.

1331. *Id.*

1332. 481 U.S. 186 (1987), *overruled by* Idaho v. Wright, 497 U.S. 805 (1990).

not accurately reported, or that it was not really true when made. In the present case, for example, the petitioner sought to establish that Norberto had a motive for falsely reporting a confession that never in fact occurred. In such circumstances a codefendant's confession that corroborates the defendant's confession significantly harms the defendant's case, whereas one that is positively incompatible gives credence to the defendant's assertion that his own alleged confession was nonexistent or false. Quite obviously, what the "interlocking" nature of the codefendant's confession pertains to is not its *harmfulness* but rather its *reliability:* If it confirms essentially the same facts as the defendant's own confession it is more likely to be true. Its reliability, however, may be relevant to whether the confession should (despite the lack of opportunity for cross-examination) be *admitted as evidence* against the defendant, *see Lee v. Illinois,* 476 U.S.__, 106 S. Ct. 2056, 90 L.Ed.2d 514 (1986), but cannot conceivably be relevant to whether, assuming it cannot be admitted, the jury is likely to obey the instruction to disregard it, or the jury's failure to obey is likely to be inconsequential.

* * *

We hold that, where a nontestifying codefendant's confession incriminating the defendant is not directly admissible against the defendant, see *Lee v. Illinios, supra,* the Confrontation Clause bars its admission at their joint trial, even if the jury is instructed not to consider it against the defendant, and even if the defendant's own confession is admitted against him.[1333]

Although *Parker v. Randolph* was not literally laid to rest in the decisions of *Cruz* and *Lee,* the Illinois Supreme Court has read Cruz as putting the iron stake through *Parker's* heart. In *People v. Jones,*[1334] Justice Ryan wrote that the Supreme Court has recently overruled *Parker:* a nontestifying co-defendant's confessions, incriminating the defendant, are inadmissible at a joint trial, even if the statements can be characterized as interlocking. Once again, therefore, in the opinion of this writer and most judges, defense attorneys, and prosecutors, a return to the *Bruton* approach to severance is the safe way to deal with confessing co-defendants.

In *People v. Rodriguez,*[1335] the court addressed the issue of joinder of two minors. Both minors were charged in connection with the same shooting. Upon motion of the state, defendant's case was joined with A.P.'s, although they were tried by two separate juries. Defendant contended that their positions were antagonists because the witnesses told one story at the time they were interviewed

---

1333.   *Cruz,* 481 U.S. 192–93.

1334.   121 Ill. 2d 21, 520 N.E.2d 325 (1988).

1335.   289 Ill. App. 3d 223, 680 N.E.2d 757 (2d Dist. 1997).

immediately after the shooting (none of them identified defendant as a shooter) and another story at the time of trial (most, if not all, identified defendant as a shooter). At trial, A.P. attempted to demonstrate that the witnesses' earlier statements were coerced and unreliable, whereas the defendant attempted to demonstrate that the initial statements were reliable.

The standard for separate trials is whether actual hostility exists between the defendants. In other words, each must profess his or her innocence and condemn the other. Inconsistent theories of the case are not sufficient. In this case, it was clear that the defendant and A.P. did not explicitly implicate each other. However, the defenses were antagonistic in a "more subtle, yet still prejudicial manner."[1336] Defendant and A.P. presented antagonistic defenses with regard to the occurrence witnesses. A.P. by arguing that the witness were telling the truth at the time of trial was pointing the finger at the defendant.[1337] Further, A.P.'s cross-examination of the witnesses reinforced the state's examination of the witnesses implicating defendant. Thus, the jury heard testimony against defendant from two parties: the state and A.P. "While A.P. did not take the stand and 'point a finger' at defendant . . . he did the next best thing: A.P. undercut defendant's defense that the occurrence witnesses initially told the truth and reinforced the State's impeachment of those witnesses."[1338] Accordingly, the state was given two bites of the apple against the defendant. A.P. and the state were on one side; defendant was on the other side. Based on the unusual facts of this case, defendant was denied a fair trial.[1339]

The *Lee-Cruz* rule also applies to the use of co-defendants' statements at a capital sentencing hearing, following an adjudication of guilt. Thus, tape-recorded confessions of two co-defendants may not be introduced in the capital sentencing hearing since accomplices' confessions that incriminate a defendant are presumptively unreliable.[1340]

However, the Fifth District recently sanctioned the admission of a co-defendant's confession in the defendant's sentencing hearing.[1341] Recognizing that *Rogers*[1342] turned on the unreliability of the co-defendant's confession, the court observed that in a sentencing hearing, hearsay is admissible,[1343] so long

---

1336. *Id.*, 680 N.E.2d at 766.

1337. *Id.*

1338. *Id.*, 680 N.E.2d at 767.

1339. *Id.*

1340. People v. Rogers, 123 Ill. 2d 487, 528 N.E.2d 667 (1988), *cert. denied,* 488 U.S. 1046 (1989).

1341. People v. Jett, 294 Ill. App. 3d 822, 691 N.E.2d 145, 151 (5th Dist. 1998).

1342. *See* People v. Rogers, 123 Ill. 2d 487, 528 N.E.2d 667 (1988), *cert. denied*, 488 U.S. 1046 (1989).

1343. *Jett,* 294 Ill. App. 3d 822, 691 N.E.2d at 151.

as it is relevant and reliable.[1344] Of particular interest is the court's analysis that the co-defendant's statement was "against his penal interest."[1345]

Although the Supreme Court has all but overruled *Bruton*,[1346] at least where the defendants had made interlocking statements, there does remain one potentially fertile area for continued application of the Bruton rule: death penalty litigation. The rationale of *Parker v. Randolph* is that co-defendants who make interlocking confessions cannot really hurt each other if tried jointly because each admits his or her own guilt for which each is subject to the same potential liability under a theory of accountability.[1347] In capital cases, however, under some circumstances only the "principal," not a person who is guilty by virtue of accountability, may be eligible for the death penalty.[1348] Thus, although interlocking statements of jointly tried co-defendants may not hurt either defendant on the question of guilt, the defendant who is guilty solely by virtue of legal accountability may be hurt in the penalty stage when his or her co-defendant's statement is used, still without the benefit of confrontation and cross-examination.

1344. *Id.; see also* People v. Turner, 128 Ill. 2d 540, 539 N.E.2d 1196 (1989), *cert. denied*, 493 U.S. 939 (1989).

1345. *Jett,* 294 Ill. App. 3d 822, 691 N.E.2d at 151.

1346. Justice Stevens dissented in *Parker,* stating that it "seriously undercut the Court's decision in *Bruton* . . . [and] squarely overrule[d] holdings in four decisions of this Court that applied the rule of *Bruton.*" Parker v. Randolph, 442 U.S. 62, 83 (1979). The four decisions Justice Stevens refers to are *Roberts v. Russell,* 392 U.S. 293 (1968) (applied *Bruton* to the state's holding that "reduction of the co-defendant's confession to omit the references to [the defendant on appeal] as well as a cautionary instruction . . . was sufficient to avoid . . . [a Sixth Amendment violation]"; *Hopper v. Louisiana,* 392 U.S. 658 (1968) (vacated conviction of two jointly tried defendants who each made full confessions); *Brown v. United States,* 411 U.S. 223 (1973) (Bruton violation recognized but held harmless); and *Harrington v. California,* 395 U.S. 250 (1969).

1347. Sec. 5-2. When accountability exists. A person is legally accountable for the conduct of another when:

(a) Having a mental state described by the statute defining the offense, he causes another to perform the conduct, and the other person in fact or by reason of legal incapacity lacks such a mental state; or

(b) the statute defining the offense makes him so accountable; or

(c) Either before or during the commission of an offense, and with the intent to promote or facilitate such commission, he solicits, aids, abets, agrees or attempts to aid, such other person in the planning or commission of the offense . . . .

720 ILCS 5/5-2.

1348. Enmund v. Florida, 458 U.S. 782 (1982).

Recognizing the inherent constitutional violation of using *Bruton*-precluded statements at a capital sentencing hearing, the Florida Supreme Court found that "[t]he consideration of the confession or statement of a co-defendant is quite different from the consideration of a presentence report . . . [A] defendant cannot require a co-defendant to waive his constitutional right to remain silent and force him to testify during the sentencing procedure."[1349]

The status of the use of such *Bruton*-precluded statements in Illinois capital sentencing hearings has not yet been resolved.

Regardless of changes in the application of Bruton, both vigorous advocacy regarding the use at trial of a co-defendant's statements (statements should be microscopically analyzed to establish differences that demonstrate that they are not interlocking) and their use in capital sentencing hearings cannot be over-emphasized. Creative lawyering in this regard may prevent a verdict adverse to the defendant; ultimately it may prevent the imposition of the death penalty.

§ 4.89 — Antagonistic Defenses

The second circumstance under which jointly charged defendants are entitled to separate trials is when the defense of one defendant is antagonistic to that of the other.[1350] The "mere apprehension" on the part of the moving defendant that he or she will be prejudiced by a joint trial is not enough to entitle that defendant to a separate trial.[1351] Rather, there must be actual hostility such that each defendant "professes his own innocence and condemns the other."[1352] "It is not sufficient to require a severance where a codefendant's theory is inconsistent or contradictory to the defendant's theory."[1353] What makes defenses antagonistic? *People v. Rodriguez*[1354] provides a good example.

In *Rodriguez*, A.P. and Rodriguez were tried together.[1355] A.P. contended that the initial statements of occurrence witnesses that identified A.P. but not Rodriguez were untruthful, while Rodriguez contended that they were truthful.[1356] At trial, the occurrence witnesses recanted their earlier statements and

---

1349.　Engle v. Florida, 438 So. 2d 803, 814 (Fla. 1983), *cert. denied*, 465 U.S. 1074 (1984).

1350.　People v. Rodriguez, 289 Ill. App. 3d 223, 680 N.E.2d 757, 765 (2d Dist. 1997).

1351.　*Id.*, 680 N.E.2d at 766.

1352.　*Id.*, quoting People v. Lovelady, 221 Ill. App. 3d 829, 582 N.E.2d 1217, 1224 (1st Dist. 1991) (citing People v. Adams, 176 Ill. App. 3d 197, 530 N.E.2d 1155, 1157 (1st Dist. 1988)).

1353.　*Rodriguez*, 289 Ill. App. 3d 223, 680 N.E.2d at 766.

1354.　*Id.*

1355.　*Id.*, 680 N.E.2d at 759.

1356.　*Id.*, 680 N.E.2d at 766.

identified Rodriguez as the shooter.[1357] Thus, at trial, A.P.'s position was that the occurrence witness who now identified Rodriguez as the shooter was telling the truth.[1358] A.P., for all practical purposes, became an additional prosecutor against Rodriguez, thus requiring a severance.[1359]

People v. Spain[1360] is another good example of antagonistic defenses justifying severance. In *Spain*, co-defendant Danny Morones's defense claimed, among other things, that he was not accountable for the actions of Gonzalez, another alleged shooter, and that Spain really was the shooter.[1361] At the same time, Spain's defense was that Morones was the shooter.[1362] Under such circumstances, where "each defendant [is] protesting his innocence at the expense of the other," the trial court's failure to sever is an abuse of discretion requiring reversal.[1363]

It should be obvious how imperative it is that trial counsel ascertain at the earliest possible moment whether jointly charged defendants have antagonistic defenses. Note, however, that "[g]enerally, a defendant must move for a severance prior to trial, demonstrating how he or she will be prejudiced in a joint trial."[1364] "[T]he trial court has a continuing duty at all stages of trial to grant severance if prejudice is apparent."[1365]

1357. *Id.*

1358. *Id. See also* People v. Bean, 109 Ill. 2d 80, 485 N.E.2d 349 (1985).

1359. *Rodriguez,* 289 Ill. App. 3d 223, 680 N.E.2d at 766.

1360. 285 Ill. App. 3d 228, 673 N.E.2d 414 (1st Dist. 1996).

1361. *Id.,* 673 N.E.2d at 418–19.

1362. *Id.,* 673 N.E.2d at 419, 420.

1363. *Id.,* 673 N.E.2d at 421.

1364. People v. Peterson, 273 Ill. App. 3d 412, 652 N.E.2d 1252, 1263 (1st Dist. 1995).

1365. People v. Blount, 220 Ill. App. 3d 732, 580 N.E.2d 1381, 1386 (1st Dist. 1991).